INDEX OF PLAYS

INDEX OF PLAYLETS

complete index of all Prefaces and Plays appears at e end of Volume VI. Most of the Prefatory and Post- ript material adjoins the play which it interprets. Vhen Prefaces are not connected, they can be located referring to the Table of Contents of the Volume in hich the play appears.

BERNARD SHAW

COMPLETE PLAYS
WITH PREFACES

VOLUME IV

TAKEN AT ADELPHI TERRACE, HIS FORMER LONDON HOME, AT THE TIME HE WAS WRITING "ST. JOAN."
PHOTOGRAPH BY HOPPE

BERNARD SHAW

COMPLETE PLAYS WITH PREFACES

Volume IV

DODD, MEAD & COMPANY
NEW YORK
1963

LIBRARY OF CONRESS CATALOG CARD NUMBER: 62-13608

PRINTED IN THE UNITED STATES OF AMERICA

CONTENTS

MISALLIANCE

A DEBATE IN ONE SITTING

Written in 1909 and 1910

First Performed London 1910

PARENTS AND CHILDREN

TRAILING CLOUDS OF GLORY

CHILDHOOD is a stage in the process of that continual remanufacture of the Life Stuff by which the human race is perpetuated. The Life Force either will not or cannot achieve immortality except in very low organisms: indeed it is by no means ascertained that even the amoeba is immortal. Human beings visibly wear out, though they last longer than their friends the dogs. Turtles, parrots, and elephants are believed to be capable of outliving the memory of the oldest human inhabitant. But the fact that new ones are born conclusively proves that they are not immortal. Do away with death and you do away with the need for birth: in fact if you went on breeding, you would finally have to kill old people to make room for young ones.

Now death is not necessarily a failure of energy on the part of the Life Force. People with no imagination try to make things which will last for ever, and even want to live for ever themselves. But the intelligently imaginative man knows very well that it is waste of labor to make a machine that will last ten years, because it will probably be superseded in half that time by an improved machine answering the same purpose. He also knows that if some devil were to convince us that our dream of personal immortality is no dream but a hard fact, such a shriek of despair would go up from the human race as no other conceivable horror could provoke. With all our perverse nonsense as to John Smith living for a thousand million eons and for ever after, we die voluntarily, knowing that it is time for us to be scrapped, to be remanufactured, to come back, as Wordsworth divined, trailing ever brightening clouds of glory. We must all be born again, and yet again and again. We should like to live a little longer just as we should like £50: that is, we should take it if we could get it for nothing; but that sort of idle liking is not will. It is amazing—considering the way we talk—how little a man will do to get £50: all the £50 notes I have ever known of have been more easily earned than a laborious sixpence; but the difficulty of inducing a man to make any serious effort to obtain £50 is nothing to the difficulty of inducing him to make a serious effort to keep alive. The moment he sees death approach, he gets into bed and sends for a doctor. He knows very well at the back of his conscience that he is rather a poor job and had better be remanufactured. He knows that his death will make room for a birth; and he hopes that it will be a birth of something that he aspired to be and fell short of. He knows that it is through death and rebirth that this corruptible shall become incorruptible, and this mortal put on immortality. Practise as you will on his ignorance, his fears, and his imagination with bribes of paradises and threats of hells, there is only one belief that can rob death of its sting and the grave of its victory; and that is the belief that we can lay down the burden of our wretched little makeshift individualities for ever at each lift towards the goal of evolution, which can only be a being that cannot be improved upon. After all, what man is capable of the insane self-conceit of believing that an eternity of himself would be tolerable even to himself? Those who try to believe it postulate that they shall be made perfect first. But if you make me perfect I shall no longer be myself, nor will it be possible for me to conceive my present imperfections (and what I cannot conceive I cannot remember); so that you may just as well give me a new name and face the fact that I am a new person and that the old Bernard Shaw is as dead as mutton. Thus, oddly enough, the conventional belief in the matter comes to this: that if you wish to live for ever you must be wicked enough to be irretrievably damned, since the saved are no longer what they were, and in hell alone do people retain their sinful nature: that is to say, their individuality. And this sort of hell, however convenient as a means of intimidating persons who have practically no honor and no conscience, is not a fact. Death is for many of us the gate of hell; but we are inside on the way out, not outside on the way in. Therefore let us give up telling one another idle stories, and rejoice in death as we rejoice in birth; for without death we cannot be born again;

and the man who does not wish to be born again and born better is fit only to represent the City of London in Parliament, or perhaps the university of Oxford.

THE CHILD IS FATHER TO THE MAN

Is he? Then in the name of common sense why do we always treat children on the assumption that the man is father to the child? Oh, these fathers! And we are not content with fathers: we must have godfathers, forgetting that the child is godfather to the man. Has it ever struck you as curious that in a country where the first article of belief is that every child is born with a godfather whom we all call "our father which art in heaven," two very limited individual mortals should be allowed to appear at its baptism and explain that they are its godparents, and that they will look after its salvation until it is no longer a child. I had a godmother who made herself responsible in this way for me. She presented me with a Bible with a gilt clasp and edges, larger than the Bibles similarly presented to my sisters, because my sex entitled me to a heavier article. I must have seen that lady at least four times in the twenty years following. She never alluded to my salvation in any way. People occasionally ask me to act as godfather to their children with a levity which convinces me that they have not the faintest notion that it involves anything more than calling the helpless child George Bernard without regard to the possibility that it may grow up in the liveliest abhorrence of my notions.

A person with a turn for logic might argue that if God is the Father of all men, and if the child is father to the man, it follows that the true representative of God at the christening is the child itself. But such posers are unpopular, because they imply that our little customs, or, as we often call them, our religion, mean something, or must originally have meant something, and that we understand and believe that something.

However, my business is not to make confusion worse confounded, but to clear it up. Only, it is as well to begin by a sample of current thought and practice which shews that on the subject of children we are very deeply confused. On the whole, whatever our theory or no theory may be, our practice is to treat the child as the property of its immediate physical parents, and to allow them to do what they like with it as far as it will let them. It has no rights and no liberties: in short, its condition is that which adults recognize as the most miserable and dangerous politically possible for themselves: namely, the condition of slavery. For its alleviation we trust to the natural affection of the parties, and to public opinion. A father cannot for his own credit let his son go in rags. Also, in a very large section of the population, parents finally become dependent on their children. Thus there are checks on child slavery which do not exist, or are less powerful, in the case of manual and industrial slavery. Sensationally bad cases fall into two classes, which are really the same class: namely, the children whose parents are excessively addicted to the sensual luxury of petting children, and the children whose parents are excessively addicted to the sensual luxury of physically torturing them. There is a Society for the Prevention of Cruelty to Children which has effectually made an end of our belief that mothers are any more to be trusted than stepmothers, or fathers than slave-drivers. And there is a growing body of law designed to prevent parents from using their children ruthlessly to make money for the household. Such legislation has always been furiously resisted by the parents, even when the horrors of factory slavery were at their worst; and the extension of such legislation at present would be impossible if it were not that the parents affected by it cannot control a majority of votes in Parliament. In domestic life a great deal of service is done by children, the girls acting as nursemaids and general servants, and the lads as errand boys. In the country both boys and girls do a substantial share of farm labor. This is why it is necessary to coerce poor parents to send their children to school, though in the relatively small class which keeps plenty of servants it is impossible to induce parents to keep their children at home instead of paying schoolmasters to take them off their hands.

It appears then that the bond of affection between parents and children does not save children from the slavery that denial of rights involves in adult political relations. It sometimes intensifies it, sometimes mitigates it; but on the whole children and parents confront one another as two classes in which all the political power is on one side; and the results are not at all unlike what they would be if there were no immediate consanguinity between them, and one were white and the other black, or one enfranchised and the other disenfranchised, or one ranked as gentle and the other simple. Not that Nature counts for nothing in the case and political rights for everything. But a denial of political rights, and the resultant delivery of one class into the mastery of another, affects their relations so extensively and profoundly that it is impossible to ascertain what the real natural relations of the two classes are until this political relation is abolished.

WHAT IS A CHILD?

An experiment. A fresh attempt to produce the just man made perfect: that is, to make humanity divine. And you will vitiate the experiment if you make the slightest attempt to abort it into some fancy figure of your own: for example, your notion of a good man or a womanly woman. If you treat it as a little wild beast to be tamed, or as a pet to be played with, or even as a means to save you trouble and to make money for you (and these are our commonest ways), it may fight its way through in spite of you and save its soul alive; for all its instincts will resist you, and possibly be strengthened in the resistance; but if you begin with its own holiest aspirations, and suborn them for your own purposes, then there is hardly any limit to the mischief you may do. Swear at a child, throw your boots at it, send it flying from the room with a cuff or a kick; and the experience will be as instructive to the child as a difficulty with a short-tempered dog or a bull. Francis Place tells us that his father always struck his children when he found one within his reach. The effect on the young Places seems to have been simply to make them keep out of their father's way, which was no doubt what he desired, as far as he desired anything at all. Francis records the habit without bitterness, having reason to thank his stars that his father respected the inside of his head whilst cuffing the outside of it; and this made it easy for Francis to do yeoman's service to his country as that rare and admirable thing, a Freethinker: the only sort of thinker, I may remark, whose thoughts, and consequently whose religious convictions, command any respect.

Now Mr Place, senior, would be described by many as a bad father; and I do not contend that he was a conspicuously good one. But as compared with the conventional good father who deliberately imposes himself on his son as a god; who takes advantage of childish credulity and parent worship to persuade his son that what he approves of is right and what he disapproves of is wrong; who imposes a corresponding conduct on the child by a system of prohibitions and penalties, rewards and eulogies, for which he claims divine sanction: compared to this sort of abortionist and monster maker, I say, Place appears almost as a Providence. Not that it is possible to live with children any more than with grown-up people without imposing rules of conduct on them. There is a point at which every person with human nerves has to say to a child "Stop that noise." But suppose the child asks why! There are various answers in use. The simplest: "Because it irritates me," may fail; for it may strike the child as being rather amusing to irritate you; also the child, having comparatively no nerves, may be unable to conceive your meaning vividly enough. In any case it may want to make a noise more than to spare your feelings. You may therefore have to explain that the effect of the irritation will be that you will do something unpleasant if the noise continues. The something unpleasant may be only a look of suffering to rouse the child's affectionate sympathy (if it has any), or it may run to forcible expulsion from the room with plenty of unnecessary violence; but the principle is the same: there are no false pretences involved: the child learns in a straightforward way that it does not pay to be inconsiderate. Also, perhaps, that Mamma, who made the child learn the Sermon on the Mount, is not really a Christian.

THE SIN OF NADAB AND ABIHU

But there is another sort of answer in wide use which is neither straightforward, instructive, nor harmless. In its simplest form it substitutes for "Stop that noise," "Dont be naughty," which means that the child, instead of annoying you by a perfectly healthy and natural infantile procedure, is offending God. This is a blasphemous lie; and the fact that it is on the lips of every nurserymaid does not excuse it in the least. Dickens tells us of a nurserymaid who elaborated it into "If you do that, angels wont never love you." I remember a servant who used to tell me that if I were not good, by which she meant if I did not behave with a single eye to her personal convenience, the cock would come down the chimney. Less imaginative but equally dishonest people told me I should go to hell if I did not make myself agreeable to them. Bodily violence, provided it be the hasty expression of normal provoked resentment and not vicious cruelty, cannot harm a child as this sort of pious fraud harms it. There is a legal limit to physical cruelty; and there are also human limits to it. There is an active Society which brings to book a good many parents who starve and torture and overwork their children, and intimidates a good many more. When parents of this type are caught, they are treated as criminals; and not infrequently the police have some trouble to save them from being lynched. The people against whom children are wholly unprotected are those who devote themselves to the very mischievous and cruel sort of abortion which is called bringing up a child in the way it should go. Now nobody knows the way a child should go. All the ways discovered so far lead to the horrors of our existing civilizations, described quite justifiably by Ruskin as heaps of agonizing human maggots, struggling with one another for scraps of food. Pious fraud is an attempt to pervert that divine mystery called the child's conscience into an instrument of our own convenience, and to use that wonderful and terrible power called Shame to grind our own axe. It is the sin of stealing fire from the altar: a sin so impudently practised by popes, parents, and pedagogues, that one can hardly expect the nurserymaids to see any harm in stealing a few cinders when they are worrited.

Into the blackest depths of this violation of children's souls one can hardly bear to look; for here we find pious fraud masking the violation of the body by obscene cruelty. Any parent or school teacher who takes a secret and abominable delight in torture is allowed to lay traps into which every child must fall, and then beat it to his or her heart's content. A gentleman once wrote to me and said, with an obvious conviction that he was being most reasonable and high-minded, that the only thing he beat his children for was failure in perfect obedience and perfect truthfulness. On these virtues, he said, he must insist. As one of them is not a virtue at all, and the other is the attribute of a god, one can imagine what the lives of this gentleman's children would have been if it had been possible for him to live down to his monstrous and foolish pretensions. And yet he might have written his letter to The Times (he very nearly did, by the way) without incurring any danger of being removed to an asylum, or even losing his reputation for taking a very proper view of his parental duties. And at least it was not a trivial view, nor an ill meant one. It was much more respectable than the general consensus of opinion that if a school teacher can devise a question a child cannot answer, or overhear it calling omega omeega, he or she may beat the child viciously. Only, the cruelty must be whitewashed by a moral excuse, and a pretence of reluctance. It must be for the child's good. The assailant must say "This hurts me more than it hurts you." There must be hypocrisy as well as cruelty. The injury to the child would be far less if the voluptuary said frankly "I beat you because I like beating you;

and I shall do it whenever I can contrive an excuse for it." But to represent this detestable lust to the child as Divine wrath, and the cruelty as the beneficent act of God, which is exactly what all our floggers do, is to add to the torture of the body, out of which the flogger at least gets some pleasure, the maiming and blinding of the child's soul, which can bring nothing but horror to anyone.

THE MANUFACTURE OF MONSTERS

This industry is by no means peculiar to China. The Chinese (they say) make physical monsters. We revile them for it and proceed to make moral monsters of our own children. The most excusable parents are those who try to correct their own faults in their offspring. The parent who says to his child: "I am one of the successes of the Almighty: therefore imitate me in every particular or I will have the skin off your back" (a quite common attitude) is a much more absurd figure than the man who, with a pipe in his mouth, thrashes his boy for smoking. If you must hold yourself up to your children as an object lesson (which is not at all necessary), hold yourself up as a warning and not as an example. But you had much better let the child's character alone. If you once allow yourself to regard a child as so much material for you to manufacture into any shape that happens to suit your fancy you are defeating the experiment of the Life Force. You are assuming that the child does not know its own business, and that you do. In this you are sure to be wrong: the child feels the drive of the Life Force (often called the Will of God); and you cannot feel it for him. Handel's parents no doubt thought they knew better than their child when they tried to prevent his becoming a musician. They would have been equally wrong and equally unsuccessful if they had tried to prevent the child becoming a great rascal had its genius lain in that direction. Handel would have been Handel, and Napoleon and Peter of Russia *them*selves in spite of all the parents in creation, because, as often happens, they were stronger than their parents. But this does not happen always. Most children can be, and many are, hopelessly warped and wasted by parents who are ignorant and silly enough to suppose that they know what a human being ought to be, and who stick at nothing in their determination to force their children into their moulds. Every child has a right to its own bent. It has a right to be a Plymouth Brother though its parents be convinced atheists. It has a right to dislike its mother or father or sister or brother or uncle or aunt if they are antipathetic to it. It has a right to find its own way and go its own way, whether that way seems wise or foolish to others, exactly as an adult has. It has a right to privacy as to its own doings and its own affairs as much as if it were its own father.

SMALL AND LARGE FAMILIES

These rights have now become more important than they used to be, because the modern practice of limiting families enables them to be more effectually violated. In a family of ten, eight, six, or even four children, the rights of the younger ones to a great extent take care of themselves and of the rights of the elder ones too. Two adult parents, in spite of a house to keep and an income to earn, can still interfere to a disastrous extent with the rights and liberties of one child. But by the time a fourth child has arrived, they are not only outnumbered two to one, but are getting tired of the thankless and mischievous job of bringing up their children in the way they think they should go. The old observation that members of large families get on in the world holds good because in large families it is impossible for each child to receive what schoolmasters call "individual attention." The children may receive a good deal of individual attention from one another in the shape of outspoken reproach, ruthless ridicule, and violent resistance to their attempts at aggression; but the parental despots are compelled by the multitude of their subjects to resort to political rather than personal rule, and to spread their attempts at moral monster-making over so many children, that each child has enough freedom, and enough sport in the prophylactic process of laughing at its elders behind their backs, to escape with much less damage than the single child. In a large school the system may be bad; but the personal influence of the head master has to be exerted, when it is exerted at all, in a public way, because he has little more power of working on the affections of the individual scholar in the intimate way that, for example, the mother of a single child can, than the prime minister has of working on the affections of any individual voter.

CHILDREN AS NUISANCES

Experienced parents, when children's rights are preached to them, very naturally ask whether children are to be allowed to do what they like. The best reply is to ask whether adults are to be allowed to do what they like. The two cases are the same. The adult who is nasty is not allowed to do what he likes: neither can the child who likes to be nasty. There is no difference in principle between the rights of a child and those of an adult: the difference in their cases is one of circumstance. An adult is not supposed to be punished except by process of law; nor, when he is so punished, is the person whom he has injured allowed to act as judge, jury, and executioner. It is true that employers do act in this way every day to their workpeople; but this is not a justified and intended part of the situation: it is an abuse of Capitalism which nobody defends in principle. As between child and parent or nurse it is not argued about because it is inevitable. You cannot hold an impartial judicial inquiry every time a child misbehaves itself. To allow the child to misbehave without instantly making it unpleasantly conscious of the fact would be to spoil it. The adult has therefore to take action of some sort with nothing but his conscience to shield the child from injustice or unkindness. The action may be a torrent of scolding culminating in a furious smack causing terror and pain, or it may be a remonstrance causing remorse, or it may be a sarcasm causing shame and humiliation, or it may be a sermon causing the child to believe that it is a little reprobate on the road to hell. The child has no defence in any case except the kindness and conscience of the adult; and the adult had better not forget this; for it involves a heavy responsibility.

And now comes our difficulty. The responsibility, being so heavy, cannot be discharged by persons of feeble character or intelligence. And yet people of high character and intelligence cannot be plagued with the care of children. A child is a restless, noisy little animal, with an insatiable appetite for knowledge, and consequently a maddening persistence in asking questions. If the child is to remain in the room with a highly intelligent and sensitive adult, it must be told, and if necessary forced, to sit still and not speak, which is injurious to its health, unnatural, unjust, and therefore cruel and selfish beyond toleration. Consequently the highly intelligent and sensitive adult hands the child over to a nurserymaid who has no nerves and can therefore stand more noise, but who has also no scruples, and may therefore be very bad company for the child.

Here we have come to the central fact of the question: a fact nobody avows, which is yet the true explanation of the monstrous system of child imprisonment and torture which we disguise under such hypocrisies as education, training, formation of character and the rest of it. This fact is simply that a child is a nuisance to a grown-up person. What is more, the nuisance becomes more and more intolerable as the grown-up person becomes more cultivated, more sensitive, and more deeply engaged in the highest methods of adult work. The child at play is noisy and ought to be noisy: Sir Isaac Newton at work is quiet and ought to be quiet. And the child should spend most of its time at play, whilst the adult should spend most of his time at work. I am not now writing on behalf of persons who coddle themselves into a ridiculous condition of nervous feebleness, and at last imagine themselves unable to work under conditions of bustle which to healthy people are cheerful and stimulating. I am sure that if people had to choose between living where the noise of children never stopped and where it was never heard, all the goodnatured and sound people would prefer the incessant noise to the incessant silence. But that choice is not thrust upon us by the nature of things. There is no reason why children and adults should not see just as much of one another as is good for them, no more and no less. Even at present you are not compelled to choose between sending your child to a boarding school (which means getting rid of it altogether on more or less hypocritical pretences) and keeping it continually at home. Most working folk today either send their children to day schools or turn them out of doors. This solves the problem for the parents. It does not solve it for the children, any more than the tethering of a goat in a field or the chasing of an unlicensed dog into the streets solves it for the goat or the dog; but it shews that in no class are people willing to endure the society of their children, and consequently that it is an error to believe that the family provides children with edifying adult society, or that the family is a social unit. The family is in that, as in so many other respects, a humbug. Old people and young people cannot walk at the same pace without distress and final loss of health to one of the parties. When they are sitting indoors they cannot endure the same degrees of temperature and the same supplies of fresh air. Even if the main factors of noise, restlessness, and inquisitiveness are left out of account, children can stand with indifference sights, sounds, smells, and disorders that would make an adult of fifty utterly miserable; whilst on the other hand such adults find a tranquil happiness in conditions which to children mean unspeakable boredom. And since our system is nevertheless to pack them all into the same house and pretend that they are happy, and that this particular sort of happiness is the foundation of virtue, it is found that in discussing family life we never speak of actual adults or actual children, or of realities of any sort, but always of ideals such as The Home, a Mother's Influence, a Father's Care, Filial Piety, Duty, Affection, Family Life, etc. etc., which are no doubt very comforting phrases, but which beg the question of what a home and a mother's influence and a father's care and so forth really come to in practice. How many hours a week of the time when his children are out of bed does the ordinary bread-winning father spend in the company of his children or even in the same building with them? The home may be a thieves' kitchen, the mother a procuress, the father a violent drunkard; or the mother and father may be fashionable people who see their children three or four times a year during the holidays, and then not oftener than they can help, living meanwhile in daily and intimate contact with their valets and lady's-maids, whose influence and care are often dominant in the household. Affection, as distinguished from simple kindliness, may or may not exist: when it does it either depends on qualities in the parties that would produce it equally if they were of no kin to one another, or it is a more or less morbid survival of the nursing passion; for affection between adults (if they are really adult in mind and not merely grown-up children) and creatures so relatively selfish and cruel as children necessarily are without knowing it or meaning it, cannot be called natural: in fact the evidence shews that it is easier to love the company of a dog than of a commonplace child between the ages of six and the beginnings of controlled maturity; for women who cannot bear to be separated from their pet dogs send their children to boarding schools cheerfully. They may say and even believe that in allowing their children to leave home they are sacrificing themselves for their children's good; but there are very few pet dogs who would not be the better for a month or two spent elsewhere than in a lady's lap or roasting on a drawingroom hearthrug. Besides, to allege that children are better continually away from home is to give up the whole popular sentimental theory of the family; yet the dogs are kept and the children are banished.

CHILD FANCIERS

There is, however, a good deal of spurious family affection. There is the clannishness that will make a dozen brothers and sisters who quarrel furiously among themselves close up their ranks and make common cause against a brother-in-law or a sister-in-law. And there is a strong sense of property in children, which often makes mothers and fathers bitterly jealous of allowing anyone else to interfere with their children, whom they may none the less treat very badly. And there is an extremely dangerous craze for children which leads certain people to establish orphanages and baby farms and schools, seizing any pretext for filling their houses with children exactly as some eccentric old ladies and gentlemen fill theirs with cats. In such places the children are the victims of all the caprices of doting affection and all the excesses of lascivious cruelty. Yet the people who have this morbid craze seldom have any difficulty in finding victims. Parents and guardians are so worried by children and so anxious to get rid of them that anyone who is willing to take them off their hands is welcomed and whitewashed. The very people who read with indignation of Squeers and Creakle in the novels of Dickens are quite ready to hand over their own children to Squeers and Creakle, and to pretend that Squeers and Creakle are monsters of the past. But read the autobiography of Stanley the traveller, or sit in the company of men talking about their schooldays, and you will soon find that fiction, which must, if it is to be sold and read, stop short of being positively sickening, dare not tell the whole truth about the people to whom children are handed over on educational pretexts. Not very long ago a schoolmaster in Ireland was murdered by his boys; and for reasons which were never made public it was at first decided not to prosecute the murderers. Yet all these flogging schoolmasters and orphanage fiends and baby farmers are "lovers of children." They are really child fanciers (like bird fanciers or dog fanciers) by irresistible natural predilection, never happy unless they are surrounded by their victims, and always certain to make their living by accepting the custody of children, no matter how many alternative occupations may be available. And bear in mind that they are only the extreme instances of what is commonly called natural affection, apparently because it is obviously unnatural.

The really natural feeling of adults for children in the long prosaic intervals between the moments of affectionate impulse is just that feeling that leads them to avoid their care and constant company as a burden beyond bearing, and to pretend that the places they send them to are well conducted, beneficial, and indispensable to the success of the children in after life. The true cry of the kind mother after her little rosary of kisses is "Run away, darling." It is nicer than "Hold your noise, you young devil; or it will be the worse for you"; but fundamentally it means the same thing: that if you compel an adult and a child to live in one another's company either the adult or the child will be miserable. There is nothing whatever unnatural or wrong or shocking in this fact; and there is no harm in it if only it be sensibly faced and provided for. The mischief that it does at present is produced by our efforts to ignore it, or to smother it under a heap of sentimental lies and false pretences.

CHILDHOOD AS A STATE OF SIN

Unfortunately all this nonsense tends to accumulate as we become more sympathetic. In many families it is still the custom to treat childhood frankly as a state of sin, and impudently proclaim the monstrous principle that little children should be seen and not heard, and to enforce a set of prison rules designed solely to make cohabitation with children as convenient as possible for adults without the smallest regard for the interests, either remote or immediate, of the children. This system tends to produce a tough, rather brutal, stupid, unscrupulous class, with a fixed idea that all enjoyment consists in undetected sinning; and in certain phases of civilization people of this kind are apt to get the upper hand of more amiable and conscientious races and classes. They have the ferocity of a chained dog, and are proud of it. But the end of it is that they are always in chains, even at the height of their military or political success: they win everything on condition that they are afraid to enjoy it. Their civilizations rest on intimidation, which is so necessary to them that when they cannot find anybody brave enough to intimidate them they intimidate themselves and live in a continual moral and political panic. In the end they get found out and bullied. But that is not the point that concerns us here, which is, that they are in some respects better brought up than the children of sentimental people who are always anxious and miserable about their duty to their children, and who end by neither making their children happy nor having a tolerable life for themselves. A selfish tyrant you know where to have, and he (or she) at least does not confuse your affections; but a conscientious and kindly meddler may literally worry you out of your senses. It is fortunate that only very few parents are capable of doing what they conceive their duty continually or even at all, and that still fewer are tough enough to ride roughshod over their children at home.

SCHOOL

But please observe the limitation "at home." What private amateur parental enterprise cannot do may be done very effectively by organized professional enterprise in large institutions established for the purpose. And it is to such professional enterprise that parents hand over their children when they can afford it. They send their children to school; and there is, on the whole, nothing on earth intended for innocent people so horrible as a school. To begin with, it is a prison. But it is in some respects more cruel than a prison. In a prison, for instance, you are not forced to read books written by the warders and the governor (who of course would not be warders and governors if they could write readable books), and beaten or otherwise tormented if you cannot remember their utterly unmemorable contents. In the prison you are not forced to sit listening to turnkeys discoursing without charm or interest on subjects that they dont understand and dont care about, and are therefore incapable of making you understand or care about. In a prison they may torture your body; but they do not torture your brains; and they protect you against violence and outrage from your fellow prisoners. In a school you have none of these advantages. With the world's bookshelves loaded with fascinating and inspired books, the very manna sent down from Heaven to feed your souls, you are forced to read a hideous imposture called a school book, written by a man who cannot write: a book from which no human being can learn anything: a book which, though you may decipher it, you cannot in any fruitful sense read, though the enforced attempt will make you loathe the sight of a book all the rest of your life. With millions of acres of woods and valleys and hills and wind and air and birds and streams and fishes and all sorts of instructive and healthy things easily accessible, or with streets and shop windows and crowds and vehicles and all sorts of city delights at the door, you are forced to sit, not in a room with some human grace and comfort of furniture and decoration, but in a stalled pound with a lot of other children, beaten if you talk, beaten if you move, beaten if you cannot prove by answering idiotic questions that even when you escaped from the pound and from the eye of your gaoler, you were still agonizing over his detestable sham books instead of daring to live. And your childish hatred of your gaoler and flogger is nothing to his adult hatred of you; for he is a slave forced to endure your society for his daily bread. You have not even the satisfaction of knowing how you are torturing him and how he loathes you; and you give yourself unnecessary pains to annoy him with furtive tricks and spiteful doing of forbidden things. No wonder he is sometimes provoked to fiendish outbursts of wrath. No wonder men of downright sense, like Dr Johnson, admit that under such circumstances children will not learn anything unless they are so cruelly beaten that they make desperate efforts to memorize words and phrases to escape flagellation. It is a ghastly business, quite beyond words, this schooling.

And now I hear cries of protest arising all round. First my own schoolmasters, or their ghosts, asking whether I was cruelly beaten at school? No; but then I did not learn anything at school. Dr Johnson's schoolmaster presumably did care enough whether Sam learned anything to beat him savagely enough to force him to lame his mind—for Johnson's great mind *was* lamed—by learning his lessons. None of my schoolmasters really cared a rap (or perhaps it would be fairer to them to say that their employers did not care a rap and therefore did not give them the necessary caning powers) whether I learnt my lessons or not, provided my father paid my schooling bill, the collection of which was the real object of the school. Consequently I did not learn my school lessons, having much more important ones in hand, with the result that I have not wasted my life trifling with literary fools in taverns as Johnson did when he should have been shaking England with the thunder of his spirit. My schooling did me a great deal of harm and no good whatever: it was simply dragging a child's soul through the dirt; but I escaped Squeers and Creakle just as I escaped Johnson and Carlyle. And this is what happens to most of us. We are not effectively coerced to learn: we stave off punishment as far as we can by lying and trickery and guessing and using our wits; and when this does not suffice we scribble impositions, or suffer extra imprisonments—"keeping in" was the phrase in my time—or let a master strike us with a cane and fall back on our pride at being able to bear it physically (he not being allowed to hit us too hard) to outface the dishonor we should have been taught to die rather than endure. And so idleness and worthlessness on the one hand and a pretence of coercion on the other became a despicable routine. If my schoolmasters had been really engaged in educating me instead of painfully earning their bread by keeping me from annoying my elders they would have turned me out of the school, telling me that I was thoroughly disloyal to it; that I had no intention of learning; that I was mocking and distracting the boys who did wish to learn; that I was a liar and a shirker and a seditious little nuisance; and that nothing could injure me in character and degrade their occupation more than allowing me (much less forcing me) to remain in the school under such conditions.

But in order to get expelled, it was necessary to commit a crime of such atrocity that the parents of the other boys would have threatened to remove their sons sooner than allow them to be schoolfellows with the delinquent. I can remember only one case in which such a penalty was threatened; and in that case the culprit, a boarder, had kissed a housemaid, or possibly, being a handsome youth, been kissed by her. She did not kiss me; and nobody ever dreamt of expelling me. The truth was, a boy meant just so much a year to the institution. That was why he was kept there against his will. That was why he was kept there when his expulsion would have been an unspeakable relief and benefit both to his teachers and himself.

It may be argued that if the uncommercial attitude had been taken, and all the disloyal wasters and idlers shewn sternly to the door, the school would not have been emptied, but filled. But so honest an attitude was impossible. The masters must have hated the school much more than the boys did. Just as you cannot imprison a man without imprisoning a warder to see that he does not escape, the warder being tied to the prison as effectually by the fear of unemployment and starvation as the prisoner is by the bolts and bars, so these poor schoolmasters, with their small salaries and large classes, were as much prisoners as we were, and much more responsible and anxious ones. They could not impose the heroic attitude on their employers; nor would they have been able to obtain places as schoolmasters if their habits had been heroic. For the best of them their employment was provisional: they looked forward to escaping from it into the pulpit. The ablest and most impatient of them were often so irritated by the awkward, slow-witted, slovenly boys: that is, the ones that required special consideration and patient treatment, that they vented their irritation on them ruthlessly, nothing being easier than to entrap or bewilder such a boy into giving a pretext for punishing him.

MY SCHOLASTIC ACQUIREMENTS

The results, as far as I was concerned, were what might

have been expected. My school made only the thinnest pretence of teaching anything but Latin and Greek. When I went there as a very small boy I knew a good deal of Latin grammar which I had been taught in a few weeks privately by my uncle. When I had been several years at school this same uncle examined me and discovered that the net result of my schooling was that I had forgotten what he had taught me, and had learnt nothing else. To this day, though I can still decline a Latin noun and repeat some of the old paradigms in the old meaningless way, because their rhythm sticks to me, I have never yet seen a Latin inscription on a tomb that I could translate throughout. Of Greek I can decipher perhaps the greater part of the Greek alphabet. In short, I am, as to classical education, another Shakespear. I can read French as easily as English; and under pressure of necessity I can turn to account some scraps of German and a little operatic Italian; but these I was never taught at school. Instead, I was taught lying, dishonorable submission to tyranny, dirty stories, a blasphemous habit of treating love and maternity as obscene jokes, hopelessness, evasion, derision, cowardice, and all the blackguard's shifts by which the coward intimidates other cowards. And if I had been a boarder at an English public school instead of a day boy at an Irish one, I might have had to add to these, deeper shames still.

SCHOOLMASTERS OF GENIUS

And now, if I have reduced the ghosts of my schoolmasters to melancholy acquiescence in all this (which everybody who has been at an ordinary school will recognize as true), I have still to meet the much more sincere protests of the handful of people who have a natural genius for "bringing up" children. I shall be asked with kindly scorn whether I have heard of Froebel and Pestalozzi, whether I know the work that is being done by Miss Mason and the Dottoressa Montessori or, best of all as I think, the Eurythmics School of Jacques Dalcroze at Hellerau near Dresden. Jacques Dalcroze, like Plato, believes in saturating his pupils with music. They walk to music, play to music, work to music, obey drill commands that would bewilder a guardsman to music, think to music, live to music, get so clearheaded about music that they can move their several limbs each in a different metre until they become complicated living magazines of cross rhythms, and, what is more, make music for others to do all these things to. Stranger still, though Jacques Dalcroze, like all these great teachers, is the completest of tyrants, knowing what is right and that he must and will have the lesson just so or else break his heart (not somebody else's, observe), yet his school is so fascinating that every woman who sees it exclaims "Oh, why was I not taught like this!" and elderly gentlemen excitedly enrol themselves as students and distract classes of infants by their desperate endeavors to beat two in a bar with one hand and three with the other, and start off on earnest walks round the room, taking two steps backward whenever Monsieur Dalcroze calls out "Hop!" Oh yes: I know all about these wonderful schools that you cannot keep children or even adults out of, and these teachers whom their pupils not only obey without coercion, but adore. And if you will tell me roughly how many Masons and Montessoris and Dalcrozes you think you can pick up in Europe for salaries of from thirty shillings to five pounds a week, I will estimate your chances of converting your millions of little scholastic hells into little scholastic heavens. If you are a distressed gentlewoman starting to make a living, you can still open a little school; and you can easily buy a secondhand brass plate inscribed PESTALOZZIAN INSTITUTE and nail it to your door, though you have no more idea of who Pestalozzi was and what he advocated or how he did it than the manager of a hotel which began as a Hydropathic has of the water cure. Or you can buy a cheaper plate inscribed KINDERGARTEN, and imagine, or leave others to imagine, that Froebel is the governing genius of your little *crèche*. No doubt the new brass plates are being inscribed Montessori Institute, and will be used when the Dottoressa is no longer with us by all the Mrs Pipchins and Mrs Wilfers throughout this unhappy land.

I will go further, and admit that the brass plates may not all be frauds. I will tell you that one of my friends was led to genuine love and considerable knowledge of classical literature by an Irish schoolmaster whom you would call a hedge schoolmaster (he would not be allowed to teach anything now) and that it took four years of Harrow to obliterate that knowledge and change the love into loathing. Another friend of mine who keeps a school in the suburbs, and who deeply deplores my "prejudice against schoolmasters," has offered to accept my challenge to tell his pupils that they are as free to get up and go out of the school at any moment as their parents are to get up and go out of a theatre where my plays are being performed. Even among my own schoolmasters I can recollect a few whose classes interested me, and whom I should certainly have pestered for information and instruction if I could have got into any decent human relationship with them, and if they had not been compelled by their position to defend themselves as carefully against such advances as against furtive attempts to hurt them accidentally in the football field or smash their hats with a clod from behind a wall. But these rare cases actually do more harm than good; for they encourage us to pretend that all schoolmasters are like that. Of what use is it to us that there are always somewhere two or three teachers of children whose specific genius for their occupation triumphs over our tyrannous system and even finds in it its opportunity? For that matter, it is possible, if difficult, to find a solicitor, or even a judge, who has some notion of what law means, a doctor with a glimmering of science, an officer who understands duty and discipline, and a clergyman with an inkling of religion, though there are nothing like enough of them to go round. But even the few who, like Ibsen's Mrs Solness, have "a genius for nursing the souls of little children" are like angels forced to work in prisons instead of in heaven; and even at that they are mostly underpaid and despised.

That friend of mine who went from the hedge schoolmaster to Harrow once saw a schoolmaster rush from an elementary school in pursuit of a boy and strike him. My friend, not considering that the unfortunate man was probably goaded beyond endurance, smote the schoolmaster and blackened his eye. The schoolmaster appealed to the law; and my friend found himself waiting nervously in the Hammersmith Police Court to answer for his breach of the peace. In his anxiety he asked a police officer what would happen to him. "What did you do?" said the officer. "I gave a man a black eye" said my friend. "Six pounds if he was a gentleman: two pounds if he wasnt" said the constable. "He was a schoolmaster" said my friend. "Two pounds" said the officer; and two pounds it was. The blood money was paid cheerfully; and I have ever since advised elementary schoolmasters to qualify themselves in the art of self-defence, as the British Constitution expresses our national estimate of them by allowing us to blacken three of their eyes for the same price as one of an ordinary professional man. How many Froebels and Pestalozzis and Miss Masons and Doctoress Montessoris would you be likely to get on these terms even if they occurred much more frequently in nature than they actually do?

No: I cannot be put off by the news that our system would be perfect if it were worked by angels. I do not admit it even at that, just as I do not admit that if the sky fell we should all catch larks. But I do not propose to bother about a supply of specific genius which does not exist, and which, if it did exist, could operate only by at once recognizing and establishing the rights of children.

WHAT WE DO NOT TEACH, AND WHY

To my mind, a glance at the subjects now taught in schools ought to convince any reasonable person that the object of the lessons is to keep children out of mischief, and not to qualify them for their part in life as responsible citizens of a free State. It is not possible to maintain freedom in any State, no matter how perfect its original constitution, unless its publicly active citizens know a good deal of constitutional history, law, and political science, with its basis of economics. If as much pains had been taken a century ago to make us all understand Ricardo's law of rent as to learn our catechisms, the face of the world would have been changed for the better. But for that very reason the greatest care is taken to keep such beneficially subversive knowledge from us, with the result that in public life we are either place-hunters, anarchists, or sheep shepherded by wolves.

But it will be observed that these are highly controversial subjects. Now no controversial subject can be taught dogmatically. He who knows only the official side of a controversy knows less than nothing of its nature. The abler a schoolmaster is, the more dangerous he is to his pupils unless they have the fullest opportunity of hearing another equally able person do his utmost to shake his authority and convict him of error.

At present such teaching is very unpopular. It does not exist in schools; but every adult who derives his knowledge of public affairs from the newspapers can take in, at the cost of an extra halfpenny, two papers of opposite politics. Yet the ordinary man so dislikes having his mind unsettled, as he calls it, that he angrily refuses to allow a paper which dissents from his views to be brought into his house. Even at his club he resents seeing it, and excludes it if it happens to run counter to the opinions of all the members. The result is that his opinions are not worth considering. A churchman who never reads The Freethinker very soon has no more real religion than the atheist who never reads The Church Times. The attitude is the same in both cases: they want to hear nothing good of their enemies; consequently they remain enemies and suffer from bad blood all their lives; whereas men who know their opponents and understand their case, quite commonly respect and like them, and always learn something from them.

Here, again, as at so many points, we come up against the abuse of schools to keep people in ignorance and error, so that they may be incapable of successful revolt against their industrial slavery. The most important simple fundamental economic truth to impress on a child in complicated civilizations like ours is the truth that whoever consumes goods or services without producing by personal effort the equivalent of what he or she consumes, inflicts on the community precisely the same injury that a thief produces, and would, in any honest State, be treated as a thief, however full his or her pockets might be of money made by other people. The nation that first teaches its children that truth, instead of flogging them if they discover it for themselves, may have to fight all the slaves of all the other nations to begin with; but it will beat them as easily as an unburdened man with his hands free and with all his energies in full play can beat an invalid who has to carry another invalid on his back.

This, however, is not an evil produced by the denial of children's rights, nor is it inherent in the nature of schools. I mention it only because it would be folly to call for a reform of our schools without taking account of the corrupt resistance which awaits the reformer.

A word must also be said about the opposition to reform of the vested interest of the classical and coercive schoolmaster. He, poor wretch, has no other means of livelihood; and reform would leave him as a workman is now left when he is superseded by a machine. He had therefore better do what he can to get the workman compensated, so as to make the public familiar with the idea of compensation before his own turn comes.

TABOO IN SCHOOLS

The suppression of economic knowledge, disastrous as it is, is quite intelligible, its corrupt motive being as clear as the motive of a burglar for concealing his jemmy from a policeman. But the other great suppression in our schools, the suppression of the subject of sex, is a case of taboo. In mankind, the lower the type, and the less cultivated the mind, the less courage there is to face important subjects objectively. The ablest and most highly cultivated people continually discuss religion, politics, and sex: it is hardly an exaggeration to say that they discuss nothing else with fully-awakened interest. Commoner and less cultivated people, even when they form societies for discussion, make a rule that politics and religion are not to be mentioned, and take it for granted that no decent person would attempt to discuss sex. The three subjects are feared because they rouse the crude passions which call for furious gratification in murder and rapine at worst, and, at best, lead to quarrels and undesirable states of consciousness.

Even when this excuse of bad manners, ill temper, and brutishness (for that is what it comes to) compels us to accept if from those adults among whom political and theological discussion does as a matter of fact lead to the drawing of knives and pistols, and sex discussion leads to obscenity, it has no application to children except as an imperative reason for training them to respect other people's opinions, and to insist on respect for their own in these as in other important matters which are equally dangerous: for example, money. And in any case there are decisive reasons, superior, like the reasons for suspending conventional reticences between doctor and patient, to all considerations of mere decorum, for giving proper instruction in the facts of sex. Those who object to it (not counting coarse people who thoughtlessly seize every opportunity of affecting and parading a fictitious delicacy) are, in effect, advocating ignorance as a safeguard against precocity. If ignorance were practicable there would be something to be said for it up to the age at which ignorance is a danger instead of a safeguard. Even as it is it seems undesirable that any special emphasis should be given to the subject, whether by way of delicacy and poetry or too impressive warning. But the plain fact is that in refusing to allow the child to be taught by qualified unrelated elders (the parents shrink from the lesson, even when they are otherwise qualified, because their own relation to the child makes the subject impossible between them) we are virtually arranging to have our children taught by other children in guilty secrets and unclean jests. And that settles the question for all sensible people.

The dogmatic objection, the sheer instinctive taboo which rules the subject out altogether as indecent, has no age limit. It means that at no matter what age a woman consents to a proposal of marriage, she should do so in ignorance of the relation she is undertaking. When this actually happens (and apparently it does happen oftener than would seem possible) a horrible fraud is being practised on both the man and the woman. He is led to believe that she knows what she is promising, and that he is in no danger of finding himself bound to a woman to whom he is eugenically antipathetic. She contemplates nothing but such affectionate relations as may exist between her and her nearest kinsmen, and has no knowledge of the condition which, if not foreseen, must come as an amazing revelation and a dangerous shock, ending possibly in the discovery that the marriage has been an irreparable mistake. Nothing can justify such a risk. There may be people incapable of understanding that the right to know all there is to know about oneself is a natural human right that sweeps away all the pretences of others to tamper with one's consciousness in order to produce what they choose to consider a good character. But they must here bow to the plain mischievousness of entrapping people into contracts on which the happiness of their whole lives depends without letting them know what they are undertaking.

ALLEGED NOVELTIES IN MODERN SCHOOLS

There is just one more nuisance to be disposed of before I come to the positive side of my case. I mean the person who tells me that my schooldays belong to a bygone order of educational ideas and institutions, and that schools are not now a bit like my old school. I reply, with Sir Walter Raleigh, by calling on my soul to give this statement the lie. Some years ago I lectured in Oxford on the subject of Education. A friend to whom I mentioned my intention said,

"You know nothing of modern education: schools are not now what they were when you were a boy." I immediately procured the time sheets of half a dozen modern schools, and found, as I expected, that they might all have been my old school: there was no real difference. I may mention, too, that I have visited modern schools, and observed that there is a tendency to hang printed pictures in an untidy and soulless manner on the walls, and occasionally to display on the mantelshelf a deplorable glass case containing certain objects which might possibly, if placed in the hands of the pupils, give them some practical experience of the weight of a pound and the length of an inch. And sometimes a scoundrel who has rifled a bird's nest or killed a harmless snake encourages the children to go and do likewise by putting his victims into an imitation nest and bottling and exhibiting them as aids to "Nature study." A suggestion that Nature is worth study would certainly have staggered my schoolmasters; so perhaps I may admit a gleam of progress here. But as any child who attempted to handle these dusty objects would probably be caned, I do not attach any importance to such modernities in school furniture. The school remains what it was in my boyhood, because its real object remains what it was. And that object, I repeat, is to keep the children out of mischief: mischief meaning for the most part worrying the grown-ups.

WHAT IS TO BE DONE?

The practical question, then, is what to do with the children. Tolerate them at home we will not. Let them run loose in the streets we dare not until our streets become safe places for children, which, to our utter shame, they are not at present, though they can hardly be worse than some homes and some schools.

The grotesque difficulty of making even a beginning was brought home to me by the lady of the manor in the little village in Hertfordshire where I write these lines. She asked me very properly what I was going to do for the village school. I did not know what to reply. As the school kept the children quiet during my working hours, I did not for the sake of my own personal convenience want to blow it up with dynamite as I should like to blow up most schools. So I asked for guidance. "You ought to give a prize" said the lady. I asked if there was a prize for good conduct. As I expected, there was: one for the best-behaved boy and another for the best-behaved girl. On reflection I offered a handsome prize for the worst-behaved boy and girl on condition that a record should be kept of their subsequent careers and compared with the records of the best-behaved, in order to ascertain whether the school criterion of good conduct was valid out of school. My offer was refused because it would not have had the effect of encouraging the children to give as little trouble as possible, which is of course the real object of all conduct prizes in schools.

I must not pretend, then, that I have a system ready to replace all the other systems. Obstructing the way of the proper organization of childhood, as of everything else, lies our ridiculous misdistribution of the national income, with its accompanying class distinctions and imposition of snobbery on children as a necessary part of their social training. The result of our economic folly is that we are a nation of undesirable acquaintances; and the first object of all our institutions for children is segregation. If, for example, our children were set free to roam and play about as they pleased, they would have to be policed; and the first duty of the police in a State like ours would be to see that every child wore a badge indicating its class in society, and that every child seen speaking to another child with a lower-class badge, or any child wearing a higher badge than that allotted to it by, say, the College of Heralds, should immediately be skinned alive with a birch rod. It might even be insisted that girls with high-class badges should be attended by footmen, grooms, or even military escorts. In short, there is hardly any limit to the follies with which our Commercialism would infect any system that it would tolerate at all. But something like a change of heart is still possible; and since all the evils of snobbery and segregation are rampant in our schools at present we may as well make the best as the worst of them.

CHILDREN'S RIGHTS AND DUTIES

Now let us ask what are a child's rights, and what are the rights of society over the child. Its rights, being clearly those of any other human being, are summed up in the right to live: that is, to have all the conclusive arguments that prove that it would be better dead, that it is a child of wrath, that the population is already excessive, that the pains of life are greater than its pleasures, that its sacrifice in a hospital or laboratory experiment might save millions of lives, etc. etc. etc., put out of the question, and its existence accepted as necessary and sacred, all theories to the contrary notwithstanding, whether by Calvin or Schopenhauer or Pasteur or the nearest person with a taste for infanticide. And this right to live includes, and in fact is, the right to be what the child likes and can, to do what it likes and can, to make what it likes and can, to think what it likes and can, to smash what it dislikes and can, and generally to behave in an altogether unaccountable manner within the limits imposed by the similar rights of its neighbors. And the rights of society over it clearly extend to requiring it to qualify itself to live in society without wasting other people's time: that is, it must know the rules of the road, be able to read placards and proclamations, fill voting papers, compose and send letters and telegrams, purchase food and clothing and railway tickets for itself, count money and give and take change, and, generally, know how many beans make five. It must know some law, were it only a simple set of commandments, some political economy, agriculture enough to shut the gates of fields with cattle in them and not to trample on growing crops, sanitation enough not to defile its haunts, and religion enough to have some idea of why it is allowed its rights and why it must respect the rights of others. And the rest of its education must consist of anything else it can pick up; for beyond this society cannot go with any certainty, and indeed can only go this far rather apologetically and provisionally, as doing the best it can on very uncertain ground.

SHOULD CHILDREN EARN THEIR LIVING?

Now comes the question how far children should be asked to contribute to the support of the community. In approaching it we must put aside the considerations that now induce all humane and thoughtful political students to agitate for the uncompromising abolition of child labor under our capitalist system. It is not the least of the curses of that system that it will bequeath to future generations a mass of legislation to prevent capitalists from "using up nine generations of men in one generation," as they began by doing until they were restrained by law at the suggestion of Robert Owen, the founder of English Socialism. Most of this legislation will become an insufferable restraint upon freedom and variety of action when Capitalism goes the way of Druidic human sacrifice (a much less slaughterous institution). There is every reason why a child should not be allowed to work for commercial profit or for the support of its parents at the expense of its own future; but there is no reason whatever why a child should not do some work for its own sake and that of the community if it can be shewn that both it and the community will be the better for it.

CHILDREN'S HAPPINESS

Also it is important to put the happiness of the children rather carefully in its place, which is really not a front place. The unsympathetic, selfish, hard people who regard happiness as a very exceptional indulgence to which children are by no means entitled, though they may be allowed a very little of it on their birthdays or at Christmas, are sometimes better parents in effect than those who imagine that children are as capable of happiness as adults. Adults habitually exaggerate their own capacity in that direction grossly; yet most adults can stand an allowance of happiness that would be quite thrown away on children. The secret of being miserable is to have leisure to bother about whether you are happy or not. The cure for it is occupation, because occupation means pre-occupation; and the pre-occupied person is neither happy nor unhappy, but simply alive and active, which is pleasanter than any happiness until you are tired of it. That is why it is necessary to happiness that one should be tired. Music after dinner is pleasant: music before breakfast is so unpleasant as to be clearly unnatural. To people who are not overworked holidays are a nuisance. To people who are, and who can afford them, they are a troublesome necessity. A perpetual holiday is a good working definition of hell.

THE HORROR OF THE PERPETUAL HOLIDAY

It will be said here that, on the contrary, heaven is always conceived as a perpetual holiday, and that whoever is not born to an independent income is striving for one or longing for one because it gives holidays for life. To which I reply, first, that heaven, as conventionally conceived, is a place so inane, so dull, so useless, so miserable, that nobody has ever ventured to describe a whole day in heaven, though plenty of people have described a day at the seaside; and that the genuine popular verdict on it is expressed in the proverb "Heaven for holiness and Hell for company." Second, I point out that the wretched people who have independent incomes and no useful occupation, do the most amazingly disagreeable and dangerous things to make themselves tired and hungry in the evening. When they are not involved in what they call sport, they are doing aimlessly what other people have to be paid to do: driving horses and motor cars; trying on dresses and walking up and down to shew them off; and acting as footmen and housemaids to royal personages. The sole and obvious cause of the notion that idleness is delightful and that heaven is a place where there is nothing to be done, is our school system and our industrial system. The school is a prison in which work is a punishment and a curse. In avowed prisons, hard labor, the only alleviation of a prisoner's lot, is treated as an aggravation of his punishment; and everything possible is done to intensify the prisoner's inculcated and unnatural notion that work is an evil. In industry we are overworked and underfed prisoners. Under such absurd circumstances our judgment of things becomes as perverted as our habits. If we were habitually underworked and overfed, our notion of heaven would be a place where everybody worked strenuously for twenty-four hours a day and never got anything to eat.

Once realize that a perpetual holiday is beyond human endurance, and that "Satan finds some mischief still for idle hands to do" and it will be seen that we have no right to impose a perpetual holiday on children. If we did, they would soon outdo the Labor Party in their claim for a Right to Work Bill.

In any case no child should be brought up to suppose that its food and clothes come down from heaven or are miraculously conjured from empty space by papa. Loathsome as we have made the idea of duty (like the idea of work) we must habituate children to a sense of repayable obligation to the community for what they consume and enjoy, and inculcate the repayment as a point of honor. If we did that today—and nothing but flat dishonesty prevents us from doing it—we should have no idle rich and indeed probably no rich, since there is no distinction in being rich if you have to pay scot and lot in personal effort like the working folk. Therefore, if for only half an hour a day, a child should do something serviceable to the community.

Productive work for children has the advantage that its discipline is the discipline of impersonal necessity, not that of wanton personal coercion. The eagerness of children in our industrial districts to escape from school to the factory is not caused by lighter tasks or shorter hours in the factory, nor altogether by the temptation of wages, nor even by the desire for novelty, but by the dignity of adult work, the exchange of the humiliating liability to personal assault from the lawless schoolmaster, from which the grown-ups are free, for the stern but entirely dignified pressure of necessity to which all flesh is subject.

UNIVERSITY SCHOOLBOYISHNESS

Older children might do a good deal before beginning their collegiate education. What is the matter with our universities is that the students are school children, whereas it is of the very essence of university education that they should be adults. The function of a university is not to teach things that can now be taught as well or better by University Extension lectures or by private tutors or modern correspondence classes with gramophones. We go to them to be socialized: to acquire the hall mark of communal training; to become citizens of the world instead of inmates of the enlarged rabbit hutches we call homes; to learn manners and become unchallengeable ladies and gentlemen. The social pressure which effects these changes should be that of persons who have faced the full responsibilities of adults as working members of the general community, not that of a rowdy rabble of half emancipated school children and unemancipable pedants. It is true that in a reasonable state of society this outside experience would do for us very completely what the university does now so corruptly that we tolerate its bad manners only because they are better than no manners at all. But the university will always exist in some form as a community of persons desirous of pushing their culture to the highest pitch they are capable of, not as solitary students reading in seclusion, but as members of a body of individuals all pursuing culture, talking culture, thinking culture, above all, criticizing culture. If such persons are to read and talk and criticize to any purpose, they must know the world outside the university at least as well as the shopkeeper in the High Street does. And this is just what they do not know at present. You may say of them, paraphrasing Mr. Kipling, "What do they know of Plato that only Plato know?" If our universities would exclude everybody who had not earned a living by his or her own exertions for at least a couple of years, their effect would be vastly improved.

THE NEW LAZINESS

The child of the future, then, if there is to be any future

but one of decay, will work more or less for its living from an early age; and in doing so it will not shock anyone, provided there be no longer any reason to associate the conception of children working for their living with infants toiling in a factory for ten hours a day or boys drudging from nine to six under gas lamps in underground city offices. Lads and lasses in their teens will probably be able to produce as much as the most expensive person now costs in his own person (it is retinue that eats up the big income) without working too hard or too long for quite as much happiness as they can enjoy. The question to be balanced then will be, not how soon people should be put to work, but how soon they should be released from any obligation of the kind. A life's work is like a day's work: it can begin early and leave off early or begin late and leave off late, or, as with us, begin too early and never leave off at all, obviously the worst of all possible plans. In any event we must finally reckon work, not as the curse our schools and prisons and capitalist profit factories make it seem today, but as a prime necessity of a tolerable existence. And if we cannot devise fresh wants as fast as we shorten the process of supplying the old ones, there will come a scarcity of work simultaneously with an excess of leisure. Work may have to be shared out among people who want more of it. Our spurious substitute, exercise, will not serve. A new sort of laziness will become the bugbear of society: the laziness that refuses to face the mental toil and adventure of making work by inventing new ideas or extending the domain of knowledge, and insists on a ready-made routine. It may come to forcing people to retire before they are willing to make way for younger ones: that is, to driving all persons of a certain age out of industry, leaving them to find something experimental to occupy them on pain of perpetual holiday. Men will then try to spend twenty thousand a year for the sake of having to earn it. Instead of being what we are now, the cheapest and nastiest of the animals, we shall be the costliest, most fastidious, and best bred. In short, there is no end to the astonishing things that may happen when the curse of Adam becomes first a blessing and then an incurable habit. And in view of that day we must not grudge children their share of it.

THE INFINITE SCHOOL TASK

The question of children's work, however, is only a question of what the child ought to do for the community. How highly it should qualify itself is another matter. But most of the difficulty of inducing children to learn would disappear if our demands became not only definite but finite. When learning is only an excuse for imprisonment, it is an instrument of torture which becomes more painful the more progress is made. Thus when you have forced a child to learn the Church Catechism, a document profound beyond the comprehension of most adults, you are sometimes at a standstill for something else to teach; and you therefore keep the wretched child repeating its catechism again and again until you hit on the plan of making it learn instalments of Bible verses, preferably from the book of Numbers. But as it is less trouble to set a lesson that you know yourself, there is a tendency to keep repeating the already learnt lesson rather than break new ground. At school I began with a fairly complete knowledge of Latin grammar in the childish sense of being able to repeat all the paradigms; and I was kept at this, or rather kept in a class where the master never asked me to do it because he knew I could, and therefore devoted himself to trapping the boys who could not, until I finally forgot most of it. But when progress took place, what did it mean? First it meant Caesar, with the foreknowledge that to master Caesar meant only being set at Virgil, with the culminating horror of Greek and Homer in reserve at the end of that. I preferred Caesar, because his statement that Gaul is divided into three parts, though neither interesting nor true, was the only Latin sentence I could translate at sight: therefore the longer we stuck at Caesar the better I was pleased. Just so do less classically educated children see nothing in the mastery of addition but the beginning of subtraction, and so on through multiplication and division and fractions, with the black cloud of algebra on the horizon. And if a boy rushes through all that, there is always the calculus to fall back on, unless indeed you insist on his learning music, and proceed to hit him if he cannot tell you the year Beethoven was born.

A child has a right to finality as regards its compulsory lessons. Also as regards physical training. At present it is assumed that the schoolmaster has a right to force every child into an attempt to become Porson and Bentley, Leibnitz and Newton, all rolled into one. This is the tradition of the oldest grammar schools. In our times an even more horrible and cynical claim has been made for the right to drive boys through compulsory games in the playing fields until they are too much exhausted physically to do anything but drop off to sleep. This is supposed to protect them from vice; but as it also protects them from poetry, literature, music, meditation and prayer, it may be dismissed with the obvious remark that if boarding schools are places whose keepers are driven to such monstrous measures lest more abominable things should happen, then the sooner boarding schools are violently abolished the better. It is true that society may make physical claims on the child as well as mental ones: the child must learn to walk, to use a knife and fork, to swim, to ride a bicycle, to acquire sufficient power of self-defence to make an attack on it an arduous and uncertain enterprise, perhaps to fly. What as a matter of common sense it clearly has not a right to do is to make this an excuse for keeping the child slaving for ten hours at physical exercises on the ground that it is not yet as dexterous as Cinquevalli and as strong as Sandow.

THE REWARDS AND RISKS OF KNOWLEDGE

In a word, we cannot completely educate a child; for its education can end only with its life and will not even then be complete. Compulsory completion of education is the last folly of a rotten and desperate civilization. All we can fairly do is to prescribe definite acquirements and accomplishments as qualifications for citizenship in general, with further specific qualifications for professional employments; and to secure them, not by the ridiculous method of inflicting artificial injuries on the persons who have not yet mastered them, but by the natural co-operation of self-respect from within with social respect from without.

Most acquirements carry their own privileges with them. Thus a baby has to be pretty closely guarded and imprisoned because it cannot take care of itself. It has even to be carried about (the most complete conceivable infringement of its liberty) until it can walk. But nobody goes on carrying children after they can walk lest they should walk into mischief, though Arab boys make their sisters carry them, as our own spoiled children sometimes make their nurses, out of mere laziness, because sisters in the East and nurses in the West are kept in servitude. But in a society of equals (the only reasonable and permanently possible sort of society) children are in much greater danger of acquiring bandy legs through being left to walk before they are strong enough than of being carried when they are well able to walk. Anyhow, freedom of movement in a nursery is the reward of learning to walk; and in precisely the same way freedom of movement in a city is the reward of learning how to read public notices, and to count and use money. The consequences are of course much larger than the mere ability to read the name of a street or the number of a railway platform and the destination of a train. When you enable a child to read these, you also enable it to read this preface, to the utter destruction, you may quite possibly think, of its morals (its docility). You also expose it to the danger of being run over by taxicabs and trains. The moral and physical risks of education are enormous: every new power a child acquires, from speaking, walking, and co-ordinating its vision, to conquering continents and founding religions, opens up immense new possibilities of mischief. Teach a child to write and you teach it how to forge: teach it to speak and you teach it how to lie: teach it to walk and you teach it how to kick its mother to death.

PARENTS AND CHILDREN

The great problem of slavery for those whose aim is to maintain it is the problem of reconciling the efficiency of the slave with the helplessness that keeps him in servitude; and this problem is fortunately not completely soluble; for it is not in fact found possible for a duke to treat his solicitor or his doctor as he treats his laborers, though they are all equally his slaves: the laborer being in fact less dependent on his favor than the professional man. Hence it is that men come to resent, of all things, protection, because it so often means restriction of their liberty lest they should make a bad use of it. If there are dangerous precipices about it, it is much easier and cheaper to forbid people to walk near the edge than to put up an effective fence: that is why both legislators and parents and the paid deputies of parents are always inhibiting and prohibiting and punishing and scolding and laming and cramping and delaying progress and growth instead of making the dangerous places as safe as possible and then boldly taking and allowing others to take the irreducible minimum of risk.

ENGLISH PHYSICAL HARDIHOOD AND SPIRITUAL COWARDICE

It is easier to convert most people to the need for allowing their children to run physical risks than moral ones. I can remember a relative of mine who, when I was a small child, unused to horses and very much afraid of them, insisted on putting me on a rather rumbustious pony with little spurs on my heels (knowing that in my agitation I would use them unconsciously), and being enormously amused at my terrors. Yet when that same lady discovered that I had found a copy of The Arabian Nights and was devouring it with avidity, she was horrified, and hid it away from me lest it should break my soul as the pony might have broken my neck. This way of producing hardy bodies and timid souls is so common in country houses that you may spend hours in them listening to stories of broken collar bones, broken backs, and broken necks without coming upon a single spiritual adventure or daring thought.

But whether the risks to which liberty exposes us are moral or physical, our right to liberty involves the right to run them. A man who is not free to risk his neck as an aviator or his soul as a heretic is not free at all; and the right to liberty begins, not at the age of 21 years but of 21 seconds.

THE RISKS OF IGNORANCE AND WEAKNESS

The difficulty with children is that they need protection from risks they are too young to understand, and attacks they can neither avoid nor resist. You may on academic grounds allow a child to snatch glowing coals from the fire once. You will not do it twice. The risks of liberty we must let everyone take; but the risks of ignorance and self-helplessness are another matter. Not only children but adults need protection from them. At present adults are often exposed to risks outside their knowledge or beyond their comprehension or powers of resistance or foresight: for example, we have to look on every day at marriages or financial speculations that may involve far worse consequences than burnt fingers. And just as it is part of the business of adults to protect children, to feed them, clothe them, shelter them, and shift for them in all sorts of ways until they are able to shift for themselves, it is coming more and more to be seen that this is true not only of the relation between adults and children, but between adults and adults. We shall not always look on indifferently at foolish marriages and financial speculations, nor allow dead men to control live communities by ridiculous wills and living heirs to squander and ruin great estates, nor tolerate a hundred other absurd liberties that we allow today because we are too lazy to find out the proper way to interfere. But the interference must be regulated by some theory of the individual's rights. Though the right to live is absolute, it is not unconditional. If a man is unbearably mischievous, he must be killed. This is a mere matter of necessity, like the killing of a man-eating tiger in a nursery, a venomous snake in the garden, or a fox in the poultry yard. No society could be constructed on the assumption that such extermination is a violation of the creature's right to live, and therefore must not be allowed. And then at once arises the danger into which morality has led us: the danger of persecution. One Christian spreading his doctrines may seem more mischievous than a dozen thieves: throw him therefore to the lions. A lying or disobedient child may corrupt a whole generation and make human Society impossible: therefore thrash the vice out of him. And so on until our whole system of abortion, intimidation, tyranny, cruelty and the rest is in full swing again.

THE COMMON SENSE OF TOLERATION

The real safeguard against this is the dogma of Toleration. I need not here repeat the compact treatise on it which I prepared for the Joint Committee on the Censorship of Stage Plays, and prefixed to The Shewing Up of Blanco Posnet. It must suffice now to say that the present must not attempt to schoolmaster the future by pretending to know good from evil in tendency, or protect citizens against shocks to their opinions and convictions, moral, political or religious: in other words it must not persecute doctrines of any kind, or what is called bad taste, and must insist on all persons facing such shocks as they face frosty weather or any of the other disagreeable, dangerous, or bracing incidents of freedom. The expediency of Toleration has been forced on us by the fact that progressive enlightenment depends on a fair hearing for doctrines which at first appear seditious, blasphemous, and immoral, and which deeply shock people who never think originally, thought being with them merely a habit and an echo. The deeper ground for Toleration is the nature of creation, which, as we now know, proceeds by evolution. Evolution finds its way by experiment; and this finding of the way varies according to the stage of development reached, from the blindest groping along the line of least resistance to conscious intellectual speculation, with its routine of hypothesis and verification, induction and deduction; or even into so rapid and intuitive an integration of all these processes in a single brain that we get the inspired guess of the man of genius and the fanatical resolution of the teacher of new truths who is first slain as a blasphemous apostate and then worshipped as a prophet.

Here the law for the child is the same as for the adult. The high priest must not rend his garments and cry "Crucify him" when he is shocked, nor the atheist clamor for the suppression of Law's Serious Call because it has for two centuries destroyed the natural happiness of innumerable children by persuading pious parents that it is a religious duty to make children miserable. It, and the Sermon on the Mount, and Machiavelli's Prince, and La Rochefoucauld's maxims, and Hymns Ancient and Modern, and De Glanville's apologue, and Dr. Watt's rhymes, and Nietzsche's Gay Science, and Ingersoll's Mistakes of Moses, and the speeches and pamphlets of the people who want us to make war on Germany, and the Noodle's Orations and articles of our politicians and journalists, must all be tolerated not only because any of them may for all we know be on the right track but because it is in the conflict of opinion that we win knowledge and wisdom. However terrible the wounds suffered in that conflict, they are better than the barren peace of death that follows when all the combatants are slaughtered or bound hand and foot.

The difficulty at present is that though this necessity for Toleration is a law of political science as well established as the law of gravitation, our rulers are never taught political science: on the contrary, they are taught in school that the master tolerates nothing that is disagreeable to him; that ruling is simply being master; and that the master's method is the method of violent punishment. And our citizens, all school taught, are walking in the same darkness. As I write these lines the Home Secretary is explaining that he must not release a man who has been imprisoned for blasphemy, as his remarks were painful to the feelings of his pious fellow townsmen. Now it happens that this very Home Secretary has driven many thousands of his fellow citizens almost beside themselves by the crudity of his notions of government, and his simple inability to understand why he should not use and make laws to torment and subdue people who do not happen to agree with him. In a word, he is not a politician, but a grown-up schoolboy who has at last got a cane in his hand. And as all the rest of us are in the same condition (except as to command of the cane) the only objection made to his proceedings takes the shape of clamorous demands that *he* should be caned instead of being allowed to cane other people.

THE SIN OF ATHANASIUS

It seems hopeless. Anarchists are tempted to preach a violent and implacable resistance to all law as the only remedy; and the result of that speedily is that people welcome any tyranny that will rescue them from chaos. But there is really no need to choose between anarchy and tyranny. A quite reasonable state of things is practicable if we proceed on human assumptions and not on academic ones. If adults will frankly give up their claim to know better than children what the purposes of the Life Force are, and treat the child as an experiment like themselves, and possibly a more successful one, and at the same time relinquish their monstrous parental claims to personal private property in children, the rest may be left to common sense. It is our attitude, our religion, that is wrong. A good beginning might be made by enacting that any person dictating a piece of conduct to a child or to anyone else as the will of God, or as absolutely right, should be dealt with as a blasphemer: as, indeed, guilty of the unpardonable sin against the Holy Ghost. If the penalty were death, it would rid us at once of that scourge of humanity, the amateur Pope. As an Irish Protestant, I raise the cry of No Popery with hereditary zest. We are overrun with Popes. From curates and governesses, who may claim a sort of professional standing, to parents and uncles and nurserymaids and school teachers and wiseacres generally, there are scores of thousands of human insects groping through our darkness by the feeble phosphorescence of their own tails, yet ready at a moment's notice to reveal the will of God on every possible subject; to explain how and why the universe was made (in my youth they added the exact date) and the circumstances under which it will cease to exist; to lay down precise rules of right and wrong conduct; to discriminate infallibly between virtuous and vicious character; and this with such certainty that they are prepared to visit all the rigors of the law, and all the ruinous penalties of social ostracism on those, however harmless their actions may be, who venture to laugh at their monstrous conceit or to pay their assumptions the extravagant compliment of criticizing them. As to children, who shall say what canings and birchings and terrifyings and threats of hell fire and impositions and humiliations and petty imprisonings and sendings to bed and standing in corners and the like they have suffered because their parents and guardians and teachers knew everything so much better than Socrates or Solon?

It is this ignorant uppishness that does the mischief. A stranger on the planet might expect that its grotesque absurdity would provoke enough ridicule to cure it; but unfortunately quite the contrary happens. Just as our ill health delivers us into the hands of medical quacks and creates a passionate demand for impudent pretences that doctors can cure the diseases they themselves die of daily, so our ignorance and helplessness set us clamoring for spiritual and moral quacks who pretend that they can save our souls from their own damnation. If a doctor were to say to his patients, "I am familiar with your symptoms, because I have seen other people in your condition; and I will bring the very little knowledge we have to your treatment; but except in that very shallow sense I dont know what is the matter with you; and I cant undertake to cure you" he would be a lost man professionally; and if a clergyman, on being called on to award a prize for good conduct in the village school, were to say, "I am afraid I cannot say who is the best-behaved child, because I really do not know what good conduct is;

but I will gladly take the teacher's word as to which child has caused least inconvenience" he would probably be unfrocked, if not excommunicated. And yet no honest and intellectually capable doctor or parson can say more. Clearly it would not be wise of the doctor to say it, because optimistic lies have such immense therapeutic value that a doctor who cannot tell them convincingly has mistaken his profession. And a clergyman who is not prepared to lay down the law dogmatically will not be of much use in a village school, though it behoves him all the more to be very careful what law he lays down. But unless both the clergyman and the doctor are in the attitude expressed by these speeches they are not fit for their work. The man who believes that he has more than a provisional hypothesis to go upon is a born fool. He may have to act vigorously on it. The world has no use for the Agnostic who wont believe anything because anything might be false, and wont deny anything because anything might be true. But there is a wide difference between saying, "I believe this; and I am going to act on it," or, "I dont believe it; and I wont act on it," and saying, "It is true; and it is my duty and yours to act on it," or, "It is false; and it is my duty and yours to refuse to act on it." The difference is as great as that between the Apostles' Creed and the Athanasian Creed. When you repeat the Apostles' Creed you affirm that you believe certain things. There you are clearly within your rights. When you repeat the Athanasian Creed, you affirm that certain things are so, and that anybody who doubts that they are so cannot be saved. And this is simply a piece of impudence on your part, as you know nothing about it except that as good men as you have never heard of your creed. The apostolic attitude is a desire to convert others to our beliefs for the sake of sympathy and light: the Athanasian attitude is a desire to murder people who dont agree with us. I am sufficient of an Athanasian to advocate a law for the speedy execution of all Athanasians, because they violate the fundamental proposition of my creed, which is, I repeat, that all living creatures are experiments.

The precise formula for the Superman, *ci-devant* The Just Man Made Perfect, has not yet been discovered. Until it is, every birth is an experiment in the Great Research which is being conducted by the Life Force to discover that formula.

THE EXPERIMENT EXPERIMENTING

And now all the modern schoolmaster abortionists will rise up beaming, and say, "We quite agree. We regard every child in our school as a subject for experiment. We are always experimenting with them. We challenge the experimental test for our system. We are continually guided by our experience in our great work of moulding the character of our future citizens, etc. etc. etc." I am sorry to seem irreconcilable; but it is the Life Force that has to make the experiment and not the schoolmaster; and the Life Force for the child's purpose is in the child and not in the schoolmaster. The schoolmaster is another experiment; and a laboratory in which all the experiments began experimenting on one another would not produce intelligible results. I admit, however, that if my schoolmasters had treated me as an experiment of the Life Force: that is, if they had set me free to do as I liked subject only to my political rights and theirs, they could not have watched the experiment very long, because the first result would have been a rapid movement on my part in the direction of the door, and my disappearance therethrough.

It may be worth inquiring where I should have gone to. I should say that practically every time I should have gone to a much more educational place. I should have gone into the country, or into the sea, or into the National Gallery, or to hear a band if there was one, or to any library where there were no schoolbooks. I should have read very dry and difficult books: for example, though nothing would have induced me to read the budget of stupid party lies that served as a text-book of history in school, I remember reading Robertson's Charles V. and his history of Scotland from end to end most laboriously. Once, stung by the airs of a schoolfellow who alleged that he had read Locke On The Human

Understanding, I attempted to read the Bible straight through, and actually got to the Pauline Epistles before I broke down in disgust at what seemed to me their inveterate crookedness of mind. If there had been a school where children were really free, I should have had to be driven out of it for the sake of my health by the teachers; for the children to whom a literary education can be of any use are insatiable: they will read and study far more than is good for them. In fact the real difficulty is to prevent them from wasting their time by reading for the sake of reading and studying for the sake of studying, instead of taking some trouble to find out what they really like and are capable of doing some good at. Some silly person will probably interrupt me here with the remark that many children have no appetite for a literary education at all, and would never open a book if they were not forced to. I have known many such persons who have been forced to the point of obtaining University degrees. And for all the effect their literary exercises has left on them they might just as well have been put on the treadmill. In fact they are actually less literate than the treadmill would have left them; for they might now by chance pick up and dip into a volume of Shakespear or a translation of Homer if they had not been driven to loathe every famous name in literature. I should probably know as much Latin as French, if Latin had not been made the excuse for my school imprisonment and degradation.

WHY WE LOATHE LEARNING AND LOVE SPORT

If we are to discuss the importance of art, learning, and intellectual culture, the first thing we have to recognize is that we have very little of them at present; and that this little has not been produced by compulsory education: nay, that the scarcity is unnatural and has been produced by the violent exclusion of art and artists from schools. On the other hand we have quite a considerable degree of bodily culture: indeed there is a continual outcry against the sacrifice of mental accomplishments to athletics. In other words a sacrifice of the professed object of compulsory education to the real object of voluntary education. It is assumed that this means that people prefer bodily to mental culture; but may it not mean that they prefer liberty and satisfaction to coercion and privation. Why is it that people who have been taught Shakespear as a school subject loathe his plays and cannot by any means be persuaded ever to open his works after they escape from school, whereas there is still, 300 years after his death, a wide and steady sale for his works to people who regard his plays as plays, not as task work? If Shakespear, or for that matter, Newton and Leibnitz, are allowed to find their readers and students they will find them. If their works are annotated and paraphrased by dullards, and the annotations and paraphrases forced on all young people by imprisonment and flogging and scolding, there will not be a single man of letters or higher mathematician the more in the country: on the contrary there will be less, as so many potential lovers of literature and mathematics will have been incurably prejudiced against them. Everyone who is conversant with the class in which child imprisonment and compulsory schooling is carried out to the final extremity of the university degree knows that its scholastic culture is a sham; that it knows little about literature or art and a great deal about point-to-point races; and that the village cobbler, who has never read a page of Plato, and is admittedly a dangerously ignorant man politically, is nevertheless a Socrates compared to the classically educated gentlemen who discuss politics in country houses at election time (and at no other time) after their day's earnest and skilful shooting. Think of the years and years of weary torment the women of the piano-possessing class have been forced to spend over the keyboard, fingering scales. How many of them could be bribed to attend a pianoforte recital by a great player, though they will rise from sick beds rather than miss Ascot or Goodwood?

Another familiar fact that teaches the same lesson is that many women who have voluntarily attained a high degree of culture cannot add up their own housekeeping books, though their education in simple arithmetic was compulsory, whereas their higher education has been wholly voluntary. Everywhere we find the same result. The imprisonment, the beating, the taming and laming, the breaking of young spirits, the arrest of development, the atrophy of all inhibitive power except the power of fear, are real: the education is sham. Those who have been taught most know least.

ANTICHRIST

Among the worst effects of the unnatural segregation of children in schools and the equally unnatural constant association of them with adults in the family is the utter defeat of the vital element in Christianity. Christ stands in the world for that intuition of the highest humanity that we, being members one of another, must not complain, must not scold, must not strike, nor revile nor persecute nor revenge nor punish. Now family life and school life are, as far as the moral training of children is concerned, nothing but the deliberate inculcation of a routine of complaint, scolding, punishment, persecution, and revenge as the natural and only possible way of dealing with evil or inconvenience. "Aint nobody to be whopped for this here?" exclaimed Sam Weller when he saw his employer's name written up on a stage coach, and conceived the phenomenon as an insult which reflected on himself. This exclamation of Sam Weller is at once the negation of Christianity and the beginning and the end of current morality; and so it will remain as long as the family and the school persist as we know them: that is, as long as the rights of children are so utterly denied that nobody will even take the trouble to ascertain what they are, and coming of age is like the turning of a convict into the streets after twenty-one years penal servitude. Indeed it is worse; for the convict, having learnt before his conviction how to live at large, may remember how to set about it, however lamed his power of initiative may have become through disuse; but the child knows no other way of life than the slave's way. Born free, as Rousseau says, he has been laid hands on by slaves from the moment of his birth and brought up as a slave. How is he, when he is at last set free, to be anything else than the slave he actually is, clamoring for war, for the lash, for police, prisons, and scaffolds in a wild panic of delusion that without these things he is lost. The grown-up Englishman is to the end of his days a badly brought-up child, beyond belief quarrelsome, petulant, selfish, destructive, and cowardly: afraid that the Germans will come and enslave him; that the burglar will come and rob him; that the bicycle or motor car will run over him; that the smallpox will attack him; and that the devil will run away with him and empty him out like a sack of coals on a blazing fire unless his nurse or his parents or his schoolmaster or his bishop or his judge or his army or his navy will do something to frighten these bad things away. And this Englishman, without the moral courage of a louse, will risk his neck for fun fifty times every winter in the hunting field, and at Badajos sieges and the like will ram his head into a hole bristling with sword blades rather than be beaten in the one department in which he has been brought up to consult his own honor. As a Sportsman (and war is fundamentally the sport of hunting and fighting the most dangerous of the beasts of prey) he feels free. He will tell you himself that the true sportsman is never a snob, a coward, a duffer, a cheat, a thief, or a liar. Curious, is it not, that he has not the same confidence in other sorts of man?

And even sport is losing its freedom. Soon everybody will be schooled, mentally and physically, from the cradle to the end of the term of adult compulsory military service, and finally of compulsory civil service lasting until the age of superannuation. Always more schooling, more compulsion. We are to be cured by an excess of the dose that has poisoned us. Satan is to cast out Satan.

UNDER THE WHIP

Clearly this will not do. We must reconcile education with liberty. We must find out some means of making men workers and, if need be, warriors, without making them slaves. We must cultivate the noble virtues that have their root in pride. Now no schoolmaster will teach these any more than a prison governor will teach his prisoners how to mutiny and escape. Self-preservation forces him to break the spirit that revolts against him, and to inculcate submission, even to obscene assault, as a duty. A bishop once had the hardihood to say that he would rather see England free than England sober. Nobody has yet dared to say that he would rather see an England of ignoramuses than an England of cowards and slaves. And if anyone did, it would be necessary to point out that the antithesis is not a practical one, as we have at present an England of ignoramuses who are also cowards and slaves, and patriotically proud of it at that, because in school they are taught to submit, with what they ridiculously call Oriental fatalism (as if any Oriental has ever submitted more helplessly and sheepishly to robbery and oppression than we Occidentals do), to be driven day after day into compounds and set to the tasks they loathe by the men they hate and fear, as if this were the inevitable destiny of mankind. And naturally, when they grow up, they helplessly exchange the prison of the school for the prison of the mine or the workshop or the office, and drudge along stupidly and miserably, with just enough gregarious instinct to turn furiously on any intelligent person who proposes a change. It would be quite easy to make England a paradise, according to our present ideas, in a few years. There is no mystery about it: the way has been pointed out over and over again. The difficulty is not the way but the will. And we have no will because the first thing done with us in childhood was to break our will. Can anything be more disgusting than the spectacle of a nation reading the biography of Gladstone and gloating over the account of how he was flogged at Eton, two of his schoolfellows being compelled to hold him down whilst he was flogged. Not long ago a public body in England had to deal with the case of a schoolmaster who, conceiving himself insulted by the smoking of a cigaret against his orders by a pupil eighteen years old, proposed to flog him publicly as a satisfaction to what he called his honor and authority. I had intended to give the particulars of this case, but find the drudgery of raking over such stuff too sickening, and the effect unjust to a man who was doing only what others all over the country were doing as part of the established routine of what is called education. The astounding part of it was the manner in which the person to whom this outrage on decency seemed quite proper and natural claimed to be a functionary of high character, and had his claim allowed. In Japan he would hardly have been allowed the privilege of committing suicide. What is to be said of a profession in which such obscenities are made points of honor, or of institutions in which they are an accepted part of the daily routine? Wholesome people would not argue about the taste of such nastinesses: they would spit them out; but we are tainted with flagellomania from our childhood. When will we realize that the fact that we can become accustomed to anything, however disgusting at first, makes it necessary for us to examine carefully everything we have become accustomed to? Before motor cars became common, necessity had accustomed us to a foulness in our streets which would have horrified us had the street been our drawing room carpet. Before long we shall be as particular about our streets as we now are about our carpets; and their condition in the nineteenth century will become as forgotten and incredible as the condition of the corridors of palaces and the courts of castles was as late as the eighteenth century. This foulness, we can plead, was imposed on us as a necessity by the use of horses and of huge retinues; but flogging has never been so imposed: it has always been a vice, craved for on any pretext by those depraved by it. Boys were flogged when criminals were hanged, to impress the awful warning on them. Boys were flogged at boundaries, to impress the boundaries on their memory. Other methods and other punishments were always available: the choice of this one betrayed the sensual impulse which makes the practice an abomination. But when its viciousness made it customary, it was practised and tolerated on all hands by people who were innocent of anything worse than stupidity, ill temper, and inability to discover other methods of maintaining order than those they had always seen practised and approved of. From children and animals it extended to slaves and criminals. In the days of Moses it was limited to 39 lashes. In the early nineteenth century it had become an open madness: soldiers were sentenced to a thousand lashes for trifling offences, with the result (among others less mentionable) that the Iron Duke of Wellington complained that it was impossible to get an order obeyed in the British army except in two or three crack regiments. Such frantic excesses of this disgusting neurosis provoked a reaction against it; but the clamor for it by depraved persons never ceased, and was tolerated by a nation trained to it from childhood in the schools until last year (1913), when, in what must be described as a paroxysm of sexual excitement provoked by the agitation concerning the White Slave Traffic (the purely commercial nature of which I was prevented from exposing on the stage by the Censorship twenty years ago), the Government yielded to an outcry for flagellation led by the Archbishop of Canterbury, and passed an Act under which a judge can sentence a man to be flogged to the utmost extremity with any instrument usable for such a purpose that he cares to prescribe. Such an Act is not a legislative phenomenon but a psychopathic one. Its effect on the White Slave Traffic was, of course, to distract public attention from its real cause and from the people who really profit by it to imaginary "foreign scoundrels," and to secure a monopoly of its organization for women.

And all this evil is made possible by the schoolmaster with his cane and birch, by the parents getting rid as best they can of the nuisance of children making noise and mischief in the house, and by the denial to children of the elementary rights of human beings.

The first man who enslaved and "broke in" an animal

with a whip would have invented the explosion engine instead could he have foreseen the curse he was laying on his race. For men and women learnt thereby to enslave and break in their children by the same means. These children, grown up, knew no other methods of training. Finally the evil that was done for gain by the greedy was refined on and done for pleasure by the lustful. Flogging has become a pleasure purchasable in our streets, and inhibition a grown-up habit that children play at. "Go and see what baby is doing; and tell him he mustnt" is the last word of the nursery; and the grimmest aspect of it is that it was first formulated by a comic paper as a capital joke.

TECHNICAL INSTRUCTION

Technical instruction tempts to violence (as a short cut) more than liberal education. The sailor in Mr Rudyard Kipling's Captains Courageous, teaching the boy the names of the ship's tackle with a rope's end, does not disgust us as our schoolmasters do, especially as the boy was a spoiled boy. But an unspoiled boy would not have needed that drastic medicine. Technical training may be as tedious as learning to skate or to play the piano or violin; but it is the price one must pay to achieve certain desirable results or necessary ends. It is a monstrous thing to force a child to learn Latin or Greek or mathematics on the ground that they are an indispensable gymnastic for the mental powers. It would be monstrous even if it were true; for there is no labor that might not be imposed on a child or an adult on the same pretext; but as a glance at the average products of our public school and university education shews that it is not true, it need not trouble us. But it is a fact that ignorance of Latin and Greek and mathematics closes certain careers to men (I do not mean artificial, unnecessary, noxious careers like those of the commercial schoolmaster). Languages, even dead ones, have their uses; and, as it seems to many of us, mathematics have their uses. They will always be learned by people who want to learn them; and people will always want to learn them as long as they are of any importance in life:

indeed the want will survive their importance: superstition is nowhere stronger than in the field of obsolete acquirements. And they will never be learnt fruitfully by people who do not want to learn them either for their own sake or for use in necessary work. There is no harder schoolmaster than experience; and yet experience fails to teach where there is no desire to learn.

Still, one must not begin to apply this generalization too early. And this brings me to an important factor in the case: the factor of evolution.

DOCILITY AND DEPENDENCE

If anyone, impressed by my view that the rights of a child are precisely those of an adult, proceeds to treat a child as if it were an adult, he (or she) will find that though the plan will work much better at some points than the usual plan, at others it will not work at all; and this discovery may provoke him to turn back from the whole conception of children's rights with a jest at the expense of bachelors' and old maids' children. In dealing with children what is needed is not logic but sense. There is no logical reason why young persons should be allowed greater control of their property the day after they are twenty-one than the day before it. There is no logical reason why I, who strongly object to an adult standing over a boy of ten with a Latin grammar, and saying "you must learn this, whether you want to or not," should nevertheless be quite prepared to stand over a boy of five with the multiplication table or a copy book or a code of elementary good manners, and practise on his docility to make him learn them. And there is no logical reason why I should do for a child a great many little offices, some of them troublesome and disagreeable, which I should not do for a boy twice its age, or support a boy or girl when I would unhesitatingly throw an adult on his own resources. But there are practical reasons, and sensible reasons, and affectionate reasons for all these illogicalities. Children do not want to be treated altogether as adults: such treatment terrifies them and overburdens them with responsibility. In truth, very few adults care to be called on for independence and originality: they also are bewildered and terrified in the absence of precedents and precepts and commandments; but modern Democracy allows them a sanctioning and cancelling power if they are capable of using it, which children are not. To treat a child wholly as an adult would be to mock and destroy it. Infantile docility and juvenile dependence are, like death, a product of Natural Selection; and though there is no viler crime than to abuse them, yet there is no greater cruelty than to ignore them. I have complained sufficiently of what I suffered through the process of assault, imprisonment, and compulsory lessons that taught me nothing, which are called my schooling. But I could say a good deal also about the things I was not taught and should have been taught, not to mention the things I was allowed to do which I should not have been allowed to do. I have no recollection of being taught to read or write; so I presume I was born with both faculties; but many people seem to have bitter recollections of being forced reluctantly to acquire them. And though I have the uttermost contempt for a teacher so ill-mannered and incompetent as to be unable to make a child learn to read and write without also making it cry, still I am prepared to admit that I had rather have been compelled to learn to read and write with tears by an incompetent and ill-mannered person than left in ignorance. Reading, writing, and enough arithmetic to use money honestly and accurately, together with the rudiments of law and order, become necessary conditions of a child's liberty before it can appreciate the importance of its liberty, or foresee that these accomplishments are worth acquiring. Nature has provided for this by evolving the instinct of docility. Children are very docile: they have a sound intuition that they must do what they are told or perish. And adults have an intuition, equally sound, that they must take advantage of this docility to teach children how to live properly or the children will not survive. The difficulty is to know where to stop. To illustrate this, let us consider the main danger of childish docility and parental officiousness.

THE ABUSE OF DOCILITY

Docility may survive as a lazy habit long after it has ceased to be a beneficial instinct. If you catch a child when it is young enough to be instinctively docile, and keep it in a condition of unremitted tutelage under the nurserymaid, the governess, the preparatory school, the secondary school, and the university, until it is an adult, you will produce, not a self-reliant, free, fully matured human being, but a grown-up schoolboy or schoolgirl, capable of nothing in the way of original or independent action except outbursts of naughtiness in the women and blackguardism in the men. That is exactly what we get at present in our rich and consequently governing classes: they pass from juvenility to senility without ever touching maturity except in body. The classes which cannot afford this sustained tutelage are notably more self-reliant and grown-up: an office boy of fifteen is often more of a man than a university student of twenty. Unfortunately this precocity is disabled by poverty, ignorance, narrowness, and a hideous power of living without art or love or beauty and being rather proud of it. The poor never escape from servitude: their docility is preserved by their slavery. And so all become the prey of the greedy, the selfish, the domineering, the unscrupulous, the predatory. If here and there an individual refuses to be docile, ten docile persons will beat him or lock him up or shoot him or hang him at the bidding of his oppressors and their own. The crux of the whole difficulty about parents, schoolmasters, priests, absolute monarchs, and despots of every sort, is the tendency to abuse natural docility. A nation should always be healthily rebellious; but rulers have yet to be found who will make trouble for themselves by cultivating that side of the national spirit. A child should begin to assert itself early, and shift for itself more and more not only in washing and dressing itself, but in opinions and conduct; yet as nothing is so exasperating and so unlovable as an uppish child, it is useless to expect parents and schoolmasters to inculcate this uppishness. Such unamiable precepts as Always contradict an authoritative statement, Always return a blow, Never lose a chance of a good fight, When you are scolded for a mistake ask the person who scolds you whether he or she supposes you did it on purpose, and follow the question with a blow or an insult or some other unmistakeable expression of resentment, Remember that the progress of the world depends on your knowing better than your elders, are just as important as those of the sermon on the mount; but no one has yet seen them written up in letters of gold in a schoolroom or nursery. The child is taught to be kind, to be respectful, to be quiet, not to answer back, to be truthful when its elders want to find out anything from it, to lie when the truth would shock or hurt its elders, to be above all things obedient, and to be seen and not heard. Here we have two sets of precepts, each of which will spoil an ordinary child if the other be omitted. Unfortunately we do not allow fair play between them. The rebellious, intractable, aggressive, selfish set provoke a corrective resistance, and do not pretend to high moral or religious sanctions; and they are never urged by grown-up people on young people. They are therefore more in danger of neglect or suppression than the other set, which have all the adults, all the laws, all the religions on their side. How is the child to be secured its due share of both bodies of doctrine?

THE SCHOOLBOY AND THE HOMEBOY

In practice what happens is that parents notice that boys brought up at home become mollycoddles, or prigs, or duffers, unable to take care of themselves. They see that boys should learn to rough it a little and to mix with children of their own age. This is natural enough. When you have preached at and punished a boy until he is a moral cripple, you are as much hampered by him as by a physical cripple; and as you do not intend to have him on your hands all your life, and are generally rather impatient for the day when he will earn his own living and leave you to attend to yourself, you sooner or later begin to talk to him about the need for self-reliance, learning to think, and so forth, with the result that your victim, bewildered by your inconsistency, concludes that there is no use trying to please you, and falls into an attitude of sulky resentment. Which is an additional inducement to pack him off to school.

In school, he finds himself in a dual world, under two dispensations. There is the world of the boys, where the point of honor is to be untameable, always ready to fight, ruthless in taking the conceit out of anyone who ventures to give himself airs of superior knowledge or taste, and generally to take Lucifer for one's model. And there is the world of the masters, the world of discipline, submission, diligence, obedience, and continual and shameless assumption of moral and intellectual authority. Thus the schoolboy hears both sides, and is so far better off than the home-bred boy who hears only one. But the two sides are not fairly presented. They are presented as good and evil, as vice and virtue, as villainy and heroism. The boy feels mean and cowardly when he obeys, and selfish and rascally when he disobeys. He loses his moral courage just as he comes to hate books and languages. In the end, John Ruskin, tied so closely to his mother's apron-string that he did not escape even when he went to Oxford, and John Stuart Mill, whose father ought to have been prosecuted for laying his son's childhood waste with lessons, were superior, as products of training, to our schoolboys. They were very conspicuously superior in moral courage; and though they did not distinguish themselves at cricket and football, they had quite as much physical hardihood as any civilized man needs. But it is to be observed that Ruskin's parents were wise people who gave John a full share in their own life, and put up with his presence both at home and abroad when they must sometimes have been very weary of him; and Mill, as it happens, was deliberately educated to challenge all the most sacred institutions of his country. The households they were brought up in were no more average households than a Montessori school is an average school.

THE COMINGS OF AGE OF CHILDREN

All this inculcated adult docility, which wrecks every civilization as it is wrecking ours, is inhuman and unnatural. We must reconsider our institution of the Coming of Age, which is too late for some purposes, and too early for others. There should be a series of Coming of Ages for every individual. The mammals have their first coming of age when they are weaned; and it is noteworthy that this rather cruel and selfish operation on the part of the parent has to be performed resolutely, with claws and teeth; for your little mammal does not want to be weaned, and yields only to a pretty rough assertion of the right of the parent to be relieved of the child as soon as the child is old enough to bear the separation. The same thing occurs with children: they hang on to the mother's apron-string and the father's coat tails as long as they can, often baffling those sensitive parents who know that children should think for themselves and fend for themselves, but are too kind to throw them on their own resources with the ferocity of the domestic cat. The child should have its first coming of age when it is weaned, another when it can talk, another when it can walk, another when it can dress itself without assistance; and when it can read, write, count money, and pass an examination in going a simple errand involving a purchase and a journey by rail or other public method of locomotion, it should have quite a majority. At present the children of laborers are soon mobile and able to shift for themselves, whereas it is possible to find grown-up women in the rich classes who are actually afraid to take a walk in the streets unattended and unprotected. It is true that this is a superstition from the time when a retinue was part of the state of persons of quality, and the unattended person was supposed to be a common person of no quality, earning a living; but this has now become so absurd that children and young women are no longer told why they are forbidden to go about alone, and have to be persuaded that the streets are dangerous places, which of course they are; but people who are not educated to live dangerously have only half a life, and are more likely to die miserably after all than those who have taken all the common risks of freedom from their childhood onward as matters of course.

THE CONFLICT OF WILLS

The world wags in spite of its schools and its families because both schools and families are mostly very largely anarchic: parents and schoolmasters are good-natured or weak or lazy; and children are docile and affectionate and very shortwinded in their fits of naughtiness; and so most families slummock along and muddle through until the children cease to be children. In the few cases when the parties are energetic and determined, the child is crushed or the parent is reduced to a cipher, as the case may be. When the opposed forces are neither of them strong enough to annihilate the other, there is serious trouble: that is how we get those feuds between parent and child which recur to our memory so ironically when we hear people sentimentalizing about natural affection. We even get tragedies; for there is nothing so tragic to contemplate or so devastating to suffer as the oppression of will without conscience; and the whole tendency of our family and school system is to set the will of the parent and the school despot above conscience as something that must be deferred to abjectly and absolutely for its own sake.

The strongest, fiercest force in nature is human will. It is the highest organization we know of the will that has created the whole universe. Now all honest civilization, religion, law, and convention is an attempt to keep this force within beneficent bounds. What corrupts civilization, religion, law, and convention (and they are at present pretty nearly as corrupt as they dare) is the constant attempts made by the wills of individuals and classes to thwart the wills and enslave the powers of other individuals and classes. The powers of the parent and the schoolmaster, and of their public analogues the lawgiver and the judge, become instruments of tyranny in the hands of those who are too narrow-minded to understand law and exercise judgment; and in their hands (with us they mostly fall into such hands) law becomes tyranny. And what is a tyrant? Quite simply a person who says to another person, young or old "You shall do as I tell you; you shall make what I want; you shall profess my creed; you shall have no will of your own; and your powers shall be at the disposal of my will." It has come to this at last: that the phrase "she has a will of her own," or "he has a will of his own" has come to denote a person of exceptional obstinacy and self-assertion. And even persons of good natural disposition, if brought up to expect such deference, are roused to unreasoning fury, and sometimes to the commission of atrocious crimes, by the slightest challenge to their authority. Thus a laborer may be dirty, drunken, untruthful, slothful, untrustworthy in every way without exhausting the indulgence of the country house. But let him dare to be "disrespectful" and he is a lost man, though he be the cleanest, soberest, most diligent, most veracious, most trustworthy man in the county. Dickens's instinct for detecting social cankers never served him better than when he shewed us Mrs Heep teaching her son to "be umble," knowing that if he carried out that precept he might be pretty well anything else he liked. The maintenance of deference to our wills becomes a mania which will carry the best of us to any extremity. We will allow a village of Egyptian fellaheen or Indian tribesmen to live the lowest life they please among themselves without molestation; but let one of them slay an Englishman or even strike him on the strongest provocation, and straightway we go stark mad, burning and destroying, shooting and shelling, flogging, and hanging, if only such survivors as we may leave are thoroughly cowed in the presence of a man with a white face. In the committee room of a local council or city corporation, the humblest employees of the committee find defenders if they complain of harsh treatment. Gratuities are voted, indulgences and holidays are pleaded for, delinquencies are excused in the most sentimental manner provided only the employee, however patent a hypocrite or incorrigible a slacker, is hat in hand. But let the most obvious measure of justice be demanded by the secretary of a Trade Union in terms which omit all expressions of subservience, and it is with the greatest difficulty that the cooler-headed can defeat angry motions that the letter be thrown into the waste paper basket and the committee proceed to the next business.

THE DEMAGOGUE'S OPPORTUNITY

And the employee has in him the same fierce impulse to impose his will without respect for the will of others. Democracy is in practice nothing but a device for cajoling from him the vote he refuses to arbitrary authority. He will not vote for Coriolanus; but when an experienced demagogue comes along and says "Sir: *you* are the dictator: the voice of the people is the voice of God; and I am only your very humble servant" he says at once "All right: tell me what to dictate" and is presently enslaved more effectually with his own silly consent than Coriolanus would ever have enslaved him without asking his leave. And the trick by which the demagogue defeats Coriolanus is played on him in his turn by *his* inferiors. Everywhere we see the cunning succeeding in the world by seeking a rich or powerful master and practising on his lust for subservience. The political adventurer who gets into parliament by offering himself to the poor voter, not as his representative but as his will-less soulless "delegate," is himself the dupe of a clever wife who repudiates Votes for Women, knowing well that whilst the man is master, the man's mistress will rule. Uriah Heep may be a crawling creature; but his crawling takes him upstairs.

Thus does the selfishness of the will turn on itself, and obtain by flattery what it cannot seize by open force. Democracy becomes the latest trick of tyranny: "womanliness" becomes the latest wile of prostitution.

Between parent and child the same conflict wages and the same destruction of character ensues. Parents set themselves to bend the will of their children to their own—to break their stubborn spirit, as they call it—with the ruthlessness of Grand Inquisitors. Cunning, unscrupulous children learn all the arts of the sneak in circumventing tyranny: children of better character are cruelly distressed and more or less lamed for life by it.

OUR QUARRELSOMENESS

As between adults, we find a general quarrelsomeness which makes political reform as impossible to most Englishmen as to hogs. Certain sections of the nation get cured of this disability. University men, sailors, and politicians are comparatively free from it, because the communal life of the University, the fact that in a ship a man must either learn to consider others or else go overboard or into irons, and the habit of working on committees and ceasing to expect more of one's own way than is included in the greatest common measure of the committee, educate the will socially. But no one who has ever had to guide a committee of ordinary private Englishmen through their first attempts at collective action, in committee or otherwise, can retain any illusions as to the appalling effects on our national manners and character of the organization of the home and the school as petty tyrannies, and the absence of all teaching of self-respect and training in self-assertion. Bullied and ordered about, the Englishman obeys like a sheep, evades like a knave, or tries to murder his oppressor. Merely criticized or opposed in committee, or invited to consider anybody's views but his own, he feels personally insulted and wants to resign or leave the room unless he is apologized to. And his panic and bewilderment when he sees that the older hands at the work have no patience with him and do not intend to treat him as infallible, are pitiable as far as they are anything but ludicrous. That is what comes of not being taught to consider other people's wills, and left to submit to them or to override them as if they were the winds and the weather. Such a state of mind is incompatible not only with the democratic introduction of high civilization, but with the comprehension and maintenance of such civilized institutions as have been introduced by benevolent and intelligent despots and aristocrats.

WE MUST REFORM SOCIETY BEFORE WE CAN REFORM OURSELVES

When we come to the positive problem of what to do with children if we are to give up the established plan, we find the difficulties so great that we begin to understand why so many people who detest the system and look back with loathing on their own schooldays, must helplessly send their children to the very schools they themselves were sent to, because there is no alternative except abandoning the children to undisciplined vagabondism. Man in society must do as everybody else does in his class: only fools and romantic novices imagine that freedom is a mere matter of the readiness of the individual to snap his fingers at convention. It is true that most of us live in a condition of quite unnecessary inhibition, wearing ugly and uncomfortable clothes, making ourselves and other people miserable by the heathen horrors of mourning, staying away from the theatre because we cannot afford the stalls and are ashamed to go to the pit, and in dozens of other ways enslaving ourselves when there are comfortable alternatives open to us without any real drawbacks. The contemplation of these petty slaveries, and of the triumphant ease with which sensible people throw them off, creates an impression that if we only take Johnson's advice to free our minds from cant, we can achieve freedom. But if we all freed our minds from cant we should find that for the most part we should have to go on doing the necessary work of the world exactly as we did it before until we organized new and free methods of doing it. Many people believed in secondary co-education (boys and girls taught together) before schools like Bedales were founded: indeed the practice was common enough in elementary schools and in Scotland; but their belief did not help them until Bedales and St George's were organized; and there are still not nearly enough co-educational schools in existence to accommodate all the children of the parents who believe in co-education up to university age, even if they could always afford the fees of these exceptional schools. It may be edifying to tell a duke that our public schools are all wrong in their constitution and methods, or a costermonger that children should be treated as in Goethe's Wilhelm Meister instead of as they are treated at the elementary school at the corner of his street; but what are the duke and the coster to do? Neither of them has any effective choice in the matter: their children must either go to the schools that are, or to no school at all. And as the duke thinks with reason that his son will be a lout or a milksop or a prig if he does not go to school, and the coster knows that his son will become an illiterate hooligan if he is left to the streets, there is no real alternative for either of them. Child life must be socially organized: no parent, rich or poor, can choose institutions that do not exist; and the private enterprise of individual schoolmasters appealing to a group of well-to-do parents, though it may shew what can be done by enthusiasts with new methods, cannot touch the mass of our children. For the average parent or child nothing is really available except the established practice; and this is what makes it so important that the established practice should be a sound one, and so useless for clever individuals to disparage it unless they can organize an alternative practice and make it, too, general.

THE PURSUIT OF MANNERS

If you cross-examine the duke and the coster, you will find that they are not concerned for the scholastic attainments of their children. Ask the duke whether he could pass the standard examination of twelve-year-old children in elementary schools, and he will admit, with an entirely placid smile, that he would almost certainly be ignominiously plucked. And he is so little ashamed of or disadvantaged by his condition that he is not prepared to spend an hour in remedying it. The coster may resent the inquiry instead of being amused by it; but his answer, if true, will be the same. What they both want for their children is the communal training, the apprenticeship to society, the lessons in holding one's own among people of all sorts with whom one is not, as in the home, on privileged terms. These can be acquired only by "mixing with the world," no matter how wicked the world is. No parent cares twopence whether his children can write Latin hexameters or repeat the dates of the accession of all the English monarchs since the Conqueror; but all parents are earnestly anxious about the manners of their children. Better Claude Duval than Kaspar Hauser. Laborers who are contemptuously anti-clerical in their opinions will send their daughters to the convent school because the nuns teach them some sort of gentleness of speech and behavior. And peers who tell you that our public schools are rotten through and through, and that our Universities ought to be razed to the foundations, send their sons to Eton and Oxford, Harrow and Cambridge, not only because there is nothing else to be done, but because these places, though they turn out blackguards and ignoramuses and boobies galore, turn them out with the habits and manners of the society they belong to. Bad as those manners are in many respects, they are better than no manners at all. And no individual or family can possibly teach them. They can be acquired only by living in an organized community in which they are traditional.

Thus we see that there are reasons for the segregation of children even in families where the great reason: namely, that children are nuisances to adults, does not press very hardly, as, for instance, in the houses of the very poor, who can send their children to play in the streets, or the houses of the very rich, which are so large that the children's quarters can be kept out of the parents' way like the servants' quarters.

NOT TOO MUCH WIND ON THE HEATH, BROTHER

What, then, is to be done? For the present, unfortunately, little except propagating the conception of Children's Rights. Only the achievement of economic equality through Socialism can make it possible to deal thoroughly with the question from the point of view of the total interest of the community, which must always consist of grown-up children. Yet economic equality, like all simple and obvious arrangements, seems impossible to people brought up as children are now. Still, something can be done even within class limits. Large communities of children of the same class are possible today; and voluntary organization of outdoor life for children has already begun in Boy Scouting and excursions of one kind or another. The discovery that anything, even school life, is better for the child than home life, will become an over-ridden hobby; and we shall presently be told by our faddists that anything, even camp life, is better than school life. Some blundering beginnings of this are already perceptible. There is a movement for making our British children into priggish little barefooted vagabonds, all talking like that born fool George Borrow, and supposed to be splendidly healthy because they would die if they slept in rooms with the windows shut, or perhaps even with a roof over their heads. Still, this is a fairly healthy folly; and it may do something to establish Mr Harold Cox's claim of a Right to Roam as the basis of a much needed law compelling proprietors of land to provide plenty of gates in their fences, and to leave them unlocked when there are no growing crops to be damaged nor bulls to be encountered, instead of, as at present, imprisoning the human race in dusty or muddy thoroughfares between walls of barbed wire.

The reaction against vagabondage will come from the children themselves. For them freedom will not mean the expensive kind of savagery now called "the simple life." Their natural disgust with the visions of cockney book fanciers blowing themselves out with "the wind on the heath, brother," and of anarchists who are either too weak to understand that men are strong and free in proportion to the social pressure they can stand and the complexity of the obligations they are prepared to undertake, or too strong to realize that what is freedom to them may be terror and bewilderment to others, will drive them back to the home and the school if these have meanwhile learned the lesson that children are independent human beings and have rights.

WANTED: A CHILD'S MAGNA CHARTA

Whether we shall presently be discussing a Juvenile Magna Charta or Declaration of Rights by way of including children in the Constitution is a question on which I leave others to speculate. But if it could once be established that a child has an adult's Right of Egress from uncomfortable places and unpleasant company, and there were children's lawyers to sue pedagogues and others for assault and imprisonment, there would be an amazing change in the behavior of schoolmasters, the quality of school books, and the amenities of school life. That Consciousness of Consent which, even in its present delusive form, has enabled Democracy to oust tyrannical systems in spite of all its vulgarities and stupidities and rancors and ineptitudes and ignorances, would operate as powerfully among children as it does now among grown-ups. No doubt the pedagogue would promptly turn demagogue, and woo his scholars by all the arts of demagogy; but none of these arts can easily be so dishonorable or mischievous as the art of caning. And, after all, if larger liberties are attached to the acquisition of knowledge, and the child finds that it can no more go to the seaside without a knowledge of the multiplication and pence tables than it can be an astronomer without mathematics, it will learn the multiplication table, which is more than it always does at present, in spite of all the canings and keepings-in.

THE PURSUIT OF LEARNING

When the Pursuit of Learning comes to mean the pursuit of learning by the child instead of the pursuit of the child by Learning, cane in hand, the danger will be precocity of the intellect, which is just as undesirable as precocity of the emotions. We still have a silly habit of talking and thinking as if intellect were a mechanical process and not a passion; and in spite of the German tutors who confess openly that three out of every five of the young men they coach for examinations are lamed for life thereby; in spite of Dickens and his picture of little Paul Dombey dying of lessons, we persist in heaping on growing children and adolescent youths and maidens tasks Pythagoras would have declined out of common regard for his own health and common modesty as to his own capacity. And this overwork is not all the effect of compulsion; for the average schoolmaster does not compel his scholars to learn: he only scolds and punishes them if they do not, which is quite a different thing, the net effect being that the school prisoners need not learn unless they like. Nay, it is sometimes remarked that the school dunce—meaning the one who does not like—often turns out well afterwards, as if idleness were a sign of ability and character. A much more sensible explanation is that the so-called dunces are not exhausted before they begin the serious business of life. It is said that boys will be boys; and one can only add one wishes they would. Boys really want to be manly, and are unfortunately encouraged thoughtlessly in this very dangerous and overstraining aspiration. All the people who have really worked (Herbert Spencer for instance) warn us against work as earnestly as some people warn us against drink. When learning is placed on the voluntary footing of sport, the teacher will find himself saying every day "Run away and play: you have worked as much as is good for you." Trying to make children leave school will be like trying to make them go to bed; and it will be necessary to surprise them with the idea that teaching is work, and that the teacher is tired and must go play or rest or eat: possibilities always concealed by that infamous humbug the current schoolmaster, who achieves a spurious divinity and a witch doctor's authority by persuading children that he is not human, just as ladies used to persuade them that they have no legs.

CHILDREN AND GAME: A PROPOSAL

Of the many wild absurdities of our existing social order perhaps the most grotesque is the costly and strictly enforced reservation of large tracts of country as deer forests and breeding grounds for pheasants whilst there is so little provision of the kind made for children. I have more than once thought of trying to introduce the shooting of children as a sport, as the children would then be preserved very carefully for ten months in the year, thereby reducing their death rate far more than the fusillades of the sportsmen during the other two would raise it. At present the killing of a fox except by a pack of foxhounds is regarded with horror; but you may and do kill children in a hundred and fifty ways provided you do not shoot them or set a pack of dogs on them. It must be admitted that the foxes have the best of it; and indeed a glance at our pheasants, our deer, and our children will convince the most sceptical that the children have decidedly the worst of it.

This much hope, however, can be extracted from the present state of things. It is so fantastic, so mad, so apparently impossible, that no scheme of reform need ever henceforth be discredited on the ground that it is fantastic or mad or apparently impossible. It is the sensible schemes, unfortunately, that are hopeless in England. Therefore I have great hopes that my own views, though fundamentally sensible, can be made to appear fantastic enough to have a chance.

First, then, I lay it down as a prime condition of sane society, obvious as such to anyone but an idiot, that in any decent community, children should find in every part of their native country, food, clothing, lodging, instruction, and parental kindness for the asking. For the matter of that, so should adults; but the two cases differ in that as these commodities do not grow on the bushes, the adults cannot have them unless they themselves organize and provide the supply, whereas the children must have them as if by magic, with nothing to do but rub the lamp, like Aladdin, and have their needs satisfied.

THE PARENTS' INTOLERABLE BURDEN

There is nothing new in this: it is how children have always had and must always have their needs satisfied. The parent has to play the part of Aladdin's djinn; and many a parent has sunk beneath the burden of this service. All the novelty we need is to organize it so that instead of the individual child fastening like a parasite on its own particular parents, the whole body of children should be thrown not only upon the whole body of parents, but upon the celibates and childless as well, whose present exemption from a full share in the social burden of children is obviously unjust and unwholesome. Today it is easy to find a widow who has at great cost to herself in pain, danger, and disablement, borne six or eight children. In the same town you will find rich bachelors and old maids, and married couples with no children or with families voluntarily limited to two or three. The eight children do not belong to the woman in any real or legal sense. When she has reared them they pass away from her into the community as independent persons, marrying strangers, working for strangers, spending on the community the life that has been built up at her expense. No more monstrous injustice could be imagined than that the burden of rearing the children should fall on her alone and not on the celibates and the selfish as well.

This is so far recognized that already the child finds, wherever it goes, a school for it, and somebody to force it into the school; and more and more these schools are being driven by the mere logic of facts to provide the children with meals, with boots, with spectacles, with dentists and doctors. In fact, when the child's parents are destitute or not to be found, bread, lodging, and clothing are provided. It is true that they are provided grudgingly and on conditions infamous enough to draw down abundant fire from Heaven upon us every day in the shape of crime and disease and vice; but still the practice of keeping children barely alive at the charge of the community is established; and there is no need for me to argue about it. I propose only two extensions of the practice. One is to provide for all the child's reasonable human wants, on which point, if you differ from me, I shall take leave to say that you are socially a fool and personally an inhuman wretch. The other is that these wants should be supplied in complete freedom from compulsory schooling or compulsory anything except restraint from crime, though, as they can be supplied only by social organization, the child must be conscious of and subject to the conditions of that organization, which may involve such portions of adult responsibility and duty as a child may be able to bear according to its age, and which will in any case prevent it from forming the vagabond and anarchist habit of mind.

One more exception might be necessary: compulsory freedom. I am sure that a child should not be imprisoned in a school. I am not so sure that it should not sometimes be driven out into the open—imprisoned in the woods and on the mountains, as it were. For there are frowsty children, just as there are frowsty adults, who dont want freedom. This morbid result of over-domestication would, let us hope, soon disappear with its cause.

MOBILIZATION

Those who see no prospect held out to them by this except a country in which all the children shall be roaming savages, should consider, first, whether their condition would be any worse than that of the little caged savages of today; and second, whether either children or adults are so apt to run wild that it is necessary to tether them fast to one neighborhood to prevent a general dissolution of society. My own observation leads me to believe that we are not half mobilized enough. True, I cannot deny that we are more mobile than we were. You will still find in the home counties old men who have never been to London, and who tell you that they once went to Winchester or St Albans much as if they had been to the South Pole; but they are not so common as the clerk who has been to Paris or to Lovely Lucerne, and who " goes away somewhere" when he has a holiday. His grandfather never had a holiday, and, if he had, would no more have dreamed of crossing the Channel than of taking a box at the Opera. But with all allowance for the Polytechnic excursion and the tourist agency, our inertia is still appalling. I confess to having once spent nine years in

London without putting my nose outside it; and though this was better, perhaps, than the restless globe-trotting vagabondage of the idle rich, wandering from hotel to hotel and never really living anywhere, yet I should no more have done it if I had been properly mobilized in my childhood than I should have worn the same suit of clothes all that time (which, by the way, I very nearly did, my professional income not having as yet begun to sprout). There are masses of people who could afford at least a trip to Margate, and a good many who could afford a trip round the world, who are more immovable than Aldgate pump. To others, who would move if they knew how, travelling is surrounded with imaginary difficulties and terrors. In short, the difficulty is not to fix people, but to root them up. We keep repeating the silly proverb that a rolling stone gathers no moss, as if moss were a desirable parasite. What we mean is that a vagabond does not prosper. Even this is not true, if prosperity means enjoyment as well as responsibility and money. The real misery of vagabondage is the misery of having nothing to do and nowhere to go, the misery of being derelict of God and Man, the misery of the idle, poor or rich. And this is one of the miseries of unoccupied childhood. The unoccupied adult, thus afflicted, tries many distractions, which are to say the least, unsuited to children. But one of them, the distraction of seeing the world, is innocent and beneficial. Also it is childish, being a continuation of what nurses call "taking notice," by which a child becomes experienced. It is pitiable nowadays to see men and women doing after the age of 45 all the travelling and sightseeing they should have done before they were 15. Mere wondering and staring at things is an important part of a child's education: that is why children can be thoroughly mobilized without making vagabonds of them. A vagabond is at home nowhere because he wanders: a child should wander because it ought to be at home everywhere. And if it has its papers and its passports, and gets what it requires not by begging and pilfering, but from responsible agents of the community as of right, and with some formal acknowledgment of the obligations it is incurring and a knowledge of the fact that these obligations are being recorded: if, further, certain qualifications are exacted before it is promoted from permission to go as far as its legs will carry it to using mechanical aids to locomotion, it can roam without much danger of gypsification.

Under such circumstances the boy or girl could always run away, and never be lost; and on no other conditions can a child be free without being also a homeless outcast. Parents could also run away from disagreeable children or drive them out of doors or even drop their acquaintance, temporarily or permanently, without inhumanity. Thus both parties would be on their good behavior, and not, as at present, on their filial or parental behavior, which, like all unfree behavior, is mostly bad behavior.

As to what other results might follow, we had better wait and see; for nobody now alive can imagine what customs and institutions would grow up in societies of free children. Child laws and child fashions, child manners and child morals are now not tolerated; but among free children there would certainly be surprising developments in this direction. I do not think there would be any danger of free children behaving as badly as grown-up people do now because they have never been free. They could hardly behave worse, anyhow.

CHILDREN'S RIGHTS AND PARENTS' WRONGS

A very distinguished man once assured a mother of my acquaintance that she would never know what it meant to be hurt until she was hurt through her children. Children are extremely cruel without intending it; and in ninety-nine cases out of a hundred the reason is that they do not conceive their elders as having any human feelings. Serve the elders right, perhaps, for posing as superhuman! The penalty of the impostor is not that he is found out (he very seldom is) but that he is taken for what he pretends to be, and treated as such. And to be treated as anything but what you really are may seem pleasant to the imagination when the treatment is above your merits; but in actual experience it is often quite the reverse. When I was a very small boy, my romantic imagination, stimulated by early doses of fiction, led me to brag to a still smaller boy so outrageously that he, being a simple soul, really believed me to be an invincible hero. I cannot remember whether this pleased me much; but I do remember very distinctly that one day this admirer of mine, who had a pet goat, found the animal in the hands of a larger boy than either of us, who mocked him and refused to restore the animal to his rightful owner. Whereupon, naturally, he came weeping to me, and demanded that I should rescue the goat and annihilate the aggressor. My terror was beyond description: fortunately for me, it imparted such a ghastliness to my voice and aspect as I, under the eye of my poor little dupe, advanced on the enemy with that hideous extremity of cowardice which is called the courage of despair, and said "You let go that goat," that he abandoned his prey and fled, to my unforgettable, unspeakable relief. I have never since exaggerated my prowess in bodily combat.

Now what happened to me in the adventure of the goat happens very often to parents, and would happen to schoolmasters if the prison door of the school did not shut out the trials of life. I remember once, at school, the resident head master was brought down to earth by the sudden illness of his wife. In the confusion that ensued it became necessary to leave one of the schoolrooms without a master. I was in the class that occupied that schoolroom. To have sent us home would have been to break the fundamental bargain with our parents by which the school was bound to keep us out of their way for half the day at all hazards. Therefore an appeal had to be made to our better feelings: that is, to our common humanity, not to make a noise. But the head master had never admitted any common humanity with us. We had been carefully broken in to regard him as a being quite aloof from and above us: one not subject to error or suffering or death or illness or mortality. Consequently sympathy was impossible; and if the unfortunate lady did not perish, it was because, as I now comfort myself with guessing, she was too much pre-occupied with her own pains, and possibly making too much noise herself, to be conscious of the pandemonium downstairs.

A great deal of the fiendishness of schoolboys and the cruelty of children to their elders is produced just in this way. Elders cannot be superhuman beings and suffering fellow-creatures at the same time. If you pose as a little god, you must pose for better for worse.

HOW LITTLE WE KNOW ABOUT OUR PARENTS

The relation between parent and child has cruel moments for the parent even when money is no object, and the material worries are delegated to servants and school teachers. The child and the parent are strangers to one another necessarily, because their ages must differ widely. Read Goethe's autobiography; and note that though he was happy in his parents and had exceptional powers of observation, divination, and story-telling, he knew less about his father and mother than about most of the other people he mentions. I myself was never on bad terms with my mother: we lived together until I was forty-two years old, absolutely without the smallest friction of any kind; yet when her death set me thinking curiously about our relations, I realized that I knew very little about her. Introduce me to a strange woman who was a child when I was a child, a girl when I was a boy, an adolescent when I was an adolescent; and if we take naturally to one another I will know more of her and she of me at the end of forty days (I had almost said of forty minutes) than I knew of my mother at the end of forty years. A contemporary stranger is a novelty and an enigma, also a possibility; but a mother is like a broomstick or like the sun in the heavens, it does not matter which as far as one's knowledge of her is concerned: the broomstick is there and the sun is there; and whether the child is beaten by it or warmed and enlightened by it, it accepts it as a fact in nature, and does not conceive it as having had youth, passions, and weaknesses, or as still growing, yearning, suffering, and learning. If I meet a widow I may ask her all about her marriage; but what son ever dreams of asking his mother about her marriage, or could endure to hear of it without violently breaking off the old sacred relationship between them, and ceasing to be her child or anything more to her than the first man in the street might be?

Yet though in this sense the child cannot realize its parent's humanity, the parent can realize the child's; for the parents with their experience of life have none of the illusions about the child that the child has about the parents; and the consequence is that the child can hurt its parents' feelings much more than its parents can hurt the child's, because the child, even when there has been none of the deliberate hypocrisy by which children are taken advantage of by their elders, cannot conceive the parent as a fellow-creature, whilst the parents know very well that the children are only themselves over again. The child cannot conceive that its blame or contempt or want of interest could possibly hurt its parent, and therefore expresses them all with an indifference which has given rise to the term *enfant terrible* (a tragic term in spite of the jests connected with it); whilst the parent can suffer from such slights and reproaches more from a child than from anyone else, even when the child is not beloved, because the child is so unmistakeably sincere in them.

OUR ABANDONED MOTHERS

Take a very common instance of this agonizing incompatibility. A widow brings up her son to manhood. He meets a strange woman, and goes off with and marries her, leaving his mother desolate. It does not occur to him that this is at all hard on her: he does it as a matter of course, and actually expects his mother to receive, on terms of special affection, the woman for whom she has been abandoned. If he shewed any sense of what he was doing, any remorse; if he mingled his tears with hers and asked her not to think too hardly of him because he had obeyed the inevitable destiny of a man to leave his father and mother and cleave to his wife, she could give him her blessing and accept her bereavement with dignity and without reproach. But the man never dreams of such considerations. To him his mother's feeling in the matter, when she betrays it, is unreasonable, ridiculous, and even odious, as shewing a prejudice against his adorable bride.

I have taken the widow as an extreme and obvious case; but there are many husbands and wives who are tired of their consorts, or disappointed in them, or estranged from them by infidelities; and these parents, in losing a son or a daughter through marriage, may be losing everything they care for. No parent's love is as innocent as the love of a child: the exclusion of all conscious sexual feeling from it does not exclude the bitterness, jealousy, and despair at loss which characterize sexual passion: in fact, what is called a pure love may easily be more selfish and jealous than a carnal one. Anyhow, it is plain matter of fact that naïvely selfish people sometimes try with fierce jealousy to prevent their children marrying.

FAMILY AFFECTION

Until the family as we know it ceases to exist, nobody will dare to analyze parental affection as distinguished from that general human sympathy which has secured to many an orphan fonder care in a stranger's house than it would have received from its actual parents. Not even Tolstoy, in The Kreutzer Sonata, has said all that we suspect about it. When it persists beyond the period at which it ceases to be necessary to the child's welfare, it is apt to be morbid; and we are probably wrong to inculcate its deliberate cultivation. The natural course is for the parents and children to cast off the specific parental and filial relation when they are no longer necessary to one another. The child does this readily enough to form fresh ties, closer and more fascinating. Parents are not always excluded from such compensations: it happens sometimes that when the children go out at the door the lover comes in at the window. Indeed it happens now oftener than it used to, because people remain much longer in the sexual arena. The cultivated Jewess no longer cuts off her hair at her marriage. The British matron has discarded her cap and her conscientious ugliness; and a bishop's wife at fifty has more of the air of a *femme galante* than an actress had at thirty-five in her grandmother's time. But as people marry later, the facts of age and time still inexorably condemn most parents to comparative solitude when their children marry. This may be a privation and may be a relief: probably in healthy circumstances it is no worse than a salutary change of habit; but even at that it is, for the moment at least, a wrench. For though parents and children sometimes dislike one another, there is an experience of succor and a habit of dependence and expectation formed in infancy which naturally attaches a child to its parent or to its nurse (a foster parent) in a quite peculiar way. A benefit to the child may be a burden to the parent; but people become attached to their burdens sometimes more than the burdens are attached to them; and to "suffer little children" has become an affectionate impulse deep in our nature.

Now there is no such impulse to suffer our sisters and brothers, our aunts and uncles, much less our cousins. If we could choose our relatives, we might, by selecting congenial ones, mitigate the repulsive effect of the obligation to like them and to admit them to our intimacy. But to have a person imposed on us as a brother merely because he happens to have the same parents is unbearable when, as may easily happen, he is the sort of person we should carefully avoid if he were anyone else's brother. All Europe (except Scotland, which has clans instead of families) draws the line at second cousins. Protestantism draws it still closer by making the first cousin a marriageable stranger; and the only reason for not drawing it at sisters and brothers is that the institution of the family compels us to spend our childhood with them, and thus imposes on us a curious relation in which familiarity destroys romantic charm, and is yet expected to create a specially warm affection. Such a relation is dangerously factitious and unnatural; and the practical moral is that the less said at home about specific family affection the better. Children, like grown-up people, get on well enough together if they are not pushed down one another's throats; and grown-up relatives will get on together in proportion to their separation and their care not to presume on their blood relationship. We should let children's feelings take their natural course without prompting. I have seen a child scolded and called unfeeling because it did not occur to it to make a theatrical demonstration of affectionate delight when its mother returned after an absence: a typical example of the way in which spurious family sentiment is stoked up. We are, after all, sociable animals; and if we are let alone in the matter of our affections, and well brought up otherwise, we shall not get on any the worse with particular people because they happen to be our brothers and sisters and cousins. The danger lies in assuming that we shall get on any better.

The main point to grasp here is that families are not kept together at present by family feeling but by human feeling. The family cultivates sympathy and mutual help and consolation as any other form of kindly association cultivates them; but the addition of a dictated compulsory affection as an attribute of near kinship is not only unnecessary, but positively detrimental; and the alleged tendency of modern social development to break up the family need alarm nobody. We cannot break up the facts of kinship nor eradicate its natural emotional consequences. What we can do and ought to do is to set people free to behave naturally and to change their behavior as circumstances change. To impose on a citizen of London the family duties of a Highland cateran in the eighteenth century is as absurd as to compel him to carry a claymore and target instead of an umbrella. The civilized man has no special use for cousins; and he may presently find that he has no special use for brothers and sisters. The parent seems likely to remain indispensable; but there is no reason why that natural tie should be made the excuse for unnatural aggravations of it, as crushing to the parent as they are oppressive to the child. The mother and father will not always have to shoulder the burthen of maintenance which should fall on the Atlas shoulders of the fatherland and motherland. Pending such reforms and emancipations, a shattering break-up of the paternal home must remain one of normal incidents of marriage. The parent is left lonely and the child is not. Woe to the old if they have no impersonal interests, no convictions, no public causes to advance, no tastes or hobbies! It is well to be a mother but not to be a mother-in-law; and if men were cut off artificially from intellectual and public interests as women are, the father-in-law would be as deplorable a figure in popular tradition as the mother-in-law.

It is not to be wondered at that some people hold that blood relationship should be kept a secret from the persons related, and that the happiest condition in this respect is that of the foundling who, if he ever meets his parents or brothers or sisters, passes them by without knowing them. And for such a view there is this to be said: that our family system does unquestionably take the natural bond between members of the same family, which, like all natural bonds, is not too tight to be borne, and superimposes on it a painful burden of forced, inculcated, suggested, and altogether unnecessary affection and responsibility which we should do well to get rid of by making relatives as independent of one another as possible.

THE FATE OF THE FAMILY

The difficulty of inducing people to talk sensibly about the family is the same as that which I pointed out in a previous volume as confusing discussions of marriage. Marriage is not a single invariable institution: it changes from civilization to civilization, from religion to religion, from civil code to civil code, from frontier to frontier. The family is still more variable, because the number of persons constituting a family, unlike the number of persons constituting a marriage, varies from one to twenty: indeed, when a widower with a family marries a widow with a family, and the two produce a third family, even that very high number may be surpassed. And the conditions may vary between opposite extremes: for example, in a London or Paris slum every child adds to the burden of poverty and helps to starve the parents and all the other children, whereas in a settlement of pioneer colonists every child, from the moment it is big enough to lend a hand to the family industry, is an investment in which the only danger is that of temporary overcapitalization. Then there are the variations in family sentiment. Sometimes the family organization is as frankly political as the organization of an army or an industry: fathers being no more expected to be sentimental about their children than colonels about soldiers, or factory owners about their employees, though the mother may be allowed a little tenderness if her character is weak. The Roman father was a despot: the Chinese father is an object of worship: the sentimental modern western father is often a playfellow looked to for toys and pocket-money. The farmer sees his children constantly: the squire sees them only during the holidays, and not then oftener than he can help: the tram conductor, when employed by a joint stock company, sometimes never sees them at all.

Under such circumstances phrases like The Influence of Home Life, The Family, The Domestic Hearth, and so on, are no more specific than The Mammals, or The Man In The Street; and the pious generalizations founded so glibly on them by our sentimental moralists are unworkable. When households average twelve persons with the sexes about equally represented, the results may be fairly good. When they average three the results may be very bad indeed; and to lump the two together under the general term The Family is to confuse the question hopelessly. The modern small family is much too stuffy: children "brought up at home" in it are unfit for society.

But here again circumstances differ. If the parents live in what is called a garden suburb, where there is a good deal of social intercourse, and the family, instead of keeping itself to itself, as the evil old saying is, and glowering at the neighbors over the blinds of the long street in which nobody knows his neighbor and everyone wishes to deceive him as to his income and social importance, is in effect broken up by school life, by out-of-door habits, and by frank neighborly intercourse through dances and concerts and theatricals and excursions and the like, families of four may turn out much less barbarous citizens than families of ten which attain the Boer ideal of being out of sight of one another's chimney smoke.

All one can say is, roughly, that the homelier the home, and the more familiar the family, the worse for everybody concerned. The family ideal is a humbug and a nuisance: one might as reasonably talk of the barrack ideal, or the forecastle ideal, or any other substitution of the machinery of social organization for the end of it, which must always be the fullest and most capable life: in short, the most godly life. And this significant word reminds us that though the popular conception of heaven includes a Holy Family, it does not attach to that family the notion of a separate home, or a private nursery or kitchen or mother-in-law, or anything that constitutes the family as we know it. Even blood relationship is miraculously abstracted from it; and the Father is the father of all children, the mother the mother of all mothers and babies, and the Son the Son of Man and the Savior of his brothers: one whose chief utterance on the subject of the conventional family was an invitation to all of us to leave our families and follow him, and to leave the dead to bury the dead, and not debauch ourselves at that gloomy festival the family funeral, with its sequel of hideous mourning and grief which is either affected or morbid.

FAMILY MOURNING

I do not know how far this detestable custom of mourning is carried in France; but judging from the appearance of the French people I should say that a Frenchwoman goes into mourning for her cousins to the seventeenth degree. The result is that when I cross the Channel I seem to have reached a country devastated by war or pestilence. It is really suffering only from the family. Will anyone pretend that England has not the better of this striking difference? It is such senseless and unnatural conventions as this that make us so impatient of what we call family feeling. Even apart from its insufferable pretensions, the family needs hearty discrediting; for there is hardly any vulnerable part of it that could not be amputated with advantage.

ART TEACHING

By art teaching I hasten to say that I do not mean giving children lessons in freehand drawing and perspective. I am simply calling attention to the fact that fine art is the only teacher except torture. I have already pointed out that nobody, except under threat of torture, can read a school book. The reason is that a school book is not a work of art. Similarly, you cannot listen to a lesson or a sermon unless the teacher or the preacher is an artist. You cannot read the Bible if you have no sense of literary art. The reason why the continental European is, to the Englishman or American, so surprisingly ignorant of the Bible, is that the authorized English version is a great work of literary art, and the continental versions are comparatively artless. To read a dull book; to listen to a tedious play or prosy sermon or lecture; to stare at uninteresting pictures or ugly buildings: nothing, short of disease, is more dreadful than this. The violence done to our souls by it leaves injuries and produces subtle maladies which have never been properly studied by psychopathologists. Yet we are so inured to it in school, where practically all the teachers are bores trying to do the work of artists, and all the books artless, that we acquire a truly frightful power of enduring boredom. We even acquire the notion that fine art is lascivious and destructive to the character. In church, in the House of Commons, at public meetings, we sit solemnly listening to bores and twaddlers because from the time we could walk or speak we have been snubbed, scolded, bullied, beaten and imprisoned whenever we dared to resent being bored or twaddled at, or to express our natural impatience and derision of bores and twaddlers. And when a man arises with a soul of sufficient native strength to break the bonds of this inculcated reverence and to expose and deride and tweak the noses of our humbugs and panjandrums, like Voltaire or Dickens, we are shocked and scandalized, even when we cannot help laughing. Worse, we dread and persecute those who can see and declare the truth, because their sincerity and insight reflects on our delusion and blindness. We are all like Nell Gwynne's footman, who defended Nell's reputation with his fists, not because he believed her to be what he called an honest woman, but because he objected to be scorned as the footman of one who was no better than she should be.

This wretched power of allowing ourselves to be bored may seem to give the fine arts a chance sometimes. People will sit through a performance of Beethoven's ninth symphony or of Wagner's Ring just as they will sit through a dull sermon or a front bench politician saying nothing for two hours whilst his unfortunate country is perishing through the delay of its business in Parliament. But their endurance is very bad for the ninth symphony, because they never hiss when it is murdered. I have heard an Italian conductor (no longer living) take the *adagio* of that symphony at a lively *allegretto*, slowing down for the warmer major sections into the speed and manner of the heroine's death song in a Verdi opera; and the listeners, far from relieving my excruciation by rising with yells of fury and hurling their programs and opera glasses at the miscreant, behaved just as they do when Richter conducts it. The mass of imposture that thrives on this combination of ignorance with despairing endurance is incalculable. Given a public trained from childhood to stand anything tedious, and so saturated with school discipline that even with the doors open and no schoolmasters to stop them they will sit there helplessly until the end of the concert or opera gives them leave to go home; and you will have in great capitals hundreds of thousands of pounds spent every night in the season on professedly artistic entertainments which have no other effect on fine art than to exacerbate the hatred in which it is already secretly held in England.

Fortunately, there are arts that cannot be cut off from the people by bad performances. We can read books for ourselves; and we can play a good deal of fine music for ourselves with the help of a pianola. Nothing stands between us and the actual handwork of the great masters of painting except distance; and modern photographic methods of reproduction are in some cases quite and in many nearly as effective in conveying the artist's message as a modern edition of Shakespear's plays is in conveying the message that first existed in his handwriting. The reproduction of great feats of musical execution is already on the way: the gramophone, for all its wheezing and snarling and braying, is steadily improving in its manners; and what with this improvement on the one hand, and on the other that blessed selective faculty which enables us to ignore a good deal of disagreeable noise if there is a thread of music in the middle of it (few critics of the gramophone seem to be conscious of the very considerable mechanical noise set up by choirs and orchestras) we have at last reached a point at which, for example, a person living in an English village where the church music is the only music, and that music is made by a few well-intentioned ladies with the help of a harmonium, can hear masses by Palestrina very passably executed, and can thereby be led to the discovery that Jackson in F and Hymns Ancient and Modern are not perhaps the last word of beauty and propriety in the praise of God.

In short, there is a vast body of art now within the reach of everybody. The difficulty is that this art, which alone can educate us in grace of body and soul, and which alone can make the history of the past live for us or the hope of the future shine for us, which alone can give delicacy and nobility to our crude lusts, which is the appointed vehicle of inspiration and the method of the communion of saints, is actually branded as sinful among us because, wherever it arises, there is resistance to tyranny, breaking of fetters, and the breath of freedom. The attempt to suppress art is not wholly successful: we might as well try to suppress oxygen. But it is carried far enough to inflict on huge numbers of people a most injurious art starvation, and to corrupt a great deal of the art that is tolerated. You will find in England plenty of rich families with little more culture than their dogs and horses. And you will find poor families, cut off by poverty and town life from the contemplation of the beauty of the earth, with its dresses of leaves, its scarves of cloud, and its contours of hill and valley, who would positively be happier as hogs, so little have they cultivated their humanity by the only effective instrument of culture: art. The dearth is artificially maintained even when there are the means of satisfying it. Story books are forbidden, picture post cards are forbidden, theatres are forbidden, operas are forbidden, circuses are forbidden, sweetmeats are forbidden, pretty colors are forbidden, all exactly as vice is forbidden. The Creator is explicitly prayed to, and implicitly convicted of indecency every day. An association of vice and sin with everything that is delightful and of goodness with everything that is wretched and detestable is set up. All the most perilous (and glorious) appetites and propensities are at once inflamed by starvation and uneducated by art. All the wholesome conditions which art imposes on appetite are waived: instead of cultivated men and women restrained by a thousand delicacies, repelled by ugliness, chilled by vulgarity, horrified by coarseness, deeply and sweetly moved by the graces that art has revealed to them and nursed in them, we get indiscriminate rapacity in pursuit of pleasure and a parade of the grossest stimulations in catering for it. We have a continual clamor for goodness, beauty, virtue, and sanctity, with such an appalling inability to recognize it or love it when it arrives that it is more dangerous to be a great prophet or poet than to promote twenty companies for swindling simple folk out of their savings. Do not for a moment suppose that uncultivated people are merely indifferent to high and noble qualities. They hate them malignantly. At best, such qualities are like rare and beautiful birds: when they appear the whole country takes down its guns; but the birds receive the statuary tribute of having their corpses stuffed.

And it really all comes from the habit of preventing children from being troublesome. You are so careful of your boy's morals, knowing how troublesome they may be, that you keep him away from the Venus of Milo only to find him in the arms of the scullery maid or someone much worse. You decide that the Hermes of Praxiteles and Wagner's Tristan are not suited for young girls; and your daughter marries somebody appallingly unlike either Hermes or Tristan solely to escape from your parental protection. You have not stifled a single passion nor averted a single danger: you have depraved the passions by starving them, and broken down all the defences which so effectively protect children brought up in freedom. You have men who imagine themselves to be ministers of religion openly declaring that when they pass through the streets they have to keep out in the wheeled traffic to avoid the temptations of the pavement. You have them organizing hunts of the women who tempt them—poor creatures whom no artist would touch without a shudder—and wildly clamoring for more clothes to disguise and conceal the body, and for the abolition of pictures, statues, theatres, and pretty colors. And incredible as it seems, these unhappy lunatics are left at large, unrebuked, even admired and revered, whilst artists have to struggle for toleration. To them an undraped human body is the most monstrous, the most blighting, the most obscene, the most unbearable spectacle in the universe. To an artist it is, at its best, the most admirable spectacle in nature, and, at its average, an object of indifference. If every rag of clothing miraculously dropped from the inhabitants of London at noon tomorrow (say as a preliminary to the Great Judgment), the artistic people would not turn a hair; but the artless people would go mad and call on the mountains to hide them. I submit that this indicates a thoroughly healthy state on the part of the artists, and a thoroughly morbid one on the part of the artless. And the healthy state is attainable in a cold country like ours only by familiarity with the undraped figure acquired through pictures, statues, and theatrical representations in which an illusion of natural clotheslessness is produced and made poetic.

In short, we all grow up stupid and mad to just the extent to which we have not been artistically educated; and the fact that this taint of stupidity and madness has to be tolerated because it is general, and is even boasted of as characteristically English, makes the situation all the worse. It is becoming exceedingly grave at present, because the last ray of art is being cut off from our schools by the discontinuance of religious education.

THE IMPOSSIBILITY OF SECULAR EDUCATION

Now children must be taught some sort of religion. Secular education is an impossibility. Secular education comes to this: that the only reason for ceasing to do evil and learning to do well is that if you do not you will be caned. This is worse than being taught in a church school that if you become a dissenter you will go to hell; for hell is presented as the instrument of something eternal, divine, and inevitable: you cannot evade it the moment the schoolmaster's back is turned. What confuses this issue and leads even highly intelligent religious persons to advocate secular education as a means of rescuing children from the strife of rival proselytizers is the failure to distinguish between the child's personal subjective need for a religion and its right to an impartially communicated historical objective knowledge of all the creeds and Churches. Just as a child, no matter what its race and color may be, should know that there are black men and brown men and yellow men, and, no matter what its political convictions may be, that there are Monarchists and Republicans and Positivists, Socialists and Unsocialists, so it should know that there are Christians and Mahometans and Buddhists and Shintoists and so forth, and that they are on the average just as honest and well-behaved as its own father. For example, it should not be told that Allah is a false god set up by the Turks and Arabs, who will all be damned for taking that liberty; but it should be told that many English people think so, and that many Turks and Arabs think the converse about English people. It should be taught that Allah is simply the name by which God is known to Turks and Arabs, who are just as eligible for salvation as any Christian. Further, that the practical reason why a Turkish child should pray in a mosque and an English child in a church is that as worship is organized in Turkey in mosques in the name of Mahomet and in England in churches in the name of Christ, a Turkish child joining the Church of England or an English child following Mahomet will find that it has no place for its worship and no organization of its religion within its reach. Any other teaching of the history and present facts of religion is false teaching, and is politically extremely dangerous in an empire in which a huge majority of the fellow subjects of the governing island do not profess the religion of that island.

But this objectivity, though intellectually honest, tells the child only what other people believe. What it should itself believe is quite another matter. The sort of Rationalism which says to a child "You must suspend your judgment until you are old enough to choose your religion" is Rationalism gone mad. The child must have a conscience and a code of honor (which is the essence of religion) even if it be only a provisional one, to be revised at its confirmation. For confirmation is meant to signalize a spiritual coming of age, and may be a repudiation. Really active souls have many confirmations and repudiations as their life deepens and their knowledge widens. But what is to guide the child before its first confirmation? Not mere orders, because orders must have a sanction of some sort or why should the child obey them? If, as a Secularist, you refuse to teach any sanction, you must say "You will be punished if you disobey."

"Yes," says the child to itself, "if I am found out; but wait until your back is turned and I will do as I like, and lie about it." There can be no objective punishment for successful fraud; and as no espionage can cover the whole range of a child's conduct, the upshot is that the child becomes a liar and schemer with an atrophied conscience. And a good many of the orders given to it are not obeyed after all. Thus the Secularist who is not a fool is forced to appeal to the child's vital impulse towards perfection, to the divine spark; and no resolution not to call this impulse an impulse of loyalty to the Fellowship of the Holy Ghost, or obedience to the Will of God, or any other standard theological term, can alter the fact that the Secularist has stepped outside Secularism and is educating the child religiously, even if he insists on repudiating that pious adverb and substituting the word metaphysically.

NATURAL SELECTION AS A RELIGION

We must make up our minds to it therefore that whatever measures we may be forced to take to prevent the recruiting sergeants of the Churches, free or established, from obtaining an exclusive right of entry to schools, we shall not be able to exclude religion from them. The most horrible of all religions: that which teaches us to regard ourselves as the helpless prey of a series of senseless accidents called Natural Selection, is allowed and even welcomed in so-called secular schools because it is, in a sense, the negation of all religion; but for school purposes a religion is a belief which affects conduct; and no belief affects conduct more radically and often so disastrously as the belief that the universe is a product of Natural Selection. What is more, the theory of Natural Selection cannot be kept out of schools, because many of the natural facts that present the most plausible appearance of design can be accounted for by Natural Selection; and it would be as absurd to keep a child in delusive ignorance of so potent a factor in evolution as to keep it in ignorance of radiation or capillary attraction. Even if you make a religion of Natural Selection, and teach the child to regard itself as the irresponsible prey of its circumstances and appetites (or its heredity as you will perhaps call them), you will none the less find that its appetites are stimulated by your encouragement and daunted by your discouragement; that one of its appetites is an appetite for perfection; that if you discourage this appetite and encourage the cruder acquisitive appetites the child will steal and lie and be a nuisance to you; and that if you encourage its appetite for perfection and teach it to attach a peculiar sacredness to it and place it before the other appetites, it will be a much nicer child and you will have a much easier job, at which point you will, in spite of your pseudo-scientific jargon, find yourself back in the old-fashioned religious teaching as deep as Dr Watts and in fact fathoms deeper.

MORAL INSTRUCTION LEAGUES

And now the voices of our Moral Instruction Leagues will be lifted, asking whether there is any reason why the appetite for perfection should not be cultivated in rationally scientific terms instead of being associated with the story of Jonah and the great fish and the thousand other tales that grow up round religions. Yes: there are many reasons; and one of them is that children all like the story of Jonah and the whale (they insist on its being a whale in spite of demonstrations by Bible smashers without any sense of humor that Jonah would not have fitted into a whale's gullet—as if the story would be credible of a whale with an enlarged throat) and that no child on earth can stand moral instruction books or catechisms or any other statement of the case for religion in abstract terms. The object of a moral instruction book is not to be rational, scientific, exact, proof against controversy, nor even credible: its object is to make children good. If it makes them sick instead its place is the waste-paper basket. And if it is to be read it must be readable.

Take for an illustration the story of Elisha and the bears. To the authors of the moral instruction books it is in the last degree reprehensible. It is obviously not true as a record of fact; and the picture it gives us of the temper of God (which is what interests an adult reader) is shocking and blasphemous. But it is a capital story for a child. It interests a child because it is about bears; and it leaves the child with an impression that children who poke fun at old gentlemen and make rude remarks about bald heads are not nice children, which is a highly desirable impression, and just as much as a child is capable of receiving from the story. When a story is about God and a child, children take God for granted and criticize the child. Adults do the opposite, and are thereby often led to talk great nonsense about the bad effect of Bible stories on infants.

But let no one think that a child or anyone else can learn religion from a teacher or a book or by any academic process whatever. It is only by an unfettered access to the whole body of Fine Art: that is, to the whole body of inspired revelation, that we can build up that conception of divinity to which all virtue is an aspiration. And to hope to find this body of art purified from all that is obsolete or dangerous or fierce or lusty, or to pick and choose what will be good for any particular child, much less for all children, is the shallowest of vanities. Such schoolmasterly selection is neither possible nor desirable. Ignorance of evil is not virtue but imbecility: admiring it is like giving a prize for honesty to a man who has not stolen your watch because he did not know you had one. Virtue chooses good from evil; and without knowledge there can be no choice. And even this is a dangerous simplification of what actually occurs. We are not choosing: we are growing. Were you to cut all of what you call the evil out of a child, it would drop dead. If you try to stretch it to full human stature when it is ten years old, you will simply pull it into two pieces and be hanged. And when you try to do this morally, which is what parents and schoolmasters are doing every day, you ought to be hanged; and some day, when we take a sensible view of the matter, you will be; and serve you right. The child does not stand between a good and a bad angel: what it has to deal with is a middling angel who, in normal healthy cases, wants to be a good angel as fast as it can without killing itself in the process, which is a dangerous one.

Therefore there is no question of providing the child with a carefully regulated access to good art. There is no good art, any more than there is good anything else in the absolute sense. Art that is too good for the child will either teach it nothing or drive it mad, as the Bible has driven many people mad who might have kept their sanity had they been allowed to read much lower forms of literature. The practical moral is that we must read whatever stories, see whatever pictures, hear whatever songs and symphonies, go to whatever plays we like. We shall not like those which have nothing to say to us; and though everyone has a right to bias our choice, no one has a right to deprive us of it by keeping us from any work of art or any work of art from us.

I may now say without danger of being misunderstood that the popular English compromise called Cowper-Templeism (unsectarian Bible education) is not so silly as it looks. It is true that the Bible inculcates half a dozen religions: some of them barbarous; some cynical and pessimistic; some amoristic and romantic; some sceptical and challenging; some kindly, simple, and intuitional; some sophistical and intellectual; none suited to the character and conditions of western civilization unless it be the Christianity which was finally suppressed by the Crucifixion, and has never been put into practice by any State before or since. But the Bible contains the ancient literature of a very remarkable Oriental race; and the imposition of this literature, on whatever false pretences, on our children left them more literate than if they knew no literature at all, which was the practical alternative. And as our Authorized Version is a great work of art as well, to know it was better than knowing no art, which also was the practical alternative. It is at least not a school book; and it is not a bad story book, horrible as some of the stories are. Therefore as between the Bible and the blank represented by secular education in its most matter-of-fact sense, the choice is with the Bible.

But the Bible is not sufficient. The real Bible of modern Europe is the whole body of great literature in which the inspiration and revelation of Hebrew Scripture has been continued to the present day. Nietzsche's Thus Spake Zoroaster is less comforting to the ill and unhappy than the Psalms; but it is much truer, subtler, and more edifying. The pleasure we get from the rhetoric of the book of Job and its tragic picture of a bewildered soul cannot disguise the ignoble irrelevance of the retort of God with which it closes, nor supply the need for such modern revelations as Shelley's Prometheus or The Niblung's Ring of Richard Wagner. There is nothing in the Bible greater in inspiration than Beethoven's ninth symphony; and the power of modern music to convey that inspiration to a modern man is far greater than that of Elizabethan English, which is, except for people steeped in the Bible from childhood like Sir Walter Scott and Ruskin, a dead language.

Besides, many who have no ear for literature or for music are accessible to architecture, to pictures, to statues, to dresses, and to the arts of the stage. Every device of art should be brought to bear on the young; so that they may discover some form of it that delights them naturally; for there will come to all of them that period between dawning adolescence and full maturity when the pleasures and emotions of art will have to satisfy cravings which, if starved or insulted, may become morbid and seek disgraceful satisfactions, and, if prematurely gratified otherwise than poetically, may destroy the stamina of the race. And it must be borne in mind that the most dangerous art for this necessary purpose is the art that presents itself as religious ecstasy. Young people are ripe for love long before they are ripe for religion. Only a very foolish person would substitute the Imitation of Christ for Treasure Island as a present for a boy or girl, or for Byron's Don Juan as a present for a swain or lass. Pickwick is the safest saint for us in our nonage. Flaubert's Temptation of St Anthony is an excellent book for a man of fifty, perhaps the best within reach as a healthy study of visionary ecstasy; but for the purposes of a boy of fifteen Ivanoe and the Templar make a much better saint and devil. And the boy of fifteen will find this out for himself if he is allowed to wander in a well-stocked literary garden, and hear bands and see pictures and spend his pennies on cinematograph shows. His choice may often be rather disgusting to his elders when they want him to choose the best before he is ready for it. The greatest Protestant Manifesto ever written, as far as I know, is Houston Chamberlain's Foundations of the Nineteenth Century: everybody capable of it should read it. Probably the History of Maria Monk is at the opposite extreme of merit (this is a guess: I have never read it); but it is certain that a boy let loose in a library would go for Maria Monk and have no use whatever for Mr. Chamberlain. I should probably have read Maria Monk myself if I had not had the Arabian Nights and their like to occupy me better. In art, children, like adults, will find their level if they are left free to find it, and not restricted to what adults think good for them. Just at present our young people are going mad over ragtimes, apparently because syncopated rhythms are new to them. If they had learnt what can be done with syncopation from Beethoven's third Leonora overture, they would enjoy the ragtimes all the more; but they would put them in their proper place as amusing vulgarities.

ARTIST IDOLATRY

But there are more dangerous influences than ragtimes waiting for people brought up in ignorance of fine art. Nothing is more pitiably ridiculous than the wild worship of artists by those who have never been seasoned in youth to the enchantments of art. Tenors and prima donnas, pianists and violinists, actors and actresses enjoy powers of seduction which in the middle ages would have exposed them to the risk of being burnt for sorcery. But as they exercise this power by singing, playing, and acting, no great harm is done except perhaps to themselves. Far graver are the powers enjoyed by brilliant persons who are also connoisseurs in art. The influence they can exercise on young people who have been brought up in the darkness and wretchedness of a home without art, and in whom a natural bent towards art has always been baffled and snubbed, is incredible to those who have not witnessed and understood it. He (or she) who reveals the world of art to them opens heaven to them. They become satellites, disciples, worshippers of the apostle. Now the apostle may be a voluptuary without much conscience. Nature may have given him enough virtue to suffice in a reasonable environment. But this allowance may not be enough to defend him against the temptation and demoralization of finding himself a little god on the strength of what ought to be a quite ordinary culture. He may find adorers in all directions in our uncultivated society among people of stronger character than himself, not one of whom, if they had been artistically educated, would have had anything to learn from him or regarded him as in any way extraordinary apart from his actual achievements as an artist. Tartuffe is not always a priest. Indeed he is not always a rascal: he is often a weak man absurdly credited with omniscience and perfection, and taking unfair advantages only because they are offered to him and he is too weak to refuse. Give everyone his culture, and no one will offer him more than his due.

In thus delivering our children from the idolatry of the artist, we shall not destroy for them the enchantment of art: on the contrary, we shall teach them to demand art everywhere as a condition attainable by cultivating the body, mind, and heart. Art, said Morris, is the expression of pleasure in work. And certainly, when work is made detestable by slavery, there is no art. It is only when learning is made a slavery by tyrannical teachers that art becomes loathsome to the pupil.

"THE MACHINE"

When we set to work at a Constitution to secure freedom for children, we had better bear in mind that the children may not be at all obliged to us for our pains. Rousseau said that men are born free; and this dangerous saying, as Rousseau meant it, was and is a great and true saying; yet let it not lead us into the error of supposing that all men long for freedom and embrace it when it is offered to them. On the contrary, it has to be forced on them; and even then they will give it the slip if it is not religiously inculcated and strongly safe-guarded.

Besides, men are born docile, and must in the nature of things remain so with regard to everything they do not understand. Now political science and the art of government are among the things they do not understand, and indeed are not at present allowed to understand. They can be enslaved by a system, as we are at present, because it happens to be there, and nobody understands it. An intelligently worked Capitalist system, as Comte saw, would give us all that most of us are intelligent enough to want. What makes it produce such unspeakably vile results is that it is an automatic system which is as little understood by those who profit by it in money as by those who are starved and degraded by it: our millionaires and statesmen are manifestly no more "captains of industry" or scientific politicians than our bookmakers are mathematicians. For some time past a significant word has been coming into use as a substitute for Destiny, Fate, and Providence. It is "The Machine": the machine that has no god in it. Why do governments do nothing in spite of reports of Royal Commissions that establish the most frightful urgency? Why do our philanthropic millionaires do nothing, though they are ready to throw bucketfuls of gold into the streets? The Machine will not let them. Always The Machine. In short, they dont know how. They try to reform Society as an old lady might try to restore a broken down locomotive by prodding it with a knitting needle. And this is not at all because they are born fools, but because they have been educated, not into manhood and freedom, but into blindness and slavery by their parents and schoolmasters, themselves the victims of a similar misdirection, and consequently of The Machine.

They do not want liberty. They have not been educated to want it. They choose slavery and inequality; and all the other evils are automatically added to them.

And yet we must have The Machine. It is only in unskilled hands under ignorant direction that machinery is dangerous. We can no more govern modern communities without political machinery than we can feed and clothe them without industrial machinery. Shatter The Machine, and you get Anarchy. And yet The Machine works so detestably at present that we have people who advocate anarchy and call themselves Anarchists.

THE PROVOCATION TO ANARCHISM

The Anarchists are right when they say that Governments, like schoolmasters, try to simplify their task by destroying liberty and glorifying authority, especially their own. But the difficulty of combining law and order with free institutions is not a natural one. It is a matter of inculcation. If people are brought up to be slaves, it is useless and dangerous to let them loose at the age of twenty-one and say "Now you are free." No one with the tamed soul and broken spirit of a slave can be free. It is like saying to a laborer brought up on a family income of thirteen shillings a week, "Here is one hundred thousand pounds: now you are wealthy." Nothing can make such a man really wealthy. Freedom and wealth are difficult and responsible conditions to which men must be accustomed and socially trained from birth. A nation that is free at twenty-one is not free at all; just as a man first enriched at fifty remains poor all his life, even if he does not curtail it by drinking himself to death in the first wild ecstasy of being able to swallow as much as he likes for the first time. You cannot govern men brought up as slaves otherwise than as slaves are governed. You may pile Bills of Right and Habeas Corpus Acts on Great Charters; promulgate American Constitutions; burn the chateaux and guillotine the seigneurs; chop off the heads of kings and queens and set up Democracy on the ruins of feudalism: the end of it all for us is that already in the twentieth century there has been as much brute coercion and savage intolerance, as much flogging and hanging, as much impudent injustice on the bench and lustful rancor in the pulpit, as much naive resort to torture, persecution, and suppression of free speech and freedom of the press, as much war, as much of the vilest excess of mutilation, rapine, and delirious indiscriminate slaughter of helpless non-combatants, old and young, as much prostitution of professional talent, literary and political, in defence of manifest wrong, as much cowardly sycophancy giving fine names to all this villainy or pretending that it is "greatly exaggerated," as we can find any record of from the days when the advocacy of liberty was a capital offence and Democracy was hardly thinkable. Democracy exhibits the vanity of Louis XIV, the savagery of Peter of Russia, the nepotism and provinciality of Napoleon, the fickleness of Catherine II: in short, all the childishnesses of all the despots without any of the qualities that enabled the greatest of them to fascinate and dominate their contemporaries.

And the flatterers of Democracy are as impudently servile to the successful, and insolent to common honest folk, as the flatterers of the monarchs. Democracy in America has led to the withdrawal of ordinary refined persons from politics; and the same result is coming in England as fast as we make Democracy as democratic as it is in America. This is true also of popular religion: it is so horribly irreligious that nobody with the smallest pretence to culture, or the least inkling of what the great prophets vainly tried to make the world understand, will have anything to do with it except for purely secular reasons.

IMAGINATION

Before we can clearly understand how baleful is this condition of intimidation in which we live, it is necessary to clear up the confusion made by our use of the word imagination to denote two very different powers of mind. One is the power to imagine things as they are not: this I call the romantic imagination. The other is the power to imagine things as they are without actually sensing them; and this I will call the realistic imagination. Take for example marriage and war. One man has a vision of perpetual bliss with a domestic angel at home, and of flashing sabres, thundering guns, victorious cavalry charges, and routed enemies in the field. That is romantic imagination; and the mischief it does is incalculable. It begins in silly and selfish expectations of the impossible, and ends in spiteful disappointment, sour grievance, cynicism, and misanthropic resistance to any attempt to better a hopeless world. The wise man knows that imagination is not only a means of pleasing himself and beguiling tedious hours with romances and fairy tales and fools' paradises (a quite defensible and delightful amusement when you know exactly what you are doing and where fancy ends and facts begin), but also a means of foreseeing and being prepared for realities as yet unexperienced, and of testing the feasibility and desirability of serious Utopias. He does not expect his wife to be an angel; nor does he overlook the facts that war depends on the rousing of all the murderous blackguardism still latent in mankind; that every victory means a defeat; that fatigue, hunger, terror, and disease are the raw material which romancers work up into military glory; and that soldiers for the most part go to war as children go to school, because they are afraid not to. They are afraid even to say they are afraid, as such candor is punishable by death in the military code.

A very little realistic imagination gives an ambitious person enormous power over the multitudinous victims of the romantic imagination. For the romancer not only pleases himself with fictitious glories: he also terrifies himself with imaginary dangers. He does not even picture what these dangers are: he conceives the unknown as always dangerous. When you say to a realist "You must do this" or "You must not do that," he instantly asks what will happen to him if he does (or does not, as the case may be). Failing an unromantic convincing answer, he does just as he pleases unless he can find for himself a real reason for refraining.

In short, though you can intimidate him, you cannot bluff him. But you can always bluff the romantic person: indeed his grasp of real considerations is so feeble that you find it necessary to bluff him even when you have solid considerations to offer him instead. The campaigns of Napoleon, with their atmosphere of glory, illustrate this. In the Russian campaign Napoleon's marshals achieved miracles of bluff, especially Ney, who, with a handful of men, monstrously outnumbered, repeatedly kept the Russian troops paralysed with terror by pure bounce. Napoleon himself, much more a realist than Ney (that was why he dominated him), would probably have surrendered; for sometimes the bravest of the brave will achieve successes never attempted by the cleverest of the clever. Wellington was a completer realist than Napoleon. It was impossible to persuade Wellington that he was beaten until he actually was beaten. He was unbluffable; and if Napoleon had understood the nature of Wellington's strength instead of returning Wellington's snobbish contempt for him by an academic contempt for Wellington, he would not have left the attack at Waterloo to Ney and D'Erlon, who, on that field, did not know when they were beaten, whereas Wellington knew precisely when he was not beaten. The unbluffable would have triumphed anyhow, probably, because Napoleon was an academic soldier, doing the academic thing (the attack in columns and so forth)with superlative ability and energy; whilst Wellington was an original soldier who, instead of outdoing the terrible academic columns with still more terrible and academic columns, outwitted them with the thin red line, not of heroes, but, as this uncompromising realist never hesitated to testify, of the scum of the earth.

GOVERNMENT BY BULLIES

These picturesque martial incidents are being reproduced every day in our ordinary life. We are bluffed by hardy simpletons and headstrong bounders as the Russians were bluffed by Ney; and our Wellingtons are threadbound by slave-democracy as Gulliver was threadbound by the

Lilliputians. We are a mass of people living in a submissive routine to which we have been drilled from our childhood. When you ask us to take the simplest step outside that routine, we say shyly, "Oh, I really couldnt," or "Oh, I shouldnt like to," without being able to point out the smallest harm that could possibly ensue: victims, not of a rational fear of real dangers, but of pure abstract fear, the quintessence of cowardice, the very negation of "the fear of God." Dotted about among us are a few spirits relatively free from this inculcated paralysis, sometimes because they are half-witted, sometimes because they are unscrupulously selfish, sometimes because they are realists as to money and unimaginative as to other things, sometimes even because they are exceptionally able, but always because they are not afraid of shadows nor oppressed with nightmares. And we see these few rising as if by magic into power and affluence, and forming, with the millionaires who have accidentally gained huge riches by the occasional windfalls of our commerce, the governing class. Now nothing is more disastrous than a governing class that does not know how to govern. And how can this rabble of the casual products of luck, cunning, and folly, be expected to know how to govern? The merely lucky ones and the hereditary ones do not owe their position to their qualifications at all. As to the rest, the realism which seems their essential qualification often consists not only in a lack of romantic imagination, which lack is a merit, but of the realistic, constructive, Utopian imagination, which lack is a ghastly defect. Freedom from imaginative illusion is therefore no guarantee whatever of nobility of character: that is why inculcated submissiveness makes us slaves to people much worse than ourselves, and why it is so important that submissiveness should no longer be inculcated.

And yet as long as you have the compulsory school as we know it, we shall have submissiveness inculcated. What is more, until the active hours of child life are organized separately from the active hours of adult life, so that adults can enjoy the society of children in reason without being tormented, disturbed, harried, burdened, and hindered in their work by them as they would be now if there were no compulsory schools and no children hypnotized into the belief that they must tamely go to them and be imprisoned and beaten and over-tasked in them, we shall have schools under one pretext or another; and we shall have all the evil consequences and all the social hopelessness that result from turning a nation of potential freemen and freewomen into a nation of two-legged spoilt spaniels with everything crushed out of their nature except dread of the whip. Liberty is the breath of life to nations; and liberty is the one thing that parents, schoolmasters, and rulers spend their lives in extirpating for the sake of an immediately quiet and finally disastrous life.

MISALLIANCE

JOHNNY TARLETON, an ordinary young business man of thirty or less, is taking his weekly Friday to Tuesday in the house of his father, John Tarleton, who has made a great deal of money out of Tarleton's Underwear. The house is in Surrey, on the slope of Hindhead; and Johnny, reclining, novel in hand, in a swinging chair with a little awning above it, is enshrined in a spacious half hemisphere of glass which forms a pavilion commanding the garden, and, beyond it, a barren but lovely landscape of hill profile with fir trees, commons of bracken and gorse, and wonderful cloud pictures.

The glass pavilion springs from a bridgelike arch in the wall of the house, through which one comes into a big hall with tiled flooring, which suggests that the proprietor's notion of domestic luxury is founded on the lounges of week-end hotels. The arch is not quite in the centre of the wall. There is more wall to Johnny's right than to his left; and this space is occupied by a hat rack and umbrella stand in which tennis rackets, white parasols, caps, Panama hats, and other summery articles are bestowed. Just through the arch at this corner stands a new portable Turkish bath, recently unpacked, with its crate beside it, and on the crate the drawn nails and the hammer used in unpacking. Near the crate are open boxes of garden games: bowls and croquet. Nearly in the middle of the glass wall of the pavilion is a door giving on the garden, with a couple of steps to surmount the hot-water pipes which skirt the glass. At intervals round the pavilion are marble pillars with specimens of Viennese pottery on them, very flamboyant in colour and florid in design. Between them are folded garden chairs flung anyhow against the pipes. In the side walls are two doors: one near the hat stand, leading to the interior of the house, the other on the opposite side and at the other end, leading to the vestibule.

There is no solid furniture except a sideboard which stands against the wall between the vestibule door and the pavilion, a small writing table with blotter, rack for telegram forms and stationery, and a wastepaper basket, standing out in the hall near the sideboard, and a lady's worktable, with two chairs at it, to-

wards the other side of the lounge. The writing table has also two chairs at it. On the sideboard there is a tantalus, liqueur bottles, a syphon, a glass jug of lemonade, tumblers, and every convenience for casual drinking. Also a plate of sponge cakes, and a highly ornate punchbowl in the same style as the keramic display in the pavilion. Wicker chairs and little bamboo tables with ash trays and boxes of matches on them are scattered in all directions. In the pavilion, which is flooded with sunshine, is the elaborate patent swing seat and awning in which Johnny reclines with his novel. There are two wicker chairs right and left of him.

Bentley Summerhays, one of those smallish, thinskinned youths, who from 17 to 70 retain unaltered the mental airs of the later and the physical appearance of the earlier age, appears in the garden and comes through the glass door into the pavilion. He is unmistakably a grade above Johnny socially; and though he looks sensitive enough, his assurance and his high voice are a little exasperating.

JOHNNY. Hallo! Wheres your luggage?

BENTLEY. I left it at the station. Ive walked up from Haslemere. [*He goes to the hat stand and hangs up his hat*].

JOHNNY [*shortly*] Oh! And whos to fetch it?

BENTLEY. Dont know. Dont care. Providence, probably. If not, your mother will have it fetched.

JOHNNY. Not her business, exactly, is it?

BENTLEY [*returning to the pavilion*] Of course not. Thats why one loves her for doing it. Look here: chuck away your silly week-end novel, and talk to a chap. After a week in that filthy office my brain is simply blue-mouldy. Lets argue about something intellectual. [*He throws himself into the wicker chair on Johnny's right*].

JOHNNY [*straightening up in the swing with a yell of protest*] No. Now seriously, Bunny, Ive come down here to have a pleasant week-end; and I'm not going to stand your confounded arguments. If you want to argue, get out of this and go over to the Congregationalist minister's. Hes a nailer at arguing. He likes it.

BENTLEY. You cant argue with a person when his livelihood depends on his not letting you convert him. And would you mind not calling me Bunny? My name is Bentley Summerhays, which you please.

JOHNNY. Whats the matter with Bunny?

BENTLEY. It puts me in a false position. Have you ever considered the fact that I was an afterthought?

JOHNNY. An afterthought? What do you mean by that?

BENTLEY. I—

JOHNNY. No, stop: I dont want to know. It's only a dodge to start an argument.

BENTLEY. Dont be afraid: it wont overtax your brain. My father was 44 when I was born. My mother was 41. There was twelve years between me and the next eldest. I was unexpected. I was probably unintentional. My brothers and sisters are not the least like me. Theyre the regular thing that you always get in the first batch from young parents: quite pleasant, ordinary, do-the-regular-thing sort: all body and no brains, like you.

JOHNNY. Thank you.

BENTLEY. Dont mention it, old chap. Now I'm different. By the time I was born, the old couple knew something. So I came out all brains and no more body than is absolutely necessary. I am really a good deal older than you, though you were born ten years sooner. Everybody feels that when they hear us talk; consequently, though it's quite natural to hear me calling you Johnny, it sounds ridiculous and unbecoming for you to call me Bunny. [*He rises*].

JOHNNY. Does it, by George? You stop me doing it if you can: thats all.

BENTLEY. If you go on doing it after Ive asked you not, youll feel an awful swine (*He strolls away carelessly to the sideboard with his eye on the sponge-cakes*]. At least I should; but I suppose youre not so particular.

JOHNNY [*rising vengefully and following Bentley, who is forced to turn and listen*] I'll tell you what it is, my boy: you want a good talking to; and I'm going to give it to you. If you think that because your father's a K.C.B., and you want to marry my sister, you can make yourself as nasty as you please and say what you like, youre mistaken. Let me tell you that except Hypatia, not one person in this house is in favor of her marrying you; and I dont believe shes happy about it herself. The match isnt settled yet: dont forget that. Youre on trial in the office because the Governor isnt giving his daughter money for an idle man to live on her. Youre on trial here because my mother thinks a girl should know what a man is like in the house before she marries him. Thats been going on for two months now; and whats the result? Youve got yourself thoroughly disliked in the office; and youre getting yourself thoroughly disliked here, all through your bad manners and your conceit, and the damned impudence you think clever.

BENTLEY [*deeply wounded and trying hard to control himself*] Thats enough, thank you. You dont suppose, I hope, that I should have come down if I had known that that was how you all feel about me. [*He makes for the vestibule door*].

JOHNNY [*collaring him*] No: you dont run away. I'm going to have this out with you. Sit down: d'y' hear? [*Bentley attempts to go with dignity. Johnny slings him into a chair at the writing table, where he sits, bitterly humiliated, but afraid to speak lest he should burst into tears*]. Thats the advantage of having more body than brains, you see: it enables me to teach you manners; and I'm going to do it too. Youre a spoilt young pup; and you need a jolly good licking. And if youre not careful youll get it: I'll see to that next time you call me a swine.

BENTLEY. I didnt call you a swine. But [*bursting into a fury of tears*] you a r e a swine: youre a beast: youre a brute: youre a cad: youre a liar: youre a bully: I should like to wring your damned neck for you.

JOHNNY [*with a derisive laugh*] Try it, my son. [*Bentley gives an inarticulate sob of rage*]. Fighting isnt in your line. Youre too small; and youre too childish. I always suspected that your cleverness wouldnt come to very much when it was brought up against something solid: some decent chap's fist, for instance.

BENTLEY. I hope your beastly fist may come up against a mad bull or a prizefighter's nose, or something solider than me. I dont care about your fist; but if everybody here dislikes me—[*he is checked by a sob*]. Well, I dont care. [*Trying to recover himself*] I'm sorry I intruded: I didnt know. [*Breaking down again*] Oh you beast! you pig! Swine, swine, swine, swine, swine! Now!

JOHNNY. All right, my lad, all right. Sling your mud as hard as you please: it wont stick to me. What I want to know is this. How is it that your father, who I suppose is the strongest man England has produced in our time—

BENTLEY. You got that out of your halfpenny paper. A lot you know about him!

JOHNNY. I dont set up to be able to do anything but admire him and appreciate him and be proud of him as an Englishman. If it wasnt for my respect for him, I wouldnt have stood your cheek for two days, let alone two months. But what I cant understand is why he didnt lick it out of you when you were a kid. For twenty-five years he kept a place twice as big as England in order: a place full of seditious coffee-colored heathens and pestilential white agitators in the middle of a lot of savage tribes. And yet he couldnt keep you in order. I dont set up to be half the man your father undoubtedly is; but, by George, it's lucky for you you were not my son. I dont hold with my own father's views about corporal punishment being wrong. It's necessary for some people; and I'd have tried it on you until you first learnt to howl and then to behave yourself.

BENTLEY [*contemptuously*] Yes: behavior wouldnt come naturally to your son, would it?

JOHNNY [*stung into sudden violence*] Now you keep a civil tongue in your head. I'll stand none of your snobbery. I'm just as proud of Tarleton's Underwear as you are of your father's title and his K.C.B., and all the rest of it. My father began in a little hole of a shop in Leeds no bigger than our pantry down the passage there. He—

BENTLEY. Oh yes: I know. Ive read it. "The Romance of Business, or The Story of Tarleton's Underwear. Please Take One!" I took one the day after I first met Hypatia. I went and bought half a dozen unshrinkable vests for her sake.

JOHNNY. Well: did they shrink?

BENTLEY. Oh, dont be a fool.

JOHNNY. Never mind whether I'm a fool or not. Did they shrink? Thats the point. Were they worth the money?

BENTLEY. I couldnt wear them: do you think my skin's as thick as your customers' hides? I'd as soon have dressed myself in a nutmeg grater.

JOHNNY. Pity your father didnt give your thin skin a jolly good lacing with a cane!

BENTLEY. Pity you havnt got more than one idea! If you want to know, they did try that on me once, when I was a small kid. A silly governess did it. I yelled fit to bring down the house, and went into convulsions and brain fever and that sort of thing for three weeks. So the old girl got the sack; and serve her right! After that, I was let do what I liked. My father didnt want me to grow up a broken-spirited spaniel, which is your idea of a man, I suppose.

JOHNNY. Jolly good thing for you that my father made you come into the office and shew what you were made of. And it didnt come to much: let me tell you that. When the Governor asked me where I thought we ought to put you, I said "Make him the Office Boy." The Governor said you were too green. And so you were.

BENTLEY. I daresay. So would you be pretty green if you were shoved into my father's set. I picked up your silly business in a fortnight. Youve been at it ten years; and you havnt picked it up yet.

JOHNNY. Dont talk rot, child. You know you simply make me pity you.

BENTLEY. "Romance of Business" indeed! The real romance of Tarleton's business is the story that you understand anything about it. You never could explain any mortal thing about it to me when I asked you. "See what was done the last time": that was the beginning and the end of your wisdom. Youre nothing but a turnspit.

JOHNNY. A what!

BENTLEY. A turnspit. If your father hadnt made a roasting jack for you to turn, youd be earning twenty-four shillings a week behind a counter.

JOHNNY. If you dont take that back and apologize for your bad manners, I'll give you as good a hiding as ever—

BENTLEY. Help! Johnny's beating me! Oh! Murder! [*He throws himself on the ground, uttering piercing yells*].

JOHNNY. Dont be a fool. Stop that noise, will you. I'm not going to touch you. Sh—sh—

Hypatia rushes in through the inner door, followed by Mrs Tarleton, and throws herself on her knees by Bentley. Mrs Tarleton, whose knees are stiffer, bends over him and tries to lift him. Mrs Tarleton is a shrewed and motherly old lady who has been pretty in her time, and is still very pleasant and likeable and unaffected. Hypatia is a typical English girl of a sort never called typical: that is, she has an opaque white skin, black hair, large dark eyes with black brows and lashes, curved lips, swift glances and movements that flash out of a waiting stillness, boundless energy and audacity held in leash.

HYPATIA [*pouncing on Bentley with no very gentle hand*] Bentley: whats the matter? Dont cry like that: whats the use? Whats happened?

MRS TARLETON. Are you ill, child? [*They get him up*]. There, there, pet! It's all right: dont cry [*they put him into a chair*]: there! there! there! Johnny will go for the doctor; and he'll give you something nice to make it well.

HYPATIA. What has happened, Johnny?

MRS TARLETON. Was it a wasp?

BENTLEY [*impatiently*] Wasp be dashed!

MRS TARLETON. Oh Bunny! that was a naughty word.

BENTLEY. Yes, I know: I beg your pardon. [*He rises, and extricates himself from them*]. Thats all right. Johnny frightened me. You know how easy it is to hurt me; and I'm too small to defend myself against Johnny.

MRS TARLETON. Johnny: how often have I told you that you must not bully the little ones. I thought youd outgrown all that.

HYPATIA [*angrily*] I do declare, mamma, that Johnny's brutality makes it impossible to live in the house with him.

JOHNNY [*deeply hurt*] It's fourteen years, mother, since you had that row with me for licking Robert and giving Hypatia a black eye because she bit me. I promised you then that I'd never raise my hand to one of them again; and Ive never broken my word. And now because this young whelp begins to cry out before he's hurt, you treat me as if I were a brute and a savage.

MRS TARLETON. No dear, not a savage; but you know you musnt call our visitor naughty names.

BENTLEY. Oh, let him alone—

JOHNNY [*fiercely*] Dont you interfere between my mother and me: d'y' hear?

HYPATIA. Johnny's lost his temper, mother. We'd better go. Come, Bentley.

MRS TARLETON. Yes: that will be best. [*To Bentley*] Johnny doesnt mean any harm, dear: he'll be himself presently. Come.

The two ladies go out through the inner door with Bentley, who turns derisively at the door to cock a snook at Johnny as he goes out.

Johnny, left alone, clenches his fists and grinds his teeth, but can find no relief in that way for his rage. After choking and stamping for a moment, he makes for the vestibule door. It opens before he reaches it; and Lord Summerhays comes in. Johnny glares at him, speechless. Lord Summerhays takes in the situation, and quickly takes the punchbowl from the sideboard and offers it to Johnny.

LORD SUMMERHAYS. Smash it. Dont hesitate: it's an ugly thing. Smash it: hard. [*Johnny, with a stifled yell, dashes it in pieces, and then sits down and mops his brow*]. Feel better now? [*Johnny nods*]. I know only one person alive who could drive me to the point of having either to break china or commit murder; and that person is my son Bentley. Was it he? [*Johnny nods again, not yet able to speak*]. As the car stopped I heard a yell which is only too familiar to me. It generally means that some infuriated person is trying to thrash Bentley. Nobody has ever succeeded, though almost everybody has tried. [*He seats himself comfortably close to the writing table, and sets to work to collect the fragments of the punchbowl in the wastepaper basket whilst Johnny, with diminishing difficulty, collects himself*]. Bentley is a problem which I confess I have never been able to solve. He was born to be a great success at the age of fifty. Most Englishmen of his class seem to be born to be great successes at the age of twenty-four at most. The domestic problem for me is how to endure Bentley until he is fifty. The problem for the nation is how to get itself governed by men whose growth is arrested when they are little more than college lads. Bentley doesnt really mean to be offensive. You can always make him cry by telling him you dont like him. Only, he cries so loud that the experiment should be made in the open air: in the middle of Salisbury Plain if possible. He has a hard and penetrating intellect and a remarkable power of looking facts in the face; but unfortunately, being very young, he has no idea of how very little of that sort of thing most of us can stand. On the other hand, he is frightfully sensitive and even affectionate; so that he probably gets as much as he gives in the way of hurt feelings. Youll excuse me rambling on like this about my son.

JOHNNY [*who has pulled himself together*] You did it on purpose. I wasnt quite myself: I needed a moment to pull round. Thank you.

LORD SUMMERHAYS. Not at all. Is your father at home?

JOHNNY. No: hes opening one of his free libraries. Thats another nice little penny gone. He's mad on reading. He promised another free library last week. It's ruinous. Itll hit you as well as me when Bunny marries Hypatia. When all Hypatia's money is thrown away on libraries, where will Bunny come in? Cant you stop him?

LORD SUMMERHAYS. I'm afraid not. Hes a perfect whirlwind. Indefatigable at public work. Wonderful man, I think.

JOHNNY. Oh, public work! He does too much of it. It's really a sort of laziness, getting away from your own serious business to amuse yourself with other people's. Mind: I dont say there isnt another side to it. It has its value as an advertisement. It makes useful acquaintances and leads to valuable business connections. But it takes his mind off the main chance; and he overdoes it.

LORD SUMMERHAYS. The danger of public business is that it never ends. A man may kill himself at it.

JOHNNY. Or he can spend more on it than it brings him in: thats how I look at it. What I say is that everybody's business is nobody's business. I hope I'm not a hard man, nor a narrow man, nor unwilling to pay reasonable taxes, and subscribe in reason to deserving charities, and even serve on a jury in my turn; and no man can say I ever refused to help a friend out of a difficulty when he was worth helping. But when you ask me to go beyond that, I tell you frankly I dont see it. I never did see it, even when I was only a boy, and had to pretend to take in all the ideas the Governor fed me up with. I didnt see it; and I dont see it.

LORD SUMMERHAYS. There is certainly no business reason why you should take more than your share of the world's work.

JOHNNY. So I say. It's really a great encouragement to me to find you agree with me. For of course if nobody agrees with you, how are you to know that youre not a fool?

LORD SUMMERHAYS. Quite so.

JOHNNY. I wish youd talk to him about it. It's no use my saying anything: I'm a child to him still: I have no influence. Besides, you know how to handle men. See how you handled me when I was making a fool of myself about Bunny!

LORD SUMMERHAYS. Not at all.

JOHNNY. Oh yes I was: I know I was. Well, if my blessed father had come in he'd have told me to control myself. As if I was losing my temper on purpose!

Bentley returns, newly washed. He beams when he sees his father, and comes affectionately behind him and pats him on the shoulders.

BENTLEY. Hel-lo, commander! have you come? Ive been making a filthy silly ass of myself here. I'm awfully sorry, Johnny, old chap: I beg your pardon. Why dont you kick me when I go on like that?

LORD SUMMERHAYS. As we came through Godalming I thought I heard some yelling—

BENTLEY. I should think you did. Johnny was rather rough on me, though. He told me nobody here liked me; and I was silly enough to believe him.

LORD SUMMERHAYS. And all the women have been kissing you and pitying you ever since to stop your crying, I suppose. Baby!

BENTLEY. I did cry. But I always feel good after crying: it relieves my wretched nerves. I feel perfectly jolly now.

LORD SUMMERHAYS. Not at all ashamed of yourself, for instance?

BENTLEY. If I started being ashamed of myself I shouldnt have time for anything else all my life. I say: I feel very fit and spry. Lets all go down and meet the Grand Cham. [*He goes to the hatstand and takes down his hat*].

LORD SUMMERHAYS. Does Mr Tarleton like to be called the Grand Cham, do you think, Bentley?

BENTLEY. Well, he thinks hes too modest for it. He calls himself Plain John. But you cant call him that in his own office: besides, it doesnt suit him: it's not flamboyant enough.

JOHNNY. Flam what?

BENTLEY. Flamboyant. Lets go and meet him. He's telephoned from Guildford to say hes on the road. The dear old son is always telephoning or telegraphing: he thinks hes hustling along like anything when hes only sending unnecessary messages.

LORD SUMMERHAYS. Thank you: I should prefer a quiet afternoon.

BENTLEY. Right o! I shant press Johnny: hes had enough

of me for one week-end. [*He goes out through the pavilion into the grounds*].

JOHNNY. Not a bad idea, that.

LORD SUMMERHAYS. What?

JOHNNY. Going to meet the Governor. You know you wouldnt think it; but the Governor likes Bunny rather. And Bunny is cultivating it. I shouldnt be surprised if he thought he could squeeze me out one of these days.

LORD SUMMERHAYS. You dont say so! Young rascal! I want to consult you about him, if you dont mind. Shall we stroll over to the Gibbet? Bentley is too fast for me as a walking companion; but I should like a short turn.

JOHNNY [*rising eagerly, highly flattered*] Right you are. Thatll suit me down to the ground. [*He takes a Panama and stick from the hat stand*].

Mrs Tarleton and Hypatia come back just as the two men are going out. Hypatia salutes Summerhays from a distance with an enigmatic lift of her eyelids in his direction and a demure nod before she sits down at the worktable and busies herself with her needle. Mrs Tarleton, hospitably fussy, goes over to him.

MRS TARLETON. Oh, Lord Summerhays, I didnt know you were here. Wont you have some tea?

LORD SUMMERHAYS. No, thank you: I'm not allowed tea. And I'm ashamed to say Ive knocked over your beautiful punch-bowl. You must let me replace it.

MRS TARLETON. Oh, it doesnt matter: I'm only too glad to be rid of it. The shopman told me it was in the best taste; but when my poor old nurse Martha got cataract, Bunny said it was a merciful provision of Nature to prevent her seeing our china.

LORD SUMMERHAYS [*gravely*] That was exceedingly rude of Bentley, Mrs Tarleton. I hope you told him so.

MRS TARLETON. Oh, bless you! I dont care what he says; so long as he says it to me and not before visitors.

JOHNNY. We're going out for a stroll, mother.

MRS TARLETON. All right: dont let us keep you. Never mind about that crock: I'll get the girl to come and take the pieces away. [*Recollecting herself*] There! Ive done it again!

JOHNNY. Done what?

MRS TARLETON. Called her the girl. You know, Lord Summerhays, it's a funny thing; but now I'm getting old, I'm dropping back into all the ways John and I had when we had barely a hundred a year. You should have known me when I was forty! I talked like a duchess; and if Johnny or Hypatia let slip a word that was like old times, I was down on them like anything. And now I'm beginning to do it myself at every turn.

LORD SUMMERHAYS. There comes a time when all that seems to matter so little. Even queens drop the mask when they reach our time of life.

MRS TARLETON. Let you alone for giving a thing a pretty turn! Youre a humbug, you know, Lord Summerhays. John doesnt know it; and Johnny doesnt know it; but you and I know it, dont we? Now thats something that even you cant answer; so be off with you for your walk without another word.

Lord Summerhays smiles; bows; and goes out through the vestibule door, followed by Johnny. Mrs Tarleton sits down at the worktable and takes out her darning materials and one of her husband's socks. Hypatia is at the other side of the table, on her mother's right. They chat as they work.

HYPATIA. I wonder whether they laugh at us when they are by themselves!

MRS TARLETON. Who?

HYPATIA. Bentley and his father and all the toffs in their set.

MRS TARLETON. Oh, thats only their way. I used to think that the aristocracy were a nasty sneering lot, and that they were laughing at me and John. Theyre always giggling and pretending not to care much about anything. But you get used to it: theyre the same to one another and to everybody. Besides, what does it matter what they think? It's far worse when theyre civil, because that always means that they want you to lend them money; and you must never do that,

Hypatia, because they never pay. How can they? They dont make anything, you see. Of course, if you can make up your mind to regard it as a gift, thats different; but then they generally ask you again; and you may as well say no first as last. You neednt be afraid of the aristocracy, dear: theyre only human creatures like ourselves after all; and youll hold your own with them easy enough.

HYPATIA. Oh, I'm not a bit afraid of them, I assure you.

MRS TARLETON. Well, no, not afraid of them, exactly; but youve got to pick up their ways. You know, dear, I never quite agreed with your father's notion of keeping clear of them, and sending you to a school that was so expensive that they couldnt afford to send their daughters there; so that all the girls belonged to big business families like ourselves. It takes all sorts to make a world; and I wanted you to see a little of all sorts. When you marry Bunny, and go among the women of his father's set, theyll shock you at first.

HYPATIA [*incredulously*] How?

MRS TARLETON. Well, the things they talk about.

HYPATIA. Oh! scandalmongering?

MRS TARLETON. Oh no: we all do that: that's only human nature. But you know theyve no notion of decency. I shall never forget the first day I spent with a marchioness, two duchesses, and no end of Ladies This and That. Of course it was only a committee: theyd put me on to get a big subscription out of John. I'd never heard such talk in my life. The things they mentioned! And it was the marchioness that started it.

HYPATIA. What sort of things?

MRS TARLETON. Drainage!! She tried three systems in her castle; and she was going to do away with them all and try another. I didnt know which way to look when she began talking about it: I thought theyd all have got up and gone out of the room. But not a bit of it, if you please. They were all just as bad as she. They all had systems; and each of them swore by her own system. I sat there with my cheeks burn ing until one of the duchesses, thinking I looked out of it, I suppose, asked me what system I had. I said I was sure I knew nothing about such things, and hadnt we better change the subject. Then the fat was in the fire, I can tell you. There was a regular terror of a countess with an anaerobic system; and she told me, downright brutally, that I'd better learn something about them before my children died of diptheria. That was just two months after I'd buried poor little Bobby; and that was the very thing he died of, poor little lamb! I burst out crying: I couldnt help it. It was as good as telling me I'd killed my own child. I had to go away; but before I was out of the door one of the duchesses—quite a young woman—began talking about what sour milk did in her inside and how she expected to live to be over a hundred if she took it regularly. And me listening to her, that had never dared to think that a duchess could have anything so common as an inside! I shouldnt have minded if it had been children's insides: we h a v e to talk about them. But grown-up people! I was glad to get away that time.

HYPATIA. There was a physiology and hygiene class started at school; but of course none of our girls were let attend it.

MRS TARLETON. If it had been an aristocratic school plenty would have attended it. Thats what theyre like: theyve nasty minds. With really nice good women a thing is either decent or indecent; and if it's indecent, we just dont mention it or pretend to know about it; and theres an end of it. But all the aristocracy cares about is whether it can get any good out of the thing. Theyre what Johnny calls cynical-like. And of course nobody can say a word to them for it. Theyre so high up that they can do and say what they like.

HYPATIA. Well, I think they might leave the drains to their husbands, I shouldnt think much of a man that left such things to me.

MRS TARLETON. Oh, dont think that, dear, whatever you do. I never let on about it to you; but it's me that takes care of the drainage here. After what that countess said to me I wasnt going to lose another child nor trust John. And I dont want my grandchildren to die any more than my children.

HYPATIA. Do you think Bentley will ever be as big a man as his father? I dont mean clever: I mean big and strong.

MRS TARLETON. Not he. He's overbred, like one of those expensive little dogs. I like a bit of a mongrel myself, whether it's a man or a dog: theyre the best for everyday. But we all have our tastes: whats one woman's meat is another woman's poison. Bunny's a dear little fellow; but I never could have fancied him for a husband when I was your age.

HYPATIA. Yes; but he has some brains. He's not like all the rest. One cant have everything.

MRS TARLETON. Oh, youre quite right, dear: quite right. It's a great thing to have brains: look what it's done for your father! Thats the reason I never said a word when you jilted poor Jerry Mackintosh.

HYPATIA [*excusing herself*] I really couldnt stick it out with Jerry, mother. I know you liked him; and nobody can deny that hes a splendid animal—

MRS TARLETON [*shocked*] Hypatia! How can you! The things that girls say nowadays!

HYPATIA. Well, what else can you call him? If I'd been deaf or he'd been dumb, I could have married him. But living with father, Ive got accustomed to cleverness. Jerry would drive me mad: you know very well hes a fool: even Johnny thinks him a fool.

MRS TARLETON [*up in arms at once in defence of her boy*] Now dont begin about my Johnny. You know it annoys me. Johnny's as clever as anybody else in his own way. I dont say hes as clever as you in some ways; but hes a man, at all events, and not a little squit of a thing like your Bunny.

HYPATIA. Oh, I say nothing against your darling: we all know Johnny's perfection.

MRS TARLETON. Dont be cross, dearie. You let Johnny alone; and I'll let Bunny alone. I'm just as bad as you. There!

HYPATIA. Oh, I dont mind your saying that about Bentley. It's true. He is a little squit of a thing. I wish he wasnt. But who else is there? Think of all the other chances Ive had! Not one of them has as much brains in his whole body as Bentley has in his little finger. Besides, theyve no distinction. It's as much as I can do to tell one from the other. They wouldnt even have money if they werent the sons of their fathers, like Johnny. Whats a girl to do? I never met anybody like Bentley before. He may be small; but he's the best of the bunch: you cant deny that.

MRS TARLETON [*with a sigh*] Well, my pet, if you fancy him, theres no more to be said.

A pause follows this remark: the two women sewing silently.

HYPATIA. Mother: do you think marriage is as much a question of fancy as it used to be in your time and father's?

MRS TARLETON. Oh, it wasnt much fancy with me, dear: your father just wouldnt take no for an answer; and I was only too glad to be his wife instead of his shop-girl. Still, it's curious; but I had more choice than you in a way, because you see, I was poor; and there are so many more poor men than rich ones that I might have had more of a pick, as you might say, if John hadnt suited me.

HYPATIA. I can imagine all sorts of men I could fall in love with; but I never seem to meet them. The real ones are too small, like Bunny, or too silly, like Jerry. Of course one can get into a state about any man: fall in love with him if you like to call it that. But who would risk marrying a man for love? *I* shouldnt. I remember three girls at school who agreed that the one man you should never marry was the man you were in love with, because it would make a perfect slave of you. Theres a sort of instinct against it, I think, thats just as strong as the other instinct. One of them, to my certain knowledge, refused a man she was in love with, and married another who was in love with her; and it turned out very well.

MRS TARLETON. Does all that mean that youre not in love with Bunny?

HYPATIA. Oh, how could anybody be in love with Bunny? I like him to kiss me just as I like a baby to kiss me. I'm fond of him; and he never bores me; and I see that he's very clever; but I'm not what you call gone about him, if thats what you mean.

MRS TARLETON. Then why need you marry him?

HYPATIA. What better can I do? I must marry somebody, I suppose. Ive realized that since I was twentythree. I always used to take it as a matter of course that I should be married before I was twenty.

BENTLEY'S VOICE [*in the garden*] Youve got to keep yourself fresh: to look at these things with an open mind.

JOHN TARLETON'S VOICE. Quite right, quite right: I always say so.

MRS TARLETON. Theres your father, and Bunny with him.

BENTLEY. Keep young. Keep your eye on me. Thats the tip for you.

Bentley and Mr Tarleton (*an immense and genial veteran of trade*) *come into view and enter the pavilion.*

JOHN TARLETON. You think youre young, do you? You think I'm old? [*energetically shaking off his motoring coat and hanging it up with his cap*].

BENTLEY [*helping him with the coat*] Of course youre old. Look at your face and look at mine. What you call your youth is nothing but your levity. Why do we get on so well together? Because I'm a young cub and youre an old josser. [*He throws a cushion at Hypatia's feet and sits down on it with his back against her knees*].

TARLETON. Old! Thats all you know about it, my lad. How do, Patsy! [*Hypatia kisses him*]. How is my Chickabiddy? [*He kisses Mrs Tarleton's hand and poses expansively in the middle of the picture*]. Look at me! Look at these wrinkles, these grey hairs, this repulsive mask that you call old age! What is it? [*Vehemently*] I ask you, what is it?

BENTLEY. Jolly nice and venerable, old man. Dont be discouraged.

TARLETON. Nice? Not a bit of it. Venerable? Venerable be

blowed! Read your Darwin, my boy. Read your Weismann. [*He goes to the sideboard for a drink of lemonade*].

MRS TARLETON. For shame, John! Tell him to read his Bible.

TARLETON [*manipulating the syphon*] Whats the use of telling children to read the Bible when you know they wont. I was kept away from the Bible for forty years by being told to read it when I was young. Then I picked it up one evening in a hotel in Sunderland when I had left all my papers in the train; and I found it wasnt half bad. [*He drinks, and puts down the glass with a smack of enjoyment*]. Better than most halfpenny papers, anyhow, if only you could make people believe it. [*He sits down by the writing-table, near his wife*]. But if you want to understand old age scientifically, read Darwin and Weismann. Of course if you want to understand it romantically, read about Solomon.

MRS TARLETON. Have you had tea, John?

TARLETON. Yes. Dont interrupt me when I'm improving the boy's mind. Where was I? This repulsive mask—Yes. [*Explosively*] What is death?

MRS TARLETON. John!

HYPATIA. Death is a rather unpleasant subject, papa.

TARLETON. Not a bit. Not scientifically. Scientifically it's a delightful subject. You think death's natural. Well, it isnt. You read Weismann. There wasnt any death to start with. You go look in any ditch outside and youll find swimming about there as fresh as paint some of the identical little live cells that Adam christened in the Garden of Eden. But if big things like us didnt die, we'd crowd one another off the face of the globe. Nothing survived, sir, except the sort of people that had the sense and good manners to die and make room for the fresh supplies. And so death was introduced by Natural Selection. You get it out of your head, my lad, that I'm going to die because I'm wearing out or decaying. There's no such thing as decay to a vital man. I shall clear out; but I shant decay.

BENTLEY. And what about the wrinkles and the almond

tree and the grasshopper that becomes a burden and the desire that fails?

TARLETON. Does it? by George! No, sir: it spiritualizes. As to your grasshopper, I can carry an elephant.

MRS TARLETON. You do say such things, Bunny! What does he mean by the almond tree?

TARLETON. He means my white hairs: the repulsive mask. That, my boy, is another invention of Natural Selection to disgust young women with me, and give the lads a turn.

MRS TARLETON. John: I wont have it. Thats a forbidden subject.

TARLETON. They talk of the wickedness and vanity of women painting their faces and wearing auburn wigs at fifty. But why shouldnt they? Why should a woman allow Nature to put a false mask of age on her when she knows that she's as young as ever? Why should she look in the glass and see a wrinkled lie when a touch of fine art will shew her a glorious truth? The wrinkles are a dodge to repel young men. Suppose she doesnt want to repel young men! Suppose she likes them!

MRS TARLETON. Bunny: take Hypatia out into the grounds for a walk: theres a good boy. John has got one of his naughty fits this evening.

HYPATIA. Oh, never mind me. I'm used to him.

BENTLEY. I'm not. I never heard such conversation: I cant believe my ears. And mind you, this is the man who objected to my marrying his daughter on the ground that a marriage between a member of the great and good middle class with one of the vicious and corrupt aristocracy would be a misalliance. A misalliance, if you please! This is the man Ive adopted as a father!

TARLETON. Eh? Whats that? Adopted me as a father, have you?

BENTLEY. Yes. Thats an idea of mine. I knew a chap named Joey Percival at Oxford (you know I was two months at Balliol before I was sent down for telling the old woman who was head of that silly college what I jolly well thought of him. He would have been glad to have me back, too, at the end of six months; but I wouldnt go: I just let him want; and serve him right!) Well, Joey was a most awfully clever fellow, and so nice! I asked him what made such a difference between him and all the other pups—they were pups, if you like. He told me it was very simple: they had only one father apiece; and he had three.

MRS TARLETON. Dont talk nonsense, child. How could that be?

BENTLEY. Oh, very simple. His father—

TARLETON. Which father?

BENTLEY. The first one: the regulation natural chap. He kept a tame philosopher in the house: a sort of Coleridge or Herbert Spencer kind of card, you know. That was the second father. Then his mother was an Italian princess; and she had an Italian priest always about. He was supposed to take charge of her conscience; but from what I could make out she jolly well took charge of his. The whole three of them took charge of Joey's conscience. He used to hear them arguing like mad about everything. You see, the philosopher was a freethinker, and always believed the latest thing. The priest didnt believe anything, because it was sure to get him into trouble with someone or another. And the natural father kept an open mind and believed whatever paid him best. Between the lot of them Joey got cultivated no end. He said if he could only have had three mothers as well, he'd have backed himself against Napoleon.

TARLETON [*impressed*] Thats an idea. Thats a most interesting idea: a most important idea.

MRS TARLETON. You always were one for ideas, John.

TARLETON. Youre right, Chickabiddy. What do I tell Johnny when he brags about Tarleton's Underwear? It's not the underwear. The underwear be hanged! Anybody can make underwear. Anybody can sell underwear. Tarleton's Ideas: thats whats done it. Ive often thought of putting that up over the shop.

BENTLEY. Take me into partnership when you do, old

man. I'm wasted on the underwear; but I shall come in strong on the ideas.

TARLETON. You be a good boy; and perhaps I will.

MRS TARLETON [*scenting a plot against her beloved Johnny*] Now, John: you promised—

TARLETON. Yes, yes. All right, Chickabiddy: dont fuss. Your precious Johnny shant be interfered with. [*Bouncing up, too energetic to sit still*] But I'm getting sick of that old shop. Thirty-five years Ive had of it: same blessed old stairs to go up and down every day: same old lot: same old game: sorry I ever started it now. I'll chuck it and try something else: something that will give a scope to all my faculties.

HYPATIA. Theres money in underwear: theres none in wild-cat ideas.

TARLETON. Theres money in me, madam, no matter what I go into.

MRS TARLETON. Dont boast, John. Dont tempt Providence.

TARLETON. Rats! You dont understand Providence. Providence likes to be tempted. Thats the secret of the successful man. Read Browning. Natural theology on an island, eh? Caliban was afraid to tempt Providence: that was why he was never able to get even with Prospero. What did Prospero do? Prospero didnt even tempt Providence: he was Providence. Thats one of Tarleton's ideas; and dont you forget it.

BENTLEY. You are full of beef today, old man.

TARLETON. Beef be blowed! Joy of life. Read Ibsen. [*He goes into the pavilion to relieve his restlessness, and stares out with his hands thrust deep in his pockets*].

HYPATIA [*thoughtful*] Bentley: couldnt you invite your friend Mr Percival down here?

BENTLEY. Not if I know it. Youd throw me over the moment you set eyes on him.

MRS TARLETON. Oh, Bunny! For shame!

BENTLEY. Well, who'd marry me, dyou suppose, if they could get my brains with a full-sized body? No, thank you.

I shall take jolly good care to keep Joey out of this until Hypatia is past praying for.

Johnny and Lord Summerhays return through the pavilion from their stroll.

TARLETON. Welcome! welcome! Why have you stayed away so long?

LORD SUMMERHAYS [*shaking hands*] Yes: I should have come sooner. But I'm still rather lost in England. [*Johnny takes his hat and hangs it up beside his own*]. Thank you. [*Johnny returns to his swing and his novel. Lord Summerhays comes to the writing table*]. The fact is that as Ive nothing to do, I never have time to go anywhere. [*He sits down next Mrs Tarleton*].

TARLETON [*following him and sitting down on his left*] Paradox, paradox. Good. Paradoxes are the only truths. Read Chesterton. But theres lots for you to do here. You have a genius for government. You learnt your job out there in Jinghiskahn. Well, we want to be governed here in England. Govern us.

LORD SUMMERHAYS. Ah yes, my friend; but in Jinghiskahn you have to govern the right way. If you dont, you go under and come home. Here everything has to be done the wrong way, to suit governors who understand nothing but partridge shooting (our English native princes, in fact) and voters who dont know what theyre voting about. I dont understand these democratic games; and I'm afraid I'm too old to learn. What can I do but sit in the window of my club, which consists mostly of retired Indian Civil servants? We look on at the muddle and the folly and amateurishness; and we ask each other where a single fortnight of it would have landed us.

TARLETON. Very true. Still, Democracy's all right, you know. Read Mill. Read Jefferson.

LORD SUMMERHAYS. Yes. Democracy reads well; but it doesnt act well, like some people's plays. No, no, my friend Tarleton: to make Democracy work, you need an aristocratic democracy. To make Aristocracy work, you need a democratic aristocracy. Youve got neither; and theres an end of it.

TARLETON. Still, you know, the superman may come. The superman's an idea. I believe in ideas. Read Whatshisname.

LORD SUMMERHAYS. Reading is a dangerous amusement, Tarleton. I wish I could persuade your free library people of that.

TARLETON. Why, man, it's the beginning of education.

LORD SUMMERHAYS. On the contrary, it's the end of it. How can you dare teach a man to read until youve taught him everything else first?

JOHNNY [*intercepting his father's reply by coming out of the swing and taking the floor*] Leave it at that. Thats good sense. Anybody on for a game of tennis?

BENTLEY. Oh, lets have some more improving conversation. Wouldnt you rather, Johnny?

JOHNNY. If you ask me, no.

TARLETON. Johnny: you dont cultivate your mind. You dont read.

JOHNNY [*coming between his mother and Lord Summerhays, book in hand*] Yes I do. I bet you what you like that, page for page, I read more than you, though I dont talk about it so much. Only, I dont read the same books. I like a book with a plot in it. You like a book with nothing in it but some idea that the chap that writes it keeps worrying, like a cat chasing its own tail. I can stand a little of it, just as I can stand watching the cat for two minutes, say, when Ive nothing better to do. But a man soon gets fed up with that sort of thing. The fact is, you look on an author as a sort of god. *I* look on him as a man that I pay to do a certain thing for me. I pay him to amuse me and to take me out of myself and make me forget.

TARLETON. No. Wrong principle. You want to remember. Read Kipling. "Lest we forget."

JOHNNY. If Kipling wants to remember, let him remember. If he had to run Tarleton's Underwear, he'd be jolly glad to forget. As he has a much softer job, and wants to keep himself before the public, his cry is, "Dont you forget the sort of things I'm rather clever at writing about." Well, I dont blame him: it's his business: I should do the same in his place. But what he wants and what I want are two different things. I want to forget; and I pay another man to make me forget. If I buy a book or go to the theatre, I want to forget the shop and forget myself from the moment I go in to the moment I come out. Thats what I pay my money for. And if I find that the author's simply getting at me the whole time, I consider that he's obtained my money under false pretences. I'm not a morbid crank: I'm a natural man; and, as such, I dont like being got at. If a man in my employment did it, I should sack him. If a member of my club did it, I should cut him. If he went too far with it, I should bring his conduct before the committee. I might even punch his head, if it came to that. Well, who and what is an author that he should be privileged to take liberties that are not allowed to other men?

MRS TARLETON. You see, John! What have I always told you? Johnny has as much to say for himself as anybody when he likes.

JOHNNY. I'm no fool, mother, whatever some people may fancy. I dont set up to have as many ideas as the Governor; but what ideas I have are consecutive, at all events. I can think as well as talk.

BENTLEY [*to Tarleton, chuckling*] Had you there, old man, hadnt he? You are rather all over the shop with your ideas, aint you?

JOHNNY [*handsomely*] I'm not saying anything against you, Governor. But I do say that the time has come for sane, healthy, unpretending men like me to make a stand against this conspiracy of the writing and talking and artistic lot to put us in the back row. It isnt a fact that we're inferior to them: it's a put-up job; and it's they that have put the job up. It's we that run the country for them; and all the thanks we get is to be told we're Philistines and vulgar tradesmen and sordid city men and so forth, and that theyre all angels of light and leading. The time has come to assert ourselves and put a stop to their stuck-up nonsense. Perhaps if we had nothing better to do than talking or writing, we could do it better than they. Anyhow, theyre the failures and refuse of business (hardly a man of them that didnt begin in an office) and we're the successes of it. Thank God I havnt failed yet at anything; and I dont believe I should fail at literature if it would pay me to turn my hand to it.

BENTLEY. Hear, hear!

MRS TARLETON. Fancy you writing a book, Johnny! Do you think he could, Lord Summerhays?

LORD SUMMERHAYS. Why not? As a matter of fact all the really prosperous authors I have met since my return to England have been very like him.

TARLETON [*again impressed*] Thats an idea. Thats a new idea. I believe I ought to have made Johnny an author. Ive never said so before for fear of hurting his feelings, because, after all, the lad cant help it; but Ive never thought Johnny worth tuppence as a man of business.

JOHNNY [*sarcastic*] Oh! You think youve always kept that to yourself, do you, Governor? I know your opinion of me as well as you know it yourself. It takes one man of business to appreciate another; and you arnt, and you never have been, a real man of business. I know where Tarleton's would have been three or four times if it hadnt been for me. [*With a snort and a nod to emphasize the implied warning, he retreats to the Turkish bath, and lolls against it with an air of good-humored indifference*].

TARLETON. Well, who denies it? Youre quite right, my boy. I dont mind confessing to you all that the circumstances that condemned me to keep a shop are the biggest tragedy in modern life. I ought to have been a writer. I'm essentially a man of ideas. When I was a young man I sometimes used to pray that I might fail, so that I should be justified in giving up business and doing something: something first-class. But it was no good: I couldnt fail. I said to myself that if I could only once go to my Chickabiddy here and shew her a chartered accountant's statement proving that I'd made £20 less than last year, I could ask her to let me chance Johnny's and Hypatia's future by going into literature. But it was no good. First it was £250 more than last year. Then it was £700. Then it was £2000. Then I saw it was no use: Prometheus was chained to his rock: read Shelley: read Mrs Browning. Well, well, it was not to be. [*He rises solemnly*]. Lord Summerhays: I ask you to excuse me for a few moments. There are times when a man needs to meditate in solitude on his destiny. A chord is touched; and he sees the drama of his life as a spectator sees a play. Laugh if you feel inclined: no man sees the comic side of it more than I. In the theatre of life everyone may be amused except the actor. [*Brightening*] Theres an idea in this: an idea for a picture. What a pity young Bentley is not a painter! Tarleton meditating on his destiny. Not in a toga. Not in the trappings of the tragedian or the philosopher. In plain coat and trousers: a man like any other man. And beneath that coat and trousers a human soul. Tarleton's Underwear! [*He goes out gravely into the vestibule*].

MRS TARLETON [*fondly*] I suppose it's a wife's partiality, Lord Summerhays; but I do think John is really great. I'm sure he was meant to be a king. My father looked down on John, because he was a rate collector and John kept a shop. It hurt his pride to have to borrow money so often from John; and he used to console himself by saying, "After all, hes only a linendraper." But at last one day he said to me, "John is a king."

BENTLEY. How much did he borrow on that occasion?

LORD SUMMERHAYS [*sharply*] Bentley!

MRS TARLETON. Oh, dont scold the child: he'd have to say something like that if it was to be his last word on earth. Besides, hes quite right: my poor father had asked for his usual five pounds; and John gave him a hundred in his big way. Just like a king.

LORD SUMMERHAYS. Not at all. I had five kings to manage

in Jinghiskahn; and I think you do your husband some injustice, Mrs Tarleton. They pretended to like me because I kept their brothers from murdering them; but I didnt like them. And I like Tarleton.

MRS TARLETON. Everybody does. I really must go and make the cook do him a Welsh rabbit. He expects one on special occasions. [*She goes to the inner door*]. Johnny: when he comes back ask him where we're to put that new Turkish bath. Turkish baths are his latest. [*She goes out*].

JOHNNY [*coming forward again*] Now that the Governor has given himself away, and the old lady's gone, I'll tell you something, Lord Summerhays. If you study men whove made an enormous pile in business without being keen on money, youll find that they all have a slate off. The Governor's a wonderful man; but he's not quite all there, you know. If you notice, he's different from me; and whatever my failings may be, I'm a sane man. Erratic: thats what he is. And the danger is that some day he'll give the whole show away.

LORD SUMMERHAYS. Giving the show away is a method like any other method. Keeping it to yourself is only another method. I should keep an open mind about it.

JOHNNY. Has it ever occurred to you that a man with an open mind must be a bit of a scoundrel? If you ask me, I like a man who makes up his mind once for all as to whats right and whats wrong and then sticks to it. At all events you know where to have him.

LORD SUMMERHAYS. That may not be his object.

BENTLEY. He may want to have you, old chap.

JOHNNY. Well, let him. If a member of my club wants to steal my umbrella, he knows where to find it. If a man put up for the club who had an open mind on the subject of property in umbrellas, I should blackball him. An open mind is all very well in clever talky-talky; but in conduct and in business give me solid ground.

LORD SUMMERHAYS. Yes: the quicksands make life difficult. Still, there they are. It's no use pretending theyre rocks.

JOHNNY. I dont know. You can draw a line and make other chaps toe it. Thats what I call morality.

LORD SUMMERHAYS. Very true. But you dont make any progress when youre toeing a line.

HYPATIA [*suddenly, as if she could bear no more of it*] Bentley: do go and play tennis with Johnny. You must take exercise.

LORD SUMMERHAYS. Do, my boy, do. [*To Johnny*] Take him out and make him skip about.

BENTLEY [*rising reluctantly*] I promised you two inches more round my chest this summer. I tried exercises with an indiarubber expander; but I wasnt strong enough: instead of my expanding it, it crumpled me up. Come along, Johnny.

JOHNNY. Do you no end of good, young chap. [*He goes out with Bentley through the pavilion*].

Hypatia throws aside her work with an enormous sigh of relief.

LORD SUMMERHAYS. At last!

HYPATIA. At last. Oh, if I might only have a holiday in an asylum for the dumb. How I envy the animals! They cant talk. If Johnny could only put back his ears or wag his tail instead of laying down the law, how much better it would be! We should know when he was cross and when he was pleased; and thats all we know now, with all his talk. It never stops: talk, talk, talk, talk. Thats my life. All the day I listen to mamma talking; at dinner I listen to papa talking; and when papa stops for breath I listen to Johnny talking.

LORD SUMMERHAYS. You make me feel very guilty. I talk too, I'm afraid.

HYPATIA. Oh, I dont mind that, because your talk is a novelty. But it must have been dreadful for your daughters.

LORD SUMMERHAYS. I suppose so.

HYPATIA. If parents would only realize how they bore their children! Three or four times in the last half hour Ive been on the point of screaming.

LORD SUMMERHAYS. Were we very dull?

HYPATIA. Not at all: you were very clever. Thats whats so hard to bear, because it makes it so difficult to avoid listening. You see, I'm young; and I do so want something to happen. My mother tells me that when I'm her age, I shall be only too glad that nothing's happened; but I'm not her age; so what good is that to me? Theres my father in the garden, meditating on his destiny. All very well for him: he's had a destiny to meditate on; but I havnt had any destiny yet. Everything's happened to him: nothing's happened to me. Thats why this unending talk is so maddeningly uninteresting to me.

LORD SUMMERHAYS. It would be worse if we sat in silence.

HYPATIA. No it wouldnt. If you all sat in silence, as if you were waiting for something to happen, then there would be hope even if nothing did happen. But this eternal cackle, cackle, cackle about things in general is only fit for old, old, OLD people. I suppose it means something to them: theyve had their fling. All I listen for is some sign of it ending in something; but just when it seems to be coming to a point, Johnny or papa just starts another hare; and it all begins over again; and I realize that it's never going to lead anywhere and never going to stop. Thats when I want to scream. I wonder how you can stand it.

LORD SUMMERHAYS. Well, I'm old and garrulous myself, you see. Besides, I'm not here of my own free will, exactly. I came because you ordered me to come.

HYPATIA. Didnt you want to come?

LORD SUMMERHAYS. My dear: after thirty years of managing other people's business, men lose the habit of considering what they want or dont want.

HYPATIA. Oh, dont begin to talk about what men do, and about thirty years experience. If you cant get off that subject, youd better send for Johnny and papa and begin it all over again.

LORD SUMMERHAYS. I'm sorry. I beg your pardon.

HYPATIA. I asked you, didnt you want to come?

LORD SUMMERHAYS. I did not stop to consider whether I wanted or not, because when I read your letter I knew I had to come.

HYPATIA. Why?

LORD SUMMERHAYS. O come, Miss Tarleton! Really! really! Dont force me to call you a blackmailer to your face. You have me in your power; and I do what you tell me very obediently. Dont ask me to pretend I do it of my own free will.

HYPATIA. I dont know what a blackmailer is. I havnt even that much experience.

LORD SUMMERHAYS. A blackmailer, my dear young lady, is a person who knows a disgraceful secret in the life of another person, and extorts money from that other person by threatening to make his secret public unless the money is paid.

HYPATIA. I havnt asked you for money.

LORD SUMMERHAYS. No; but you asked me to come down here and talk to you; and you mentioned casually that if I didnt youd have nobody to talk about me to but Bentley. That was a threat, was it not?

HYPATIA. Well, I wanted you to come.

LORD SUMMERHAYS. In spite of my age and my unfortunate talkativeness?

HYPATIA. I like talking to you. I can let myself go with you. I can say things to you I cant say to other people.

LORD SUMMERHAYS. I wonder why?

HYPATIA. Well, you are the only really clever, grown-up, high-class, experienced man I know who has given himself away to me by making an utter fool of himself with me. You cant wrap yourself up in your toga after that. You cant give yourself airs with me.

LORD SUMMERHAYS. You mean you can tell Bentley about me if I do.

HYPATIA. Even if there wasnt any Bentley: even if you didnt care (and I really dont see why you should care so much) still, we never could be on conventional terms with one another again. Besides, Ive got a feeling for you: almost a ghastly sort of love for you.

LORD SUMMERHAYS [*shrinking*] I beg you—no, please.

HYPATIA. Oh, it's nothing at all flattering; and, of course, nothing wrong, as I suppose youd call it.

LORD SUMMERHAYS. Please believe that I know that. When men of my age—

HYPATIA [*impatiently*] Oh, do talk about yourself when you mean yourself, and not about men of your age.

LORD SUMMERHAYS. I'll put it as bluntly as I can. When, as you say, I made an utter fool of myself, believe me, I made a poetic fool of myself. I was seduced, not by appetites which, thank Heaven, Ive long outlived: not even by the desire of second childhood for a child companion, but by the innocent impulse to place the delicacy and wisdom and spirituality of my age at the affectionate service of your youth for a few years, at the end of which you would be a grown, strong, formed—widow. Alas, my dear, the delicacy of age reckoned, as usual, without the derision and cruelty of youth. You told me that you didnt want to be an old man's nurse, and that you didnt want to have undersized children like Bentley. It served me right: I dont reproach you: I was an old fool. But how you can imagine, after that, that I can suspect you of the smallest feeling for me except the inevitable feeling of early youth for late age, or imagine that I have any feeling for you except one of shrinking humiliation, I cant understand.

HYPATIA. I dont blame you for falling in love with me. I shall be grateful to you all my life for it, because that was the first time that anything really interesting happened to me.

LORD SUMMERHAYS. Do you mean to tell me that nothing of that kind had ever happened before? that no man had ever—

HYPATIA. Oh, lots. Thats part of the routine of life here: the very dullest part of it. The young man who comes a-courting is as familiar an incident in my life as coffee for breakfast. Of course, he's too much of a gentleman to misbehave himself; and I'm too much of a lady to let him; and he's shy and sheepish; and I'm correct and self-possessed; and at last, when I can bear it no longer, I either frighten him off or give him a chance of proposing, just to see how he'll do it, and refuse him because he does it in the same silly way as all the rest. You dont call that an event in one's life, do you? With you it was different. I should as soon have expected the North Pole to fall in love with me as you. You know I'm only a linendraper's daughter when all's said. I was afraid of you: you, a great man! a lord! and older than my father. And then, what a situation it was! Just think of it! I was engaged to your son; and you knew nothing about it. He was afraid to tell you: he brought you down here because he thought if he could throw us together I could get round you because I was such a ripping girl. We arranged it all: he and I. We got Papa and Mamma and Johnny out of the way splendidly; and then Bentley took himself off, and left us—you and me!—to take a walk through the heather and admire the scenery of Hindhead. You never dreamt that it was all a plan: that what made me so nice was the way I was playing up to my destiny as the sweet girl that was to make your boy happy. And then! and then! [*She rises to dance and clap her hands in her glee*].

LORD SUMMERHAYS [*shuddering*] Stop, stop. Can no woman understand a man's delicacy?

HYPATIA [*revelling in the recollection*] And then—ha, ha! —you proposed. You! A father! For your son's girl!

LORD SUMMERHAYS. Stop, I tell you. Dont profane what you dont understand.

HYPATIA. That was something happening at last with a vengeance. It was splendid. It was my first peep behind the scenes. If I'd been seventeen I should have fallen in love with you. Even as it is, I feel quite differently towards you from what I do towards other old men. So [*offering her hand*] you may kiss my hand if that will be any fun for you.

LORD SUMMERHAYS [*rising and recoiling to the table, deeply revolted*] No, no, no. How dare you? [*She laughs mischiev-*

ously]. How callous youth is! How coarse! How cynical! How ruthlessly cruel!

HYPATIA. Stuff! It's only that youre tired of a great many things Ive never tried.

LORD SUMMERHAYS. It's not alone that. Ive not forgotten the brutality of my own boyhood. But do try to learn, glorious young beast that you are, that age is squeamish, sentimental, fastidious. If you cant understand my holier feelings, at least you know the bodily infirmities of the old. You know that I darent eat all the rich things you gobble up at every meal; that I cant bear the noise and racket and clatter that affect you no more than they affect a stone. Well, my soul is like that too. Spare it: be gentle with it [*he involuntarily puts out his hands to plead: she takes them with a laugh*]. If you could possibly think of me as half an angel and half an invalid, we should get on much better together.

HYPATIA. We get on very well, I think. Nobody else ever called me a glorious young beast. I like that. Glorious young beast expresses exactly what I like to be.

LORD SUMMERHAYS [*extricating his hands and sitting down*] Where on earth did you get these morbid tastes? You seem to have been well brought up in a normal, healthy, respectable, middle-class family. Yet you go on like the most unwholesome product of the rankest Bohemianism.

HYPATIA. Thats just it. I'm fed up with—

LORD SUMMERHAYS. Horrible expression. Dont.

HYPATIA. Oh, I daresay it's vulgar; but theres no other word for it. I'm fed up with nice things: with respectability, with propriety! When a woman has nothing to do, money and respectability mean that nothing is ever allowed to happen to her. I dont want to be good; and I dont want to be bad: I just dont want to be bothered about either good or bad: I want to be an active verb.

LORD SUMMERHAYS. An active verb? Oh, I see. An active verb signifies to be, to do, or to suffer.

HYPATIA. Just so: how clever of you! I want to be; I want to do; and I'm game to suffer if it costs that. But stick here doing nothing but being good and nice and ladylike I simply wont. Stay down here with us for a week; and I'll shew you what it means: shew it to you going on day after day, year after year, lifetime after lifetime.

LORD SUMMERHAYS. Shew me what?

HYPATIA. Girls withering into ladies. Ladies withering into old maids. Nursing old women. Running errands for old men. Good for nothing else at last. Oh, you cant imagine the fiendish selfishness of the old people and the maudlin sacrifice of the young. It's more unbearable than any poverty: more horrible than any regular-right-down wickedness. Oh, home! home! parents! family! duty! how I loathe them! How I'd like to see them all blown to bits! The poor escape. The wicked escape. Well, I cant be poor: we're rolling in money: it's no use pretending we're not. But I can be wicked; and I'm quite prepared to be.

LORD SUMMERHAYS. You think that easy?

HYPATIA. Well, isnt it? Being a man, you ought to know.

LORD SUMMERHAYS. It requires some natural talent, which can no doubt be cultivated. It's not really easy to be anything out of the common.

HYPATIA. Anyhow, I mean to make a fight for living.

LORD SUMMERHAYS. Living your own life, I believe the Suffragist phrase is.

HYPATIA. Living *any* life. Living, instead of withering without even a gardener to snip you off when youre rotten.

LORD SUMMERHAYS. Ive lived an active life; but Ive withered all the same.

HYPATIA. No: youve worn out: thats quite different. And youve some life in you yet or you wouldnt have fallen in love with me. You can never imagine how delighted I was to find that instead of being the correct sort of big panjandrum you were supposed to be, you were really an old rip like papa.

LORD SUMMERHAYS. No, no: not about your father: I really cant bear it. And if you must say these terrible things: these heart-wounding shameful things, at least find something prettier to call me than an old rip.

HYPATIA. Well, what would you call a man proposing to a girl who might be—

LORD SUMMERHAYS. His daughter: yes, I know.

HYPATIA. I was going to say his granddaughter.

LORD SUMMERHAYS. You always have one more blow to get in.

HYPATIA. Youre too sensitive. Did you ever make mud pies when you were a kid—beg pardon: a child.

LORD SUMMERHAYS. I hope not.

HYPATIA. It's a dirty job; but Johnny and I were vulgar enough to like it. I like young people because theyre not too afraid of dirt to live. Ive grown out of the mud pies; but I like slang; and I like bustling you up by saying things that shock you; and I'd rather put up with swearing and smoking than with dull respectability; and there are lots of things that would just shrivel you up that I think rather jolly. Now!

LORD SUMMERHAYS. Ive not the slightest doubt of it. Dont insist.

HYPATIA. It's not your ideal, is it?

LORD SUMMERHAYS. No.

HYPATIA. Shall I tell you why? Your ideal is an old woman. I daresay she's got a young face; but she's an old woman. Old, old, old. Squeamish. Cant stand up to things. Cant enjoy things: not real things. Always on the shrink.

LORD SUMMERHAYS. On the shrink! Detestable expression.

HYPATIA. Bah! you cant stand even a little thing like that. What good are you? Oh, what good are you?

LORD SUMMERHAYS. Dont ask me. I dont know. I dont know.

Tarleton returns from the vestibule. Hypatia sits down demurely.

HYPATIA. Well, papa: have you meditated on your destiny?

TARLETON [*puzzled*] What? Oh! my destiny. Gad, I forgot all about it: Jock started a rabbit and put it clean out of my head. Besides, why should I give way to morbid introspection? It's a sign of madness. Read Lombroso. [*To Lord Summerhays*] Well, Summerhays, has my little girl been entertaining you?

LORD SUMMERHAYS. Yes. She is a wonderful entertainer.

TARLETON. I think my idea of bringing up a young girl has been rather a success. Dont you listen to this, Patsy: it might make you conceited. She's never been treated like a child. I always said the same thing to her mother. Let her read what she likes. Let her do what she likes. Let her go where she likes. Eh, Patsy?

HYPATIA. Oh yes, if there had only been anything for me to do, any place for me to go, anything I wanted to read.

TARLETON. There, you see! She's not satisfied. Restless. Wants things to happen. Wants adventures to drop out of the sky.

HYPATIA [*gathering up her work*] If youre going to talk about me and my education, I'm off.

TARLETON. Well, well, off with you. [*To Lord Summerhays*] She's active, like me. She actually wanted me to put her into the shop.

HYPATIA. Well, they tell me that the girls there have adventures sometimes. [*She goes out through the inner door*].

TARLETON. She had me there, though she doesnt know it, poor innocent lamb! Public scandal exaggerates enormously, of course; but moralize as you will, superabundant vitality is a physical fact that cant be talked away. [*He sits down between the writing table and the sideboard*]. Difficult question this, of bringing up children. Between ourselves, it has beaten me. I never was so surprised in my life as when I came to know Johnny as a man of business and found out what he was really like. How did you manage with your sons?

LORD SUMMERHAYS. Well, I really hadnt time to be a father: thats the plain truth of the matter. Their poor dear mother did the usual thing while they were with us. Then of course Eton, Oxford, the usual routine of their class. I saw very little of them, and thought very little about them: how could I? with a whole province on my hands. They and I are—acquaintances. Not, perhaps, quite ordinary acquaintances: theres a sort of—er—I should almost call it a sort of remorse about the way we shake hands (when we do shake hands) which means, I suppose, that we're sorry we dont care more for one another; and I'm afraid we dont meet oftener than we can help. We put each other too much out of countenance. It's really a very difficult relation. To my mind not altogether a natural one.

TARLETON [*impressed, as usual*] Thats an idea, certainly. I dont think anybody has ever written about that.

LORD SUMMERHAYS. Bentley is the only one who was really my son in any serious sense. He was completely spoilt. When he was sent to a preparatory school he simply yelled until he was sent home. Eton was out of the question; but we managed to tutor him into Oxford. No use: he was sent down. By that time my work was over; and I saw a good deal of him. But I could do nothing with him—except look on. I should have thought your case was quite different. You keep up the middle-class tradition: the day school and the business training instead of the university. I believe in the day school part of it. At all events, you know your own children.

TARLETON. Do we? I'm not so sure of it. Fact is, my dear Summerhays, once childhood is over, once the little animal has got past the stage at which it acquires what you might call a sense of decency, it's all up with the relation between parent and child. You cant get over the fearful shyness of it.

LORD SUMMERHAYS. Shyness?

TARLETON. Yes, shyness. Read Dickens.

LORD SUMMERHAYS [*surprised*] Dickens!! Of all authors, Charles Dickens! Are you serious?

TARLETON. I dont mean his books. Read his letters to his family. Read any man's letters to his children. Theyre not human. Theyre not about himself or themselves. Theyre about hotels, scenery, about the weather, about getting wet and losing the train and what he saw on the road and all that. Not a word about himself. Forced. Shy. Duty letters. All fit to be published: that says everything. I tell you theres a wall ten feet thick and ten miles high between parent and child. I know what I'm talking about. Ive girls in my employment: girls and young men. I had ideas on the subject. I used to go to the parents and tell them not to let their children go out into the world without instruction in the dangers and temptations they were going to be thrown into. What did every one of the mothers say to me? "Oh, sir, how could I speak of such things to my own daughter?" The men said I was quite right; but they didnt do it, any more than I'd been able to do it myself to Johnny. I had to leave books in his way; and I felt just awful when I did it. Believe me, Summerhays, the relation between the young and the old should be an innocent relation. It should be something they could talk about. Well, the relation between parent and child may be an affectionate relation. It may be a useful relation. It may be a necessary relation. But it can never be an innocent relation. Youd die rather than allude to it. Depend on it, in a thousand years itll be considered bad form to know who your father and mother are. Embarrassing. Better hand Bentley over to me. I can look him in the face and talk to him as man to man. You can have Johnny.

LORD SUMMERHAYS. Thank you. Ive lived so long in a country where a man may have fifty sons, who are no more to him than a regiment of soldiers, that I'm afraid Ive lost the English feeling about it.

TARLETON [*restless again*] You mean Jinghiskahn. Ah yes. Good thing the empire. Educates us. Opens our minds. Knocks the Bible out of us. And civilizes the other chaps.

LORD SUMMERHAYS. Yes: it civilizes t h e m. And it uncivilizes us. Their gain. Our loss, Tarleton, believe me, our loss.

TARLETON. Well, why not? Averages out the human race. Makes the nigger half an Englishman. Makes the Englishman half a nigger.

LORD SUMMERHAYS. Speaking as the unfortunate Englishman in question, I dont like the process. If I had my life to live over again, I'd stay at home and supercivilize myself.

TARLETON. Nonsense! dont be selfish. Think how youve improved the other chaps. Look at the Spanish empire! Bad job for Spain, but splendid for South America. Look at what the Romans did for Britain! They burst up and had to clear out; but think of all they taught us! They were the making of us: I believe there was a Roman camp on Hindhead: I'll shew it to you tomorrow. Thats the good side of Imperialism: it's unselfish. I despise the Little Englanders: theyre always thinking about England. Smallminded. I'm for the Parliament of man, the federation of the world. Read Tennyson. [*He settles down again*]. Then theres the great food question.

LORD SUMMERHAYS [*apprehensively*] Need we go into that this afternoon?

TARLETON. No; but I wish youd tell the Chickabiddy that the Jinghiskahns eat no end of toasted cheese, and that it's the secret of their amazing health and long life!

LORD SUMMERHAYS. Unfortunately they are neither healthy nor long lived. And they dont eat toasted cheese.

TARLETON. There you are! They would be if they ate it. Anyhow, say what you like, provided the moral is a Welsh rabbit for my supper.

LORD SUMMERHAYS. British morality in a nutshell!

TARLETON [*hugely amused*] Yes. Ha ha! Awful hypocrites, aint we?

They are interrupted by excited cries from the grounds.

HYPATIA } Papa! Mamma! Come out as fast as you can. Quick. Quick.

BENTLEY } Hello, governor! Come out. An aeroplane. Look, look.

TARLETON [*starting up*] Aeroplane! Did he say an aeroplane?

LORD SUMMERHAYS. Aeroplane! [*A shadow falls on the pavilion; and some of the glass at the top is shattered and falls on the floor*].

Tarleton and Lord Summerhays rush out through the pavilion into the garden.

HYPATIA | Take care. Take care of the chimney.
BENTLEY | Come this side: it's coming right where youre standing.
TARLETON | Hallo! where the devil are you coming? youll have my roof off.
LORD SUMMERHAYS | He's lost control.

MRS. TARLETON. Look, look, Hypatia. There are two people in it.

BENTLEY. Theyve cleared it. Well steered!

TARLETON | Yes; but theyre coming slam into the greenhouse.
LORD SUMMERHAYS | Look out for the glass.
MRS. TARLETON | Theyll break all the glass. Theyll spoil all the grapes.
BENTLEY | Mind where youre coming. He'll save it. No: theyre down.

An appalling crash of breaking glass is heard. Everybody shrieks.

MRS. TARLETON | Oh, are they killed? John: are they killed?
LORD SUMMERHAYS | Are you hurt? Is anything broken? Can you stand?
HYPATIA | Oh, you must be hurt. Are you sure? Shall I get you some water? Or some wine?
TARLETON | Are you all right? Sure you wont have some brandy just to take off the shock.

THE AVIATOR. No, thank you. Quite right. Not a scratch. I assure you I'm all right.

BENTLEY. What luck! And what a smash! You *are* a lucky chap, I can tell you.

The Aviator and Tarleton come in through the pavilion, followed by Lord Summerhays and Bentley, the Aviator on Tarleton's right. Bentley passes the Aviator and turns to have an admiring look at him. Lord Summerhays overtakes Tarleton less pointedly on the opposite side with the same object.

THE AVIATOR. I'm really very sorry. I'm afraid Ive knocked your vinery into a cocked hat. (*Effusively*) You dont mind, do you?

TARLETON. Not a bit. Come in and have some tea. Stay to dinner. Stay over the week-end. All my life Ive wanted to fly.

THE AVIATOR [*taking off his goggles*] Youre really more than kind.

BENTLEY. Why, it's Joey Percival.

PERCIVAL. Hallo, Ben! That you?

TARLETON. What! The man with three fathers!

PERCIVAL. Oh! has Ben been talking about me?

TARLETON. Consider yourself as one of the family—if you will do me the honor. And your friend too. Wheres your friend?

PERCIVAL. Oh, by the way! before he comes in: let me explain. I dont know him.

TARLETON. Eh?

PERCIVAL. Havnt even looked at him. I'm trying to make a club record with a passenger. The club supplied the passenger. He just got in; and Ive been too busy handling the aeroplane to look at him. I havnt said a word to him; and I cant answer for him socially; but he's an ideal passenger for a flyer. He saved me from a smash.

LORD SUMMERHAYS. I saw it. It was extraordinary. When you were thrown out he held on to the top bar with one hand. You came past him in the air, going straight for the glass. He caught you and turned you off into the flower bed, and then lighted beside you like a bird.

PERCIVAL. How he kept his head I cant imagine. Frankly, *I* didnt.

The Passenger, also begoggled, comes in through the pavilion with Johnny and the two ladies. The Passenger comes between Percival and Tarleton, Mrs. Tarleton between Lord Summerhays and her husband, Hypatia between Percival and Bentley, and Johnny to Bentley's right.

TARLETON. Just discussing your prowess, my dear sir.

Magnificent. Youll stay to dinner. Youll stay the night. Stay over the week. The Chickabiddy will be delighted.

MRS TARLETON. Wont you take off your goggles and have some tea?

The passenger begins to remove the goggles.

TARLETON. Do. Have a wash. Johnny: take the gentleman to your room: I'll look after Mr Percival. They must—

By this time the passenger has got the goggles off, and stands revealed as a remarkably good-looking woman.

MRS TARLETON	Well I never ! ! !	*All together.*
BENTLEY	[*in a whisper*] Oh, I say!	
JOHNNY	By George!	
LORD SUMMERHAYS	A lady!	
HYPATIA	A woman!	
TARLETON	[*to Percival*] You never told me—	
PERCIVAL	I hadnt the least idea—	

An embarrassed pause.

PERCIVAL. I assure you if I'd had the faintest notion that my passenger was a lady I shouldnt have left you to shift for yourself in that selfish way.

LORD SUMMERHAYS. The lady seems to have shifted for both very effectually, sir.

PERCIVAL. Saved my life. I admit it most gratefully.

TARLETON. I must apologize, madam, for having offered you the civilities appropriate to the opposite sex. And yet, why opposite? We are all human: males and females of the same species. When the dress is the same the distinction vanishes. I'm proud to receive in my house a lady of evident refinement and distinction. Allow me to introduce myself: Tarleton: John Tarleton (*seeing conjecture in the passenger's eye*)—yes, yes: Tarleton's Underwear. My wife, Mrs Tarleton: youll excuse me for having in what I had taken to be a confidence between man and man alluded to her as the Chickabiddy. My daughter Hypatia, who has always wanted some adventure to drop out of the sky, and is now, I hope, satisfied at last. Lord Summerhays: a man known wherever the British flag waves. His son Bentley, engaged to Hypatia. Mr Joseph Percival, the promising son of three highly intellectual fathers.

HYPATIA [*startled*] Bentley's friend? [*Bentley nods*].

TARLETON [*continuing, to the passenger*] May I now ask to be allowed the pleasure of knowing your name?

THE PASSENGER. My name is Lina Szczepanowska [*pronouncing it Sh-Chepanovska*].

PERCIVAL. Sh— I beg your pardon?

LINA. Szczepanowska.

PERCIVAL [*dubiously*] Thank you.

TARLETON [*very politely*] Would you mind saying it again?

LINA. Say fish.

TARLETON. Fish.

LINA. Say church.

TARLETON. Church.

LINA. Say fish church.

TARLETON [*remonstrating*] But it's not good sense.

LINA [*inexorable*] Say fish church.

TARLETON. Fish church.

LINA. Again.

TARLETON. No, but—[*resigning himself*] fish church.

LINA. Now say Szczepanowska.

TARLETON. Szczepanowska. Got it, by Gad. [*A sibilant whispering becomes audible: they are all saying Sh-ch to themselves*]. Szczepanowska! Not an English name, is it?

LINA. Polish. I'm a Pole.

TARLETON [*dithyrambically*] Ah yes. What other nation, madame, could have produced your magical personality? Your countrywomen have always appealed to our imagination. Women of Destiny! beautiful! musical! passionate! tragic! You will be at home here: my own temperament is pre-eminently Polish. Wont you sit down?

The group breaks up. Johnny and Bentley hurry to the pavilion and fetch the two wicker chairs. Johnny gives his to Lina. Hypatia and Percival take the chairs at the worktable. Lord Summerhays gives the chair at the vestibule end of the writing table to Mrs Tarleton; and Bentley replaces it with a wicker chair, which Lord Summerhays takes. Johnny remains standing behind the worktable, Bentley behind his father.

MRS TARLETON [*to Lina*] Have some tea now, wont you?

LINA. I never drink tea.

TARLETON [*sitting down at the end of the writing table nearest Lina*] Bad thing to aeroplane on, I should imagine. Too jumpy. Been up much?

LINA. Not in an aeroplane. Ive parachuted; but thats child's play.

MRS TARLETON. But arnt you very foolish to run such a dreadful risk?

LINA. You cant live without running risks.

MRS TARLETON. Oh, what a thing to say! Didnt you know you might have been killed?

LINA. That was why I went up.

HYPATIA. Of course. Cant you understand the fascination of the thing? the novelty! the daring! the sense of something happening!

LINA. Oh no. It's too tame a business for that. I went up for family reasons.

TARLETON. Eh? What? Family reasons?

MRS TARLETON. I hope it wasnt to spite your mother?

PERCIVAL [*quickly*] Or your husband?

LINA. I'm not married. And why should I want to spite my mother?

HYPATIA [*aside to Percival*] That was clever of you, Mr Percival.

PERCIVAL. What?

HYPATIA. To find out.

TARLETON. I'm in a difficulty. I cant understand a lady going up in an aeroplane for family reasons. It's rude to be curious and ask questions; but then it's inhuman to be indifferent, as if you didnt care.

LINA. I'll tell you with pleasure. For the last hundred and fifty years, not a single day has passed without some member of my family risking his life—or her life. It's a point of honor with us to keep up that tradition. Usually several of us do it; but it happens that just at this moment it is being kept up by one of my brothers only. Early this morning I got a telegram from him to say that there had been a fire, and that he could do nothing for the rest of the week. Fortunately I had an invitation from the Aerial League to see this gentleman try to break the passenger record. I appealed to the President of the League to let me save the honor of my family. He arranged it for me.

TARLETON. Oh, I must be dreaming. This is stark raving nonsense.

LINA [*quietly*] You are quite awake, sir.

JOHNNY. We cant all be dreaming the same thing, Governor.

TARLETON. Of course not, you duffer; but then I'm dreaming you as well as the lady.

MRS TARLETON. Dont be silly, John. The lady is only joking, I'm sure. [*To Lina*] I suppose your luggage is in the aeroplane.

PERCIVAL. Luggage was out of the question. If I stay to dinner I'm afraid I cant change unless youll lend me some clothes.

MRS TARLETON. Do you mean neither of you?

PERCIVAL. I'm afraid so.

MRS TARLETON. Oh well, never mind: Hypatia will lend the lady a gown.

LINA. Thank you: I'm quite comfortable as I am. I am not accustomed to gowns: they hamper me and make me feel ridiculous; so if you dont mind I shall not change.

MRS TARLETON. Well, I'm beginning to think I'm doing a bit of dreaming myself.

HYPATIA [*impatiently*] Oh, it's all right, mamma. Johnny: look after Mr Percival. [*To Lina, rising*] Come with me.

Lina follows her to the inner door. They all rise.

JOHNNY [*to Percival*] I'll shew you.

PERCIVAL. Thank you.

Lina goes out with Hypatia, and Percival with Johnny.

MRS TARLETON. Well, this is a nice thing to happen! And look at the greenhouse! Itll cost thirty pounds to mend it. People have no right to do such things. And you invited them to dinner too! What sort of woman is that to have in our house when you know that all Hindhead will be calling on us to see that aeroplane? Bunny: come with me and help me to get all the people out of the grounds: I declare they came running as if theyd sprung up out of the earth [*she makes for the inner door*].

TARLETON. No: dont you trouble, Chickabiddy: I'll tackle em.

MRS TARLETON. Indeed youll do nothing of the kind: youll stay here quietly with Lord Summerhays. Youd invite them all to dinner. Come, Bunny. [*She goes out, followed by Bentley. Lord Summerhays sits down again*].

TARLETON. Singularly beautiful woman, Summerhays. What do you make of her? She must be a princess. Whats this family of warriors and statesmen that risk their lives every day?

LORD SUMMERHAYS. They are evidently not warriors and statesmen, or they wouldnt do that.

TARLETON. Well, then, what the devil are they?

LORD SUMMERHAYS. I think I know. The last time I saw that lady, she did something I should not have thought possible.

TARLETON. What was that?

LORD SUMMERHAYS. Well, she walked backwards along a taut wire without a balancing pole and turned a somersault in the middle. I remember that her name was Lina, and that the other name was foreign; though I dont recollect it.

TARLETON. Szcz! You couldnt have forgotten that if youd heard it.

LORD SUMMERHAYS. I didnt hear it: I only saw it on a program. But it's clear she's an acrobat. It explains how she saved Percival. And it accounts for her family pride.

TARLETON. An acrobat, eh? Good! good! good! Summerhays: that brings her within reach. Thats better than a princess. I steeled this evergreen heart of mine when I thought she was a princess. Now I shall let it be touched. She is accessible. Good.

LORD SUMMERHAYS. I hope you are not serious. Remember: you have a family. You have a position. You are not in your first youth.

TARLETON. No matter.

Theres magic in the night
When the heart is young.

My heart is young. Besides, I'm a married man, not a widower like you. A married man can do anything he likes if his wife dont mind. A widower cant be too careful. Not that I would have you think me an unprincipled man or a bad husband. I'm not. But Ive a superabundance of vitality. Read Pepys' Diary.

LORD SUMMERHAYS. The woman is your guest, Tarleton.

TARLETON. Well, is she? A woman I bring into my house is my guest. A woman y o u bring into my house is my guest. But a woman who drops bang down out of the sky into my greenhouse and smashes every blessed pane of glass in it must take her chance.

LORD SUMMERHAYS. Still, you know that my name must not be associated with any scandal. Youll be careful, wont you?

TARLETON. Oh Lord, yes! Yes, yes, yes, yes, yes. I was only joking, of course.

Mrs Tarleton comes back through the inner door.

MRS TARLETON. Well I never! John: I dont think that young woman's right in her head. Do you know what she's just asked for?

TARLETON. Champagne?

MRS TARLETON. No. She wants a Bible and six oranges.

TARLETON. What?

MRS TARLETON. A Bible and six oranges.

TARLETON. I understand the oranges: she's doing an orange cure of some sort. But what on earth does she want the Bible for?

MRS TARLETON. I'm sure I cant imagine. She cant be right in her head.

LORD SUMMERHAYS. Perhaps she wants to read it.

MRS TARLETON. But why should she? on a weekday at all events. What would you advise me to do, Lord Summerhays?

LORD SUMMERHAYS. Well, is there a Bible in the house?

TARLETON. Stacks of em. Theres the family Bible, and the Doré Bible, and the parallel revised version Bible, and the Doves Press Bible, and Johnny's Bible and Bobby's Bible and Patsy's Bible and the Chickabiddy's Bible and my Bible; and I daresay the servants could raise a few more between them. Let her have the lot.

MRS TARLETON. Dont talk like that before Lord Summerhays, John.

LORD SUMMERHAYS. It doesnt matter, Mrs Tarleton: in Jinghiskahn it was a punishable offense to expose a Bible for sale. The empire has no religion.

Lina comes in. She has left her cap in Hypatia's room, but has made no other change. She stops just inside the door, holding it open, evidently not intending to stay.

LINA. Oh, Mrs Tarleton, shall I be making myself very troublesome if I ask for a music-stand in my room as well?

TARLETON. Not at all. You can have the piano if you like. Or the gramophone. Have the gramophone?

LINA. No, thank you: no music.

MRS TARLETON [*going towards her*] Do you think it's good for you to eat so many oranges? Arnt you afraid of getting jaundice?

LINA. Not in the least. But billiard balls will do quite as well.

MRS TARLETON. But you cant eat billiard balls, child!

TARLETON. Get em, Chickabiddy. I understand. [*He imitates a juggler tossing up balls*]. Eh?

LINA [*going to him, past his wife*] Just so.

TARLETON. Billiard balls and cues? Plates, knives, and forks? Two paraffin lamps and a hatstand?

LINA. No: that is popular low-class business. In our family we touch nothing but classical work. Anybody can do lamp and hatstands. *I* can do silver bullets. That is really hard. [*She passes on to Lord Summerhays, and looks gravely down at him as he sits by the writing table*].

MRS TARLETON. Well, I'm sure I dont know what youre talking about; and I only hope you know yourselves. However, you shall have what you want, of course. [*She goes out through the inner door*].

LORD SUMMERHAYS. Will you forgive my curiosity? What is the Bible for?

LINA. To quiet my soul.

LORD SUMMERHAYS [*with a sigh*] Ah yes, yes. It no longer quiets mine, I am sorry to say.

LINA. That is because you do not know how to read it. Put it up before you on a stand; and open it at the Psalms. When you can read them and understand them, quite quietly and happily, and keep six balls in the air all the time, you are in perfect condition; and youll never make a mistake that evening. If you find you cant do that, then go and pray until you can. And be very careful that evening.

LORD SUMMERHAYS. Is that the usual form of test in your profession?

LINA. Nothing that we Szczepanowskis do is usual, my lord.

LORD SUMMERHAYS. Are you all so wonderful?

LINA. It is our profession to be wonderful.

LORD SUMMERHAYS. Do you never condescend to do as common people do? For instance, do you not pray as common people pray?

LINA. Common people do not pray, my lord: they only beg.

LORD SUMMERHAYS. You never ask for anything?

LINA. No.

LORD SUMMERHAYS. Then why do you pray?

LINA. To remind myself that I have a soul.

TARLETON [*walking about*] True. Fine. Good. Beautiful.

All this damned materialism: what good is it to anybody? Ive got a soul: dont tell me I havnt. Cut me up and you cant find it. Cut up a steam engine and you cant find the steam. But, by George, it makes the engine go. Say what you will, Summerhays, the divine spark is a fact.

LORD SUMMERHAYS. Have I denied it?

TARLETON. Our whole civilization is a denial of it. Read Walt Whitman.

LORD SUMMERHAYS. I shall go to the billiard room and get the balls for you.

LINA. Thank you.

Lord Summerhays goes out through the vestibule door.

TARLETON [*going to her*] Listen to me. [*She turns quickly*]. What you said just now was beautiful. You touch chords. You appeal to the poetry in a man. You inspire him. Come now! Youre a woman of the world: youre independent: you must have driven lots of men crazy. You know the sort of man I am, dont you? See through me at a glance, eh?

LINA. Yes. [*She sits down quietly in the chair Lord Summerhays has just left*].

TARLETON. Good. Well, do you like me? Dont misunderstand me: I'm perfectly aware that youre not going to fall in love at first sight with a ridiculous old shopkeeper. I cant help that ridiculous old shopkeeper. I have to carry him about with me whether I like it or not. I have to pay for his clothes, though I hate the cut of them: especially the waistcoat. I have to look at him in the glass while I'm shaving. I loathe him because he's a living lie. My soul's not like that: it's like yours. I want to make a fool of myself. About you. Will you let me?

LINA [*very calm*] How much will you pay?

TARLETON. Nothing. But I'll throw as many sovereigns as you like into the sea to shew you that I'm in earnest.

LINA. Are those your usual terms?

TARLETON. No. I never made that bid before.

LINA [*producing a dainty little book and preparing to write in it*] What did you say your name was?

TARLETON. John Tarleton. The great John Tarleton of Tarleton's Underwear.

LINA [*writing*] T-a-r-l-e-t-o-n. Er—? [*She looks up at him inquiringly*].

TARLETON [*promptly*] Fifty-eight.

LINA. Thank you. I keep a list of all my offers. I like to know what I'm considered worth.

TARLETON. Let me look.

LINA [*offering the book to him*] It's in Polish.

TARLETON. Thats no good. Is mine the lowest offer?

LINA. No: the highest.

TARLETON. What do most of them come to? Diamonds? Motor cars? Furs? Villa at Monte Carlo?

LINA. Oh yes: all that. And sometimes the devotion of a lifetime.

TARLETON. Fancy that! A young man offering a woman his old age as a temptation!

LINA. By the way, you did not say how long.

TARLETON. Until you get tired of me.

LINA. Or until you get tired of me?

TARLETON. I never get tired. I never go on long enough for that. But when it becomes so grand, so inspiring that I feel that everything must be an anti-climax after that, then I run away.

LINA. Does she let you go without a struggle?

TARLETON. Yes. Glad to get rid of me. When love takes a man as it takes me—when it makes him great—it frightens a woman.

LINA. The lady here is your wife, isnt she? Dont you care for her?

TARLETON. Yes. And mind! she comes first always. I reserve her dignity even when I sacrifice my own. Youll respect that point of honor, wont you?

LINA. Only a point of honor?

TARLETON [*impulsively*] No, by God! a point of affection as well.

LINA [*smiling, pleased with him*] Shake hands, old pal.

[*She rises and offers him her hand frankly*].

TARLETON [*giving his hand rather dolefully*] Thanks. That means no, doesnt it?

LINA. It means something that will last longer than yes. I like you. I admit you to my friendship. What a pity you were not trained when you were young! Youd be young still.

TARLETON. I suppose, to an athlete like you, I'm pretty awful, eh?

LINA. Shocking.

TARLETON. Too much crumb. Wrinkles. Yellow patches that wont come off. Short wind. I know. I'm ashamed of myself. I could do nothing on the high rope.

LINA. Oh yes: I could put you in a wheelbarrow and run you along, two hundred feet up.

TARLETON [*shuddering*] Ugh! Well, I'd do even that for you. Read The Master Builder.

LINA. Have you learnt everything from books?

TARLETON. Well, have you learnt everything from the flying trapeze?

LINA. On the flying trapeze there is often another woman; and her life is in your hands every night and your life in hers.

TARLETON. Lina: I'm going to make a fool of myself. I'm going to cry. [*He crumples into the nearest chair*].

LINA. Pray instead: dont cry. Why should you cry? Youre not the first Ive said no to.

TARLETON. If you had said yes, should I have been the first then?

LINA. What right have you to ask? Have I asked am *I* the first?

TARLETON. Youre right: a vulgar question. To a man like me, everybody is the first. Life renews itself.

LINA. The youngest child is the sweetest.

TARLETON. Dont probe too deep, Lina. It hurts.

LINA. You must get out of the habit of thinking that these things matter so much. It's linendraperish.

TARLETON. Youre quite right. Ive often said so. All the

same, it does matter; for I want to cry. [*He buries his face in his arms on the worktable and sobs*].

LINA [*going to him*] O la la! [*She slaps him vigorously, but not unkindly, on the shoulder*]. Courage, old pal, courage! Have you a gymnasium here?

TARLETON. Theres a trapeze and bars and things in the billiard room.

LINA. Come. You need a few exercises. I'll teach you how to stop crying. [*She takes his arm and leads him off into the vestibule*].

A young man, cheaply dressed and strange in manner, appears in the garden; steals to the pavilion door; and looks in. Seeing that there is nobody, he enters cautiously until he has come far enough to see into the hatstand corner. He draws a revolver, and examines it, apparently to make sure that it is loaded. Then his attention is caught by the Turkish bath. He looks down the lunette, and opens the panels.

HYPATIA [*calling in the garden*] Mr Percival! Mr Percival! Where are you?

The young man makes for the door, but sees Percival coming. He turns and bolts into the Turkish bath, which he closes upon himself just in time to escape being caught by Percival, who runs in through the pavilion, bareheaded. He also, it appears, is in search of a hiding-place; for he stops and turns between the two tables to take a survey of the room; then runs into the corner between the end of the sideboard and the wall. Hypatia, excited, mischievous, her eyes glowing, runs in, precisely on his trail; turns at the same spot; and discovers him just as he makes a dash for the pavilion door. She flies back and intercepts him.

HYPATIA. Aha! Arnt you glad Ive caught you?

PERCIVAL [*illhumoredly turning away from her and coming towards the writing table*] No I'm not. Confound it, what sort of girl are you? What sort of house is this? Must I throw all good manners to the winds?

HYPATIA [*following him*] Do, do, do, do, do. This is the house of a respectable shopkeeper, enormously rich. This is the respectable shopkeeper's daughter, tired of good manners. [*Slipping her left hand into his right*] Come, handsome young man, and play with the respectable shopkeeper's daughter.

PERCIVAL [*withdrawing quickly from her touch*] No, no: dont you know you mustnt go on like this with a perfect stranger?

HYPATIA. Dropped down from the sky. Dont you know that you must always go on like this when you get the chance? You must come to the top of the hill and chase me through the bracken. You may kiss me if you catch me.

PERCIVAL. I shall do nothing of the sort.

HYPATIA. Yes, you will: you cant help yourself. Come along. [*She seizes his sleeve*]. Fool, fool: come along. Dont you want to?

PERCIVAL. No: certainly not. I should never be forgiven if I did it.

HYPATIA. Youll never forgive yourself if you dont.

PERCIVAL. Nonsense. Youre engaged to Ben. Ben's my friend. What do you take me for?

HYPATIA. Ben's old. Ben was born old. Theyre all old here, except you and me and the man-woman or woman-man or whatever you call her that came with you. They never do anything: they only discuss whether what other people do is right. Come and give them something to discuss.

PERCIVAL. I will do nothing incorrect.

HYPATIA. Oh, dont be afraid, little boy: youll get nothing but a kiss; and I'll fight like the devil to keep you from getting that. But we must play on the hill and race through the heather.

PERCIVAL. Why?

HYPATIA. Because we want to, handsome young man.

PERCIVAL. But if everybody went on in this way—

HYPATIA. How happy! oh how happy the world would be!

PERCIVAL. But the consequences may be serious.

HYPATIA. Nothing is worth doing unless the consequences may be serious. My father says so; and I'm my father's daughter.

PERCIVAL. I'm the son of three fathers. I mistrust these wild impulses.

HYPATIA. Take care. Youre letting the moment slip. I feel the first chill of the wave of prudence. Save me.

PERCIVAL. Really, Miss Tarleton! [*She strikes him across the face*]. Damn you! [*Recovering himself, horrified at his lapse*] I beg your pardon; but since weve both forgotten ourselves, youll please allow me to leave the house. [*He turns towards the inner door, having left his cap in the bedroom*].

HYPATIA [*standing in his way*] Are you ashamed of having said "Damn you" to me?

PERCIVAL. I had no right to say it. I'm very much ashamed of it. I have already begged your pardon.

HYPATIA. And youre not ashamed of having said "Really, Miss Tarleton!"?

PERCIVAL. Why should I?

HYPATIA. O man, man! mean, stupid, cowardly, selfish, masculine male man! You ought to have been a governess. I was expelled from school for saying that the very next person that said "Really, Miss Tarleton!" to me, I would strike across the face. You were the next.

PERCIVAL. I had no intention of being offensive. Surely there is nothing that can wound any lady in—[*He hesitates, not quite convinced*]. At least—er—I really didnt mean to be disagreeable.

HYPATIA. Liar.

PERCIVAL. Of course if youre going to insult me, I am quite helpless. Youre a woman: you can say what you like.

HYPATIA. And you can only say what you dare. Poor wretch: it isnt much. [*He bites his lip, and sits down, very much annoyed*]. Really, Mr Percival! You sit down in the presence of a lady and leave her standing. [*He rises hastily*]. Ha, ha! Really, Mr Percival! Oh really, really, really, really, really, Mr Percival! How do you like it? Wouldnt you rather I damned you?

PERCIVAL. Miss Tarleton—

HYPATIA [*caressingly*] Hypatia, Joey. Patsy, if you like.

PERCIVAL. Look here: this is no good. You want to do what you like?

HYPATIA. Dont you!

PERCIVAL. No. Ive been too well brought up. Ive argued all through this thing; and I tell you I'm not prepared to cast off the social bond. It's like a corset: it's a support to the figure even if it does squeeze and deform it a bit. I want to be free.

HYPATIA. Well, I'm tempting you to be free.

PERCIVAL. Not at all. Freedom, my good girl, means being able to count on how other people will behave. If every man who dislikes me is to throw a handful of mud in my face, and every woman who likes me is to behave like Potiphar's wife, then I shall be a slave: the slave of uncertainty: the slave of fear: the worst of all slaveries. How would you like it if every laborer you met in the road were to make love to you? No. Give me the blessed protection of a good stiff conventionality among thoroughly well-brought up ladies and gentlemen.

HYPATIA. Another talker! Men like conventions because men made them. I didnt make them: I dont like them: I wont keep them. Now, what will you do?

PERCIVAL. Bolt. [*He runs out through the pavilion*].

HYPATIA. I'll catch you. [*She dashes off in pursuit*].

During this conversation the head of the scandalized man in the Turkish bath has repeatedly risen from the lunette, with a strong expression of moral shock. It vanishes abruptly as the two turn towards it in their flight. At the same moment Tarleton comes back through the vestibule door, exhausted by severe and unaccustomed exercise.

TARLETON [*looking after the flying figures with amazement*] Hallo, Patsy: whats up? Another aeroplane? [*They are far too preoccupied to hear him; and he is left staring after them as they rush away through the garden. He goes to the pavilion door and looks up; but the heavens are empty. His exhaustion disables him from further inquiry. He dabs his brow with his handker-*

chief, and walks stiffly to the nearest convenient support, which happens to be the Turkish bath. He props himself upon it with his elbow, and covers his eyes with his hand for a moment. After a few sighing breaths, he feels a little better, and uncovers his eyes. The man's head rises from the lunette a few inches from his nose. He recoils from the bath with a violent start]. Oh Lord! My brain's gone. [*Calling piteously*] Chickabiddy! [*He staggers down to the writing table*].

THE MAN [*coming out of the bath, pistol in hand*] Another sound; and youre a dead man.

TARLETON [*braced*] Am I? Well, youre a live one: thats one comfort. I thought you were a ghost. [*He sits down, quite undisturbed by the pistol*] Who are you; and what the devil were you doing in my new Turkish bath?

THE MAN [*with tragic intensity*] I am the son of Lucinda Titmus.

TARLETON [*the name conveying nothing to him*] Indeed? And how is she? Quite well, I hope, eh?

THE MAN. She is dead. Dead, my God! and you are alive.

TARLETON [*unimpressed by the tragedy, but sympathetic*] Oh! Lost your mother? Thats sad. I'm sorry. But we cant all have the luck to die before our mothers, and be nursed out of the world by the hands that nursed us into it.

THE MAN. Much you care, damn you!

TARLETON. Oh, dont cut up rough. Face it like a man. You see I didnt know your mother; but Ive no doubt she was an excellent woman.

THE MAN. Not know her! Do you dare to stand there by her open grave and deny that you knew her?

TARLETON [*trying to recollect*] What did you say her name was?

THE MAN. Lucinda Titmus.

TARLETON. Well, I ought to remember a rum name like that if I ever heard it. But I dont. Have you a photograph or anything?

THE MAN. Forgotten even the name of your victim!

TARLETON. Oh! she was my victim, was she?

THE MAN. She was. And you shall see her face again before you die, dead as she is. I have a photograph.

TARLETON. Good.

THE MAN. Ive two photographs.

TARLETON. Still better. Treasure the mother's pictures. Good boy!

THE MAN. One of them as you knew her. The other as she became when you flung her aside, and she withered into an old woman.

TARLETON. She'd have done that anyhow, my lad. We all grow old. Look at me! [*Seeing that the man is embarrassed by his pistol in fumbling for the photographs with his left hand in his breast pocket*] Let me hold the gun for you.

THE MAN [*retreating to the worktable*] Stand back. Do you take me for a fool?

TARLETON. Well, youre a little upset, naturally. It does you credit.

THE MAN. Look here, upon this picture and on this. [*He holds out the two photographs like a hand at cards, and points to them with the pistol*].

TARLETON. Good. Read Shakespear: he has a word for every occasion. [*He takes the photographs, one in each hand, and looks from one to the other, pleased and interested, but without any sign of recognition*] What a pretty girl! Very pretty. I can imagine myself falling in love with her when I was your age. I wasnt a bad-looking young fellow myself in those days. [*Looking at the other*] Curious that we should both have gone the same way.

THE MAN. You and she the same way! What do you mean?

TARLETON. Both got stout, I mean.

THE MAN. Would you have had her deny herself food?

TARLETON. No: it wouldnt have been any use. It is constitutional. No matter how little you eat you put on flesh if youre made that way. [*He resumes his study of the earlier photograph*].

THE MAN. Is that all the feeling that rises in you at the

sight of the face you once knew so well?

TARLETON [*too much absorbed in the portrait to heed him*] Funny that I cant remember! Let this be a lesson to you, young man. I could go into court tomorrow and swear I never saw that face before in my life if it wasnt for that brooch [*pointing to the photograph*]. Have you got that brooch, by the way? [*The man again resorts to his breast pocket*]. You seem to carry the whole family property in that pocket.

THE MAN [*producing a brooch*] Here it is to prove my bona fides.

TARLETON [*pensively putting the photographs on the table and taking the brooch*] I bought that brooch in Cheapside from a man with a yellow wig and a cast in his left eye. Ive never set eyes on him from that day to this. And yet I remember that man; and I cant remember your mother.

THE MAN. Monster! Without conscience! without even memory! You left her to her shame—

TARLETON [*throwing the brooch on the table and rising pepperily*] Come, come, young man! none of that. Respect the romance of your mother's youth. Dont you start throwing stones at her. I dont recall her features just at this moment; but Ive no doubt she was kind to me and we were happy together. If you have a word to say against her, take yourself out of my house and say it elsewhere.

THE MAN. What sort of a joker are you? Are you trying to put me in the wrong, when you have to answer to me for a crime that would make every honest man spit at you as you passed in the street if I were to make it known?

TARLETON. You read a good deal, dont you?

THE MAN. What if I do? What has that to do with your infamy and my mother's doom?

TARLETON. There, you see! Doom! Thats not good sense; but it's literature. Now it happens that I'm a tremendous reader: always was. When I was your age I read books of that sort by the bushel: the Doom sort, you know. It's odd, isnt it, that you and I should be like one another in that respect? Can you account for it in any way?

THE MAN. No. What are you driving at?

TARLETON. Well, do you know who your father was?

THE MAN. I see what you mean now. You dare set up to be my father! Thank heaven Ive not a drop of your vile blood in my veins.

TARLETON [*sitting down again with a shrug*] Well, if you wont be civil, theres no pleasure in talking to you, is there? What do you want? Money?

THE MAN. How dare you insult me?

TARLETON. Well, what do you want?

THE MAN. Justice.

TARLETON. Youre quite sure thats all?

THE MAN. It's enough for me.

TARLETON. A modest sort of demand, isnt it? Nobody ever had it since the world began, fortunately for themselves; but you must have it, must you? Well, youve come to the wrong shop for it: youll get no justice here: we dont keep it. Human nature is what we stock.

THE MAN. Human nature! Debauchery! gluttony! selfishness! robbery of the poor! Is that what you call human nature?

TARLETON. No: thats what you call it. Come, my lad! Whats the matter with you? You dont look starved; and youve a decent suit of clothes.

THE MAN. Forty-two shillings.

TARLETON. They can do you a very decent suit for forty-two shillings. Have you paid for it?

THE MAN. Do you take me for a thief? And do you suppose I can get credit like you?

TARLETON. Then you were able to lay your hand on forty-two shillings. Judging from your conversational style, I should think you must spend at least a shilling a week on romantic literature.

THE MAN. Where would I get a shilling a week to spend on books when I can hardly keep myself decent? I get books at the Free Library.

TARLETON [*springing to his feet*] What!!!

THE MAN [*recoiling before his vehemence*] The Free Library. Theres no harm in that.

TARLETON. Ingrate! I supply you with free books; and the use you make of them is to persuade yourself that it's a fine thing to shoot me. [*He throws himself doggedly back into his chair*]. I'll never give another penny to a Free Library.

THE MAN. Youll never give another penny to anything. This is the end: for you and me.

TARLETON. Pooh! Come, come, man! talk business. Whats wrong? Are you out of employment?

THE MAN. No. This is my Saturday afternoon. Dont flatter yourself that I'm a loafer or a criminal. I'm a cashier; and I defy you to say that my cash has ever been a farthing wrong. Ive a right to call you to account because my hands are clean.

TARLETON. Well, call away. What have I to account for? Had you a hard time with your mother? Why didnt she ask me for money?

THE MAN. She'd have died first. Besides, who wanted your money? Do you suppose we lived in the gutter? My father maynt have been in as large a way as you; but he was better connected; and his shop was as respectable as yours.

TARLETON. I suppose your mother brought him a little capital.

THE MAN. I dont know. Whats that got to do with you?

TARLETON. Well, you say she and I knew one another and parted. She must have had something off me then, you know. One doesnt get out of these things for nothing. Hang it, young man: do you suppose Ive no heart? Of course she had her due; and she found a husband with it, and set him up in business with it, and brought you up respectably; so what the devil have you to complain of?

THE MAN. Are women to be ruined with impunity?

TARLETON. I havnt ruined any woman that I'm aware of. Ive been the making of you and your mother.

THE MAN. Oh, I'm a fool to listen to you and argue with you. I came here to kill you and then kill myself.

TARLETON. Begin with yourself, if you dont mind. Ive a good deal of business to do still before I die. Havnt you?

THE MAN. No. Thats just it: Ive no business to do. Do you know what my life is? I spend my days from nine to six—nine hours of daylight and fresh air—in a stuffy little den counting another man's money. Ive an intellect: a mind and a brain and a soul; and the use he makes of them is to fix them on his tuppences and his eighteenpences and his two pound seventeen and tenpences and see how much they come to at the end of the day and take care that no one steals them. I enter and enter, and add and add, and take money and give change, and fill cheques and stamp receipts; and not a penny of that money is my own: not one of those transactions has the smallest interest for me or anyone else in the world but him; and even he couldnt stand it if he had to do it all himself. And I'm envied: aye, envied for the variety and liveliness of my job, by the poor devil of a bookkeeper that has to copy all my entries over again. Fifty thousand entries a year that poor wretch makes; and not ten out of the fifty thousand ever has to be referred to again; and when all the figures are counted up and the balance sheet made out, the boss isnt a penny the richer than he'd be if bookkeeping had never been invented. Of all the damnable waste of human life that ever was invented, clerking is the very worst.

TARLETON. Why not join the territorials?

THE MAN. Because the boss wont let me. He hasnt the sense to see that it would pay him to get some cheap soldiering out of me. How can a man tied to a desk from nine to six be anything—be even a man, let alone a soldier? But I'll teach him and you a lesson. Ive had enough of living a dog's life and despising myself for it. Ive had enough of being talked down to by hogs like you, and wearing my life out for a salary that wouldnt keep you in cigars. Youll never believe that a clerk's a man until one of us makes an example of one of you.

TARLETON. Despotism tempered by assassination, eh?

THE MAN. Yes. Thats what they do in Russia. Well, a business office is Russia as far as the clerks are concerned. So dont you take it so coolly. You think I'm not going to do it; but I am.

TARLETON [*rising and facing him*] Come, now, as man to man! It's not my fault that youre poorer than I am; and it's not your fault that I'm richer than you. And if you could undo all that passed between me and your mother, you wouldnt undo it; and neither would she. But youre sick of your slavery; and you want to be the hero of a romance and to get into the papers. Eh? A son revenges his mother's shame. Villain weltering in his gore. Mother: look down from heaven and receive your unhappy son's last sigh.

THE MAN. Oh, rot! do you think I read novelettes? And do you suppose I believe such superstitions as heaven? I go to church because the boss told me I'd get the sack if I didnt. Free England! Ha! [*Lina appears at the pavilion door, and comes swiftly and noiselessly forward on seeing the man with a pistol in his hand*].

TARLETON. Youre afraid of getting the sack; but youre not afraid to shoot yourself.

THE MAN. Damn you! youre trying to keep me talking until somebody comes. [*He raises the pistol desperately, but not very resolutely*].

LINA [*at his right elbow*] Somebody has come.

THE MAN [*turning on her*] Stand off. I'll shoot you if you lay a hand on me. I will, by God.

LINA. You cant cover me with that pistol. Try.

He tries, presenting the pistol at her face. She moves round him in the opposite direction to the hands of a clock with a light dancing step. He finds it impossible to cover her with the pistol: she is always too far to his left. Tarleton, behind him, grips his wrist and drags his arm straight up, so that the pistol points to the ceiling. As he tries to turn on his assailant, Lina grips his other wrist.

LINA. Please stop. I cant bear to twist anyone's wrist; but I must if you dont let the pistol go.

THE MAN [*letting Tarleton take it from him*] All right: I'm done. Couldnt even do that job decently. Thats a clerk all over. Very well: send for your damned police and make an end of it. I'm accustomed to prison from nine to six: I daresay I can stand from six to nine as well.

TARLETON. Dont swear. Thats a lady. [*He throws the pistol on the writing table*].

THE MAN [*looking at Lina in amazement*] Beaten by a female! It needed only this. [*He collapses in the chair near the worktable, and hides his face. They cannot help pitying him*].

LINA. Old pal: dont call the police. Lend him a bicycle and let him get away.

THE MAN. I cant ride a bicycle. I never could afford one. I'm not even that much good.

TARLETON. If I gave you a hundred pound note now to go and have a good spree with, I wonder would you know how to set about it. Do you ever take a holiday?

THE MAN. Take! I got four days last August.

TARLETON. What did you do?

THE MAN. I did a cheap trip to Folkestone. I spent sevenpence on dropping pennies into silly automatic machines and peepshows of rowdy girls having a jolly time. I spent a penny on the lift and fourpence on refreshments. That cleaned me out. The rest of the time I was so miserable that I was glad to get back to the office. Now you know.

LINA. Come to the gymnasium: I'll teach you how to make a man of yourself. [*The man is about to rise irresolutely, from the mere habit of doing what he is told, when Tarleton stops him*].

TARLETON. Young man: dont. Youve tried to shoot me; but I'm not vindictive. I draw the line at putting a man on the rack. If you want every joint in your body stretched until it's an agony to live—until you have an unnatural feeling that all your muscles are singing and laughing with pain—then go to the gymnasium with that lady. But youll be more comfortable in jail.

LINA [*greatly amused*] Was that why you went away, old

pal? Was that the telegram you said you had forgotten to send?

Mrs Tarleton comes in hastily through the inner door.

MRS TARLETON [*on the steps*] Is anything the matter, John? Nurse says she heard you calling me a quarter of an hour ago; and that your voice sounded as if you were ill. [*She comes between Tarleton and the man*]. Is anything the matter?

TARLETON. This is the son of an old friend of mine. Mr —er—Mr Gunner. [*To the man, who rises awkwardly*]. My wife.

MRS TARLETON. Good evening to you.

GUNNER. Er— [*He is too nervous to speak, and makes a shambling bow*].

Bentley looks in at the pavilion door, very peevish, and too preoccupied with his own affairs to pay any attention to those of the company.

BENTLEY. I say: has anybody seen Hypatia? She promised to come out with me; and I cant find her anywhere. And wheres Joey?

GUNNER [*suddenly breaking out aggressively, being incapable of any middle way between submissiveness and violence*] I can tell you where Hypatia is. I can tell you where Joey is. And I say it's a scandal and an infamy. If people only knew what goes on in this so-called respectable house it would be put a stop to. These are the morals of our pious capitalist class! This is your rotten bourgeoisie! This—

MRS TARLETON. Dont you dare use such language in company. I wont allow it.

TARLETON. All right, Chickabiddy: it's not bad language: it's only Socialism.

MRS TARLETON. Well, I wont have any Socialism in my house.

TARLETON [*to Gunner*] You hear what Mrs Tarleton says. Well, in this house everybody does what she says or out they go.

GUNNER. Do you suppose I want to stay? Do you think

I would breathe this polluted atmosphere a moment longer than I could help?

BENTLEY [*running forward between Lina and Gunner*] But what did you mean by what you said about Miss Tarleton and Mr Percival, you beastly rotter, you?

GUNNER [*to Tarleton*] Oh! is Hypatia your daughter? And Joey is Mister Percival, is he? One of your set, I suppose. One of the smart set! One of the bridge-playing, eighty-horse-power, week-ender set! One of the johnnies I slave for! Well, Joey has more decency than your daughter, anyhow. The women are the worst. I never believed it til I saw it with my own eyes. Well, it wont last for ever. The writing is on the wall. Rome fell. Babylon fell. Hindhead's turn will come.

MRS TARLETON [*naively looking at the wall for the writing*] Whatever are you talking about, young man?

GUNNER. I know what I'm talking about. I went into that Turkish bath a boy: I came out a man.

MRS TARLETON. Good gracious! he's mad. [*To Lina*] Did John make him take a Turkish bath?

LINA. No. He doesnt need Turkish baths: he needs to put on a little flesh. I dont understand what it's all about. I found him trying to shoot Mr Tarleton.

MRS TARLETON [*with a scream*] Oh! and John encouraging him, I'll be bound! Bunny: you go for the police. [*To Gunner*] I'll teach you to come into my house and shoot my husband.

GUNNER. Teach away. I never asked to be let off. I'm ashamed to be free instead of taking my part with the rest. Women—beautiful women of noble birth—are going to prison for their opinions. Girl students in Russia go to the gallows; let themselves be cut in pieces with the knout, or driven through the frozen snows of Siberia, sooner than stand looking on tamely at the world being made a hell for the toiling millions. If you were not all skunks and cowards youd be suffering with them instead of battening here on the plunder of the poor.

MRS TARLETON [*much vexed*] Oh, did you ever hear such silly nonsense? Bunny: go and tell the gardener to send over one of his men to Grayshott for the police.

GUNNER. I'll go with him. I intend to give myself up. I'm going to expose what Ive seen here, no matter what the consequences may be to my miserable self.

TARLETON. Stop. You stay where you are, Ben. Chickabiddy: youve never had the police in. If you had, youd not be in a hurry to have them in again. Now, young man: cut the cackle; and tell us, as short as you can, what did you see?

GUNNER. I cant tell you in the presence of ladies.

MRS TARLETON. Oh, you are tiresome. As if it mattered to anyone what you saw. Me! A married woman that might be your mother. [*To Lina*] And I'm sure youre not particular, if youll excuse my saying so.

TARLETON. Out with it. What did you see?

GUNNER. I saw your daughter with my own eyes—oh well, never mind what I saw.

BENTLEY [*almost crying with anxiety*] You beastly rotter. I'll get Joey to give you such a hiding—

TARLETON. You cant leave it at that, you know. What did you see my daughter doing?

GUNNER. After all, why shouldnt she do it? The Russian students do it. Women should be as free as men. I'm a fool. I'm so full of your bourgeois morality that I let myself be shocked by the application of my own revolutionary principles. If she likes the man why shouldnt she tell him so?

MRS TARLETON. I do wonder at you, John, letting him talk like this before everybody. [*Turning rather tartly to Lina*] Would you mind going away to the drawing room just for a few minutes, Miss Chipenoska. This is a private family matter, if you dont mind.

LINA. I should have gone before, Mrs Tarleton, if there had been anyone to protect Mr Tarleton and the young gentleman. [*She goes out through the inner door*].

GUNNER. There you are! It's all of a piece here. The men effeminate, the women unsexed—

TARLETON. Dont begin again, old chap. Keep it for Trafalgar Square.

HYPATIA'S VOICE OUTSIDE. No, no. [*She breaks off in a stifled half laugh, half scream, and is seen darting across the garden with Percival in hot pursuit. Immediately afterwards she appears again, and runs into the pavilion. Finding it full of people, including a stranger, she stops; but Percival, flushed and reckless, rushes in and seizes her before he, too, realizes that they are not alone. He releases her in confusion*].

Dead silence. They are all afraid to look at one another except Mrs Tarleton, who stares sternly at Hypatia. Hypatia is the first to recover her presence of mind.

HYPATIA. Excuse me rushing in like this. Mr Percival has been chasing me down the hill.

GUNNER. Who chased him up it? Dont be ashamed. Be fearless. Be truthful.

TARLETON. Gunner: will you go to Paris for a fortnight? I'll pay your expenses.

HYPATIA. What do you mean?

GUNNER. There was a silent witness in the Turkish bath.

TARLETON. I found him hiding there. Whatever went on here, he saw and heard. Thats what he means.

PERCIVAL [*sternly approaching Gunner, and speaking with deep but contained indignation*] Am I to understand you as daring to put forward the monstrous and blackguardly lie that this lady behaved improperly in my presence?

GUNNER [*turning white*] You know what I saw and heard.

Hypatia, with a gleam of triumph in her eyes, slips noiselessly into the swing chair, and watches Percival and Gunner, swinging slightly, but otherwise motionless.

PERCIVAL. I hope it is not necessary for me to assure you all that there is not one word of truth—not one grain of substance—in this rascally calumny, which no man with a spark of decent feeling would have uttered even if he had been ignorant enough to believe it. Miss Tarleton's conduct, since I have had the honor of knowing her, has been, I need hardly say, in every respect beyond reproach. [*To Gunner*] As for you, sir, youll have the goodness to come out with me immediately. I have some business with you which cant be settled in Mrs Tarleton's presence or in her house.

GUNNER [*painfully frightened*] Why should I go out with you?

PERCIVAL. Because I intend that you shall.

GUNNER. I wont be bullied by you. [*Percival makes a threatening step towards him*]. Police! [*He tries to bolt; but Percival seizes him*]. Leave me go, will you? What right have you to lay hands on me?

TARLETON. Let him run for it, Mr Percival. He's very poor company. We shall be well rid of him. Let him go.

PERCIVAL. Not until he has taken back and made the fullest apology for the abominable lie he has told. He shall do that, or he shall defend himself as best he can against the most thorough thrashing I'm capable of giving him. [*Releasing Gunner, but facing him ominously*] Take your choice. Which is it to be?

GUNNER. Give me a fair chance. Go and stick at a desk from nine to six for a month, and let me have your grub and your sport and your lessons in boxing, and I'll fight you fast enough. You know I'm no good or you darent bully me like this.

PERCIVAL. You should have thought of that before you attacked a lady with a dastardly slander. I'm waiting for your decision. I'm rather in a hurry, please.

GUNNER. I never said anything against the lady.

MRS TARLETON } { Oh, listen to that!
BENTLEY } { What a liar!
HYPATIA } { Oh!
TARLETON } { Oh, come!

PERCIVAL. We'll have it in writing, if you dont mind. [*Pointing to the writing table*] Sit down; and take that pen in your hand. [*Gunner looks irresolutely a little way round; then obeys*]. Now write. "I," whatever your name is—

GUNNER [*after a vain attempt*] I cant. My hand's shaking too much. You see it's no use. I'm doing my best. I cant.

PERCIVAL. Mr Summerhays will write it: you can sign it.

BENTLEY [*insolently to Gunner*] Get up. [*Gunner obeys; and Bentley, shouldering him aside towards Percival, takes his place and prepares to write*].

PERCIVAL. Whats your name?

GUNNER. John Brown.

TARLETON. Oh come! Couldnt you make it Horace Smith? or Algernon Robinson?

GUNNER [*agitatedly*] But my name is John Brown. There are really John Browns. How can I help it if my name's a common one?

BENTLEY. Shew us a letter addressed to you.

GUNNER. How can I? I never get any letters: I'm only a clerk. I can shew you J. B. on my handkerchief. [*He takes out a not very clean one*].

BENTLEY [*with disgust*] Oh, put it up again. Let it go at John Brown.

PERCIVAL. Where do you live?

GUNNER. 4 Chesterfield Parade, Kentish Town, N. W.

PERCIVAL [*dictating*] I, John Brown, of 4 Chesterfield Parade, Kentish Town, do hereby voluntarily confess that on the 31st May 1909 I— [*To Tarleton*] What did he do exactly?

TARLETON [*dictating*]—I trespassed on the land of John Tarleton at Hindhead, and effected an unlawful entry into his house, where I secreted myself in a portable Turkish bath—

BENTLEY. Go slow, old man. Just a moment. "Turkish bath"—yes?

TARLETON [*continuing*]—with a pistol, with which I threatened to take the life of the said John Tarleton—

MRS TARLETON. Oh, John! You might have been killed.

TARLETON. —and was prevented from doing so only by

the timely arrival of the celebrated Miss Lina Szczepanowska.

MRS TARLETON. Is she celebrated? [*Apologetically*] I never dreamt—

BENTLEY. Look here: I'm awfully sorry; but I cant spell Szczepanowska.

PERCIVAL. I think it's S, z, c, z—Better say the Polish lady.

BENTLEY [*writing*] "the Polish lady"?

TARLETON [*to Percival*] Now it's your turn.

PERCIVAL [*dictating*] I further confess that I was guilty of uttering an abominable calumny concerning Miss Hypatia Tarleton, for which there was not a shred of foundation.

Impressive silence whilst Bentley writes.

BENTLEY. "foundation"?

PERCIVAL. I apologize most humbly to the lady and her family for my conduct—[*he waits for Bentley to write*].

BENTLEY. "conduct"?

PERCIVAL. —and I promise Mr Tarleton not to repeat it, and to amend my life—

BENTLEY. "amend my life"?

PERCIVAL. —and to do what in me lies to prove worthy of his kindness in giving me another chance—

BENTLEY. "another chance"?

PERCIVAL. —and refraining from delivering me up to the punishment I so richly deserve.

BENTLEY. "richly deserve."

PERCIVAL [*to Hypatia*] Does that satisfy you, Miss Tarleton?

HYPATIA. Yes: that will teach him to tell lies next time.

BENTLEY [*rising to make place for Gunner and handing him the pen*] You mean it will teach him to tell the truth next time.

TARLETON. Ahem! Do you, Patsy?

PERCIVAL. Be good enough to sign. [*Gunner sits down helplessly and dips the pen in the ink*]. I hope what you are signing is no mere form of words to you, and that you not only say you are sorry, but that you a r e sorry.

Lord Summerhays and Johnny come in through the pavilion door.

MRS TARLETON. Stop. Mr Percival: I think, on Hypatia's account, Lord Summerhays ought to be told about this.

Lord Summerhays, wondering what the matter is, comes forward between Percival and Lina. Johnny stops beside Hypatia.

PERCIVAL. Certainly.

TARLETON [*uneasily*] Take my advice and cut it short. Get rid of him.

MRS TARLETON. Hypatia ought to have her character cleared.

TARLETON. You let well alone, Chickabiddy. Most of our characters will bear a little careful dusting; but they wont bear scouring. Patsy is jolly well out of it. What does it matter, anyhow?

PERCIVAL. Mr Tarleton: we have already said either too much or not enough. Lord Summerhays: will you be kind enough to witness the declaration this man has just signed?

GUNNER. I havnt yet. Am I to sign now?

PERCIVAL. Of course. [*Gunner, who is now incapable of doing anything on his own initiative, signs*]. Now stand up and read your declaration to this gentleman. [*Gunner makes a vague movement and looks stupidly round. Percival adds peremptorily*] Now, please.

GUNNER [*rising apprehensively and reading without punctuation in a hardly audible voice, like a very sick man*] I John Brown of 4 Chesterfield Parade Kentish Town do hereby voluntarily confess that on the 31st May 1909 I trespassed on the land of John Tarleton at Hindhead and effected an unlawful entry into his house where I secreted myself in a portable Turkish bath with a pistol with which I threatened to take the life of the said John Tarleton and was prevented from doing so only by the timely arrival of the Polish lady. I further confess that I was guilty of uttering an abominable calumny concerning Miss Hypatia Tarleton for which there was not a shred of foundation I apologize most humbly to the lady and her family for my conduct and I promise Mr Tarleton not to repeat it and to amend my life and to do what in me lies to prove worthy of his kindness in giving me another chance and refraining from delivering me up to the punishment I so richly deserve.

A short and painful silence follows. Then Percival speaks.

PERCIVAL. Do you consider that sufficient, Lord Summerhays?

LORD SUMMERHAYS. Oh quite, quite.

PERCIVAL [*to Hypatia*] Lord Summerhays would probably like to hear you say that you are satisfied, Miss Tarleton.

HYPATIA [*coming out of the swing, and advancing between Percival and Lord Summerhays*] I must say that you have behaved like a perfect gentleman, Mr Percival.

PERCIVAL [*first bowing to Hypatia, and then turning with cold contempt to Gunner, who is standing helpless*] We need not trouble you any further. [*Gunner turns vaguely towards the pavilion*].

JOHNNY [*with less refined offensiveness, pointing to the pavilion*] Thats your way. The gardener will shew you the shortest way into the road. Go the shortest way.

GUNNER [*oppressed and disconcerted, hardly knows how to get out of the room*] Yes, sir. I— [*He turns again, appealing to Tarleton*] Maynt I have my mother's photographs back again? [*Mrs Tarleton pricks up her ears*].

TARLETON. Eh? What? Oh, the photographs! Yes, yes, yes: take them. [*Gunner takes them from the table, and is creeping away, when Mrs Tarleton puts out her hand and stops him*].

MRS TARLETON. Whats this, John? What were you doing with his mother's photographs?

TARLETON. Nothing, nothing. Never mind, Chickabiddy: it's all right.

MRS TARLETON [*snatching the photographs from Gunner's irresolute fingers, and recognizing them at a glance*] Lucy Titmus! Oh John, John!

TARLETON [*grimly, to Gunner*] Young man: youre a fool;

but youve just put the lid on this job in a masterly manner. I knew you would. I told you all to let well alone. You wouldnt; and now you must take the consequences—or rather *I* must take them.

MRS TARLETON [*maternally*] Are you Lucy's son?

GUNNER. Yes!

MRS TARLETON. And why didnt you come to me? I didnt turn my back on your mother when she came to me in her trouble. Didnt you know that?

GUNNER. No. She never talked to me about anything.

TARLETON. How could she talk to her own son? Shy, Summerhays, shy. Parent and child. Shy. [*He sits down at the end of the writing table nearest the sideboard like a man resigned to anything that fate may have in store for him*].

MRS TARLETON. Then how did you find out?

GUNNER. From her papers after she died.

MRS TARLETON [*shocked*] Is Lucy dead? And I never knew! [*With an effusion of tenderness*] And you here being treated like that, poor orphan, with nobody to take your part! Tear up that foolish paper, child; and sit down and make friends with me.

JOHNNY { Hallo, mother: this is all very well, you know—
PERCIVAL { But may I point out, Mrs Tarleton, that—
BENTLEY { Do you mean that after what he said of—
HYPATIA { Oh, look here, mamma: this is really—

MRS TARLETON. Will you please speak one at a time? *Silence.*

PERCIVAL [*in a very gentlemanly manner*] Will you allow me to remind you, Mrs Tarleton, that this man has uttered a most serious and disgraceful falsehood concerning Miss Tarleton and myself?

MRS TARLETON. I dont believe a word of it. If the poor lad was there in the Turkish bath, who has a better right to say what was going on here than he has? You ought to be ashamed of yourself, Patsy; and so ought you too, Mr Percival, for encouraging her. [*Hypatia retreats to the pavilion, and exchanges grimaces with Johnny, shamelessly enjoying Percival's sudden reverse. They know their mother*].

PERCIVAL [*gasping*] Mrs Tarleton: I give you my word of honor—

MRS TARLETON. Oh, go along with you and your word of honor. Do you think I'm a fool? I wonder you can look the lad in the face after bullying him and making him sign those wicked lies; and all the time you carrying on with my daughter before youd been half an hour in my house. Fie, for shame!

PERCIVAL. Lord Summerhays: I appeal to you. Have I done the correct thing or not?

LORD SUMMERHAYS. Youve done your best, Mr Percival. But the correct thing depends for its success on everybody playing the game very strictly. As a single-handed game, it's impossible.

BENTLEY [*suddenly breaking out lamentably*] Joey: have you taken Hypatia away from me?

LORD SUMMERHAYS [*severely*] Bentley! Bentley! Control yourself, sir.

TARLETON. Come, Mr Percival! the shutters are up on the gentlemanly business. Try the truth.

PERCIVAL. I am in a wretched position. If I tell the truth nobody will believe me.

TARLETON. Oh yes they will. The truth makes everybody believe it.

PERCIVAL. It also makes everybody pretend not to believe it. Mrs Tarleton: youre not playing the game.

MRS TARLETON. I dont think youve behaved at all nicely, Mr Percival.

BENTLEY. I wouldnt have played you such a dirty trick, Joey. [*Struggling with a sob*] You beast.

LORD SUMMERHAYS. Bentley: you must control yourself. Let me say at the same time, Mr Percival, that my son seems to have been mistaken in regarding you either as his friend or as a gentleman.

PERCIVAL. Miss Tarleton: I'm suffering this for your

sake. I ask you just to say that I am not to blame. Just that and nothing more.

HYPATIA [*gloating mischievously over his distress*] You chased me through the heather and kissed me. You shouldnt have done that if you were not in earnest.

PERCIVAL. Oh, this is really the limit. [*Turning desperately to Gunner*] Sir: I appeal to you. As a gentleman! as a man of honor! as a man bound to stand by another man! You were in that Turkish bath. You saw how it began. Could any man have behaved more correctly than I did? Is there a shadow of foundation for the accusations brought against me?

GUNNER [*sorely perplexed*] Well, what do you want me to say?

JOHNNY. He has said what he had to say already, hasnt he? Read that paper.

GUNNER. When I tell the truth, you make me go back on it. And now you want me to go back on myself! What is a man to do?

PERCIVAL [*patiently*] Please try to get your mind clear, Mr Brown. I pointed out to you that you could not, as a gentleman, disparage a lady's character. You agree with me, I hope.

GUNNER. Yes: that sounds all right.

PERCIVAL. But youre also bound to tell the truth. Surely youll not deny that.

GUNNER. Who's denying it? I say nothing against it.

PERCIVAL. Of course not. Well, I ask you to tell the truth simply and unaffectedly. Did you witness any improper conduct on my part when you were in the bath?

GUNNER. No, sir.

JOHNNY } Then what do you mean by saying that—
HYPATIA } Do you mean to say that I—
BENTLEY } Oh, you are a rotter. Youre afraid—

TARLETON [*rising*] Stop. [*Silence*]. Leave it at that. Enough said. You keep quiet, Johnny. Mr Percival: youre whitewashed. So are you, Patsy. Honors are easy. Lets drop the subject. The next thing to do is to open a subscription to start this young man on a ranch in some far country thats accustomed to be in a disturbed state. He—

MRS TARLETON. Now stop joking the poor lad, John: I wont have it. He's been worried to death between you all. [*To Gunner*] Have you had your tea?

GUNNER. Tea? No: it's too early. I'm all right; only I had no dinner: I didnt think I'd want it. I didnt think I'd be alive.

MRS TARLETON. Oh, what a thing to say! You mustnt talk like that.

JOHNNY. He's out of his mind. He thinks it's past dinnertime.

MRS TARLETON. Oh, youve no sense, Johnny. He calls his lunch his dinner, and has his tea at half-past six. Havnt you, dear?

GUNNER [*timidly*] Hasnt everybody?

JOHNNY [*laughing*] Well, by George, thats not bad.

MRS TARLETON. Now dont be rude, Johnny: you know I dont like it. [*To Gunner*] A cup of tea will pick you up.

GUNNER. I'd rather not. I'm all right.

TARLETON [*going to the sideboard*] Here! try a mouthful of sloe gin.

GUNNER. No, thanks. I'm a teetotaler. I cant touch alcohol in any form.

TARLETON. Nonsense! This isnt alcohol. Sloe gin. Vegetarian, you know.

GUNNER [*hesitating*] Is it a fruit beverage?

TARLETON. Of course it is. Fruit beverage. Here you are. [*He gives him a glass of sloe gin*].

GUNNER [*going to the sideboard*] Thanks. [*He begins to drink it confidently; but the first mouthful startles and almost chokes him*]. It's rather hot.

TARLETON. Do you good. Dont be afraid of it.

MRS TARLETON [*going to him*] Sip it, dear. Dont be in a hurry.

Gunner sips slowly, each sip making his eyes water.

JOHNNY [*coming forward into the place left vacant by Gunner's visit to the sideboard*] Well, now that the gentleman has been attended to, I should like to know where we are. It may be a vulgar business habit; but I confess I like to know where I am.

TARLETON. I dont. Wherever you are, youre there anyhow. I tell you again, leave it at that.

BENTLEY. I want to know too. Hypatia's engaged to me.

HYPATIA. Bentley: if you insult me again: if you say another word, I'll leave the house and not enter it until you leave it.

JOHNNY. Put that in your pipe and smoke it, my boy.

BENTLEY [*inarticulate with fury and suppressed tears*] Oh! Beasts! Brutes!

MRS TARLETON. Now dont hurt his feelings, poor little lamb!

LORD SUMMERHAYS [*very sternly*] Bentley: you are not behaving well. You had better leave us until you have recovered yourself.

Bentley goes out in disgrace, but gets no further than half way to the pavilion door, when, with a wild sob, he throws himself on the floor and begins to yell.

MRS TARLETON [*running to him*] Oh, poor child, poor child! Dont cry, duckie: he didnt mean it: dont cry.

LORD SUMMERHAYS Stop that infernal noise, sir: do you hear? Stop it instantly.

JOHNNY Thats the game he tried on me. There you are! Now, mother! Now, Patsy! You see for yourselves.

HYPATIA [*covering her ears*] Oh you little wretch! Stop him, Mr Percival. Kick him.

TARLETON Steady on, steady on. Easy, Bunny, easy.

LINA [*appearing at the door*] Leave him to me, Mrs Tarleton. [*Clear and authoritative*] Stand clear, please.

She quickly lifts the upper half of Bentley from the ground;

dives under him; rises with his body hanging across her shoulders; and runs out with him.

BENTLEY [*in scared, sobered, humble tones as he is borne off*] What are you doing? Let me down. Please, Miss Szczepanowska—[*they pass out of hearing*].

An awestruck silence falls on the company as they speculate on Bentley's fate.

JOHNNY. I wonder what she's going to do with him.

HYPATIA. Spank him, I hope. Spank him hard.

LORD SUMMERHAYS. I hope so. I hope so. Tarleton: I'm beyond measure humiliated and annoyed by my son's behavior in your house. I had better take him home.

TARLETON. Not at all: not at all. Now, Chickabiddy: as Miss Lina has taken away Ben, suppose you take away Mr Brown for a while.

GUNNER [*with unexpected aggressiveness*] My name isnt Brown. [*They stare at him: he meets their stare defiantly, pugnacious with sloe gin; drains the last drop from his glass; throws it on the sideboard; and advances to the writing table*]. My name's Baker: Julius Baker. Mister Baker. If any man doubts it, I'm ready for him.

MRS TARLETON. John: you shouldnt have given him that sloe gin. It's gone to his head.

GUNNER. Dont you think it. Fruit beverages dont go to the head; and what matter if they did? I say nothing to you, maam: I regard you with respect and affection. [*Lachrymosely*] You were very good to my mother: my poor mother! [*Relapsing into his daring mood*] But I say my name's Baker; and I'm not to be treated as a child or made a slave of by any man. Baker is my name. Did you think I was going to give you my real name? Not likely! Not me!

TARLETON. So you thought of John Brown. That was clever of you.

GUNNER. Clever! yes: we're not all such fools as you think: we clerks. It was the bookkeeper put me up to that. It's the only name that nobody gives as a false name, he said. Clever, eh? I should think so.

MRS TARLETON. Come now, Julius—

GUNNER [*reassuring her gravely*] Dont you be alarmed, maam. I know what is due to you as a lady and to myself as a gentleman. I regard you with respect and affection. If you had been my mother, as you ought to have been, I should have had more chance. But you shall have no cause to be ashamed of me. The strength of a chain is no greater than its weakest link; but the greatness of a poet is the greatness of his greatest moment. Shakespear used to get drunk. Frederick the Great ran away from a battle. But it was what they could rise to, not what they could sink to, that made them great. They werent good always; but they were good on their day. Well, on my day—on my day, mind you—I'm good for something too. I know that Ive made a silly exhibition of myself here. I know I didnt rise to the occasion. I know that if youd been my mother, youd have been ashamed of me. I lost my presence of mind: I was a contemptible coward. But [*slapping himself on the chest*] I'm not the man I was then. This is my day. Ive seen the tenth possessor of a foolish face carried out kicking and screaming by a woman. [*To Percival*] You crowed pretty big over me. You hypnotized me. But when you were put through the fire yourself, you were found wanting. I tell you straight I dont give a damn for you.

MRS TARLETON. No: thats naughty. You shouldnt say that before me.

GUNNER. I would cut my tongue out sooner than say anything vulgar in your presence; for I regard you with respect and affection. I was not swearing. I was affirming my manhood.

MRS TARLETON. What an idea! What puts all these things into your head?

GUNNER. Oh, dont think, because I'm only a clerk, that I'm not one of the intellectuals. I'm a reading man, a thinking man. I read in a book—a high class six shilling book—this precept: Affirm your manhood. It appealed to me. Ive always remembered it. I believe in it. I feel I must do it to recover your respect after my cowardly behavior. Therefore I affirm it in your presence. I tell that man who insulted me that I dont give a damn for him. And neither I do.

TARLETON. I say, Summerhays: did you have chaps of this sort in Jinghiskahn?

LORD SUMMERHAYS. Oh yes: they exist everywhere: they are a most serious modern problem.

GUNNER. Yes. Youre right. [*Conceitedly*] I'm a problem. And I tell you that when we clerks realize that we're problems! well, look out: thats all.

LORD SUMMERHAYS [*suavely, to Gunner*] You read a great deal, you say?

GUNNER. Ive read more than any man in this room, if the truth were known, I expect. Thats whats going to smash up your Capitalism. The problems are beginning to read. Ha! We're free to do that here in England. What would you do with me in Jinghiskahn if you had me there?

LORD SUMMERHAYS. Well, since you ask me so directly, I'll tell you. I should take advantage of the fact that you have neither sense enough nor strength enough to know how to behave yourself in a difficulty of any sort. I should warn an intelligent and ambitious policeman that you are a troublesome person. The intelligent and ambitious policeman would take an early opportunity of upsetting your temper by ordering you to move on, and treading on your heels until you were provoked into obstructing an officer in the discharge of his duty. Any trifle of that sort would be sufficient to make a man like you lose your self-possession and put yourself in the wrong. You would then be charged and imprisoned until things quieted down.

GUNNER. And you call that justice!

LORD SUMMERHAYS. No. Justice was not my business. I had to govern a province; and I took the necessary steps to maintain order in it. Men are not governed by justice, but by law or persuasion. When they refuse to be governed by law or persuasion, they have to be governed by force or fraud, or both. I used both when law and persuasion failed me.

Every ruler of men since the world began has done so, even when he has hated both fraud and force as heartily as I do. It is as well that you should know this, my young friend; so that you may recognize in time that anarchism is a game at which the police can beat you. What have you to say to that?

GUNNER. What have I to say to it! Well, I call it scandalous: thats what I have to say to it.

LORD SUMMERHAYS. Precisely: thats all anybody has to say to it, except the British public, which pretends not to believe it. And now let me ask you a sympathetic personal question. Havnt you a headache?

GUNNER. Well, since you ask me, I have. Ive overexcited myself.

MRS TARLETON. Poor lad! No wonder, after all youve gone through! You want to eat a little and to lie down. You come with me. I want you to tell me about your poor dear mother and about yourself. Come along with me. [*She leads the way to the inner door*].

GUNNER [*following her obediently*] Thank you kindly, madam. [*She goes out. Before passing out after her, he partly closes the door and lingers for a moment to whisper*] Mind: I'm not knuckling down to any man here. I knuckle down to Mrs Tarleton because she's a woman in a thousand. I affirm my manhood all the same. Understand: I dont give a damn for the lot of you. [*He hurries out, rather afraid of the consequences of this defiance, which has provoked Johnny to an impatient movement towards him*].

HYPATIA. Thank goodness he's gone! Oh, what a bore! WHAT a bore!!! Talk! talk! talk!

TARLETON. Patsy: it's no good. We're going to talk. And we're going to talk about you.

JOHNNY. It's no use shirking it, Pat. We'd better know where we are.

LORD SUMMERHAYS. Come, Miss Tarleton. Wont you sit down? I'm very tired of standing. [*Hypatia comes from the pavilion and takes a chair at the worktable. Lord Summerhays takes the opposite chair, on her right. Percival takes the chair*

Johnny placed for Lina on her arrival. Tarleton sits down at the end of the writing table. Johnny remains standing. Lord Summerhays continues, with a sigh of relief at being seated] We shall now get the change of subject we are all pining for.

JOHNNY [*puzzled*] Whats that?

LORD SUMMERHAYS. The great question. The question that men and women will spend hours over without complaining. The question that occupies all the novel readers and all the playgoers. The question they never get tired of.

JOHNNY. But what question?

LORD SUMMERHAYS. The question which particular young man some young woman will mate with.

PERCIVAL. As if it mattered!

HYPATIA [*sharply*] Whats that you said?

PERCIVAL. I said: As if it mattered.

HYPATIA. I call that ungentlemanly.

PERCIVAL. Do you care about that? you who are so magnificently unladylike!

JOHNNY. Look here, Mr Percival: youre not supposed to insult my sister.

HYPATIA. Oh, shut up, Johnny. I can take care of myself. Dont you interfere.

JOHNNY. Oh, very well. If you choose to give yourself away like that—to allow a man to call you unladylike and then to be unladylike, Ive nothing more to say.

HYPATIA. I think Mr Percival is most ungentlemanly; but I wont be protected. I'll not have my affairs interfered with by men on pretence of protecting me. I'm not your baby. If I interfered between you and a woman, you would soon tell me to mind my own business.

TARLETON. Children: dont squabble. Read Dr Watts. Behave yourselves.

JOHNNY. Ive nothing more to say; and as I dont seem to be wanted here, I shall take myself off. [*He goes out with affected calm through the pavilion*].

TARLETON. Summerhays: a family is an awful thing, an impossible thing. Cat and dog. Patsy: I'm ashamed of you.

HYPATIA. I'll make it up with Johnny afterwards; but I really cant have him here sticking his clumsy hoof into my affairs.

LORD SUMMERHAYS. The question is, Mr Percival, are you really a gentleman, or are you not?

PERCIVAL. Was Napoleon really a gentleman or was he not? He made the lady get out of the way of the porter and said, "Respect the burden, madam." That was behaving like a very fine gentleman; but he kicked Volney for saying that what France wanted was the Bourbons back again. That was behaving rather like a navvy. Now I, like Napoleon, am not all one piece. On occasion, as you have all seen, I can behave like a gentleman. On occasion, I can behave with a brutal simplicity which Miss Tarleton herself could hardly surpass.

TARLETON. Gentleman or no gentleman, Patsy: what are your intentions?

HYPATIA. My intentions! Surely it's the gentleman who should be asked his intentions.

TARLETON. Come now, Patsy! none of that nonsense. Has Mr Percival said anything to you that I ought to know or that Bentley ought to know? Have you said anything to Mr Percival?

HYPATIA. Mr Percival chased me through the heather and kissed me.

LORD SUMMERHAYS. As a gentleman, Mr Percival, what do you say to that?

PERCIVAL. As a gentleman, I do not kiss and tell. As a mere man: a mere cad, if you like, I say that I did so at Miss Tarleton's own suggestion.

HYPATIA. Beast!

PERCIVAL. I dont deny that I enjoyed it. But I did not initiate it. And I began by running away.

TARLETON. So Patsy can run faster than you, can she?

PERCIVAL. Yes, when she is in pursuit of me. She runs faster and faster. I run slower and slower. And these woods of yours are full of magic. There was a confounded fern owl.

Did you ever hear the churr of a fern owl? Did you ever hear it create a sudden silence by ceasing? Did you ever hear it call its mate by striking its wings together twice and whistling that single note that no nightingale can imitate? That is what happened in the woods when I was running away. So I turned; and the pursuer became the pursued.

HYPATIA. I had to fight like a wild cat.

LORD SUMMERHAYS. Please dont tell us this. It's not fit for old people to hear.

TARLETON. Come: how did it end?

HYPATIA. It's not ended yet.

TARLETON. How is it going to end?

HYPATIA. Ask him.

TARLETON. How is it going to end, Mr Percival?

PERCIVAL. I cant afford to marry, Mr Tarleton. Ive only a thousand a year until my father dies. Two people cant possibly live on that.

TARLETON. Oh, cant they? When *I* married, I should have been jolly glad to have felt sure of the quarter of it.

PERCIVAL. No doubt; but I am not a cheap person, Mr Tarleton. I was brought up in a household which cost at least seven or eight times that; and I am in constant money difficulties because I simply dont know how to live on the thousand a year scale. As to ask a woman to share my degrading poverty, it's out of the question. Besides, I'm rather young to marry. I'm only 28.

HYPATIA. Papa: buy the brute for me.

LORD SUMMERHAYS [*shrinking*] My dear Miss Tarleton: dont be so naughty. I know how delightful it is to shock an old man; but there is a point at which it becomes barbarous. Dont. Please dont.

HYPATIA. Shall I tell Papa about you?

LORD SUMMERHAYS. Tarleton: I had better tell you that I once asked your daughter to become my widow.

TARLETON [*to Hypatia*] Why didnt you accept him, you young idiot?

LORD SUMMERHAYS. I was too old.

TARLETON. All this has been going on under my nose, I suppose. You run after young men; and old men run after you. And I'm the last person in the world to hear of it.

HYPATIA. How could I tell you?

LORD SUMMERHAYS. Parents and children, Tarleton.

TARLETON. Oh, the gulf that lies between them! the impassable, eternal gulf! And so I'm to buy the brute for you, eh?

HYPATIA. If you please, papa.

TARLETON. Whats the price, Mr Percival?

PERCIVAL. We might do with another fifteen hundred if my father would contribute. But I should like more.

TARLETON. It's purely a question of money with you, is it?

PERCIVAL [*after a moment's consideration*] Practically yes: it turns on that.

TARLETON. I thought you might have some sort of preference for Patsy, you know.

PERCIVAL. Well, but does that matter, do you think? Patsy fascinates me, no doubt. I apparently fascinate Patsy. But, believe me, all that is not worth considering. One of my three fathers (the priest) has married hundreds of couples: couples selected by one another, couples selected by the parents, couples forced to marry one another by circumstances of one kind or another; and he assures me that if marriages were made by putting all the men's names into one sack and the women's names into another, and having them taken out by a blindfolded child like lottery numbers, there would be just as high a percentage of happy marriages as we have here in England. He said Cupid was nothing but the blindfolded child: pretty idea that, I think! I shall have as good a chance with Patsy as with anyone else. Mind: I'm not bigoted about it. I'm not a doctrinaire: not the slave of a theory. You and Lord Summerhays are experienced married men. If you can tell me of any trustworthy method of selecting a wife, I shall be happy to make use of it. I await your suggestions. [*He looks with polite attention to Lord Summerhays, who, having nothing to say, avoids his eye. He looks to Tarleton, who purses his lips glumly and rattles his money in his pockets without a word*]. Apparently neither of you has anything to suggest. Then Patsy will do as well as another, provided the money is forthcoming.

HYPATIA. Oh, you beauty! you beauty!

TARLETON. When I married Patsy's mother, I was in love with her.

PERCIVAL. For the first time?

TARLETON. Yes: for the first time.

PERCIVAL. For the last time?

LORD SUMMERHAYS [*revolted*] Sir: you are in the presence of his daughter.

HYPATIA. Oh, dont mind me. I dont care. I'm accustomed to Papa's adventures.

TARLETON [*blushing painfully*] Patsy, my child: that was not—not delicate.

HYPATIA. Well, papa, youve never shewn any delicacy in talking to me about my conduct; and I really dont see why I shouldnt talk to you about yours. It's such nonsense! Do you think young people dont know?

LORD SUMMERHAYS. I'm sure they dont feel. Tarleton: this is too horrible, too brutal. If neither of these young people have any—any—any—

PERCIVAL. Shall we say paternal sentimentality? I'm extremely sorry to shock you; but you must remember that Ive been educated to discuss human affairs with three fathers simultaneously. I'm an adult person. Patsy is an adult person. You do not inspire me with veneration. Apparently you do not inspire Patsy with veneration. That may surprise you. It may pain you. I'm sorry. It cant be helped. What about the money?

TARLETON. You dont inspire me with generosity, young man.

HYPATIA [*laughing with genuine amusement*] He had you there, Joey.

TARLETON. I havnt been a bad father to you, Patsy.

HYPATIA. I dont say you have, dear. If only I could persuade you Ive grown up, we should get along perfectly.

TARLETON. Do you remember Bill Burt?

HYPATIA. Why?

TARLETON [*to the others*] Bill Burt was a laborer here. I was going to sack him for kicking his father. He said his father had kicked him until he was big enough to kick back. Patsy begged him off. I asked that man what it felt like the first time he kicked his father, and found that it was just like kicking any other man. He laughed and said that it was the old man that knew what it felt like. Think of that, Summerhays! think of that!

HYPATIA. I havnt kicked you, papa.

TARLETON. Youve kicked me harder than Bill Burt ever kicked.

LORD SUMMERHAYS. It's no use, Tarleton. Spare yourself. Do you seriously expect these young people, at their age, to sympathize with what this gentleman calls your paternal sentimentality?

TARLETON [*wistfully*] Is it nothing to you but paternal sentimentality, Patsy?

HYPATIA. Well, I greatly prefer your superabundant vitality, papa.

TARLETON [*violently*] Hold your tongue, you young devil. The young are all alike: hard, coarse, shallow, cruel, selfish, dirty-minded. You can clear out of my house as soon as you can coax him to take you; and the sooner the better. [*To Percival*] I think you said your price was fifteen hundred a year. Take it. And I wish you joy of your bargain.

PERCIVAL. If you wish to know who I am—

TARLETON. I dont care a tinker's curse who you are or what you are. Youre willing to take that girl off my hands for fifteen hundred a year: thats all that concerns me. Tell her who you are if you like: it's her affair, not mine.

HYPATIA. Dont answer him, Joey: it wont last. Lord Summerhays, I'm sorry about Bentley; but Joey's the only man for me.

LORD SUMMERHAYS. It may—

HYPATIA. Please dont say it may break your poor boy's heart. It's much more likely to break yours.

LORD SUMMERHAYS. Oh!

TARLETON [*springing to his feet*] Leave the room. Do you hear: leave the room.

PERCIVAL. Arnt we getting a little cross? Dont be angry, Mr Tarleton. Read Marcus Aurelius.

TARLETON. Dont you dare make fun of me. Take your aeroplane out of my vinery and yourself out of my house.

PERCIVAL [*rising, to Hypatia*] I'm afraid I shall have to dine at the Beacon, Patsy.

HYPATIA [*rising*] Do. I dine with you.

TARLETON. Did you hear me tell you to leave the room?

HYPATIA. I did. [*To Percival*] You see what living with one's parents means, Joey. It means living in a house where you can be ordered to leave the room. Ive got to obey: it's his house, not mine.

TARLETON. Who pays for it? Go and support yourself as I did if you want to be independent.

HYPATIA. I wanted to and you wouldnt let me. How can I support myself when I'm a prisoner?

TARLETON. Hold your tongue.

HYPATIA. Keep your temper.

PERCIVAL [*coming between them*] Lord Summerhays: youll join me, I'm sure, in pointing out to both father and daughter that they have now reached that very common stage in family life at which anything but a blow would be an anti-climax. Do you seriously want to beat Patsy, Mr Tarleton?

TARLETON. Yes. I want to thrash the life out of her. If she doesnt get out of my reach, I'll do it. [*He sits down and grasps the writing table to restrain himself*].

HYPATIA [*coolly going to him and leaning with her breast on his writhing shoulders*] Oh, if you want to beat me just to relieve your feelings—just really and truly for the fun of it and the satisfaction of it, beat away. I dont grudge you that.

TARLETON [*almost in hysterics*] I used to think that this sort of thing went on in other families but that it never could happen in ours. And now—[*He is broken with emotion, and continues lamentably*] I cant say the right thing. I cant do the right thing. I dont know what i s the right thing. I'm beaten; and she knows it. Summerhays: tell me what to do.

LORD SUMMERHAYS. When my council in Jinghiskahn reached the point of coming to blows, I used to adjourn the sitting. Let us postpone the discussion. Wait until Monday: we shall have Sunday to quiet down in. Believe me, I'm not making fun of you; but I think theres something in this young gentleman's advice. Read something.

TARLETON. I'll read King Lear.

HYPATIA. Dont. I'm very sorry, dear.

TARLETON. Youre not. Youre laughing at me. Serve me right! Parents and children! No man should know his own child. No child should know its own father. Let the family be rooted out of civilization! Let the human race be brought up in institutions!

HYPATIA. Oh yes. How jolly! You and I might be friends then; and Joey could stay to dinner.

TARLETON. Let him stay to dinner. Let him stay to breakfast. Let him spend his life here. Dont you say I drove him out. Dont you say I drove you out.

PERCIVAL. I really have no right to inflict myself on you. Dropping in as I did—

TARLETON. Out of the sky. Ha! Dropping in. The new sport of aviation. You just see a nice house; drop in; scoop up the man's daughter; and off with you again.

Bentley comes back, with his shoulders hanging as if he too had been exercised to the last pitch of fatigue. He is very sad. They stare at him as he gropes to Percival's chair.

BENTLEY. I'm sorry for making a fool of myself. I beg your pardon. Hypatia: I'm awfully sorry; but Ive made up my mind that I'll never marry. [*He sits down in deep depression*].

HYPATIA [*running to him*] How nice of you, Bentley! Of course you guessed I wanted to marry Joey. What did the Polish lady do to you?

BENTLEY [*turning his head away*] I'd rather not speak of her, if you dont mind.

HYPATIA. Youve fallen in love with her. [*She laughs*].

BENTLEY. It's beastly of you to laugh.

LORD SUMMERHAYS. You are not the first to fall today under the lash of that young lady's terrible derision, Bentley.

Lina, her cap on, and her goggles in her hand, comes impetuously through the inner door.

LINA [*on the steps*] Mr Percival: can we get that aeroplane started again? [*She comes down and runs to the pavilion door*]. I must get out of this into the air: right up into the blue.

PERCIVAL. Impossible. The frame's twisted. The petrol has given out: thats what brought us down. And how can we get a clear run to start with among these woods?

LINA [*swooping back through the middle of the pavilion*] We can straighten the frame. We can buy petrol at the Beacon. With a few laborers we can get her out on to the Portsmouth Road and start her along that.

TARLETON [*rising*] But why do you want to leave us, Miss Szcz?

LINA. Old pal: this is a stuffy house. You seem to think of nothing but making love. All the conversation here is about love-making. All the pictures are about love-making. The eyes of all of you are sheep's eyes. You are steeped in it, soaked in it: the very texts on the walls of your bedrooms are the ones about love. It is disgusting. It is not healthy. Your women are kept idle and dressed up for no other purpose than to be made love to. I have not been here an hour; and already everybody makes love to me as if because I am a woman it were my profession to be made love to. First you, old pal. I forgave you because you were nice about your wife.

HYPATIA. Oh! oh! oh! Oh, papa!

LINA. Then you, Lord Summerhays, come to me; and all you have to say is to ask me not to mention that you made love to me in Vienna two years ago. I forgave you because I thought you were an ambassador; and all ambassadors make love and are very nice and useful to people who travel. Then this young gentleman. He is engaged to this young lady; but no matter for that: he makes love to me because I carry him off in my arms when he cries. All these I bore in silence. But now comes your Johnny and tells me I'm a ripping fine woman, and asks to me marry him. I, Lina Szczepanowska, MARRY him!!!!! I do not mind this boy: he is a child: he loves me: I should have to give him money and take care of him: that would be foolish, but honorable. I do not mind you, old pal: you are what you call an old—ouf! but you do not offer to buy me: you say until we are tired—until you are so happy that you dare not ask for more. That is foolish too, at your age; but it is an adventure: it is not dishonorable. I do not mind Lord Summerhays: it was in Vienna: they had been toasting him at a great banquet: he was not sober. That is bad for the health; but it is not dishonorable. But your Johnny! Oh, your Johnny! with his marriage. He will do the straight thing by me. He will give me a home, a position. He tells me I must know that my present position is not one for a nice woman. This to me, Lina Szczepanowska! I am an honest woman: I earn my living. I am a free woman: I live in my own house. I am a woman of the world: I have thousands of friends: every night crowds of people applaud me, delight in me, buy my picture, pay hard-earned money to see me. I am strong: I am skilful: I am brave: I am independent: I am unbought: I am all that a woman ought to be; and in my family there has not been a single drunkard for four generations. And this Englishman! this linendraper! he dares to ask me to come and live with him in this rrrrrrrabbit hutch, and take my bread from his hand, and ask him for pocket money, and wear soft clothes, and be his woman! his wife! Sooner than that, I would stoop to the lowest depths of my profession. I would stuff lions with food and pretend to tame them. I would deceive honest people's eyes with conjuring tricks instead of real feats of strength and skill. I would be a clown and set bad examples of conduct to little children. I would sink yet lower and be an actress or an opera singer, imperilling my soul by the wicked lie of pretending to be somebody else. All this I would do sooner than take my bread from the hand of a man and make him the master of my body and soul. And so you may tell your Johnny to buy an Englishwoman: he shall not buy Lina Szczepanowska; and I will not stay in the house where such dishonor is offered me. Adieu. [*She turns precipitately to go, but is faced in the pavilion doorway by Johnny, who comes in slowly, his hands in his pockets, meditating deeply*].

JOHNNY [*confidentially to Lina*] You wont mention our little conversation, Miss Shepanoska. It'll do no good; and I'd rather you didnt.

TARLETON. Weve just heard about it, Johnny.

JOHNNY [*shortly, but without ill-temper*] Oh: is that so?

HYPATIA. The cat's out of the bag, Johnny, about everybody. They were all beforehand with you: papa, Lord Summerhays, Bentley and all. Dont you let them laugh at you.

JOHNNY [*a grin slowly overspreading his countenance*] Well, theres no use my pretending to be surprised at you, Governor, is there? I hope you got it as hot as I did. Mind, Miss Shepanoska: it wasnt lost on me. I'm a thinking man. I kept my temper. Youll admit that.

LINA [*frankly*] Oh yes. I do not quarrel. You are what is called a chump; but you are not a bad sort of chump.

JOHNNY. Thank you. Well, if a chump may have an opinion, I should put it at this. You make, I suppose, ten pounds a night off your own bat, Miss Lina?

LINA [*scornfully*] Ten pounds a night! I have made ten pounds a minute.

JOHNNY [*with increased respect*] Have you indeed? I didnt know: youll excuse my mistake, I hope. But the principle is the same. Now I trust you wont be offended at what I'm going to say; but Ive thought about this and watched it in daily experience; and you may take it from me that the moment a woman becomes pecuniarily independent, she gets hold of the wrong end of the stick in moral questions.

LINA. Indeed! And what do you conclude from that, Mister Johnny?

JOHNNY. Well, obviously, that independence for women is wrong and shouldnt be allowed. For their own good, you know. And for the good of morality in general. You agree with me, Lord Summerhays, dont you?

LORD SUMMERHAYS. It's a very moral moral, if I may so express myself.

Mrs Tarleton comes in softly through the inner door.

MRS TARLETON. Dont make too much noise. The lad's asleep.

TARLETON. Chickabiddy: we have some news for you.

JOHNNY [*apprehensively*] Now theres no need, you know, Governor, to worry mother with everything that passes.

MRS TARLETON [*coming to Tarleton*] Whats been going on? Dont you hold anything back from me, John. What have you been doing?

TARLETON. Patsy isnt going to marry Bentley.

MRS TARLETON. Of course not. Is that your great news? I never believed she'd marry him.

TARLETON. Theres something else. Mr Percival here—

MRS TARLETON [*to Percival*] Are you going to marry Patsy?

PERCIVAL [*diplomatically*] Patsy is going to marry me, with your permission.

MRS TARLETON. Oh, she has my permission: she ought to have been married long ago.

HYPATIA. Mother!

TARLETON. Miss Lina here, though she has been so short a time with us, has inspired a good deal of attachment in— I may say in almost all of us. Therefore I hope she'll stay to dinner, and not insist on flying away in that aeroplane.

PERCIVAL. You must stay, Miss Szczepanowska. I cant go up again this evening.

LINA. Ive seen you work it. Do you think I require any help? And Bentley shall come with me as a passenger.

BENTLEY [*terrified*] Go up in an aeroplane! I darent.

LINA. You must learn to dare.

BENTLEY [*pale but heroic*] All right. I'll come.

LORD SUMMERHAYS } No, no, Bentley, impossible. I shall not allow it.

MRS TARLETON } Do you want to kill the child? He shant go.

BENTLEY. I will. I'll lie down and yell until you let me go. I'm not a coward. I wont be a coward.

LORD SUMMERHAYS. Miss Szczepanowska; my son is very dear to me. I implore you to wait until tomorrow morning.

LINA. There may be a storm tomorrow. And I'll go: storm or no storm. I must risk my life tomorrow.

BENTLEY. I hope there will be a storm.

LINA [*grasping his arm*] You are trembling.

BENTLEY. Yes: it's terror, sheer terror. I can hardly see. I can hardly stand. But I'll go with you.

LINA [*slapping him on the back and knocking a ghastly white smile into his face*] You shall. I like you, my boy. We go tomorrow, together.

BENTLEY. Yes: together: tomorrow.

TARLETON. Well, sufficient unto the day is the evil thereof. Read the old book.

MRS TARLETON. Is there anything else?

TARLETON. Well, I—er [*he addresses Lina, and stops*]. I—er [*he addresses Lord Summerhays, and stops*]. I—er [*he gives it up*]. Well, I suppose—er—I suppose theres nothing more to be said.

HYPATIA [*fervently*] Thank goodness!

THE APPLE CART

A POLITICAL EXTRAVAGANZA IN
TWO ACTS AND AN INTERLUDE

Written in 1929

First Performed (in Polish) Warsaw 1929

PREFACE

THE first performances of this play at home and abroad provoked several confident anticipations that it would be published with an elaborate prefatory treatise on Democracy to explain why I, formerly a notorious democrat, have apparently veered round to the opposite quarter and become a devoted Royalist. In Dresden the performance was actually prohibited as a blasphemy against Democracy.

What was all this pother about? I had written a comedy in which a King defeats an attempt by his popularly elected Prime Minister to deprive him of the right to influence public opinion through the press and the platform: in short, to reduce him to a cipher. The King's reply is that rather than be a cipher he will abandon his throne and take his obviously very rosy chance of becoming a popularly elected Prime Minister himself. To those who believe that our system of votes for everybody produces parliaments which represent the people it should seem that this solution of the difficulty is completely democratic, and that the Prime Minister must at once accept it joyfully as such. He knows better. The change would rally the anti-democratic royalist vote against him, and impose on him a rival in the person of the only public man whose ability he has to fear. The comedic paradox of the situation is that the King wins, not by exercising his royal authority, but by threatening to resign it and go to the democratic poll.

That so many critics who believe themselves to be ardent democrats should take the entirely personal triumph of the hereditary king over the elected minister to be a triumph of autocracy over democracy, and its dramatization an act of political apostasy on the part of the author, convinces me that our professed devotion to political principles is only a mask for our idolatry of eminent persons. The Apple Cart exposes the unreality of both democracy and royalty as our idealists conceive them. Our Liberal democrats believe in a figment called a constitutional monarch, a sort of Punch puppet who cannot move until his Prime Minister's fingers are in his sleeves. They believe in another figment called a responsible minister, who moves only when similarly actuated by the million fingers of the electorate. But the most superficial inspection of any two such figures shews that they are not puppets but living men, and that the supposed control of one by the other and of both by the electorate amounts to no more than a not very deterrent fear of uncertain and under ordinary circumstances quite remote consequences. The nearest thing to a puppet in our political system is a Cabinet minister at the head of a great public office. Unless he possesses a very exceptional share of dominating ability and relevant knowledge he is helpless in the hands of his officials. He must sign whatever documents they present to him, and repeat whatever words they put into his mouth when answering questions in parliament, with a docility which cannot be imposed on a king who works at his job; for the king works continuously whilst his ministers are in office for spells only, the spells being few and brief, and often occurring for the first time to men of advanced age with little or no training for and experience of supreme responsibility. George the Third and Queen Victoria were not, like Queen Elizabeth, the natural superiors of their ministers in political genius and general capacity; but they were for many purposes of State necessarily superior to them in experience, in cunning, in exact knowledge of the limits of their responsibility and consequently of the limits of their irresponsibility: in short, in the authority and practical power that these superiorities produce. Very clever men who have come into contact with monarchs have been so impressed that they have attributed to them extraordinary natural qualifications which they, as now visible to us in historical perspective, clearly did not possess. In conflicts between monarchs and popularly elected ministers the monarchs win every time when personal ability and good sense are at all equally divided.

In The Apple Cart this equality is assumed. It is masked

by a strong contrast of character and methods which has led my less considerate critics to complain that I have packed the cards by making the King a wise man and the minister a fool. But that is not at all the relation between the two. Both play with equal skill; and the King wins, not by greater astuteness, but because he has the ace of trumps in his hand and knows when to play it. As the prettier player of the two he has the sympathy of the audience. Not being as pampered and powerful as an operatic prima donna, and depending as he does not on some commercially valuable talent but on his conformity to the popular ideal of dignity and perfect breeding, he has to be trained, and to train himself, to accept good manners as an indispensable condition of his intercourse with his subjects, and to leave to the less highly placed such indulgences as tempers, tantrums, bullyings, sneerings, swearings, kickings: in short, the commoner violences and intemperances of authority.

His ministers have much laxer standards. It is open to them, if it will save their time, to get their own way by making scenes, flying into calculated rages, and substituting vulgar abuse for argument. A clever minister, not having had a royal training, will, if he finds himself involved in a duel with his king, be careful not to choose the weapons at which the king can beat him. Rather will he in cold blood oppose to the king's perfect behavior an intentional misbehavior and apparently childish petulance which he can always drop at the right moment for a demeanor as urbane as that of the king himself, thus employing two sets of weapons to the king's one. This gives him the advantages of his own training as a successful ambitious man who has pushed his way from obscurity to celebrity: a process involving a considerable use of the shorter and more selfish methods of dominating the feebly recalcitrant, the unreasonable, the timid, and the stupid, as well as a sharp sense of the danger of these methods when dealing with persons of strong character in strong positions.

In this light the style of fighting adopted by the antagonists in the scrap between King Magnus and Mr Joseph Proteus is seen to be a plain deduction from their relative positions and antecedents, and not a manufactured contrast between democracy and royalty to the disadvantage of the former. Those who so mistook it are out of date. They still regard democracy as the under dog in the conflict. But to me it is the king who is doomed to be tragically in that position in the future into which the play is projected: in fact, he is visibly at least half in it already; and the theory of constitutional monarchy assumes that he is wholly in it, and has been so since the end of the seventeenth century.

Besides, the conflict is not really between royalty and democracy. It is between both and plutocracy, which, having destroyed the royal power by frank force under democratic pretexts, has bought and swallowed democracy. Money talks: money prints: money broadcasts: money reigns; and kings and labor leaders alike have to register its decrees, and even, by a staggering paradox, to finance its enterprises and guarantee its profits. Democracy is no longer bought: it is bilked. Ministers who are Socialists to the backbone are as helpless in the grip of Breakages Limited as its acknowledged henchmen: from the moment when they attain to what is with unintentional irony called power (meaning the drudgery of carrying on for the plutocrats) they no longer dare even to talk of nationalizing any industry, however socially vital, that has a farthing of profit for plutocracy still left in it, or that can be made to yield a farthing for it by subsidies.

King Magnus' little tactical victory, which bulks so largely in the playhouse, leaves him in a worse plight than his defeated opponent, who can always plead that he is only the instrument of the people's will, whereas the unfortunate monarch, making a desperate bid for dictatorship on the perfectly true plea that democracy has destroyed all other responsibility (has not Mussolini said that there is a vacant throne in every country in Europe waiting for a capable man to fill it?), is compelled to assume full responsibility himself, and face all the reproaches that Mr Proteus can shirk. In his

Cabinet there is only one friendly man who has courage, principle, and genuine good manners when he is courteously treated; and that man is an uncompromising republican, his rival for the dictatorship. The splendidly honest and devoted Die-hard lady is too scornfully tactless to help much; but with a little more experience in the art of handling effective men and women as distinguished from the art of handling mass meetings Mr Bill Boanerges might surprise those who, because he makes them laugh, see nothing in him but a caricature.

In short, those critics of mine who have taken The Apple Cart for a story of a struggle between a hero and a roomful of guys have been grossly taken in. It is never safe to take my plays at their suburban face value: it ends in your finding in them only what you bring to them, and so getting nothing for your money.

On the subject of Democracy generally I have nothing to say that can take the problem farther than I have already carried it in my Intelligent Woman's Guide to Socialism and Capitalism. We have to solve two inseparable main problems: the economic problem of how to produce and distribute our subsistence, and the political problem of how to select our rulers and prevent them from abusing their authority in their own interests or those of their class or religion. Our solution of the economic problem is the Capitalist system, which achieves miracles in production, but fails so ludicrously and disastrously to distribute its products rationally, or to produce in the order of social need, that it is always complaining of being paralysed by its "overproduction" of things of which millions of us stand in desperate want. Our solution of the political problem is Votes for Everybody and Every Authority Elected by Vote, an expedient originally devised to prevent rulers from tyrannizing by the very effectual method of preventing them from doing anything, and thus leaving everything to irresponsible private enterprise. But as private enterprise will do nothing that is not profitable to its little self, and the very existence of civilization now depends on the swift and unhampered public execution of enterprises that supersede private enterprise and are not merely profitable but vitally necessary to the whole community, this purely inhibitive check on tyranny has become a stranglehold on genuine democracy. Its painfully evolved machinery of parliament and Party System and Cabinet is so effective in obstruction that we take thirty years by constitutional methods to do thirty minutes work, and shall presently be forced to clear up thirty years arrears in thirty minutes by unconstitutional ones unless we pass a Reform Bill that will make a complete revolution in our political machinery and procedure. When we see parliaments like ours kicked into the gutter by dictators, both in kingdoms and republics, it is foolish to wait until the dictator dies or collapses, and then do nothing but pick the poor old things up and try to scrape the mud off them: the only sane course is to take the step by which the dictatorship could have been anticipated and averted, and construct a political system for rapid positive work instead of slow nugatory work, made to fit into the twentieth century instead of into the sixteenth.

Until we face this task and accomplish it we shall not be able to produce electorates capable of doing anything by their votes except pave the way to their own destruction. An election at present, considered as a means of selecting the best qualified rulers, is so absurd that if the last dozen parliaments had consisted of the candidates who were at the foot of the poll instead of those who were at the head of it there is no reason to suppose that we should have been a step more or less advanced than we are today. In neither case would the electorate have had any real choice of representatives. If it had, we might have had to struggle with parliaments of Titus Oateses and Lord George Gordons dominating a few generals and artists, with Cabinets made up of the sort of orator who is said to carry away his hearers by his eloquence because, having first ascertained by a few cautious feelers what they are ready to applaud, he gives it to them a dozen times over in an overwhelming crescendo, and is in effect carried away by them. As it is, the voters have no real choice of candidates: they have to take what they can get and make the best of it according to their lights, which is often the worst of it by the light of heaven. By chance rather than by judgment they find themselves represented in parliament by a fortunate proportion of reasonably honest and public spirited persons who happen to be also successful public speakers. The rest are in parliament because they can afford it and have a fancy for it or an interest in it.

Last October (1929) I was asked to address the enormous audience created by the new invention of Wireless Broadcast on a range of political and cultural topics introduced by a previous speaker under the general heading of Points of View. Among the topics was Democracy, presented, as usual, in a completely abstract guise as an infinitely beneficent principle in which we must trust though it slay us. I was determined that this time Votes for Everybody and Every Authority Elected by Vote should not escape by wearing its imposing mask. I delivered myself as follows:

Your Majesties, your Royal Highnesses, your Excellencies, your Graces and Reverences, my Lords, Ladies and Gentlemen, fellow-citizens of all degrees: I am going to talk to you about Democracy objectively: that is, as it exists and as we must all reckon with it equally, no matter what our points of view may be. Suppose I were to talk to you not about Democracy, but about the sea, which is in some respects rather like Democracy! We all have our own views of the sea. Some of us hate it and are never well when we are at it or on it. Others love it, and are never so happy as when they are in it or on it or looking at it. Some of us regard it as Britain's natural realm and surest bulwark: others want a Channel Tunnel. But certain facts about the sea are quite independent of our feelings towards it. If I take it for granted that the sea exists, none of you will contradict me. If I say that the sea is sometimes furiously violent and always uncertain, and that those who are most familiar with it trust it least, you will not immediately shriek out that I do not believe in the sea; that I am an enemy of the sea; that I want to abolish the sea; that I am going to make bathing illegal; that I am out to ruin our carrying trade and lay waste all our seaside resorts and scrap the British Navy. If I tell you that you cannot breathe in the sea, you will not take that as a personal insult and ask me indignantly if I consider you inferior to a fish. Well, you must please be equally sensible when I tell you some hard facts about Democracy. When I tell you that it is sometimes furiously violent and always dangerous and treacherous, and that those who are familiar with it as practical statesmen trust it least, you must not at once denounce me as a paid agent of Benito Mussolini, or declare that I have become a Tory Die-hard in my old age, and accuse me of wanting to take away your votes and make an end of parliament, and the franchise, and free speech, and public meeting, and trial by jury. Still less must you rise in your places and give me three rousing cheers as a champion of medieval monarchy and feudalism. I am quite innocent of any such extravagances. All I mean is that whether we are Democrats or Tories, Catholics or Protestants, Communists or Fascists, we are all face to face with a certain force in the world called Democracy; and we must understand the nature of that force whether we want to fight it or to forward it. Our business is not to deny the perils of Democracy, but to provide against them as far as we can, and then consider whether the risks we cannot provide against are worth taking.

Democracy, as you know it, is seldom more than a long word beginning with a capital letter, which we accept reverently or disparage contemptuously without asking any questions. Now we should never accept anything reverently until we have asked it a great many very searching questions, the first two being What are you? and Where do you live? When I put these questions to Democracy the answer I get is "My name is Demos; and I live in the British Empire, the United States of America, and wherever the love of liberty burns in the heart of man. You, my friend Shaw, are a unit of Democracy: your name is also Demos: you are a citizen of a great democratic community: you are a potential constituent of the Parliament of Man, the Federation of the World." At this I usually burst into loud cheers, which do credit to my enthusiastic nature. To-night, however, I shall do nothing of the sort: I shall say "Dont talk nonsense. My name is not Demos: it is Bernard Shaw. My address is not the British Empire, nor the United States of America, nor wherever the love of liberty burns in the heart of man: it is at such and such a number in such and such a street in London; and it will be time enough to discuss my seat in the Parliament of Man when that celebrated institution comes into existence. I dont believe your name is Demos: nobody's name is Demos; and all I can make of your address is that you have no address, and are just a tramp—if indeed you exist at all."

You will notice that I am too polite to call Demos a windbag or a hot air merchant; but I am going to ask you to begin our study of Democracy by considering it first as a big balloon, filled with gas or hot air, and sent up so that you shall be kept looking up at the sky whilst other people are picking your pockets. When the balloon comes down to earth every five years or so you are invited to get into the basket if you can throw out one of the people who are sitting tightly in it; but as you can afford neither the time nor the money, and there are forty millions of you and hardly room for six hundred in the basket, the balloon goes up again with much the same lot in it and leaves you where you were before. I think you will admit that the balloon as an image of Democracy corresponds to the parliamentary facts.

Now let us examine a more poetic conception of Democracy. Abraham Lincoln is represented as standing amid the carnage of the battlefield of Gettysburg, and declaring that all that slaughter of Americans by Americans occurred in order that Democracy, defined as government *of* the people *for* the people *by* the people, should not perish from the earth. Let us pick this famous peroration to pieces and see what there really is inside it. (By the way, Lincoln did not really declaim it on the field of Gettysburg; and the American Civil War was not fought in defence of any such principle, but, on the contrary, to enable one half of the United States to force the other half to be governed as they did not wish to be governed. But never mind that. I mentioned it only to remind you that it seems impossible for statesmen to make speeches about Democracy, or journalists to report them, without obscuring it in a cloud of humbug).

Now for the three articles of the definition. Number One: Government *of* the people: that, evidently, is necessary: a human community can no more exist without a government than a human being can exist without a co-ordinated control of its breathing and blood circulation. Number Two: Government *for* the people, is most important. Dean Inge put it perfectly for us when he called Democracy a form of society which means equal consideration for all. He added that it is a Christian principle, and that, as a Christian, he believes in it. So do I. That is why I insist on equality of income. Equal consideration for a person with a hundred a year and one with a hundred thousand is impossible. But Number Three: Government *by* the people, is quite a different matter. All the monarchs, all the tyrants, all the dictators, all the Die-hard Tories are agreed that we must be governed. Democrats like the Dean and myself are agreed that we must be governed with equal consideration for everybody. But we repudiate Number Three on the ground that the people cannot govern. The thing is a physical impossibility. Every citizen cannot be a ruler any more than every boy can be an engine driver or a pirate king. A nation of prime ministers or dictators is as absurd as an army of field marshals. Government by the people is not and never can be a reality: it is only a cry by which demagogues humbug us into voting for them. If you doubt this—if you ask me "Why should not the people make their own laws?" I need only ask you "Why should not the people write their own plays?" They cannot. It is much easier to write a good play than to make a good law. And there are not a hundred men in the world who can write a play good enough to stand daily wear and tear as long as a law must.

Now comes the question, If we cannot govern ourselves, what can we do to save ourselves from being at the mercy of those who *can* govern, and who may quite possibly be thoroughpaced grafters and scoundrels? The primitive answer is that as we are always in a huge majority we can, if rulers oppress us intolerably, burn their houses and tear them to pieces. This is not satisfactory. Decent people never do it until they have quite lost their heads; and when they have lost their heads they are as likely as not to burn the wrong house and tear the wrong man to pieces. When we have what is called a popular movement very few people who take part in it know what it is all about. I once saw a real popular movement in London. People were running excitedly through the streets. Everyone who saw them doing it immediately joined in the rush. They ran simply because everyone else was doing it. It was most impressive to see thousands of people sweeping along at full speed like that. There could be no doubt that it was literally a popular movement. I ascertained afterwards that it was started by a runaway cow. That cow had an important share in my education as a political philosopher; and I can assure you that if you will study crowds, and lost and terrified animals, and things like that, instead of reading books and newspaper articles, you will learn a great deal about politics from them. Most general elections, for instance, are nothing but stampedes. Our last but one was a conspicuous example of this. The cow was a Russian one.

I think we may take it that neither mob violence nor popular movements can be depended on as checks upon the abuse of power by governments. One might suppose that at least they would act as a last resort when an autocrat goes mad and commits outrageous excesses of tyranny and cruelty. But it is a curious fact that they never do. Take two famous cases: those of Nero and Tsar Paul the First of Russia. If Nero had been an ordinary professional fiddler he would probably have been no worse a man than any member of the wireless orchestra. If Paul had been a lieutenant in a line regiment we should never have heard of him. But when these two poor fellows were invested with absolute powers over their fellow-creatures they went mad, and did such appalling things that they had to be killed like mad dogs. Only, it was not the people that rose up and killed them. They were dispatched quite privately by a very select circle of their own bodyguards. For a genuinely democratic execution of unpopular statesmen we must turn to the brothers De Witt, who were torn to pieces by a Dutch mob in the seventeenth century. They were neither tyrants nor autocrats. On the contrary, one of them had been imprisoned and tortured for his resistance to the despotism of William of Orange; and the other had come to meet him as he came out of prison. The mob was on the side of the autocrat. We may take it that the shortest way for a tyrant to get rid of a troublesome champion of liberty is to raise a hue and cry against him as an unpatriotic person, and leave the mob to do the rest after supplying them with a well tipped ringleader. Nowadays this is called direct action by the revolutionary proletariat. Those who put their faith in it soon find that proletariats are never revolutionary, and that their direct action, when it is controlled at all, is usually controlled by police agents.

Democracy, then, cannot be government by the people: it can only be government by consent of the governed. Unfortunately, when democratic statesmen propose to govern us by our own consent, they find that we dont want to be governed at all, and that we regard rates and taxes and rents and death duties as intolerable burdens. What we want to know is how little government we can get along with without being murdered in our beds. That question cannot be answered until we have explained what we mean by getting along. Savages manage to get along. Unruly Arabs and Tartars get along. The only rule in the matter is that the civilized way of getting along is the way of corporate action, not individual action; and corporate action involves more government than individual action.

Thus government, which used to be a comparatively simple affair, today has to manage an enormous development of Socialism and Communism. Our industrial and social life is set in a huge communistic framework of public roadways, streets, bridges, water supplies, power supplies, lighting, tramways, schools, dockyards, and public aids and conveniences, employing a prodigious army of police, inspectors, teachers, and officials of all grades in hundreds of departments. We have found by bitter experience that it is impossible to trust factories, workshops, and mines to private management. Only by stern laws enforced by constant inspection have we stopped the monstrous waste of human life and welfare it cost when it was left uncontrolled by the Government. During the war our attempt to leave the munitioning of the army to private enterprise led us to the verge of defeat and caused an appalling slaughter of our soldiers. When the Government took the work out of private hands and had it done in national factories it was at once successful. The private firms were still allowed to do what little they could; but they had to be taught to do it economically, and to keep their accounts properly, by Government officials. Our big capitalist enterprises now run to the Government for help as a lamb runs to its mother. They cannot even make an extension of the Tube railway in London without Government aid. Unassisted private capitalism is breaking down or getting left behind in all directions. If all our Socialism and Communism and the drastic taxation of unearned incomes which finances it were to stop, our private enterprises would drop like shot stags, and we should all be dead in a month. When Mr Baldwin tried to win the last election by declaring that Socialism had been a failure whenever and wherever it had been tried, Socialism went over him like a steam roller and handed his office to a Socialist

Prime Minister. Nothing could save us in the war but a great extension of Socialism; and now it is clear enough that only still greater extensions of it can repair the ravages of the war and keep pace with the growing requirements of civilization.

What we have to ask ourselves, then, is not whether we will have Socialism and Communism or not, but whether Democracy can keep pace with the developments of both that are being forced on us by the growth of national and international corporate action.

Now corporate action is impossible without a governing body. It may be the central Government: it may be a municipal corporation, a county council, a district council, or a parish council. It may be the board of directors of a joint stock company, or of a trust made by combining several joint stock companies. Such boards, elected by the votes of the shareholders, are little States within the State, and very powerful ones, too, some of them. If they have not laws and kings, they have by-laws and chairmen. And you and I, the consumers of their services, are more at the mercy of the boards that organize them than we are at the mercy of parliament. Several active politicians who began as Liberals and are now Socialists have said to me that they were converted by seeing that the nation had to choose, not between governmental control of industry and control by separate private individuals kept in order by their competition for our custom, but between governmental control and control by gigantic trusts wielding great power without responsibility, and having no object but to make as much money out of us as possible. Our Government is at this moment having much more trouble with the private corporations on whom we are dependent for our coals and cotton goods than with France or the United States of America. We are in the hands of our corporate bodies, public or private, for the satisfaction of our everyday needs. Their powers are life and death powers. I need not labor this point: we all know it.

But what we do not all realize is that we are equally dependent on corporate action for the satisfaction of our religious needs. Dean Inge tells us that our general elections have become public auctions at which the contending parties bid against one another for our votes by each promising us a larger share than the other of the plunder of the minority. Now that is perfectly true. The contending parties do not as yet venture to put it exactly in those words; but that is what it comes to. And the Dean's profession obliges him to urge his congregation, which is much wider than that of St Paul's (it extends across the Atlantic), always to vote for the party which pledges itself to go farthest in enabling those of us who have great possessions to sell them and give the price to the poor. But we cannot do this as private persons. It must be done by the Government or not at all. Take my own case. I am not a young man with great possessions; but I am an old man paying enough in income tax and surtax to provide doles for some hundreds of unemployed and old age pensioners. I have not the smallest objection to this: on the contrary, I advocated it strongly for years before I had any income worth taxing. But I could not do it if the Government did not arrange it for me. If the Government ceased taxing my superfluous money and redistributing it among people who have no incomes at all, I could do nothing by myself. What could I do? Can you suggest anything? I could send my war bonds to the Chancellor of the Exchequer and invite him to cancel the part of the National Debt that they represent; and he would undoubtedly thank me in the most courteous official terms for my patriotism. But the poor would not get any of it. The other payers of surtax and income tax and death duties would save the interest they now have to pay on it: that is all. I should only have made the rich richer and myself poorer. I could burn all my share certificates and inform the secretaries of the companies that they might write off that much of their capital indebtedness. The result would be a bigger dividend for the rest of the shareholders, with the poor out in the cold as before. I might sell my war bonds and share certificates for cash, and throw the money into the street to be scrambled for; but it would be snatched up, not by the poorest, but by the best fed and most able-bodied of the scramblers. Besides, if we all tried to sell our bonds and shares—and this is what you have to consider; for Christ's advice was not addressed to me alone but to all who have great possessions—the result would be that their value would fall to nothing, as the Stock Exchange would immediately become a market in which there were all sellers and no buyers. Accordingly, any spare money that the Government leaves me is invested where I can get the highest interest and the best security, as thereby I can make sure that it goes where it is most wanted and gives immediate employment. This is the best I can do without Government interference: indeed any other way of dealing with my spare money would be foolish and demoralizing; but the result is that I become richer and richer, and the poor become relatively poorer and poorer. So you see I cannot even be a Christian except through Government action; and neither can the Dean.

Now let us get down to our problem. We cannot govern ourselves; yet if we entrust the immense powers and revenues which are necessary in an effective modern Government to an absolute monarch or dictator, he goes more or less mad unless he is a quite extraordinary and therefore very seldom obtainable person. Besides, modern government is not a one-man job: it is too big for that. If we resort to a committee or parliament of superior persons, they will set up an oligarchy and abuse their power for their own benefit. Our dilemma is that men in the lump cannot govern themselves; and yet, as William Morris put it, no man is good enough to be another man's master. We need to be governed, and yet to control our governors. But the best governors will not accept any control except that of their own consciences; and, as we who are governed are also apt to abuse any power of control we have, our ignorance, our passions, our private and immediate interests are constantly in conflict with the knowledge, the wisdom, and the public spirit and regard for the future of our best qualified governors.

Still, if we cannot control our governors, can we not at least choose them and change them if they do not suit?

Let me invent a primitive example of democratic choice. It is always best to take imaginary examples: they offend nobody. Imagine then that we are the inhabitants of a village. We have to elect somebody for the office of postman. There are several candidates; but one stands out conspicuously, because he has frequently treated us at the public-house, has subscribed a shilling to our little flower show, has a kind word for the children when he passes, and is a victim of oppression by the squire because his late father was one of our most successful poachers. We elect him triumphantly; and he is duly installed, uniformed, provided with a red bicycle, and given a batch of letters to deliver. As his motive in seeking the post has been pure ambition, he has not thought much beforehand about his duties; and it now occurs to him for the first time that he cannot read. So he hires a boy to come round with him and read the addresses. The boy conceals himself in the lane whilst the postman delivers the letters at the house, takes the Christmas boxes, and gets the whole credit of the transaction. In course of time he dies with a high reputation for efficiency in the discharge of his duties; and we elect another equally illiterate successor on similar grounds. But by this time the boy has grown up and become an institution. He presents himself to the new postman as an established and indispensable feature of the postal system, and finally becomes recognized and paid by the village as such.

Here you have the perfect image of a popularly elected Cabinet Minister and the Civil Service department over which he presides. It may work very well; for our postman, though illiterate, may be a very capable fellow; and the boy who reads the addresses for him may be quite incapable of doing anything more. But this does not always happen. Whether it happens or not, the system is not a democratic reality: it is a democratic illusion. The boy, when he has ability enough to take advantage of the situation, is the master of the man. The person elected to do the work is not really doing it: he is a popular humbug who is merely doing what a permanent official tells him to do. That is how it comes about that we are now governed by a Civil Service which has such enormous power that its regulations are taking the place of the laws of England, though some of them are made for the convenience of the officials without the slightest regard to the convenience or even the rights of the public. And how are our Civil Servants selected? Mostly by an educational test which nobody but an expensively schooled youth can pass, thus making the most powerful and effective part of our government an irresponsible class government.

Now, what control have you or I over the Services? We have votes. I have used mine a few times to see what it is like. Well, it is like this. When the election approaches, two or three persons of whom I know nothing write to me soliciting my vote and enclosing a list of meetings, an election address, and a polling card. One of the addresses reads like an article in The Morning Post, and has a Union Jack on it. Another is like The Daily News or Manchester Guardian. Both might have been compiled from the editorial waste paper baskets of a hundred years ago. A third address, more up-to-date and much better phrased, convinces me that the sender has had it written for him at the headquarters of the Labor Party. A fourth, the most hopelessly out of date of them all, contains scraps of the early English translations of the Communist Manifesto of 1848. I have no guarantee that any of these documents were written by the candidates. They convey nothing whatever to me as to their character or political capacity. The half-tone photographic portraits which adorn the front pages do not even tell me their ages, having been taken twenty years ago. If I go to one of the meetings I find a schoolroom packed with people who find an election meeting cheaper and funnier than a theatre. On the platform sit one or two poor men who have worked hard to keep party politics alive in the constituency. They ought to be the candidates; but they have no more chance of such eminence than they have of possessing a Rolls-Royce car. They move votes of confidence in the candidate, though as the candidate is a stranger to them and to everybody else present nobody can possibly feel any such confidence. They lead the applause for him; they prompt him when questions are asked; and when he is completely floored they jump up and cry "Let me answer that, Mr Chairman!" and then pretend that he has answered it. The old shibboleths are droned over; and nothing has any sense or reality in it except the vituperation of the opposition party, which is received with shouts of relief by the audience. Yet it is nothing but an exhibition of bad manners. If I vote for one of these candidates, and he or she is elected, I am supposed to be enjoying a democratic control of the government—to be exercising government *of* myself, *for* myself, *by* myself. Do you wonder that the Dean cannot believe such nonsense? If I believed it I should not be fit to vote at all. If this is Democracy, who can blame Signor Mussolini for describing it as a putrefying corpse?

The candidates may ask me what more they can do for me but present themselves and answer any questions I may put to them. I quite admit that they can do nothing; but that does not mend matters. What I should like is a real test of their capacity. Shortly before the war a doctor in San Francisco discovered that if a drop of a candidate's blood can be obtained on a piece of blotting paper it is possible to discover within half an hour what is wrong with him physically. What I am waiting for is the discovery of a process by which on delivery of a drop of his blood or a lock of his hair we can ascertain what is right with him mentally. We could then have a graded series of panels of capable persons for all employments, public or private, and not allow any person, however popular, to undertake the employment of governing us unless he or she were on the appropriate panel. At the lower end of the scale there would be a panel of persons qualified to take part in a parish meeting; at the higher end a panel of persons qualified to act as Secretaries of State for Foreign

Affairs or Finance Ministers. At present not more than two per thousand of the population would be available for the highest panel. I should then be in no danger of electing a postman and finding that he could neither read nor write. My choice of candidates would be perhaps more restricted than at present; but I do not desire liberty to choose windbags and nincompoops to represent me in parliament; and my power to choose between one qualified candidate and another would give me as much control as is either possible or desirable. The voting and counting would be done by machinery: I should connect my telephone with the proper office; touch a button; and the machinery would do the rest.

Pending such a completion of the American doctor's discovery, how are we to go on? Well, as best we can, with the sort of government that our present system produces. Several reforms are possible without any new discovery. Our present parliament is obsolete: it can no more do the work of a modern State than Julius Cæsar's galley could do the work of an Atlantic liner. We need in these islands two or three additional federal legislatures, working on our municipal committee system instead of our parliamentary party system. We need a central authority to co-ordinate the federal work. Our obsolete little internal frontiers must be obliterated, and our units of local government enlarged to dimensions compatible with the recent prodigious advances in facility of communication and co-operation. Commonwealth affairs and supernational activities through the League of Nations or otherwise will have to be provided for, and Cabinet function to be transformed. All the pseudo-democratic obstructive functions of our political machinery must be ruthlessly scrapped, and the general problem of government approached from a positive viewpoint at which mere anarchic national sovereignty as distinguished from self-government will have no meaning.

I must conclude by warning you that when everything has been done that can be done, civilization will still be dependent on the consciences of the governors and the governed. Our natural dispositions may be good; but we have been badly brought up, and are full of anti-social personal ambitions and prejudices and snobberies. Had we not better teach our children to be better citizens than ourselves? We are not doing that at present. The Russians *are*. That is my last word. Think over it.

So much for my broadcast on Democracy! And now a word about Breakages, Limited. Like all Socialists who know their business I have an exasperated sense of the mischief done by our system of private Capitalism in setting up huge vested interests in destruction, waste, and disease. The armament firms thrive on war; the glaziers gain by broken windows; the operating surgeons depend on cancer for their children's bread; the distillers and brewers build cathedrals to sanctify the profits of drunkenness; and the prosperity of Dives costs the privation of a hundred Lazaruses.

The title Breakages, Limited, was suggested to me by the fate of that remarkable genius, the late Alfred Warwick Gattie, with whom I was personally acquainted. I knew him first as the author of a play. He was a disturbing man, afflicted—or, as it turned out, gifted—with chronic hyperæsthesia, feeling everything violently and expressing his feelings vehemently and on occasion volcanically. I concluded that he was not sufficiently cold-blooded to do much as a playwright; so that when, having lost sight of him for some years, I was told that he had made an invention of first-rate importance, I was incredulous, and concluded that the invention was only a Utopian project. Our friend Henry Murray was so provoked by my attitude that to appease him I consented to investigate the alleged great invention in person on Gattie's promising to behave like a reasonable being during the process, a promise which he redeemed with the greatest dignity, remaining silent whilst an engineer explained his miracles to me, and contenting himself with the reading of a brief statement shewing that the adoption of his plan would release from industry enough men to utterly overwhelm the Central Empires with whom we were then at war.

I approached the investigation very sceptically. Our friend spoke of "the works." I could not believe that Gattie had any works, except in his fervid imagination. He mentioned "the company." That was more credible: anyone may form a company; but that it had any resources seemed to me doubtful. However, I suffered myself to be taken to Battersea; and there, sure enough, I found a workshop, duly labelled as the premises of The New Transport Company, Limited, and spacious enough to accommodate a double railway line with a platform. The affair was unquestionably real, so far. The platform was not provided with a station: its sole equipment was a table with a row of buttons on it for making electrical contacts. Each line of railway had on it a truck with a steel lid. The practical part of the proceedings began by placing an armchair on the lid of one of the trucks and seating me in it. A brimming glass of water was then set at my feet. I could not imagine what I was expected to do with the water or what was going to happen; and there was a suggestion of electrocution about the chair which made me nervous. Gattie then sat down majestically at the table on the platform with his hand hovering over the buttons. Intimating that the miracle would take place when my truck passed the other truck, he asked me to choose whether it should occur at the first passage or later, and to dictate the order in which it should be repeated. I was by that time incapable of choosing; so I said the sooner the better; and the two trucks started. When the other truck had passed mine I found myself magically sitting on it, chair and all, with the glass of water unspilled at my feet.

The rest of the story is a tragi-comedy. When I said to Gattie apologetically (I felt deeply guilty of having underrated him) that I had never known that he was an engineer, and had taken him to be the usual amateur inventor with no professional training, he told me that this was exactly what he was: just like Sir Christopher Wren. He had been concerned in an electric lighting business, and had been revolted by the prodigious number of breakages of glass bulbs involved by the handling of the crates in which they were packed for transport by rail and road. What was needed was a method of transferring the crates from truck to truck, and from truck to road lorry, and from road lorry to warehouse lift without shock, friction, or handling. Gattie, being, I suppose, by natural genius an inventor though by mistaken vocation a playwright, solved the mechanical problem without apparent difficulty, and offered his nation the means of effecting an enormous saving of labor and smash. But instead of being received with open arms as a social benefactor he found himself up against Breakages, Limited. The glass blowers whose employment was threatened, the exploiters of the great industry of repairing our railway trucks (every time a goods train is stopped a series of 150 violent collisions is propagated from end to end of the train, as those who live within earshot know to their cost), and the railway porters who dump the crates from truck to platform and then hurl them into other trucks, shattering bulbs, battering cans, and too often rupturing themselves in the process, saw in Gattie an enemy of the human race, a wrecker of homes and a starver of innocent babes. He fought them undauntedly; but they were too strong for him; and in due time his patents expired and he died almost unrecognized, whilst Unknown Soldiers were being canonized throughout the world. So far, The Apple Cart is his only shrine; and as it does not even bear his name, I have written it here pending its tardy appearance in the roll of fame.

I must not leave my readers to assume that Gattie was an easy man to deal with, or that he handled the opposition in a conciliatory manner with due allowance for the inertia of a somewhat unimaginative officialdom which had not, like myself, sat on his trucks, and probably set him down as a Utopian (a species much dreaded in Government departments) and thus missed the real point, which was that he was an inventor. Like many men of genius he could not understand why things obvious to him should not be so at once to other people, and found it easier to believe that they were corrupt than that they could be so stupid. Once, after I had urged him to be more diplomatic, he brought me, with some pride, a letter to the Board of Trade which he considered a masterpiece of tact and good temper. It contained not a word descriptive of his invention; and it began somewhat in this fashion: "Sir: If you are an honest man you cannot deny that among the worst abuses of this corrupt age is the acceptance of city directorships by retired members of the Board of Trade." Clearly it was not easy for the Board of Trade to deal with an inventor who wished to interest them, not in his new machines, but in the desirability of its abolishing itself as infamous.

The last time I saw him he called on me to unfold a new scheme of much greater importance, as he declared, than his trucks. He was very interesting on that occasion. He began by giving me a vivid account of the pirates who used to infest the Thames below London Bridge before the docks were built. He described how the docks had come into existence not as wharves for loading and unloading but as strongholds in which ships and their cargoes could be secure from piracy. They are now, he declared, a waste of fabulously valuable ground; and their work should be done in quite another way. He then produced plans of a pier to be built in the middle of the river, communicating directly by rail and road with the shore and the great main lines. The ships would come alongside the pier; and by a simple system of hoists the contents of their holds would be lifted out and transferred (like myself in the armchair) to railway trucks or motor lorries without being touched by a human hand and therefore without risk of breakage. It was all so masterly, so simple in its complexity, so convincing as to its practicability, and so prodigiously valuable socially, that I, taking it very seriously, proceeded to discuss what could be done to interest the proper people in it.

To my amazement Gattie began to shew unmistakeable

signs of disappointment and indignation. "You do not seem to understand me," he said. "I have shewn you all this mechanical stuff merely by way of illustration. What I have come to consult you about is a great melodrama I am going to write, the scene of which will be the Pool of London in the seventeenth century among the pirates!"

What could I or anyone do with a man like that? He was naïvely surprised when I laughed; and he went away only half persuaded that his scheme for turning the docks into building land; expediting the Thames traffic; saving much dangerous and demoralizingly casual labor; and transfiguring the underpaid stevedore into a fullfed electrician, was stupendously more important than any ridiculous melodrama. He admitted that there was of course all that in it; but I could see that his heart was in the melodrama.

As it was evident that officialdom, writhing under his insults and shocked by his utter lack of veneration for bigwigs, besides being hampered as all our Government departments are by the vested interests of Breakages, Limited, would do nothing for him, I induced some less embarrassed public persons to take a ride in the trucks and be convinced that they really existed and worked. But here again the parallel between Gattie and his fellow-amateur Sir Christopher Wren came in. Wren was not content to redesign and rebuild St Paul's: he wanted to redesign London as well. He was quite right: what we have lost by not letting him do it is incalculable. Similarly, Gattie was not content to improve the luggage arrangements of our railways: he would not listen to you if your mind was not large enough to grasp the immediate necessity for a new central clearing house in Farringdon Market, connected with the existing railways by a system of new tubes. He was of course right; and we have already lost by sticking to our old ways more than the gigantic sum his scheme would have cost. But neither the money nor the enterprise was available just then, with the war on our hands. The Clearing House, like the Thames pier, remains on paper; and Gattie is in his grave. But I still hold that there must have been something great in a man who, having not only imagined them but invented their machinery, could, far from being crushed by their rejection, exclaim "Perish all my mechanical trash if only it provides material for one bad play!"

This little history will explain how it actually did provide material for Breakages, Limited, and for the bitter cry of the Powermistress General. Not until Breakages is itself broken will it cease to have a message for us.

AYOT ST LAWRENCE,

March 1930.

THE APPLE CART

ACT I

AN office in the royal palace. Two writing tables face each other from opposite sides of the room, leaving plenty of room between them. Each table has a chair by it for visitors. The door is in the middle of the farthest wall. The clock shews that it is a little past 11; *and the light is that of a fine summer morning.*

Sempronius, smart and still presentably young, shews his right profile as he sits at one of the tables opening the Kings' letters. Pamphilius, middle aged, shews his left as he leans back in his chair at the other table with a pile of the morning papers at his elbow, reading one of them. This goes on silently for some time. Then Pamphilius, putting down his paper, looks at Sempronius for a moment before speaking.

PAMPHILIUS. What was your father?

SEMPRONIUS [*startled*] Eh?

PAMPHILIUS. What was your father?

SEMPRONIUS. My father?

PAMPHILIUS. Yes. What was he?

SEMPRONIUS. A Ritualist.

PAMPHILIUS. I dont mean his religion. I mean his profession. And his politics.

SEMPRONIUS. He was a Ritualist by profession, a Ritualist in politics, a Ritualist in religion: a raging emotional Die Hard Ritualist right down to his boots.

PAMPHILIUS. Do you mean that he was a parson?

SEMPRONIUS. Not at all. He was a sort of spectacular artist. He got up pageants and Lord Mayors' Shows and military tattoos and big public ceremonies and things like that. He arranged the last two coronations. That was how I got my job here in the palace. All our royal people knew him quite well: he was behind the scenes with them.

PAMPHILIUS. Behind the scenes and yet believed they were all real!

SEMPRONIUS. Yes. Believed in them with all his soul.

PAMPHILIUS. Although he manufactured them himself?

SEMPRONIUS. Certainly. Do you suppose a baker cannot believe sincerely in the sacrifice of the Mass or in holy communion because he has baked the consecrated wafer himself?

PAMPHILIUS. I never thought of that.

SEMPRONIUS. My father might have made millions in the theatres and film studios. But he refused to touch them because the things they represented hadnt really happened. He didnt mind doing the christening of Queen Elizabeth in Shakespear's Henry the Eighth because that had really happened. It was a celebration of royalty. But not anything romantic: not though they offered him thousands.

PAMPHILIUS. Did you ever ask him what he really thought about it all? But of course you didnt: one cant ask one's father anything about himself.

SEMPRONIUS. My dear Pam: my father never thought. He didnt know what thought meant. Very few people do, you know. He had vision: actual bodily vision, I mean; and he had an oddly limited sort of imagination. What I mean is that he couldnt imagine anything he didnt see; but he could imagine that what he did see was divine and holy and omniscient and omnipotent and eternal and everything that is impossible if only it looked splendid enough, and the organ was solemn enough, or the military bands brassy enough.

PAMPHILIUS. You mean that he had to get everything from outside.

SEMPRONIUS. Exactly. He'd never have felt anything if he hadnt had parents to feel about in his childhood, and a wife and babies to feel about when he grew up. He'd never have known anything if he hadnt been taught at school. He couldnt amuse himself: he had to pay oceans of money to other people to amuse him with all sorts of ghastly sports and pleasures that would have driven me into a monastery to escape from them. You see it was all ritual: he went to the Riviera every winter just as he went to church.

PAMPHILIUS. By the way, is he alive? I should like to know him.

SEMPRONIUS. No. He died in 1962, of solitude.

PAMPHILIUS. What do you mean? of solitude?

SEMPRONIUS. He couldnt bear to be alone for a moment: it was death to him. Somebody had to be with him always.

PAMPHILIUS. Oh well, come! That was friendly and kindly. It shews he had something inside him after all.

SEMPRONIUS. Not a bit. He never talked to his friends. He played cards with them. They never exchanged a thought.

PAMPHILIUS. He must have been a rum old bird.

SEMPRONIUS. Not rum enough to be noticed. There are millions like him.

PAMPHILIUS. But what about his dying of solitude? Was he imprisoned?

SEMPRONIUS. No. His yacht struck a reef and sank somewhere off the north of Scotland; and he managed to swim to an uninhabited island. All the rest were drowned; and he was not taken off for three weeks. When they found him he was melancholy mad, poor old boy; and he never got over it. Simply from having no one to play cards with, and no church to go to.

PAMPHILIUS. My dear Sem: one isnt alone on an uninhabited island. My mother used to stand me on the table and make me recite about it.

[*He declaims*]

To sit on rocks; to muse o'er flood and fell;
To slowly trace the forest's shady scene
Where things that own not man's dominion dwell
And mortal foot hath ne'er or rarely been;
To climb the trackless mountain all unseen
With the wild flock that never needs a fold;
Alone o'er steeps and foaming falls to lean:
This is not solitude: 'tis but to hold
Converse with Nature's charms, and view her stores
unrolled.

SEMPRONIUS. Now you have hit the really funny thing about my father. All that about the lonely woods and the rest of it—what you call Nature—didnt exist for him. It had to be something artificial to get at him. Nature to him meant nakedness; and nakedness only disgusted him. He wouldnt look at a horse grazing in a field; but put splendid trappings on it and stick it into a procession and he just loved it. The same with men and women: they were nothing to him until they were dressed up in fancy costumes and painted and wigged and titled. To him the sacredness of the priest was the beauty of his vestment, the loveliness of women the dazzle of their jewels and robes, the charm of the countryside not in its hills and trees, nor in the blue smoke from its cottages in the winter evenings, but of its temples, palaces, mansions, park gates, and porticoed country houses. Think of the horror of that island to him! A void! a place where he was deaf and dumb and blind and lonely! If only there had been a peacock with its tail in full bloom it might have saved his reason; but all the birds were gulls; and gulls are not decorative. Our King could have lived there for thirty years with nothing but his own thoughts. You would have been all right with a fishing rod and a golf ball with a bag of clubs. I should have been as happy as a man in a picture gallery looking at the dawns and sunsets, the changing seasons, the continual miracle of life ever renewing itself. Who could be dull with pools in the rocks to watch? Yet my father, with all that under his nose, was driven mad by its nothingness. They say that where there is nothing the king loses his rights. My father found that where there is nothing a man loses his reason and dies.

PAMPHILIUS. Let me add that in this palace, when the king's letters are not ready for him at 12 o'clock, a secretary loses his job.

SEMPRONIUS [*hastily resuming his work*] Yes, devil take you: why did you start me talking before I had finished my work? You have nothing to do but pretend to read the newspapers for him; and when you say "Nothing particular this morning, Sir," all he says is "Thank Heaven!" But if I missed a note from one of his aunts inviting herself to tea, or a little line from Orinthia the Beloved marked "Strictly private and confidential: to be opened by His Majesty alone," I should never hear the end of it. He had six love letters yesterday; and all he said when I told him was "Take them to the Queen." He thinks they amuse her. I believe they make her as sick as they make me.

PAMPHILIUS. Do Orinthia's letters go to the Queen?

SEMPRONIUS. No, by George! Even I dont read Orinthia's letters. My instructions are to read everything; but I take care to forget to open hers. And I notice that I am not rebuked for my negligence.

PAMPHILIUS [*thoughtfully*] I suppose—

SEMPRONIUS. Oh shut up, Pam. I shall never get through if you go on talking.

PAMPHILIUS. I was only going to say that I suppose—

SEMPRONIUS. Something about Orinthia. Dont. If you indulge in supposition on that subject, you will lose your job, old chap. So stow it.

PAMPHILIUS. Dont cry out before Orinthia is hurt, young chap. I was going to say that I suppose you know that that bull-roarer Boanerges has just been taken into the Cabinet as President of the Board of Trade, and that he is coming here today to give the King a piece of his mind, or what he calls his mind, about the crisis.

SEMPRONIUS. What does the King care about the crisis? There has been a crisis every two months since he came to the throne; but he has always been too clever for them. He'll turn Boanerges inside out after letting him roar the palace down.

Boanerges enters, dressed in a Russian blouse and peaked cap, which he keeps on. He is fifty, heavily built and aggressively self-assertive.

BOANERGES. Look here. The King has an appointment with me at a quarter to twelve. How long more am I to be kept waiting?

SEMPRONIUS [*with cheerful politeness*] Good morning. Mr Boanerges, I think.

BOANERGES [*shortly, but a little taken aback*] Oh, good

morning to you. They say that politeness is the punctuality of kings—

SEMPRONIUS. The other way about, Mr Boanerges. Punctuality is the politeness of kings; and King Magnus is a model in that respect. Your arrival cannot have been announced to His Majesty. I will see about it. [*He hurries out*].

PAMPHILIUS. Be seated, Mr Boanerges.

BOANERGES [*seating himself by Pamphilius's writing table*] A nice lot of young upstarts you have in this palace, Mr—?

PAMPHILIUS. Pamphilius is my name.

BOANERGES. Oh yes: Ive heard of you. Youre one of the king's private secretaries.

PAMPHILIUS. I am. And what have our young upstarts been doing to you, Mr Boanerges?

BOANERGES. Well, I told one of them to tell the king I was here, and to look sharp about it. He looked at me as if I was a performing elephant, and took himself off after whispering to another flunkey. Then this other chap comes over to me and pretends he doesnt know who I am! asks me can he have my name! "My lad" I said: "not to know me argues yourself unknown. You know who I am as well as I do myself. Go and tell the king I'm waiting for him, d'ye see?" So he took himself off with a flea in his ear. I waited until I was fed up with it, and then opened the nearest door and came in here.

PAMPHILIUS. Young rascals! However, my friend Mr Sempronius will make it all right for you.

BOANERGES. Oh: that was Sempronius, was it. Ive heard of him too.

PAMPHILIUS. You seem to have heard of all of us. You will be quite at home in the palace now that you are a Cabinet Minister. By the way, may I congratulate you on your appointment—or rather congratulate the Cabinet on your accession?

SEMPRONIUS [*returning*] The King. [*He goes to his table and takes the visitor's chair in his hand, ready for the king's instructions as to where to place it*].

Pamphilius rises. Boanerges turns to the door in his chair without rising. King Magnus, a tallish studious looking gentleman of 45 or thereabouts, enters, and comes quickly down the middle of the room to Boanerges, proffering his hand cordially.

MAGNUS. You are very welcome to my little palace, Mr Boanerges. Wont you sit down?

BOANERGES. I am sitting down.

MAGNUS. True, Mr Boanerges. I had not noticed it. Forgive me: force of habit.

He indicates to Sempronius that he wishes to sit near Boanerges, on his right. Sempronius places the chair accordingly.

MAGNUS. You will allow me to be seated?

BOANERGES. Oh, sit down, man, sit down. Youre in your own house: ceremony cuts no ice with me.

MAGNUS [*gratefully*] Thank you.

The King sits. Pamphilius sits. Sempronius returns to his table and sits.

MAGNUS. It is a great pleasure to meet you at last, Mr Boanerges. I have followed your career with interest ever since you contested Northampton twenty-five years ago.

BOANERGES [*pleased and credulous*] I should just think you have, King Magnus. I have made you sit up once or twice, eh?

MAGNUS [*smiling*] Your voice has shaken the throne oftener than that.

BOANERGES [*indicating the secretaries with a jerk of his head*] What about these two? Are they to overhear everything that passes?

MAGNUS. My private secretaries. Do they incommode you?

BOANERGES. Oh, they dont incommode me. I am ready to have our talk out in Trafalgar Square if you like, or have it broadcast on the wireless.

MAGNUS. That would be a treat for my people, Mr Boanerges. I am sorry we have not arranged for it.

BOANERGES [*gathering himself together formidably*] Yes; but do you realize that I am going to say things to you that have never been said to a king before?

MAGNUS. I am very glad indeed to hear it, Mr Boanerges.

I thought I had already heard everything that could possibly be said to a king. I shall be grateful for the smallest novelty.

BOANERGES. I warn you it wont be agreeable. I am a plain man, Magnus: a very plain man.

MAGNUS. Not at all, I assure you—

BOANERGES [*indignantly*] I was not alluding to my personal appearance.

MAGNUS [*gravely*] Nor was I. Do not deceive yourself, Mr Boanerges. You are very far from being a plain man. To me you have always been an Enigma.

BOANERGES [*surprised and enormously flattered: he cannot help smiling with pleasure*] Well, perhaps I am a bit of an enigma. Perhaps I am.

MAGNUS [*humbly*] I wish I could see through you, Mr Boanerges. But I have not your sort of cleverness. I can only ask you to be frank with me.

BOANERGES [*now convinced that he has the upper hand*] You mean about the crisis. Well, frank is just what I have come here to be. And the first thing I am going to tell you frankly about it is that this country has got to be governed, not by you, but by your ministers.

MAGNUS. I shall be only too grateful to them for taking a very difficult and thankless job off my hands.

BOANERGES. But it's not on your hands. It's on your ministers' hands. You are only a constitutional monarch. Do you know what they call that in Belgium?

MAGNUS. An indiarubber stamp, I think. Am I right?

BOANERGES. You are, King Magnus. An indiarubber stamp. Thats what you have got to be; and dont you forget it.

MAGNUS. Yes: thats what we are most of the time: both of us.

BOANERGES [*outraged*] What do you mean? both of us?

MAGNUS. They bring us papers. We sign. You have no time to read them, luckily for you. But I am expected to read everything. I do not always agree; but I must sign: there is nothing else to be done. For instance, death warrants. Not only have I to sign the death warrants of persons who in my opinion ought not to be killed; but I may not even issue death warrants for a great many people who in my opinion ought to be killed.

BOANERGES [*sarcastic*] Youd like to be able to say "Off with his head!" wouldnt you?

MAGNUS. Many men would hardly miss their heads, there is so little in them. Still, killing is a serious business: at least the person who is to be killed is usually conceited enough to think so. I think that if there were a question of killing me—

BOANERGES [*grimly*] There may be, someday. I have heard it discussed.

MAGNUS. Oh, quite. I have not forgotten King Charles's head. Well, I hope it will be settled by a living person and not by an indiarubber stamp.

BOANERGES. It will be settled by the Home Secretary, your duly constituted democratic minister.

MAGNUS. Another indiarubber stamp, eh?

BOANERGES. At present, perhaps. But not when I am Home Secretary, by Jingo! Nobody will make an indiarubber stamp of Bill Boanerges: take that from me.

MAGNUS. Of course not. Is it not curious how people idealize their rulers? In the old days the king—poor man!—was a god, and was actually called God and worshipped as infallible and omniscient. That was monstrous—

BOANERGES. It was silly: just silly.

MAGNUS. But was it half so silly as our pretence that he is an indiarubber stamp? The ancient Roman emperor-god had not infinite wisdom, infinite knowledge, infinite power; but he had some: perhaps even as much as his ministers. He was alive, not dead. What man has ever approached either a king or a minister and been able to pick him up from the table and use him as one picks up and uses a piece of wood and brass and rubber? Permanent officials of your department will try to pick you up and use you like that. Nineteen times out of twenty you will have to let them do it, because you cannot know everything; and even if you could you cannot do everything and be everywhere. But what about the twentieth time?

BOANERGES. The twentieth time they will find they are up against Bill Boanerges, eh?

MAGNUS. Precisely. The indiarubber stamp theory will not work, Mr. Boanerges. The old divine theory worked because there is a divine spark in us all; and the stupidest or worst monarch or minister, if not wholly god, is a bit of a god—an attempt at a god—however little the bit and unsuccessful the attempt. But the indiarubber stamp theory breaks down in every real emergency, because no king or minister is the very least little bit like a stamp: he is a living soul.

BOANERGES. A soul, eh? You kings still believe in that, I suppose.

MAGNUS. I find the word convenient: it is short and familiar. But if you dislike being called a soul, let us say that you are animate matter as distinguished from inanimate.

BOANERGES [*not quite liking this*] I think I'd rather you called me a soul, you know, if you must call me anything at all. I know I have too much matter about me: the doctor says I ought to knock off a stone or two; but there's something more to me than beef. Call it a soul if you like; only not in a superstitious sense, if you understand me.

MAGNUS. Perfectly. So you see, Mr Boanerges, that though we have been dealing with one another for less than ten minutes, you have already led me into an intellectual discussion which shews that we are something more than a pair of indiarubber stamps. You are up against my brains, such as they are.

BOANERGES. And you are up against mine.

MAGNUS [*gallantly*] There can be no doubt of that.

BOANERGES [*grinning*] Such as they are, eh?

MAGNUS. It is not for me to make that qualification, except in my own case. Besides, you have given your proofs. No common man could have risen as you have done. As for me, I am a king because I was the nephew of my uncle, and because my two elder brothers died. If I had been the stupidest man in the country I should still be its king. I have not won my position by my merits. If I had been born as you were in the—in the—

BOANERGES. In the gutter. Out with it. Picked up by a policeman at the foot of Captain Coram's statue. Adopted by the policeman's grandmother, bless her!

MAGNUS. Where should *I* have been if the policeman had picked me up?

BOANERGES. Ah! Where? Not, mind you, that you mightnt have done pretty well for yourself. Youre no fool, Magnus: I will say that for you.

MAGNUS. You flatter me.

BOANERGES. Flatter a king! Never. Not Bill Boanerges.

MAGNUS. Yes, yes: everybody flatters the King. But everybody has not your tact, and, may I say? your good nature.

BOANERGES [*beaming with self-satisfaction*] Perhaps not. Still, I am a Republican, you know.

MAGNUS. That is what has always surprised me. Do you really think that any man should have as much personal power as the presidents of the republican States have? Ambitious kings envy them.

BOANERGES. What's that? I dont follow that.

MAGNUS [*smiling*] You cannot humbug me, Mr Boanerges. I see why you are a Republican. If the English people send me packing and establish a republic, no man has a better chance of being the first British president than you.

BOANERGES [*almost blushing*] Oh! I dont say that.

MAGNUS. Come come! You know it as well as I do. Well, if it happens you will have ten times more power than I have ever had.

BOANERGES [*not quite convinced*] How can that be? Youre King.

MAGNUS. And what is the King? An idol set up by a group of plutocrats so that they can rule the country with the king as their scapegoat and puppet. Presidents, now, are chosen by the people, who always want a Strong Man to protect them against the rich.

BOANERGES. Well, speaking as a bit of a Strong Man myself, there may be something in that. But honestly, Magnus, as man to man, do you tell me youd rather be a president than what you are?

MAGNUS. By no means. You wouldnt believe me if I did; and you would be quite right. You see, my security is very comfortable.

BOANERGES Security, eh? You admitted just now that even a modest individual like myself had given your throne a shake or two.

MAGNUS. True. You are quite right to remind me of it. I know that the monarchy may come to an end at any moment. But while the monarchy lasts—while it lasts, mark you—I am very secure. I escape the dreadful and demoralizing drudgery of electioneering. I have no voters to please. Ministers come and ministers go; but I go on for ever. The terrible precariousness of your position—

BOANERGES. What's that? How is my position precarious?

MAGNUS. The vote may go against you. Yours is a Trade Union seat, is it not? If the Hydro-Electric Workers Federation throw you over, where would you be?

BOANERGES [*confidently*] They wont throw me over. You dont know the workers, Magnus: you have never been a worker.

MAGNUS [*lifts his eyebrows*]!

BOANERGES [*continuing*] No king on earth is as safe in his job as a Trade Union official. There is only one thing that can get him sacked; and that is drink. Not even that, as long as he doesnt actually fall down. I talk democracy to these men and women. I tell them that they have the vote, and that theirs is the kingdom and the power and the glory. I say to them "You are supreme: exercise your power." They say, "That's right: tell us what to do"; and I tell them. I say "Exercise your vote intelligently by voting for me." And they do. That's democracy; and a splendid thing it is too for putting the right men in the right place.

MAGNUS. Magnificent! I have never heard it better described. You certainly have a head on you, Mr Boanerges. You should write an essay on democracy. But—

BOANERGES. But what?

MAGNUS. Suppose a man with a bigger voice comes along! Some fool! Some windbag! Some upstart with a platform trick of gulling the multitude!

BOANERGES. Youre thinking of Iky Jacobus? He is only a talker. [*Snapping his fingers*] I dont give that for him.

MAGNUS. I never even heard of Mr Jacobus. But why do you say "only a talker." Talkers are very formidable rivals for popular favor. The multitude understands talk: it does not understand work. I mean brain work, like yours and mine.

BOANERGES. That's true. But I can talk Iky's head off.

MAGNUS. Lucky man: you have all the trumps in your hand. But I, who cannot pretend to your gifts, am very glad that Iky cannot upset me as long as I am the nephew of my uncle.

A young lady, dressed for walking, rushes in impetuously.

THE YOUNG LADY. Papa: I cannot find the address—

MAGNUS [*cutting her short*] No, no, no, dear: not now. Go away. Dont you see that I am particularly engaged with the President of the Board of Trade? You must excuse my unruly daughter, Mr Boanerges. May I present her to you? Alice, my eldest girl. Mr Boanerges, dear.

ALICE. Oh! Are you the great Mr Boanerges?

BOANERGES [*rising in a glow of gratification*] Well, I dont call myself that, you know. But I believe the expression is in use, as you might say. I am very pleased indeed to make the acquaintance of the Princess Royal.

They shake hands.

ALICE. Why do you wear such awful clothes, Mr Boanerges?

MAGNUS [*remonstrating*] My dear—!

ALICE [*continuing*] I cant go out walking with you in that [*pointing to his blouse*].

BOANERGES. The uniform of Labor, your Royal Highness. I'm proud of it.

ALICE. Oh yes, I know all that, Mr Boanerges. But you dont look the part, you know. Anyone can see that you belong naturally to the governing class.

BOANERGES [*struck by this view*] In a way, perhaps. But I have earned my bread by my hands. Not as a laborer, though. I am a skilled mechanic, or was until my country called on me to lead it.

MAGNUS [*to Alice*] Well, my dear, you have broken up a most interesting conversation, and to me a most instructive one. It's no use our trying to go on, Mr Boanerges: I must go and find what my daughter wants, though I strongly suspect that what she really came in for was to see my wonderful new minister. We shall meet again presently: you know that the Prime Minister is calling on me today with some of his colleagues—including, I hope, yourself—to discuss the crisis. [*Taking Alice's arm and turning towards the door*] You will excuse us, wont you?

BOANERGES [*graciously*] Oh, thats all right. Thats quite all right.

The King and the Princess go out, apparently much pleased.

BOANERGES [*to Sempronius and Pamphilius comprehensively*] Well, say what you will, the King is no fool. Not when you know how to handle him.

PAMPHILIUS. Of course, that makes all the difference.

BOANERGES. And the girl hasnt been spoilt. I was glad to see that. She doesnt seem to know that she is the Princess Royal, eh?

SEMPRONIUS. Well, she wouldnt dream of giving herself any airs with you.

BOANERGES. What! Isnt she always like that?

SEMPRONIUS. Oh no. It's not everybody who is received as you have been. I hope you have enjoyed your visit.

BOANERGES. Well, I pulled Magnus through it pretty well: eh? Dont you think so?

SEMPRONIUS. He was pleased. You have a way with you, Mr President.

BOANERGES. Well, perhaps I have, perhaps I have.

A bevy of six Cabinet Ministers, resplendent in diplomatic uniforms, enters. Proteus the Prime Minister has on his left, Pliny, Chancellor of the Exchequer, goodhumored and conciliatory, and Nicobar, Foreign Secretary, snaky and censorious. On his right Crassus, Colonial Secretary, elderly and anxious, and Balbus, Home Secretary, rude and thoughtless.

BALBUS. Holy snakes! look at Bill. [*To Boanerges*] Go home and dress yourself properly, man.

NICOBAR. Where do you think you are?

CRASSUS. Who do you think you are?

PLINY [*fingering the blouse*] Where did you buy it, Bill?

BOANERGES [*turning on them like a baited bear*] Well, if you come to that, who do you think *you* are, the lot of you?

PROTEUS [*conciliatory*] Never mind them, Bill: theyre jealous because they didnt think of it themselves. How did you get on with the King?

BOANERGES. Right as rain, Joe. You leave the king to me. I know how to handle him. If I'd been in the Cabinet these last three months there'd have been no crisis.

NICOBAR. He put you through it, did he?

BOANERGES. What do you mean? put me through it? Is this a police office?

PLINY. The third degree is not unknown in this palace, my boy. [*To Pamphilius*] Did the matron take a hand?

PAMPHILIUS. No. But the Princess Alice happened to drop in. She was greatly impressed by the President.

They all laugh uproariously at Boanerges.

BOANERGES. What in hell are you laughing at?

PROTEUS. Take no notice of them, Bill: they are only having their bit of fun with you as a new comer. Come, lads! enough of fooling: lets get to business. [*He takes the chair vacated by the King*].

Sempronius and Pamphilius at once rise and go out busily, taking some of their papers with them. Pliny takes Boanerges' chair, Balbus that of Sempronius, Boanerges that of Pamphilius, whilst Nicobar and Crassus take chairs from the wall and sit down at the ends of the writing tables, left and right of the Prime Minister respectively.

PROTEUS. Now to start with, do you chaps all fully realize that though we wiped out every other party at the last election, and have been in power for the last three years, this country has been governed during that time by the King?

NICOBAR. I dont see that. We—

PROTEUS [*impatiently*] Well, if you dont, then for Heaven's sake either resign and get out of the way of men who can see facts and look them in the face, or else take my job and lead the party yourself.

NICOBAR. The worst of you is that you wont face the fact that though youre Prime Minister youre not God Almighty. The king cant do anything except what we advise him to do. How can he govern the country if we have all the power and he has none?

BOANERGES. Dont talk silly, Nick. This indiarubber stamp theory doesnt work. What man has ever approached a king or a minister and been able to pick him up from the table and use him as youd use a bit of wood and brass and rubber? The king's a live man; and what more are you, with your blessed advice?

PLINY. Hullo, Bill! You have been having your mind improved by somebody.

BOANERGES. What do you mean? Isnt it what I have always said?

PROTEUS [*whose nerves are on edge*] Oh, will you stop squabbling. What are we going to say to the king when he comes in? If you will only hold together and say the same thing—or let me say it—he must give way. But he is as artful as the very devil. He'll have a pin to stick into the seat of every man of you. If you all start quarrelling and scolding and bawling, which is just what he wants you to do, it will end in his having his own way as usual, because one man that has a mind and knows it can always beat ten men who havnt and dont.

PLINY. Steady, Prime Minister. Youre overwrought.

PROTEUS. It's enough to drive a man mad. I am sorry.

PLINY [*changing the subject*] Where's Mandy?

NICOBAR. And Lizzie?

PROTEUS. Late as usual. Come! Business, business, business.

BOANERGES [*thunderously*] Order order!

PROTEUS. The King is working the Press against us. The King is making speeches. Things have come to a head. He said yesterday on the opening of the new Chamber of Commerce building that the king's veto is the only remaining defence of the people against corrupt legislation.

BOANERGES. So it is, by Jingo. What other defence is there? Democracy? Yah! We know what Democracy is worth. What we need is a Strong Man.

NICOBAR [*sneering*] Yourself, for instance.

BOANERGES. I should stand a better chance than you, my lad, if we were a Republic, and the people could choose. And let me tell you that a republican president has more power than a king because the people know that they need a Strong Man to protect them against the rich.

PROTEUS [*flinging himself back in his chair in desperation*] This is a nice thing. Two Labor papers have leading articles this morning supporting the King; and the latest addition to the Cabinet here is a King's man. I resign.

General consternation except on the part of Nicobar, who displays cheerful unconcern, and of Boanerges, who squares himself with an iron face.

PLINY. } No: dont do that, Joe.
BALBUS. } What! Now! You cant. You mustnt.
CRASSUS. } Of course not. Out of the question.

PROTEUS. No use. [*Rising*] I resign, I tell you. You can all go to the devil. I have lost my health, and almost lost my reason, trying to keep this Cabinet together in the face of the cunningest enemy popular government has ever had to face. I have had enough of it. [*Sitting down again*] I resign.

CRASSUS. But not at such a moment as this. Dont let us swop horses when crossing a stream.

NICOBAR. Why not, if the horse you have got is subject to hysterics?

BOANERGES. Not to mention that you may have more than one horse at your disposal.

PROTEUS. Right you are. Perfectly true. Take my job, Nick. It's vacant for you, Bill. I wish you joy of it.

PLINY. Now boys, boys, boys: be good. We cant make a new Cabinet before Magnus comes in. You have something in your pocket, Joe. Out with it. Read it to them.

PROTEUS [*taking a paper from his pocket*] What I was going to propose—and you can take it or leave it—is an ultimatum.

CRASSUS. Good!

PROTEUS. Either he signs this, or—[*he pauses significantly*]!

NICOBAR. Or what?

PROTEUS [*disgusted*] Oh, you make me sick.

NICOBAR. Youre sick already, by your own account. I only ask, suppose he refuses to sign your ultimatum?

PROTEUS. You call yourself a Cabinet Minister, and you cant answer that!

NICOBAR. No I cant. I press my question. You said he must sign, OR. I ask, or what?

PROTEUS. Or we resign and tell the country that we cant carry on the King's Government under conditions which destroy our responsibility.

BALBUS. Thatll do it. He couldnt face that.

CRASSUS. Yes: thatll bunker him.

PROTEUS. Is that agreed?

PLINY.
CRASSUS.
BALBUS. } Yes, yes, yes, 'greed 'greed 'greed.

BOANERGES. I retain an open mind. Let us hear the ultimatum.

NICOBAR. Yes: lets hear it.

PROTEUS. Memorandum of understanding arrived at—

The king enters, with Amanda, Postmistress General, a merry lady in uniform like the men, on his left, and Lysistrata,

Powermistress General, a grave lady in academic robes, on his right. All rise. The Prime Minister's face darkens.

MAGNUS. Welcome, gentlemen. I hope I am not too early. [*Noting the Prime Minister's scowl*] Am I intruding?

PROTEUS. I protest. It is intolerable. I call a conference of my Cabinet to consider our position in regard to the prerogative; and I find the two lady members, the Postmistress General and the Powermistress General, closeted with your majesty instead of being in their places to confer with me.

LYSISTRATA. You mind your own business, Joe.

MAGNUS. Oh no: really, really, my dear Lysistrata, you must not take that line. Our business is to meddle in everybody's business. A Prime Minister is a busybody by profession. So is a monarch. So are we all.

LYSISTRATA. Well, they say everybody's business is nobody's business, which is just what Joe is fit for. [*She takes a chair from the wall with a powerful hand, and swings it forward to the inside corner of Sempronius's table, where she stands waiting for the King to sit down*].

PROTEUS. This is what I have to put up with when I am on the verge of a nervous breakdown [*he sits down distractedly, and buries his face in his hands*].

AMANDA [*going to him and petting him*] Come, Joe! dont make a scene. You asked for it, you know.

NICOBAR. What do you go provoking Lizzie for like that? You know she has a temper.

LYSISTRATA. There is nothing whatever wrong with my temper. But I am not going to stand any of Joe's nonsense; and the sooner he makes up his mind to that the smoother our proceedings are likely to be.

BOANERGES. I protest. I say, let us be dignified. I say, let us respect ourselves and respect the throne. All this Joe and Bill and Nick and Lizzie: we might as well be hobnobbing in a fried fish shop. The Prime Minister is the prime minister: he isnt Joe. The Powermistress isnt Lizzie: she's Lysis Traitor.

LYSISTRATA [*who has evidently been a schoolmistress*] Certainly not, Bill. She is Ly Siśtrata. You had better say Lizzie: it is easier to pronounce.

BOANERGES [*scornfully*] Ly Siśtrata! A more foolish affectation I never heard: you might as well call me Bo Annerjeeze [*he flings himself into his chair*].

MAGNUS [*sweetly*] Shall we sit, ladies and gentlemen?

Boanerges hastily rises and sits down again. The King sits in Pliny's chair. Lysistrata and the rest of the men resume their seats, leaving Pliny and Amanda standing. Amanda takes an empty chair in each hand and plants them side by side between the King and the table of Pamphilius.

AMANDA. There you are, Plin. [*She sits next the table*].

PLINY. Ta ta, Mandy. Pardon me: I should have said Amanda. [*He sits next the King*].

AMANDA. Dont mention it, darling.

BOANERGES. Order, order!

AMANDA [*waves him a kiss*]!!

MAGNUS. Prime Minister: the word is with you. Why have you all simultaneously given me the great pleasure of exercising your constitutional right of access to the sovereign?

LYSISTRATA. Have I that right, sir; or havnt I?

MAGNUS. Most undoubtedly you have.

LYSISTRATA. You hear that, Joe?

PROTEUS. I——

BALBUS. Oh for Heaven's sake dont contradict her, Joe. We shall never get anywhere at this rate. Come to the crisis.

NICOBAR. } [*together*] { Yes yes: the crisis!
CRASSUS. } { Yes yes: come along!
PLINY. } { The crisis: out with it!

BALBUS. The ultimatum. Lets have the ultimatum.

MAGNUS. Oh, there is an ultimatum! I gathered from yesterday's evening papers that there is a crisis—another crisis. But the ultimatum is new to me. [*To Proteus*] Have you an ultimatum?

PROTEUS. Your Majesty's allusion to the royal veto in a speech yesterday has brought matters to a head.

MAGNUS. It was perhaps indelicate. But you all allude so freely to your own powers—to the supremacy of Parliament and the voice of the people and so forth—that I fear I have lost any little delicacy I ever possessed. If you may flourish your thunderbolts why may I not shoulder my little popgun of a veto and strut up and down with it for a moment?

NICOBAR. This is not a subject for jesting—

MAGNUS [*interrupting him quickly*] I am not jesting, Mr Nicobar. But I am certainly trying to discuss our differences in a goodhumored manner. Do you wish me to lose my temper and make scenes?

AMANDA. Oh please no, your Majesty. We get enough of that from Joe.

PROTEUS. I pro—

MAGNUS [*his hand persuasively on the Prime Minister's arm*] Take care, Prime Minister: take care: do not let your wily Postmistress General provoke you to supply the evidence against yourself.

All the rest laugh.

PROTEUS [*coolly*] I thank your Majesty for the caution. The Postmistress General has never forgiven me for not making her First Lady of the Admiralty. She has three nephews in the navy.

AMANDA. Oh you—[*She swallows the epithet, and contents herself with shaking her fist at the Premier*].

MAGNUS. Tch-tch-tch! Gently, Amanda, gently. Three very promising lads: they do you credit.

AMANDA. I never wanted them to go to sea. I could have found them better jobs in the Post Office.

MAGNUS. Apart from Amanda's family relations, am I face to face with a united Cabinet?

PLINY. No, sir. You are face to face with a squabbling Cabinet; but, on the constitutional question, united we stand: divided we fall.

BALBUS. That is so.

NICOBAR. Hear hear!

MAGNUS. What is the constitutional question? Do you

deny the royal veto? or do you object only to my reminding my subjects of its existence?

NICOBAR. What we say is that the king has no right to remind his subjects of anything constitutional except by the advice of the Prime Minister, and in words which he has read and approved.

MAGNUS. Which Prime Minister? There are so many of them in the Cabinet.

BOANERGES. There! Serves you all right! Arnt you ashamed of yourselves? But I am not surprised, Joseph Proteus. I own I like a Prime Minister that knows how to be a Prime Minister. Why do you let them take the word out of your mouth every time?

PROTEUS. If His Majesty wants a Cabinet of dumb dogs he will not get it from my party.

BALBUS. Hear hear, Joe!

MAGNUS. Heaven forbid! The variety of opinion in the Cabinet is always most instructive and interesting. Who is to be its spokesman today?

PROTEUS. I know your Majesty's opinion of me; but let—

MAGNUS [*before he can proceed*] Let me state it quite frankly. My opinion of you is that no man knows better than you when to speak and when to let others speak for you; when to make scenes and threaten resignation; and when to be as cool as a cucumber.

PROTEUS [*not altogether displeased*] Well, sir, I hope I am not such a fool as some fools think me. I may not always keep my temper. You would not be surprised at that if you knew how much temper I have to keep. [*He straightens up and becomes impressively eloquent*]. At this moment my cue is to shew you, not my own temper, but the temper of my Cabinet. What the Foreign Secretary and the Chancellor of the Exchequer and the Home Secretary have told you is true. If we are to carry on your government we cannot have you making speeches that express your own opinions and not ours. We cannot have you implying that everything that is of any value in our legislation is your doing and not ours.

We cannot have you telling people that their only safeguard against the political encroachments of big business whilst we are doing nothing but bungling and squabbling is your power of veto. It has got to stop, once for all.

BALBUS.
NICOBAR. } Hear hear!

PROTEUS. Is that clear?

MAGNUS. Far clearer than I have ever dared to make it, Mr Proteus. Except, by the way, on one point. When you say that all this of which you complain must cease once for all, do you mean that henceforth I am to agree with you or you with me?

PROTEUS. I mean that when you disagree with us you are to keep your disagreement to yourself.

MAGNUS. That would be a very heavy responsibility for me. If I see you leading the nation over the edge of a precipice may I not warn it?

BALBUS. It is our business to warn it, not yours.

MAGNUS. Suppose you dont do your business! Suppose you dont see the danger! That has happened. It may happen again.

CRASSUS [*insinuating*] As democrats, I think we are bound to proceed on the assumption that such a thing cannot happen.

BOANERGES. Rot! It's happening all the time until somebody has the gumption to put his foot down and stop it.

CRASSUS. Yes: I know. But that is not democracy.

BOANERGES. Democracy be— [*he leaves the word unspoken*]! I have thirty years experience of democracy. So have most of you. I say no more.

BALBUS. Wages are too high, if you ask me. Anybody can earn from five to twenty pounds a week now, and a big dole when there is no job for him. And what Englishman will give his mind to politics as long as he can afford to keep a motor car?

NICOBAR. How many voted at the last election? Not seven per cent of the register.

BALBUS. Yes; and the seven per cent were only a parcel of sillies playing at ins and outs. To make democracy work in Crassus's way we need poverty and hardship.

PROTEUS [*emphatically*] And we have abolished poverty and hardship. That is why the people trust us. [*To the King*] And that is why you will have to give way to us. We have the people of England in comfort—solid middle class comfort—at our backs.

MAGNUS. No: we have not abolished poverty and hardship. Our big business men have abolished them. But how? By sending our capital abroad to places where poverty and hardship still exist: in other words, where labor is cheap. We live in comfort on the imported profits of that capital. We are all ladies and gentlemen now.

NICOBAR. Well, what more do you want?

PLINY. You surely dont grudge us our wonderful prosperity, sir.

MAGNUS. I want it to last.

NICOBAR. Why shouldnt it last? [*Rising*] Own the truth. You had rather have the people poor, and pose as their champion and savior, than have to admit that the people are better off under our government—under our squabbling and bungling, as you call it.

MAGNUS. No: it was the Prime Minister who used those expressions.

NICOBAR. Dont quibble: he was quoting them from your reptile press. What I say is that we stand for high wages, and you are always belittling and opposing the men that pay them. Well, the voters like high wages. They know when they are well off; and they dont know what you are grumbling about; and thats what will beat you every time you try to stir them against us [*he resumes his seat*].

PLINY. There is no need to rub it in like that, Nick. We're all good friends. Nobody objects to prosperity.

MAGNUS. You think this prosperity is safe?

NICOBAR. Safe!

PLINY. Oh come, sir! Really!

BALBUS. Safe! Look at my constituency: Northeast-by-north Birmingham, with its four square miles of confectionery works! Do you know that in the Christmas cracker trade Birmingham is the workshop of the world?

CRASSUS. Take Gateshead and Middlesborough alone! Do you know that there has not been a day's unemployment there for five years past, and that their daily output of chocolate creams totals up to twenty thousand tons?

MAGNUS. It is certainly a consoling thought that if we were peacefully blockaded by the League of Nations we could live for at least three weeks on our chocolate creams.

NICOBAR. You neednt sneer at the sweets: we turn out plenty of solid stuff. Where will you find the equal of the English golf club?

BALBUS. Look at the potteries: the new crown Derby! the new Chelsea! Look at the tapestries! Why, Greenwich Goblin has chased the French stuff out of the market.

CRASSUS. Dont forget our racing motor boats and cars, sir: the finest on earth, and all individually designed. No cheap mass production stuff there.

PLINY. And our live stock! Can you beat the English polo pony?

AMANDA. Or the English parlormaid? She wins in all the international beauty shows.

PLINY. Now Mandy, Mandy! None of your triviality.

MAGNUS. I am not sure that the British parlormaid is not the only real asset in your balance sheet.

AMANDA [*triumphant*] Aha! [*To Pliny*] You go home to bed and reflect on that, old man.

PROTEUS. Well, sir? Are you satisfied that we have the best paid proletariat in the world on our side?

MAGNUS [*gravely*] I dread revolution.

All except the two women laugh uproariously at this.

BOANERGES. I must join them there, sir. I am as much against chocolate creams as you are: they never agree with me. But a revolution in England!!! Put that out of your head sir. Not if you were to tear up Magna Carta in Trafalgar

Square, and light the fires of Smithfield to burn every mem ber of the House of Commons.

MAGNUS. I was not thinking of a revolution in England, I was thinking of the countries on whose tribute we are living. Suppose it occurs to them to stop paying it! That has happened before.

PLINY. Oh no, sir: no, no, no. What would become of their foreign trade with us?

MAGNUS. At a pinch, I think they could do without the Christmas crackers.

CRASSUS. Oh, thats childish.

MAGNUS. Children in their innocence are sometimes very practical, Mr Colonial Secretary. The more I see of the sort of prosperity that comes of your leaving our vital industries to big business men as long as they keep your constituents quiet with high wages, the more I feel as if I were sitting on a volcano.

LYSISTRATA [*who has been listening with implacable contempt to the discussion, suddenly breaks in in a sepulchral contralto*] Hear hear! My department was perfectly able and ready to deal with the supply of power from the tides in the north of Scotland, and you gave it away, like the boobs you are, to the Pentland Forth Syndicate: a gang of foreign capitalists who will make billions out of it at the people's expense while we are bungling and squabbling. Crassus worked that. His uncle is chairman.

CRASSUS. A lie. A flat lie. He is not related to me. He is only my stepson's father-in-law.

BALBUS. I demand an explanation of the words bungling and squabbling. We have had quite enough of them here today. Who are you getting at? It was not I who bungled the Factory Bill. I found it on my desk when I took office, with all His Majesty's suggestions in the margin; and you know it.

PROTEUS. Have you all done playing straight into His Majesty's hand, and making my situation here impossible?

Guilty silence.

PROTEUS [*proceeding deliberately and authoritatively*] The

question before us is not one of our manners and our abilities. His Majesty will not press that question, because if he did he would oblige us to raise the question of his own morals.

MAGNUS [*starts*] What!

BALBUS. Good, Joe!

CRASSUS [*aside to Amanda*] Thats got him.

MAGNUS. Am I to take that threat seriously, Mr Proteus?

PROTEUS. If you try to prejudice what is a purely constitutional question by personal scandal, it will be easy enough for us to throw your mud back. In this conflict we are the challengers. You have the choice of weapons. If you choose scandal, we'll take you on at that. Personally I shall deplore it if you do. No good will come of washing our dirty linen in public. But dont make any mistake as to what will happen. I will be plain with you: I will dot the Is and cross the Ts. You will say that Crassus is a jobber.

CRASSUS [*springing up*] I—

PROTEUS [*fiercely crushing him*] Sit down. Leave this to me.

CRASSUS [*sits*] I a jobber! Well!

PROTEUS [*continuing*] You will say that I should never have given the Home Office to a bully like Balbus—

BALBUS [*intimidated by the fate of Crassus, but unable to forbear a protest*] Look here, Joe—

PROTEUS. You shut up, Bert. It's true.

BALBUS [*subsides with a shrug*]!

PROTEUS. Well, what will happen? There will be no denials, no excuses, no vindications. We shall not fall into that trap, clever as you are at setting it. Crassus will say just simply that you are a freethinker. And Balbus will say that you are a libertine.

THE MALE CABINET [*below their breaths*] Aha-a-a-a-h!!!

PROTEUS. Now, King Magnus! Our cards are on the table. What have you to say?

MAGNUS. Admirably put! People ask how it is that with all these strong characters around you hold your own as the only possible Prime Minister, in spite of your hysterics and tantrums, your secretiveness and your appalling laziness—

BALBUS [*delighted*] Hear hear! Youre getting it now, Joe.

MAGNUS [*continuing*] But when the decisive moment comes, they find out what a wonderful man you are.

PROTEUS. I am not a wonderful man. There is not a man or woman here whose job I could do as well as they do it. I am Prime Minister for the same reason that all Prime Ministers have been Prime Ministers: because I am good for nothing else. But I can keep to the point—when it suits me. And I can keep you to the point, sir, whether it suits you or not.

MAGNUS. At all events you do not flatter kings. One of them, at least, is grateful to you for that.

PROTEUS. Kings, as you and I very well know, rule their ministers by flattering them; and now that you are the only king left in the civilized half of Europe Nature seems to have concentrated in you all the genius for flattery that she used to have to divide between half a dozen kings, three emperors, and a Sultan.

MAGNUS. But what interest has a king in flattering a subject?

AMANDA. Suppose she's a goodlooking woman, sir!

NICOBAR. Suppose he has a lot of money, and the king's hard up!

PROTEUS. Suppose he is a Prime Minister, and you can do nothing except by his advice.

MAGNUS [*smiling with his utmost charm*] Ah, there you have hit the nail on the head. Well, I suppose I must surrender. I am beaten. You are all too clever for me.

BOANERGES. Well, nothing can be fairer than that.

PLINY [*rubbing his hands*] You are a gentleman, sir. We shant rub it in, you know.

BALBUS. Ever the best of friends. I am the last to kick a man when he's down.

CRASSUS. I may be a jobber; but nobody shall say that I am an ungenerous opponent.

BOANERGES [*suddenly overwhelmed with emotion, rises and begins singing in stentorian tones*]

Should auld acquaintance be forgot,
And never brought to mind—

Amanda bursts into uncontrollable laughter. The King looks reproachfully at her, struggling hard to keep his countenance. The others are beginning to join in the chorus when Proteus rises in a fury.

PROTEUS. Are you all drunk?

Dead silence. Boanerges sits down hastily. The other singers pretend that they have disapproved of his minstrelsy.

PROTEUS. You are at present engaged in a tug of war with the King: the tug of your lives. You think you have won. You havnt. All that has happened is that the King has let go the rope. You are sprawling on your backs; and he is laughing at you. Look at him! [*He sits down contemptuously*].

MAGNUS [*making no further attempt to conceal his merriment*] Come to my rescue, Amanda. It was you who set me off.

AMANDA [*wreathed with smiles*] You got me so nicely, sir. [*To Boanerges*] Bill: you are a great boob.

BOANERGES. I dont understand this. I understood His Majesty to give way to us in, I must say, the handsomest manner. Cant we take our victory like gentlemen?

MAGNUS. Perhaps I had better explain. I quite appreciate the frank and magnanimous spirit—may I say the English spirit?—in which my little concession has been received, especially by you, Mr Boanerges. But in truth it leaves matters just where they were; for I should never have dreamt of entering on a campaign of recrimination such as the Prime Minister suggested. As he has reminded you, my own character is far too vulnerable. A king is not allowed the luxury of a good character. Our country has produced millions of blameless greengrocers, but not one blameless monarch. I have to rule over more religious sects than I can count. To rule them impartially I must not belong to any of them; and they all regard people who do not belong to them as atheists. My court includes several perfectly respectable wives and mothers whose strange vanity it is to be talked about as abandoned females. To gain the reputation of being the king's mistress they would do almost anything except give the unfortunate monarch the pleasure of substantiating their claim. Side by side with them are the ladies who are really unscrupulous. They are so careful of their reputations that they lose no opportunity of indignantly denying that they have ever yielded to solicitations which have in fact never been made to them. Thus every king is supposed to be a libertine; and as, oddly enough, he owes a great part of his popularity to this belief, he cannot deny it without deeply disappointing his subjects.

There is a rather grim silence, during which the King looks round in vain for some encouraging response.

LYSISTRATA [*severely*] Your Majesty's private affairs do not concern us, in any case.

AMANDA [*splutters into an irrepressible laugh*]!!

MAGNUS [*looks reproachfully at Amanda*]!

AMANDA [*composing her features as best she can*] Excuse me.

CRASSUS. I hope your Majesty recognizes that kings are not the only people to whom certain sorts of mud always stick, no matter what fool throws them. Call a minister a jobber—

BALBUS. Or a bungler.

CRASSUS. Yes, or a bungler, and everybody believes it. Jobbery and incompetence are the two sorts of mud that stick to us, no matter how honest or capable we are; and we havnt the royal advantage that you enjoy, that the more the ladies take away your character the better the people like you.

BOANERGES [*suddenly*] Prime Minister: will you tell me what the Postmistress General is sniggering at?

AMANDA. This is a free country, Bill. A sense of humor is not a crime. And when the King is not setting me off, you are.

BOANERGES. Where is the joke? I dont see it.

AMANDA. If you could see a joke, Bill, you wouldnt be the great popular orator you are.

BOANERGES. Thank Heaven, I am not a silly giggler like some I could mention.

AMANDA. Thanks, dearest Bill. Now Joe: dont you think

you have let us run loose long enough? What about that ultimatum?

MAGNUS [*shaking his head at her*] Traitor!

PROTEUS. I am in no hurry. His Majesty's speeches are very wise and interesting; and your back chat amuses both you and him. But the ultimatum is here all the time; and I shall not leave this room until I have His Majesty's signed pledge that its conditions will be observed.

All become gravely attentive.

MAGNUS. What are its terms?

PROTEUS. First, no more royal speeches.

MAGNUS. What! Not even if you dictate them?

PROTEUS. Not even if we dictate them. Your Majesty has a way of unrolling the manuscript and winking—

MAGNUS. Winking!

PROTEUS. You know what I mean. The best speech in the world can be read in such a way as to set the audience laughing at it. We have had enough of that. So, in future, no speeches.

MAGNUS. A dumb king?

PROTEUS. Of course we cannot object to such speeches as "We declare this foundation stone well and truly laid" and so forth. But politically, yes: a dumb king.

PLINY [*to soften it*] A constitutional king.

PROTEUS [*implacably*] A dumb king.

MAGNUS. Hm! What next?

PROTEUS. The working of the Press from the palace back stairs must cease.

MAGNUS. You know that I have no control of the Press. The Press is in the hands of men much richer than I, who would not insert a single paragraph against their own interests even if it were signed by my own hand and sent to them with a royal command.

PROTEUS. We know that. But though these men are richer than you, they are not cleverer. They get amusing articles, spiced with exclusive backstairs information, that dont seem to them to have anything to do with politics. The next thing they know is that their pet shares have dropped fifteen points; that capital is frightened off their best prospectuses; and that some of the best measures in our party program are made to look like city jobs.

MAGNUS. Am I supposed to write these articles?

NICOBAR. Your man Sempronius does. I can spot his fist out of fifty columns.

CRASSUS. So can I. When he is getting at me he always begins the sentence with "Singularly enough."

PLINY [*chuckling*] Thats his trademark. "Singularly enough." Ha! ha!

MAGNUS. Is there to be any restriction on the other side? I have noticed, for instance, that in a certain newspaper which loses no opportunity of disparaging the throne, the last sentence of the leading article almost invariably begins with the words "Once for all." Whose trademark is that?

PROTEUS. Mine.

MAGNUS. Frank, Mr Proteus.

PROTEUS. I know when to be frank. I learnt the trick from Your Majesty.

AMANDA [*tries not to laugh*]!

MAGNUS [*gently reproachful*] Amanda: what is the joke now? I am surprised at you.

AMANDA. Joe frank! When I want to find out what he is up to I have to come and ask your Majesty.

LYSISTRATA. That is perfectly true. In this Cabinet there is no such thing as a policy. Every man plays for his own hand.

NICOBAR. It's like a game of cards.

BALBUS. Only there are no partners.

LYSISTRATA. Except Crassus and Nicobar.

PLINY. Good, Lizzie! He! he! he!

NICOBAR. What do you mean?

LYSISTRATA. You know quite well what I mean. When will you learn, Nicobar, that it is no use trying to browbeat me. I began life as a schoolmistress; and I can browbeat any man in this Cabinet or out of it if he is fool enough to try to compete with me in that department.

BOANERGES. Order! order! Cannot the Prime Minister check these unseemly personalities?

PROTEUS. They give me time to think, Bill. When you have had as much parliamentary experience as I have you will be very glad of an interruption occasionally. May I proceed?

Silence.

PROTEUS. His Majesty asks whether the restriction on press campaigning is to be entirely onesided. That, I take it, sir, is your question.

MAGNUS [*nods assent*]!

PROTEUS. The answer is in the affirmative.

BALBUS. Good!

MAGNUS. Anything more?

PROTEUS. Yes: one thing more. The veto must not be mentioned again. That can apply to both sides, if you like. The veto is dead.

MAGNUS. May we not make a historical reference to the corpse?

PROTEUS. No. I cannot carry on the King's government unless I can give pledges and carry them out. What is my pledge worth if our constituents are reminded every day that the King may veto anything that Parliament does? Do you expect me to say, when I am asked for a pledge, "You must ask the King"?

MAGNUS. I have to say "You must ask the Prime Minister."

PLINY [*consoling him*] Thats the constitution, you know.

MAGNUS. Quite. I only mention it to shew that the Prime Minister does not really wish to kill the veto. He only wishes to move it to next door.

PROTEUS. The people live next door. The name on the brass plate is Public Opinion.

MAGNUS [*gravely*] Admirably turned, Mr Prime Minister; but unreal. I am far more subject to public opinion than you, because, thanks to the general belief in democracy, you can always pretend that what you do is done by the will of the people, who, God knows, never dreamt of it, and would not have understood it if they had; whereas, for what a king does, he, and he alone, is held responsible. A demagogue may steal a horse where a king dare not look over a hedge.

LYSISTRATA. I doubt if that is any longer true, sir. I know that I get blamed for everything that goes wrong in my department.

MAGNUS. Ah! But what a despot you are, Lysistrata! Granted, however, that the people have found out long ago that democracy is humbug, and that instead of establishing responsible government it has abolished it, do you not see what this means?

BOANERGES [*scandalized*] Steady, steady! I cannot sit here and listen to such a word as humbug being applied to democracy. I am sorry, sir; but with all respect for you, I really must draw the line at that.

MAGNUS. You are right, Mr Boanerges, as you always are. Democracy is a very real thing, with much less humbug about it than many older institutions. But it means, not that the people govern, but that the responsibility and the veto now belong neither to kings nor demagogues as such, but to whoever is clever enough to get them.

LYSISTRATA. Yourself, sir, for example?

MAGNUS. I think I am in the running. That is why I do not feel bound to accept this ultimatum. By signing it I put myself out of the running. Why should I?

BALBUS. Because youre the king: thats why.

MAGNUS. Does it follow?

PROTEUS. If two men ride the same horse, one must ride behind.

LYSISTRATA. Which?

PROTEUS [*turning to her sharply*] What was that you said?

LYSISTRATA [*with placid but formidable obstinacy and ironical explicitness*] I said Which? You said that if two men rode the same horse one of them must ride behind. I said Which? [*Explanatorily*] Which man must ride behind?

AMANDA. Got it, Joe?

PROTEUS. That is exactly the question that has to be settled here and now.

AMANDA. "Once for all."

Everybody laughs except Proteus, who rises in a fury.

PROTEUS. I will not stand this perpetual tomfooling. I had rather be a dog than the Prime Minister of a country where the only things the inhabitants can be serious about are football and refreshments. Lick the king's boots: that is all you are fit for. [*He dashes out of the room*].

BALBUS. Youve done it now, Mandy. I hope youre proud of yourself.

MAGNUS. It is you, Amanda, who should go and coax him back. But I suppose I must do it myself, as usual. Excuse me, ladies and gentlemen.

He rises. The rest rise. He goes out.

BOANERGES. I told you. I told you what would come of conducting a conference with His Majesty as if it were a smoking concert. I am disgusted. [*He flings himself back into his chair*].

BALBUS. We'd just cornered the old fox; and then Amanda must have her silly laugh and lets him out of it [*he sits*].

NICOBAR. What are we to do now? thats what I want to know.

AMANDA [*incorrigible*] I suggest a little community singing [*she makes conductorlike gestures*].

NICOBAR. Yah!! [*he sits down very sulkily*].

AMANDA [*sits down with a little splutter of laughter*]!

CRASSUS [*thoughtful*] Take it easy, friends. Joe knows what he is about.

LYSISTRATA. Of course he does. I can excuse you, Bill, because it's your first day in the Cabinet. But if the rest of you havnt found out by this time that Joe's rages are invariably calculated, then nothing will ever teach you anything [*she sits down contemptuously*].

BOANERGES [*in his grandest manner*] Well, madam, I know I am a newcomer: everything must have a beginning. I am open to argument and conviction. The Prime Minister brought this conference, in what I admit was a very able and resolute manner, to the verge of a decision. Then, in a fit of childish temper he breaks up the conference, leaving us looking like fools with nothing done. And you tell me he did it on purpose! Where was the advantage to him in such a display? answer me that.

LYSISTRATA. He is settling the whole business with the King behind our backs. That is what Joe always contrives to do, by hook or crook.

PLINY. You didnt arrange it with him, Mandy: did you?

AMANDA. There wasnt any need to arrange it. Joe can always depend on one or other of us saying something that will give him an excuse for flying out.

CRASSUS. In my opinion, ladies and gentlemen, we have done our bit, and may leave the rest to Joe. Matters had reached a point at which it was yes or no between the Cabinet and the Crown. There is only one sort of committee that is better than a committee of two; and that is a committee of one. Like the family in Wordsworth's poem, we are seven—

LYSISTRATA. Eight.

CRASSUS. Well, seven or eight, we were too many for the final grapple. Two persons sticking to the point are worth eight all over the shop. So my advice is that we just sit here quietly until Joe comes back and tells us whats been settled. Perhaps Amanda will oblige with a song. [*He resumes his seat*].

The King returns with Proteus, who looks glum. All rise. The two resume their seats in silence. The rest sit down.

MAGNUS [*very grave*] The Prime Minister has been good enough to pursue the discussion with me in private to a point at which the issue is now clear. If I do not accept the ultimatum I shall receive your resignations and his; and the country will learn from his explanatory speech in the House of Commons that it is to choose between Cabinet government and monarchical government: an issue on which I frankly say that I should be very sorry to win, as I cannot carry on without the support of a body of ministers whose existence gives the English people a sensation of self-government.

AMANDA [*splutters*]!

CRASSUS [*whispers*] Shut up, will you?

MAGNUS [*continuing*] Naturally I want to avert a conflict in which success would damage me and failure disable me. But you tell me that I can do so only by signing pledges which would make me a mere Lord Chamberlain, without even the despotism which he exercises over the theatre. I should sink below the level of the meanest of my subjects, my sole privilege being that of being shot at when some victim of misgovernment resorts to assassination to avenge himself. How am I to defend myself? You are many: I oppose you single-handed. There was a time when the king could depend on the support of the aristocracy and the cultivated bourgeoisie. Today there is not a single aristocrat left in politics, not a single member of the professions, not a single leading personage in big business or finance. They are richer than ever, more powerful than ever, more able and better educated than ever. But not one of them will touch this drudgery of government, this public work that never ends because we cannot finish one job without creating ten fresh ones. We get no thanks for it because ninety nine hundredths of it is unknown to the people, and the remaining hundredth is resented by them as an invasion of their liberty or an increase in their taxation. It wears out the strongest man, and even the strongest woman, in five or six years. It slows down to nothing when we are fresh from our holidays and best able to bear it, and rises in an overwhelming wave through some unforeseen catastrophe when we are on the verge of nervous breakdown from overwork and fit for rest and sleep only. And this drudgery, remember, is a sweated trade, the only one now left in this country. My civil list leaves me a poor man among multi-millionaires. Your salaries can be earned ten times over in the city by anyone with outstanding organizing or administrative ability. History tells us that the first Lord Chancellor who abandoned the woolsack for the city boardroom struck the nation with amazement: today the nation would be equally amazed if a man of his ability thought it worth his while to prefer the woolsack even to the stool of an office boy as a jumping-off place for his ambition. Our work is no longer even respected. It is looked down on by our men of genius as dirty work. What great actor would exchange his stage? what great barrister his court? what great preacher his pulpit? for the squalor of the political arena in which we have to struggle with foolish factions in parliament and with ignorant voters in the constituencies? The scientists will have nothing to do with us; for the atmosphere of politics is not the atmosphere of science. Even political science, the science by which civilization must live or die, is busy explaining the past whilst we have to grapple with the present: it leaves the ground before our feet in black darkness whilst it lights up every corner of the landscape behind us. All the talent and genius of the country is bought up by the flood of unearned money. On that poisoned wealth talent and genius live far more luxuriously in the service of the rich than we in the service of our country. Politics, once the centre of attraction for ability, public spirit, and ambition, has now become the refuge of a few fanciers of public speaking and party intrigue who find all the other avenues to distinction closed to them either by their lack of practical ability, their comparative poverty and lack of education, or, let me hasten to add, their hatred of oppression and injustice, and their contempt for the chicaneries and false pretences of commercialized professionalism. History tells us of a gentleman-statesman who declared that such people were not fit to govern. Within a year it was discovered that they could govern at least as well as anyone else who could be persuaded to take on the job. Then began that abandonment of politics by the old governing class which has ended in all Cabinets, conservative no less than progressive, being what were called in the days of that rash statesman Labor Cabinets. Do not misunderstand me: I do not want the old governing class back. It governed so selfishly that the people would have perished if democracy had not swept it out of politics. But evil as it was in many ways, at least it stood above the tyranny of popular ignorance and popular poverty. Today only the King stands above that tyranny. You are dangerously subject to it. In spite of my urgings and remonstrances you have not yet dared to take command of our schools and put a stop to the inculcation upon your unfortunate children of superstitions and prejudices that stand like stone walls across every forward path. Are you well advised in trying to reduce me to your own slavery to them? If I do not stand above them there is no longer any reason for my existence at all. I stand for the future and the past, for the posterity that has no vote and the tradition that never had any. I stand for the great abstractions: for conscience and virtue; for the eternal against the expedient; for the evolutionary appetite against the day's gluttony; for intellectual integrity, for humanity, for the rescue of industry from commercialism and of science from professionalism, for everything that you desire as sincerely as I, but which in you is held in leash by the Press, which can organize against you the ignorance and superstition, the timidity and credulity, the gullibility and prudery, the hating and hunting instinct of the voting mob, and cast you down from power if you utter a word to alarm or displease the adventurers who have the Press in their pockets. Between you and that tyranny stands the throne. I have no elections to fear; and if any newspaper magnate dares offend me, that magnate's fashionable wife and marriageable daughters will soon make him understand that the King's displeasure is still a sentence of social death within range of St James's Palace. Think of the things you dare not do! the persons you dare not offend! Well, a King with a little courage may tackle them for you. Responsibilities which would break your backs may still be borne on a King's shoulders. But he must be a king, not a puppet. You would be responsible for a puppet: remember that. But whilst you continue to support me as a separate and independent estate of the realm, I am your scapegoat: you get the credit of all our popular legislation whilst you put the odium of all our resistance to ignorant popular clamor on me. I ask you, before you play your last card and destroy me, to consider where you will be without me. Think once: think twice; for your danger is, not that I may defeat you, but that your success is certain if you insist.

LYSISTRATA. Splendid!

AMANDA. You did speak that piece beautifully, sir.

BALBUS [*grumbling*] All very well; but what about my brother-in-law Mike?

LYSISTRATA [*maddened*] Oh, confound your brother-in-law Mike!

BOANERGES. Order! order!

LYSISTRATA [*to the King*] I beg your pardon, sir; but really —at a moment like this—[*words fail her*].

MAGNUS [*to Balbus*] If I had not put my foot down, Mr Balbus, the Prime Minister would have been unable to keep your brother-in-law out of the Cabinet.

BALBUS [*aggressively*] And why should he not be in the Cabinet?

AMANDA. Booze, my Balby: booze. Raising the elbow!

BALBUS [*bullying*] Who says so?

AMANDA. I do, darling.

BALBUS [*subsiding*] Well, perhaps it would surprise you all to know that Mike doesnt drink as much as I do.

AMANDA. You carry it better, Bert.

PLINY. Mike never knows when to stop.

CRASSUS. The time for Mike to stop is before he begins, if you ask me.

LYSISTRATA [*impetuously*] What sort of animals are you—you men? The king puts before us the most serious question of principle we shall ever have to deal with; and off you start discussing whether this drunken wretch takes honest whisky like Balbus or methylated spirit or petrol or whatever he can lay his hands on when the fit takes him.

BALBUS. I agree with that. What does it matter what Mike drinks? What does it matter whether he drinks or not? Mike would strengthen the Cabinet because he represents Breakages, Limited, the biggest industrial corporation in the country.

LYSISTRATA [*letting herself go*] Just so! Breakages, Limited! just so! Listen to me, sir; and judge whether I have not reason to feel everything you have just said to the very marrow of my bones. Here am I, the Powermistress Royal. I have to organize and administer all the motor power in the country for the good of the country. I have to harness the winds and the tides, the oils and the coal seams. I have to see that every little sewing machine in the Hebrides, every dentist's drill in Shetland, every carpet sweeper in Margate, has its stream of driving power on tap from a switch in the wall as punctually as the great thundering dynamos of our big industrial plants. I do it; but it costs twice as much as it should. Why? Because every new invention is bought up and suppressed by Breakages, Limited. Every breakdown, every accident, every smash and crash, is a job for them. But for them we should have unbreakable glass, unbreakable steel, imperishable materials of all sorts. But for them our goods trains could be started and stopped without battering and tearing the vitals out of every wagon and sending it to their repair shops once a week instead of once a year. Our national repair bill runs up to hundreds of millions. I could name you a dozen inventions within my own term of office which would have effected enormous economies in breakages and breakdowns; but these people can afford to pay an inventor more for his machine or his process or whatever it may be than he could hope to make by a legitimate use of it; and when they have bought it they smother it. When the inventor is poor and not good at defending himself they make bogus trials of his machine and report that it is no use. I have been shot at twice by inventors driven crazy by this sort of thing: they blamed me for it—as if I could stand up against this monster with its millions and its newspapers and its fingers in every pie. It is heartbreaking. I love my department: I dream of nothing but its efficiency: with me it comes before every personal tie, every happiness that common women run after. I would give my right hand to see these people in the bankruptcy court with half their business abolished and the other half done in public workshops where public losses are not private gains. You stand for that, sir; and I would be with you to the last drop of my blood if I dared. But what can I do? If I said one word of this in public, not a week would pass in the next two years without an article on the inefficiency and corruption of all Government departments, especially departments managed, like mine, by females. They would dig up the very machines they have buried, and make out that it is my fault that they have never been brought into use. They would set their private police to watch me day and night to get something against my private character. One of their directors told me to my face that by lifting up his finger he could get my windows broken by the mob; and that Breakages, Limited, would get the job of putting in new glass. And it is true. It is infamous; it is outrageous; but if I attempt to fight them I shall be hounded out of public life, and they will shove Mouldy Mike into the Cabinet to run my department in their interests: that is, to make such a failure of it that Joe will have to sell it to Breakages, Limited, at scrap iron prices. I—I—oh, it is beyond bearing [*she breaks down*].

There is a troubled silence for a moment. Then the voice of the Prime Minister breaks it impressively as he addresses the King.

PROTEUS. You hear that, sir. Your one supporter in the Cabinet admits that the industrial situation is too strong for her. I do not pretend to be able to control the women in my Cabinet; but not one of them dare support you.

AMANDA [*springing up*] Whats that? Not dare! What do you bet that I dont go down to Mouldy Mike's constituency and say everything that Lizzie has said and a lot more too, if I choose? I tell you, Breakages, Limited, never interferes in my department. I'd like to catch them at it.

MAGNUS. I am afraid that that is only because the efficiency of the Post Office is as important to them as to the general public.

AMANDA. Stuff! They could get rid of me without shutting up the Post Office. Theyre afraid of me—of me, Amanda Postlethwaite.

MAGNUS. You coax them, I am afraid.

AMANDA. Coax! What do you think they care for coaxing? They can have all the coaxing they want from younger and prettier women than I by paying for it. No use trying to coax that lot. Intimidate them: thats the way to handle them.

LYSISTRATA [*her voice still broken*] I wish I could intimidate them.

MAGNUS. But what can Amanda do that you cannot do?

AMANDA. I'll tell you. She cant mimic people. And she cant sing funny songs. I can do both; and that—with all respect, sir—makes me the real queen of England.

BOANERGES. Oh, come! Disgraceful! Shame!

AMANDA. If you provoke me, Bill, I'll drive you out of your constituency inside of two months.

BOANERGES. Ho! You will, will you? How?

AMANDA. Just as I drove the Chairman of Breakages out of my own constituency when he came down there and tried to take my seat from me.

MAGNUS. I never quite understood why he turned tail. How did you do it?

AMANDA. I'll tell you. He opened his campaign with a great Saturday night speech against me in the Home Lovers' Hall to five thousand people. In that same hall a week later, I faced a meeting of the very same people. I didnt argue. I mimicked him. I took all the highfalutin passages in his speech, and repeated them in his best manner until I had the whole five thousand laughing at him. Then I asked them would they like me to sing; and their Yes nearly lifted the roof off. I had two songs. They both had choruses. One went "She lets me go out on Saturday night, on Saturday night, on Saturday night"—like that. The other went "Boo! Hoo! I want Amanda's Teddy bear to play with." They sang it under the windows of his hotel next time he came. He cancelled his meeting and left. And thats how England is governed by yours truly, sir. Lucky for England that Queen Amanda is a good sort, in spite of some surface faults. [*She resumes her seat with triumphant self-satisfaction*].

BALBUS. Lucky for England theres only one of you: thats what *I* say.

AMANDA [*wafts him a kiss*]!

MAGNUS. Should not the Queen support the King, your Majesty?

AMANDA. Sorry, sir; but there isnt room for two monarchs in my realm. I am against you on principle because the talent for mimicry isnt hereditary.

PROTEUS. Now, anybody else? We have heard why the two ladies cannot support the King. Is there anybody who can?

Silence.

MAGNUS. I see that my appeal has been in vain. I do not reproach you, ladies and gentlemen, because I perceive that your situation is a difficult one. The question is, how to change it.

NICOBAR. Sign the ultimatum: that is how.

MAGNUS. I am not quite convinced of that. The Home Secretary's brother-in-law was quite willing to sign the pledge of total abstinence if I would admit him to the Cabinet. His offer was not accepted, because, though none of us doubted that he would sign the pledge, we were not equally certain that the infirmities of his nature would allow him to keep it. My nature is also subject to infirmity. Are you satisfied, Mr Proteus, that if I sign this ultimatum, I shall not inevitably relapse into the conduct that my nature dictates?

PROTEUS [*his patience strained*] What is the use of going on like this? You are like a man on the scaffold, spinning out his prayers to put off the inevitable execution as long as possible. Nothing that you can say will make any difference. You know you must sign. Why not sign and have done with it?

NICOBAR. Now youre talking, Joe.

BALBUS. Thats the stuff to give him.

PLINY. Gulp it down, sir. It wont get any sweeter by keeping: what?

LYSISTRATA. Oh, for God's sake, sign, sir. This is torture to me.

MAGNUS. I perceive, gentlemen, that I have come to the end of your patience. I will tax it no further: you have been very forbearing; and I thank you for it. I will say no more by way of discussion; but I must have until five o'clock this evening to consider my decision. At that hour, if I can find no other way out, I will sign without another word. Meanwhile, ladies and gentlemen, au revoir!

He rises. All rise. He marches out.

PROTEUS. His last wriggle. Never mind: we have him safe enough. What about lunch? I am starving. Will you lunch with me, Lizzie?

LYSISTRATA. Dont speak to me. [*She rushes out distractedly*].

AMANDA. Poor darling Lizzie! She's a regular old true blue Diehard. If only I had her brains and education! or if she had my variety talent! what a queen she'd make! Like old Queen Elizabeth, eh? Dont grieve, Joe: I'll lunch with you since your so pressing.

CRASSUS. Come and lunch with me—all of you.

AMANDA. What opulence! Can you afford it?

CRASSUS. Breakages will pay. They have a standing account at the Ritz. Over five thousand a year, it comes to.

PROTEUS. Right. Let us spoil the Egyptians.

BOANERGES [*with Roman dignity*] My lunch will cost me one and sixpence; and I shall pay for it myself [*he stalks out*].

AMANDA [*calling after him*] Dont make a beast of yourself, Bill. Ta ta!

PROTEUS. Come on, come on: it's ever so late.

They all hurry out. Sempronius and Pamphilius, entering, have to stand aside to let them pass before returning to their desks. Proteus, with Amanda on his arm, stops in the doorway on seeing them.

PROTEUS. Have you two been listening, may I ask?

PAMPHILIUS. Well, it would be rather inconvenient, wouldnt it, if we had to be told everything that passed?

SEMPRONIUS. Once for all, Mr Proteus, the King's private secretaries must hear everything, see everything, and know everything.

PROTEUS. Singularly enough, Mr Sempronius, I havnt the slightest objection [*he goes*].

AMANDA [*going with him*] Goodbye, Semmy. So long, Pam.

SEMPRONIUS } PAMPHILIUS } [*seating themselves at their writing tables and yawning prodigiously*] Ou-ou-ou-ou-ou-fff!!!

AN INTERLUDE

ORINTHIA'S boudoir at half-past fifteen on the same day. She is at her writing table scribbling notes. She is romantically beautiful, and beautifully dressed. As the table is against the wall near a corner, with the other wall on her left, her back alone is visible from the middle of the room. The door is near the corner diagonally opposite. There is a large settee in the middle of the room.

The King enters and waits on the threshold.

ORINTHIA [*crossly, without looking round*] Who is that?

MAGNUS. His Majesty the King.

ORINTHIA. I dont want to see him.

MAGNUS. How soon will you be disengaged?

ORINTHIA. I didnt say I was engaged. Tell the king I dont want to see him.

MAGNUS. He awaits your pleasure [*he comes in and seats himself on the settee*].

ORINTHIA. Go away. [*A pause*]. I wont speak to you. [*Another pause*]. If my private rooms are to be broken into at any moment because they are in the palace, and the king is not a gentleman, I must take a house outside. I am writing to the agents about one now.

MAGNUS. What is our quarrel today, belovéd?

ORINTHIA. Ask your conscience.

MAGNUS. I have none when you are concerned. You must tell me.

She takes a book from the table and rises; then sweeps superbly forward to the settee and flings the book into his hands.

ORINTHIA. There!

MAGNUS. What is this?

ORINTHIA. Page 16. Look at it.

MAGNUS [*looking at the title on the back of the book*] "Songs of our Great Great Grandparents." What page did you say?

ORINTHIA [*between her teeth*] Six-teen.

MAGNUS [*opening the book and finding the page, his eye lighting up with recognition as he looks at it*] Ah! The Pilgrim of

Love!

ORINTHIA. Read the first three words—if you dare.

MAGNUS [*smiling as he caresses the phrase*] "Orinthia, my belovéd".

ORINTHIA. The name you pretended to invent specially for me, the only woman in the world for you. Picked up out of the rubbish basket in a secondhand bookseller's! And I thought you were a poet!

MAGNUS. Well, one poet may consecrate a name for another. Orinthia is a name full of magic for me. It could not be that if I had invented it myself. I heard it at a concert of ancient music when I was a child; and I have treasured it ever since.

ORINTHIA. You always have a pretty excuse. You are the King of liars and humbugs. You cannot understand how a falsehood like that wounds me.

MAGNUS [*remorsefully, stretching out his arms towards her*] Belovéd: I am sorry.

ORINTHIA. Put your hands in your pockets: they shall not touch me ever again.

MAGNUS [*obeying*] Dont pretend to be hurt unless you really are, dearest. It wrings my heart.

ORINTHIA. Since when have you set up a heart? Did you buy that, too, secondhand?

MAGNUS. I have something in me that winces when you are hurt—or pretend to be.

ORINTHIA [*contemptuously*] Yes: I have only to squeal, and you will take me up and pet me as you would a puppy run over by a car. [*Sitting down beside him, but beyond arm's length*] That is what you give me when my heart demands love. I had rather you kicked me.

MAGNUS. I should like to kick you sometimes, when you are specially aggravating. But I shouldnt do it well. I should be afraid of hurting you all the time.

ORINTHIA. I believe you would sign my death warrant without turning a hair.

MAGNUS. That is true, in a way. It is wonderful how

subtle your mind is, as far as it goes.

ORINTHIA. It does not go as far as yours, I suppose.

MAGNUS. I dont know. Our minds go together half way. Whether it is that your mind stops there or else that the road forks, and you take the high road and I take the low road, I cannot say; but somehow after a certain point we lose one another.

ORINTHIA. And then you go back to your Amandas and Lysistratas: creatures whose idea of romance is a minister in love with a department, and whose bedside books are blue books.

MAGNUS. They are not always thinking of some man or other. That is a rather desirable extension of their interests, in my opinion. If Lysistrata had a lover I should not be interested in him in the least; and she would bore me to distraction if she could talk of nothing else. But I am very much interested in her department. Her devotion to it gives us a topic of endless interest.

ORINTHIA. Well, go to her: I am not detaining you. But dont tell her that I have nothing to talk about but men; for that is a lie; and you know it.

MAGNUS. It is, as you say, a lie; and I know it. But I did not say it.

ORINTHIA. You implied it. You meant it. When those ridiculous political women are with us you talk to them all the time, and never say a word to me.

MAGNUS. Nor you to me. We cannot talk to one another in public: we have nothing to say that could be said before other people. Yet we find enough to say to one another when we are alone together. Would you change that if you could?

ORINTHIA. You are as slippery as an eel; but you shall not slip through my fingers. Why do you surround yourself with political bores and frumps and dowdy busybodies who cant talk: they can only debate about their dull departments and their fads and their election chances. [*Rising impatiently*] Who could talk to such people? If it were not for the nonentities of wives and husbands they drag about with them, there would be nobody to talk to at all. And even they can talk of nothing but the servants and the baby. [*Suddenly returning to her seat*] Listen to me, Magnus. Why can you not be a real king?

MAGNUS. In what way, belovédest?

ORINTHIA. Send all these stupid people packing. Make them do their drudgeries in their departments without bothering you about it, as you make your servants here sweep the floors and dust the furniture. Live a really noble and beautiful life—a kingly life—with me. What you need to make you a real king is a real queen.

MAGNUS. But I have got one.

ORINTHIA. Oh, you are blind. You are worse than blind: you have low tastes. Heaven is offering you a rose; and you cling to a cabbage.

MAGNUS [*laughing*] That is a very apt metaphor, belovéd. But what wise man, if you force him to choose between doing without roses and doing without cabbages, would not secure the cabbages? Besides, all these old married cabbages were once roses; and, though young things like you dont remember that, their husbands do. They dont notice the change. Besides, you should know better than anyone else that when a man gets tired of his wife and leaves her it is never because she has lost her good looks. The new love is often older and uglier than the old.

ORINTHIA. Why should I know it better than anyone else?

MAGNUS. Why, because you have been married twice; and both your husbands have run away from you to much plainer and stupider women. When I begged your present husband to come back to court for a while for the sake of appearances he said no man could call his soul his own in the same house with you. And yet that man was utterly infatuated with your beauty when he married you. Your first husband actually forced a good wife to divorce him so that he might marry you; but before two years were out he went back to her and died in her arms, poor chap.

ORINTHIA. Shall I tell you why these men could not live with me? It was because I am a thoroughbred, and they are only hacks. They had nothing against me: I was perfectly faithful to them. I kept their houses beautifully: I fed them better than they had ever been fed in their lives. But because I was higher than they were, and greater, they could not stand the strain of trying to live up to me. So I let them go their way, poor wretches, back to their cabbages. Look at the old creature Ignatius is living with now! She gives you his real measure.

MAGNUS. An excellent woman. Ignatius is quite happy with her. I never saw a man so changed.

ORINTHIA. Just what he is fit for. Commonplace. Bourgeoise. She trots through the streets shopping. [*Rising*] *I* tread the plains of Heaven. Common women cannot come where I am; and common men find themselves out and slink away.

MAGNUS. It must be magnificent to have the consciousness of a goddess without ever doing a thing to justify it.

ORINTHIA. Give me a goddess's work to do; and I will do it. I will even stoop to a queen's work if you will share the throne with me. But do not pretend that people become great by doing great things. They do great things because they are great, if the great things come along. But they are great just the same when the great things do not come along. If I never did anything but sit in this room and powder my face and tell you what a clever fool you are, I should still be heavens high above the millions of common women who do their domestic duty, and sacrifice themselves, and run Trade departments and all the rest of the vulgarities. Has all the tedious public work you have done made you any the better? I have seen you before and after your boasted strokes of policy; and you were the same man, and would have been the same man to me and to yourself if you had never done them. Thank God my self-consciousness is something nobler than vulgar conceit in having done something. It is what I am, not what I do, that you must worship in me. If you want deeds, go to your men and women of action, as you call them, who are all in a conspiracy to pretend that the mechanical things they do, the foolhardy way they risk their worthless lives, or their getting up in the morning at four and working sixteen hours a day for thirty years, like coral insects, make them great. What are they for? these dull slaves? To keep the streets swept for me. To enable me to reign over them in beauty like the stars without having anything to do with their slavery except to console it, to dazzle it, to enable them to forget it in adoring dreams of me. Am I not worth it? [*She sits, fascinating him*]. Look into my eyes and tell the truth. Am I worth it or not?

MAGNUS. To me, who love beauty, yes. But you should hear the speeches Balbus makes about your pension.

ORINTHIA. And my debts: do not forget my debts, my mortgages, the bill of sale on my furniture, the thousands I have had from the moneylenders to save me from being sold up because I will not borrow from my friends. Lecture me again about them; but do not dare pretend that the people grudge me my pension. They glory in it, and in my extravagance, as you call it.

MAGNUS [*more gravely*] By the way, Orinthia, when your dressmakers took up that last bill for you, they were speculating, were they not, in your chances of becoming my queen some day?

ORINTHIA. Well, what if they were?

MAGNUS. They would hardly have ventured on that without a hint from somebody. Was it from you?

ORINTHIA. You think me capable of that! You have a very low side to you, Magnus.

MAGNUS. No doubt: like other mortal fabrics I have a wrong side and a right side. But it is no use your giving yourself airs, belovédest. You are capable of anything. Do you deny that there was some suggestion of the kind?

ORINTHIA. How dare you challenge me to deny it? I never deny. Of course there was a suggestion of the kind.

MAGNUS. I thought so.

ORINTHIA. Oh, stupid! stupid! Go keep a grocer's shop: that is what you are fit for. Do you suppose that the suggestion came from me? Why, you great oaf, it is in the air: when my dressmaker hinted at it I told her that if she ever dared to repeat such a thing she should never get another order from me. But can I help people seeing what is as plain as the sun in the heavens? [*Rising again*] Everyone knows that I am the real queen. Everyone treats me as the real queen. They cheer me in the streets. When I open one of the art exhibitions or launch a new ship they crowd the place out. I am one of Nature's queens; and they know it. If you do not, you are not one of Nature's kings.

MAGNUS. Sublime! Nothing but genuine inspiration could give a woman such cheek.

ORINTHIA. Yes: inspiration, not cheek. [*Sitting as before*] Magnus: when are you going to face my destiny, and your own?

MAGNUS. But my wife? the queen? What is to become of my poor dear Jemima?

ORINTHIA. Oh, drown her: shoot her: tell your chauffeur to drive her into the Serpentine and leave her there. The woman makes you ridiculous.

MAGNUS. I dont think I should like that. And the public would think it illnatured.

ORINTHIA. Oh, you know what I mean. Divorce her. Make her divorce you. It is quite easy. That was how Ronny married me. Everybody does it when they need a change.

MAGNUS. But I cant imagine what I should do without Jemima.

ORINTHIA. Nobody else can imagine what you do with her. But you need not do without her. You can see as much of her as you like when we are married. I shall not be jealous and make scenes.

MAGNUS. That is very magnanimous of you. But I am afraid it does not settle the difficulty. Jemima would not think it right to keep up her present intimacy with me if I were married to you.

ORINTHIA. What a woman! Would she be in any worse position then than I am in now?

MAGNUS. No.

ORINTHIA. You mean, then, that you do not mind placing me in a position that you do not think good enough for her?

MAGNUS. Orinthia: I did not place you in your present position. You placed yourself in it. I could not resist you. You gathered me like a daisy.

ORINTHIA. Did you want to resist me?

MAGNUS. Oh no. I never resist temptation, because I have found that things that are bad for me do not tempt me.

ORINTHIA. Well, then, what are we talking about?

MAGNUS. I forget. I think I was explaining the impossibility of my wife changing places with you.

ORINTHIA. Why impossible, pray?

MAGNUS. I cannot make you understand: you see you have never been really married, though you have led two captives to the altar, and borne children to one of them. Being your husband is only a job for which one man will do as well as another, and which the last man holds subject to six months notice in the divorce court. Being my wife is something quite different. The smallest derogation to Jemima's dignity would hit me like the lash of a whip across the face. About yours, somehow, I do not care a rap.

ORINTHIA. Nothing can derogate from my dignity: it is divine. Hers is only a convention: that is why you tremble when it is challenged.

MAGNUS. Not a bit. It is because she is a part of my real workaday self. You belong to fairyland.

ORINTHIA. Suppose she dies! Will you die too?

MAGNUS. Not immediately. I shall have to carry on as best I can without her, though the prospect terrifies me.

ORINTHIA. Might not carrying on without her include marrying me?

MAGNUS. My dear Orinthia, I had rather marry the devil. Being a wife is not your job.

ORINTHIA. You think so because you have no imagination. And you dont know me because I have never let you really possess me. I should make you more happy than any man has ever yet been on earth.

MAGNUS. I defy you to make me more happy than our strangely innocent relations have already made me.

ORINTHIA [*rising restlessly*] You talk like a child or a saint. [*Turning on him*] I can give you a new life: one of which you have no conception. I can give you beautiful, wonderful children: have you ever seen a lovelier boy than my Basil?

MAGNUS. Your children are beautiful; but they are fairy children; and I have several very real ones already. A divorce would not sweep them out of the way of fairies.

ORINTHIA. In short, when your golden moment comes—when the gates of heaven open before you, you are afraid to come out of your pigsty.

MAGNUS. If I am a pig, a pigsty is the proper place for me.

ORINTHIA. I cannot understand it. All men are fools and moral cowards when you come to know them. But you are less of a fool and less of a moral coward than any man I have ever known. You have almost the makings of a first rate woman in you. When I leave the earth and soar up to the regions which are my real eternal home, you can follow me: I can speak to you as I can speak to no one else; and you can say things to me that would just make your stupid wife cry. There is more of you in me than of any other man within my reach. There is more of me in you than of any other woman within your reach. We are meant for one another: it is written across the sky that you and I are queen and king. How can you hesitate? What attraction is there for you in your common healthy jolly lumps of children and your common housekeeper wife and the rabble of dowdies and upstarts and intriguers and clowns that think they are governing the country when they are only squabbling with you? Look again at me, man: again and again. Am I not worth a million such? Is not life with me as high above them as the sun is above the gutter?

MAGNUS. Yes yes yes yes, of course. You are lovely: you

are divine [*she cannot restrain a gesture of triumph*]. And you are enormously amusing.

This anti-climax is too much for Orinthia's exaltation; but she is too clever not to appreciate it. With another gesture, this time of deflation, she sits down at his left hand with an air of suffering patience, and listens in silence to the harangue which follows.

MAGNUS. Some day perhaps Nature will graft the roses on the cabbages and make every woman as enchanting as you; and then what a glorious lark life will be! But at present, what I come here for is to enjoy talking to you like this when I need an hour's respite from royalty: when my stupid wife has been worrying me, or my jolly lumps of children bothering me, or my turbulent Cabinet obstructing me: when, as the doctors say, what I need is a change. You see, my dear, there is no wife on earth so precious, no children so jolly, no Cabinet so tactful that it is impossible ever to get tired of them. Jemima has her limitations, as you have observed. And I have mine. Now if our limitations exactly corresponded I should never want to talk to anyone else; and neither would she. But as that never happens, we are like all other married couples: that is, there are subjects which can never be discussed between us because they are sore subjects. There are people we avoid mentioning to oneanother because one of us likes them and the other doesnt. Not only individuals, but whole sorts of people. For instance, your sort. My wife doesnt like your sort, doesnt understand it, mistrusts and dreads it. Not without reason; for women like you are dangerous to wives. But I dont dislike your sort: I understand it, being a little in that line myself. At all events I am not afraid of it; though the least allusion to it brings a cloud over my wife's face. So when I want to talk freely about it I come and talk to you. And I take it she talks to friends of hers about people of whom she never talks to me. She has men friends from whom she can get some things that she cannot get from me. If she didnt do so she would be limited by my limitations, which would end in her hating me. So I always do my best to make her men friends feel at home with us.

ORINTHIA. A model husband in a model household! And when the model household becomes a bore, I am the diversion.

MAGNUS. Well, what more can you ask? Do not let us fall into the common mistake of expecting to become one flesh and one spirit. Every star has its own orbit; and between it and its nearest neighbor there is not only a powerful attraction but an infinite distance. When the attraction becomes stronger than the distance the two do not embrace: they crash together in ruin. We two also have our orbits, and must keep an infinite distance between us to avoid a disastrous collision. Keeping our distance is the whole secret of good manners; and without good manners human society is intolerable and impossible.

ORINTHIA. Would any other woman stand your sermons, and even like them?

MAGNUS. Orinthia: we are only two children at play; and you must be content to be my queen in fairyland. And [*rising*] I must go back to my work.

ORINTHIA. What work have you that is more important than being with me?

MAGNUS. None.

ORINTHIA. Then sit down.

MAGNUS. Unfortunately, this silly business of government must be carried on. And there is a crisis this evening, as usual.

ORINTHIA. But the crisis is not until five: I heard all about it from Sempronius. Why do you encourage that greedy schemer Proteus? He humbugs you. He humbugs everybody. He even humbugs himself; and of course he humbugs that Cabinet which is a disgrace to you: it is like an overcrowded third class carriage. Why do you allow such riffraff to waste your time? After all, what are you paid for? To be a king: that is, to wipe your boots on common people.

MAGNUS. Yes; but this king business, as the Americans call it, has got itself so mixed up with democracy that half the country expects me to wipe my perfectly polished boots on the Cabinet, and the other half expects me to let the Cabinet wipe its muddy boots on me. The Crisis at five o'clock is to decide which of us is to be the doormat.

ORINTHIA. And you will condescend to fight with Proteus for power?

MAGNUS. Oh no: I never fight. But I sometimes win.

ORINTHIA. If you let yourself be beaten by that trickster and poseur, never dare to approach me again.

MAGNUS. Proteus is a clever fellow: even on occasion a fine fellow. It would give me no satisfaction to beat him: I hate beating people. But there would be some innocent fun in outwitting him.

ORINTHIA. Magnus: you are a mollycoddle. If you were a real man you would just delight in beating him to a jelly.

MAGNUS. A real man would never do as a king. I am only an idol, my love; and all I can do is to draw the line at being a cruel idol. [*He looks at his watch*] Now I must really be off. Au revoir.

ORINTHIA [*looking at her wrist watch*] But it is only twentyfive minutes past four. You have heaps of time before five.

MAGNUS. Yes; but tea is at half-past four.

ORINTHIA [*catching him by the arm with a snakelike dart*] Never mind your tea. I will give you your tea.

MAGNUS. Impossible, belovéd. Jemima does not like to be kept waiting.

ORINTHIA. Oh, bother Jemima! You shall not leave me to go to Jemima [*she pulls him back so vigorously that he falls into the seat beside her*].

MAGNUS. My dear, I must.

ORINTHIA. No, not today. Listen, Magnus. I have something very particular to say to you.

MAGNUS. You have not. You are only trying to make me late to annoy my wife. [*He tries to rise, but is pulled back*]. Let me go, please.

ORINTHIA [*holding on*] Why are you so afraid of your wife? You are the laughing stock of London, you poor henpecked darling.

MAGNUS. Henpecked! What do you call this? At least my wife does not restrain me by bodily violence.

ORINTHIA. I will not be deserted for your old Dutch.

MAGNUS. Listen, Orinthia. Dont be absurd. You know I must go. Do be good.

ORINTHIA. Only ten minutes more.

MAGNUS. It is half-past already.

He tries to rise; but she holds him back.

MAGNUS [*pausing for breath*] You are doing this out of sheer devilment. You are so abominably strong that I cannot break loose without hurting you. Must I call the guard?

ORINTHIA. Do, do. It will be in all the papers tomorrow.

MAGNUS. Fiend [*Summoning all his dignity*] Orinthia: I command you.

ORINTHIA [*laughs wildly*]!!!

MAGNUS [*furious*] Very well, then, you she devil: you shall let go.

He tackles her in earnest. She flings her arms round him and holds on with mischievous enjoyment. There is a tapping at the door; but they do not hear it. As he is breaking loose she suddenly shifts her grip to his waist and drags him on to the floor, where they roll over one another. Sempronius enters. He stares at the scandalous scene for a moment; then hastily slips out; shuts the door; clears his throat and blows his nose noisily; and knocks loudly and repeatedly. The two combatants cease hostilities and scramble hastily to their feet.

MAGNUS. Come in.

SEMPRONIUS [*entering*] Her Majesty sent me to remind you that tea is waiting, sir.

MAGNUS. Thank you. [*He goes quickly out*].

ORINTHIA [*panting but greatly pleased with herself*] The King forgets everything when he is here. So do I, I am afraid. I am so sorry.

SEMPRONIUS [*stiffly*] No explanations are needed. I saw what happened. [*He goes out*].

ORINTHIA. The beast! He must have looked through the keyhole. [*She throws her hand up with a gesture of laughing defiance, and dances back to her seat at the writing table*].

ACT II

LATER in the afternoon. The Terrace of the Palace. A low balustrade separates it from the lawn. Terrace chairs in abundance, ranged along the balustrade. Some dining room chairs also, not ranged, but standing about as if they had just been occupied. The terrace is accessible from the lawn by a central flight of steps.

The King and Queen are sitting apart near the corners of the steps, the Queen to the King's right. He is reading the evening paper: she is knitting. She has a little work table on her right, with a small gong on it.

THE QUEEN. Why did you tell them to leave the chairs when they took away the tea?

MAGNUS. I shall receive the Cabinet here.

THE QUEEN. Here! Why?

MAGNUS. Well, I think the open air and the evening light will have a quieting effect on them. They cannot make speeches at me so easily as in a room.

THE QUEEN. Are you sure? When Robert asked Boanerges where he learnt to speak so beautifully, he said "In Hyde Park."

MAGNUS. Yes; but with a crowd to stimulate him.

THE QUEEN. Robert says you have tamed Boanerges.

MAGNUS. No: I have not tamed him. I have taught him how to behave. I have to valet all the beginners; but that does not tame them: it teaches them how to use their strength instead of wasting it in making fools of themselves. So much the worse for me when I have to fight them.

THE QUEEN. You get no thanks for it. They think you are only humbugging them.

MAGNUS. Well, so I am, in the elementary lessons. But when it comes to real business humbug is no use: they pick it up themselves too quickly.

Pamphilius enters along the terrace, from the Queen's side.

MAGNUS [*looking at his watch*] Good Heavens! They havnt come, have they? It's not five yet.

PAMPHILIUS. No, sir. It's the American ambassador.

THE QUEEN [*resenting this a little*] Has he an audience?

PAMPHILIUS. No, maam. He is rather excited about something, I think. I cant get anything out of him. He says he must see His Majesty at once.

THE QUEEN. Must!! An American must see the King at once, without an audience! Well!

MAGNUS [*rising*] Send him in, Pam.

Pamphilius goes out.

THE QUEEN. *I* should have told him to write for an audience, and then kept him waiting a week for it.

MAGNUS. What! When we still owe America that old war debt. And with a mad imperialist president like Bossfield! No you wouldnt, my dear: you would be crawlingly civil to him, as I am going to be, confound him!

PAMPHILIUS [*re-appearing*] His Excellency the American Ambassador. Mr Vanhattan.

He retires as Mr Vanhattan enters in an effusive condition, and, like a man assured of an enthusiastic welcome, hurries to the Queen, and salutes her with a handshake so prolonged that she stares in astonishment, first at him, and then appealingly at the King, with her hands being vigorously wrung and waved up and down all the time.

MAGNUS. What on earth is the matter, Mr Vanhattan? You are shaking Her Majesty's rings off.

VANHATTAN [*desisting*] Her Majesty will excuse me when she learns the nature of my errand here. This, King Magnus, is a great historic scene: one of the greatest, perhaps, that history has ever recorded or will ever again record.

MAGNUS. Have you had tea?

VANHATTAN. Tea! Who can think of tea at such a moment as this?

THE QUEEN [*rather coldly*] It is hard for us to share your enthusiasm in complete ignorance of its cause.

VANHATTAN. That is true, maam. I am just behaving like a crazy man. But you shall hear. You shall judge. And then you shall say whether I exaggerate the importance—the immensity—of an occasion that cannot be exaggerated.

MAGNUS. Goodness gracious! Wont you sit down?

VANHATTAN [*taking a chair and placing it between them*] I thank your Majesty. [*He sits*].

MAGNUS. You have some exciting news for us, apparently. Is it private or official?

VANHATTAN. Official, sir. No mistake about it. What I am going to tell you is authentic from the United States of America to the British Empire.

THE QUEEN. Perhaps I had better go.

VANHATTAN. No, maam: you shall not go. Whatever may be the limits of your privileges as the consort of your sovereign, it is your right as an Englishwoman to learn what I have come here to communicate.

MAGNUS. My dear Vanhattan, what the devil is the matter?

VANHATTAN. King Magnus: between your country and mine there is a debt.

MAGNUS. Does that matter, now that our capitalists have invested so heavily in American concerns that after paying yourselves the interest on the debt you have to send us two thousand million dollars a year to balance the account.

VANHATTAN. King Magnus: for the moment, forget figures. Between your country and mine there is not only a debt but a frontier: the frontier that has on it not a single gun nor a single soldier, and across which the American citizen every day shakes the hand of the Canadian subject of your throne.

MAGNUS. There is also the frontier of the ocean, which is somewhat more expensively defended at our joint expense by the League of Nations.

VANHATTAN [*rising to give his words more impressiveness*] Sir: the debt is cancelled. The frontier no longer exists.

THE QUEEN. How can that be?

MAGNUS. Am I to understand, Mr Vanhattan, that by some convulsion of Nature the continent of North America has been submerged in the Atlantic?

VANHATTAN. Something even more wonderful than that has happened. One may say that the Atlantic Ocean has been submerged in the British Empire.

MAGNUS. I think you had better tell us as succinctly as possible what has happened. Pray sit down.

VANHATTAN [*resuming his seat*] You are aware, sir, that the United States of America at one time formed a part of your empire.

MAGNUS. There is a tradition to that effect.

VANHATTAN. No mere tradition, sir. An undoubted historical fact. In the eighteenth century—

MAGNUS. That is a long time ago.

VANHATTAN. Centuries count for but little in the lifetimes of great nations, sir. Let me recall the parable of the prodigal son.

MAGNUS. Oh really, Mr Vanhattan, that was a very very long time ago. I take it that something important has happened since yesterday.

VANHATTAN. It has. It has indeed, King Magnus.

MAGNUS. Then what is it? I have not time to attend to the eighteenth century and the prodigal son at this moment.

THE QUEEN. The King has a Cabinet meeting in ten minutes, Mr Vanhattan.

VANHATTAN. I should like to see the faces of your Cabinet ministers, King Magnus, when they hear what I have to tell you.

MAGNUS. So should I. But I am not in a position to tell it to them, because I dont know what it is.

VANHATTAN. The prodigal, sir, has returned to his father's house. Not poor, not hungry, not ragged, as of old. Oh no. This time he returns bringing with him the riches of the earth to the ancestral home.

MAGNUS [*starting from his chair*] You dont mean to say—

VANHATTAN [*rising also, blandly triumphant*] I do, sir. The Declaration of Independence is cancelled. The treaties which endorsed it are torn up. We have decided to rejoin the British Empire. We shall of course enjoy Dominion Home Rule under the Presidency of Mr Bossfield. I shall revisit you here shortly, not as the Ambassador of a foreign power, but as

High Commissioner for the greatest of your dominions, ana your very loyal and devoted subject, sir.

MAGNUS [*collapsing into his chair*] The devil you will! [*He stares haggardly into futurity, now for the first time utterly at a loss*].

THE QUEEN. What a splendid thing, Mr Vanhattan!

VANHATTAN. I thought your Majesty would say so. The most splendid thing that has ever happened. [*He resumes his seat*].

THE QUEEN [*looking anxiously at the king*] Dont you think so, Magnus?

MAGNUS [*pulling himself together with a visible effort*] May I ask, Mr Vanhattan, with whom did this—this—this masterstroke of American policy originate? Frankly, I have been accustomed to regard your President as a statesman whose mouth was the most efficient part of his head. He cannot have thought of this himself. Who suggested it to him?

VANHATTAN. I must accept your criticism of Mr Bossfield with all doo reserve, but I may mention that we Americans will probably connect the good news with the recent visit to our shores of the President of the Irish Free State. I cannot pronounce his name in its official Gaelic form; and there is only one typist in our bureau who can spell it; but he is known to his friends as Mick O'Rafferty.

MAGNUS. The rascal! Jemima: we shall have to live in Dublin. This is the end of England.

VANHATTAN. In a sense that may be so. But England will not perish. She will merge—merge, sir—into a bigger and brighter concern. Perhaps I should have mentioned that one of our conditions will be that you shall be Emperor. King may be good enough for this little island; but if we come in we shall require something grander.

MAGNUS. This little island! "This little gem set in a silver sea!" Has it occurred to you, Mr Vanhattan, that rather than be reduced to a mere appendage of a big American concern, we might raise the old warcry of Sinn Fein, and fight for our independence to the last drop of our blood?

VANHATTAN. I should be right sorry to contemplate such a reversion to a barbarous past. Fortunately, it's impossible —imm-pawsibl. The old warcry would not appeal to the cosmopolitan crews of the fleet of the League of Nations in the Atlantic. That fleet would blockade you, sir. And I fear we should be obliged to boycott you. The two thousand million dollars a year would stop.

MAGNUS. But the continental Powers! Do you suppose they would consent for a moment to such a change in the balance of power?

VANHATTAN. Why not? The change would be only nominal.

MAGNUS. Nominal! You call an amalgamation of the British Commonwealth with the United States a nominal change! What will France and Germany call it?

VANHATTAN [*shaking his head indulgently*] France and Germany? These queer old geographical expressions which you use here from old family habit do not trouble us. I suppose you mean by Germany the chain of more or less Soviet Republics between the Ural Mountains and the North Sea. Well, the clever people at Moscow and Berlin and Geneva are trying to federate them; and it is fully understood between us that if we dont object to their move they will not object to ours. France, by which I take it you mean the Government at New Timgad, is too busy in Africa to fuss about what is happening at the ends of your little Channel Tube. So long as Paris is full of Americans, and Americans are full of money, all's well in the west from the French point of view. One of the great attractions of Paris for Americans is the excursion to Old England. The French want us to feel at home here. And so we do. Why shouldnt we? After all, we are at home here.

MAGNUS. In what sense, may I ask?

VANHATTAN. Well, we find here everything we are accustomed to: our industrial products, our books, our plays, our sports, our Christian Science churches, our osteopaths, our movies and talkies. Put it in a small parcel and say our goods and our ideas. A political union with us will be just the official recognition of an already accomplished fact. A union of hearts, you might call it.

THE QUEEN. You forget, Mr Vanhattan. We have a great national tradition.

VANHATTAN. The United States, maam, have absorbed all the great national traditions, and blended them with their own glorious tradition of Freedom into something that is unique and universal.

THE QUEEN. We have a civilized culture which is peculiar to ourselves. It may not be better than yours; but it is different.

VANHATTAN. Well, is it? We found that culture enshrined in British material works of art: in the stately country homes of your nobility, in the cathedrals our common forefathers built as the country houses of God. What did you do with them? You sold them to us. I was brought up in the shade of Ely cathedral, the removal of which from the county of Cambridge to New Jersey was my dear old father's first big professional job. The building which stands on its former site is a very fine one: in my opinion the best example of reinforced concrete of its period; but it was designed by an American architect, and built by the Synthetic Building Materials Trust, an international affair. Believe me, the English people, the real English people who take things as they come instead of reading books about them, will be more at home with us than they are with the old English notions which our tourists try to keep alive. When you find some country gentleman keeping up the old English customs at Christmas and so forth, who is he? An American who has bought the place. Your people get up the show for him because he pays for it, not because it is natural to them.

THE QUEEN [*with a sigh*] Our own best families go so much to Ireland nowadays. People should not be allowed to go from England to Ireland. They never come back.

VANHATTAN. Well, can you blame them, maam? Look at the climate!

THE QUEEN. No: it is not the climate. It is the Horse Show.

The King rises very thoughtfully; and Vanhattan follows his example.

MAGNUS. I must think over this. I have known for years past that it was on the cards. When I was young, and under the influence of our family tradition, which of course never recognized the rebellion of the American colonies as valid, I actually dreamt of a reunited English speaking empire at the head of civilization.

VANHATTAN. Fine! Great! And now come true.

MAGNUS. Not yet. Now that I am older and wiser I find the reality less attractive than the dream.

VANHATTAN. And is that all I am to report to the President, sir? He will be disappointed. I am a little taken aback, myself.

MAGNUS. For the present, that is all. This may be a great idea—

VANHATTAN. Surely, surely.

MAGNUS. It may also be a trap in which England will perish.

VANHATTAN [*encouragingly*] Oh, I shouldnt look at it that way. Besides, nothing—not even dear old England—can last for ever. Progress, you know, sir, progress, progress!

MAGNUS. Just so, just so. We may survive only as another star on your flag. Still, we cling to the little scrap of individuality you have left us. If we must merge, as you call it—or did you say submerge?—some of us will swim to the last. [*To the Queen*] My dear.

The Queen strikes her gong.

Pamphilius returns.

MAGNUS. You shall hear from me after the Cabinet meets. Not tonight: you must not sit up waiting for a message. Early tomorrow, I hope. Thank you for bringing me the news before the papers got it: that seldom happens now. Pamphilius: you will reconduct his Excellency. Good evening. [*He shakes hands*].

VANHATTAN. I thank your Majesty. [*To the Queen*] Good evening, maam. I look forward to presenting myself in court dress soon.

THE QUEEN. You will look very nice in it, Mr Vanhattan. Good evening.

The Ambassador goes out with Pamphilius.

MAGNUS [*striding grimly to and fro*] The scoundrels! That blackguard O'Rafferty! That booby bullroarer Bossfield! Breakages, Limited, have taken it into their heads to mend the British Commonwealth.

THE QUEEN [*quietly*] I think it is a very good thing. You will make a very good emperor. We shall civilize these Americans.

MAGNUS. How can we when we have not yet civilized ourselves? They have come to regard us as a mere tribe of redskins. England will be just a reservation.

THE QUEEN. Nonsense, dear! They know that we are their natural superiors. You can see it by the way their women behave at court. They really love and reverence royalty; while our English peeresses are hardly civil—when they condescend to come at all.

MAGNUS. Well, my dear, I do many things to please you that I should never do to please myself; and I suppose I shall end as American Emperor just to keep you amused.

THE QUEEN. I never desire anything that is not good for you, Magnus. You do not always know what is good for you.

MAGNUS. Well, well, well, well! Have it your own way, dearest. Where are these infernal ministers? Theyre late.

THE QUEEN [*looking out into the garden*] Coming across the lawn with Sempronius.

The Cabinet arrives. The men take off their hats as they come up the steps. Boanerges has taken advantage of the interval to procure a brilliant uniform and change into it. Proteus, with Sempronius, heads the procession, followed immediately by the two lady ministers. The Queen rises as Proteus turns to her. Sempronius moves the little table quickly back to the balustrade out of the way, and puts the Queen's chair in the centre for the King.

THE QUEEN [*shaking hands*] How do you do, Mr Proteus?

PROTEUS. May I present the President of the Board of Trade, Mr Boanerges?

THE QUEEN. I remember seeing you, Mr Boanerges, at the opening of the Transport Workers' Summer Palace. You wore a most becoming costume then. I hope you have not given it up.

BOANERGES. But the Princess told me I looked ridiculous in it!

THE QUEEN. That was very naughty of the Princess. You looked particularly well in it. However, you look well in anything. And now I leave you all to your labors.

She goes out along the terrace. Sempronius follows with her knitting.

MAGNUS [*sitting down*] Be seated, ladies and gentlemen.

They take chairs of one sort or another where they can find them, first leaving their hats on the balustrade. When they are seated, their order from the King's right to his left is Nicobar, Crassus, Boanerges, Amanda, the King, Proteus, Lysistrata, Pliny, and Balbus.

A pause, Proteus waiting for the King to begin. He, deep in thought, says nothing. The silence becomes oppressive.

PLINY [*chattily*] Nice weather we're having, these evenings.

AMANDA [*splutters*]!!!

MAGNUS. There is rather a threatening cloud on the western horizon, Mr Pliny. [*To Proteus*] Have you heard the news from America?

PROTEUS. I have, sir.

MAGNUS. Am I to be favored with the advice of my ministers on that subject?

PROTEUS. By your Majesty's leave, we will take the question of the ultimatum first.

MAGNUS. Do you think the ultimatum will matter much when the capital of the British Commonwealth is shifted to Washington?

NICOBAR. We'll see it shifted to Melbourne or Montreal

or Johannesburg first.

MAGNUS. It would not stay there. It will stay at a real centre of gravity only.

PROTEUS. We are agreed about that. If it shifts at all it will shift either west to Washington or east to Moscow.

BOANERGES. Moscow thinks a lot of itself. But what has Moscow to teach us that we cannot teach ourselves? Moscow is built on English history, written in London by Karl Marx.

PROTEUS. Yes; and the English king has sidetracked you again. [*To Magnus*] What about the ultimatum, sir? You promised us your decision at five o'clock. It is now a quarter past.

MAGNUS. Are you inexorably determined to force this issue to its logical end? You know how unEnglish it is to do that?

PROTEUS. My people came from Scotland.

LYSISTRATA. I wish they had stayed there. I am English: every bone in my body.

BOANERGES [*vociferously*] Same here!

PROTEUS. God help England if she had no Scots to think for her!

MAGNUS. What does the Cabinet say to that?

AMANDA. All their people came from Scotland or Ireland or Wales or Jerusalem or somewhere, sir. It is no use appealing to English sentiment here.

CRASSUS. Politics are not suited to the English, if you ask me.

MAGNUS. Then I, the only Englishman left in politics, apparently, am to be reduced to complete nullity?

PROTEUS [*bluntly*] Yes. You cannot frighten us out of our position by painting it red. I could paint your position black if I liked. In plain terms we require from you an unconditional surrender. If you refuse it then I go to the country on the question whether England is to be an absolute monarchy or a constitutional one. We are all agreed on that: there will be no resignations. I have letters from the absent members of the Government: those present will speak for themselves.

ALL THE OTHER MEN. Agreed, agreed.

PROTEUS. Now, what is your answer?

MAGNUS. The day for absolute monarchies is past. You think you can do without me; and I know that I cannot do without you. I decide, of course, in favor of a constitutional monarchy.

THE MEN [*greatly relieved and delighted*] Hear! hear!

MAGNUS. Wait a moment.

Sudden silence and mistrust.

PROTEUS. So! There is a catch in it, is there?

MAGNUS. Not exactly a catch. But you have driven me to face the fact that I am unfitted to be a constitutional monarch. I am by nature incapable of the necessary self-effacement.

AMANDA. Well, thats true, at all events. You and I are a pair, sir.

MAGNUS. Thank you. Therefore, whilst accepting your constitutional principle without the slightest reserve, I cannot sign your ultimatum, because by doing so I should be making personal promises which I know I should break—which in fact I must break because I have forces within me which your constitutional limits cannot hold in check.

BALBUS. How can you accept our principle if you dont sign the ultimatum?

MAGNUS. Oh, there is no difficulty about that. When an honest man finds himself incapable of discharging the duties of a public post, he resigns.

PROTEUS [*alarmed*] Resigns! What are you driving at?

CRASSUS. A king cannot resign.

NICOBAR. You might as well talk of beheading yourself. You cant behead yourself.

BOANERGES. Other people can, though.

MAGNUS. Do not let us quarrel about words, gentlemen. I cannot resign. But I can abdicate.

ALL THE REST [*starting to their feet*] Abdicate! [*They stare at him in consternation*].

AMANDA [*whistling a descending minor scale very expressively*] !!!!!!!![*She sits down*].

MAGNUS. Of course, abdicate. Lysistrata: you have been a teacher of history. You can assure your colleagues that there is nothing unprecedented in an abdication. The Emperor Charles the Fifth, for instance—

LYSISTRATA. Oh, Charles the Fifth be—be bothered! he's not good enough. Sir: I have stood by you as far as I dared. Dont throw me over. You must not abdicate. [*She sits down, distressed*].

PROTEUS. You cannot abdicate except by my advice.

MAGNUS. I am acting upon your advice.

PROTEUS. Nonsense! [*He sits down*].

BALBUS. Ridiculous! [*He sits down*].

PLINY. Youre not serious, you know. [*He sits down*].

NICOBAR. You cant upset the apple cart like this. [*He sits down*].

CRASSUS. I must say this is not playing the game. [*He sits down*].

BOANERGES [*powerfully*] Well, why not? Why not? Though as an old Republican I have no respect for His Majesty as a King, I have a great respect for him as a Strong Man. But he is not the only pebble on the beach. Why not have done with this superstition of monarchy, and bring the British Commonwealth into line with all the other great Powers today as a republic? [*He sits down*].

MAGNUS. My abdication does not involve that, Mr Boanerges. I am abdicating to save the monarchy, not to destroy it. I shall be succeeded by my son Robert, Prince of Wales. He will make an admirable constitutional monarch.

PLINY. Oh, come! Dont be hard on the lad, sir. He has plenty of brains.

MAGNUS. Oh yes, yes, yes: I did not mean that he is a nonentity: quite the contrary: he is much cleverer than I am. But I have never been able to induce him to take any interest in parliamentary politics. He prefers intellectual pursuits.

NICOBAR. Dont you believe it. He is up to his neck in business.

MAGNUS. Just so. He asks me why I waste my time with you here pretending to govern the country when it is really governed by Breakages, Limited. And really I hardly know how to answer him.

CRASSUS. Things are like that nowadays. My son says just the same.

LYSISTRATA. Personally I get on very well with the Prince; but somehow I do not feel that he is interested in what I am doing.

BALBUS. He isnt. He wont interfere with you as long as you dont interfere with him. Just the right king for us. Not pig-headed. Not meddlesome. Thinks that nothing we do matters a rap. What do you say, Joe?

PROTEUS. After all, why not? if your Majesty is in earnest.

MAGNUS. I assure you I am very much in earnest.

PROTEUS. Well, I confess I did not foresee this turn of events. But I ought to have foreseen it. What your Majesty proposes is the straightforward, logical, intellectually honest solution of our difficulty. Consequently it is the last solution I could have expected in politics. But I reckoned without your Majesty's character. The more I think of it the more clearly I see that you are right—that you are taking the only course open to you.

CRASSUS. I never said I was against it, Joe.

BALBUS. Neither did I.

NICOBAR. I think theres a great deal to be said for it. *I* have no objection.

PLINY. One king is no worse than another, is he?

BOANERGES. Is he any better? The way you fellows scuttle backward and forward from one mind to another whenever Joe holds up his finger is disgusting. This is a Cabinet of sheep.

PROTEUS. Well, give the flock a better lead if you can. Have you anything else to propose?

BOANERGES. I dont know that I have on the spur of the moment. We should have had notice of this. But I suppose the King must do as he thinks right.

PROTEUS. Then the goat goes with the sheep; so thats all right.

BOANERGES. Who are you calling a goat?

NICOBAR. If you come to that, who are *you* calling sheep?

AMANDA. Steady there, children! steady! steady! [*To the King*] You have brought us all round, sir, as usual.

PROTEUS. There is nothing more to be said.

AMANDA. That means another half hour at least.

BOANERGES. Woman: this is not the moment for your tomfooleries.

PROTEUS [*impressively*] Bill is right, Amanda. [*He rises and becomes the conventional House of Commons orator*].

Ministers compose themselves to listen with grave attention, as if in church; but Lysistrata is contemptuous and Amanda amused.

PROTEUS [*continuing*] It is a solemn moment. It is a moment in which an old tie is being broken. I am not ashamed to confess that it is a tie from which I have learned something.

MALE MINISTERS [*murmur*] Hear hear! Hear hear!

PROTEUS. For my own part—and I think I may speak for others here as well—it has been no mere political tie, but a tie of sincere friendship.

Renewed murmurs of sympathy. Increasing emotion.

PROTEUS. We have had our disagreements—as which of us has not?—but they have been family quarrels.

CRASSUS. Thats all. Nothing more.

PROTEUS. May I say lovers' quarrels?

PLINY [*wiping his eyes*] You may, Joe. You may.

PROTEUS. My friends, we came here to a meeting. We find, alas! that the meeting is to be a leavetaking. [*Crassus sniffs tearfully*]. It is a sad leavetaking on our part, but a cordial one.[Hear Hear *from Pliny*]. We are cast down, but not discouraged. Looking back to the past with regret, we can still look forward to the future with hope. That future has its dangers and its difficulties. It will bring us new problems; and it will bring us face to face with a new king. But the new problems and the new king will not make us forget our old counsellor, monarch, and—he will allow me to say—comrade. [Hear Hears *ad libitum*]. I know my words will find an echo in all your hearts when I conclude by saying that whatsoever king shall reign—

AMANDA. Youll be the Vicar of Bray, Joe.

Uproar. Proteus flings himself into his chair indignantly.

BALBUS. Shame!

NICOBAR. Shut up, you b—

PLINY. A joke's a joke; but really—

CRASSUS. Too bad, Amanda! Behave yourself.

LYSISTRATA. She has a perfect right to speak. You are a parcel of sentimental fools.

BOANERGES [*rising*] Silence. Order.

AMANDA. Sorry.

BOANERGES. So you ought to be. Where's your manners? Where's your education? King Magnus: we part; but we part as strong men part: as friends. The Prime Minister has correctly represented the sentiments of all the men present. I call on them to express those sentiments in the good old English fashion. [*Singing in stentorian tones*] Fo-o-o-o-r-r-r

MALE MINISTERS EXCEPT PROTEUS [*rising and singing*]

— he's a jolly good fel-low
For he's a jolly good fel-low
For he's—

MAGNUS [*peremptorily*] Stop. Stop.

Sudden silence and misgiving. They sit down furtively.

MAGNUS. I thank you with all my heart; but there is a misapprehension. We are not taking leave of one another. I have no intention of withdrawing from an active part in politics.

PROTEUS. What!!

MAGNUS. You are looking on me, with an emotion which has deeply touched me, as a man with a political past. But I look on myself rather as a man with a political future. I have not yet told you my plans.

NICOBAR. What plans?

BALBUS. A retired king cant have plans and a future.

MAGNUS. Why not? I am looking forward to a most exciting and enjoyable time. As I shall of course dissolve parliament, the fun will begin with a general election.

BOANERGES [*dismayed*] But Ive only just been elected. Do you mean that I shall have to stand two elections in one month? Have you thought of the expenses?

MAGNUS. Surely your expenses will be paid by the State.

BOANERGES. Paid by the State! Is that all you know about electioneering in England?

PROTEUS. You will get your whack out of the party funds, Bill; and if you cant find the extras you must put up with straight votes. Go on, sir: we want to hear about those plans of yours.

MAGNUS. My last act of royal authority will be to divest myself of all titles and dignities; so that I may step down at once into the position of a commoner.

BOANERGES. Step up, you mean. The common man is the superior, not the inferior, of the titled man.

MAGNUS. That is why I am going to make myself a common man, Mr Boanerges.

PLINY. Well, it does you honor.

CRASSUS. Not all of us would be capable of a sacrifice like that.

BOANERGES. A fine gesture, sir. A fine gesture. I admit it.

PROTEUS [*suspicious*] And since when, pray, has your Majesty taken to making gestures? Whats the game this time?

BOANERGES. Shame!

PROTEUS. Shut up, you gaby. [*To the King*] I say, whats the game?

MAGNUS. There is no imposing on you, Prime Minister. The game is, of course, that when I come back into politics I shall be in a better position as a commoner than as a peer. I shall seek a parliamentary seat.

PROTEUS. You in the House of Commons!

MAGNUS [*blandly*] It is my intention to offer myself to the Royal Borough of Windsor as a candidate at the forthcoming General Election.

All the rest except Boanerges and the ladies rise in consternation.

PROTEUS. This is treachery.

BALBUS. A dirty trick.

NICOBAR. The meanest on record.

PLINY. He'll be at the top of the poll.

CRASSUS. There wont be any poll: it will be a walk-over.

BALBUS. This shews what all your fine manners and friendly ways are worth.

NICOBAR. Hypocrite!

CRASSUS. Humbug!

LYSISTRATA. I wish your Majesty every success.

AMANDA. Hear hear! Fair play, boys. Why shouldnt he go into parliament with us?

BOANERGES. Well said! well said! Why not?

THE OTHER MALE MINISTERS. Ya-a-a-ah! [*They sit down in utter disgust*].

PROTEUS [*very sullen*] And when you are in Parliament, what then?

MAGNUS. There are several possibilities. I shall naturally endeavour to form a party. My son King Robert will have to call on some Party leader who can depend on the support of the House of Commons to form a Government. He may call on you. He may even call on me.

AMANDA [*breaks the glum silence by whistling a bar or two of the National Anthem*]!!

MAGNUS. Whatever happens, it will be a great relief to us to be able to speak out quite frankly about oneanother in public. You have never been able to tell the British people what you really think of me: no real criticism of the King is possible. I have never been able to speak my mind as to your various capacities and characters. All that reserve, that tedious affectation, that unwholesome concealment will end. I hope you look forward to our new footing as pleasurably as I do.

LYSISTRATA. I am delighted, sir. You will fight Breakages for me.

AMANDA. It will be awful fun.

BOANERGES. Now, Mr Prime Minister, we are waiting

for you. What have you to say about it?

PROTEUS [*rising and speaking slowly, with his brows deeply knitted*] Has Your Majesty got that ultimatum on you?

MAGNUS [*produces it from his breast pocket and presents it to him*]!

PROTEUS [*with measured emphasis, after tearing the paper up into four pieces at two deliberate strokes, and throwing the pieces away*] There is not going to be any abdication. There is not going to be any general election. There is not going to be any ultimatum. We go on as before. The crisis is a wash-out. [*To the King, with deadly concentration*] I will never forgive you for this. You stole your ace of trumps from the hand I played this morning. [*He takes his hat from the balustrade and goes away through the park*].

BOANERGES [*rising*] That was a very deplorable exhibition of temper on the part of the Prime Minister, sir. It was not the gesture of a Strong Man. I will remonstrate with him. You may depend on me. [*He takes his hat and follows Proteus in a serious and dignified manner*].

NICOBAR [*rising*] Well, I shall not say what I think. [*He is taking his hat when the King addresses him*].

MAGNUS. So I have not upset the apple cart after all, Mr Nicobar.

NICOBAR. You can upset it as soon as you like for all I care. I am going out of politics. Politics is a mug's game. [*He goes*].

CRASSUS [*rising reluctantly and taking his hat*] If Nick goes, I shall have to go too.

MAGNUS. Can you really tear yourself away from politics?

CRASSUS. Only too glad to be well out of them, if Breakages will let me. They shoved me into it; and I daresay theyll find another job for me. [*He goes*].

PLINY [*cheerful to the last as he, too, goes for his hat*] Well, I am glad nothing's happened. You know, sir, nothing ever really does happen in the Cabinet. Never mind their bit of temper. Theyll feed out of your hand tomorrow. [*He goes*].

BALBUS [*after taking his hat*] Now that theyre all gone I dont mind saying that if anything should ever happen to the throne, and your Majesty should become a President with a Cabinet to pick, you might easily find a worse Home Secretary than me, with all my faults.

MAGNUS. I shall bear it in mind. By the way, if you should happen to overtake the Prime Minister, will you be so good as to remind him that we quite forgot to settle that little affair of the proposal of America to annex the British Commonwealth.

BALBUS. By the Lord, so we did! Well, thats a good one! Ha ha! Ha ha ha ha ha! [*He goes out laughing heartily*].

MAGNUS. They dont take it in, Lizzie: not one bit. It is as if another planet were crashing into us. The kingdom and the power and the glory will pass from us and leave us naked face to face with our real selves at last.

LYSISTRATA. So much the better, if by our real selves you mean the old English stock that was unlike any other. Nowadays men all over the world are as much alike as hotel dinners. It's no use pretending that the America of George Washington is going to swallow up the England of Queen Anne. The America of George Washington is as dead as Queen Anne. What they call an American is only a wop pretending to be a Pilgrim Father. He is no more Uncle Jonathan than you are John Bull.

MAGNUS. Yes: we live in a world of wops, all melting into one another; and when all the frontiers are down London may be outvoted by Tennessee, and all the other places where we still madly teach our children the mentality of an eighteenth century village school.

LYSISTRATA. Never fear, sir. It is not the most ignorant national crowd that will come out on top, but the best power station; for you cant do without power stations, and you cant run them on patriotic songs and hatred of the foreigner, and guff and bugaboo, though you can run nationalism on nothing else. But I am heartbroken at your not coming into the House with us to keep old England in front and lead a new Party against Breakages [*tears come into her eyes*].

MAGNUS [*patting her consolingly on the back*] That would

have been splendid, wouldnt it? But I am too old fashioned. This is a farce that younger men must finish.

AMANDA [*taking her arm*] Come home with me, dear. I will sing to you until you cant help laughing. Come.

Lysistrata pockets her handkerchief; shakes the King's hands impulsively; and goes with Amanda. The King plunges into deep thought. Presently the Queen comes back.

THE QUEEN. Now Magnus: it's time to dress for dinner.

MAGNUS [*much disturbed*] Oh, not now. I have something very big to think about. I dont want any dinner.

THE QUEEN [*peremptorily*] No dinner! Did anyone ever hear of such a thing! You know you will not sleep if you think after seven o'clock.

MAGNUS [*worried*] But really, Jemima—

THE QUEEN [*going to him and taking his arm*] Now, now, now! dont be naughty. I mustnt be late for dinner. Come on, like a good little boy.

The King, with a grimace of hopeless tenderness, allows himself to be led away.

GETTING MARRIED

A CONVERSATION
(A DISQUISITORY PLAY)

Written in 1908

First Performed London 1908

PREFACE TO GETTING MARRIED

THE REVOLT AGAINST MARRIAGE

THERE is no subject on which more dangerous nonsense is talked and thought than marriage. If the mischief stopped at talking and thinking it would be bad enough; but it goes further, into disastrous anarchical action. Because our marriage law is inhuman and unreasonable to the point of downright abomination, the bolder and more rebellious spirits form illicit unions, defiantly sending cards round to their friends announcing what they have done. Young women come to me and ask me whether I think they ought to consent to marry the man they have decided to live with; and they are perplexed and astonished when I, who am supposed (heaven knows why!) to have the most advanced views attainable on the subject, urge them on no account to compromize themselves without the security of an authentic wedding ring. They cite the example of George Eliot, who formed an illicit union with Lewes. They quote a saying attributed to Nietzsche, that a married philosopher is ridiculous, though the men of their choice are not philosophers. When they finally give up the idea of reforming our marriage institutions by private enterprise and personal righteousness, and consent to be led to the Registry or even to the altar, they insist on first arriving at an explicit understanding that both parties are to be perfectly free to sip every flower and change every hour, as their fancy may dictate, in spite of the legal bond. I do not observe that their unions prove less monogamic than other people's: rather the contrary, in fact; consequently, I do not know whether they make less fuss than ordinary people when either party claims the benefit of the treaty; but the existence of the treaty shews the same anarchical notion that the law can be set aside by any two private persons by the simple process of promising one another to ignore it.

MARRIAGE NEVERTHELESS INEVITABLE

Now most laws are, and all laws ought to be, stronger than the strongest individual. Certainly the marriage law is.

The only people who successfully evade it are those who actually avail themselves of its shelter by pretending to be married when they are not, and by Bohemians who have no position to lose and no career to be closed. In every other case open violation of the marriage laws means either downright ruin or such inconvenience and disablement as a prudent man or woman would get married ten times over rather than face. And these disablements and inconveniences are not even the price of freedom; for, as Brieux has shewn so convincingly in Les Hannetons, an avowedly illicit union is often found in practice to be as tyrannical and as hard to escape from as the worst legal one.

We may take it then that when a joint domestic establishment, involving questions of children or property, is contemplated, marriage is in effect compulsory upon all normal people; and until the law is altered there is nothing for us but to make the best of it as it stands. Even when no such establishment is desired, clandestine irregularities are negligible as an alternative to marriage. How common they are nobody knows; for in spite of the powerful protection afforded to the parties by the law of libel, and the readiness of society on various other grounds to be hoodwinked by the keeping up of the very thinnest appearances, most of them are probably never suspected. But they are neither dignified nor safe and comfortable, which at once rules them out for normal decent people. Marriage remains practically inevitable; and the sooner we acknowledge this, the sooner we shall set to work to make it decent and reasonable.

WHAT DOES THE WORD MARRIAGE MEAN?

However much we may all suffer through marriage, most of us think so little about it that we regard it as a fixed part of the order of nature, like gravitation. Except for this error, which may be regarded as constant, we use the word with reckless looseness, meaning a dozen different things by it, and yet always assuming that to a respectable man it can have only one meaning. The pious citizen, suspecting the Socialist (for example) of unmentionable things, and asking him heatedly whether he wishes to abolish marriage, is infuriated by a sense of unanswerable quibbling when the Socialist asks him what particular variety of marriage he means: English civil marriage, sacramental marriage, indissoluble Roman Catholic marriage, marriage of divorced persons, Scotch marriage, Irish marriage, French, German, Turkish, or South Dakotan marriage. In Sweden, one of the most highly civilized countries in the world, a marriage is dissolved if both parties wish it, without any question of conduct. That is what marriage means in Sweden. In Clapham that is what they call by the senseless name of Free Love. In the British Empire we have unlimited Kulin polygamy, Muslim polygamy limited to four wives, child marriages, and, nearer home, marriages of first cousins: all of them abominations in the eyes of many worthy persons. Not only may the respectable British champion of marriage mean any of these widely different institutions; sometimes he does not mean marriage at all. He means monogamy, chastity, temperance, respectability, morality, Christianity, anti-socialism, and a dozen other things that have no necessary connection with marriage. He often means something that he dare not avow: ownership of the person of another human being, for instance. And he never tells the truth about his own marriage either to himself or anyone else.

With those individualists who in the nineteenth century dreamt of doing away with marriage altogether on the ground that it is a private concern between the two parties with which society has nothing to do, there is now no need to deal. The vogue of "the self-regarding action" has passed; and it may be assumed without argument that unions for the purpose of establishing a family will continue to be registered and regulated by the State. Such registration is marriage, and will continue to be called marriage long after the conditions of the registration have changed so much that no citizen now living would recognize them as marriage conditions at all if he revisited the earth. There is therefore no question of abolishing marriage; but there is a very pressing question of improving its conditions. I have never met anybody really in favor of maintaining marriage as it exists in England today. A Roman Catholic may obey his Church by assenting verbally to the doctrine of indissoluble marriage. But nobody worth counting believes directly, frankly, and instinctively that when a person commits a murder and is put into prison for twenty years for it, the free and innocent husband or wife of that murderer should remain bound by the marriage. To put it briefly, a contract for better for worse is a contract that should not be tolerated. As a matter of fact it is not tolerated fully even by the Roman Catholic Church; for Roman Catholic marriages can be dissolved, if not by the temporal Courts, by the Pope. Indissoluble marriage is an academic figment, advocated only by celibates and by comfortably married people who imagine that if other couples are uncomfortable it must be their own fault, just as rich people are apt to imagine that if other people are poor it serves them right. There is always some means of dissolution. The conditions of dissolution may vary widely, from those on which Henry VIII. procured his divorce from Katharine of Aragon to the pleas on which American wives obtain divorces (for instance, "mental anguish" caused by the husband's neglect to cut his toe-nails); but there is always some point at which the theory of the inviolable better-for-worse marriage breaks down in practice. South Carolina has indeed passed what is called a freak law declaring that a marriage shall not be dissolved under any circumstances; but such an absurdity will probably be repealed or amended by sheer force of circumstances before these words are in print. The only question to be considered is, What shall the conditions of the dissolution be?

SURVIVALS OF SEX SLAVERY

If we adopt the common romantic assumption that the object of marriage is bliss, then the very strongest reason for dissolving a marriage is that it shall be disagreeable to one or other or both of the parties. If we accept the view that the object of marriage is to provide for the production and rearing of children, then childlessness should be a conclusive reason for dissolution. As neither of these causes entitles married persons to divorce it is at once clear that our marriage law is not founded on either assumption. What it is really founded on is the morality of the tenth commandment, which Englishwomen will one day succeed in obliterating from the walls of our churches by refusing to enter any building where they are publicly classed with a man's house, his ox, and his ass, as his purchased chattels. In this morality female adultery is malversation by the woman and theft by the man, whilst male adultery with an unmarried woman is not an offence at all. But though this is not only the theory of our marriage laws, but the practical morality of many of us, it is no longer an avowed morality, nor does its persistence depend on marriage; for the abolition of marriage would, other things remaining unchanged, leave women more effectually enslaved than they now are. We shall come to the question of the economic dependence of women on men later on; but at present we had better confine ourselves to the theories of marriage which we are not ashamed to acknowledge and defend, and upon which, therefore, marriage reformers will be obliged to proceed.

We may, I think, dismiss from the field of practical politics the extreme sacerdotal view of marriage as a sacred and indissoluble covenant, because, though reinforced by unhappy marriages as all fanaticisms are reinforced by human sacrifices, it has been reduced to a private and socially inoperative eccentricity by the introduction of civil marriage and divorce. Theoretically, our civilly married couples are to a Catholic as unmarried couples are: that is, they are living in open sin. Practically, civilly married couples are received in society, by Catholics and everyone else, precisely as sacramentally married couples are; and so are people who have divorced their wives or husbands and married again. And yet marriage is enforced by public opinion with such ferocity that the least suggestion of laxity in its support is fatal to even the highest and strongest reputations, although laxity of conduct is winked at with grinning indulgence; so that we find the austere Shelley denounced as a fiend in human form, whilst Nelson, who openly left his wife and formed a *menage à trois* with Sir William and Lady Hamilton, was idolized. Shelley might have had an illegitimate child in every county in England if he had done so frankly as a sinner. His unpardonable offence was that he attacked marriage as an institution. We feel a strange anguish of terror and hatred against him, as against one who threatens us with a mortal injury. What is the element in his proposals that produces this effect?

The answer of the specialists is the one already alluded to: that the attack on marriage is an attack on property; so that Shelley was something more hateful to a husband than a horse thief: to wit, a wife thief, and something more hateful to a wife than a burglar: namely, one who would steal her husband's house from over her head, and leave her destitute and nameless on the streets. Now, no doubt this accounts for a good deal of anti-Shelleyan prejudice: a prejudice so deeply rooted in our habits that, as I have shewn in my play, men who are bolder freethinkers than Shelley himself can no more bring themselves to commit adultery than to commit any common theft, whilst women who loathe sex slavery more fiercely than Mary Wollstonecraft are unable to face the insecurity and discredit of the vagabondage which is the masterless woman's only alternative to celibacy. But in spite of all this there is a revolt against marriage which has spread so rapidly within my recollection that though we all still assume the existence of a huge and dangerous majority which regards the least hint of scepticism as to the beauty and holiness of marriage as infamous and abhorrent, I sometimes wonder why it is so difficult to find an authentic living member of this dreaded army of convention outside the ranks of the people who never think about public questions at all, and who, for all their numerical weight and apparently invincible prejudices, accept social changes today as tamely as their forefathers accepted the Reformation under Henry and Edward, the Restoration under Mary, and, after Mary's death, the shandygaff which Elizabeth compounded from both doctrines and called the Articles of the Church of England. If matters were left to these simple folk, there would never be any changes at all; and society would perish like a snake that could not cast its skins. Nevertheless the snake does change its skin in spite of them; and there are signs that our marriage-law skin is causing discomfort to thoughtful people and will presently be cast whether the others are satisfied with it or not. The question therefore arises: What is there in marriage that makes the thoughtful people so uncomfortable?

THE NEW ATTACK ON MARRIAGE

The answer to this question is an answer which everybody knows and nobody likes to give. What is driving our ministers of religion and statesmen to blurt it out at last is the plain fact that marriage is now beginning to depopulate the country with such alarming rapidity that we are forced to throw aside our modesty like people who, awakened by an alarm of fire, rush into the streets in their nightdresses or in no dresses at all. The fictitious Free Lover, who was supposed to attack marriage because it thwarted his inordinate affections and prevented him from making life a carnival, has vanished and given place to the very real, very strong, very austere avenger of outraged decency who declares that the licentiousness of marriage, now that it no longer recruits the race, is destroying it.

As usual, this change of front has not yet been noticed by our newspaper controversialists and by the suburban season-ticket holders whose minds the newspapers make. They still defend the citadel on the side on which nobody is attacking it, and leave its weakest front undefended.

The religious revolt against marriage is a very old one. Christianity began with a fierce attack on marriage; and to this day the celibacy of the Roman Catholic priesthood is a standing protest against its compatibility with the higher life. St Paul's reluctant sanction of marriage; his personal protest that he countenanced it of necessity and against his own conviction; his contemptuous "better to marry than to burn" is only out of date in respect of his belief that the end of the world was at hand and that there was therefore no longer any population question. His instinctive recoil from its worst aspect as a slavery to pleasure which induces two people to accept slavery to one another has remained an active force in the world to this day, and is now stirring more uneasily than ever. We have more and more Pauline celibates whose objection to marriage is the intolerable indignity of being supposed to desire or live the married life as ordinarily conceived. Every thoughtful and observant minister of religion is troubled by the determination of his flock to regard marriage as a sanctuary for pleasure, seeing as he does that the known libertines of his parish are visibly suffering much less from intemperance than many of the married people who stigmatize them as monsters of vice.

A FORGOTTEN CONFERENCE OF MARRIED MEN

The late Hugh Price Hughes, an eminent Methodist divine, once organized in London a conference of respectable men to consider the subject. Nothing came of it (nor indeed could have come of it in the absence of women); but it had its value as giving the young sociologists present, of whom I was one, an authentic notion of what a picked audience of respectable men understood by married life. It was certainly a staggering revelation. Peter the Great would have been shocked; Byron would have been horrified; Don Juan would have fled from the conference into a monastery. The respectable men all regarded the marriage ceremony as a rite which absolved them from the laws of health and temperance; inaugurated a life-long honeymoon; and placed their pleasures on exactly the same footing as their prayers. It seemed entirely proper and natural to them that out of every twenty-four hours of their lives they should pass eight shut up in one room with their wives alone, and this, not birdlike, for the mating season, but all the year round and every year. How they settled even such minor questions as to which party should decide whether and how much the window should be open and how many blankets should be on the bed, and at what hour they should go to bed and get up so as to avoid disturbing one another's sleep, seemed insoluble questions to me. But the members of the conference did not seem to mind. They were content to have the whole national housing problem treated on a basis of one room for two people. That was the essence of marriage for them.

Please remember, too, that there was nothing in their circumstances to check intemperance. They were men of business; that is, men for the most part engaged in routine work which exercized neither their minds nor their bodies to the full pitch of their capacities. Compared with statesmen, first-rate professional men, artists, and even with laborers and artisans as far as muscular exertion goes, they were underworked, and could spare the fine edge of their faculties and the last few inches of their chests without being any the less fit for their daily routine. If I had adopted their habits, a startling deterioration would have appeared in my writing before the end of a fortnight, and frightened me back to what they would have considered an impossible asceticism. But they paid no penalty of which they were conscious. They had as much health as they wanted: that is, they did not feel the need of a doctor. They enjoyed their smokes, their meals, their respectable clothes, their affectionate games with their children, their prospects of larger profits or higher salaries, their Saturday half holidays and Sunday walks, and the rest of it. They did less than two hours work a day and took from seven to nine office hours to do it in. And they were no good for any mortal purpose except to go on doing it. They were respectable only by the standard they themselves had set. Considered seriously as electors governing an empire through their votes, and choosing and maintaining its religious and moral institutions by their powers of social persecution, they were a black-coated army of calamity. They were incapable of comprehending the industries they were engaged in, the laws under which they lived, or the relation of their country to other countries. They lived the lives of old men contentedly. They were timidly conservative at the age at which every healthy human being ought to be obstreperously revolutionary. And their wives went through the routine of the kitchen, nursery, and drawing-room just as they went through the routine of the office. They had all, as they called it, settled down, like balloons that had lost their lifting margin of gas; and it was evident that the process of settling down would go on until they settled into their graves. They read old-fashioned newspapers with effort, and were just taking with avidity to a new sort of paper, costing a halfpenny, which they believed to be extraordinarily bright and attractive, and which never really succeeded until it became extremely dull, discarding all serious news and replacing it by vapid tittle-tattle, and substituting for political articles informed by at least some pretence of knowledge of economics, history, and constitutional law, such paltry follies and sentimentalities, snobberies and partisaneries, as ignorance can understand and irresponsibility relish.

What they called patriotism was a conviction that because they were born in Tooting or Camberwell, they were the natural superiors of Beethoven, of Rodin, of Ibsen, of Tolstoy and all other benighted foreigners. Those of them who did not think it wrong to go to the theatre liked above everything a play in which the hero was called Dick; was continually fingering a briar pipe; and, after being overwhelmed with admiration and affection through three acts, was finally rewarded with the legal possession of a pretty heroine's person on the strength of a staggering lack of virtue. Indeed their only conception of the meaning of the word virtue was abstention from stealing other men's wives or from refusing to marry their daughters.

As to law, religion, ethics, and constitutional government, any counterfeit could impose on them. Any atheist could pass himself off on them as a bishop, any anarchist as a judge, any despot as a Whig, any sentimental socialist as a Tory, any philtre-monger or witch-finder as a man of science, any phrase-maker as a statesman. Those who did not believe the story of Jonah and the great fish were all the readier to believe that metals can be transmuted and all diseases cured by radium, and that men can live for two hundred years by drinking sour milk. Even these credulities involved too severe an intellectual effort for many of them: it was easier to grin and believe nothing. They maintained their respect for themselves by "playing the game" (that is, doing what everybody else did), and by being good judges of hats, ties, dogs, pipes, cricket, gardens, flowers, and the like. They were capable of discussing each other's solvency and respectability with some shrewdness, and could carry out quite complicated systems of paying visits and "knowing" one another. They felt a little vulgar when they spent a day at Margate, and quite distinguished and travelled when they spent it at Boulogne. They were, except as to their clothes, "not particular": that is, they could put up with ugly sights and sounds, unhealthy smells, and inconvenient houses, with inhuman apathy and callousness. They had, as to adults, a theory that human nature is so poor that it is useless to try to make the world any better, whilst as to children they believed that if they were only sufficiently lectured and whipped, they could be brought to a state of moral perfection such as no fanatic has ever ascribed to his deity. Though they were not intentionally malicious, they practised the most appalling cruelties from mere thoughtlessness, thinking nothing of imprisoning men and women for periods up to twenty years for breaking into their houses; of treating their children as wild beasts to be tamed by a system of blows and imprisonment which they called education; and of keeping pianos in their houses, not for musical purposes, but to torment their daughters with a senseless stupidity that would have revolted an inquisitor.

In short, dear reader, they were very like you and me. I could fill a hundred pages with the tale of our imbecilities and still leave much untold; but what I have set down here haphazard is enough to condemn the system that produced us. The corner-stone of that system was the family and the institution of marriage as we have it today in England.

HEARTH AND HOME

There is no shirking it: if marriage cannot be made to produce something better than we are, marriage will have to go, or else the nation will have to go. It is no use talking of honor, virtue, purity, and wholesome, sweet, clean English home lives when what is meant is simply the habits I have described. The flat fact is that English home life today is neither honorable, virtuous, wholesome, sweet, clean, nor in any creditable way distinctively English. It is in many respects conspicuously the reverse; and the result of withdrawing children from it completely at an early age, and sending them to a public school and then to a university, does, in spite of the fact that these institutions are class warped and in some respects quite abominably corrupt, produce sociabler men. Women, too, are improved by the escape from home provided by women's colleges; but as very few of them are fortunate enough to enjoy this advantage, most women are so thoroughly home-bred as to be unfit for human society. So little is expected of them that in Sheridan's School for Scandal we hardly notice that the heroine is a female cad, as detestable and dishonorable in her repentance as she is vulgar and silly in her naughtiness. It was left to an abnormal critic like George Gissing to point out the glaring fact that in the collection of life studies of Victorian women to be found in the novels of Dickens, the most convincingly real ones are either vilely unamiable or comically contemptible; whilst his attempts to manufacture admirable heroines by idealizations of home-bred womanhood are not only absurd but not even pleasantly absurd: one has no patience with them.

As all this is corrigible by reducing home life and domestic sentiment to something like reasonable proportions in the life of the individual, the danger of it does not lie in human nature. Home life as we understand it is no more natural to us than a cage is natural to a cockatoo. Its grave danger to the nation lies in its narrow views, its unnaturally sustained and spitefully jealous concupiscences, its petty tyrannies, its false social pretences, its endless grudges and squabbles, its sacrifice of the boy's future by setting him to earn money to help the family when he should be in training for his adult life (remember the boy Dickens and the blacking factory), and of the girl's chances by making her a slave to sick or selfish parents, its unnatural packing into little brick boxes of little parcels of humanity of ill-assorted ages, with the old scolding or beating the young for behaving like young people, and the young hating and thwarting the old for behaving like old people, and all the other ills, mentionable and unmentionable, that arise from excessive segregation. It sets these evils up as benefits and blessings representing the highest attainable degree of honor and virtue, whilst any criticism of or revolt against them is savagely persecuted as the extremity of vice. The revolt, driven under ground and exacerbated, produces debauchery veiled by hyprocisy, an overwhelming demand for licentious theatrical entertainments which no censorship can stem, and, worst of all, a confusion of virtue with the mere morality that steals its name until the real thing is loathed because the imposture is loathsome. Literary traditions spring up in which the libertine and profligate—Tom Jones and Charles Surface—are the heroes, and decorous, law-abiding persons—Blifil and Joseph Surface—are the villains and butts. People like to believe that Nell Gwynne has every amiable quality and the Bishop's wife every odious one. Poor Mr Pecksniff, who is generally no worse than a humbug with a turn for pompous talking, is represented as a criminal instead of as a very typical English paterfamilias keeping a roof over the head of himself and his daughters by inducing people to pay him more for his services than they are worth. In the extreme instances of reaction against convention, female murderers get sheaves of offers of marriage; and when Nature throws up that rare phenomenon, an unscrupulous libertine, his success among "well brought-up" girls is so easy, and the devotion he inspires so extravagant, that it is impossible not to see that the revolt against conventional respectability has transfigured a commonplace rascal into a sort of Anarchist Savior. As to the respectable voluptuary, who joins Omar Khayyam clubs and vibrates to Swinburne's invocation of Dolores to "come down and redeem us from virtue," he is to be found in every suburb.

TOO MUCH OF A GOOD THING

We must be reasonable in our domestic ideals. I do not think that life at a public school is altogether good for a boy any more than barrack life is altogether good for a soldier. But neither is home life altogether good. Such good as it does, I should say, is due to its freedom from the very atmosphere it professes to supply. That atmosphere is usually described as an atmosphere of love; and this definition should be sufficient to put any sane person on guard against it. The people who talk and write as if the highest attainable state is that of a family stewing in love continuously from the cradle to the grave, can hardly have given five minutes serious consideration to so outrageous a proposition. They cannot have even made up their minds as to what they mean by love; for when they expatiate on their thesis they are sometimes talking about kindness, and sometimes about mere appetite. In either sense they are equally far from the realities of life. No healthy man or animal is occupied with love in any sense for more than a very small fraction indeed of the time he devotes to business and to recreations wholly unconnected with love. A wife entirely preoccupied with her affection for her husband, a mother entirely preoccupied with her affection for her children, may be all very well in a book (for people who like that kind of book); but in actual life she is a nuisance. Husbands may escape from her when their business compels them to be away from home all day; but young children may be, and quite often are, killed by her cuddling and coddling and doctoring and preaching: above all, by her continuous attempts to excite precocious sentimentality, a practice as objectionable, and possibly as mischievous, as the worst tricks of the worst nursemaids.

LARGE AND SMALL FAMILIES

In most healthy families there is a revolt against this tendency. The exchanging of presents on birthdays and the like is barred by general consent, and the relations of the parties are placed by express treaty on an unsentimental footing.

Unfortunately this mitigation of family sentimentality is much more characteristic of large families than small ones. It used to be said that members of large families get on in the world; and it is certainly true that for purposes of social training a household of twenty surpasses a household of five as an Oxford College surpasses an eight-roomed house in a cheap street. Ten children, with the necessary adults, make a community in which an excess of sentimentality is impossible. Two children make a doll's house, in which both parents and children become morbid if they keep to themselves. What is more, when large families were the fashion, they were organized as tyrannies much more than as "atmospheres of love." Francis Place tells us that he kept out of his father's way because his father never passed a child within his reach without striking it; and though the case was an extreme one, it was an extreme that illustrated a tendency. Sir Walter Scott's father, when his son incautiously expressed some relish for his porridge, dashed a handful of salt into it with an instinctive sense that it was his duty as a father to prevent his son enjoying himself. Ruskin's mother gratified the sensual side of her maternal passion, not by cuddling her son, but by whipping him when he fell downstairs or was slack in learning the Bible off by heart; and this grotesque safety-valve for voluptuousness, mischievous as it was in many ways, had at least the advantage that the child did not enjoy it and was not debauched by it, as he would have been by transports of sentimentality.

But nowadays we cannot depend on these safeguards, such as they were. We no longer have large families: all the families are too small to give the children the necessary social training. The Roman father is out of fashion; and the whip and the cane are becoming discredited, not so much by the old arguments against corporal punishment (sound as these were) as by the gradual wearing away of the veil from the fact that flogging is a form of debauchery. The advocate of flogging as a punishment is now exposed to very disagreeable suspicions; and ever since Rousseau rose to the effort of making a certain very ridiculous confession on the subject, there has been a growing perception that child whipping, even for the children themselves, is not always the innocent and highminded practice it professes to be. At all events there is no getting away from the facts that families are smaller than they used to be, and that passions which formerly took effect in tyranny have been largely diverted into sentimentality. And though a little sentimentality may be a very good thing, chronic sentimentality is a horror, more dangerous, because more possible, than the erotomania which we all condemn when we are not thoughtlessly glorifying it as the ideal married state.

THE GOSPEL OF LAODICEA

Let us try to get at the root error of these false domestic doctrines. Why was it that the late Samuel Butler with a conviction that increased with his experience or life, preached the gospel of Laodicea, urging people to be temperate in what they called goodness as in everything else? Why is it that I, when I hear some well-meaning person exhort young people to make it a rule to do at least one kind action every day, feel very much as I should if I heard them persuade children to get drunk at least once every day? Apart from the initial absurdity of accepting as permanent a state of things in which there would be in this country misery enough to supply occasion for several thousand million kind actions per annum, the effect on the character of the doers of the actions would be so appalling, that one month of any serious attempt to carry out such counsel would probably bring about more stringent legislation against actions going beyond the strict letter of the law in the way of kindness than we have now against excess in the opposite direction.

There is no more dangerous mistake than the mistake of supposing that we cannot have too much of a good thing. The truth is, an immoderately good man is very much more dangerous than an immoderately bad man: that is why Savonarola was burnt and John of Leyden torn to pieces with red-hot pincers whilst multitudes of unredeemed rascals were being let off with clipped ears, burnt palms, a flogging, or a few years in the galleys. That is why Christianity never got any grip of the world until it virtually reduced its claims on the ordinary citizen's attention to a couple of hours every seventh day, and let him alone on week-days. If the fanatics who are preoccupied day in and day out with their salvation were healthy, virtuous, and wise, the Laodiceanism of the ordinary man might be regarded as a deplorable shortcoming; but, as a matter of fact, no more frightful misfortune could threaten us than a general spread of fanaticism. What people call goodness has to be kept in check just as carefully as what they call badness; for the human constitution will not stand very much of either without serious psychological mischief, ending in insanity or crime. The fact that the insanity may be privileged, as Savonarola's was up to the point of wrecking the social life of Florence, does not alter the case. We always hesitate to treat a dangerously good man as a lunatic because he may turn out to be a prophet in the true sense: that is, a man of exceptional sanity who is in the right when we are in the wrong. However necessary it may have been to get rid of Savonarola, it was foolish to poison Socrates and burn St Joan of Arc. But it is none the less necessary to take a firm stand against the monstrous proposition that because certain attitudes and sentiments may be heroic and admirable at some momentous crisis, they should or can be maintained at the same pitch continuously through life. A life spent in prayer and almsgiving is really as insane as a life spent in cursing and picking pockets: the effect of everybody doing it would be equally disastrous. The superstitious tolerance so long accorded to monks and nuns is inevitably giving way to a very general and very natural practice of confiscating their retreats and expelling them from their country, with the result that they come to England and Ireland, where they are partly unnoticed and partly encouraged because they conduct technical schools and teach our girls softer speech and gentler manners than our comparatively ruffianly elementary teachers. But they are still full of the notion that because it is possible for men to attain the summit of Mont Blanc and stay there for an hour, it is possible for them to live there. Children are punished and scolded for not living there; and adults take serious offence if it is not assumed that they live there.

As a matter of fact, ethical strain is just as bad for us as physical strain. It is desirable that the normal pitch of conduct at which men are not conscious of being particularly virtuous, although they feel mean when they fall below it, should be raised as high as possible; but it is not desirable that they should attempt to live above this pitch any more than that they should habitually walk at the rate of five miles an hour or carry a hundredweight continually on their backs. Their normal condition should be in nowise difficult or remarkable; and it is a perfectly sound instinct that leads us to mistrust the good man as much as the bad man, and to object to the clergyman who is pious extra-professionally as much as to the professional pugilist who is quarrelsome and violent in private life. We do not want good men and bad men any more than we want giants and dwarfs. What we do want is a high quality for our normal: that is, people who can be much better than what we now call respectable without self-sacrifice. Conscious goodness, like conscious muscular effort, may be of use in emergencies; but for everyday national use it is negligible; and its effect on the character of the individual may easily be disastrous.

FOR BETTER FOR WORSE

It would be hard to find any document in practical daily

use in which these obvious truths seem so stupidly overlooked as they are in the marriage service. As we have seen, the stupidity is only apparent: the service was really only an honest attempt to make the best of a commercial contract of property and slavery by subjecting it to some religious restraint and elevating it by some touch of poetry. But the actual result is that when two people are under the influence of the most violent, most insane, most delusive, and most transient of passions, they are required to swear that they will remain in that excited, abnormal, and exhausting condition continuously until death do them part. And though of course nobody expects them to do anything so impossible and so unwholesome, yet the law that regulates their relations, and the public opinion that regulates that law, is actually founded on the assumption that the marriage vow is not only feasible but beautiful and holy, and that if they are false to it, they deserve no sympathy and no relief. If all married people really lived together, no doubt the mere force of facts would make an end to this inhuman nonsense in a month, if not sooner; but it is very seldom brought to that test. The typical British husband sees much less of his wife than he does of his business partner, his fellow clerk, or whoever works beside him day by day. Man and wife do not, as a rule, live together: they only breakfast together, dine together, and sleep in the same room. In most cases the woman knows nothing of the man's working life and he knows nothing of her working life (he calls it her home life). It is remarkable that the very people who romance most absurdly about the closeness and sacredness of the marriage tie are also those who are most convinced that the man's sphere and the woman's sphere are so entirely separate that only in their leisure moments can they ever be together. A man as intimate with his own wife as a magistrate is with his clerk, or a Prime Minister with the leader of the Opposition, is a man in ten thousand. The majority of married couples never get to know one another at all: they only get accustomed to having the same house, the same children, and the same income, which is quite a different matter. The comparatively few men who work at home—writers, artists, and to some extent clergymen—have to effect some sort of segregation within the house or else run a heavy risk of overstraining their domestic relations. When the pair is so poor that it can afford only a single room, the strain is intolerable: violent quarrelling is the result. Very few couples can live in a single-roomed tenement without exchanging blows quite frequently. In the leisured classes there is often no real family life at all. The boys are at a public school; the girls are in the schoolroom in charge of a governess; the husband is at his club or in a set which is not his wife's; and the institution of marriage enjoys the credit of a domestic peace which is hardly more intimate than the relations of prisoners in the same gaol or guests at the same garden party. Taking these two cases of the single room and the unearned income as the extremes, we might perhaps locate at a guess whereabout on the scale between them any particular family stands. But it is clear enough that the one-roomed end, though its conditions enable the marriage vow to be carried out with the utmost attainable exactitude, is far less endurable in practice, and far more mischievous in its effect on the parties concerned, and through them on the community, than the other end. Thus we see that the revolt against marriage is by no means only a revolt against its sordidness as a survival of sex slavery. It may even plausibly be maintained that this is precisely the part of it that works most smoothly in practice. The revolt is also against its sentimentality, its romance, its Amorism, even against its enervating happiness.

WANTED: AN IMMORAL STATESMAN

We now see that the statesman who undertakes to deal with marriage will have to face an amazingly complicated public opinion. In fact, he will have to leave opinion as far as possible out of the question, and deal with human nature instead. For even if there could be any real public opinion in a society like ours, which is a mere mob of classes, each with its own habits and prejudices, it would be at best a jumble of superstitions and interests, taboos and hypocrisies, which could not be reconciled in any coherent enactment. It would probably proclaim passionately that it does not matter in the least what sort of children we have, or how few or how many, provided the children are legitimate. Also that it does not matter in the least what sort of adults we have, provided they are married. No statesman worth the name can possibly act on these views. He is bound to prefer one healthy illegitimate child to ten rickety legitimate ones, and one energetic and capable unmarried couple to a dozen inferior apathetic husbands and wives. If it could be proved that illicit unions produce three children each and marriages only one and a half, he would be bound to encourage illicit unions and discourage and even penalize marriage. The common notion that the existing forms of marriage are not political contrivances, but sacred ethical obligations to which everything, even the very existence of the human race, must be sacrificed if necessary (and this is what the vulgar morality we mostly profess on the subject comes to) is one on which no sane Government could act for a moment; and yet it influences, or is believed to influence, so many votes, that no Government will touch the marriage question if it can possibly help it, even when there is a demand for the extension of marriage, as in the case of the recent long-delayed Act legalizing marriage with a deceased wife's sister. When a reform in the other direction is needed (for example, an extension of divorce), not even the existence of the most unbearable hardships will induce our statesmen to move so long as the victims submit sheepishly, though when they take the remedy into their own hands an inquiry is soon begun. But what is now making some action in the matter imperative is neither the sufferings of those who are tied for life to criminals, drunkards, physically unsound and dangerous mates, and worthless and unamiable people generally, nor the immorality of the couples condemned to celibacy by separation orders which do not annul their marriages, but the fall in the birth-rate. Public opinion will not help us out of this difficulty: on the contrary, it will, if it be allowed, punish anybody who mentions it. When Zola tried to repopulate France by writing a novel in praise of parentage, the only comment made here was that the book could not possibly be translated into English, as its subject was too improper.

THE LIMITS OF DEMOCRACY

Now if England had been governed in the past by statesmen willing to be ruled by such public opinion as that, she would have been wiped off the political map long ago. The modern notion that democracy means governing a country according to the ignorance of its majorities is never more disastrous than when there is some question of sexual morals to be dealt with. The business of a democratic statesman is not, as some of us seem to think, to convince the voters that he knows no better than they as to the methods of attaining their common ends, but on the contrary to convince them that he knows much better than they do, and therefore differs from them on every possible question of method. The voter's duty is to take care that the Government consists of men whom he can trust to devize or support institutions making for the common welfare. This is highly skilled work; and to be governed by people who set about it as the man in the street would set about it is to make straight for "red ruin and the breaking up of laws." Voltaire said that Mr Everybody is wiser than anybody; and whether he is or not, it is his will that must prevail; but the will and the way are two very different things. For example, it is the will of the people on a hot day that the means of relief from the effects of the heat should be within the reach of everybody. Nothing could be more innocent, more hygienic, more important to the social welfare. But the way of the people on such occasions is mostly to drink large quantities of beer, or, among the more luxurious classes, iced claret cup, lemon squashes, and the like. To take a moral illustration, the will to suppress misconduct and secure efficiency in work is general and salutary; but the notion that the best and only effective way is by complaining, scolding, punishing, and revenging is equally general. When Mrs Squeers opened an abscess on her pupil's head with an inky penknife, her object was entirely laudable: her heart was in the right place: a statesman interfering with her on the ground that he did not want the boy cured would have deserved impeachment for gross tyranny. But a statesman tolerating amateur surgical practice with inky penknives in school would be a very bad Minister of Education. It is on the question of method that your expert comes in; and though I am democrat enough to insist that he must first convince a representative body of amateurs that his way is the right way and Mrs Squeers's way the wrong way, yet I would not have them assume that Mrs Squeers's amateur way is likely to be the right way because shc belongs to the democracy and the Minister to the bureaucracy, or that any other test is to be applied to it except the test of its effect on human welfare.

THE SCIENCE AND ART OF POLITICS

Political Science means nothing else than the devizing of the best ways of fulfilling the will of the world; and, I repeat, it is skilled work. Once the way is discovered, the methods laid down, and the machinery provided, the work of the statesman is done, and that of the official begins. To illustrate, there is no need for the police officer who governs the street traffic to be or to know any better than the people who obey the wave of his hand. All concerted action involves subordination and the appointment of directors at whose signal the others will act. There is no more need for them to be superior to the rcst than for the keystone of an arch to be of harder stone than the coping. But when it comes to devizing the directions which are to be obeyed: that is, to making new institutions and scrapping old ones, then you need aristocracy in the sense of government by the best. A military state organized so as to carry out exactly the impulses of the average soldier would not last a year. The result of trying to make the Church of England reflect the notions of the average churchgoer has reduced it to a cipher except for the purposes of a petulantly irreligious social and political club. Democracy as to the thing to be done may be inevitable (hence the vital need for a democracy of supermen); but democracy as to the way to do it is like letting the passengers drive the train: it can only end in collision and wreck. As a matter of fact, we obtain reforms (such as they are), not by allowing the electorate to draft statutes, but by persuading it that a certain minister and his cabinet are gifted with sufficient political sagacity to find out how to produce the desired result. And the usual penalty of taking advantage of this power to reform our institutions is defeat by a vehement "swing of the pendulum" at the next election. Therein lies the peril and the glory of democratic statesmanship. A statesman who confines himself to popular legislation—or, for the matter of that, a playwright who confines himself to popular plays—is like a blind man's dog who goes wherever the blind man pulls him, on the ground that both of them want to go to the same place.

WHY STATESMEN SHIRK THE MARRIAGE QUESTION

The reform of marriage, then, will be a very splendid and very hazardous adventure for the Prime Minister who takes it in hand. He will be posted on every hoarding and denounced in every Opposition paper, especially in the sporting papers, as the destroyer of the home, the family, of decency, of morality, of chastity and what not. All the commonplaces of the modern anti-Socialist Noodle's Oration will be hurled at him. And he will have to proceed without the slightest concession to it, giving the noodles nothing but their due in the assurance "I know how to attain our ends better than you," and staking his political life on the conviction carried by that assurance, which conviction will depend a good deal on the certainty with which it is made, which again can be attained only by studying the facts of marriage and understanding the needs of the nation. And, after all, he will find that the pious commonplaces on which he and the electorate are agreed conceal an utter difference in the real ends in view: his being public, far-sighted, and impersonal, and those of multitudes of the electorate narrow, personal, jealous, and corrupt. Under such circumstances, it is not to be wondered at that the mere mention of the marriage question makes a British Cabinet shiver with apprehension and hastily pass on to safer business. Nevertheless the reform of marriage cannot be put off for ever. When its hour comes, what are the points the Cabinet will have to take up?

THE QUESTION OF POPULATION

First, it will have to make up its mind as to how many people we want in the country. If we want less than at present, we must ascertain how many less; and if we allow the reduction to be made by the continued operation of the present sterilization of marriage, we must settle how the process is to be stopped when it has gone far enough. But if we desire to maintain the population at its present figure, or to increase it, we must take immediate steps to induce people of moderate means to marry earlier and to have more children. There is less urgency in the case of the very poor and the very rich. They breed recklessly: the rich because they can afford it, and the poor because they cannot afford the precautions by which the artisans and the middle classes avoid big families. Nevertheless the population declines, because the high birth-rate of the very poor is counterbalanced by a huge infantile-mortality in the slums, whilst the very rich are also the very few, and are becoming sterilized by the spreading revolt of their women against excessive childbearing—sometimes against any childbearing.

This last cause is important. It cannot be removed by any economic readjustment. If every family were provided with £10,000 a year tomorrow, women would still refuse more and more to continue bearing children until they are exhausted whilst numbers of others are bearing no children at all. Even if every woman bearing and rearing a valuable child received a handsome series of payments, thereby making motherhood a real profession as it ought to be, the number of women able or willing to give more of their lives to gestation and nursing than three or four children would cost them might not be very large if the advance in social organization and conscience indicated by such payments involved also the opening up of other means of livelihood to women. And it must be remembered that urban civilization itself, insofar as it is a method of evolution (and when it is not this, it is simply a nuisance), is a sterilizing process as far as numbers go. It is harder to keep up the supply of elephants than of sparrows and rabbits; and for the same reason it will be harder to keep up the supply of highly cultivated men and women than it now is of agricultural laborers. Bees get out of this difficulty by a special system of feeding which enables a queen bee to produce 4000 eggs a day whilst the other females lose their sex altogether and become workers supporting the males in luxury and idleness until the queen has found her mate, when the queen kills him and the quondam females kill all the rest (such at least are the accounts given by romantic naturalists of the matter).

THE RIGHT TO MOTHERHOOD

This system certainly shews a much higher development of social intelligence than our marriage system; but if it were physically possible to introduce it into human society it would be wrecked by an opposite and not less important revolt of women: that is, the revolt against compulsory barrenness. In this two classes of women are concerned: those who, though they have no desire for the presence or care of children, nevertheless feel that motherhood is an experience necessary to their complete psychical development and understanding of themselves and others, and those who, though unable to find or unwilling to entertain a husband, would like to occupy themselves with the rearing of children. My own experience of discussing this question leads me to believe that the one point on which all women are in furious secret rebellion against the existing law is the saddling of the right to a child with the obligation to become the servant of a man. Adoption, or the begging or buying or stealing of another woman's child, is no remedy: it does not provide the supreme experience of bearing the child. No political constitution will ever succeed or deserve to succeed unless it includes the recognition of an absolute right to sexual experience, and is untainted by the Pauline or romantic view of such experience as sinful in itself. And since this experience in its fullest sense must be carried in the case of women to the point of childbearing, it can only be reconciled with the acceptance of marriage with the child's father by legalizing polygyny, because there are more adult women in the country than men. Now though polygyny prevails throughout the greater part of the British Empire, and is as practicable here as in India, there is a good deal to be said against it, and still more to be felt. However, let us put our feelings aside for a moment, and consider the question politically.

MONOGAMY, POLYGYNY, AND POLYANDRY

The number of wives permitted to a single husband or of husbands to a single wife under a marriage system, is not an ethical problem: it depends solely on the proportion of the sexes in the population. If in consequence of a great war three-quarters of the men in this country were killed, it would be absolutely necessary to adopt the Mohammedan allowance of four wives to each man in order to recruit the population. The fundamental reason for not allowing women to risk their lives in battle and for giving them the first chance of escape in all dangerous emergencies: in short, for treating their lives as more valuable than male lives, is not in the least a chivalrous reason, though men may consent to it under the illusion of chivalry. It is a simple matter of necessity; for if a large proportion of women were killed or disabled, no possible readjustment of our marriage law could avert the depopulation and consequent political ruin of the country, because a woman with several husbands bears fewer children than a woman with one, whereas a man can produce as many families as he has wives. The natural foundation of the institution of monogamy is not any inherent viciousness in polygyny or polyandry, but the hard fact that men and women are born in about equal numbers. Unfortunately, we kill so many of our male children in infancy that we are left with a surplus of adult women which is sufficiently large to claim attention, and yet not large enough to enable every man to have two wives. Even if it were, we should be met by an economic difficulty. A Kaffir is rich in proportion to the number of his wives, because the women are the breadwinners. But in our civilization women are not paid for their social work in the bearing and rearing of children and the ordering of households: they are quartered on the wages of their husbands. At least four out of five of our men could not afford two wives unless their wages were nearly doubled. Would it not then be well to try unlimited polygyny; so that the remaining fifth could have as many wives apiece as they could afford? Let us see how this would work.

THE MALE REVOLT AGAINST POLYGYNY

Experience shews that women do not object to polygyny when it is customary: on the contrary, they are its most ardent supporters. The reason is obvious. The question, as it presents itself in practice to a woman, is whether it is better to have, say, a whole share in a tenth-rate man or a tenth share in a first-rate man. Substitute the word Income for the word Man, and you will have the question as it presents itself economically to the dependent woman. The woman whose instincts are maternal, who desires superior children more than anything else, never hesitates. She would take a thousandth share, if necessary, in a husband who was a man in a thousand, rather than have some comparatively weedy weakling all to herself. It is the comparatively weedy weakling, left mateless by polygyny, who objects. Thus, it was not the women of Salt Lake City nor even of America who attacked Mormon polygyny. It was the men. And very naturally. On the other hand, women object to polyandry, because polyandry enables the best women to monopolize all the men, just as polygyny enables the best men to monopolize all the women. That is why all our ordinary men and women are unanimous in defence of monogamy, the men because it excludes polygyny, and the women because it excludes polyandry. The women, left to themselves, would tolerate polygyny. The men, left to themselves, would tolerate polyandry. But polygyny would condemn a great many men, and polyandry a great many women, to the celibacy of neglect. Hence the resistance any attempt to establish unlimited polygyny always provokes, not from the best people but from the mediocrities and the inferiors. If we could get rid of our inferiors and screw up our average quality until mediocrity ceased to be a reproach, thus making every man reasonably eligible as a father and every woman reasonably desirable as a mother, polygyny and polyandry would immediately fall into sincere disrepute, because monogamy is so much more convenient and economical that nobody would want to share a husband or wife if he (or she) could have a sufficiently good one all to himself (or herself). Thus it appears that it is the scarcity of husbands or wives of high quality that leads women to polygyny and men to polyandry, and that if this scarcity were cured, monogamy, in the sense of having only one husband or wife at a time (facilities for changing are another matter), would be found satisfactory.

DIFFERENCE BETWEEN ORIENTAL AND OCCIDENTAL POLYGYNY

It may now be asked why the polygynist nations have not gravitated to monogamy, like the latter-day saints of Salt Lake City. The answer is not far to seek: their polygyny is limited. By the Mohammedan law a man cannot marry more than four wives; and by the unwritten law of necessity no man can keep more wives than he can afford; so that a man with four wives must be quite as exceptional in Asia as a man with a carriage-and-pair or a motor car is in Europe, where, nevertheless, we may all have as many carriages and motors as we can afford to pay for. Kulin polygyny, though unlimited, is not really a popular institution: if you are a person of high caste you pay another person of very august caste indeed to make your daughter momentarily one of his sixty or seventy momentary wives for the sake of ennobling your grandchildren; but this fashion of a small and intensely snobbish class is negligible as a general precedent. In any case, men and women in the East do not marry anyone they fancy, as in England and America. Women are secluded and marriages are arranged. In Salt Lake City the free unsecluded woman could see and meet the ablest man of the community, and tempt him to make her his tenth wife by all the arts peculiar to women in English-speaking countries. No Eastern woman can do anything of the sort. The man alone has any initiative; but he has no access to the woman; besides, as we have seen, the difficulty created by male licence is not polygyny but polyandry, which is not allowed.

Consequently, if we are to make polygyny a success, we must limit it. If we have two women to every one man, we must allow each man only two wives. That is simple; but unfortunately our own actual proportion is, roughly, something like $1\frac{1}{11}$ women to 1 man. Now you cannot enact that each man shall be allowed $1\frac{1}{11}$ wives, or that each woman who cannot get a husband all to herself shall divide herself between eleven already married husbands. Thus there is no way out for us through polygyny. There is no way at all out of the present system of condemning the superfluous women to barrenness, except by legitimizing the children of women who are not married to the fathers.

THE OLD MAID'S RIGHT TO MOTHERHOOD

Now the right to bear children without taking a husband could not be confined to women who are superfluous in the monogamic reckoning. There is the practical difficulty that although in our population there are about a million monogamically superfluous women, yet it is quite impossible to say of any given unmarried woman that she is one of the superfluous. And there is the difficulty of principle. The right to bear a child, perhaps the most sacred of all women's rights, is not one that should have any conditions attached to it except in the interests of race welfare. There are many women of admirable character, strong, capable, independent, who dislike the domestic habits of men; have no natural turn for mothering and coddling them; and find the concession of conjugal rights to any person under any conditions intolerable by their self-respect. Yet the general sense of the community recognizes in these very women the fittest people to have charge of children, and trusts them, as schoolmistresses and matrons of institutions, more than women of any other type when it is possible to procure them for such work. Why should the taking of a husband be imposed on these women as the price of their right to maternity? I am quite unable to answer that question. I see a good deal of first-rate maternal ability and sagacity spending itself on bees and poultry and village schools and cottage hospitals; and I find myself repeatedly asking myself why this valuable strain in the national breed should be sterilized. Unfortunately, the very women whom we should tempt to become mothers for the good of the race are the very last people to press their services on their country in that way. Plato long ago pointed out the importance of being governed by men with sufficient sense of responsibility and comprehension of public duties to be very reluctant to undertake the work of governing; and yet we have taken his instruction so little to heart that we are at present suffering acutely from government by gentlemen who will stoop to all the mean shifts of electioneering and incur all its heavy expenses for the sake of a seat in Parliament. But what our sentimentalists have not yet been told is that exactly the same thing applies to maternity as to government. The best mothers are not those who are so enslaved by their primitive instincts that they will bear children no matter how hard the conditions are, but precisely those who place a very high price on their services, and are quite prepared to become old maids if the price is refused, and even to feel relieved at their escape. Our democratic and matrimonial institutions may have their merits: at all events they are mostly reforms of something worse; but they put a premium on want of self-respect in certain very important matters; and the consequence is that we are very badly governed and are, on the whole, an ugly, mean, ill-bred race.

IBSEN'S CHAIN STITCH

Let us not forget, however, in our sympathy for the superfluous women, that their children must have fathers as well as mothers. Who are the fathers to be? All monogamists and married women will reply hastily: either bachelors or widowers; and this solution will serve as well as another; for it would be hypocritical to pretend that the difficulty is a practical one. None the less, the monogamists, after due reflection, will point out that if there are widowers enough the superfluous women are not really superfluous, and therefore there is no reason why the parties should not marry respectably like other people. And they might in that case be right if the reasons were purely numerical: that is, if every woman were willing to take a husband if one could be found for her, and every man willing to take a wife on the same terms; also, please remember, if widows would remain celibate to give the unmarried woman a chance. These ifs will not work. We must recognize two classes of old maids: one, the really superfluous women, and the other, the women who refuse to accept maternity on the (to them) unbearable condition of taking a husband. From both classes may, perhaps, be subtracted for the present the large proportion of women who could not afford the extra expense of one or more children. I say "perhaps," because it is by no means sure that within reasonable limits mothers do not make a better fight for subsistence, and have not, on the whole, a better time than single women. In any case, we have two distinct cases to deal with: the superfluous and the voluntary; and it is the voluntary whose grit we are most concerned to fertilize. But here, again, we cannot put our finger on any particular case and pick out Miss Robinson's as superfluous, and Miss Wilkinson's as voluntary. Whether we legitimize the child of the unmarried woman as a duty to the superfluous or as a bribe to the voluntary, the practical result must be the same: to wit, that the condition of marriage now attached to legitimate parentage will be withdrawn from all women, and fertile unions outside marriage recognized by society. Now clearly the consequences would not stop there. The strong-minded ladies who are resolved to be mistresses in their own houses would not be the only ones to take advantage of the new law. Even women to whom a home without a man in it would be no home at all, and who fully intended, if the man turned out to be the right one, to live with him exactly as married couples live, would, if they were possessed of independent means, have every inducement to adopt the new conditions instead of the old ones. Only the women whose sole means of livelihood was wifehood would insist on marriage: hence a tendency would set in to make marriage more and more one of the customs imposed by necessity on the poor, whilst the freer form of union, regulated, no doubt, by settlements and private contracts of various kinds, would become the practice of the rich: that is, would become the fashion. At which point nothing but the achievement of economic independence by women, which is already seen clearly ahead of us, would be needed to make marriage disappear altogether, not by formal abolition, but by simple disuse. The private contract stage of this process was reached in ancient Rome. The only practicable alternative to it seems to be such an extension of divorce as will reduce the risks and obligations of marriage to a degree at which they will be no worse than those of the alternatives to marriage. As we shall see, this is the solution to which all the arguments tend. Meanwhile, note how much reason a statesman has to pause before meddling with an institution which, unendurable as its drawbacks are, threatens to come to pieces in all directions if a single thread of it be cut. Ibsen's similitude of the machine-made chain stitch, which unravels the whole seam at the first pull when a single stitch is ripped, is very applicable to the knot of marriage.

REMOTENESS OF THE FACTS FROM THE IDEAL

But before we allow this to deter us from touching the sacred fabric, we must find out whether it is not already coming to pieces in all directions by the continuous strain of circumstances. No doubt, if it were all that it pretends to be, and human nature were working smoothly within its limits, there would be nothing more to be said: it would be let alone as it always is let alone during the cruder stages of civilization. But the moment we refer to the facts, we discover that the ideal matrimony and domesticity which our bigots implore us to preserve as the corner-stone of our society is a figment: what we have really got is something very different, questionable at its best, and abominable at its worst. The word pure, so commonly applied to it by thoughtless people, is absurd; because if they do not mean celibate by it, they mean nothing; and if they do mean celibate, then marriage is legalized impurity, a conclusion which is offensive and inhuman. Marriage as a fact is not in the least like marriage as an ideal. If it were, the sudden changes which have been made on the Continent from indissoluble Roman Catholic marriage to marriage that can be dissolved by a box on the ear as in France, by an epithet as in Germany, or simply at the wish of both parties as in Sweden, not to mention the experiments made by some of the American States, would have shaken society to its foundations. Yet they have produced so little effect that Englishmen open their eyes in surprise when told of their existence.

DIFFICULTY OF OBTAINING EVIDENCE

As to what actual marriage is, one would like evidence instead of guesses; but as all departures from the ideal are regarded as disgraceful, evidence cannot be obtained; for when the whole community is indicted, nobody will go into the witness-box for the prosecution. Some guesses we can make with some confidence. For example, if it be objected to any change that our bachelors and widowers would no longer be Galahads, we may without extravagance or cynicism reply that many of them are not Galahads now, and that the only change would be that hypocrisy would no longer be compulsory. Indeed, this can hardly be called guessing: the evidence is in the streets. But when we attempt to find out the truth about our marriages, we cannot even guess with any confidence. Speaking for myself, I can say that I know the inside history of perhaps half a dozen marriages. Any family solicitor knows more than this; but even a family solicitor, however large his practice, knows nothing of the million households which have no solicitors, and which nevertheless make marriage what it really is. And all he can say comes to no more than I can say: to wit, that no marriage of which I have any knowledge is in the least like the ideal marriage. I do not mean that it is worse: I mean simply that it is different. Also, far from society being organized in a defence of its ideal so jealous and implacable that the least step from the straight path means exposure and ruin, it is almost impossible by any extravagance of misconduct to provoke society to relax its steady pretence of blindness, unless you do one or both of two fatal things. One is to get into the newspapers; and the other is to confess. If you confess misconduct to respectable men or women, they must either disown you or become virtually your accomplices: that is why they are so angry with you for confessing. If you get into the papers, the pretence of not knowing becomes impossible. But it is hardly too much to say that if you avoid these two perils, you can do anything you like, as far as your neighbors are concerned. And since we can hardly flatter ourselves that this is the effect of charity, it is difficult not to suspect that our extraordinary forbearance in the matter of stone throwing is that suggested in the well-known parable of the woman taken in adultery which some early freethinker slipped into the Gospel of St John: namely, that we all live in glass houses. We may take it, then, that the ideal husband and the ideal wife are no more real human beings than the cherubim. Possibly the great majority keeps its marriage vows in the technical divorce court sense. No husband or wife yet born keeps them or ever can keep them in the ideal sense.

MARRIAGE AS A MAGIC SPELL

The truth which people seem to overlook in this matter is that the marriage ceremony is quite useless as a magic spell for changing in an instant the nature of the relations of two human beings to one another. If a man marries a woman after three weeks acquaintance, and the day after meets a woman he has known for twenty years, he finds, sometimes to his own irrational surprise and his wife's equally irrational indignation, that his wife is a stranger to him, and the other woman an old friend. Also, there is no hocus pocus that can possibly be devized with rings and veils and vows and benedictions that can fix either a man's or woman's affection for twenty minutes, much less twenty years. Even the most affectionate couples must have moments during which they are far more conscious of one another's faults than of one another's attractions. There are couples who dislike one another furiously for several hours at a time; there are couples who dislike one another permanently; and there are couples who never dislike one another; but these last are people who are incapable of disliking anybody. If they do not quarrel, it is not because they are married, but because they are not quarrelsome. The people who are quarrelsome quarrel with their husbands and wives just as easily as with their servants and relatives and acquaintances: marriage makes no difference. Those who talk and write and legislate as if all this could be prevented by making solemn vows that it shall not happen, are either insincere, insane, or hopelessly stupid. There is some sense in a contract to perform or abstain from actions that are reasonably within voluntary control; but such contracts are only needed to provide against the possibility of either party being no longer desirous of the specified performance or abstention. A person proposing or accepting a contract not only to do something but to like doing it would be certified as mad. Yet popular superstition credits the wedding rite with the power of fixing our fancies or affections for life even under the most unnatural conditions.

THE IMPERSONALITY OF SEX

It is necessary to lay some stress on these points, because few realize the extent to which we proceed on the assumption that marriage is a short cut to perfect and permanent intimacy and affection. But there is a still more unworkable assumption which must be discarded before discussions of marriage can get into any sort of touch with the facts of life. That assumption is that the specific relation which marriage authorizes between the parties is the most intimate and personal of human relations, and embraces all the other high human relations. Now this is violently untrue. Every adult knows that the relation in question can and does exist between entire strangers, different in language, color, tastes, class, civilization, morals, religion, character: in everything, in short, except their bodily homology and the reproductive appetite common to all living organisms. Even hatred, cruelty, and contempt are not incompatible with it; and jealousy and murder are as near to it as affectionate friendship. It is true that it is a relation beset with wildly extravagant illusions for inexperienced people, and that even the most experienced people have not always sufficient analytic faculty to disentangle it from the sentiments, sympathetic or abhorrent, which may spring up through the other relations which are compulsorily attached to it by our laws, or sentimentally associated with it in romance. But the fact remains that the most disastrous marriages are those founded exclusively on it, and the most successful those in which it has been least considered, and in which the decisive considerations have had nothing to do with sex, such as liking, money, congeniality of tastes, similarity of habits, suitability of class, &c., &c.

It is no doubt necessary under existing circumstances for a woman without property to be sexually attractive, because she must get married to secure a livelihood; and the illusions of sexual attraction will cause the imagination of young men to endow her with every accomplishment and virtue that can make a wife a treasure. The attraction being thus constantly and ruthlessly used as a bait, both by individuals and by society, any discussion tending to strip it of its illusions and get at its real natural history is nervously discouraged. But nothing can well be more unwholesome for everybody than the exaggeration and glorification of an instinctive function which clouds the reason and upsets the judgment more than all the other instincts put together. The process may be pleasant and romantic; but the consequences are not. It would be far better for everyone, as well as far honester, if young people were taught that what they call love is an appetite which, like all other appetites, is destroyed for the moment by its gratification; that no profession, promise, or proposal made under its influence should bind anybody; and that its great natural purpose so completely transcends the personal interests of any individual or even of any ten generations of individuals that it should be held to be an act of prostitution and even a sort of blasphemy to attempt to turn it to account by exacting a personal return for its gratification, whether by process of law or not. By all means let it be the subject of contracts with society as to its consequences; but to make marriage an open trade in it as at present, with money, board and lodging, personal slavery, vows of eternal exclusive personal sentimentalities and the rest of it as the price, is neither virtuous, dignified, nor decent. No husband ever secured his domestic happiness and honor, nor has any wife ever secured hers, by relying on it. No private claims of any sort should be founded on it: the real point of honor is to take no corrupt advantage of it. When we hear of young women being led astray and the like, we find that what has led them astray is a sedulously inculcated false notion that the relation they are tempted to contract is so intensely personal, and the vows made under the influence of its transient infatuation so sacred and enduring, that only an atrociously wicked man could make light of or forget them. What is more, as the same fantastic errors are inculcated in men, and the conscientious ones therefore feel bound in honor to stand by what they have promised, one of the surest methods to obtain a husband is to practise on his susceptibilities until he is either carried away into a promise of marriage to which he can be legally held, or else into an indiscretion which he must repair by marriage on pain of having to regard himself as a scoundrel and a seducer, besides facing the utmost damage the lady's relatives can do him.

Such a transaction is not an entrance into a "holy state of matrimony": it is as often as not the inauguration of a lifelong squabble, a corroding grudge, that causes more misery and degradation of character than a dozen entirely natural "desertions" and "betrayals." Yet the number of marriages effected more or less in this way must be enormous. When people say that love should be free, their words, taken literally, may be foolish; but they are only expressing inaccurately a very real need for the disentanglement of sexual relations from a mass of exorbitant and irrelevant conditions imposed on them on false pretences to enable needy parents to get their daughters "off their hands" and to keep those who are already married effectually enslaved by one another.

THE ECONOMIC SLAVERY OF WOMEN

One of the consequences of basing marriage on the considerations stated with cold abhorrence by Saint Paul in the seventh chapter of his epistle to the Corinthians, as being made necessary by the unlikeness of most men to himself, is that the sex slavery involved has become complicated by economic slavery; so that whilst the man defends marriage because he is really defending his pleasures, the woman is even more vehement on the same side because she is defending her only means of livelihood. To a woman without property or marketable talent a husband is more necessary than a master to a dog. There is nothing more wounding to our sense of human dignity than the husband hunting that begins in every family when the daughters become marriageable; but it is inevitable under existing circumstances; and the parents who refuse to engage in it are bad parents, though they may be superior individuals. The cubs of a humane tigress would starve; and the daughters of women who cannot bring themselves to devote several years of their lives to the pursuit of sons-in-law often have to expiate their mother's squeamishness by lifelong celibacy and indigence. To ask a young man his intentions when you know he has no intentions, but is unable to deny that he has paid attentions; to threaten an action for breach of promise of marriage; to pretend that your daughter is a musician when she has with the greatest difficulty been coached into playing three pianoforte pieces which she loathes; to use your own mature charms to attract men to the house when your daughters have no aptitude for that department of sport; to coach them, when they have, in the arts by which men can be led to compromize themselves; and to keep all the skeletons carefully locked up in the family cupboard until the prey is duly hunted down and bagged: all this is a mother's duty today; and a very revolting duty it is: one that disposes of the conventional assumption that it is in the faithful discharge of her home duties that a woman finds her self-respect. The truth is that family life will never be decent, much less ennobling, until this central horror of the dependence of women on men is done away with. At present it reduces the difference between marriage and prostitution to the difference between Trade Unionism and unorganized casual labor: a huge difference, no doubt, as to order and comfort, but not a difference in kind.

However, it is not by any reform of the marriage laws that this can be dealt with. It is in the general movement for the prevention of destitution that the means for making women independent of the compulsory sale of their persons, in marriage or otherwise, will be found; but meanwhile those who deal specifically with the marriage laws should never allow themselves for a moment to forget this abomination that "plucks the rose from the fair forehead of an innocent love, and sets a blister there", and then calmly calls itself purity, home, motherhood, respectability, honor, decency, and any other fine name that happens to be convenient, not to mention the foul epithets it hurls freely at those who are ashamed of it.

UNPOPULARITY OF IMPERSONAL VIEWS

Unfortunately it is very hard to make an average citizen take impersonal views of any sort in matters affecting personal comfort or conduct. We may be enthusiastic Liberals or Conservatives without any hope of seats in Parliament, knighthoods, or posts in the Government, because party politics do not make the slightest difference in our daily lives and therefore cost us nothing. But to take a vital process in which we are keenly interested personal instruments and ask us to regard it, and feel about it, and legislate on it, wholly as if it were an impersonal one, is to make a higher demand than most people seem capable of responding to. We all have personal interests in marriage which we are not prepared to sink. It is not only the women who want to get married: the men do too, sometimes on sentimental grounds, sometimes on the more sordid calculation that bachelor life is less comfortable and more expensive, since a wife pays for her status with domestic service as well as with the other services expected of her. Now that children are avoidable, this calculation is becoming more common and conscious than it was: a result which is regarded as "a steady improvement in general morality."

IMPERSONALITY IS NOT PROMISCUITY

There is, too, a really appalling prevalence of the superstition that the sexual instinct in men is utterly promiscuous and that the least relaxation of law and custom must produce a wild outbreak of licentiousness. As far as our moralists can grasp the proposition that we should deal with the sexual relation as impersonal, it seems to them to mean that we should encourage it to be promiscuous: hence their recoil from it. But promiscuity and impersonality are not the same thing. No man ever yet fell in love with the entire female sex, nor any woman with the entire male sex. We often do not fall in love at all; and when we do we fall in love with one person, and remain indifferent to thousands of others who pass before our eyes every day. Selection, carried even to such fastidiousness as to induce people to say quite commonly that there is only one man or woman in the world for them, is the rule in nature. If anyone doubts this, let him open a shop for the sale of picture post-cards, and, when an enamoured lady customer demands a portrait of her favorite actor or a gentleman of his favorite actress, try to substitute some other portrait on the ground that since the sexual instinct is promiscuous, one portrait is as pleasing as another. I suppose no shopkeeper has ever been foolish enough to do such a thing; and yet all our shopkeepers, the moment a discussion arises on marriage, will passionately argue against all reform on the ground that nothing but the most severe coercion can save their wives and daughters from quite indiscriminate rapine.

DOMESTIC CHANGE OF AIR

Our relief at the morality of the reassurance that man is not promiscuous in his fancies must not blind us to the fact that he is (to use the word coined by certain American writers to describe themselves) something of a Varietist. Even those who say there is only one man or woman in the world for them, find that it is not always the same man or woman. It happens that our law permits us to study this phenomenon among entirely law-abiding people. I know one lady who has been married five times. She is, as might be expected, a wise, attractive, and interesting woman. The question is, Is she wise, attractive, and interesting because she has been married five times, or has she been married five times because she is wise, attractive, and interesting? Probably some of the truth lies both ways. I also know of a household consisting of three families, A having married first B, and then C, who afterwards married D. All three unions were fruitful; so that the children had a change both of fathers and mothers. Now I cannot honestly say that these and similar cases have convinced me that people are the worse for a change. The lady who has married and managed five husbands must be much more expert at it than most monogamic ladies; and as a companion and counsellor she probably leaves them nowhere. Mr. Kipling's question

What can they know of England that only England know?

disposes not only of the patriots who are so patriotic that they never leave their own country to look at another, but of the citizens who are so domestic that they have never married again and never loved anyone except their own husbands and wives. The domestic doctrinaires are also the dull people. The impersonal relation of sex may be judicially reserved for one person; but any such reservation of friendship, affection, admiration, sympathy and so forth is only possible to a wretchedly narrow and jealous nature; and neither history nor contemporary society shews us a single amiable and respectable character capable of it. This has always been recognized in cultivated society: that is why poor people accuse cultivated society of profligacy, poor people being often so ignorant and uncultivated that they have nothing to offer each other but the sex relationship, and cannot conceive why men and women should associate for any other purpose.

As to the children of the triple household, they were not only on excellent terms with one another, and never thought of any distinction between their full and their half brothers and sisters; but they had the superior sociability which distinguishes people who live in communities from those who live in small families.

The inference is that changes of partners are not in themselves injurious or undesirable. People are not demoralized by them when they are effected according to law. Therefore we need not hesitate to alter the law merely because the alteration would make such changes easier.

HOME MANNERS ARE BAD MANNERS

On the other hand, we have all seen the bonds of marriage vilely abused by people who are never classed with shrews and wife-beaters: they are indeed sometimes held up as models of domesticity because they do not drink nor gamble nor neglect their children nor tolerate dirt and untidiness, and because they are not amiable enough to have what are called amiable weaknesses. These terrors conceive marriage as a dispensation from all the common civilities and delicacies which they have to observe among strangers, or, as they put it, "before company." And here the effects of indissoluble marriage-for-better-for-worse are very plainly and disagreeably seen. If such people took their domestic manners into general society, they would very soon find themselves without a friend or even an acquaintance in the world. There are women who, through total disuse, have lost the power of kindly human speech and can only scold and complain: there are men who grumble and nag from inveterate habit even when they are comfortable. But their unfortunate spouses and children cannot escape from them.

SPURIOUS "NATURAL" AFFECTION

What is more, they are protected from even such discomfort as the dislike of his prisoners may cause to a gaoler by the hypnotism of the convention that the natural relation between husband and wife and parent and child is one of intense affection, and that to feel any other sentiment towards a member of one's family is to be a monster. Under the influence of the emotion thus manufactured the most detestable people are spoilt with entirely undeserved deference, obedience, and even affection whilst they live, and mourned when they die by those whose lives they wantonly or maliciously made miserable. And this is what we call natural conduct. Nothing could well be less natural. That such a convention should have been established shews that the indissolubility of marriage creates such intolerable situations that only by beglamoring the human imagination with a hypnotic suggestion of wholly unnatural feelings can it be made to keep up appearances.

If the sentimental theory of family relationship encourages bad manners and personal slovenliness and uncleanness in the home, it also, in the case of sentimental people, encourages the practice of rousing and playing on the affections of children prematurely and far too frequently. The lady who says that as her religion is love, her children shall be brought up in an atmosphere of love, and institutes a system of sedulous endearments and exchanges of presents and conscious and studied acts of artificial kindness, may be defeated in a large family by the healthy derision and rebellion of children who have acquired hardihood and common sense in their conflicts with one another. But the small families, which are the rule just now, succumb more easily; and in the case of a single sensitive child the effect of being forced in a hothouse atmosphere of unnatural affection may be disastrous.

In short, whichever way you take it, the convention that marriage and family relationship produce special feelings which alter the nature of human intercourse is a mischievous one. The whole difficulty of bringing up a family well is the difficulty of making its members behave as considerately at home as on a visit in a strange house, and as frankly, kindly, and easily in a strange house as at home. In the middle classes, where the segregation of the artificially limited family in its little brick box is horribly complete, bad manners, ugly dresses, awkwardness, cowardice, peevishness, and all the petty vices of unsociability flourish like mushrooms in a cellar. In the upper class, where families are not limited for money reasons; where at least two houses and sometimes three or four are the rule (not to mention the clubs); where there is travelling and hotel life; and where the men are brought up, not in the family, but in public schools, universities, and the naval and military services, besides being constantly in social training in other people's houses, the result is to produce a set that, in comparison with the middle class, counts as a different and much more sociable species. And in the very poorest class, where people have no homes, only sleeping places crowded with lodgers, and consequently live practically in the streets, sociability again appears, leaving the middle class despised and disliked for its helpless and offensive unsociability as much by those below it as those above it, and yet ignorant enough to be proud of it, and to hold itself up as a model for the reform of the (as it considers) elegantly vicious rich and profligate poor alike.

CARRYING THE WAR INTO THE ENEMY'S COUNTRY

Without pretending to exhaust the subject, I have said enough to make it clear that the moment we lose the desire to defend our present matrimonial and family arrangements, there will be no difficulty in making out an overwhelming case against them. No doubt until then we shall continue to hold up the British home as the Holy of Holies in the temple of honorable motherhood, innocent childhood, manly virtue, and sweet and wholesome national life. But with a clever turn of the hand this holy of holies can be exposed as an Augean stable, so filthy that it would seem more hopeful to burn it down than to attempt to sweep it out. And this latter view will perhaps prevail if the idolaters of marriage persist in refusing all proposals for reform and treating those who advocate it as infamous delinquents. Neither view is of any use except as a poisoned arrow in a fierce fight between two parties determined to discredit each other with a view to obtaining powers of legal coercion over one another.

SHELLEY AND QUEEN VICTORIA

The best way to avert such a struggle is to open the eyes of the thoughtlessly conventional people to the weakness of their position in a mere contest of recrimination. Hitherto they have assumed that they have the advantage of coming into the field without a stain on their characters to combat libertines who have no character at all. They conceive it to be their duty to throw mud; and they feel that even if the enemy can find any mud to throw, none of it will stick. They are mistaken. There will be plenty of that sort of ammunition in the other camp; and most of it will stick very hard indeed. The moral is, do not throw any. If we can imagine Shelley and Queen Victoria arguing out their differences in another world, we may be sure that the Queen has long ago found out that she cannot settle the question by classing Shelley with George IV. as a bad man; and Shelley is not likely to have called her vile names on the general ground that as the economic dependence of women makes marriage a money bargain in which the man is the purchaser and the woman the purchased, there is no essential difference between a married woman and the woman of the streets. Unfortunately, all the people whose methods of controversy are represented by our popular newspapers are not Queen Victorias and Shelleys. A great mass of them, when their prejudices are challenged, have no other impulse than to call the challenger names, and, when the crowd seems to be on their side, to maltreat him personally or hand him over to the law, if he is vulnerable to it. Therefore I cannot say that I have any certainty that the marriage question will be dealt with decently and tolerantly. But dealt with it will be, decently or indecently; for the present state of things in England is too strained and mischievous to last. Europe and America have left us a century behind in this matter.

A PROBABLE EFFECT OF GIVING WOMEN THE VOTE

The political emancipation of women is likely to lead to a comparatively stringent enforcement by law of sexual morality (that is why so many of us dread it); and this will soon compel us to consider what our sexual morality shall be. At present a ridiculous distinction is made between vice and crime, in order that men may be vicious with impunity. Adultery, for instance, though it is sometimes fiercely punished by giving an injured husband crushing damages in a divorce suit (injured wives are not considered in this way), is not now directly prosecuted; and this impunity extends to illicit relations between unmarried persons who have reached what is called the age of consent. There are other matters, such as notification of contagious disease and solicitation, in which the hand of the law has been brought down on one sex only. Outrages which were capital offences within the memory of persons still living when committed on women outside marriage, can still be inflicted by men on their wives without legal remedy. At all such points the code will be screwed up by the operation of Votes for Women, if there be any virtue in the franchise at all. The result will be that men will find the more ascetic side of our sexual morality taken seriously by the law. It is easy to foresee the consequences. No man will take much trouble to alter laws which he can evade, or which are either not enforced or enforced on women only. But when these laws take him by the collar and thrust him into prison, he suddenly becomes keenly critical of them, and of the arguments by which they are supported. Now we have seen that our marriage laws will not stand criticism, and that they have held out so far only because they are so worked as to fit roughly our state of society, in which women are neither politically nor personally free, in which indeed women are called womanly only when they regard themselves as existing solely for the use of men. When Liberalism enfranchises them politically, and Socialism emancipates them economically, they will no longer allow the law to take immorality so easily. Both men and women will be forced to behave morally in sex matters; and when they find that this is inevitable they will raise the question of what behavior really should be established as moral. If they decide in favor of our present professed morality, they will have to make a revolutionary change in their habits by becoming in fact what they only pretend to be at present. If, on the other hand, they find that this would be an unbearable tyranny, without even the excuse of justice or sound eugenics, they will reconsider their morality and remodel the law.

THE PERSONAL SENTIMENTAL BASIS OF MONOGAMY

Monogamy has a sentimental basis which is quite distinct from the political one of equal numbers of the sexes. Equal numbers in the sexes are quite compatible with a change of partners every day or every hour. Physically there is nothing to distinguish human society from the farm-yard except that children are more troublesome and costly than chickens and calves, and that men and women are not so completely enslaved as farm stock. Accordingly, the people whose conception of marriage is a farm-yard or slave-quarter conception are always more or less in a panic lest the slightest relaxation of the marriage laws should utterly demoralize society; whilst those to whom marriage is a matter of more highly evolved sentiments and needs (sometimes said to be distinctively human, though birds and animals in a state of freedom evince them quite as touchingly as we) are much more liberal, knowing as they do that monogamy will take care of itself provided the parties are free enough, and that promiscuity is a product of slavery and not of liberty.

The solid foundation of their confidence is the fact that the relationship set up by a comfortable marriage is so intimate and so pervasive of the whole life of the parties to it, that nobody has room in his or her life for more than one such relationship at a time. What is called a household of three is never really of three except in the sense that every household becomes a household of three when a child is born, and may in the same way become a household of four or fourteen if the union be fertile enough. Now no doubt the marriage tie means so little to some people that the addition to the household of half a dozen more wives or husbands would be as possible as the addition of half a dozen governesses or tutors or visitors or servants. A Sultan may have fifty wives as easily as he may have fifty dishes on his table, because in the English sense he has no wives at all; nor have his wives any husband: in short, he is not what we call a married man. And there are sultans and sultanas and seraglios existing in England under English forms. But when you come to the real modern marriage of sentiment, a relation is created which has never to my knowledge been shared by three persons except when all three have been extraordinarily fond of one another. Take for example the famous case of Nelson and Sir William and Lady Hamilton. The secret of this household of three was not only that both the husband and Nelson were devoted to Lady Hamilton, but that they were also apparently devoted to one another. When Hamilton died both Nelson and Emma seem to have been equally heartbroken. When there is a successful household of one man and two women the same unusual condition is fulfilled: the two women not only cannot live happily without the man but cannot live happily without each other. In every other case known to me, either from observation or record, the experiment is a hopeless failure: one of the two rivals for the really intimate affection of the third inevitably drives out the other. The driven-out party may accept the situation and remain in the house as a friend to save appearances, or for the sake of the children, or for economic reasons; but such an arrangement can subsist only when the forfeited relation is no longer really valued; and this indifference, like the triple bond of affection which carried Sir William Hamilton through, is so rare as to be practicably negligible in the establishment of a conventional morality of marriage. Therefore sensible and experienced people always assume that when a declaration of love is made to an already married person, the declaration binds the parties in honor never to see one another again unless they contemplate divorce and remarriage. And this is a sound convention, even for unconventional people. Let me illustrate by reference to a fictitious case: the one imagined in my own play Candida will do as well as another. Here a young man who has been received as a friend into the house of a clergyman falls in love with the clergyman's wife, and being young and inexperienced, declares his feelings, and claims that he, and not the clergyman, is the more suitable mate for the lady. The clergyman, who has a temper, is first tempted to hurl the youth into the street by bodily violence: an impulse natural, perhaps, but vulgar and improper, and not open, on consideration, to decent men. Even coarse and inconsiderate men are restrained from it by the fact that the sympathy of the woman turns naturally to the victim of physical brutality and against the bully, the Thackerayan notion to the contrary being one of the illusions of literary masculinity. Besides, the husband is not necessarily the stronger man: and appeal to force has resulted in the ignominious defeat of the husband quite as often as in poetic justice as conceived in the conventional novelet. What an honorable and sensible man does when his household is invaded is what the Reverend James Mavor Morell does in my play. He recognizes that just as there is not room for two women in that sacredly intimate relation of sentimental domesticity which is what marriage means to him, so there is no room for two men in that relation with his wife; and he accordingly tells her firmly that she must choose which man will occupy the place that is large enough for one only. He is so far shrewdly unconventional as to recognize that if she chooses the other man, he must give way, legal tie or no legal tie; but he knows that either one or the other must go. And a sensible wife would act in the same way. If a romantic young lady came into her house and proposed to adore her husband on a tolerated footing, she would say "My husband has not room in his life for two wives: either you go out of the house or I go out of it." The situation is not at all unlikely: I had almost said not at all unusual. Young ladies and gentlemen in the greensickly condition which is called calf-love, associating with married couples at dangerous periods of mature life, quite often find themselves in it; and the extreme reluctance of proud and sensitive people to make any assertion of matrimonial rights, or to condescend to jealousy, sometimes make the threatened husband or wife hesitate to take prompt steps and do the apparently conventional thing. But whether they hesitate or act the result is always the same. In a real marriage of sentiment the wife or husband cannot be supplanted by halves; and such a marriage will break very soon under the strain of polygyny or polyandry. What we want at present is a sufficiently clear teaching of this fact to ensure that prompt and decisive action shall always be taken in such cases without any false shame of seeming conventional (a shame to which people capable of such real marriage are specially susceptible), and a rational divorce law to enable the marriage to be dissolved and the parties honorably resorted and recoupled without disgrace and scandal if that should prove the proper solution.

It must be repeated here that no law, however stringent, can prevent polygamy among groups of people who choose to live loosely and be monogamous only in appearance. But such cases are not now under consideration. Also, affectionate husbands like Samuel Pepys, and affectionate wives of the corresponding temperament, may, it appears, engage in transient casual adventures out of doors without breaking up their home life. But within doors that home life may be regarded as naturally monogamous. It does not need to be protected against polygamy; it protects itself.

DIVORCE

All this has an important bearing on the question of divorce. Divorce reformers are so much preoccupied with the injustice of forbidding a woman to divorce her husband for unfaithfulness to his marriage vow, whilst allowing him that power over her, that they are apt to overlook the pressing need for admitting other and far more important grounds for divorce. If we take a document like Pepys' Diary, we learn that a woman may have an incorrigibly unfaithful husband, and yet be much better off than if she had an ill-tempered, peevish, maliciously sarcastic one, or was chained for life to a criminal, a drunkard, a lunatic, an idle vagrant, or a person whose religious faith was contrary to her own. Imagine being married to a liar, a borrower, a mischief maker, a teaser or tormentor of children and animals, or even simply to a bore! Conceive yourself tied for life to one of the perfectly "faithful" husbands who are sentenced to a month's imprisonment occasionally for idly leaving their wives in childbirth without food, fire, or attendance! What woman would not rather marry ten Pepyses? what man a dozen Nell Gwynnes? Adultery, far from being the first and only ground for divorce, might more reasonably be made the last, or wholly excluded. The present law is perfectly logical only if you once admit (as no decent person ever does) its fundamental assumption that there can be no companionship between men and women because the woman has a "sphere" of her own, that of housekeeping, in which the man must not meddle, whilst he has all the rest of human activity for his sphere: the only point at which the two spheres touch being that of replenishing the population. On this assumption the man naturally asks for a guarantee that the children shall be his because he has to find the money to support them. The power of divorcing a woman for adultery is this guarantee, a guarantee that she does not need to protect her against a similar imposture on his part, because he cannot bear children. No doubt he can spend the money that ought to be spent on her children on another woman and her children; but this is desertion, which is a separate matter. The fact for us to seize is that in the eye of the law, adultery without consequences is merely a sentimental grievance, whereas the planting on one man of another man's offspring is a substantial one. And so, no doubt, it is; but the day has gone by for basing laws on the assumption that a woman is less to a man than his dog, and thereby encouraging and accepting the standards of the husbands who buy meat for their bull-pups and leave their wives and children hungry. That basis is the penalty we pay for having borrowed our religion from the East, instead of building up a religion of our own out of our western inspiration and western sentiment. The result is that we all believe that our religion is on its last legs, whereas the truth is that it is not yet born, though the age walks visibly pregnant with it. Meanwhile, as women are dragged down by their oriental servitude to our men, and as, further, women drag down those who degrade them quite as effectually as men do, there are moments when it is difficult to see anything in our sex institutions except a *police des mœurs* keeping the field for a competition as to which sex shall corrupt the other most.

IMPORTANCE OF SENTIMENTAL GRIEVANCES

Any tolerable western divorce law must put the sentimental grievances first, and should carefully avoid singling out any ground of divorce in such a way as to create a convention that persons having that ground are bound in honor to avail themselves of it. It is generally admitted that people should not be encouraged to petition for a divorce in a fit of petulance. What is not so clearly seen is that neither should they be encouraged to petition in a fit of jealousy, which is certainly the most detestable and mischievous of all the passions that enjoy public credit. Still less should people who are not jealous be urged to behave as if they were jealous, and to enter upon duels and divorce suits in which they have no desire to be successful. There should be no publication of the grounds on which a divorce is sought or granted; and as this would abolish the only means the public now has of ascertaining that every possible effort has been made to keep the couple united against their wills, such privacy will only be tolerated when we at last admit that the sole and sufficient reason why people should be granted a divorce is that they want one. Then there will be no more reports of divorce cases, no more letters read in court with an indelicacy that makes every sensitive person shudder and recoil as from a profanation, no more washing of household linen, dirty or clean, in public. We must learn in these matters to mind our own business and not impose our individual notions of propriety on one another, even if it carries us to the length of openly admitting what we are now compelled to assume silently, that every human being has a right to sexual experience, and that the law is concerned only with parentage, which is now a separate matter.

DIVORCE WITHOUT ASKING WHY

The one question that should never be put to a petitioner for divorce is "Why?" When a man appeals to a magistrate for protection from someone who threatens to kill him, on the simple ground that he desires to live, the magistrate might quite reasonably ask him why he desires to live, and why the person who wishes to kill him should not be gratified. Also whether he can prove that his life is a pleasure to himself or a benefit to anyone else, and whether it is good for him to be encouraged to exaggerate the importance of his short span in this vale of tears rather than to keep himself constantly ready to meet his God.

The only reason for not raising these very weighty points is that we find society unworkable except on the assumption that every man has a natural right to live. Nothing short of his own refusal to respect that right in others can reconcile the community to killing him. From this fundamental right many others are derived. The American Constitution, one of the few modern political documents drawn up by men who were forced by the sternest circumstances to think out what they really had to face instead of chopping logic in a university class-room, specifies "liberty and the pursuit of happiness" as natural rights. The terms are too vague to be of much practical use; for the supreme right to life, extended as it now must be to the life of the race, and to the quality of life as well as to the mere fact of breathing, is making short work of many ancient liberties, and exposing the pursuit of happiness as perhaps the most miserable of human occupations. Nevertheless, the American Constitution roughly expresses the conditions to which modern democracy commits us. To impose marriage on two unmarried people who do not desire to marry one another would be admittedly an act of enslavement. But it is no worse than to impose a continuation of marriage on people who have ceased to desire to be married. It will be said that the parties may not agree on that; that one may desire to maintain the marriage the other wishes to dissolve. But the same hardship arises whenever a man in love proposes marriage to a woman and is refused. The refusal is so painful to him that he often threatens to kill himself and sometimes even does it. Yet we expect him to face his ill luck, and never dream of forcing the woman to accept him. His case is the same as that of the husband whose wife tells him she no longer cares for him, and desires the marriage to be dissolved. You will say, perhaps, if you are superstitious, that it is not the same—that marriage makes a difference. You are wrong: there is no magic in marriage.

If there were, married couples would never desire to separate. But they do. And when they do, it is simple slavery to compel them to remain together.

ECONOMIC SLAVERY AGAIN THE ROOT DIFFICULTY

The husband, then, is to be allowed to discard his wife when he is tired of her, and the wife the husband when another man strikes her fancy? One must reply unhesitatingly in the affirmative; for if we are to deny every proposition that can be stated in offensive terms by its opponents, we shall never be able to affirm anything at all. But the question reminds us that until the economic independence of women is achieved, we shall have to remain impaled on the other horn of the dilemma and maintain marriage as a slavery. And here let me ask the Government of the day (1910) a question with regard to the Labor Exchanges it has very wisely established throughout the country. What do these Exchanges do when a woman enters and states that her occupation is that of a wife and mother; that she is out of a job; and that she wants an employer? If the Exchanges refuse to entertain her application, they are clearly excluding nearly the whole female sex from the benefit of the Act. If not, they must become matrimonial agencies, unless, indeed, they are prepared to become something worse by putting the woman down as a housekeeper and introducing her to an employer without making marriage a condition of the hiring.

LABOR EXCHANGES AND THE WHITE SLAVERY

Suppose, again, a woman presents herself at the Labor Exchange, and states her trade as that of a White Slave, meaning the unmentionable trade pursued by many thousands of women in all civilized cities. Will the Labor Exchange find employers for her? If not, what will it do with her? If it throws her back destitute and unhelped on the streets to starve, it might as well not exist as far as she is concerned; and the problem of unemployment remains unsolved at its most painful point. Yet if it finds honest employment for her and for all the unemployed wives and mothers, it must find new places in the world for women; and in so doing it must achieve for them economic independence of men. And when this is done, can we feel sure that any woman will consent to be a wife and mother (not to mention the less respectable alternative) unless her position is made as eligible as that of the women for whom the Labor Exchanges are finding independent work? Will not many women now engaged in domestic work under circumstances which make it repugnant to them, abandon it and seek employment under other circumstances? As unhappiness in marriage is almost the only discomfort sufficiently irksome to induce a woman to break up her home, and economic dependence the only compulsion sufficiently stringent to force her to endure such unhappiness, the solution of the problem of finding independent employment for women may cause a great number of childless unhappy marriages to break up spontaneously, whether the marriage laws are altered or not. And here we must extend the term childless marriages to cover households in which the children have grown up and gone their own way, leaving the parents alone together: a point at which many worthy couples discover for the first time that they have long since lost interest in one another, and have been united only by a common interest in their children. We may expect, then, that marriages which are maintained by economic pressure alone will dissolve when that pressure is removed; and as all the parties to them will certainly not accept a celibate life, the law must sanction the dissolution in order to prevent a recurrence of the scandal which has moved the Government to appoint the Commission now sitting to investigate the marriage question: the scandal, that is, of a great number of persons, condemned to celibacy by magisterial separation orders, and, of course, refusing to submit to the condemnation, forming illicit connections to an extent which threatens to familiarize the working classes with an open disuse of marriage. In short, once set women free from their economic slavery, and you will find that unless divorce is made as easy as the dissolution of a business partnership, the practice of dispensing with marriage will presently become so common that conventional couples will be ashamed to get married.

DIVORCE FAVORABLE TO MARRIAGE

Divorce, in fact, is not the destruction of marriage, but the first condition of its maintenance. A thousand indissoluble marriages mean a thousand marriages and no more. A thousand divorces may mean two thousand marriages; for the couples may marry again. Divorce only re-assorts the couples: a very desirable thing when they are ill-assorted. Also, it makes people much more willing to marry, especially prudent people and proud people with a high sense of self-respect. Further, the fact that a divorce is possible often prevents its being petitioned for, not only because it puts married couples on their good behaviour towards one another, but because, as no room feels like a prison if the door is left open, the removal of the sense of bondage would at once make marriage much happier than it is now. Also, if the door were always open, there would be no need to rush through it as there is now when it opens for one moment in a lifetime, and may never open again.

From this point of view England has the worst civil marriage law in the world, with the exception of silly South Carolina. In every other reasonably civilized country the grounds on which divorce can be granted admit of so wide an interpretation that all unhappy marriages can be dissolved without resorting to the shameful shifts imposed by our law. Yet the figures just given to the Royal Commission shew that in the State of Washington, where there are eleven different grounds of divorce, and where, in fact, divorce can be had for the asking at a negligible cost, the divorce rate is only 184 per 100,000 of the population, which, if we assume that the 100,000 people represent 20,000 families, means less than one per cent of domestic failures. In Japan the rate is 215, which is said to be the highest on record. This is not very alarming: what is quite hideous is that the rate in England is only 2, a figure which, if we assume that human nature is much the same in Walworth as in Washington, must represent a frightful quantity of useless unhappiness and clandestine polygamy. I am not forgetting my own demonstration that the rate is kept down in Washington by the economic slavery of women; but I must point out that this is at its worst in the middle classes only, because a woman of the working class can turn to and support herself, however poorly; and a woman of the upper classes usually has some property. And in all classes we may guess that the object of many divorces is not the resumption of a single life, but a change of partners. As this change can be affected easily under the existing law in the State of Washington it is not certain that the economic emancipation of women would alter the rate there to any startling extent. What is certain is that it could not conceivably raise it to a figure at which even the most panicky alarmist could persuade sensible people that the whole social fabric was tumbling to pieces. When journalists and bishops and American Presidents and other simple people describe this Washington result as alarming, they are speaking as a peasant speaks of a motor car or an aeroplane when he sees one for the first time. All he means is that he is not used to it and therefore fears that it may injure him. Every advance in civilization frightens these honest folk. This is a pity; but if we were to spare their feelings we should never improve the world at all. To let them frighten us, and then pretend that their stupid timidity is virtue and purity and so forth, is simply moral cowardice.

MALE ECONOMIC SLAVERY AND THE RIGHTS OF BACHELORS

It must not be forgotten that the refusal to accept the indignities, risks, hardships, softships, and divided duties of marriage is not confined to our voluntary old maids. There are men of the mould of Beethoven and Samuel Butler, whom one can hardly conceive as married men. There are the great ecclesiastics, who will not own two loyalties: one to the Church and one to the earth. There are men like Goethe, who marry late and reluctantly solely because they feel that they cannot in honest friendship refuse the status of marriage to any woman of whose attachment to them they have taken any compromizing advantage, either in fact or in appearance. No sensible man can, under existing circumstances, advise a woman to keep house with a man without insisting on his marrying her, unless he is independent of conventional society (a state of things which can occur only very exceptionally); and a man of honor cannot advise a woman to do for his sake what he would not advise her to do for anyone else's. The result is that our Beethovens and Butlers—of whom, in their ordinary human aspect, there are a good many—become barren old bachelors, and rather savage ones at that.

Another difficulty which we always think of in connection with women, but which is by no means without its application to men, is the economic one. The number of men who cannot afford to marry is large enough to produce very serious social results; and the higher the work the man is doing, the more likely he is to find himself in this class until he has reached or passed middle age. The higher departments of science, law, philosophy, poetry, and the fine arts are notoriously starved in youth and early manhood: the marriageable age there, economically speaking, is nearer fifty than twenty. Even in business the leading spirits seldom reach a position of security until they are far beyond the age at which celibacy is tolerable. Account must also be taken of the younger sons of the propertied classes, brought up in households in which the rate of expenditure, though ten times that possible on a younger son's portion, yet represents the only habit of life he has learnt.

Taking all these cases as representing a bachelor class, and bearing in mind that though a man who marries at forty is not called a bachelor, yet he has for twenty years of his adult life been one, and therefore produced all the social problems that arise out of the existence of unmarried men, we must not shrink from asking whether all these gentlemen are celibates, even though we know that the question must be answered very emphatically in the negative. Some of them marry women of property, thereby reproducing the economic dependence of women on men with the sexes reversed. But there are so few women of property available for this purpose in comparison with the number of bachelors who cannot afford to marry, that this resource does not solve the problem of the bachelor who cannot afford a wife. If there were no other resources available, bachelors would make love to the wives and daughters of their friends. This being morally inadmissible, a demand arises for a cheap temporary substitute for marriage. A class of women must be found to protect the wives and daughters of the married by keeping company with the bachelors for hire for as long or as short a time as the bachelor can afford, on the understanding that no claim is to be made on him after the hiring is ended. And such an institution, as we know, exists among us. It is commonly spoken of and thought of as an offence against our marriage morality; but all the experts who write scientific treatises on marriage seem to be agreed that it is, on the contrary, a necessary part of that morality, and must stand and fall with it.

I do not myself think that this view will bear examination. In my play, Mrs Warren's Profession, I have shewn that the institution in question is an economic phenomenon, produced by our underpayment and ill-treatment of women who try to earn an honest living. I am aware that for some reason scientific writers are perversely impatient of this view, and, to discredit it, quote police lists of the reasons given by the victims for adopting their trade, and insist on the fact that poverty is not often alleged. But this means only that the actual word is seldom used. If a prisonful of thieves were asked what induced them to take to thieving, and some replied Poverty, and others Hunger, and others Desire for Excitement, no one would deny that the three answers were really one answer—that poverty means hunger, an intolerable lack of variety and pleasure, and, in short, all sorts of privations. When a girl, similarly interrogated, says she wanted fine clothes, or more fun, or the like, she is really saying that she lacked what no woman with plenty of money need lack. The fact that, according to the testimony of men who profess experience in such matters, you may search Europe in vain for a woman in this trade who has the table manners of a lady, shews that prostitution is not a vocation but a slavery to which women are driven by the miseries of honest poverty. When every young woman has an honorable and comfortable livelihood open to her on reasonable terms, the streets will make no more recruits. When every young man can afford to marry, and marriage reform makes it easy to dissolve unions contracted by young and inexperienced people in the event of their turning out badly, or of one of the pair achieving a position neither comfortable nor suitable for the other, both prostitution and bachelordom will die a natural death. Until then, all talk of "purification" is idle. It is for that reason that I lay little stress on prostitution here, and refer readers who are curious about the psychopathy of bachelordom and spinsterhood to the monumental work of my friend Havelock Ellis.

THE PATHOLOGY OF MARRIAGE

I shall also say as little as possible of the pathology of marriage and its kerbstone breakwater. Only, as there seems to be no bottom to the abyss of public ignorance on the subject, I am compelled to warn my readers that marriage has a pathology and even a criminology. But they are both so frightful that they have been dealt with not only in such treatises as those of Havelock Ellis, Fournier, Duclaux, and many German writers, but in such comparatively popular works as The Heavenly Twins by Sarah Grand, and several of the plays of Brieux: notably Les Avariés, Les Trois Filles de M. Dupont, and Maternité. I purposely pass them by quickly, not only because attention has already been called to them by these devoted writers, but because my mission is not to deal with obvious horrors, but to open the eyes of normal respectable men to evils which are escaping their consideration.

PREFACE

As to the evils of disease and contagion, our consciences are sound enough: what is wrong with us is ignorance of the facts. No doubt this is a very formidable ignorance in a country where the first cry of the soul is "Dont tell me: I dont want to know," and where frantic denials and furious suppressions indicate everywhere the cowardice and want of faith which conceives life as something too terrible to be faced. In this particular case "I dont want to know" takes a righteous air, and becomes "I dont want to know anything about the diseases which are the just punishment of wretches who should not be mentioned in my presence or in any book that is intended for family reading." Wicked and foolish as the spirit of this attitude is, the practice of it is so easy and lazy and uppish that it is very common. But its cry is drowned by a louder and more sincere one. We who do not want to know also do not want to go blind, to go mad, to be disfigured, to be barren, to become pestiferous, or to see such things happening to our children. We learn, at last, that the majority of the victims are not the people of whom we so glibly say "Serve them right," but quite innocent children and innocent parents, smitten by a contagion which, no matter in what vice it may or may not have originated, contaminates the innocent and the guilty alike once it is launched exactly as any other contagious disease does; that indeed it often hits the innocent and misses the guilty because the guilty know the danger and take elaborate precautions against it, whilst the innocent, who have been either carefully kept from any knowledge of their danger, or erroneously led to believe that contagion is possible through misconduct only, run into danger blindfold. Once knock this fact into people's minds, and their self-righteous indifference and intolerance soon change into lively concern for themselves and their families.

THE CRIMINOLOGY OF MARRIAGE

The pathology of marriage involves the possibility of the most horrible crime imaginable: that of the person who, when suffering from contagious disease, forces the contagion on another person by an act of violence. Such an act occurring between unmarried people would, within the memory of persons now living, have exposed the aggressor to the penalty of death; and it is still punished unmercifully by an extreme term of penal servitude when it occurs, as it sometimes does, through the hideous countryside superstition that it effects a cure when the victim is a virgin. Marriage makes this outrage absolutely legal. You may with impunity do to the person to whom you are married what you may not do to the most despised outcast of the streets. And this is only the extreme instance of the outlawry which our marriage laws effect. In our anxiety to provide for ourselves a little private Alsatia in which we can indulge ourselves as we please without reproach or interference from law, religion, or even conscience (and this is what marriage has come to mean to many of us), we have forgotten that we cannot escape restraints without foregoing rights; that all the laws that are needed to compel strangers to respect us are equally if not more necessary to compel our husbands and wives to respect us; and that society without law, whether between two or two million persons, means tyranny and slavery.

If the incorrigible sentimentalists here raise their little pipe of "Not if they love one another," I tell them, with such patience as is possible, that if they had ever had five minutes experience of love they would know that love is itself a tyranny requiring special safeguards; that people will perpetrate "for the sake of" those they love, exactions and submissions that they would never dream of proposing to or suffering from those they dislike or regard with indifference; that healthy marriages are partnerships of companionable and affectionate friendship; that cases of chronic lifelong love, whether sentimental or sensual, ought to be sent to the doctor if not to the executioner; and that honorable men and women, when their circumstances permit it, are so far from desiring to be placed helplessly at one another's mercy that they employ every device the law now admits of, from the most stringent marriage settlements to the employment of separate legal advisers, to neutralize the Alsatian evils of the marriage law.

DOES IT MATTER?

A less obviously silly evasion, and one which has a greater air of common sense, is "After all, seeing that most couples get on very well together, does it matter so much?" The same reply might be made by a lazy magistrate when asked for a warrant to arrest a burglar, or by a sleepy fireman wakened by a midnight call for his fire-escape. "After all, very few people have their houses broken into; and fewer still have them burnt. Does it matter?" But tell the magistrate or fireman that it is *his* house that has been broken into, or *his* house that has been burnt; and you will be startled by the change in his attitude. Because a mass of people have shaken down into comfort enough to satisfy them, or at least to cause them no more discomfort than they are prepared to put up with for the sake of a quiet life, less lucky and more sensitive and conscientious people should not be condemned to expose themselves to intolerable wrongs. Besides, people ought not to be content with the marriage law as it is merely because it is not often unbearably uncomfortable. Slaves are very often much more comfortable both in body and mind than fully responsible free men. That does not excuse anybody for embracing slavery. It is no doubt a great pity, from many points of view, that we were not conquered by Napoleon, or even by Bismarck and Moltke. None the less we should have been rightly despised if we had not been prepared to fight them for the right to misgovern ourselves.

But, as I have said, I am content, in this matter of the evils of our marriage law, to take care of the pence and let the pounds take care of themselves. The crimes and diseases of marriage will force themselves on public attention by their own virulence. I mention them here only because they reveal certain habits of thought and feeling with regard to marriage of which we must rid ourselves if we are to act sensibly when we take the necessary reforms in hand.

CHRISTIAN MARRIAGE

First among these is the habit of allowing ourselves to be bound not only by the truths of the Christian religion but by the excesses and extravagances which the Christian movement acquired in its earlier days as a violent reaction against what it still calls paganism. By far the most dangerous of these, because it is a blasphemy against life, and, to put it in Christian terms, an accusation of indecency against God, is the notion that sex, with all its operations, is in itself absolutely an obscene thing, and that an immaculate conception is a miracle. So unwholesome an absurdity could only have gained ground under two conditions: one, a reaction against a society in which sensual luxury had been carried to revolting extremes, and, two, a belief that the world was coming to an end, and that therefore sex was no longer a necessity. Christianity, because it began under these conditions, made sexlessness and Communism the two main practical articles of its propaganda; and it has never quite lost its original bias in these directions. In spite of the putting off of the Second Coming from the lifetime of the apostles to the millennium, and of the great disappointment of the year 1000 A.D., in which multitudes of Christians seriously prepared for the end of the world, the prophet who announces that the end is at hand is still popular. Many of the people who ridicule his demonstrations that the fantastic monsters of the book of Revelation are among us in the persons of our own political contemporaries, and who proceed sanely in all their affairs on the assumption that the world is going to last, really do believe that there will be a Judgment Day, and that it *might* even be in their own time. A thunderstorm, an eclipse, or any very unusual weather will make them apprehensive and uncomfortable.

This explains why, for a long time, the Christian Church refused to have anything to do with marriage. The result was, not the abolition of sex, but its excommunication. And, of course, the consequences of persuading people that matrimony was an unholy state were so grossly carnal, that the

Church had to execute a complete right-about-face, and try to make people understand that it was a holy state: so holy indeed that it could not be validly inaugurated without the blessing of the Church. And by this teaching it did something to atone for its earlier blasphemy. But the mischief of chopping and changing your doctrine to meet this or that practical emergency instead of keeping it adjusted to the whole scheme of life, is that you end by having half-a-dozen contradictory doctrines to suit half-a-dozen different emergencies. The Church solemnized and sanctified marriage without ever giving up its original Pauline doctrine on the subject. And it soon fell into another confusion. At the point at which it took up marriage and endeavored to make it holy, marriage was, as it still is, largely a survival of the custom of selling women to men. Now in all trades a marked difference is made in price between a new article and a second-hand one. The moment we meet with this difference in value between human beings, we may know that we are in the slave-market, where the conception of our relations to the persons sold is neither religious nor natural nor human nor superhuman, but simply commercial. The Church, when it finally gave its blessing to marriage, did not, in its innocence, fathom these commercial traditions. Consequently it tried to sanctify them too, with grotesque results. The slave-dealer having always asked more money for virginity, the Church, instead of detecting the money-changer and driving him out of the temple, took him for a sentimental and chivalrous lover, and, helped by its only half-discarded doctrine of celibacy, gave virginity a heavenly value to ennoble its commercial pretensions. In short, Mammon, always mighty, put the Church in his pocket, where he keeps it to this day, in spite of the occasional saints and martyrs who contrive from time to time to get their heads and souls free to testify against him.

DIVORCE A SACRAMENTAL DUTY

But Mammon overreached himself when he tried to impose his doctrine of inalienable property on the Church under the guise of indissoluble marriage. For the Church tried to shelter this inhuman doctrine and flat contradiction of the gospel by claiming, and rightly claiming, that marriage is a sacrament. So it is; but that is exactly what makes divorce a duty when the marriage has lost the inward and spiritual grace of which the marriage ceremony is the outward and visible sign. In vain do bishops stoop to pick up the discarded arguments of the atheists of fifty years ago by pleading that the words of Jesus were in an obscure Aramic dialect, and were probably misunderstood, as Jesus, they think, could not have said anything a bishop would disapprove of. Unless they are prepared to add that the statement that those who take the sacrament with their lips but not with their hearts eat and drink their own damnation is also a mistranslation from the Aramaic, they are most solemnly bound to shield marriage from profanation, not merely by permitting divorce, but by making it compulsory in certain cases as the Chinese do.

When spiritual revolt broke out in the sixteenth century, and the Church was reformed in several countries, the Reformation was so largely a rebellion against sacerdotalism that marriage was very nearly excommunicated again: our modern civil marriage, round which so many fierce controversies and political conflicts have raged, would have been thoroughly approved of by Calvin, and hailed with relief by Luther. But the instinctive doctrine that there is something holy and mystic in sex, a doctrine which many of us now easily dissociate from any priestly ceremony, but which in those days seemed to all who felt it to need a ritual affirmation, could not be thrown on the scrap-heap with the sale of Indulgences and the like; and so the Reformation left marriage where it was: a curious mixture of commercial sex slavery, early Christian sex abhorrence, and later Christian sex sanctification.

OTHELLO AND DESDEMONA

How strong was the feeling that a husband or a wife is an article of property, greatly depreciated in value at secondhand, and not to be used or touched by any person but the proprietor, may be learnt from Shakespear. His most infatuated and passionate lovers are Antony and Othello; yet both of them betray the commercial and proprietary instinct the moment they lose their tempers. "I found you," says Antony, reproaching Cleopatra, "as a morsel cold upon dead Cæsar's trencher." Othello's worst agony is the thought of "keeping a corner in the thing he loves for others' uses." But this is not what a man feels about the thing he loves, but about the thing he owns. I never understood the full significance of Othello's outburst until I one day heard a lady, in the course of a private discussion as to the feasibility of "group marriage," say with cold disgust that she would as soon think of lending her toothbrush to another woman as her husband. The sense of outraged manhood with which I felt myself and all other husbands thus reduced to the rank of a toilet appliance gave me a very unpleasant taste of what Desdemona might have felt had she overheard Othello's outburst. I was so dumbfounded that I had not the presence of mind to ask the lady whether she insisted on having a doctor, a nurse, a dentist, and even a priest and solicitor all to herself as well. But I had too often heard men speak of women as if they were mere personal conveniences to feel surprised that exactly the same view is held, only more fastidiously, by women.

All these views must be got rid of before we can have any healthy public opinion (on which depends our having a healthy population) on the subject of sex, and consequently of marriage. Whilst the subject is considered shameful and sinful we shall have no systematic instruction in sexual hygiene, because such lectures as are given in Germany, France, and even prudish America (where the great Miltonic tradition in this matter still lives) will be considered a corruption of that youthful innocence which now subsists on nasty stories and whispered traditions handed down from generation to generation of school-children: stories and traditions which conceal nothing of sex but its dignity, its honor, its sacredness, its rank as the first necessity of society and the deepest concern of the nation. We shall continue to maintain the White Slave Trade and protect its exploiters by, on the one hand, tolerating the white slave as the necessary breakwater of marriage; and, on the other, trampling on her and degrading her until she has nothing to hope from our Courts; and so, with policemen at every corner, and law triumphant all over Europe, she will still be smuggled and cattle-driven from one end of the civilized world to the other, cheated, beaten, bullied, and hunted into the streets to disgusting overwork, without daring to utter the cry for help that brings, not rescue, but exposure and infamy, yet revenging herself terribly in the end by scattering blindness and sterility, pain and disfigurement, insanity and death among us with the certainty that we are much too pious and genteel to allow such things to be mentioned with a view to saving either her or ourselves from them. And all the time we shall keep enthusiastically investing her trade with every allurement that the art of the novelist, the playwright, the dancer, the milliner, the painter, the limelight man, and the sentimental poet can devize, after which we shall continue to be very much shocked and surprised when the cry of the youth, of the young wife, of the mother, of the infected nurse, and of all the other victims, direct and indirect, arises with its invariable refrain: "Why did nobody warn me?"

WHAT IS TO BECOME OF THE CHILDREN?

I must not reply flippantly, Make them all Wards in Chancery; yet that would be enough to put any sensible person on the track of the reply. One would think, to hear the way in which people sometimes ask the question, that not only does marriage prevent the difficulty from ever arising, but that nothing except divorce can ever raise it. It is true that if you divorce the parents, the children have to be disposed of. But if you hang the parents, or imprison the parents, or take the children out of the custody of the parents because they hold Shelley's opinions, or if the parents die, the same difficulty arises. And as these things have happened again and again, and as we have had plenty of experience of divorce decrees and separation orders, the attempt to use children as an obstacle to divorce is hardly worth arguing with. We shall deal with the children just as we should deal with them if their homes were broken up by any other cause. There is a sense in which children are a real obstacle to divorce: they give parents a common interest which keeps together many a couple who, if childless, would separate. The marriage law is superfluous in such cases. This is shewn by the fact that the proportion of childless divorces is much larger than the proportion of divorces from all causes. But it must not be forgotten that the interest of the children forms one of the most powerful arguments for divorce. An unhappy household is a bad nursery. There is something to be said for the polygynous or polyandrous household as a school for children: children really do suffer from having too few parents: this is why uncles and aunts and tutors and governesses are often so good for children. But it is just the polygamous household which our marriage law allows to be broken up, and which, as we have seen, is not possible as a typical institution in a democratic country where the numbers of the sexes are about equal. Therefore polygyny and polyandry as a means of educating children fall to the ground, and with them, I think, must go the opinion which has been expressed by Gladstone and others, that an extension of divorce, whilst admitting many new grounds for it, might exclude the ground of adultery. There are, however, clearly many things that make some of our domestic interiors little private hells for children (especially when the children are quite content in them) which would justify any intelligent State in breaking up the home and giving the custody of the children either to the parent whose conscience had revolted against the corruption of the children, or to neither.

Which brings me to the point that divorce should no longer be confined to cases in which one of the parties petitions for it. If, for instance, you have a thoroughly rascally couple making a living by infamous means and bringing up their children to their trade, the king's proctor, instead of pursuing his present purely mischievous function of preventing couples from being divorced by proving that they both desire it, might very well intervene and divorce these children from their parents. At present, if the Queen herself were to rescue some unfortunate child from degradation and misery and place her in a respectable home, and some unmentionable pair of blackguards claimed the child and proved that they were its father and mother, the child would be given to them in the name of the sanctity of the home and the holiness of parentage, after perpetrating which crime, the law would calmly send an education officer to take the child out of the parents' hands several hours a day in the still more sacred name of compulsory education. (Of course what would really happen would be that the couple would blackmail the Queen for their consent to the salvation of the child, unless, indeed, a hint from a police inspector convinced them that bad characters cannot always rely on pedantically constitutional treatment when they come into conflict with persons in high station.)

The truth is, not only must the bond between man and wife be made subject to a reasonable consideration of the welfare of the parties concerned and of the community, but the whole family bond as well. The theory that the wife is the property of the husband or the husband of the wife is not a whit less abhorrent and mischievous than the theory that the child is the property of the parent. Parental bondage will go the way of conjugal bondage: indeed the order of reform should rather be put the other way about; for the helplessness of children has already compelled the State to intervene between parent and child more than between husband and wife. If you pay less than £40 a year rent, you will sometimes feel tempted to say to the vaccination officer, the school attendance officer, and the sanitary inspector: "Is this child mine or yours?" The answer is that as the child is a vital part of the nation, the nation cannot afford to leave it at the irresponsible disposal of any individual or couple of individuals as a mere small parcel of private property. The only solid ground that the parent can take is that as the State, in spite of its imposing name, can, when all is said, do nothing with the child except place it in the charge of some human being or another, the parent is no worse a custodian than a stranger. And though this proposition may seem highly questionable at first sight to those who imagine that only parents spoil children, yet those who realize that children are as often spoilt by severity and coldness as by indulgence, and that the notion that natural parents are any worse than adopted parents is probably as complete an illusion as the notion that they are any better, see no serious likelihood that State action will detach children from their parents more than it does at present: nay, it is even likely that the present system of taking the children out of the parents' hands and having the parental duty performed by officials, will, as poverty and ignorance become the exception instead of the rule, give way to the system of simply requiring certain results, beginning with the baby's weight and ending perhaps with some sort of practical arts degree, but leaving parents and children to achieve the results as they best may. Such freedom is, of course, impossible in our present poverty-stricken circumstances. As long as the masses of our people are too poor to be good parents or good anything else except beasts of burden, it is no use requiring much more from them but hewing of wood and drawing of water: whatever is to be done must be done *for* them, mostly, alas! by people whose superiority is merely technical. Until we abolish poverty it is impossible to push rational measures of any kind very far: the wolf at the door will compel us to live in a state of siege and to do everything by a bureaucratic martial law that would be quite unnecessary and indeed intolerable in a prosperous community. But, however we settle the question, we must make the parent justify his custody of the child exactly as we should make a stranger justify it. If a family is not achieving the purposes of a family it should be dissolved just as a marriage should when it, too, is not achieving the purposes of marriage. The notion that there is or ever can be anything magical and inviolable in the legal relations of domesticity, and the curious confusion of ideas which makes some of our bishops imagine that in the phrase "Whom God hath joined," the word God means the district registrar or the Reverend John Smith or William Jones, must be got rid of. Means of breaking up undesirable families are as necessary to the preservation of the family as means of dissolving undesirable marriages are to the preservation of marriage. If our domestic laws are kept so inhuman that they at last provoke a furious general insurrection against them as they already provoke many private ones, we shall in a very literal sense empty the baby out with the bath by abolishing an institution which needs nothing more than a little obvious and easy rationalizing to make it not only harmless but comfortable, honorable, and useful.

THE COST OF DIVORCE

But please do not imagine that the evils of indissoluble marriage can be cured by divorce laws administered on our present plan. The very cheapest undefended divorce, even when conducted by a solicitor for its own sake and that of humanity, costs at least £30 out-of-pocket expenses. To a client on business terms it costs about three times as much. Until divorce is as cheap as marriage, marriage will remain indissoluble for all except the handful of people to whom £100 is a procurable sum. For the enormous majority of us there is no difference in this respect between a hundred and a quadrillion. Divorce is the one thing you may not sue for *in formâ pauperis*.

Let me, then, recommend as follows:

1. Make divorce as easy, as cheap, and as private as marriage.

2. Grant divorce at the request of either party, whether the other consents or not; and admit no other ground than the request, which should be made without stating any

reasons.

3. Confine the power of dissolving marriage for misconduct to the State acting on the petition of the king's proctor or other suitable functionary, who may, however, be moved by either party to intervene in ordinary request cases, not to prevent the divorce taking place, but to enforce alimony if it be refused and the case is one which needs it.

4. Make it impossible for marriage to be used as a punishment as it is at present. Send the husband and wife to penal servitude if you disapprove of their conduct and want to punish them; but do not send them back to perpetual wedlock.

5. If, on the other hand, you think a couple perfectly innocent and well conducted, do not condemn them also to perpetual wedlock against their wills, thereby making the treatment of what you consider innocence on both sides the same as the treatment of what you consider guilt on both sides.

6. Place the work of a wife and mother on the same footing as other work: that is, on the footing of labor worthy of its hire; and provide for unemployment in it exactly as for unemployment in shipbuilding or any other recognized bread-winning trade.

7. And take and deal with all the consequences of these acts of justice instead of letting yourself be frightened out of reason and good sense by fear of consequences. We must finally adapt our institutions to human nature. In the long run our present plan of trying to force human nature into a mould of existing abuses, superstitions, and corrupt interests, produces the explosive forces that wreck civilization.

8. Never forget that if you leave your law to judges and your religion to bishops you will presently find yourself without either law or religion. If you doubt this, ask any decent judge or bishop. Do *not* ask somebody who does not know what a judge is, or what a bishop is, or what the law is, or what religion is. In other words, do not ask your newspaper. Journalists are too poorly paid in this country to

know anything that is fit for publication.

CONCLUSIONS

To sum up, we have to depend on the solution of the problem of unemployment, probably on the principles laid down in the Minority Report of the Royal Commission on the Poor Law, to make the sexual relations between men and women decent and honorable by making women economically independent of men, and (in the younger son section of the upper classes) men economically independent of women. We also have to bring ourselves into line with the rest of Protestant civilization by providing means for dissolving all unhappy, improper, and inconvenient marriages. And, as it is our cautious custom to lag behind the rest of the world to see how their experiments in reform turn out before venturing ourselves, and then take advantage of their experience to get ahead of them, we should recognize that the ancient system of specifying grounds for divorce, such as adultery, cruelty, drunkenness, felony, insanity, vagrancy, neglect to provide for wife and children, desertion, public defamation, violent temper, religious heterodoxy, contagious disease, outrages, indignities, personal abuse, "mental anguish," conduct rendering life burdensome and so forth (all these are examples from some code actually in force at present), is a mistake, because the only effect of compelling people to plead and prove misconduct is that cases are manufactured and clean linen purposely smirched and washed in public, to the great distress and disgrace of innocent children and relatives, whilst the grounds have at the same time to be made so general that any sort of human conduct may be brought within them by a little special pleading and a little mental reservation on the part of witnesses examined on oath. When it comes to "conduct rendering life burdensome," it is clear that no marriage is any longer indissoluble; and the sensible thing to do then is to grant divorce whenever it is desired, without asking why.

GETTING MARRIED

ON a fine morning in the spring of 1908 *the Norman kitchen in the Palace of the Bishop of Chelsea looks very spacious and clean and handsome and healthy.*

The Bishop is lucky enough to have a XII century palace. The palace itself has been lucky enough to escape being carved up into XV century Gothic, or shaved into XVIII century ashlar, or "restored" by a XIX century builder and a Victorian architect with a deep sense of the umbrella-like gentlemanliness of XIV century vaulting. The present occupant, A. Chelsea, unofficially Alfred Bridgenorth, appreciates Norman work. He has, by adroit complaints of the discomfort of the place, induced the Ecclesiastical Commissioners to give him some money to spend on it; and with this he has got rid of the wall papers, the paint, the partitions, the exquisitely planed and moulded casings with which the Victorian cabinet-makers enclosed and hid the huge black beams of hewn oak, and of all the other expedients of his predecessors to make themselves feel at home and respectable in a Norman fortress. It is a house built to last for ever. The walls and beams are big enough to carry the tower of Babel, as if the builders, anticipating our modern ideas and instinctively defying them, had resolved to shew how much material they could lavish on a house built for the glory of God, instead of keeping a competitive eye on the advantage of sending in the lowest tender, and scientifically calculating how little material would be enough to prevent the whole affair from tumbling down by its own weight.

The kitchen is the Bishop's favorite room. This is not at all because he is a man of humble mind; but because the kitchen is one of the finest rooms in the house. The Bishop has neither the income nor the appetite to have his cooking done there. The windows, high up in the wall, look north and south. The north window is the largest; and if we look into the kitchen through it we see facing us the south wall with small Norman windows and an open door near the corner to the left. Through this door we have a glimpse of the garden, and of a garden chair in the sunshine. In the right-hand corner is an entrance to a vaulted circular chamber with a winding stair leading up through a tower to the upper floors of the palace. In the wall to our right is the immense fire-

place, with its huge spit like a baby crane, and a collection of old iron and brass instruments which pass as the original furniture of the fire, though as a matter of fact they have been picked up from time to time by the Bishop at secondhand shops. In the near end of the left-hand wall a small Norman door gives access to the Bishop's study, formerly a scullery. Farther along, a great oak chest stands against the wall. Across the middle of the kitchen is a big timber table surrounded by eleven stout rush-bottomed chairs: four on the far side, three on the near side, and two at each end. There is a big chair with railed back and sides on the hearth. On the floor is a drugget of thick fibre matting. The only other piece of furniture is a clock with a wooden dial about as large as the bottom of a washtub, the weights, chains, and pendulum being of corresponding magnitude; but the Bishop has long since abandoned the attempt to keep it going. It hangs above the oak chest.

The kitchen is occupied at present by the Bishop's lady, Mrs Bridgenorth, who is talking to Mr William Collins, the greengrocer. He is in evening dress, though it is early forenoon. Mrs Bridgenorth is a quiet happy-looking woman of fifty or thereabouts, placid, gentle, and humorous, with delicate features and fine grey hair with many white threads. She is dressed as for some festivity; but she is taking things easily as she sits in the big chair by the hearth, reading The Times.

Collins is an elderly man with a rather youthful waist. His muttonchop whiskers have a coquettish touch of Dundreary at their lower ends. He is an affable man, with those perfect manners which can be acquired only in keeping a shop for the sale of necessaries of life to ladies whose social position is so unquestionable that they are not anxious about it. He is a reassuring man, with a vigilant grey eye, and the power of saying anything he likes to you without offence, because his tone always implies that he does it with your kind permission. Withal by no means servile: rather gallant and compassionate, but never without a conscientious recognition, on public grounds, of social distinctions. He is at the oak chest counting a pile of napkins.

Mrs Bridgenorth reads placidly: Collins counts: a blackbird sings in the garden. Mrs Bridgenorth puts The Times down in her lap and considers Collins for a moment.

MRS BRIDGENORTH. Do you never feel nervous on these occasions, Collins?

COLLINS. Lord bless you, no, maam. It would be a joke, after marrying five of your daughters, if I was to get nervous over marrying the last of them.

MRS BRIDGENORTH. I have always said you were a wonderful man, Collins.

COLLINS [*almost blushing*] Oh, maam!

MRS BRIDGENORTH. Yes, I never could arrange anything—a wedding or even a dinner—without some hitch or other.

COLLINS. Why should you give yourself the trouble, maam? Send for the greengrocer, maam: thats the secret of easy housekeeping. Bless you, it's his business. It pays him and you, let alone the pleasure in a house like this [*Mrs Bridgenorth bows in acknowledgment of the compliment*]. They joke about the greengrocer, just as they joke about the mother-in-law. But they cant get on without both.

MRS BRIDGENORTH. What a bond between us, Collins!

COLLINS. Bless you, maam, theres all sorts of bonds between all sorts of people. You are a very affable lady, maam, for a Bishop's lady. I have known Bishops' ladies that would fairly provoke you to up and cheek them; but nobody would ever forget himself and his place with you, maam.

MRS BRIDGENORTH. Collins: you are a flatterer. You will superintend the breakfast yourself as usual, of course, wont you?

COLLINS. Yes, yes, bless you, maam, of course. I always do. Them fashionable caterers send down such people as I never did set eyes on. Dukes you would take them for. You see the relatives shaking hands with them and asking them about the family—actually ladies saying "Where have we met before?" and all sorts of confusion. Thats my secret in business, maam. You can always spot me as the greengrocer. It's a fortune to me in these days, when you cant hardly tell who anyone is or isnt. [*He goes out through the tower, and immediately returns for a moment to announce*] The General, maam.

Mrs Bridgenorth rises to receive her brother-in-law, who enters resplendent in full-dress uniform, with many medals and orders. General Bridgenorth is a well set up man of fifty, with large brave nostrils, an iron mouth, faithful dog's eyes, and much natural simplicity and dignity of character. He is ignorant, stupid, and prejudiced, having been carefully trained to be so; and it is not always possible to be patient with him when his unquestionably good intentions become actively mischievous; but one blames society, not himself, for this. He would be no worse a man than Collins, had he enjoyed Collins's social opportunities. He comes to the hearth, where Mrs Bridgenorth is standing with her back to the fireplace.

MRS BRIDGENORTH. Good morning, Boxer. [*They shake hands*]. Another niece to give away. This is the last of them.

THE GENERAL [*very gloomy*] Yes, Alice. Nothing for the old warrior uncle to do but give away brides to luckier men than himself. Has—[*he chokes*] has your sister come yet?

MRS BRIDGENORTH. Why do you always call Lesbia my sister? Dont you know that it annoys her more than any of the rest of your tricks?

THE GENERAL. Tricks! Ha! Well, I'll try to break myself of it; but I think she might bear with me in a little thing like that. She knows that her name sticks in my throat. Better call her your sister than try to call her L—[*he almost breaks down*] L— well, call her by her name and make a fool of myself by crying. [*He sits down at the near end of the table*].

MRS BRIDGENORTH [*going to him and rallying him*] Oh come, Boxer! Really, really! We are no longer boys and girls. You cant keep up a broken heart all your life. It must be nearly twenty years since she refused you. And you know that it's not because she dislikes you, but only that she's not a marrying woman.

THE GENERAL. It's no use. I love her still. And I cant help telling her so whenever we meet, though I know it makes her avoid me. [*He all but weeps*].

MRS BRIDGENORTH. What does she say when you tell her?

THE GENERAL. Only that she wonders when I am going to grow out of it. I know now that I shall never grow out of it.

MRS BRIDGENORTH. Perhaps you would if you married her. I believe youre better as you are, Boxer.

THE GENERAL. I'm a miserable man. I'm really sorry to be a ridiculous old bore, Alice; but when I come to this house for a wedding—to these scenes—to—to—recollections of the past—always to give the bride to somebody else, and never to have my bride given to me—[*he rises abruptly*] May I go into the garden and smoke it off?

MRS BRIDGENORTH. Do, Boxer.

Collins returns with the wedding cake.

MRS BRIDGENORTH. Oh, heres the cake. I believe it's the same one we had for Florence's wedding.

THE GENERAL. I cant bear it [*he hurries out through the garden door*].

COLLINS [*putting the cake on the table*] Well, look at that, maam! Aint it odd that after all the weddings he's given away at, the General cant stand the sight of a wedding cake yet. It always seems to give him the same shock.

MRS BRIDGENORTH. Well, it's his last shock. You have married the whole family now, Collins. [*She takes up The Times again and resumes her seat*].

COLLINS. Except your sister, maam. A fine character of a lady, maam, is Miss Grantham. I have an ambition to arrange her wedding breakfast.

MRS BRIDGENORTH. She wont marry, Collins.

COLLINS. Bless you, maam, they all say that. You and me said it, I'll lay. I did, anyhow.

MRS BRIDGENORTH. No: marriage came natural to me. I should have thought it did to you too.

COLLINS [*pensive*] No, maam: it didnt come natural. My wife had to break me into it. It came natural to her: she's what you might call a regular old hen. Always wants to have her family within sight of her. Wouldnt go to bed unless she knew they was all safe at home and the door locked, and the lights out. Always wants her luggage in the carriage with her. Always goes and makes the engine driver promise her to be careful. She's a born wife and mother, maam. Thats why my children all ran away from home.

MRS BRIDGENORTH. Did you ever feel inclined to run away, Collins?

COLLINS. Oh yes maam, yes: very often. But when it came to the point I couldnt bear to hurt her feelings. She's a sensitive, affectionate, anxious soul; and she was never brought up to know what freedom is to some people. You see, family life is all the life she knows: she's like a bird born in a cage, that would die if you let it loose in the woods. When I thought how little it was to a man of my easy temper to put up with her, and how deep it would hurt her to think it was because I didnt care for her, I always put off running away til next time; and so in the end I never ran away at all. I daresay it was good for me to be took such care of; but it cut me off from all my old friends something dreadful, maam: especially the women, maam. She never gave them a chance: she didnt indeed. She never understood that married people should take holidays from one another if they are to keep at all fresh. Not that I ever got tired of her, maam; but my! how I used to get tired of home life sometimes. I used to catch myself envying my brother George: I positively did, maam.

MRS BRIDGENORTH. George was a bachelor then, I suppose?

COLLINS. Bless you, no, maam. He married a very fine figure of a woman; but she was that changeable and what you might call susceptible, you would not believe. She didnt seem to have any control over herself when she fell in love. She would mope for a couple of days, crying about nothing; and then she would up and say—no matter who was there to hear her—"I must go to him, George"; and away she would go from her home and her husband without with-your-leave or by-your-leave.

MRS BRIDGENORTH. But do you mean that she did this more than once? That she came back?

COLLINS. Bless you, maam, she done it five times to my own knowledge; and then George gave up telling us about it, he got so used to it.

MRS BRIDGENORTH. But did he always take her back?

COLLINS. Well, what could he do, maam? Three times out of four the men would bring her back the same evening and no harm done. Other times theyd run away from her. What could any man with a heart do but comfort her when she came back crying at the way they dodged her when she threw herself at their heads, pretending they was too noble to accept the sacrifice she was making. George told her again and again that if she'd only stay at home and hold off a bit theyd be at her feet all day long. She got sensible at last and took his advice. George always liked change of company.

MRS BRIDGENORTH. What an odious woman, Collins! Dont you think so?

COLLINS [*judicially*] Well, many ladies with a domestic turn thought so and said so, maam. But I will say for Mrs George that the variety of experience made her wonderful interesting. Thats where the flighty ones score off the steady ones, maam. Look at my old woman! She's never known any man but me; and she cant properly know me, because she dont know other men to compare me with. Of course she knows her parents in—well, in the way one does know one's parents: not knowing half their lives as you might say, or ever thinking that they was ever young; and she knew her children as children, and never thought of them as independent human beings til they ran away and nigh broke her heart for a week or two. But Mrs George she came to know a lot about men of all sorts and ages; for the older she got the younger she liked em; and it certainly made her interesting, and gave her a lot of sense. I have often taken her advice on things when my own poor old woman wouldnt have been a bit of use to me.

MRS BRIDGENORTH. I hope you dont tell your wife that

you go elsewhere for advice.

COLLINS. Lord bless you, maam, I'm that fond of my old Matilda that I never tell her anything at all for fear of hurting her feelings. You see, she's such an out-and-out wife and mother that she's hardly a responsible human being out of her house, except when she's marketing.

MRS BRIDGENORTH. Does she approve of Mrs George?

COLLINS. Oh, Mrs George gets round her. Mrs George can get round anybody if she wants to. And then Mrs George is very particular about religion. And she's a clairvoyant.

MRS BRIDGENORTH [*surprised*] A clairvoyant!

COLLINS [*calm*] Oh yes, maam, yes. All you have to do is to mesmerize her a bit; and off she goes into a trance, and says the most wonderful things! not things about herself, but as if it was the whole human race giving you a bit of its mind. Oh, wonderful, maam, I assure you. You couldnt think of a game that Mrs George isnt up to.

Lesbia Grantham comes in through the tower. She is a tall, handsome, slender lady in her prime: that is, between 36 and 55. She has what is called a well-bred air, dressing very carefully to produce that effect without the least regard for the latest fashions, sure of herself, very terrifying to the young and shy, fastidious to the ends of her long finger-tips, and tolerant and amused rather than sympathetic.

LESBIA. Good morning, dear big sister.

MRS BRIDGENORTH. Good morning, dear little sister. [*They kiss*].

LESBIA. Good morning, Collins. How well you are looking! And how young! [*She turns the middle chair away from the table and sits down*].

COLLINS. Thats only my professional habit at a wedding, Miss. You should see me at a political dinner. I look nigh seventy. [*Looking at his watch*] Time's getting along, maam. May I send up word from you to Miss Edith to hurry a bit with her dressing?

MRS BRIDGENORTH. Do, Collins.

Collins goes out through the tower, taking the cake with him.

LESBIA. Dear old Collins! Has he told you any stories this morning?

MRS BRIDGENORTH. Yes. You were just late for a particularly thrilling invention of his.

LESBIA. About Mrs George?

MRS BRIDGENORTH. Yes. He says she's a clairvoyant.

LESBIA. I wonder whether he really invented Mrs George, or stole her out of some book.

MRS BRIDGENORTH. I wonder!

LESBIA. Wheres the Barmecide?

MRS BRIDGENORTH. In the study, working away at his new book. He thinks no more now of having a daughter married than of having an egg for breakfast.

The General, soothed by smoking, comes in from the garden.

THE GENERAL [*with resolute bonhomie*] Ah, Lesbia! How do you do? [*They shake hands; and he takes the chair on her right*].

Mrs Bridgenorth goes out through the tower.

LESBIA. How are you, Boxer? You look almost as gorgeous as the wedding cake.

THE GENERAL. I make a point of appearing in uniform whenever I take part in any ceremony, as a lesson to the subalterns. It is not the custom in Engand; but it ought to be.

LESBIA. You look very fine, Boxer. What a frightful lot of bravery all these medals must represent!

THE GENERAL. No, Lesbia. They represent despair and cowardice. I won all the early ones by trying to get killed. You know why.

LESBIA. But you had a charmed life?

THE GENERAL. Yes, a charmed life. Bayonets bent on my buckles. Bullets passed through me and left no trace: thats the worst of modern bullets: Ive never been hit by a dum-dum. When I was only a company officer I had at least the right to expose myself to death in the field. Now I'm a General even that resource is cut off. [*Persuasively drawing his chair nearer to her*] Listen to me, Lesbia. For the tenth and last time—

LESBIA [*interrupting*] On Florence's wedding morning, two years ago, you said "For the ninth and last time."

THE GENERAL. We are two years older, Lesbia. I'm fifty: you are—

LESBIA. Yes. I know. It's no use, Boxer. When will you be old enough to take no for an answer?

THE GENERAL. Never, Lesbia, never. You have never given me a real reason for refusing me yet. I once thought it was somebody else. There were lots of fellows after you; but now theyve all given it up and married. [*Bending still nearer to her*] Lesbia: tell me your secret. Why—

LESBIA [*sniffing disgustedly*] Oh! Youve been smoking. [*She rises and goes to the chair on the hearth*] Keep away, you wretch.

THE GENERAL. But for that pipe, I could not have faced you without breaking down. It has soothed me and nerved me.

LESBIA [*sitting down with The Times in her hand*] Well, it has nerved me to tell you why I'm going to be an old maid.

THE GENERAL [*impulsively approaching her*] Dont say that, Lesbia. It's not natural: it's not right: it's—

LESBIA [*fanning him off*] No: no closer, Boxer, please. [*He retreats, discouraged*]. It may not be natural; but it happens all the same. Youll find plenty of women like me, if you care to look for them: women with lots of character and good looks and money and offers, who wont and dont get married. Cant you guess why?

THE GENERAL. I can understand when there is another.

LESBIA. Yes; but there isnt another. Besides, do you suppose I think, at my time of life, that the difference between one decent sort of man and another is worth bothering about?

THE GENERAL. The heart has its preferences, Lesbia. One image, and one only, gets indelibly—

LESBIA. Yes. Excuse my interrupting you so often; but

your sentiments are so correct that I always know what you are going to say before you finish. You see, Boxer, everybody is not like you. You are a sentimental noodle: you dont see women as they really are. You dont see me as I really am. Now I do see men as they really are. I see you as you really are.

THE GENERAL [*murmuring*] No: dont say that, Lesbia.

LESBIA. I'm a regular old maid. I'm very particular about my belongings. I like to have my own house, and to have it to myself. I have a very keen sense of beauty and fitness and cleanliness and order. I am proud of my independence and jealous for it. I have a sufficiently well-stocked mind to be very good company for myself if I have plenty of books and music. The one thing I never could stand is a great lout of a man smoking all over my house and going to sleep in his chair after dinner, and untidying everything. Ugh!

THE GENERAL. But love—

LESBIA. Oh, love! Have you no imagination? Do you think I have never been in love with wonderful men? heroes! archangels! princes! sages! even fascinating rascals! and had the strangest adventures with them? Do you know what it is to look at a mere real man after that? a man with his boots in every corner, and the smell of his tobacco in every curtain?

THE GENERAL [*somewhat dazed*] Well but—excuse my mentioning it—dont you want children?

LESBIA. I ought to have children. I should be a good mother to children. I believe it would pay the country very well to pay ME very well to have children. But the country tells me that I cant have a child in my house without a man in it too; so I tell the country that it will have to do without my children. If I am to be a mother, I really cannot have a man bothering me to be a wife at the same time.

THE GENERAL. My dear Lesbia: you know I dont wish to be impertinent; but these are not correct views for an English lady to express.

LESBIA. That is why I dont express them, except to

gentlemen who wont take any other answer. The difficulty, you see, is that I really am an English lady, and am particularly proud of being one.

THE GENERAL. I'm sure of that, Lesbia: quite sure of it. I never meant—

LESBIA [*rising impatiently*] Oh, my dear Boxer, do please try to think of something else than whether you have offended me, and whether you are doing the correct thing as an English gentleman. You are faultless, and very dull. [*She shakes her shoulders intolerantly and walks across to the other side of the kitchen*].

THE GENERAL [*moodily*] Ha! thats whats the matter with me. Not clever. A poor silly soldier man.

LESBIA. The whole matter is very simple. As I say, I am an English lady, by which I mean that I have been trained to do without what I cant have on honorable terms, no matter what it is.

THE GENERAL. I really dont understand you, Lesbia.

LESBIA [*turning on him*] Then why on earth do you want to marry a woman you dont understand?

THE GENERAL. I dont know. I suppose I love you.

LESBIA. Well, Boxer, you can love me as much as you like, provided you look happy about it and dont bore me. But you cant marry me; and thats all about it.

THE GENERAL. It's so frightfully difficult to argue the matter fairly with you without wounding your delicacy by overstepping the bounds of good taste. But surely there are calls of nature—

LESBIA. Dont be ridiculous, Boxer.

THE GENERAL. Well how am I to express it? Hang it all, Lesbia, dont you want a husband?

LESBIA. No. I want children; and I want to devote myself entirely to my children, and not to their father. The law will not allow me to do that; so I have made up my mind to have neither husband nor children.

THE GENERAL. But, great Heavens, the natural appetites—

LESBIA. As I said before, an English lady is not the slave

of her appetites. That is what an English gentleman seems incapable of understanding. [*She sits down at the end of the table, near the study door*].

THE GENERAL [*huffily*] Oh well, if you refuse, you refuse. I shall not ask you again. I'm sorry I returned to the subject. [*He retires to the hearth and plants himself there, wounded and lofty*].

LESBIA. Dont be cross, Boxer.

THE GENERAL. I'm not cross, only wounded, Lesbia. And when you talk like that, I dont feel convinced: I only feel utterly at a loss.

LESBIA. Well, you know our family rule. When at a loss consult the greengrocer. [*Opportunely Collins comes in through the tower*]. Here he is.

COLLINS. Sorry to be so much in and out, Miss. I thought Mrs Bridgenorth was here. The table is ready now for the breakfast, if she would like to see it.

LESBIA. If you are satisfied, Collins, I am sure she will be.

THE GENERAL. By the way, Collins: I thought theyd made you an alderman.

COLLINS. So they have, General.

THE GENERAL. Then wheres your gown?

COLLINS. I dont wear it in private life, General.

THE GENERAL. Why? Are you ashamed of it?

COLLINS. No, General. To tell you the truth, I take a pride in it. I cant help it.

THE GENERAL. Attention, Collins. Come here. [*Collins comes to him*]. Do you see my uniform—all my medals?

COLLINS. Yes, General. They strike the eye, as it were.

THE GENERAL. They are meant to. Very well. Now you know, dont you, that your services to the community as a greengrocer are as important and as dignified as mine as a soldier?

COLLINS. I'm sure it's very honorable of you to say so, General.

THE GENERAL [*emphatically*] You know also, dont you, that any man who can see anything ridiculous, or unmanly, or unbecoming in your work or in your civic robes is not a gentleman, but a jumping, bounding, snorting cad?

COLLINS. Well, strictly between ourselves, that is my opinion, General.

THE GENERAL. Then why not dignify my niece's wedding by wearing your robes?

COLLINS. A bargain's a bargain, General. Mrs Bridgenorth sent for the greengrocer, not for the alderman. It's just as unpleasant to get more than you bargain for as to get less.

THE GENERAL. I'm sure she will agree with me. I attach importance to this as an affirmation of solidarity in the service of the community. The Bishop's apron, my uniform, your robes: the Church, the Army, and the Municipality.

COLLINS [*retiring*] Very well, General. [*He turns dubiously to Lesbia on his way to the tower*]. I wonder what my wife will say, Miss?

THE GENERAL. What! Is your wife ashamed of your robes?

COLLINS. No, sir, not ashamed of them. But she grudged the money for them; and she will be afraid of my sleeves getting into the gravy.

Mrs Bridgenorth, her placidity quite upset, comes in with a letter; hurries past Collins; and comes between Lesbia and the General.

MRS BRIDGENORTH. Lesbia: Boxer: heres a pretty mess!

Collins goes out discreetly.

THE GENERAL. Whats the matter?

MRS BRIDGENORTH. Reginald's in London, and wants to come to the wedding.

THE GENERAL [*stupended*] Well, dash my buttons!

LESBIA. Oh, all right, let him come.

THE GENERAL. Let him come! Why, the decree has not been made absolute yet. Is he to walk in here to Edith's wedding, reeking from the Divorce Court?

MRS BRIDGENORTH [*vexedly sitting down in the middle chair*] It's too bad. No: I cant forgive him, Lesbia, really. A man of Reginald's age, with a young wife—the best of girls, and as pretty as she can be—to go off with a common woman from the streets! Ugh!

LESBIA. You must make allowances. What can you expect? Reginald was always weak. He was brought up to be weak. The family property was all mortgaged when he inherited it. He had to struggle along in constant money difficulties, hustled by his solicitors, morally bullied by the Barmecide, and physically bullied by Boxer, while they two were fighting their own way and getting well trained. You know very well he couldnt afford to marry until the mortgages were cleared and he was over fifty. And then of course he made a fool of himself marrying a child like Leo.

THE GENERAL. But to hit her! Absolutely to hit her! He knocked her down—knocked her flat down on a flowerbed in the presence of his gardener. He! the head of the family! the man that stands before the Barmecide and myself as Bridgenorth of Bridgenorth! to beat his wife and go off with a low woman and be divorced for it in the face of all England! in the face of my uniform and Alfred's apron! I can never forget what I felt: it was only the King's personal request —virtually a command—that stopped me from resigning my commission. I'd cut Reginald dead if I met him in the street.

MRS BRIDGENORTH. Besides, Leo's coming. Theyd meet. It's impossible, Lesbia.

LESBIA. Oh, I forgot that. That settles it. He mustnt come.

THE GENERAL. Of course he mustnt. You tell him that if he enters this house, I'll leave it; and so will every decent man and woman in it.

COLLINS [*returning for a moment to announce*] Mr Reginald, maam. [*He withdraws when Reginald enters*].

THE GENERAL [*beside himself*] Well, dash my buttons!!

Reginald is just the man Lesbia has described. He is hardened and tough physically, and hasty and boyish in his manner and speech, belonging as he does to the large class of English gentlemen of property (solicitor-managed) who have never developed intellectually since their schooldays. He is a muddled, rebellious, hasty, untidy, forgetful, always late sort of man, who very evidently needs the care of a capable woman, and has never been lucky or attractive enough to get it. All the same, a likeable man, from whom nobody apprehends any malice nor expects any achievement. In everything but years he is younger than his brother the General.

REGINALD [*coming forward between the General and Mrs Bridgenorth*] Alice: it's no use. I cant stay away from Edith's wedding. Good morning, Lesbia. How are you, Boxer? [*He offers the General his hand*].

THE GENERAL [*with crushing stiffness*] I was just telling Alice, sir, that if you entered this house, I should leave it.

REGINALD. Well, dont let me detain you, old chap. When you start calling people Sir, youre not particularly good company.

LESBIA. Dont you two begin to quarrel. That wont improve the situation.

MRS BRIDGENORTH. I think you might have waited until you got my answer, Rejjy.

REGINALD. It's so jolly easy to say No in a letter. Wont you let me stay?

MRS BRIDGENORTH. How can I? Leo's coming.

REGINALD. Well, she wont mind.

THE GENERAL. Wont mind!!!!!

LESBIA. Dont talk nonsense, Rejjy; and be off with you.

THE GENERAL [*with biting sarcasm*] At school you had a theory that women liked being knocked down, I remember.

REGINALD. Youre a nice, chivalrous, brotherly sort of swine, you are.

THE GENERAL. Mr Bridgenorth: are you going to leave this house or am I?

REGINALD. You are, I hope. [*He emphasizes his intention to stay by sitting down*].

THE GENERAL. Alice: will you allow me to be driven from Edith's wedding by this—

LESBIA [*warningly*] Boxer!

THE GENERAL. —by this Respondent? Is Edith to be given away by him?

MRS BRIDGENORTH. Certainly not. Reginald: you were not asked to come; and I have asked you to go. You know how fond I am of Leo; and you know what she would feel if she came in and found you here.

COLLINS [*again appearing in the tower*] Mrs Reginald, maam.

LESBIA	No, no. Ask her to—	[*All three*
MRS BRIDGENORTH	Oh how unfortunate!	*clamoring*
THE GENERAL	Well, dash my buttons!	*together*].

It is too late: Leo is already in the kitchen. Collins goes out, mutely abandoning a situation which he deplores but has been unable to save.

Leo is very pretty, very youthful, very restless, and consequently very charming to people who are touched by youth and beauty, as well as to those who regard young women as more or less appetizing lollipops, and dont regard old women at all. Coldly studied, Leo's restlessness is much less lovable than the kittenishness which comes from a rich and fresh vitality. She is a born fusser about herself and everybody else for whom she feels responsible; and her vanity causes her to exaggerate her responsibilities officiously. All her fussing is about little things; but she often calls them by big names, such as Art, the Divine Spark, the world, motherhood, good breeding, the Universe, the Creator, or anything else that happens to strike her imagination as sounding intellectually important. She has more than common imagination and no more than common conception and penetration; so that she is always on the high horse about words and always in the perambulator about things. Considering herself clever, thoughtful, and superior to ordinary weaknesses and prejudices, she recklessly attaches herself to clever men on that understanding, with the result that they are first delighted, then exasperated, and finally bored. When marrying Reginald she told her friends that there was a great deal in him which needed bringing out. If she were a middle-aged man she would be the terror of his club. Being a pretty young woman, she is forgiven everything, proving that "Tout comprendre, c'est tout pardonner" is an error, the fact being that the secret of forgiving everything is to understand nothing.

She runs in fussily, full of her own importance, and swoops on Lesbia, who is much less disposed to spoil her than Mrs Bridgenorth is. But Leo affects a special intimacy with Lesbia, as of two thinkers among the Philistines.

LEO [*to Lesbia, kissing her*] Good morning. [*Coming to Mrs Bridgenorth*] How do, Alice? [*Passing on towards the hearth*] Why so gloomy, General? [*Reginald rises between her and the General*] Oh, Rejjy! What will the King's Proctor say?

REGINALD. Damn the King's Proctor!

LEO. Naughty. Well, I suppose I must kiss you; but dont any of you tell. [*She kisses him. They can hardly believe their eyes*]. Have you kept all your promises?

REGINALD. Oh, dont begin bothering about those—

LEO [*insisting*] Have? You? Kept? Your? Promises? Have you rubbed your head with the lotion every night.

REGINALD. Yes, yes. Nearly every night.

LEO. Nearly! I know what that means. Have you worn your liver pad?

THE GENERAL [*solemnly*] Leo: forgiveness is one of the most beautiful traits in a woman's nature; but there are things that should not be forgiven to a man. When a man knocks a woman down [*Leo gives a little shriek of laughter and collapses on a chair next Mrs Bridgenorth, on her left*]—

REGINALD [*sardonically*] The man that would raise his hand to a woman, save in the way of kindness, is unworthy the name of Bridgenorth. [*He sits down at the end of the table nearest the hearth.*]

THE GENERAL [*much huffed*] Oh, well, if Leo does not mind, of course I have no more to say. But I think you might out of consideration for the family, beat your wife in private and not in the presence of the gardener.

REGINALD [*out of patience*] Whats the good of beating your wife unless theres a witness to prove it afterwards? You dont suppose a man beats his wife for the fun of it, do you? How could she have got her divorce if I hadnt beaten her? Nice state of things, that!

THE GENERAL [*gasping*] Do you mean to tell me that you did it in cold blood? simply to get rid of your wife?

REGINALD. No, I didnt: I did it to get her rid of me. What would you do if you were fool enough to marry a woman thirty years younger than yourself, and then found that she didnt care for you, and was in love with a young fellow with a face like a mushroom?

LEO. He has not. [*Bursting into tears*] And you are most unkind to say I didnt care for you. Nobody could have been fonder of you.

REGINALD. A nice way of shewing your fondness! I had to go out and dig that flower bed all over with my own hands to soften it. I had to pick all the stones out of it. And then she complained that I hadnt done it properly, because she got a worm down her neck. I had to go to Brighton with a poor creature who took a fancy to me on the way down, and got conscientious scruples about committing perjury after dinner. I had to put her down in the hotel book as Mrs Reginald Bridgenorth: Leo's name! Do you know what that feels like to a decent man? Do you know what a decent man feels about his wife's name? How would you like to go into a hotel before all the waiters and people with—with that on your arm? Not that it was the poor girl's fault, of course; only she started crying because I couldnt stand her touching me; and now she keeps writing to me. And then I'm held up in the public court for cruelty and adultery, and turned away from Edith's wedding by Alice, and lectured by you! a bachelor, and a precious green one at that. What do you know about it?

THE GENERAL. Am I to understand that the whole case was one of collusion?

REGINALD. Of course it was. Half the cases are collusions: what are people to do? [*The General, passing his hand dazedly over his bewildered brow, sinks into the railed chair*]. And what do you take me for, that you should have the cheek to pretend to believe all that rot about my knocking Leo about and leaving her for—for a—a—Ugh! you should have seen her.

THE GENERAL. This is perfectly astonishing to me. Why did you do it? Why did Leo allow it?

REGINALD. Youd better ask her.

LEO [*still in tears*] I'm sure I never thought it would be so horrid for Rejjy. I offered honorably to do it myself, and let him divorce me; but he wouldnt. And he said himself that it was the only way to do it—that it was the law that he should do it that way. I never saw that hateful creature until that day in Court. If he had only shewn her to me before, I should never have allowed it.

MRS BRIDGENORTH. You did all this for Leo's sake, Rejjy?

REGINALD [*with an unbearable sense of injury*] I shouldnt mind a bit if it were for Leo's sake. But to have to do it to make room for that mushroom-faced serpent—!

THE GENERAL [*jumping up*] What right had he to be made room for? Are you in your senses? What right?

REGINALD. The right of being a young man, suitable to a young woman. I had no right at my age to marry Leo: she knew no more about life than a child.

LEO. I knew a great deal more about it than a great baby like you. I'm sure I dont know how youll get on with no one to take care of you: I often lie awake at night thinking about it. And now youve made me thoroughly miserable.

REGINALD. Serve you right! [*She weeps*]. There: dont get into a tantrum, Leo?

LESBIA. May one ask who is the mushroom-faced serpent?

LEO. He isnt.

REGINALD. Sinjon Hotchkiss, of course.

MRS BRIDGENORTH. Sinjon Hotchkiss! Why, he's coming to the wedding!

REGINALD. What! In that case I'm off [*he makes for the tower*].

LEO	[*all four rushing after him and capturing him on the threshold*]	[*seizing him*] No you shant. You promised to be nice to him.
THE GENERAL		No, dont go, old chap. Not from Edith's wedding.
MRS BRIDGENORTH		Oh, do stay, Rejjy. I shall really be hurt if you desert us.
LESBIA		Better stay, Reginald. You must meet him sooner or later.

REGINALD. A moment ago, when I wanted to stay, you were all shoving me out of the house. Now that I want to go, you wont let me.

MRS BRIDGENORTH. I shall send a note to Mr Hotchkiss not to come.

LEO [*weeping again*] Oh, Alice! [*She comes back to her chair, heartbroken*].

REGINALD [*out of patience*] Oh well, let her have her way. Let her have her mushroom. Let him come. Let them all come.

He crosses the kitchen to the oak chest and sits sulkily on it. Mrs Bridgenorth shrugs her shoulders and sits at the table in Reginald's neighborhood listening in placid helplessness. Lesbia, out of patience with Leo's tears, goes into the garden and sits there near the door, snuffing up the open air in her relief from the domestic stuffiness of Reginald's affairs.

LEO. It's so cruel of you to go on pretending that I dont care for you, Rejjy.

REGINALD [*bitterly*] She explained to me that it was only that she had exhausted my conversation.

THE GENERAL [*coming paternally to Leo*] My dear girl: all the conversation in the world has been exhausted long ago. Heaven knows I have exhausted the conversation of the British Army these thirty years; but I dont leave it on that account.

LEO. It's not that Ive exhausted it; but he will keep on repeating it when I want to read or go to sleep. And Sinjon amuses me. He's so clever.

THE GENERAL [*stung*] Ha! The old complaint. You all want geniuses to marry. This demand for clever men is ridiculous. Somebody must marry the plain, honest, stupid fellows. Have you thought of that?

LEO. But there are such lots of stupid women to marry. Why do they want to marry us? Besides, Rejjy knows that I'm quite fond of him. I like him because he wants me; and I like Sinjon because I want him. I feel that I have a duty to Rejjy.

THE GENERAL. Precisely: you have.

LEO. And, of course, Sinjon has the same duty to me.

THE GENERAL. Tut, tut!

LEO. Oh, how silly the law is! Why cant I marry them both?

THE GENERAL [*shocked*] Leo!

LEO. Well, I love them both. I should like to marry a lot of men. I should like to have Rejjy for every day, and Sinjon for concerts and theatres and going out in the evenings, and some great austere saint for about once a year at the end of the season, and some perfectly blithering idiot of a boy to be quite wicked with. I so seldom feel wicked; and, when I do, it's such a pity to waste it merely because it's too silly to confess to a real grown-up man.

REGINALD. This is the kind of thing, you know—[*Helplessly*] Well, there it is!

THE GENERAL [*decisively*] Alice: this is a job for the Barmecide. He's a Bishop: it's his duty to talk to Leo. I can stand a good deal; but when it comes to flat polygamy and polyandry, we ought to do something.

MRS BRIDGENORTH [*going to the study door*] Do come here a moment, Alfred. We're in a difficulty.

THE BISHOP [*within*] Ask Collins. I'm busy.

MRS BRIDGENORTH. Collins wont do. It's something very serious. Do come just a moment, dear. [*When she hears him coming she takes a chair at the nearest end of the table*].

The Bishop comes out of his study. He is still a slim active man, spare of flesh, and younger by temperament than his brothers. He has a delicate skin, fine hands, a salient nose with chin to match, a short beard which accentuates his sharp chin by bristling forward, clever humorous eyes, not without a glint of mischief in them, ready bright speech, and the ways of a successful man who is always interested in himself and generally rather well pleased with himself. When Lesbia hears his voice she turns her chair towards him, and presently rises and stands in the doorway listening to the conversation.

THE BISHOP [*going to Leo*] Good morning, my dear. Hullo! Youve brought Reginald with you. Thats very nice of you. Have you reconciled them, Boxer?

THE GENERAL. Reconciled them! Why, man, the whole divorce was a put-up job. She wants to marry some fellow named Hotchkiss.

REGINALD. A fellow with a face like—

LEO. You shant, Rejjy. He has a very fine face.

MRS BRIDGENORTH. And now she says she wants to marry both of them, and a lot of other people as well.

LEO. I didnt say I wanted to marry them: I only said I should like to marry them.

THE BISHOP. Quite a nice distinction, Leo.

LEO. Just occasionally, you know.

THE BISHOP [*sitting down cosily beside her*] Quite so. Sometimes a poet, sometimes a Bishop, sometimes a fairy prince, sometimes somebody quite indescribable, and sometimes nobody at all.

LEO. Yes: thats just it. How did you know?

THE BISHOP. Oh, I should say most imaginative and cultivated young women feel like that. I wouldnt give a rap for one who didnt. Shakespear pointed out long ago that a woman wanted a Sunday husband as well as a weekday one. But, as usual, he didnt follow up the idea.

THE GENERAL [*aghast*] Am I to understand—

THE BISHOP [*cutting him short*] Now, Boxer, am I the Bishop or are you?

THE GENERAL [*sulkily*] You.

THE BISHOP. Then dont ask me are you to understand. "Yours not to reason why: yours but to do and die"—

THE GENERAL. Oh, very well: go on. I'm not clever. Only a silly soldier man. Ha! Go on. [*He throws himself into the railed chair, as one prepared for the worst*].

MRS BRIDGENORTH. Alfred: dont tease Boxer.

THE BISHOP. If we are going to discuss ethical questions we must begin by giving the devil fair play. Boxer never does. England never does. We always assume that the devil is guilty: and we wont allow him to prove his innocence, because it would be against public morals if he succeeded. We used to do the same with prisoners accused of high treason. And the consequence is that we overreach ourselves; and the devil gets the better of us after all. Perhaps thats what most of us intend him to do.

THE GENERAL. Alfred: we asked you here to preach to Leo. You are preaching at me instead. I am not conscious of having said or done anything that calls for that unsolicited attention.

THE BISHOP. But poor little Leo has only told the simple truth; whilst you, Boxer, are striking moral attitudes.

THE GENERAL. I suppose thats an epigram. I dont understand epigrams. I'm only a silly soldier man. Ha! But I can put a plain question. Is Leo to be encouraged to be a polygamist?

THE BISHOP. Remember the British Empire, Boxer. Youre a British General, you know.

THE GENERAL. What has that to do with polygamy?

THE BISHOP. Well, the great majority of our fellow-subjects are polygamists. I cant as a British Bishop insult them by speaking disrespectfully of polygamy. It's a very interesting question. Many very interesting men have been polygamists: Solomon, Mahomet, and our friend the Duke of—of—hm! I never can remember his name.

THE GENERAL. It would become you better, Alfred, to send that silly girl back to her husband and her duty than to talk clever and mock at your religion. "What God hath joined together let not man put asunder." Remember that.

THE BISHOP. Dont be afraid, Boxer. What God hath joined together no man ever shall put asunder: God will take care of that. [*To Leo*] By the way, who was it that joined you and Reginald, my dear?

LEO. It was that awful little curate that afterwards drank, and travelled first class with a third-class ticket, and then tried to go on the stage. But they wouldnt have him. He called himself Egerton Fotheringay.

THE BISHOP. Well, whom Egerton Fotheringay hath joined, let Sir Gorell Barnes put asunder by all means.

THE GENERAL. I may be a silly soldier man; but I call this blasphemy.

THE BISHOP [*gravely*] Better for me to take the name of Mr Egerton Fotheringay in earnest than for you to take a higher name in vain.

LESBIA. Cant you three brothers ever meet without quarrelling?

THE BISHOP [*mildly*] This is not quarrelling, Lesbia: it's only English family life. Good morning.

LEO. You know, Bishop, it's very dear of you to take my part; but I'm not sure that I'm not a little shocked.

THE BISHOP. Then I think Ive been a little more successful than Boxer in getting you into a proper frame of mind.

THE GENERAL [*snorting*] Ha!

LEO. Not a bit; for now I'm going to shock you worse than ever. I think Solomon was an old beast.

THE BISHOP. Precisely what you ought to think of him, my dear. Dont apologize.

THE GENERAL [*more shocked*] Well, but hang it! Solomon was in the Bible. And, after all, Solomon was Solomon.

LEO. And I stick to it: I still want to have a lot of interesting men to know quite intimately—to say everything I think of to them, and have them say everything they think of to me.

THE BISHOP. So you shall, my dear, if you are lucky. But

you know you neednt marry them all. Think of all the buttons you would have to sew on. Besides, nothing is more dreadful than a husband who keeps telling you everything he thinks, and always wants to know what you think.

LEO [*struck by this*] Well, thats very true of Rejjy: in fact, thats why I had to divorce him.

THE BISHOP [*condoling*] Yes: he repeats himself dreadfully, doesnt he?

REGINALD. Look here, Alfred. If I have my faults, let her find them out for herself without your help.

THE BISHOP. She has found them all out already, Reginald.

LEO [*a little huffily*] After all, there are worse men than Reginald. I daresay he's not so clever as you; but still he's not such a fool as you seem to think him!

THE BISHOP. Quite right, dear: stand up for your husband. I hope you will always stand up for all your husbands. [*He rises and goes to the hearth, where he stands complacently with his back to the fireplace, beaming at them all as at a roomful of children*].

LEO. Please dont talk as if I wanted to marry a whole regiment. For me there can never be more than two. I shall never love anybody but Rejjy and Sinjon.

REGINALD. A man with a face like a—

LEO. I wont have it, Rejjy. It's disgusting.

THE BISHOP. You see, my dear, youll exhaust Sinjon's conversation too in a week or so. A man is like a phonograph with half-a-dozen records. You soon get tired of them all; and yet you have to sit at table whilst he reels them off to every new visitor. In the end you have to be content with his common humanity; and when you come down to that, you find out about men what a great English poet of my acquaintance used to say about women: that they all taste alike. Marry whom you please: at the end of a month he'll be Reginald over again. It wasnt worth changing: indeed it wasnt.

LEO. Then it's a mistake to get married.

THE BISHOP. It is, my dear; but it's a much bigger mistake not to get married.

THE GENERAL [*rising*] Ha! You hear that, Lesbia? [*He joins her at the garden door*].

LESBIA. Thats only an epigram, Boxer.

THE GENERAL. Sound sense, Lesbia. When a man talks rot, thats epigram: when he talks sense, then I agree with him.

REGINALD [*coming off the oak chest and looking at his watch*] It's getting late. Wheres Edith? Hasnt she got into her veil and orange blossoms yet?

MRS BRIDGENORTH. Do go and hurry her, Lesbia.

LESBIA [*going out through the tower*] Come with me, Leo.

LEO [*following Lesbia out*] Yes, certainly.

The Bishop goes over to his wife and sits down, taking her hand and kissing it by way of beginning a conversation with her.

THE BISHOP. Alice: Ive had another letter from the mysterious lady who cant spell. I like that woman's letters. Theres an intensity of passion in them that fascinates me.

MRS BRIDGENORTH. Do you mean Incognita Appassionata?

THE BISHOP. Yes.

THE GENERAL [*turning abruptly: he has been looking out into the garden*] Do you mean to say that women write love-letters to you?

THE BISHOP. Of course.

THE GENERAL. They never do to me.

THE BISHOP. The Army doesnt attract women: the Church does.

REGINALD. Do you consider it right to let them? They may be married women, you know.

THE BISHOP. They always are. This one is. [*To Mrs Bridgenorth*] Dont you think her letters are quite the best love-letters I get? [*To the two men*] Poor Alice has to read my love-letters aloud to me at breakfast, when theyre worth it.

MRS BRIDGENORTH. There really is something fascinating about Incognita. She never gives her address. Thats a good sign.

THE GENERAL. Mf! No assignations, you mean?

THE BISHOP. Oh yes: she began the correspondence by making a very curious but very natural assignation. She wants me to meet her in heaven. I hope I shall.

THE GENERAL. Well, I must say I hope not, Alfred. I hope not.

MRS BRIDGENORTH. She says she is happily married, and that love is a necessary of life to her, but that she must have, high above all her lovers—

THE BISHOP. She has several apparently—

MRS BRIDGENORTH. —some great man who will never know her, never touch her, as she is on earth, but whom she can meet in heaven when she has risen above all the everyday vulgarities of earthly love.

THE BISHOP [*rising*] Excellent. Very good for her; and no trouble to me. Everybody ought to have one of these idealizations, like Dante's Beatrice. [*He clasps his hands behind him, and strolls to the hearth and back, singing*].

Lesbia appears in the tower, rather perturbed.

LESBIA. Alice: will you come upstairs? Edith is not dressed.

MRS BRIDGENORTH [*rising*] Not dressed! Does she know what hour it is?

LESBIA. She has locked herself into her room, reading.

The Bishop's song ceases: he stops dead in his stroll.

THE GENERAL. Reading!

THE BISHOP. What is she reading?

LESBIA. Some pamphlet that came by the eleven o'clock post. She wont come out. She wont open the door. And she says she doesn't know whether she's going to be married or not til she's finished the pamphlet. Did you ever hear such a thing? Do come and speak to her.

MRS BRIDGENORTH. Alfred: you had better go.

THE BISHOP. Try Collins.

LESBIA. Weve tried Collins already. He got all that Ive told you out of her through the keyhole. Come, Alice [*She vanishes. Mrs Bridgenorth hurries after her*].

THE BISHOP. This means a delay. I shall go back to my work [*he makes for the study door*].

REGINALD. What are you working at now?

THE BISHOP [*stopping*] A chapter in my history of marriage. I'm just at the Roman business, you know.

THE GENERAL [*coming from the garden door to the chair Mrs Bridgenorth has just left, and sitting down*] Not more Ritualism, I hope, Alfred?

THE BISHOP. Oh no. I mean ancient Rome. [*He seats himself on the edge of the table*]. Ive just come to the period when the propertied classes refused to get married and went in for marriage settlements instead. A few of the oldest families stuck to the marriage tradition so as to keep up the supply of vestal virgins, who had to be legitimate; but nobody else dreamt of getting married. It's all very interesting, because we're coming to that here in England; except that as we dont require any vestal virgins, nobody will get married at all, except the poor, perhaps.

THE GENERAL. You take it devilishly coolly. Reginald: do you think the Barmecide's quite sane?

REGINALD. No worst than ever he was.

THE GENERAL [*to the Bishop*] Do you mean to say you believe such a thing will ever happen in England as that respectable people will give up being married?

THE BISHOP. In England especially they will. In other countries the introduction of reasonable divorce laws will save the situation; but in England we always let an institution strain itself until it breaks. Ive told our last four Prime Ministers that if they didnt make our marriage laws reasonable there would be a strike against marriage, and that it would begin among the propertied classes, where no Government would dare to interfere with it.

REGINALD. What did they say to that?

THE BISHOP. The usual thing. Quite agreed with me, but were sure that they were the only sensible men in the world and that the least hint of marriage reform would lose them the next election. And then lost it all the same: on cordite, on drink, on Chinese labor in South Africa, on all sorts of trumpery.

REGINALD [*lurching across the kitchen towards the hearth with his hands in his pockets*] It's no use: they wont listen to our sort. [*Turning on them*] Of course they have to make you a Bishop and Boxer a General, because, after all, their blessed rabble of snobs and cads and half-starved shopkeepers cant do government work; and the bounders and week-enders are too lazy and vulgar. Theyd simply rot without us; but what do they ever do for us? what attention do they ever pay to what we say and what we want? I take it that we Bridgenorths are a pretty typical English family of the sort that has always set things straight and stuck up for the right to think and believe according to our conscience. But nowadays we are expected to dress and eat as the week-end bounders do, and to think and believe as the converted cannibals of Central Africa do, and to lie down and let every snob and every cad and every halfpenny journalist walk over us. Why, theres not a newspaper in England today that represents what I call solid Bridgenorth opinion and tradition. Half of them read as if they were published at the nearest mothers' meeting, and the other half at the nearest motor garage. Do you call these chaps gentlemen? Do you call them Englishmen? I dont. [*He throws himself disgustedly into the nearest chair*].

THE GENERAL [*excited by Reginald's eloquence*] Do you see my uniform? What did Collins say? It strikes the eye. It was meant to. I put it on expressly to give the modern army bounder a smack in the eye. Somebody has to set a right example by beginning. Well, let it be a Bridgenorth. I believe in family blood and tradition, by George.

THE BISHOP [*musing*] I wonder who will begin the stand against marriage. It must come some day. I was married myself before I'd thought about it; and even if I had thought about it I was too much in love with Alice to let anything stand in the way. But, you know, Ive seen one of our daughters after another—Ethel, Jane, Fanny, and Christina and

Florence—go out at that door in their veils and orange blossoms; and Ive always wondered whether theyd have gone quietly if theyd known what they were doing. Ive a horrible misgiving about that pamphlet. All progress means war with Society. Heaven forbid that Edith should be one of the combatants!

St John Hotchkiss comes into the tower ushered by Collins. He is a very smart young gentleman of twenty-nine or thereabouts, correct in dress to the last thread of his collar, but too much pre-occupied with his ideas to be embarrassed by any concern as to his appearance. He talks about himself with energetic gaiety. He talks to other people with a sweet forbearance (implying a kindly consideration for their stupidity) which infuriates those whom he does not succeed in amusing. They either lose their tempers with him or try in vain to snub him.

COLLINS [*announcing*] Mr Hotchkiss. [*He withdraws*].

HOTCHKISS [*clapping Reginald gaily on the shoulder as he passes him*] Tootle loo, Rejjy.

REGINALD [*curtly, without rising or turning his head*] Morning.

HOTCHKISS. Good morning, Bishop.

THE BISHOP [*coming off the table*]. What on earth are you doing here, Sinjon? You belong to the bridegroom's party: youve no business here until after the ceremony.

HOTCHKISS. Yes, I know: thats just it. May I have a word with you in private? Rejjy or any of the family wont matter; but—[*he glances at the General, who has risen rather stiffly, as he strongly disapproves of the part played by Hotchkiss in Reginald's domestic affairs*].

THE BISHOP. All right, Sinjon. This is our brother, General Bridgenorth. [*He goes to the hearth and posts himself there, with his hands clasped behind him*].

HOTCHKISS. Oh, good! [*He turns to the General, and takes out a card-case*]. As you are in the service, allow me to introduce myself. Read my card, please. [*He presents his card to the astonished General*].

THE GENERAL [*reading*] "Mr St John Hotchkiss, the Celebrated Coward, late Lieutenant in the 165th Fusiliers."

REGINALD [*with a chuckle*] He was sent back from South Africa because he funked an order to attack, and spoiled his commanding officer's plan.

THE GENERAL [*very gravely*] I remember the case now. I had forgotten the name. I'll not refuse your acquaintance, Mr Hotchkiss; partly because youre my brother's guest, and partly because Ive seen too much active service not to know that every man's nerve plays him false at one time or another, and that some very honorable men should never go into action at all, because theyre not built that way. But if I were you I should not use that visiting card. No doubt it's an honorable trait in your character that you dont wish any man to give you his hand in ignorance of your disgrace; but you had better allow us to forget. We wish to forget. It isnt your disgrace alone: it's a disgrace to the army and to all of us. Pardon my plain speaking.

HOTCHKISS [*sunnily*] My dear General, I dont know what fear means in the military sense of the word. Ive fought seven duels with the sabre in Italy and Austria, and one with pistols in France, without turning a hair. There was no other way in which I could vindicate my motives in refusing to make that attack at Smutsfontein. I dont pretend to be a brave man. I'm afraid of wasps. I'm afraid of cats. In spite of the voice of reason, I'm afraid of ghosts; and twice Ive fled across Europe from false alarms of cholera. But afraid to fight I am not. [*He turns gaily to Reginald and slaps him on the shoulder*]. Eh, Rejjy? [*Reginald grunts*].

THE GENERAL. Then why did you not do your duty at Smutsfontein?

HOTCHKISS. I did my duty—my higher duty. If I had made that attack, my commanding officer's plan would have been successful, and he would have been promoted. Now I happen to think that the British Army should be commanded by gentlemen, and by gentlemen alone. This man was not a gentleman. I sacrificed my military career—I faced disgrace and social ostracism—rather than give that man his chance.

THE GENERAL [*generously indignant*] Your commanding officer, sir, was my friend Major Billiter.

HOTCHKISS. Precisely. What a name!

THE GENERAL. And pray, sir, on what ground do you dare allege that Major Billiter is not a gentleman?

HOTCHKISS. By an infallible sign: one of those trifles that stamp a man. He eats rice pudding with a spoon.

THE GENERAL [*very angry*] Confound you, *I* eat rice pudding with a spoon. Now!

HOTCHKISS. Oh, so do I, frequently. But there are ways of doing these things. Billiter's way was unmistakable.

THE GENERAL. Well, *I*'ll tell you something now. When I thought you were only a coward, I pitied you, and would have done what I could to help you back to your place in Society—

HOTCHKISS [*interrupting him*] Thank you: I havnt lost it. My motives have been fully appreciated. I was made an honorary member of two of the smartest clubs in London when the truth came out.

THE GENERAL. Well, sir, those clubs consist of snobs; and you are a jumping, bounding, prancing, snorting snob yourself.

THE BISHOP [*amused but hospitably remonstrant*] My dear Boxer!

HOTCHKISS [*delighted*] How kind of you to say so, General! Youre quite right: I am a snob. Why not? The whole strength of England lies in the fact that the enormous majority of the English people are snobs. They insult poverty. They despise vulgarity. They love nobility. They admire exclusiveness. They will not obey a man risen from the ranks. They never trust one of their own class. I agree with them. I share their instincts. In my undergraduate days I was a Republican—a Socialist. I tried hard to feel toward a common man as I do towards a duke. I couldnt. Neither can you. Well, why should we be ashamed of this aspiration towards what is above us? Why dont I say that an honest man's the noblest work of God? Because I dont think so. If he's not a gentleman, I dont care whether he's honest or not: I shouldnt let his son marry my daughter. And thats the test, mind. Thats the test. You feel as I do. You are a snob in fact: I am a snob, not only in fact, but on principle. I shall go down in history, not as the first snob, but as the first avowed champion of English snobbery, and its first martyr in the army. The navy boasts two such martyrs in Captains Kirby and Wade, who were shot for refusing to fight under Admiral Benbow, a promoted cabin boy. I have always envied them their glory.

THE GENERAL. As a British General, sir, I have to inform you that if any officer under my command violated the sacred equality of our profession by putting a single jot of his duty or his risk on the shoulders of the humblest drummer boy, I'd shoot him with my own hand.

HOTCHKISS. That sentiment is not your equality, General, but your superiority. Ask the Bishop. [*He seats himself on the edge of the table*].

THE BISHOP. I cant support you, Sinjon. My profession also compels me to turn my back on snobbery. You see, I have to do such a terribly democratic thing to every child that is brought to me. Without distinction of class I have to confer on it a rank so high and awful that all the grades in Debrett and Burke seem like the medals they give children in Infant Schools in comparison. I'm not allowed to make any class distinction. They are all soldiers and servants, not officers and masters.

HOTCHKISS. Ah, youre quoting the Baptism service. Thats not a bit real, you know. If I may say so, you would both feel so much more at peace with yourselves if you would acknowledge and confess your real convictions. You know you dont really think a Bishop the equal of a curate, or a lieutenant in a line regiment the equal of a general.

THE BISHOP. Of course I do. I was a curate myself.

THE GENERAL. And I was a lieutenant in a line regiment.

REGINALD. And I was nothing. But we're all our own and one another's equals, arnt we? So perhaps when youve quite done talking about yourselves, we shall get to whatever business Sinjon came about.

HOTCHKISS [*coming off the table hastily*] Oh! true, my dear fellow. I beg a thousand pardons. It's about the wedding!

THE GENERAL. What about the wedding?

HOTCHKISS. Well, we cant get our man up to the scratch. Cecil has locked himself in his room and wont see or speak to anyone. I went up to his room and banged at the door. I told him I should look through the keyhole if he didnt answer. I looked through the keyhole. He was sitting on his bed, reading a book. [*Reginald rises in consternation. The General recoils*]. I told him not to be an ass, and so forth. He said he was not going to budge until he had finished the book. I asked him did he know what time it was, and whether he happened to recollect that he had a rather important appointment to marry Edith. He said the sooner I stopped interrupting him, the sooner he'd be ready. Then he stuffed his fingers in his ears; turned over on his elbows; and buried himself in his beastly book. I couldnt get another word out of him; so I thought I'd better come here and warn you.

REGINALD. This looks to me like a practical joke. Theyve arranged it between them.

THE BISHOP. No. Edith has no sense of humor. And Ive never seen a man in a jocular mood on his wedding morning.

Collins appears in the tower, ushering in the bridegroom, a young gentleman with good looks of the serious kind, somewhat careworn by an exacting conscience, and just now distracted by insoluble problems of conduct.

COLLINS [*announcing*] Mr Cecil Sykes. [*He retires*].

HOTCHKISS. Look here, Cecil: this is all wrong. Youve no business here until after the wedding. Hang it, man! youre the bridegroom.

SYKES [*coming to the Bishop, and addressing him with dogged desperation*] Ive come here to say this. When I proposed to Edith I was in utter ignorance of what I was letting myself in for legally. Having given my word, I will stand to it. You have me at your mercy: marry me if you insist. But take notice that I protest. [*He sits down distractedly in the railed chair*].

THE GENERAL } [*Both highly incensed*] { What the devil do you mean by this? What the—
REGINALD } { Confound your impertinence, what do you—

HOTCHKISS. } { Easy, Rejjy. Easy, old man. Steady, steady, steady. [*Reginald subsides into his chair. Hotchkiss sits on his right, appeasing him*].
THE BISHOP. } { No, please, Rej. Control yourself, Boxer, I beg you.

THE GENERAL. I tell you I cant control myself. Ive been controlling myself for the last half-hour until I feel like bursting. [*He sits down furiously at the end of the table next the study*].

SYKES [*pointing to the simmering Reginald and the boiling General*] Thats just it, Bishop. Edith is her uncles' niece. She cant control herself any more than they can. And she's a Bishop's daughter. That means that she's engaged in social work of all sorts: organizing shop assistants and sweated work girls and all that. When her blood boils about it (and it boils at least once a week) she doesnt care what she says.

REGINALD. Well: you knew that when you proposed to her.

SYKES. Yes; but I didnt know that when we were married I should be legally responsible if she libelled anybody, though all her property is protected against me as if I were the lowest thief and cadger. This morning somebody sent me Belfort Bax's essays on Men's Wrongs; and they have been a perfect eye-opener to me. Bishop: I'm not thinking of myself: I would face anything for Edith. But my mother and sisters are wholly dependent on my property. I'd rather have to cut off an inch from my right arm than a hundred a year from my mother's income. I owe everything to her care of me.

Edith, in dressing-jacket and petticoat, comes in through the tower, swiftly and determinedly, pamphlet in hand, principles up in arms, more of a bishop than her father, yet as much a gentlewoman as her mother. She is the typical spoilt child of a clerical household: almost as terrible a product as the typical spoilt child of a Bohemian household: that is, all her childish affectations of conscientious scruple and religious impulse have been applauded and deferred to until she has become an ethical snob of the first water. Her father's sense of humor and her mother's placid balance have done something to save her humanity; but her impetuous temper and energetic will, unrestrained by any touch of humor or scepticism, carry everything before them. Imperious and dogmatic, she takes command of the party at once.

EDITH [*standing behind Cecil's chair*] Cecil: I heard your voice. I must speak to you very particularly. Papa: go away. Go away everybody.

THE BISHOP [*crossing to the study door*] I think there can be no doubt that Edith wishes us to retire. Come. [*He stands in the doorway, waiting for them to follow*].

SYKES. Thats it, you see. It's just this outspokenness that makes my position hard, much as I admire her for it.

EDITH. Do you want me to flatter and be untruthful?

SYKES. No, not exactly that.

EDITH. Does anybody want me to flatter and be untruthful?

HOTCHKISS. Well, since you ask me, I do. Surely it's the very first qualification for tolerable social intercourse.

THE GENERAL [*markedly*] I hope you will always tell me the truth, my darling, at all events.

EDITH [*complacently coming to the fireplace*] You can depend on me for that, Uncle Boxer.

HOTCHKISS. Are you sure you have any adequate idea of what the truth about a military man really is?

REGINALD [*aggressively*] Whats the truth about you, I wonder?

HOTCHKISS. Oh, quite unfit for publication in its entirety. If Miss Bridgenorth begins telling it, I shall have to leave the room.

REGINALD. I'm not at all surprised to hear it. [*Rising*] But whats it got to do with our business here today? Is it you thats going to be married or is it Edith?

HOTCHKISS. I'm so sorry. I get so interested in myself that I thrust myself into the front of every discussion in the most insufferable way. [*Reginald, with an exclamation of disgust, crosses the kitchen towards the study door*]. But, my dear Rejjy, are you quite sure that Miss Bridgenorth is going to be married? Are you, Miss Bridgenorth?

Before Edith has time to answer her mother returns with Leo and Lesbia.

LEO. Yes, here she is, of course. I told you I heard her dash downstairs. [*She comes to the end of the table next the fireplace*].

MRS BRIDGENORTH [*transfixed in the middle of the kitchen*] And Cecil!!

LESBIA. And Sinjon!

THE BISHOP. Edith wishes to speak to Cecil. [*Mrs Bridgenorth comes to him. Lesbia goes into the garden, as before*]. Let us go into my study.

LEO. But she must come and dress. Look at the hour!

MRS BRIDGENORTH. Come, Leo dear. [*Leo follows her reluctantly. They are about to go into the study with the Bishop*].

HOTCHKISS. Do you know, Miss Bridgenorth, I should most awfully like to hear what you have to say to poor Cecil.

REGINALD [*scandalized*] Well!

EDITH. Who is poor Cecil, pray?

HOTCHKISS. One always calls a man that on his wedding morning: I dont know why. I'm his best man, you know. Dont you think it gives me a certain right to be present in Cecil's interest?

THE GENERAL [*gravely*] There is such a thing as delicacy, Mr Hotchkiss.

HOTCHKISS. There is such a thing as curiosity, General.

THE GENERAL [*furious*] Delicacy is thrown away here, Alfred. Edith: you had better take Sykes into the study.

The group at the study door breaks up. The General flings himself into the last chair on the long side of the table, near the garden door. Leo sits at the end, next him, and Mrs Bridgenorth next Leo. Reginald returns to the oak chest, to be near Leo; and the Bishop goes to his wife and stands by her.

HOTCHKISS [*to Edith*] Of course I'll go if you wish me to. But Cecil's objection to go through with it was so entirely on public grounds—

EDITH [*with quick suspicion*] His objection?

SYKES. Sinjon: you have no right to say that. I expressly said that I'm ready to go through with it.

EDITH. Cecil: do you mean to say that you have been raising difficulties about our marriage?

SYKES. I raise no difficulty. But I do beg you to be careful what you say about people. You must remember, my dear, that when we are married I shall be responsible for everything you say. Only last week you said on a public platform that Slattox and Chinnery were scoundrels. They could have got a thousand pounds damages apiece from me for that if we'd been married at the time.

EDITH [*austerely*] I never said anything of the sort. I never stoop to mere vituperation: what would my girls say of me if I did? I chose my words most carefully. I said they were tyrants, liars, and thieves; and so they are. Slattox is even worse.

HOTCHKISS. I'm afraid that would be at least five thousand pounds.

SYKES. If it were only myself, I shouldnt care. But my mother and sisters! Ive no right to sacrifice them.

EDITH. You neednt be alarmed. I'm not going to be married.

ALL THE REST. Not!

SYKES [*in consternation*] Edith! Are you throwing me over?

EDITH. How can I? you have been beforehand with me.

SYKES. On my honor, no. All I said was that I didnt know the law when I asked you to be my wife.

EDITH. And you wouldnt have asked me if you had. Is that it?

SYKES. No. I should have asked you for my sake to be a

little more careful—not to ruin me uselessly.

EDITH. You think the truth useless?

HOTCHKISS. Much worse than useless, I assure you. Frequently most mischievous.

EDITH. Sinjon: hold your tongue. You are a chatterbox and a fool!

MRS BRIDGENORTH } [*shocked*] { Edith!
THE BISHOP } [*shocked*] { My love!

HOTCHKISS [*mildly*] I shall not take an action, Cecil.

EDITH [*to Hotchkiss*] Sorry; but you are old enough to know better. [*To the others*] And now since there is to be no wedding, we had better get back to our work. Mamma: will you tell Collins to cut up the wedding cake into thirty-three pieces for the club girls. My not being married is no reason why they should be disappointed. [*She turns to go*].

HOTCHKISS [*gallantly*] If youll allow me to take Cecil's place, Miss Bridgenorth—

LEO. Sinjon!

HOTCHKISS. Oh, I forgot. I beg your pardon. [*To Edith, apologetically*] A prior engagement.

EDITH. What! You and Leo! I thought so. Well, hadnt you two better get married at once? I dont approve of long engagements. The breakfast's ready: the cake's ready: everything's ready. I'll lend Leo my veil and things.

THE BISHOP. I'm afraid they must wait until the decree is made absolute, my dear. And the license is not transferable.

EDITH. Oh well, it cant be helped. Is there anything else before I go off to the Club?

SYKES. You dont seem much disappointed, Edith. I cant help saying that much.

EDITH. And you cant help looking enormously relieved, Cecil. We shant be any worse friends, shall we?

SYKES [*distractedly*] Of course not. Still—I'm perfectly ready—at least—if it were not for my mother—Oh, I dont know what to do. Ive been so fond of you; and when the worry of the wedding was over I should have been so fond of you again—

EDITH [*petting him*] Come, come! dont make a scene, dear. Youre quite right. I dont think a woman doing public work ought to get married unless her husband feels about it as she does. I dont blame you at all for throwing me over.

REGINALD [*bouncing off the chest, and passing behind the General to the other end of the table*] No: dash it! I'm not going to stand this. Why is the man always to be put in the wrong? Be honest, Edith. Why werent you dressed? Were you going to throw him over? If you were, take your fair share of the blame; and dont put it all on him.

HOTCHKISS [*sweetly*] Would it not be better—

REGINALD [*violently*] Now look here, Hotchkiss. Who asked you to cut in? Is your name Edith? Am I your uncle?

HOTCHKISS. I wish you were: I should like to have an uncle Reginald.

REGINALD. Yah! Sykes: are you ready to marry Edith or are you not?

SYKES. Ive already said that I'm quite ready. A promise is a promise.

REGINALD. We dont want to know whether a promise is a promise or not. Cant you answer yes or no without spoiling it and setting Hotchkiss here grinning like a Cheshire cat? If she puts on her veil and goes to Church, will you marry her?

SYKES. Certainly. Yes.

REGINALD. Thats all right. Now, Edie, put on your veil and off with you to Church. The bridegroom's waiting. [*He sits down at the table*].

EDITH. Is it understood that Slattox and Chinnery are liars and thieves, and that I hope by next Wednesday to have in my hands conclusive evidence that Slattox is something much worse?

SYKES. I made no conditions as to that when I proposed to you; and now I cant go back. I hope Providence will spare my poor mother. I say again I'm ready to marry you.

EDITH. Then I think you shew great weakness of character; and instead of taking advantage of it I shall set you a better example. I want to know is this true. [*She produces a pamphlet and takes it to the Bishop; then sits down between Hotchkiss and her mother*].

THE BISHOP [*reading the title*] DO YOU KNOW WHAT YOU ARE GOING TO DO? BY A WOMAN WHO HAS DONE IT. May I ask, my dear, what she did?

EDITH. She got married. When she had three children—the eldest only four years old—her husband committed a murder, and then attempted to commit suicide, but only succeeded in disfiguring himself. Instead of hanging him, they sent him to penal servitude for life, for the sake, they said, of his wife and infant children. And she could not get a divorce from that horrible murderer. They would not even keep him imprisoned for life. For twenty years she had to live singly, bringing up her children by her own work, and knowing that just when they were grown up and beginning life, this dreadful creature would be let out to disgrace them all, and prevent the two girls getting decently married, and drive the son out of the country perhaps. Is that really the law? Am I to understand that if Cecil commits a murder, or forges, or steals, or becomes an athiest, I cant get divorced from him?

THE BISHOP. Yes, my dear. That is so. You must take him for better for worse.

EDITH. Then I most certainly refuse to enter into any such wicked contract. What sort of servants? what sort of friends? what sort of Prime Ministers should we have if we took them for better for worse for all their lives? We should simply encourage them in every sort of wickedness. Surely my husband's conduct is of more importance to me than Mr Balfour's or Mr Asquith's. If I had known the law I would never have consented. I dont believe any woman would if she realized what she was doing.

SYKES. But I'm not going to commit murder.

EDITH. How do you know? Ive sometimes wanted to murder Slattox. Have you never wanted to murder somebody, Uncle Rejjy?

REGINALD [*at Hotchkiss, with intense expression*] Yes.

LEO. Rejjy!

REGINALD. I said yes; and I mean yes. There was one night, Hotchkiss, when I jolly nearly shot you and Leo and finished up with myself; and thats the truth.

LEO [*suddenly whimpering*] Oh Rejjy [*she runs to him and kisses him*].

REGINALD [*wrathfully*] Be off. [*She returns weeping to her seat*].

MRS BRIDGENORTH [*petting Leo, but speaking to the company at large*] But isnt all this great nonsense? What likelihood is there of any of us committing a crime?

HOTCHKISS. Oh yes, I assure you. I went into the matter once very carefully; and I found that things I have actually done—things that everybody does, I imagine—would expose me, if I were found out and prosecuted, to ten years penal servitude, two years hard labor, and the loss of all civil rights. Not counting that I'm a private trustee, and, like all private trustees, a fraudulent one. Otherwise, the widow for whom I am trustee would starve occasionally, and the children get no education. And I'm probably as honest a man as any here.

THE GENERAL [*outraged*] Do you imply that I have been guilty of conduct that would expose me to penal servitude?

HOTCHKISS. I should think it quite likely. But of course I dont know.

MRS BRIDGENORTH. But bless me! marriage is not a question of law, is it? Have you children no affection for one another? Surely thats enough?

HOTCHKISS. If it's enough, why get married?

MRS BRIDGENORTH. Stuff, Sinjon! Of course people must get married. [*Uneasily*] Alfred: why dont you say something? Surely youre not going to let this go on?

THE GENERAL. Ive been waiting for the last twenty minutes, Alfred, in amazement! in stupefaction! to hear you put a stop to all this. We look to you: it's your place, your office, your duty. Exert your authority at once.

THE BISHOP. You must give the devil fair play, Boxer.

Until you have heard and weighed his case you have no right to condemn him. I'm sorry you have been kept waiting twenty minutes; but I myself have waited twenty years for this to happen. Ive often wrestled with the temptation to pray that it might not happen in my own household. Perhaps it was a presentiment that it might become a part of our old Bridgenorth burden that made me warn our Governments so earnestly that unless the law of marriage were first made human, it could never become divine.

MRS BRIDGENORTH. Oh, do be sensible about this. People must get married. What would you have said if Cecil's parents had not been married?

THE BISHOP. They were not, my dear.

HOTCHKISS.	Hallo!
REGINALD.	What d'ye mean?
THE GENERAL.	Eh?
LEO.	Not married!
MRS BRIDGENORTH.	What!

SYKES [*rising in amazement*] What on earth do you mean, Bishop? My parents were married.

HOTCHKISS. You cant remember, Cecil.

SYKES. Well, I never asked my mother to shew me her marriage lines, if thats what you mean. What man ever has? I never suspected—I never knew—Are you joking? Or have we all gone mad?

THE BISHOP. Dont be alarmed, Cecil. Let me explain. Your parents were not Anglicans. You were not, I think, Anglican yourself, until your second year at Oxford. They were Positivists. They went through the Positivist ceremony at Newton Hall in Fetter Lane after entering into the civil contract before the Registrar of the West Strand District. I ask you, as an Anglican Catholic, was that a marriage?

SYKES [*overwhelmed*] Great Heavens, no! a thousand times, no. I never thought of that. I'm a child of sin. [*He collapses into the railed chair*].

THE BISHOP. Oh, come, come! You are no more a child of sin than any Jew, or Mahometan, or Nonconformist, or anyone else born outside the Church. But you see how it affects my view of the situation. To me there is only one marriage that is holy: the Church's sacrament of marriage. Outside that, I can recognize no distinction between one civil contract and another. There was a time when all marriages were made in Heaven. But because the Church was unwise and would not make its ordinances reasonable, its power over men and women was taken away from it; and marriages gave place to contracts at a registry office. And now that our Governments refuse to make these contracts reasonable, those whom we in our blindness drove out of the Church will be driven out of the registry office; and we shall have the history of Ancient Rome repeated. We shall be joined by our solicitors for seven, fourteen, or twenty-one years—or perhaps months. Deeds of partnership will replace the old vows.

THE GENERAL. Would you, a Bishop, approve of such partnerships?

THE BISHOP. Do you think that I, a Bishop, approve of the Deceased Wife's Sister Act? That did not prevent its becoming law.

THE GENERAL. But when the Government sounded you as to whether youd marry a man to his deceased wife's sister you very naturally and properly told them youd see them damned first.

THE BISHOP [*horrified*] No, no, really, Boxer! You must not—

THE GENERAL [*impatiently*] Oh, of course I dont mean that you used those words. But that was the meaning and the spirit of it.

THE BISHOP. Not the spirit, Boxer, I protest. But never mind that. The point is that State marriage is already divorced from Church marriage. The relations between Leo and Rejjy and Sinjon are perfectly legal; but do you expect me, as a Bishop, to approve of them?

THE GENERAL. I dont defend Reginald. He should have kicked you out of the house, Mr Hotchkiss.

REGINALD [*rising*] How could I kick him out of the house? He's stronger than me: he could have kicked me out if it came to that. He did kick me out: what else was it but kicking out, to take my wife's affections from me and establish himself in my place? [*He comes to the hearth*].

HOTCHKISS. I protest, Reginald, I said all that a man could to prevent the smash.

REGINALD. Oh, I know you did: I dont blame you: people dont do these things to one another: they happen and they cant be helped. What was I to do? I was old: she was young. I was dull: he was brilliant. I had a face like a walnut: he had a face like a mushroom. I was as glad to have him in the house as she was: he amused me. And we were a couple of fools: he gave us good advice—told us what to do when we didnt know. She found out that I wasnt any use to her and he was; so she nabbed him and gave me the chuck.

LEO. If you dont stop talking in that disgraceful way about our married life, I'll leave the room and never speak to you again.

REGINALD. Youre not going to speak to me again, anyhow, are you? Do you suppose I'm going to visit you when you marry him?

HOTCHKISS. I hope so. Surely youre not going to be vindictive, Rejjy. Besides, youll have all the advantages I formerly enjoyed. Youll be the visitor, the relief, the new face, the fresh news, the hopeless attachment: *I* shall only be the husband.

REGINALD [*savagely*] Will you tell me this, any of you? how is it that we always get talking about Hotchkiss when our business is about Edith? [*He fumes up the kitchen to the tower and back to his chair*].

MRS BRIDGENORTH. Will somebody tell me how the world is to get on if nobody is to get married?

SYKES. Will somebody tell me what an honorable man and a sincere Anglican is to propose to a woman whom he loves and who loves him and wont marry him?

LEO. Will somebody tell me how I'm to arrange to take

care of Rejjy when I'm married to Sinjon. Rejjy must not be allowed to marry anyone else, especially that odious nasty creature that told all those wicked lies about him in Court.

HOTCHKISS. Let us draw up the first English partnership deed.

LEO. For shame, Sinjon!

THE BISHOP. Somebody must begin, my dear. Ive a very strong suspicion that when it is drawn up it will be so much worse than the existing law that you will all prefer getting married. We shall therefore be doing the greatest possible service to morality by just trying how the new system would work.

LESBIA [*suddenly reminding them of her forgotten presence as she stands thoughtfully in the garden doorway*] Ive been thinking.

THE BISHOP [*to Hotchkiss*] Nothing like making people think: is there, Sinjon?

LESBIA [*coming to the table, on the General's left*] A woman has no right to refuse motherhood. That is clear, after the statistics given in The Times by Mr Sidney Webb.

THE GENERAL. Mr Webb has nothing to do with it. It is the Voice of Nature.

LESBIA. But if she is an English lady it is her right and her duty to stand out for honorable conditions. If we can agree on the conditions, I am willing to enter into an alliance with Boxer.

The General staggers to his feet, momentarily stupent and speechless.

EDITH [*rising*] And I with Cecil.

LEO [*rising*] And I with Rejjy and St John.

THE GENERAL [*aghast*] An alliance! Do you mean a—a—a—

REGINALD. She only means bigamy, as I understand her.

THE GENERAL. Alfred: how long more are you going to stand there and countenance this lunacy? Is it a horrible dream or am I awake? In the name of common sense and sanity, let us get back to real life—

Collins comes in through the tower, in alderman's robes. The ladies who are standing sit down hastily, and look as unconcerned as possible.

COLLINS. Sorry to hurry you, my lord; but the Church has been full this hour past; and the organist has played all the wedding music in *Lohengrin* three times over.

THE GENERAL. The very man we want. Alfred: I'm not equal to this crisis. Y o u are not equal to it. The Army has failed. The Church has failed. I shall put aside all idle social distinctions and appeal to the Municipality.

MRS BRIDGENORTH. Do, Boxer. He is sure to get us out of this difficulty.

Collins, a little puzzled, comes forward affably to Hotchkiss's left.

HOTCHKISS [*rising, impressed by the aldermanic gown*] Ive not had the pleasure. Will you introduce me?

COLLINS [*confidentially*] All right, sir. Only the greengrocer, sir, in charge of the wedding breakfast. Mr Alderman Collins, sir, when I'm in my gown.

HOTCHKISS [*staggered*] Very pleased indeed [*he sits down again*].

THE BISHOP. Personally I value the counsel of my old friend, Mr Alderman Collins, very highly. If Edith and Cecil will allow him—

EDITH. Collins has known me from my childhood: I'm sure he will agree with me.

COLLINS. Yes, miss: you may depend on me for that. Might I ask what the difficulty is?

EDITH. Simply this. Do you expect me to get married in the existing state of the law?

SYKES [*rising and coming to Collins's elbow*] I put it to you as a sensible man: is it any worse for her than for me?

REGINALD [*leaving his place and thrusting himself between Collins and Sykes, who returns to his chair*] Thats not the point. Let this be understood, Mr Collins. It's not the man who is backing out: it's the woman. [*He posts himself on the hearth*].

LESBIA. We do not admit that, Collins. The women are

perfectly ready to make a reasonable arrangement.

LEO. With both men.

THE GENERAL. The case is now before you, Mr Collins. And I put it to you as one man to another: did you ever hear such crazy nonsense?

MRS BRIDGENORTH. The world must go on, mustnt it, Collins?

COLLINS [*snatching at this, the first intelligible proposition he has heard*] Oh, the world will go on, maam: dont you be afraid of that. It aint so easy to stop it as the earnest kind of people think.

EDITH. I knew you would agree with me, Collins. Thank you.

HOTCHKISS. Have you the least idea of what they are talking about, Mr Alderman?

COLLINS. Oh, thats all right, sir. The particulars dont matter. I never read the report of a Committee: after all, what can they say that you dont know? You pick it up as they go on talking. [*He goes to the corner of the table and speaks across it to the company*]. Well, my Lord and Miss Edith and Madam and Gentlemen, it's like this. Marriage is tolerable enough in its way if youre easygoing and dont expect too much from it. But it doesnt bear thinking about. The great thing is to get the young people tied up before they know what theyre letting themselves in for. Theres Miss Lesbia now. She waited til she started thinking about it; and then it was all over. If you once start arguing, Miss Edith and Mr Sykes, youll never get married. Go and get married first: youll have plenty of arguing afterwards, miss, believe me.

HOTCHKISS. Your warning comes too late. Theyve started arguing already.

THE GENERAL. But you dont take in the full—well, I dont wish to exaggerate; but the only word I can find is the full horror of the situation. These ladies not only refuse our honorable offers, but as I understand it—and I'm sure I beg your pardon most heartily, Lesbia, if I'm wrong, as I hope I am—they actually call on us to enter into—I'm sorry to use the expression; but what can I say?—into ALLIANCES with them under contracts to be drawn up by our confounded solicitors.

COLLINS. Dear me, General: thats something new when the parties belong to the same class.

THE BISHOP. Not new, Collins. The Romans did it.

COLLINS. Yes: they would, them Romans. When youre in Rome do as the Romans do, is an old saying. But we're not in Rome at present, my lord.

THE BISHOP. We have got into many of their ways. What do you think of the contract system, Collins?

COLLINS. Well, my lord, when theres a question of a contract, I always say, shew it to me on paper. If it's to be talk, let it be talk; but if it's to be a contract, down with it in black and white; and then we shall know what we're about.

HOTCHKISS. Quite right, Mr Alderman. Let us draft it at once. May I go into the study for writing materials, Bishop?

THE BISHOP. Do, Sinjon.

Hotchkiss goes into the library.

COLLINS. If I might point out a difficulty, my lord—

THE BISHOP. Certainly. [*He goes to the fourth chair from the General's left, but before sitting down, courteously points to the chair at the end of the table next the hearth*]. Wont you sit down, Mr Alderman? [*Collins, very appreciative of the Bishop's distinguished consideration, sits down. The Bishop then takes his seat*].

COLLINS. We are at present six men to four ladies. Thats not fair.

REGINALD. Not fair to the men, you mean.

LEO. Oh! Rejjy has said something clever! Can I be mistaken in him?

Hotchkiss comes back with a blotter and some paper. He takes the vacant place in the middle of the table between Lesbia and the Bishop.

COLLINS. I tell you the truth, my lord and ladies and gentlemen: I dont trust my judgment on this subject. Theres a certain lady that I always consult on delicate points like this. She has a very exceptional experience, and a wonderful temperament and instinct in affairs of the heart.

HOTCHKISS. Excuse me, Mr Alderman: I'm a snob, and I warn you that theres no use consulting anyone who will not advise us frankly on class lines. Marriage is good enough for the lower classes: they have facilities for desertion that are denied to us. What is the social position of this lady?

COLLINS. The highest in the borough, sir. She is the Mayoress. But you need not stand in awe of her, sir. She is my sister-in-law. [*To the Bishop*] Ive often spoken of her to your lady, my lord. [*To Mrs Bridgenorth*] Mrs George, maam.

MRS BRIDGENORTH [*startled*] Do you mean to say, Collins, that Mrs George is a real person?

COLLINS [*equally startled*] Didnt you believe in her, maam?

MRS BRIDGENORTH. Never for a moment.

THE BISHOP. We always thought that Mrs George was too good to be true. I still dont believe in her, Collins. You must produce her if you are to convince me.

COLLINS [*overwhelmed*] Well, I'm so taken aback by this that—Well I never! ! ! Why! she's at the church at this moment, waiting to see the wedding.

THE BISHOP. Then produce her. [*Collins shakes his head*]. Come, Collins! confess. Theres no such person.

COLLINS. There is, my lord: there is, I assure you. You ask George. It's true *I* cant produce her; but you can, my lord.

THE BISHOP. I!

COLLINS. Yes, my lord, you. For some reason that I never could make out, she has forbidden me to talk about you, or to let her meet you. Ive asked her to come here of a wedding morning to help with the flowers or the like; and she has always refused. But if you order her to come as her Bishop, she'll come. She has some very strange fancies, has Mrs George. Send your ring to her, my lord—the official ring—send it by some very stylish gentleman—perhaps Mr Hotchkiss here would be good enough to take it—and she'll come.

THE BISHOP [*taking off his ring and handing it to Hotchkiss*] Oblige me by undertaking the mission.

HOTCHKISS. But how am I to know the lady?

COLLINS. She has gone to the church in state, sir, and will be attended by a Beadle with a mace. He will point her out to you; and he will take the front seat of the carriage on the way back.

HOTCHKISS. No, by heavens! Forgive me, Bishop; but you are asking too much. I ran away from the Boers because I was a snob. I run away from the Beadle for the same reason. I absolutely decline the mission.

THE GENERAL [*rising impressively*] Be good enough to give me that ring, Mr Hotchkiss.

HOTCHKISS. With pleasure. [*He hands it to him*].

THE GENERAL. I shall have great pleasure, Mr Alderman, in waiting on the Mayoress with the Bishop's orders; and I shall be proud to return with municipal honors. [*He stalks out gallantly, Collins rising for a moment to bow to him with marked dignity*].

REGINALD. Boxer is rather a fine old josser in his way.

HOTCHKISS. His uniform gives him an unfair advantage. He will take all the attention off the Beadle.

COLLINS. I think it would be as well, my lord, to go on with the contract while we're waiting. The truth is, we shall none of us have much of a look-in when Mrs George comes; so we had better finish the writing part of the business before she arrives.

HOTCHKISS. I think I have the preliminaries down all right. [*Reading*] 'Memorandum of Agreement made this day of blank blank between blank blank of blank blank in the County of blank, Esquire, hereinafter called the Gentleman, of the one part, and blank blank of blank in the County of blank, hereinafter called the Lady, of the other part, whereby it is declared and agreed as follows.'

LEO [*rising*] You might remember your manners, Sinjon. The lady comes first. [*She goes behind him and stoops to look at the draft over his shoulder*].

HOTCHKISS. To be sure. I beg your pardon. [*He alters the draft*].

LEO. And you have got only one lady and one gentleman. There ought to be two gentlemen.

COLLINS. Oh, thats a mere matter of form, maam. Any number of ladies or gentlemen can be put in.

LEO. Not any number of ladies. Only one lady. Besides, that creature wasnt a lady.

REGINALD. You shut your head, Leo. This is a general sort of contract for everybody: it's not your contract.

LEO. Then what use is it to me?

HOTCHKISS. You will get some hints from it for your own contract.

EDITH. I hope there will be no hinting. Let us have the plain straightforward truth and nothing but the truth.

COLLINS. Yes, yes, miss: it will be all right. Theres nothing underhand, I assure you. It's a model agreement, as it were.

EDITH [*unconvinced*] I hope so.

HOTCHKISS. What is the first clause in an agreement, usually? You know, Mr Alderman.

COLLINS [*at a loss*] Well, sir, the Town Clerk always sees to that. Ive got out of the habit of thinking for myself in these little matters. Perhaps his lordship knows.

THE BISHOP. I'm sorry to say I dont. But Soames will know. Alice: where is Soames?

HOTCHKISS. He's in there [*pointing to the study*].

THE BISHOP [*to his wife*] Coax him to join us, my love. [*Mrs Bridgenorth goes into the study*]. Soames is my chaplain, Mr Collins. The great difficulty about Bishops in the Church of England to-day is that the affairs of the diocese make it necessary that a Bishop should be before everything a man of business, capable of sticking to his desk for sixteen hours a day. But the result of having Bishops of this sort is that the spiritual interests of the Church, and its influence on the souls and imaginations of the people, very soon begin to go rapidly to the devil—

EDITH [*shocked*] Papa!

THE BISHOP. I am speaking technically, not in Boxer's manner. Indeed the Bishops themselves went so far in that direction that they gained a reputation for being spiritually the stupidest men in the country and commercially the sharpest. I found a way out of this difficulty. Soames was my solicitor. I found that Soames, though a very capable man of business, had a romantic secret history. His father was an eminent Nonconformist divine who habitually spoke of the Church of England as The Scarlet Woman. Soames became secretly converted to Anglicanism at the age of fifteen. He longed to take holy orders, but didnt dare to, because his father had a weak heart and habitually threatened to drop dead if anybody hurt his feelings. You may have noticed that people with weak hearts are the tyrants of English family life. So poor Soames had to become a solicitor. When his father died—by a curious stroke of poetic justice he died of scarlet fever, and was found to have had a perfectly sound heart—I ordained Soames and made him my chaplain. He is now quite happy. He is a celibate; fasts strictly on Fridays and throughout Lent; wears a cassock and biretta; and has more legal business to do than ever he had in his old office in Ely Place. And he sets me free for the spiritual and scholarly pursuits proper to a Bishop.

MRS BRIDGENORTH [*coming back from the study with a knitting basket*] Here he is. [*She resumes her seat, and knits*].

Soames comes in in cassock and biretta. He salutes the company by blessing them with two fingers.

HOTCHKISS. Take my place, Mr Soames. [*He gives up his chair to him, and retires to the oak chest, on which he seats himself*].

THE BISHOP. No longer Mr Soames, Sinjon. Father Anthony.

SOAMES [*taking his seat*] I was christened Oliver Cromwell Soames. My father had no right to do it. I have taken the name of Anthony. When you become parents, young gentlemen, be very careful not to label a helpless child with views which it may come to hold in abhorrence.

THE BISHOP. Has Alice explained to you the nature of the documents we are drafting?

SOAMES. She has indeed.

LESBIA. That sounds as if you disapproved.

SOAMES. It is not for me to approve or disapprove. I do the work that comes to my hand from my ecclesiastical superior.

THE BISHOP. Dont be uncharitable, Anthony. You must give us your best advice.

SOAMES. My advice to you all is to do your duty by taking the Christian vows of celibacy and poverty. The Church was founded to put an end to marriage and to put an end to property.

MRS BRIDGENORTH. But how could the world go on, Anthony?

SOAMES. Do your duty and see. Doing your duty is y o u r business: keeping the world going is in higher hands.

LESBIA. Anthony: youre impossible.

SOAMES [*taking up his pen*] You wont take my advice. I didnt expect you would. Well, I await your instructions.

REGINALD. We got stuck on the first clause. What should we begin with?

SOAMES. It is usual to begin with the term of the contract.

EDITH. What does that mean?

SOAMES. The term of years for which it is to hold good.

LEO. But this is a marriage contract.

SOAMES. Is the marriage to be for a year, a week, or a day?

REGINALD. Come, I say, Anthony! Youre worse than any of us. A day!

SOAMES. Off the path is off the path. An inch or a mile: what does it matter?

LEO. If the marriage is not to be for ever, I'll have nothing to do with it. I call it immoral to have a marriage for a term of years. If the people dont like it they can get divorced.

REGINALD. It ought to be for just as long as the two people like. Thats what I say.

COLLINS. They may not agree on the point, sir. It's often

fast with one and loose with the other.

LESBIA. I should say for as long as the man behaves himself.

THE BISHOP. Suppose the woman doesnt behave herself?

MRS BRIDGENORTH. The woman may have lost all her chances of a good marriage with anybody else. She should not be cast adrift.

REGINALD. So may the man! What about his home?

LEO. The wife ought to keep an eye on him, and see that he is comfortable and takes care of himself properly. The other man wont want her all the time.

LESBIA. There may not be another man.

LEO. Then why on earth should she leave him?

LESBIA. Because she wants to.

LEO. Oh, if people are going to be let do what they want to, then I call it simple immorality. [*She goes indignantly to the oak chest, and perches herself on it close beside Hotchkiss*].

REGINALD [*watching them sourly*] You do it yourself, dont you?

LEO. Oh, thats quite different. Dont make foolish witticisms, Rejjy.

THE BISHOP. We dont seem to be getting on. What do you say, Mr Alderman?

COLLINS. Well my lord, you see people do persist in talking as if marriages was all of one sort. But theres almost as many different sorts of marriages as theres different sorts of people. Theres the young things that marry for love, not knowing what theyre doing, and the old things that marry for money and comfort and companionship. Theres the people that marry for children. Theres the people that dont intend to have children and that arnt fit to have them. Theres the people that marry because theyre so much run after by the other sex that they have to put a stop to it somehow. Theres the people that want to try a new experience, and the people that want to have done with experiences. How are you to please them all? Why, youll want half a dozen different sorts of contract.

THE BISHOP. Well, if so, let us draw them all up. Let us

face it.

REGINALD. Why should we be held together whether we like it or not? Thats the question thats at the bottom of it all.

MRS BRIDGENORTH. Because of the children, Rejjy.

COLLINS. But even then, maam, why should we be held together when thats all over—when the girls are married and the boys out in the world and in business for themselves? When thats done with, the real work of the marriage is done with. If the two like to stay together, let them stay together. But if not, let them part, as old people in the workhouses do. Theyve had enough of one another. Theyve found one another out. Why should they be tied together to sit there grudging and hating and spiting one another like so many do? Put it twenty years from the birth of the youngest child.

SOAMES. How if there be no children?

COLLINS. Let em take one another on liking.

MRS BRIDGENORTH. Collins!

LEO. You wicked old man!

THE BISHOP [*remonstrating*] My dear, my dear!

LESBIA. And what is a woman to live on, pray, when she is no longer liked, as you call it?

SOAMES [*with sardonic formality*] It is proposed that the term of the agreement be twenty years from the birth of the youngest child when there are children. Any amendment?

LEO. I protest. It must be for life. It would not be a marriage at all if it were not for life.

SOAMES. Mrs Reginald Bridgenorth proposes life. Any seconder?

LEO. Dont be soulless, Anthony.

LESBIA. I have a very important amendment. If there are any children, the man must be cleared completely out of the house for two years on each occasion. At such times he is superfluous, importunate, and ridiculous.

COLLINS. But where is he to go, miss?

LESBIA. He can go where he likes as long as he does not bother the mother.

REGINALD. And is she to be left lonely—

LESBIA. Lonely! With her child. The poor woman would be only too glad to have a moment to herself. Dont be absurd, Rejjy.

REGINALD. The father is to be a wandering wretched outcast, living at his club, and seeing nobody but his friends' wives!

LESBIA [*ironically*] Poor fellow!

HOTCHKISS. The friends' wives are perhaps the solution of the problem. You see, their husbands will also be outcasts; and the poor ladies will occasionally pine for male society.

LESBIA. There is no reason why a mother should not have male society. What she clearly should not have is a husband.

SOAMES. Anything else, Miss Grantham?

LESBIA. Yes: I must have my own separate house, or my own separate part of a house. Boxer smokes: I cant endure tobacco. Boxer believes that an open window means death from cold and exposure to the night air: I must have fresh air always. We can be friends; but we cant live together; and that must be put in the agreement.

EDITH. Ive no objection to smoking; and as to opening the windows, Cecil will of course have to do what is best for his health.

THE BISHOP. Who is to be the judge of that, my dear? You or he?

EDITH. Neither of us. We must do what the doctor orders.

REGINALD. Doctors be—!

LEO [*admonitorily*] Rejjy!

REGINALD [*to Soames*] You take my tip, Anthony. Put a clause into that agreement that the doctor is to have no say in the job. It's bad enough for the two people to be married to one another without their both being married to the doctor as well.

LESBIA. That reminds me of something very important. Boxer believes in vaccination: I do not. There must be a clause that I am to decide on such questions as I think best.

LEO [*to the Bishop*] Baptism is nearly as important as vaccination: isnt it?

THE BISHOP. It used to be considered so, my dear.

LEO. Well, Sinjon scoffs at it: he says that godfathers are ridiculous. I must be allowed to decide.

REGINALD. Theyll be his children as well as yours, you know.

LEO. Dont be indelicate, Rejjy.

EDITH. You are forgetting the very important matter of money.

COLLINS. Ah! Money! Now we're coming to it!

EDITH. When I'm married I shall have practically no money except what I shall earn.

THE BISHOP. I'm sorry, Cecil. A Bishop's daughter is a poor man's daughter.

SYKES. But surely you dont imagine that I'm going to let Edith work when we're married. I'm not a rich man; but Ive enough to spare her that; and when my mother dies—

EDITH. What nonsense! Of course I shall work when I'm married. I shall keep your house.

SYKES. Oh, that!

REGINALD. You call that work?

EDITH. Dont *you*? Leo used to do it for nothing; so no doubt you thought it wasnt work at all. Does your present housekeeper do it for nothing?

REGINALD. But it will be part of your duty as a wife.

EDITH. Not under this contract. I'll not have it so. If I'm to keep the house, I shall expect Cecil to pay me at least as well as he would pay a hired housekeeper. I'll not go begging to him every time I want a new dress or a cab fare, as many women have to do.

SYKES. You know very well I would grudge you nothing, Edie.

EDITH. Then dont grudge me my self-respect and independence. I insist on it in fairness to you, Cecil, because in this way there will be a fund belonging solely to me; and if Slattox takes an action against you for anything I say, you can pay the damages and stop the interest out of my salary.

SOAMES. You forget that under this contract he will not

be liable, because you will not be his wife in law.

EDITH. Nonsense! Of course I shall be his wife.

COLLINS [*his curiosity roused*] Is Slattox taking an action against you, miss? Slattox is on the Council with me. Could I settle it?

EDITH. He has not taken an action; but Cecil says he will.

COLLINS. What for, miss, if I may ask?

EDITH. Slattox is a liar and a thief; and it is my duty to expose him.

COLLINS. You surprise me, miss. Of course Slattox is in a manner of speaking a liar. If I may say so without offence, we're all liars, if it was only to spare one another's feelings. But I shouldnt call Slattox a thief. He's not all that he should be, perhaps; but he pays his way.

EDITH. If that is only your nice way of saying that Slattox is entirely unfit to have two hundred girls in his power as absolute slaves, then I shall say that about him at the very next public meeting I address. He steals their wages under pretence of fining them. He steals their food under pretence of buying it for them. He lies when he denies having done it. And he does other things, as you evidently know, Collins. Therefore I give you notice that I shall expose him before all England without the least regard to the consequences to myself.

SYKES. Or to me?

EDITH. I take equal risks. Suppose you felt it to be your duty to shoot Slattox, what would become of me and the children? I'm sure I dont want anybody to be shot: not even Slattox; but if the public never will take any notice of even the most crying evil until somebody is shot, what are people to do but shoot somebody?

SOAMES [*inexorably*] I'm waiting for my instructions as to the term of the agreement.

REGINALD [*impatiently, leaving the hearth and going behind Soames*] It's no good talking all over the shop like this. We shall be here all day. I propose that the agreement holds good until the parties are divorced.

SOAMES. They cant be divorced. They will not be married.

REGINALD. But if they cant be divorced, then this will be worse than marriage.

MRS BRIDGENORTH. Of course it will. Do stop this nonsense. Why, who are the children to belong to?

LESBIA. We have already settled that they are to belong to the mother.

REGINALD. No: I'm dashed if you have. I'll fight for the ownership of my own children tooth and nail; and so will a good many other fellows, I can tell you.

EDITH. It seems to me that they should be divided between the parents. If Cecil wishes any of the children to be his exclusively, he should pay me a certain sum for the risk and trouble of bringing them into the world: say a thousand pounds apiece. The interest on this could go towards the support of the child as long as we live together. But the principal would be my property. In that way, if Cecil took the child away from me, I should at least be paid for what it had cost me.

MRS BRIDGENORTH [*putting down her knitting in amazement*] Edith! Who ever heard of such a thing! !

EDITH. Well, how else do you propose to settle it?

THE BISHOP. There is such a thing as a favorite child. What about the youngest child—the Benjamin—the child of its parents' matured strength and charity, always better treated and better loved than the unfortunate eldest children of their youthful ignorance and wilfulness? Which parent is to own the youngest child, payment or no payment?

COLLINS. Theres a third party, my lord. Theres the child itself. My wife is so fond of her children that they cant call their lives their own. They all run away from home to escape from her. A child hasnt a grown-up person's appetite for affection. A little of it goes a long way with them; and they like a good imitation of it better than the real thing, as every nurse knows.

SOAMES. Are you sure that any of us, young or old, like the real thing as well as we like an artistic imitation of it? Is not the real thing accursed? Are not the best beloved always the good actors rather than the true sufferers? Is not love always falsified in novels and plays to make it endurable? I have noticed in myself a great delight in pictures of the Saints and of Our Lady; but when I fall under that most terrible curse of the priest's lot, the curse of Joseph pursued by the wife of Potiphar, I am invariably repelled and terrified.

HOTCHKISS. Are you now speaking as a saint, Father Anthony, or as a solicitor?

SOAMES. There is no difference. There is not one Christian rule for solicitors and another for saints. Their hearts are alike; and their way of salvation is along the same road.

THE BISHOP. But "few there be that find it." Can you find it for us, Anthony?

SOAMES. It lies broad before you. It is the way to destruction that is narrow and tortuous. Marriage is an abomination which the Church was founded to cast out and replace by the communion of saints. I learnt that from every marriage settlement I drew up as a solicitor no less than from inspired revelation. You have set yourselves here to put your sin before you in black and white; and you cant agree upon or endure one article of it.

SYKES. It's certainly rather odd that the whole thing seems to fall to pieces the moment you touch it.

THE BISHOP. You see, when you give the devil fair play he loses his case. He has not been able to produce even the first clause of a working agreement; so I'm afraid we cant wait for him any longer.

LESBIA. Then the community will have to do without my children.

EDITH. And Cecil will have to do without me.

LEO [*getting off the chest*] And I positively will not marry Sinjon if he is not clever enough to make some provision for my looking after Rejjy. [*She leaves Hotchkiss, and goes back to her chair at the end of the table behind Mrs Bridgenorth.*]

MRS BRIDGENORTH. And the world will come to an end with this generation, I suppose.

COLLINS. Cant nothing be done, my lord?

THE BISHOP. You can make divorce reasonable and decent: that is all.

LESBIA. Thank you for nothing. If you will only make marriage reasonable and decent, you can do as you like about divorce. I have not stated my deepest objection to marriage; and I dont intend to. There are certain rights I will not give any person over me.

REGINALD. Well, I think it jolly hard that a man should support his wife for years, and lose the chance of getting a really good wife, and then have her refuse to be a wife to him.

LESBIA. I'm not going to discuss it with you, Rejjy. If your sense of personal honor doesnt make you understand, nothing will.

SOAMES [*implacably*] I'm still awaiting my instructions.

They look at one another, each waiting for one of the others to suggest something. Silence.

REGINALD [*blankly*] I suppose, after all, marriage is better than—well, than the usual alternative.

SOAMES [*turning fiercely on him*] What right have you to say so? You know that the sins that are wasting and maddening this unhappy nation are those committed in wedlock.

COLLINS. Well, the single ones cant afford to indulge their affections the same as married people.

SOAMES. Away with it all, I say. You have your Master's commandments. Obey them.

HOTCHKISS [*rising and leaning on the back of the chair left vacant by the General*] I really must point out to you, Father Anthony, that the early Christian rules of life were not made to last, because the early Christians did not believe that the world itself was going to last. Now we know that we shall have to go through with it. We have found that there are millions of years behind us; and we know that there are millions before us. Mrs Bridgenorth's question remains unanswered. How is the world to go on? You say that that is not our business—that it is the business of Providence. But the modern Christian view is that we are here to do the business of Providence and nothing else. The question is, how? Am I not to use my reason to find out why? Isnt that what my reason is for? Well, all my reason tells me at present is that you are an impracticable lunatic.

SOAMES. Does that help?

HOTCHKISS. No.

SOAMES. Then pray for light.

HOTCHKISS. No: I am a snob, not a beggar. [*He sits down in the General's chair*].

COLLINS. We dont seem to be getting on, do we? Miss Edith: you and Mr Sykes had better go off to church and settle the right and wrong of it afterwards. Itll ease your minds, believe me: I speak from experience. You will burn your boats, as one might say.

SOAMES. We should never burn our boats. It is death in life.

COLLINS. Well, Father, I will say for you that you have views of your own and are not afraid to out with them. But some of us are of a more cheerful disposition. On the Borough Council now, you would be in a minority of one. You must take human nature as it is.

SOAMES. Upon what compulsion must I? I'll take divine nature as it is. I'll not hold a candle to the devil.

THE BISHOP. Thats a very unchristian way of treating the devil.

REGINALD. Well, we dont seem to be getting any further, do we?

THE BISHOP. Will you give it up and get married, Edith?

EDITH. No. What I propose seems to me quite reasonable.

THE BISHOP. And you, Lesbia?

LESBIA. Never.

MRS BRIDGENORTH. Never is a long word, Lesbia. Dont say it.

LESBIA [*with a flash of temper*] Dont pity me, Alice, please. As I said before, I am an English lady, quite prepared to do without anything I cant have on honorable conditions.

SOAMES [*after a silence expressive of utter deadlock*] I am still awaiting my instructions.

REGINALD. Well, we dont seem to be getting along, do we?

LEO [*out of patience*] You said that before, Rejjy. Do not repeat yourself.

REGINALD. Oh, bother! [*He goes to the garden door and looks out gloomily*].

SOAMES [*rising with the paper in his hands*] Psha! [*He tears it in pieces*]. So much for your contract!

THE VOICE OF THE BEADLE. By your leave there, gentlemen. Make way for the Mayoress. Way for the worshipful the Mayoress, my lords and gentlemen. [*He comes in through the tower, in cocked hat and gold-braided overcoat, bearing the borough mace, and posts himself at the entrance*]. By your leave, gentlemen, way for the worshipful the Mayoress.

COLLINS [*moving back towards the wall*] Mrs George, my lord.

Mrs George is every inch a Mayoress in point of stylish dressing; and she does it very well indeed. There is nothing quiet about Mrs George: she is not afraid of colors, and knows how to make the most of them. Not at all a lady in Lesbia's use of the term as a class label, she proclaims herself to the first glance as the triumphant, pampered, wilful, intensely alive woman who has always been rich among poor people. In a historical museum she would explain Edward the Fourth's taste for shopkeepers' wives. Her age which is certainly 40, and might be 50, is carried off by her vitality, her resilient figure, and her confident carriage. So far, a remarkably well-preserved woman. But her beauty is wrecked, like an ageless landscape ravaged by long and fierce war. Her eyes are alive, arresting, and haunting; and there is still a turn of delicate beauty and pride in her indomitable chin; but her cheeks are wasted and lined, her mouth writhen and piteous. The whole face is a battle-field of the passions, quite deplorable until she speaks, when an alert sense of fun rejuvenates her in a moment, and makes her company irresistible.

All rise except Soames, who sits down. Leo joins Reginald at the garden door. Mrs Bridgenorth hurries to the tower to receive her guest, and gets as far as Soames's chair when Mrs George appears. Hotchkiss, apparently recognizing her, recoils in consternation to the study door at the furthest corner of the room from her.

MRS GEORGE [*coming straight to the Bishop with the ring in her hand*] Here is your ring, my lord; and here am I. It's your doing, remember: not mine.

THE BISHOP. Good of you to come.

MRS BRIDGENORTH. How do you do, Mrs Collins?

MRS GEORGE [*going to her past the Bishop, and gazing intently at her*] Are you his wife?

MRS BRIDGENORTH. The Bishop's wife? Yes.

MRS GEORGE. What a destiny! And you look like any other woman!

MRS BRIDGENORTH [*introducing Lesbia*] My sister, Miss Grantham.

MRS GEORGE. So strangely mixed up with the story of the General's life?

THE BISHOP. You know the story of his life, then?

MRS GEORGE. Not all. We reached the house before he brought it up to the present day. But enough to know the part played in it by Miss Grantham.

MRS BRIDGENORTH [*introducing Leo*] Mrs Reginald Bridgenorth.

REGINALD. The late Mrs Reginald Bridgenorth.

LEO. Hold your tongue, Rejjy. At least have the decency to wait until the decree is made absolute.

MRS GEORGE [*to Leo*] Well, youve more time to get married again than he has, havnt you?

MRS BRIDGENORTH [*introducing Hotchkiss*] Mr St John Hotchkiss.

Hotchkiss, still far aloof by the study door, bows.

MRS GEORGE. What! That! [*She makes a half tour of the kitchen and ends right in front of him*]. Young man: do you remember coming into my shop and telling me that my husband's coals were out of place in your cellar, as Nature evidently intended them for the roof?

HOTCHKISS. I remember that deplorable impertinence

with shame and confusion. You were kind enough to answer that Mr Collins was looking out for a clever young man to write advertisements, and that I could take the job if I liked.

MRS GEORGE. It's still open. [*She turns to Edith*].

MRS BRIDGENORTH. My daughter Edith. [*She comes towards the study door to make the introduction*].

MRS GEORGE. The bride! [*Looking at Edith's dressing-jacket*] Youre not going to get married like that, are you?

THE BISHOP [*coming round the table to Edith's left*] Thats just what we are discussing. Will you be so good as to join us and allow us the benefit of your wisdom and experience?

MRS GEORGE. Do you want the Beadle as well? He's a married man.

They all turn involuntarily and contemplate the Beadle, who sustains their gaze with dignity.

THE BISHOP. We think there are already too many men to be quite fair to the women.

MRS GEORGE. Right, my lord. [*She goes back to the tower and addresses the Beadle*] Take away that bauble, Joseph. Wait for me wherever you find yourself most comfortable in the neighbourhood. [*The Beadle withdraws. She notices Collins for the first time*]. Hullo, Bill: youve got em all on too. Go and hunt up a drink for Joseph: theres a dear. [*Collins goes out. She looks at Soames's cassock and biretta*]. What! Another uniform! Are you the sexton? [*He rises*].

THE BISHOP. My chaplain, Father Anthony.

MRS GEORGE. Oh Lord! [*To Soames, coaxingly*] You dont mind, do you?

SOAMES. I mind nothing but my duties.

THE BISHOP. You know everybody now, I think.

MRS GEORGE [*turning to the railed chair*] Who's this?

THE BISHOP. Oh, I beg your pardon, Cecil. Mr Sykes. The bridegroom.

MRS GEORGE [*to Sykes*] Adorned for the sacrifice, arnt you?

SYKES. It seems doubtful whether there is going to be any sacrifice.

MRS GEORGE. Well, I want to talk to the women first. Shall we go upstairs and look at the presents and dresses?

MRS BRIDGENORTH. If you wish, certainly.

REGINALD. But the men want to hear what you have to say too.

MRS GEORGE. I'll talk to them afterwards: one by one.

HOTCHKISS [*to himself*] Great heavens!

MRS BRIDGENORTH. This way, Mrs Collins. [*She leads the way out through the tower, followed by Mrs George, Lesbia, Leo, and Edith*].

THE BISHOP. Shall we try to get through the last batch of letters whilst they are away, Soames?

SOAMES. Yes, certainly. [*To Hotchkiss, who is in his way*] Excuse me.

The Bishop and Soames go into the study, disturbing Hotchkiss, who, plunged in a strange reverie, has forgotten where he is. Awakened by Soames, he stares distractedly; then, with sudden resolution, goes swiftly to the middle of the kitchen.

HOTCHKISS. Cecil. Rejjy. [*Startled by his urgency, they hurry to him*]. I'm frightfully sorry to desert on this day; but I must bolt. This time it really is pure cowardice. I cant help it.

REGINALD. What are you afraid of?

HOTCHKISS. I dont know. Listen to me. I was a young fool living by myself in London. I ordered my first ton of coals from that woman's husband. At that time I did not know that it is not true economy to buy the lowest priced article: I thought all coals were alike, and tried the thirteen shilling kind because it seemed cheap. It proved unexpectedly inferior to the family Silkstone; and in the irritation into which the first scuttle threw me, I called at the shop and made an idiot of myself as she described.

SYKES. Well, suppose you did! Laugh at it, man.

HOTCHKISS. At that, yes. But there was something worse. Judge of my horror when, calling on the coal merchant to make a trifling complaint at finding my grate acting as a battery of quick-firing guns, and being confronted by his vulgar wife, I felt in her presence an extraordinary sensation of unrest, of emotion, of unsatisfied need. I'll not disgust you with details of the madness and folly that followed that meeting. But it went as far as this: that I actually found myself prowling past the shop at night under a sort of desperate necessity to be near some place where she had been. A hideous temptation to kiss the doorstep because her foot had pressed it made me realize how mad I was. I tore myself away from London by a supreme effort; but I was on the point of returning like a needle to the lodestone when the outbreak of the war saved me. On the field of battle the infatuation wore off. The Billiter affair made a new man of me: I felt that I had left the follies and puerilities of the old days behind me for ever. But half-an-hour ago—when the Bishop sent off that ring—a sudden grip at the base of my heart filled me with a nameless terror—me, the fearless! I recognized its cause when she walked into the room. Cecil: this woman is a harpy, a siren, a mermaid, a vampire. There is only one chance for me: flight, instant precipitate flight. Make my excuses. Forget me. Farewell. [*He makes for the door and is confronted by Mrs George entering*]. Too late: I'm lost. [*He turns back and throws himself desperately into the chair nearest the study door: that being the furthest away from her*].

MRS GEORGE [*coming to the hearth and addressing Reginald*] Mr Bridgenorth: will you oblige me by leaving me with this young man. I want to talk to him like a mother, on your business.

REGINALD. Do, maam. He needs it badly. Come along, Sykes. [*He goes into the study*].

SYKES [*looks irresolutely at Hotchkiss*]—?

HOTCHKISS. Too late: you cant save me now, Cecil. Go.

Sykes goes into the study. Mrs George strolls across to Hotchkiss and contemplates him curiously.

HOTCHKISS. Useless to prolong this agony. [*Rising*] Fatal woman—if woman you are indeed and not a fiend in human form—

MRS GEORGE. Is this out of a book? Or is it your usual society small talk?

HOTCHKISS [*recklessly*] Jibes are useless: the force that is sweeping me away will not spare you. I must know the worst at once. What was your father?

MRS GEORGE. A licensed victualler who married his barmaid. You would call him a publican, most likely.

HOTCHKISS. Then you are a woman totally beneath me. Do you deny it? Do you set up any sort of pretence to be my equal in rank, in age, or in culture?

MRS GEORGE. Have you eaten anything that has disagreed with you?

HOTCHKISS [*witheringly*] Inferior!

MRS GEORGE. Thank you. Anything else?

HOTCHKISS. This. I love you. My intentions are not honorable. [*She shews no dismay*]. Scream. Ring the bell. Have me turned out of the house.

MRS GEORGE [*with sudden depth of feeling*] Oh, if you could restore to this wasted exhausted heart one ray of the passion that once welled at the glance—at the touch of a lover! It's *you* who would scream then, young man. Do you see this face, once fresh and rosy like your own, now scarred and riven by a hundred burnt-out fires?

HOTCHKISS [*wildly*] Slate fires. Thirteen shillings a ton. Fires that shoot out destructive meteors, blinding and burning, sending men into the streets to make fools of themselves.

MRS GEORGE. You seem to have got it pretty bad, Sinjon.

HOTCHKISS. Dont dare call me Sinjon.

MRS GEORGE. My name is Zenobia Alexandrina. You may call me Polly for short.

HOTCHKISS. Your name is Ashtoreth—Durga—there is no name yet invented malign enough for you.

MRS GEORGE [*sitting down comfortably*] Come! Do you really think youre better suited to that young saucebox than her husband? You enjoyed her company when you were only the friend of the family—when there was the husband there to shew off against and to take all the responsibility. Are you sure youll enjoy it as much when you are the husband? She isnt clever, you know. She's only silly-clever.

HOTCHKISS [*uneasily leaning against the table and holding on to it to control his nervous movements*] Need you tell me? fiend that you are!

MRS GEORGE. You amused the husband, didnt you?

HOTCHKISS. He has more real sense of humor than she. He's better bred. That was not my fault.

MRS GEORGE. My husband has a sense of humor too.

HOTCHKISS. The coal merchant?—I mean the slate merchant.

MRS GEORGE [*appreciatively*] He would just love to hear you talk. He's been dull lately for want of a change of company and a bit of fresh fun.

HOTCHKISS [*flinging a chair opposite her and sitting down with an overdone attempt at studied insolence*] And pray what is your wretched husband's vulgar conviviality to me?

MRS GEORGE. You love me?

HOTCHKISS. I loathe you.

MRS GEORGE. It's the same thing.

HOTCHKISS. Then I'm lost.

MRS GEORGE. You may come and see me if you promise to amuse George.

HOTCHKISS. I'll insult him, sneer at him, wipe my boots on him.

MRS GEORGE. No you wont, dear boy. Youll be a perfect gentleman.

HOTCHKISS [*beaten; appealing to her mercy*] Zenobia—

MRS GEORGE. Polly, please.

HOTCHKISS. Mrs Collins—

MRS GEORGE. Sir?

HOTCHKISS. Something stronger than my reason and common sense is holding my hands and tearing me along. I make no attempt to deny that it can drag me where you please and make me do what you like. But at least let me know your soul as you seem to know mine. Do you love this absurd coal merchant.

MRS GEORGE. Call him George.

HOTCHKISS. Do you love your Jorjy Porjy?

MRS GEORGE. Oh, I dont know that I love him. He's my husband, you know. But if I got anxious about George's health, and I thought it would nourish him, I would fry you with onions for his breakfast and think nothing of it. George and I are good friends. George belongs to me. Other men may come and go; but George goes on for ever.

HOTCHKISS. Yes: a husband soon becomes nothing but a habit. Listen: I suppose this detestable fascination you have for me is love.

MRS GEORGE. Any sort of feeling for a woman is called love nowadays.

HOTCHKISS. Do you love me?

MRS GEORGE [*promptly*] My love is not quite so cheap an article as that, my lad. I wouldnt cross the street to have another look at you—not yet. *I'*m not starving for love like the robins in winter, as the good ladies youre accustomed to are. Youll have to be very clever, and very good, and very real, if you are to interest me. If George takes a fancy to you, and you amuse him enough, I'll just tolerate you coming in and out occasionally for—well, say a month. If you can make a friend of me in that time so much the better for you. If you can touch my poor dying heart even for an instant, I'll bless you, and never forget you. You may try—if George takes to you.

HOTCHKISS. I'm to come on liking for the month?

MRS GEORGE. On condition that you drop Mrs Reginald.

HOTCHKISS. But she wont drop me. Do you suppose I ever wanted to marry her? I was a homeless bachelor; and I felt quite happy at their house as their friend. Leo was an amusing little devil; but I liked Reginald much more than I liked her. She didnt understand. One day she came to me and told me that the inevitable had happened. I had tact enough not to ask her what the inevitable was; and I gathered presently that she had told Reginald that their marriage was a mistake and that she loved me and could no longer see me breaking my heart for her in suffering silence. What could I say? What could I do? What can I say now? What can I do now?

MRS GEORGE. Tell her that the habit of falling in love with other men's wives is growing on you; and that I'm your latest.

HOTCHKISS. What! Throw her over when she has thrown Reginald over for me!

MRS GEORGE [*rising*] You wont then? Very well. Sorry we shant meet again: I should have liked to see more of you for George's sake. Good-bye [*she moves away from him towards the hearth*].

HOTCHKISS [*appealing*] Zenobia

MRS GEORGE. I thought I had made a difficult conquest. Now I see you are only one of those poor petticoat-hunting creatures that any woman can pick up. Not for me, thank you. [*Inexorable, she turns towards the tower to go*].

HOTCHKISS [*following*] Dont be an ass, Polly.

MRS GEORGE [*stopping*] Thats better.

HOTCHKISS. Cant you see that I maynt throw Leo over just because I should be only too glad to. It would be dishonorable.

MRS GEORGE. Will you be happy if you marry her?

HOTCHKISS. No, great heavens, NO!

MRS GEORGE. Will she be happy when she finds you out?

HOTCHKISS. She's incapable of happiness. But she's not incapable of the pleasure of holding a man against his will.

MRS GEORGE. Right, young man. You will tell her, please, that you love me: before everybody, mind, the very next time you see her.

HOTCHKISS. But—

MRS GEORGE. Those are my orders, Sinjon. I cant have you marry another woman until George is tired of you.

HOTCHKISS. Oh, if only I didnt selfishly want to obey you!

The General comes in from the garden. Mrs George goes half way to the garden door to speak to him. Hotchkiss posts himself on the hearth.

MRS GEORGE. Where have you been all this time?

THE GENERAL. I'm afraid my nerves were a little upset by our conversation. I just went into the garden and had a smoke. I'm all right now [*he strolls down to the study door and presently takes a chair at that end of the big table*].

MRS GEORGE. A smoke! Why, you said she couldnt bear it.

THE GENERAL. Good heavens! I forgot! It's such a natural thing to do, somehow.

Lesbia comes in through the tower.

MRS GEORGE. He's been smoking again.

LESBIA. So my nose tells me. [*She goes to the end of the table nearest the hearth, and sits down*].

THE GENERAL. Lesbia: I'm very sorry. But if I gave it up, I should become so melancholy and irritable that you would be the first to implore me to take to it again.

MRS GEORGE. Thats true. Women drive their husbands into all sorts of wickedness to keep them in good humor. Sinjon: be off with you: this doesnt concern you.

LESBIA. Please dont disturb yourself, Sinjon. Boxer's broken heart has been worn on his sleeve too long for any pretence of privacy.

THE GENERAL. You are cruel, Lesbia: devilishly cruel. [*He sits down, wounded*].

LESBIA. You are vulgar, Boxer.

HOTCHKISS. In what way? I ask, as an expert in vulgarity.

LESBIA. In two ways. First, he talks as if the only thing of any importance in life was which particular woman he shall marry. Second, he has no self-control.

THE GENERAL. Women are not all the same to me, Lesbia.

MRS GEORGE. Why should they be, pray? Women are all different: it's the men who are all the same. Besides, what does Miss Grantham know about either men or women? She's got too much self-control.

LESBIA. [*widening her eyes and lifting her chin haughtily*] And pray how does that prevent me from knowing as much about men and women as people who have no self-control?

MRS GEORGE. Because it frightens people into behaving themselves before you; and then how can you tell what they really are? Look at me! I was a spoilt child. My brothers and sisters were well brought up, like all children of respectable publicans. So should I have been if I hadnt been the youngest: ten years younger than my youngest brother. My parents were tired of doing their duty by their children by that time; and they spoilt me for all they were worth. I never knew what it was to want money or anything that money could buy. When I wanted my own way, I had nothing to do but scream for it til I got it. When I was annoyed *I* didnt control myself: I scratched and called names. Did you ever, after you were grown up, pull a grown-up woman's hair? Did you ever bite a grown-up man? Did you ever call both of them every name you could lay your tongue to?

LESBIA [*shivering with disgust*] No.

MRS GEORGE. Well, I did. I know what a woman is like when her hair's pulled. I know what a man is like when he's bit. I know what theyre both like when you tell them what you really feel about them. And thats how I know more of the world than you.

LESBIA. The Chinese know what a man is like when he is cut into a thousand pieces, or boiled in oil. That sort of knowledge is of no use to me. I'm afraid we shall never get on with one another, Mrs George. I live like a fencer, always on guard. I like to be confronted with people who are always on guard. I hate sloppy people, slovenly people, people who cant sit up straight, sentimental people!

MRS GEORGE. Oh, sentimental your grandmother! You dont learn to hold your own in the world by standing on guard, but by attacking, and getting well hammered yourself.

LESBIA. I'm not a prize-fighter, Mrs Collins. If I cant get a thing without the indignity of fighting for it, I do without it.

MRS GEORGE. Do you? Does it strike you that if we were all as clever as you at doing without, there wouldnt be much to live for, would there?

THE GENERAL. I'm afraid, Lesbia, the things you do without are the things you dont want.

LESBIA [*surprised at his wit*] Thats not bad for the silly soldier man. Yes, Boxer: the truth is, I dont want you enough to make the very unreasonable sacrifices required by marriage. And yet that is exactly why I ought to be married. Just because I have the qualities my country wants most I shall go barren to my grave; whilst the women who have neither the strength to resist marriage nor the intelligence to understand its infinite dishonor will make the England of the future. [*She rises and walks towards the study*].

THE GENERAL [*as she is about to pass him*] Well, I shall not ask you again, Lesbia.

LESBIA. Thank you, Boxer. [*She passes on to the study door*]

MRS GEORGE. Youre quite done with him, are you?

LESBIA. As far as marriage is concerned, yes. The field is clear for you, Mrs. George. [*She goes into the study*].

The General buries his face in his hands. Mrs George comes round the table to him.

MRS GEORGE [*sympathetically*] She's a nice woman, that. And a sort of beauty about her too, different from anyone else.

THE GENERAL [*overwhelmed*] Oh Mrs Collins, thank you, thank you a thousand times. [*He rises effusively*]. You have thawed the long-frozen springs [*he kisses her hand*], forgive me; and thank you: bless you—[*he again takes refuge in the garden, choked with emotion*].

MRS GEORGE [*looking after him triumphantly*] Just caught the dear old warrior on the bounce, eh?

HOTCHKISS. Unfaithful to me already!

MRS GEORGE. I'm not your property, young man: dont you think it. [*She goes over to him and faces him*]. You understand that? [*He suddenly snatches her into his arms and kisses her*]. Oh! You dare do that again, you young blackguard;

and I'll jab one of these chairs in your face [*she seizes one and holds it in readiness*]. Now you shall not see me for another month.

HOTCHKISS [*deliberately*] I shall pay my first visit to your husband this afternoon.

MRS GEORGE. Youll see what he'll say to you when I tell him what youve just done.

HOTCHKISS. What can he say? What dare he say?

MRS GEORGE. Suppose he kicks you out of the house?

HOTCHKISS. How can he? I've fought seven duels with sabres. I've muscles of iron. Nothing hurts me: not even broken bones. Fighting is absolutely uninteresting to me because it doesn't frighten me or amuse me; and I always win. Your husband is in all these respects an average man, probably. He will be horribly afraid of me; and if under the stimulus of your presence, and for your sake, and because it is the right thing to do among vulgar people, he were to attack me, I should simply defeat him and humiliate him [*he gradually gets his hand on the chair and takes it from her, as his words go home phrase by phrase*]. Sooner than expose him to that, you would suffer a thousand stolen kisses, wouldnt you?

MRS GEORGE [*in utter consternation*] You young viper!

HOTCHKISS. Ha! ha! You are in my power. That is one of the oversights of your code of honor for husbands: the man who can bully them can insult their wives with impunity. Tell him if you dare. If I choose to take ten kisses, how will you prevent me?

MRS GEORGE. You come within reach of me and I'll not leave a hair on your head.

HOTCHKISS [*catching her wrists dexterously*] Ive got your hands.

MRS GEORGE. Youve not got my teeth. Let go; or I'll bite. I will, I tell you. Let go.

HOTCHKISS. Bite away: I shall taste quite as nice as George.

MRS GEORGE. You beast. Let me go. Do you call yourself

a gentleman, to use your brute strength against a woman?

HOTCHKISS. You are stronger than me in every way but this. Do you think I will give up my one advantage? Promise youll receive me when I call this afternoon.

MRS GEORGE. After what youve just done? Not if it was to save my life.

HOTCHKISS. I'll amuse George.

MRS GEORGE. He wont be in.

HOTCHKISS [*taken aback*] Do you mean that we should be alone?

MRS GEORGE [*snatching away her hands triumphantly as his grasp relaxes*] Aha! Thats cooled you, has it?

HOTCHKISS [*anxiously*] When will George be at home?

MRS GEORGE. It wont matter to you whether he's at home or not. The door will be slammed in your face whenever you call.

HOTCHKISS. No servant in London is strong enough to close a door that I mean to keep open. You cant escape me. If you persist, I'll go into the coal trade; make George's acquaintance on the coal exchange: and coax him to take me home with him to make your acquaintance.

MRS GEORGE. We have no use for you, young man: neither George nor I [*she sails away from him and sits down at the end of the table near the study door*].

HOTCHKISS [*following her and taking the next chair round the corner of the table*] Yes you have. George cant fight for you: I can.

MRS GEORGE [*turning to face him*] You bully. You low bully.

HOTCHKISS. You have courage and fascination: I have courage and a pair of fists. We're both bullies, Polly.

MRS GEORGE. You have a mischievous tongue. Thats enough to keep you out of my house.

HOTCHKISS. It must be rather a house of cards. A word from me to George—just the right word, said in the right way—and down comes your house.

MRS GEORGE. Thats why I'll die sooner than let you into it.

HOTCHKISS. Then as surely as you live, I enter the coal trade tomorrow. George's taste for amusing company will deliver him into my hands. Before a month passes your home will be at my mercy.

MRS GEORGE [*rising, at bay*] Do you think I'll let myself be driven into a trap like this?

HOTCHKISS. You are in it already. Marriage is a trap. You are married. Any man who has the power to spoil your marriage has the power to spoil your life. I have that power over you.

MRS GEORGE [*desperate*] You mean it?

HOTCHKISS. I do.

MRS GEORGE [*resolutely*] Well, spoil my marriage and be—

HOTCHKISS [*springing up*] Polly!

MRS GEORGE. Sooner than be your slave I'd face any unhappiness.

HOTCHKISS. What! Even for George?

MRS GEORGE. There must be honor between me and George, happiness or no happiness. Do your worst.

HOTCHKISS [*admiring her*] Are you really game, Polly? Dare you defy me?

MRS GEORGE. If you ask me another question I shant be able to keep my hands off you [*she dashes distractedly past him to the other end of the table, her fingers crisping*].

HOTCHKISS. That settles it. Polly: I adore you: we were born for one another. As I happen to be a gentleman, I'll never do anything to annoy or injure you except that I reserve the right to give you a black eye if you bite me; but youll never get rid of me now to the end of your life.

MRS GEORGE. I shall get rid of you if the beadle has to brain you with the mace for it [*she makes for the tower*].

HOTCHKISS [*running between the table and the oak chest and across to the tower to cut her off*] You shant.

MRS GEORGE [*panting*] Shant I though?

HOTCHKISS. No you shant. I have one card left to play that youve forgotten. Why were you so unlike yourself when you spoke to the Bishop?

MRS GEORGE [*agitated beyond measure*] Stop. Not that. You shall respect that if you respect nothing else. I forbid you. [*He kneels at her feet*]. What are you doing? Get up: dont be a fool.

HOTCHKISS. Polly: I ask you on my knees to let me make George's acquaintance in his home this afternoon; and I shall remain on my knees til the Bishop comes in and sees us. What will he think of you then?

MRS GEORGE [*beside herself*] Wheres the poker?

She rushes to the fireplace; seizes the poker; and makes for Hotchkiss, who flies to the study door. The Bishop enters just then and finds himself between them, narrowly escaping a blow from the poker.

THE BISHOP. Dont hit him, Mrs Collins. He is my guest.

Mrs George throws down the poker; collapses into the nearest chair; and bursts into tears. The Bishop goes to her and pats her consolingly on the shoulder. She shudders all through at his touch.

THE BISHOP. Come! you are in the house of your friends. Can we help you?

MRS GEORGE [*to Hotchkiss, pointing to the study*] Go in there, you. Youre not wanted here.

HOTCHKISS. You understand, Bishop, that Mrs Collins is not to blame for this scene. I'm afraid Ive been rather irritating.

THE BISHOP. I can quite believe it, Sinjon.

Hotchkiss goes into the study.

THE BISHOP [*turning to Mrs George with great kindness of manner*] I'm sorry you have been worried [*he sits down on her left*]. Never mind him. A little pluck, a little gaiety of heart, a little prayer; and youll be laughing at him.

MRS GEORGE. Never fear. I have all that. It was as much my fault as his; and I should have put him in his place with a clip of that poker on the side of his head if you hadnt come in.

THE BISHOP. You might have put him in his coffin that way, Mrs Collins. And I should have been very sorry; because we are all fond of Sinjon.

MRS GEORGE. Yes: it's your duty to rebuke me. But do you think I dont know?

THE BISHOP. I dont rebuke you. Who am I that I should rebuke you? Besides, I know there are discussions in which the poker is the only possible argument.

MRS GEORGE. My lord: be earnest with me. I'm a very funny woman, I daresay; but I come from the same workshop as you. I heard you say that yourself years ago.

THE BISHOP. Quite so; but then I'm a very funny Bishop. Since we are both funny people, let us not forget that humor is a divine attribute.

MRS GEORGE. I know nothing about divine attributes or whatever you call them; but I can feel when I am being belittled. It was from you that I learnt first to respect myself. It was through you that I came to be able to walk safely through many wild and wilful paths. Dont go back on your own teaching.

THE BISHOP. I'm not a teacher: only a fellow-traveller of whom you asked the way. I pointed ahead—ahead of myself as well as of you.

MRS GEORGE [*rising and standing over him almost threateningly*] As I'm a living woman this day, if I find you out to be a fraud, I'll kill myself.

THE BISHOP. What! Kill yourself for finding out something! For becoming a wiser and therefore a better woman! What a bad reason!

MRS GEORGE. I have sometimes thought of killing you, and then killing myself.

THE BISHOP. Why on earth should you kill yourself—not to mention me?

MRS GEORGE. So that we might keep our assignation in Heaven.

THE BISHOP [*rising and facing her, breathless*] Mrs Collins! You are Incognita Appassionata!

MRS GEORGE. You read my letters, then? [*With a sigh of grateful relief, she sits down quietly, and says*] Thank you.

THE BISHOP [*remorsefully*] And I have broken the spell by

making you come here [*sitting down again*]. Can you ever forgive me?

MRS GEORGE. You couldnt know that it was only the coal merchant's wife, could you?

THE BISHOP. Why do you say only the coal merchant's wife?

MRS GEORGE. Many people would laugh at it.

THE BISHOP. Poor people! It's so hard to know the right place to laugh, isnt it?

MRS GEORGE. I didnt mean to make you think the letters were from a fine lady. I wrote on cheap paper; and I never could spell.

THE BISHOP. Neither could I. So that told me nothing.

MRS GEORGE. One thing I should like you to know.

THE BISHOP. Yes?

MRS GEORGE. We didnt cheat your friend. They were as good as we could do at thirteen shillings a ton.

THE BISHOP. Thats important. Thank you for telling me.

MRS GEORGE. I have something else to say; but will you please ask somebody to come and stay here while we talk? [*He rises and turns to the study door*]. Not a woman, if you dont mind. [*He nods understandingly and passes on*]. Not a man either.

THE BISHOP [*stopping*] Not a man and not a woman! We have no children left, Mrs Collins. They are all grown up and married.

MRS GEORGE. That other clergyman would do.

THE BISHOP. What! The sexton?

MRS GEORGE. Yes. He didnt mind my calling him that, did he? It was only my ignorance.

THE BISHOP. Not at all. [*He opens the study door and calls*] Soames! Anthony! [*To Mrs George*] Call him Father: he likes it. [*Soames appears at the study door*]. Mrs Collins wishes you to join us, Anthony.

Soames looks puzzled.

MRS GEORGE. You dont mind, Dad, do you? [*As this greeting visibly gives him a shock that hardly bears out the Bishop's advice, she says anxiously*] That was what you told me to call him, wasnt it?

SOAMES. I am called Father Anthony, Mrs Collins. But it does not matter what you call me. [*He comes in, and walks past her to the hearth*].

THE BISHOP. Mrs Collins has something to say to me that she wants you to hear.

SOAMES. I am listening.

THE BISHOP [*going back to his seat next her*] Now.

MRS GEORGE. My lord: you should never have married.

SOAMES. This woman is inspired. Listen to her, my lord.

THE BISHOP [*taken aback by the directness of the attack*] I married because I was so much in love with Alice that all the difficulties and doubts and dangers of marriage seemed to me the merest moonshine.

MRS GEORGE. Yes: it's mean to let poor young things in for so much while theyre in that state. Would you marry now that you know better if you were a widower?

THE BISHOP. I'm old now. It wouldnt matter.

MRS GEORGE. But would you if it did matter?

THE BISHOP. I think I should marry again lest anyone should imagine I had found marriage unhappy with Alice.

SOAMES [*sternly*] Are you fonder of your wife than of your salvation?

THE BISHOP. Oh, very much. When you meet a man who is very particular about his salvation, look out for a woman who is very particular about her character; and marry them to one another: theyll make a perfect pair. I advise you to fall in love, Anthony.

SOAMES [*with horror*] I!!

THE BISHOP. Yes, you! think of what it would do for you. For her sake you would come to care unselfishly and diligently for money instead of being selfishly and lazily indifferent to it. For her sake you would come to care in the same way for preferment. For her sake you would come to care for your health, your appearance, the good opinion of your fellow creatures, and all the really important things that make men work and strive instead of mooning and nursing their salvation.

SOAMES. In one word, for the sake of one deadly sin I should come to care for all the others.

THE BISHOP. Saint Anthony! Tempt him, Mrs Collins: tempt him.

MRS GEORGE [*rising and looking strangely before her*] Take care, my lord: you still have the power to make me obey your commands. And do you, Mr Sexton, beware of an empty heart.

THE BISHOP. Yes. Nature abhors a vacuum, Anthony. I would not dare go about with an empty heart: why, the first girl I met would fly into it by mere atmospheric pressure. Alice keeps them out now. Mrs Collins knows.

MRS GEORGE [*a faint convulsion passing like a wave over her*] I know more than either of you. One of you has not yet exhausted his first love: the other has not yet reached it. But I—I— [*she reels and is again convulsed*].

THE BISHOP [*saving her from falling*] Whats the matter? Are you ill, Mrs Collins? [*He gets her back into her chair*]. Soames: theres a glass of water in the study—quick. [*Soames hurries to the study door*].

MRS GEORGE. No. [*Soames stops*]. Dont call. Dont bring anyone. Cant you hear anything?

THE BISHOP. Nothing unusual. [*He sits by her, watching her with intense surprise and interest*].

MRS GEORGE. No music?

SOAMES. No. [*He steals to the end of the table and sits on her right, equally interested*].

MRS GEORGE. Do you see nothing—not a great light?

THE BISHOP. We are still walking in darkness.

MRS GEORGE. Put your hand on my forehead: the hand with the ring. [*He does so. Her eyes close*].

SOAMES [*inspired to prophesy*] There was a certain woman, the wife of a coal merchant, which had been a great sinner—

The Bishop, startled, takes his hand away. Mrs George's eyes open vividly as she interrupts Soames.

MRS GEORGE. You prophesy falsely, Anthony: never in all my life have I done anything that was not ordained for me. [*More quietly*] Ive been myself. Ive not been afraid of myself. And at last I have escaped from myself, and am become a voice for them that are afraid to speak, and a cry for the hearts that break in silence.

SOAMES [*whispering*] Is she inspired?

THE BISHOP. Marvellous. Hush.

MRS GEORGE. I have earned the right to speak. I have dared: I have gone through: I have not fallen withered in the fire: I have come at last out beyond, to the back of Godspeed.

THE BISHOP. And what do you see there, at the back of Godspeed?

SOAMES [*hungrily*] Give us your message.

MRS GEORGE [*with intensely sad reproach*] When you loved me I gave you the whole sun and stars to play with. I gave you eternity in a single moment, strength of the mountains in one clasp of your arms, and the volume of all the seas in one impulse of your souls. A moment only; but was it not enough? Were you not paid then for all the rest of your struggle on earth? Must I mend your clothes and sweep your floors as well? Was it not enough? I paid the price without bargaining: I bore the children without flinching: was that a reason for heaping fresh burdens on me? I carried the child in my arms: must I carry the father too? When I opened the gates of paradise, were you blind? was it nothing to you? When all the stars sang in your ears and all the winds swept you into the heart of heaven, were you deaf? were you dull? was I no more to you than a bone to a dog? Was it not enough? We spent eternity together; and you ask me for a little lifetime more. We possessed all the universe together; and you ask me to give you my scanty wages as well. I have given you the greatest of all things; and you ask me to give you little things. I gave you your own soul: you ask me for my body as a plaything. Was it not enough? Was it not enough?

SOAMES. Do you understand this, my lord?

THE BISHOP. I have that advantage over you, Anthony, thanks to Alice. [*He takes Mrs George's hand*]. Your hand is very cold. Can you come down to earth? Do you remember who I am, and who you are?

MRS GEORGE. It was enough for me. I did not ask to meet you—to touch you—[*the Bishop quickly releases her hand*]. When you spoke to my soul years ago from your pulpit, you opened the doors of my salvation to me; and now they stand open for ever. It was enough. I have asked you for nothing since: I ask you for nothing now. I have lived: it is enough. I have had my wages; and I am ready for my work. I thank you and bless you and leave you. You are happier in that than I am; for when I do for men what you did for me, I have no thanks, and no blessing: I am their prey; and there is no rest from their loving and no mercy from their loathing.

THE BISHOP. You must take us as we are, Mrs Collins.

SOAMES. No. Take us as we are capable of becoming.

MRS GEORGE. Take me as I am: I ask no more. [*She turns her head to the study door and cries*] Yes: come in, come in.

Hotchkiss comes softly in from the study.

HOTCHKISS. Will you be so kind as to tell me whether I am dreaming? In there I have heard Mrs Collins saying the strangest things, and not a syllable from you two.

SOAMES. My lord: is this possession by the devil?

THE BISHOP. Or the ecstasy of a saint?

HOTCHKISS. Or the convulsion of the pythoness on the tripod?

THE BISHOP. May not the three be one?

MRS GEORGE [*troubled*] You are paining and tiring me with idle questions. You are dragging me back to myself. You are tormenting me with your evil dreams of saints and devils and—what was it?—[*striving to fathom it*] the pythoness—the pythoness—[*giving it up*] I dont understand. I am a woman: a human creature like yourselves. Will you not take me as I am?

SOAMES. Yes; but shall we take you and burn you?

THE BISHOP. Or take you and canonize you?

HOTCHKISS [*gaily*] Or take you as a matter of course? [*Swiftly to the Bishop*] We must get her out of this: it's dangerous. [*Aloud to her*] May I suggest that you shall be Anthony's devil and the Bishop's saint and my adored Polly? [*Slipping behind her, he picks up her hand from her lap and kisses it over her shoulder*].

MRS GEORGE [*waking*] What was that? Who kissed my hand? [*To the Bishop, eagerly*] Was it you? [*He shakes his head. She is mortified*]. I beg your pardon.

THE BISHOP. Not at all. I'm not repudiating that honor. Allow me [*he kisses her hand*].

MRS GEORGE. Thank you for that. It was not the sexton, was it?

SOAMES. I!

HOTCHKISS. It was I, Polly, your ever faithful.

MRS GEORGE [*turning and seeing him*] Let me catch you doing it again: thats all. How do you come there? I sent you away. [*With great energy, becoming quite herself again*] What the goodness gracious has been happening?

HOTCHKISS. As far as I can make out, you have been having a very charming and eloquent sort of fit.

MRS GEORGE [*delighted*] What! My second sight! [*To the Bishop*] Oh, how I have prayed that it might come to me if ever I met you! And now it has come. How stunning! You may believe every word I said: I cant remember it now; but it was something that was just bursting to be said; and so it laid hold of me and said itself. Thats how it is, you see.

Edith and Cecil Sykes come in through the tower. She has her hat on. Leo follows. They have evidently been out together. Sykes, with an unnatural air, half foolish, half rakish, as if he had lost all his self-respect and were determined not to let it prey on his spirits, throws himself into a chair at the end of the table near the hearth and thrusts his hands into his pockets, like Hogarth's Rake, without waiting for Edith to sit down. She sits in the railed chair. Leo takes the chair nearest the tower on the long side of the table, brooding, with closed lips.

THE BISHOP. Have you been out, my dear?

EDITH. Yes.

THE BISHOP. With Cecil?

EDITH. Yes.

THE BISHOP. Have you come to an understanding?

No reply. Blank silence.

SYKES. You had better tell them, Edie.

EDITH. Tell them yourself.

The General comes in from the garden.

THE GENERAL [*coming forward to the table*] Can anybody oblige me with some tobacco? Ive finished mine; and my nerves are still far from settled.

THE BISHOP. Wait a moment, Boxer. Cecil has something important to tell us.

SYKES. Weve done it. Thats all.

HOTCHKISS. Done what, Cecil?

SYKES. Well, what do you suppose?

EDITH. Got married, of course.

THE GENERAL. Married! Who gave you away?

SYKES [*jerking his head towards the tower*] This gentleman did. [*Seeing that they do not understand, he looks round and sees that there is no one there*]. Oh! I thought he came in with us. He's gone downstairs, I suppose. The Beadle.

THE GENERAL. The Beadle! What the devil did he do that for?

SYKES. Oh, I dont know: I didnt make any bargain with him. [*To Mrs George*] How much ought I to give him, Mrs Collins?

MRS GEORGE. Five shillings. [*To the Bishop*] I want to rest for a moment: there! in your study. I saw it here [*she touches her forehead*].

THE BISHOP [*opening the study door for her*] By all means. Turn my brother out if he disturbs you. Soames: bring the letters out here.

SYKES. He wont be offended at my offering it, will he?

MRS GEORGE. Not he! He touches children with the mace to cure them of ringworm for fourpence apiece. [*She goes into the study. Soames follows her*].

THE GENERAL. Well, Edith, I'm a little disappointed, I must say. However, I'm glad it was done by somebody in a public uniform.

Mrs Bridgenorth and Lesbia come in through the tower. Mrs Bridgenorth makes for the Bishop. He goes to her, and they meet near the oak chest. Lesbia comes between Sykes and Edith.

THE BISHOP. Alice, my love, theyre married.

MRS BRIDGENORTH [*placidly*] Oh, well, thats all right. Better tell Collins.

Soames comes back from the study with his writing materials. He seats himself at the nearest end of the table and goes on with his work. Hotchkiss sits down in the next chair round the table corner, with his back to him.

LESBIA. You have both given in, have you?

EDITH. Not at all. We have provided for everything.

SOAMES. How?

EDITH. Before going to the church, we went to the office of that insurance company—whats its name, Cecil?

SYKES. The British Family Insurance Corporation. It insures you against poor relations and all sorts of family contingencies.

EDITH. It has consented to insure Cecil against libel actions brought against him on my account. It will give us specially low terms because I am a Bishop's daughter.

SYKES. And I have given Edie my solemn word that if I ever commit a crime I'll knock her down before a witness and go off to Brighton with another lady.

LESBIA. Thats what you call providing for everything! [*She goes to the middle of the table on the garden side and sits down*].

LEO. Do make him see that there are no worms before he knocks you down, Edith. Wheres Rejjy?

REGINALD [*coming in from the study*] Here. Whats the matter?

LEO [*springing up and flouncing round to him*] Whats the matter! You may well ask. While Edie and Cecil were at the insurance office I took a taxy and went off to your lodgings;

and a nice mess I found everything in. Your clothes are in a disgraceful state. Your liver-pad has been made into a kettle-holder. Youre no more fit to be left to yourself than a one-year-old baby.

REGINALD. Oh, I cant be bothered looking after things like that. I'm all right.

LEO. Youre not: youre a disgrace. You never consider that youre a disgrace to me: you think only of yourself. You must come home with me and be taken proper care of: my conscience will not allow me to let you live like a pig. [*She arranges his necktie*]. You must stay with me until I marry Sinjon; and then we can adopt you or something.

REGINALD [*breaking loose from her and stumping off past Hotchkiss towards the hearth*] No, I'm dashed if I'll be adopted by Sinjon. You can adopt him if you like.

HOTCHKISS [*rising*] I suggest that that would really be the better plan, Leo. Ive a confession to make to you. I'm not the man you took me for. Your objection to Rejjy was that he had low tastes.

REGINALD [*turning*] Was it? by George!

LEO. I said slovenly habits. I never thought he had really low tastes until I saw that woman in court. How he could have chosen such a creature and let her write to him after—

REGINALD. Is this fair? I never—

HOTCHKISS. Of course you didnt, Rejjy. Dont be silly, Leo. It's I who really have low tastes.

LEO. You!

HOTCHKISS. Ive fallen in love with a coal merchant's wife. I adore her. I would rather have one of her boot-laces than a lock of your hair. [*He folds his arms and stands like a rock*].

REGINALD. You damned scoundrel, how dare you throw my wife over like that before my face? [*He seems on the point of assaulting Hotchkiss when Leo gets between them and draws Reginald away towards the study door*].

LEO. Dont take any notice of him, Rejjy. Go at once and get that odious decree demolished or annulled or whatever it is. Tell Sir Gorell Barnes that I have changed my mind.

[*To Hotchkiss*] I might have known that you were too clever to be really a gentleman. [*She takes Reginald away to the oak chest and seats him there. He chuckles. Hotchkiss resumes his seat, brooding*].

THE BISHOP. All the problems appear to be solving themselves.

LESBIA. Except mine.

THE GENERAL. But, my dear Lesbia, you see what has happened here today. [*Coming a little nearer and bending his face towards hers*] Now I put it to you, does it not shew you the folly of not marrying?

LESBIA. No: I cant say it does. And [*rising*] you have been smoking again.

THE GENERAL. You drive me to it, Lesbia. I cant help it.

LESBIA [*standing behind her chair with her hands on the back of it and looking radiant*] Well, I wont scold you today. I feel in particularly good humor just now.

THE GENERAL. May I ask why, Lesbia?

LESBIA [*drawing a large breath*] To think that after all the dangers of the morning I am still unmarried! still independent! still my own mistress! still a glorious strong-minded old maid of old England!

Soames silently springs up and makes a long stretch from his end of the table to shake her hand across it.

THE GENERAL. Do you find any real happiness in being your own mistress? Would it not be more generous—would you not be happier as someone else's mistress—

LESBIA. Boxer!

THE GENERAL [*rising, horrified*] No, no, you must know, my dear Lesbia, that I was not using the word in its improper sense. I am sometimes unfortunate in my choice of expressions; but you know what I mean. I feel sure you would be happier as my wife.

LESBIA. I daresay I should, in a frowsty sort of way. But I prefer my dignity and my independence. I'm afraid I think this rage for happiness rather vulgar.

THE GENERAL. Oh, very well, Lesbia. I shall not ask you

again. [*He sits down huffily*].

LESBIA. You will, Boxer; but it will be no use. [*She also sits down again and puts her hand almost affectionately on his*]. Some day I hope to make a friend of you; and then we shall get on very nicely.

THE GENERAL [*starting up again*] Ha! I think you are hard, Lesbia. I shall make a fool of myself if I remain here. Alice: I shall go into the garden for a while.

COLLINS [*appearing in the tower*] I think everything is in order now, maam.

THE GENERAL [*going to him*] Oh, by the way, could you oblige me—[*the rest of the sentence is lost in a whisper*].

COLLINS. Certainly, General. [*He takes out a tobacco pouch and hands it to the General, who takes it and goes into the garden*].

LESBIA. I dont believe theres a man in England who really and truly loves his wife as much as he loves his pipe.

THE BISHOP. By the way, what has happened to the wedding party?

SYKES. I dont know. There wasnt a soul in the church when we were married except the pew opener and the curate who did the job.

EDITH. They had all gone home.

MRS BRIDGENORTH. But the bridesmaids?

COLLINS. Me and the beadle have been all over the place in a couple of taxies, maam; and weve collected them all. They were a good deal disappointed on account of their dresses, and thought it all rather irregular; but theyve agreed to come to the breakfast. The truth is, theyre wild with curiosity to know how it all happened. The organist held on until the organ was nigh worn out, and himself worse than the organ. He asked me particularly to tell you, my lord, that he held back Mendelssohn til the very last; but when that was gone he thought he might as well go too. So he played God Save The King and cleared out the church. He's coming to the breakfast to explain.

LEO. Please remember, Collins, that there is no truth whatever in the rumor that I am separated from my husband, or that there is, or ever has been, anything between me and Mr Hotchkiss.

COLLINS. Bless you, maam! one could always see that. [*To Mrs Bridgenorth*] Will you receive here or in the hall, maam?

MRS BRIDGENORTH. In the hall. Alfred: you and Boxer must go there and be ready to keep the first arrivals talking til we come. We have to dress Edith. Come, Lesbia: come, Leo: we must all help. Now, Edith. [*Lesbia, Leo, and Edith go out through the tower*]. Collins: we shall want you when Miss Edith's dressed to look over her veil and things and see that theyre all right.

COLLINS. Yes, maam. Anything you would like mentioned about Miss Lesbia, maam?

MRS BRIDGENORTH. No. She wont have the General. I think you may take that as final.

COLLINS. What a pity, maam! A fine lady wasted, maam. [*They shake their heads sadly; and Mrs Bridgenorth goes out through the tower*].

THE BISHOP. I'm going to the hall, Collins, to receive. Rejjy: go and tell Boxer; and come both of you to help with the small talk. Come, Cecil. [*He goes out through the tower, followed by Sykes*].

REGINALD [*to Hotchkiss*] Youve always talked a precious lot about behaving like a gentleman. Well, if you think youve behaved like a gentleman to Leo, youre mistaken. And I shall have to take her part, remember that.

HOTCHKISS. I understand. Your doors are closed to me.

REGINALD [*quickly*] Oh no. Dont be hasty. I think I should like you to drop in after a while, you know. She gets so cross and upset when theres nobody to liven up the house a bit.

HOTCHKISS. I'll do my best.

REGINALD [*relieved*] Righto. You dont mind, old chap, do you?

HOTCHKISS. It's Fate. Ive touched coal; and my hands are black; but theyre clean. So long, Rejjy. [*They shake hands; and Reginald goes into the garden to collect Boxer*].

COLLINS. Excuse me, sir; but do you stay to breakfast? Your name is on one of the covers; and I should like to change it if youre not remaining.

HOTCHKISS. How do I know? Is my destiny any longer in my own hands? Go: ask SHE WHO MUST BE OBEYED.

COLLINS [*awestruck*] Has Mrs George taken a fancy to you, sir?

HOTCHKISS. Would she had! Worse, man, worse: Ive taken a fancy to Mrs George.

COLLINS. Dont despair, sir: if George likes your conversation youll find their house a very pleasant one: livelier than Mr Reginald's was, I daresay.

HOTCHKISS [*calling*] Polly.

COLLINS [*promptly*] Oh, if it's come to Polly already, sir, I should say you were all right.

Mrs George appears at the door of the study.

HOTCHKISS. Your brother-in-law wishes to know whether I'm to stay for the wedding breakfast. Tell him.

MRS GEORGE. He stays, Bill, if he chooses to behave himself.

HOTCHKISS [*to Collins*] May I, as a friend of the family, have the privilege of calling you Bill?

COLLINS. With pleasure, sir, I'm sure, sir.

HOTCHKISS. My own pet name in the bosom of my family is Sonny.

MRS GEORGE. Why didnt you tell me that before? Sonny is just the name I wanted for you. [*She pats his cheek familiarly: he rises abruptly and goes to the hearth, where he throws himself moodily into the railed chair*]. Bill: I'm not going into the hall until there are enough people there to make a proper little court for me. Send the Beadle for me when you think it looks good enough.

COLLINS. Right, maam. [*He goes out through the tower*].

Mrs George, left alone with Hotchkiss and Soames, suddenly puts her hands on Soames's shoulders and bends over him].

MRS GEORGE. The Bishop said I was to tempt you, Anthony.

SOAMES [*without looking round*] Woman: go away.

MRS GEORGE. Anthony:

"When other lips and other hearts
Their tale of love shall tell

HOTCHKISS [*sardonically*]

In language whose excess imparts
The power they feel so well.

MRS GEORGE.

Though hollow hearts may wear a mask
Twould break your own to see,
In such a moment I but ask
That youll remember me."

And you will, Anthony. I shall put my spell on you.

SOAMES. Do you think that a man who has sung the Magnificat and adored the Queen of Heaven has any ears for such trash as that or any eyes for such trash as you—saving your poor little soul's presence. Go home to your duties, woman.

MRS GEORGE [*highly approving his fortitude*] Anthony: I adopt you as my father. Thats the talk! Give me a man whose whole life doesnt hang on some scrubby woman in the next street; and I'll never let him go [*she slaps him heartily on the back*].

SOAMES. Thats enough. You have another man to talk to. I'm busy.

MRS GEORGE [*leaving Soames and going a step or two nearer Hotchkiss*] Why arnt you like him, Sonny? Why do you hang on to a scrubby woman in the next street?

HOTCHKISS [*thoughtfully*] I must apologize to Billiter.

MRS GEORGE. Who is Billiter?

HOTCHKISS. A man who eats rice pudding with a spoon. Ive been eating rice pudding with a spoon ever since I saw you first. [*He rises*]. We all eat our rice pudding with a spoon, dont we, Soames?

SOAMES. We are members of one another. There is no need to refer to me. In the first place, I'm busy: in the second, youll find it all in the Church Catechism, which contains most of the new discoveries with which the age is bursting. Of course you should apologize to Billiter. He is your equal. He will go to the same heaven if he behaves himself and to the same hell if he doesnt.

MRS GEORGE [*sitting down*] And so will my husband the coal merchant.

HOTCHKISS. If I were your husband's superior here I should be his superior in heaven or hell: equality lies deeper than that. The coal merchant and I are in love with the same woman. That settles the question for me for ever. [*He prowls across the kitchen to the garden door, deep in thought*].

SOAMES. Psha!

MRS GEORGE. You dont believe in women, do you, Anthony? He might as well say that he and George both like fried fish.

HOTCHKISS. I do not like fried fish. Dont be low, Polly.

SOAMES. Woman: do not presume to accuse me of unbelief. And do you, Hotchkiss, not despise this woman's soul because she speaks of fried fish. Some of the victims of the Miraculous Draught of Fishes were fried. And I eat fried fish every Friday and like it. You are as ingrained a snob as ever.

HOTCHKISS [*impatiently*] My dear Anthony: I find you merely ridiculous as a preacher, because you keep referring me to places and documents and alleged occurrences in which, as a matter of fact, I dont believe. I dont believe in anything but my own will and my own pride and honor. Your fishes and your catechisms and all the rest of it make a charming poem which you call your faith. It fits you to perfection; but it doesnt fit me. I happen, like Napoleon, to prefer Mahometanism. [*Mrs George, associating Mahometanism with polygamy, looks at him with quick suspicion*]. I believe the whole British Empire will adopt a reformed Mahometanism before the end of the century. The character of Mahomet is congenial to me. I admire him, and share his views of life to a considerable extent. That beats you, you see, Soames. Religion is a great force: the only real motive force in the world; but what you fellows dont understand is that you must get at a man through his own religion and not through yours. Instead of facing that fact, you persist in trying to convert all men to your own little sect, so that you can use it against them afterwards. You are all missionaries and proselytizers trying to uproot the native religion from your neighbor's flowerbeds and plant your own in its place. You would rather let a child perish in ignorance than have it taught by a rival sectary. You talk to me of the quintessential equality of coal merchants and British officers; and yet you cant see the quintessential equality of all the religions. Who are you, anyhow, that you should know better than Mahomet or Confucius or any of the other Johnnies who have been on this job since the world existed?

MRS GEORGE [*admiring his eloquence*] George will like you, Sonny. You should hear him talking about the Church.

SOAMES. Very well, then: go to your doom, both of you. There is only one religion for me: that which my soul knows to be true; but even irreligion has one tenet; and that is the sacredness of marriage. You two are on the verge of deadly sin. Do you deny that?

HOTCHKISS. You forget, Anthony: the marriage itself is the deadly sin according to you.

SOAMES. The question is not now what I believe, but what you believe. Take the vows with me; and give up that woman if you have the strength and the light. But if you are still in the grip of this world, at least respect its institutions. Do you believe in marriage or do you not?

HOTCHKISS. My soul is utterly free from any such superstition. I solemnly declare that between this woman, as you impolitely call her, and me, I see no barrier that my conscience bids me respect. I loathe the whole marriage morality of the middle classes with all my instincts. If I were an eighteenth century marquis I could not feel more free with regard to a Parisian citizen's wife than I do with regard to Polly. I despise all this domestic purity business as the lowest depth of narrow, selfish, sensual, wife-grabbing vulgarity.

MRS GEORGE [*rising promptly*] Oh, indeed. Then youre not coming home with me, young man. I'm sorry; for it's refreshing to have met once in my life a man who wasnt frightened by my wedding ring; but I'm looking out for a friend and not for a French marquis; so youre not coming home with me.

HOTCHKISS [*inexorably*] Yes, I am.

MRS GEORGE. No.

HOTCHKISS. Yes. Think again. You know your set pretty well, I suppose, your petty tradesmen's set. You know all its scandals and hypocrisies, its jealousies and squabbles, its hundreds of divorce cases that never come into court, as well as its tens that do.

MRS GEORGE. We're not angels. I know a few scandals; but most of us are too dull to be anything but good.

HOTCHKISS. Then you must have noticed that just as all murderers, judging by their edifying remarks on the scaffold, seem to be devout Christians, so all libertines, both male and female, are invariably people overflowing with domestic sentimentality and professions of respect for the conventions they violate in secret.

MRS GEORGE. Well, you dont expect them to give themselves away, do you?

HOTCHKISS. They are people of sentiment, not of honor. Now, I'm not a man of sentiment, but a man of honor. I know well what will happen to me when once I cross the threshold of your husband's house and break bread with him. This marriage bond which I despise will bind me as it never seems to bind the people who believe in it, and whose chief amusement is to go to the theatres where it is laughed at. Soames: youre a Communist, arnt you?

SOAMES. I am a Christian. That obliges me to be a Communist.

HOTCHKISS. And you believe that many of our landed

estates were stolen from the Church by Henry the eighth?

SOAMES. I do not merely believe that: I know it as a lawyer.

HOTCHKISS. Would you steal a turnip from one of the landlords of those stolen lands?

SOAMES [*fencing with the question*] They have no right to their lands.

HOTCHKISS. Thats not what I ask you. Would you steal a turnip from one of the fields they have no right to?

SOAMES. I do not like turnips.

HOTCHKISS. As you are a lawyer, answer me.

SOAMES. I admit that I should probably not do so. I should perhaps be wrong not to steal the turnip: I cant defend my reluctance to do so; but I think I should not do so. I know I should not do so.

HOTCHKISS. Neither shall I be able to steal George's wife. I have stretched out my hand for that forbidden fruit before; and I know that my hand will always come back empty. To disbelieve in marriage is easy: to love a married woman is easy; but to betray a comrade, to be disloyal to a host, to break the covenant of bread and salt, is impossible. You may take me home with you, Polly: you have nothing to fear.

MRS GEORGE. And nothing to hope?

HOTCHKISS. Since you put it in that more than kind way, Polly, absolutely nothing.

MRS GEORGE. Hm! Like most men, you think you know everything a woman wants, dont you? But the thing one wants most has nothing to do with marriage at all. Perhaps Anthony here has a glimmering of it. Eh, Anthony?

SOAMES. Christian fellowship?

MRS GEORGE. You call it that, do you?

SOAMES. What do you call it?

COLLINS [*appearing in the tower with the Beadle*] Now, Polly, the hall's full; and theyre waiting for you.

THE BEADLE. Make way there, gentlemen, please. Way for the worshipful the Mayoress. If you please, my lords and gentlemen. By your leave, ladies and gentlemen: way for the Mayoress.

Mrs George takes Hotchkiss's arm, and goes out, preceded by the Beadle.

Soames resumes his writing tranquilly.

WIDOWERS' HOUSES

AN ORIGINAL DIDACTIC REALISTIC PLAY

Begun 1885, laid aside, finished 1892

First Performed London 1892

See Preface to the First Volume of Plays: Pleasant and Unpleasant (*Volume III, page vii*)

WIDOWERS' HOUSES

ACT I

IN the garden restaurant of a hotel at Remagen on the Rhine, on a fine afternoon in August in the eighteen-eighties. Looking down the Rhine towards Bonn, the gate leading from the garden to the riverside is seen on the right. The hotel is on the left. It has a wooden annexe with an entrance marked Table d'Hôte. A waiter is in attendance.

A couple of English tourists come out of the hotel. The younger, Dr Harry Trench, is about 24, *stoutly built, thick in the neck, close-cropped and black in the hair, with undignified medical-student manners, frank, hasty, rather boyish. The other, Mr William de Burgh Cokane, is probably over* 40, *possibly* 50: *an ill-nourished, scanty-haired gentleman, with affected manners: fidgety, touchy, and constitutionally ridiculous in uncompassionate eyes.*

COKANE [*on the threshold of the hotel, calling peremptorily to the waiter*] Two beers for us out here. [*The waiter goes for the beer. Cokane comes into the garden*]. We have secured the room with the best view in the hotel, Harry, thanks to my tact. We'll leave in the morning, and do Mainz and Frankfurt. There is a very graceful female statue in the private house of a nobleman in Frankfurt. Also a zoo. Next day, Nuremberg! finest collection of instruments of torture in the world.

TRENCH. All right. You look out the trains, will you? [*He takes a Continental Bradshaw from his pocket, and tosses it on one of the tables*].

COKANE [*baulking himself in the act of sitting down*] Pah! the seat is all dusty. These foreigners are deplorably unclean in their habits.

TRENCH [*buoyantly*] Never mind: it dont matter, old chappie. Buck up, Billy, buck up. Enjoy yourself. [*He throws Cokane into the chair, and sits down opposite him, taking out his pipe, and singing noisily*]

Pour out the Rhine wine: let it flow
Like a free and bounding river—

COKANE [*scandalized*] In the name of common decency, Harry, will you remember that you are a Gentleman, and not a coster on Hamstead Heath on Bank Holiday? Would you dream of behaving like this in London?

TRENCH. Oh, rot! Ive come abroad to enjoy myself. So would you if youd just passed an examination after four years in the medical school and walking the hospital. [*He again bursts into song*].

COKANE [*rising*] Trench: either you travel as a gentleman, or you travel alone. This is what makes Englishmen unpopular on the Continent. It may not matter before the natives; but the people who came on board the steamer at Bonn are English. I have been uneasy all the afternoon about what they must think of us. Look at our appearance.

TRENCH. Whats wrong with our appearance?

COKANE. Négligé, my dear fellow, négligé. On the steamboat a little négligé was quite en règle; but here, in this hotel, some of them are sure to dress for dinner; and you have nothing but that Norfolk jacket. How are they to know that you are well connected if you do not shew it by your costume?

TRENCH. Pooh! the steamboat people were the scum of the earth: Americans and all sorts. They may go hang themselves, Billy. I shall not bother about them. [*He strikes a match, and proceeds to light his pipe*].

COKANE. Do drop calling me Billy in public, Trench. My name is Cokane. I am sure they were persons of consequence: you were struck with the distinguished appearance of the father yourself.

TRENCH [*sobered at once*] What! those people? [*He blows out the match and puts up his pipe*].

COKANE [*following up his advantage triumphantly*] Here, Harry, here: at this hotel. I recognized the father's umbrella in the hall.

TRENCH [*with a touch of genuine shame*] I suppose I ought to have brought a change. But a lot of luggage is such a nuisance; and [*rising abruptly*] at all events we can go and have a wash. [*He turns to go into the hotel, but stops in consternation, seeing some people coming up to the riverside gate*]. Oh, I say! Here they are.

A lady and gentleman, followed by a porter with some light parcels, not luggage, but shop purchases, come into the garden. They are apparently father and daughter. The gentleman is 50, tall, well preserved, and of upright carriage. His incisive, domineering utterance and imposing style, with his strong aquiline nose and resolute clean-shaven mouth, give him an air of importance. He wears a light grey frock-coat with silk linings, a white hat, and a field-glass slung in a new leather case. A self-made man, formidable to servants, not easily accessible to anyone. His daughter is a well-dressed, well-fed, good-looking, strongminded young woman, presentably ladylike, but still her father's daughter. Nevertheless fresh and attractive, and none the worse for being vital and energetic rather than delicate and refined.

COKANE [*quickly taking the arm of Trench, who is staring as if transfixed*] Recollect yourself, Harry: presence of mind, presence of mind! [*He strolls with him towards the hotel. The waiter comes out with the beer*]. Kellner: ceci-la est notre table. Est ce que vous comprenez Français?

WAITER. Yes, zare. Oll right, zare.

THE GENTLEMAN [*to his porter*] Place those things on that table. [*The porter does not understand*].

WAITER [*interposing*] Zese zhentellmen are using zis table, zare. Vould you mind—

THE GENTLEMAN [*severely*] You should have told me so before. [*To Cokane, with fierce condescension*] I regret the mistake, sir.

COKANE. Dont mention it, my dear sir: dont mention it. Retain the place, I beg.

THE GENTLEMAN [*coldly turning his back on him*] Thank you. [*To the porter*] Place them on that table. [*The porter makes no movement until the gentleman points to the parcels and peremptorily raps on another table, nearer the gate*].

PORTER. Ja wohl, gnäd'g' Herr. [*He puts down the parcels*].

THE GENTLEMAN [*taking out a handful of money*] Waiter.

WAITER [*awestruck*] Yes, zare.

THE GENTLEMAN. Tea. For two. Out here.

WAITER. Yes, zare. [*He goes into the hotel*].

The gentleman selects a small coin from his handful of money, and gives it to the porter, who receives it with a submissive touch to his cap, and goes out, not daring to speak. His daughter sits down and opens a parcel of photographs. The gentleman takes out a Baedeker; places a chair for himself; and then, before sitting down, looks truculently at Cokane, as if waiting for him to take himself off. Cokane, not at all abashed, resumes his place at the other table with an air of modest good breeding, and calls to Trench, who is prowling irresolutely in the background.

COKANE. Trench, my dear fellow: your beer is waiting for you. [*He drinks*].

TRENCH [*glad of the excuse to come back to his chair*] Thank you, Cokane. [*He also drinks*].

COKANE. By the way, Harry, I have often meant to ask you: is Lady Roxdale your mother's sister or your father's?

This shot tells immediately. The gentleman is perceptibly interested.

TRENCH. My mother's, of course. What put that into your head?

COKANE. Nothing. I was just thinking—hm! She will expect you to marry, Harry: a doctor ought to marry.

TRENCH. What has she got to do with it?

COKANE. A great deal, dear boy. She looks forward to floating your wife in society in London.

TRENCH. What rot!

COKANE. Ah, you are young, dear boy: you dont know the importance of these things: apparently idle ceremonial trifles, really the springs and wheels of a great aristocratic system. [*The waiter comes back with the tea things, which he brings to the gentleman's table. Cokane rises and addresses the gentleman*]. My dear sir, excuse my addressing you; but I cannot help feeling that you prefer this table, and that we are in your way.

THE GENTLEMAN [*graciously*] Thank you. Blanche: this gentleman very kindly offers us his table, if you would prefer it.

BLANCHE. Oh, thanks: it makes no difference.

THE GENTLEMAN [*to Cokane*] We are fellow travellers, I believe, sir.

COKANE. Fellow travellers and fellow countrymen. Ah, we rarely feel the charm of our own tongue until it reaches our ears under a foreign sky. You have no doubt noticed that?

THE GENTLEMAN [*a little puzzled*] Hm! From a romantic point of view, possibly, very possibly. As a matter of fact, the sound of English makes me feel at home; and I dislike feeling at home when I am abroad. It is not precisely what one goes to the expense for. [*He looks at Trench*]. I think this gentleman travelled with us also.

COKANE [*acting as master of the ceremonies*] My valued friend, Dr Trench. [*The gentleman and Trench rise*]. Trench, my dear fellow, allow me to introduce you to—er—? [*He looks inquiringly at the gentleman, waiting for the name*].

THE GENTLEMAN. Permit me to shake your hand, Dr Trench. My name is Sartorius; and I have the honor of being known to Lady Roxdale, who is, I believe, a near relative of yours. Blanche. [*She looks up*]. Dr Trench. [*They bow*].

TRENCH. Perhaps I should introduce my friend Cokane to you, Mr Sartorius: Mr William de Burgh Cokane. [*Cokane makes an elaborate bow. Sartorius accepts it with dignity. The waiter meanwhile returns with the tea things.*].

SARTORIUS [*to the waiter*] Two more cups.

WAITER. Yes, zare. [*He goes into the hotel*].

BLANCHE. Do you take sugar, Mr Cokane?

COKANE. Thank you. [*To Sartorius*] This is really too kind. Harry: bring your chair round.

SARTORIUS. You are very welcome. [*Trench brings his chair to the tea table; and they all sit round it. The waiter returns with two more cups*].

WAITER. Table d'hôte at alf pass zeex, zhentellmenn.

Somesing else now, zare?

SARTORIUS. No. You can go. [*The waiter goes*].

COKANE [*very agreeably*] Do you contemplate a long stay here, Miss Sartorius?

BLANCHE. We were thinking of going on to Rolandseck. Is it as nice as this place?

COKANE. Harry: the Baedeker. [*Trench produces it from the other pocket*]. Thank you. [*He consults the index for Rolandseck*].

BLANCHE. Sugar, Dr Trench?

TRENCH. Thanks. [*She hands him the cup, and looks meaningly at him for an instant. He looks down hastily, and glances apprehensively at Sartorius, who is preoccupied with the bread and butter*].

COKANE. Rolandseck appears to be an extremely interesting place. [*He reads*] "It is one of the most beautiful and frequented spots on the river, and is surrounded with numerous villas and pleasant gardens, chiefly belonging to wealthy merchants from the Lower Rhine, and extending along the wooded slopes at the back of the village."

BLANCHE. That sounds civilized and comfortable. I vote we go there.

SARTORIUS. Quite like our place at Surbiton, my dear.

BLANCHE. Quite.

COKANE. You have a place down the river? Ah, I envy you.

SARTORIUS. No: I have merely taken a furnished villa at Surbiton for the summer. I live in Bedford Square. I am a vestryman, and must reside in the parish.

BLANCHE. Another cup, Mr Cokane?

COKANE. Thank you, no. [*To Sartorius*] I presume you have been round this little place. Not much to see here, except the Apollinaris Church.

SARTORIUS [*scandalized*] The what!

COKANE. The Apollinaris Church.

SARTORIUS. A strange name to give a church. Very continental, I must say.

COKANE. Ah, yes, yes, yes. That is where our neighbors fall short sometimes, Mr Sartorius. Taste! taste is what they occasionally fail in. But in this instance they are not to blame. The water is called after the church, not the church after the water.

SARTORIUS [*as if this were an extenuating circumstance, but not a complete excuse*] I am glad to hear it. Is the church a celebrated one?

COKANE. Baedeker stars it.

SARTORIUS [*respectfully*] Oh, in that case I should like to see it.

COKANE [*reading*] "—erected in 1839 by Zwirner, the late eminent architect of the cathedral of Cologne, at the expense of Count Fürstenberg-Stammheim."

SARTORIUS [*much impressed*] We must certainly see that, Mr Cokane. I had no idea that the architect of Cologne cathedral lived so recently.

BLANCHE. Dont let us bother about any more churches, papa: theyre all the same. I'm tired to death of them.

SARTORIUS. Well, my dear, if you think it sensible to take a long and expensive journey to see what there is to be seen, and then go away without seeing it—

BLANCHE. Not this afternoon, papa, please.

SARTORIUS. My dear: I should like you to see everything. It is part of your education—

BLANCHE [*rising, with a petulant sigh*] Oh, my education! Very well, very well: I suppose I must go through with it. Are you coming, Dr Trench? [*With a grimace*] I'm sure the Johannis Church will be a treat for you.

COKANE [*laughing softly and archly*] Ah, excellent, excellent: very good indeed. [*Seriously*] But do you know, Miss Sartorius, there actually are Johannis churches here—several of them—as well as Apollinaris ones?

SARTORIUS [*sententiously, taking out his field-glass and leading the way to the gate*] There is many a true word spoken in jest, Mr Cokane.

COKANE [*accompanying him*] How true! How true!

They go out together, ruminating profoundly. Blanche makes no movement to follow them. She watches until they are safely out of sight, and then posts herself before Trench, looking at him with an enigmatic smile, which he returns with a half sheepish, half conceited grin.

BLANCHE. Well! So you *have* done it at last.

TRENCH. Yes. At least Cokane's done it. I told you he'd manage it. He's rather an ass in some ways; but he has tremendous tact.

BLANCHE [*contemptuously*] Tact! Thats not tact: thats inquisitiveness. Inquisitive people always have a lot of practice in getting into conversation with strangers. Why didnt you speak to my father yourself on the boat? You were ready enough to speak to me without any introduction.

TRENCH. I didnt particularly want to talk to him.

BLANCHE. It didnt occur to you, I suppose, that you put me in a false position by that.

TRENCH. Oh, I dont see that, exactly. Besides, your father isnt an easy man to tackle. Of course, now that I know him, I see that he's pleasant enough; but then youve got to know him first, havnt you?

BLANCHE [*impatiently*] Everybody is afraid of papa: I'm sure I dont know why. [*She sits down again, pouting a little*].

TRENCH [*tenderly*] However, it's all right now: isnt it? [*He sits near her*].

BLANCHE [*sharply*] I dont know. How should I? You had no right to speak to me that day on board the steamer. You thought I was alone, because [*with false pathos*] I had no mother with me.

TRENCH [*protesting*] Oh, I say! Come! It was you who spoke to me. Of course I was only too glad of the chance; but on my word I shouldnt have moved an eyelid if you hadnt given me a lead.

BLANCHE. I only asked you the name of a castle. There was nothing unlady like in that.

TRENCH. Of course not. Why shouldnt you? [*With renewed tenderness*] But it's all right now: isnt it?

BLANCHE [*softly, looking subtly at him*] Is it?

TRENCH [*suddenly becoming shy*] I—I suppose so. By the way, what about the Apollinaris Church? Your father expects us to follow him, doesnt he?

BLANCHE [*with suppressed resentment*] Dont let me detain you if you wish to see it.

TRENCH. Wont you come?

BLANCHE. No. [*She turns her face away moodily*].

TRENCH [*alarmed*] I say: youre not offended, are you? [*She looks round at him for a moment with a reproachful film on her eyes*]. Blanche. [*She bristles instantly; overdoes it; and frightens him*]. I beg your pardon for calling you by your name; but I—er— [*She corrects her mistake by softening her expression eloquently. He responds with a gush*] You dont mind, do you? I felt sure you wouldnt, somehow. Well, look here. I have no idea how you will receive this: it must seem horribly abrupt; but the circumstances do not admit of—the fact is, my utter want of tact—[*he flounders more and more, unable to see that she can hardly contain her eagerness*]. Now, if it were Cokane—

BLANCHE [*impatiently*] Cokane!

TRENCH [*terrified*] No, not Cokane. Though I assure you I was only going to say about him that—

BLANCHE. That he will be back presently with papa.

TRENCH [*stupidly*] Yes: they cant be very long now. I hope I'm not detaining you.

BLANCHE. I thought you were detaining me because you had something to say.

TRENCH [*totally unnerved*] Not at all. At least, nothing very particular. That is, I'm afraid you wouldnt think it very particular. Another time, perhaps—

BLANCHE. What other time? How do you know that we shall ever meet again? [*Desperately*] Tell me now. I want you to tell me now.

TRENCH. Well, I was thinking that if we could make up our minds to—or not to—at least—er— [*His nervousness deprives him of the power of speech*].

BLANCHE [*giving him up as hopeless*] I dont think theres much danger of *your* making up your mind, Dr Trench.

TRENCH [*stammering*] I only thought— [*He stops and looks at her piteously. She hesitates a moment, and then puts her hands into his with calculated impulsiveness. He snatches her into his arms with a cry of relief*] Dear Blanche! I thought I should never have said it. I believe I should have stood stuttering here all day if you hadnt helped me out with it.

BLANCHE [*indignantly trying to break loose from him*] I didnt help you out with it.

TRENCH [*holding her*] I dont mean that you did it on purpose, of course. Only instinctively.

BLANCHE [*still a little anxious*] But you havnt said anything.

TRENCH. What more can I say than this? [*He kisses her again*].

BLANCHE [*overcome by the kiss, but holding on to her point*] But Harry—

TRENCH [*delighted at the name*] Yes.

BLANCHE. When shall we bc married?

TRENCH. At the first church we meet: the Apollinaris Church, if you like.

BLANCHE. No, but seriously. This is serious, Harry: you musnt joke about it.

TRENCH [*looking suddenly round to the riverside gate and quickly releasing her*] Sh! Here they are back again.

BLANCHE. Oh, d— [*The word is drowned by the clangor of a bell from within the hotel. The waiter appears on the steps, ringing it. Cokane and Sartorius are seen returning by the river gate*].

WAITER. Table d'hôte in dwendy minutes, ladies and zhentellmenn. [*He goes into the hotel*].

SARTORIUS [*gravely*] I intended you to accompany us, Blanche.

BLANCHE. Yes, papa. We were just about to start.

SARTORIUS. We are rather dusty: we must make ourselves presentable at the table d'hôte. I think you had better come in with me, my child. Come.

He offers Blanche his arm. The gravity of his manner overawes them all. Blanche silently takes his arm and goes into the hotel with him. Cokane, hardly less momentous than Sartorius himself, contemplates Trench with the severity of a judge.

COKANE [*with reprobation*] No, my dear boy. No, no. Never. I blush for you. I was never so ashamed in my life. You have been taking advantage of that unprotected girl.

TRENCH [*hotly*] Cokane!

COKANE [*inexorable*] Her father seems to be a perfect gentleman. I obtained the privilege of his acquaintance: I introduced you: I allowed him to believe that he might leave his daughter in your charge with absolute confidence. And what did I see on our return? what did her father see? Oh, Trench, Trench! No, my dear fellow, no, no. Bad taste, Harry, bad form!

TRENCH. Stuff! There was nothing to see.

COKANE. Nothing to see! She, a perfect lady, a person of the highest breeding, actually in your arms; and you say there was nothing to see! with a waiter there actually ringing a heavy bell to call attention to his presence! [*Lecturing him with redoubled severity*] Have you no principles, Trench? Have you no religious convictions? Have you no acquaintance with the usages of society? You actually kissed—

TRENCH. You didnt see me kiss her.

COKANE. We not only saw but heard it: the report positively reverberated down the Rhine. Dont condescend to subterfuge, Trench.

TRENCH. Nonsense, my dear Billy. You—

COKANE. There you go again. Dont use that low abbreviation. How am I to preserve the respect of fellow travellers of position and wealth, if I am to be Billied at every turn? My name is William: William de Burgh Cokane.

TRENCH. Oh, bother! There: dont be offended, old chap. Whats the use of putting your back up at every trifle? It comes natural to me to call you Billy: it suits you, somehow.

COKANE [*mortified*] You have no delicacy of feeling, Trench: no tact. I never mention it to any one; but nothing, I am afraid, will ever make a true gentleman of you. [*Sartorius appears on the threshold of the hotel*]. Here is my friend Sartorius, coming, no doubt, to ask you for an explanation of your conduct. I really should not have been surprised to see him bring a horsewhip with him. I shall not intrude on the painful scene.

TRENCH. Dont go, confound it. I dont want to meet him alone just now.

COKANE [*shaking his head*] Delicacy, Harry, delicacy! Good taste! Savoir faire! [*He walks away. Trench tries to escape in the opposite direction by strolling off towards the garden entrance*].

SARTORIUS [*mesmerically*] Dr Trench.

TRENCH [*stopping and turning*] Oh, is that you, Mr Sartorius? How did you find the church?

Sartorius, without a word, points to a seat. Trench, half hypnotized by his own nervousness and the impressiveness of Sartorius, sits down helplessly.

SARTORIUS [*also seating himself*] You have been speaking to my daughter, Dr Trench.

TRENCH [*with an attempt at ease of manner*] Yes: we had a conversation—quite a chat, in fact—while you were at the church with Cokane. How did you get on with Cokane, Mr Sartorius? I always think he has such wonderful tact.

SARTORIUS [*ignoring the digression*] I have just had a word with my daughter, Dr Trench; and I find her under the impression that something has passed between you which it is my duty as a father—the father of a motherless girl—to inquire into at once. My daughter, perhaps foolishly, has taken you quite seriously; and—

TRENCH. But—

SARTORIUS. One moment, if you will be so good. I have been a young man myself: younger, perhaps, than you would suppose from my present appearance. I mean, of course, in character. If you were not serious—

TRENCH [*ingenuously*] But I was perfectly serious. I want to marry your daughter, Mr Sartorius. I hope you dont object.

SARTORIUS [*condescending to Trench's humility from the mere instinct to seize an advantage, and yet deferring to Lady Roxdale's relative*] So far, no. I may say that your proposal seems to be an honorable and straightforward one, and that it is very gratifying to me personally.

TRENCH [*agreeably surprised*] Then I suppose we may consider the affair as settled. It's really very good of you.

SARTORIUS. Gently, Dr Trench, gently. Such a transaction as this cannot be settled off-hand.

TRENCH. Not off-hand, no. There are settlements and things, of course. But it may be regarded as settled between ourselves, maynt it?

SARTORIUS. Hm! Have you nothing further to mention?

TRENCH. Only that—that—No: I dont know that I have, except that I love—

SARTORIUS [*interrupting*] Anything about your family, for example? You do not anticipate any objection on their part, do you?

TRENCH. Oh, they have nothing to do with it.

SARTORIUS [*warmly*] Excuse me, sir: they have a great deal to do with it. [*Trench is abashed*]. I am resolved that my daughter shall approach no circle in which she will not be received with the full consideration to which her education and her breeding [*here his self-control slips a little; and he repeats, as if Trench had contradicted him*]—I say, her breeding—entitle her.

TRENCH [*bewildered*] Of course not. But what makes you think my family wont like Blanche? Of course my father was a younger son; and Ive had to take to a profession and all that; so my people wont expect us to entertain them: theyll know we cant afford it. But theyll entertain us: they always ask me.

SARTORIUS. That wont do for me, sir. Families often think it due to themselves to turn their backs on newcomers whom they may not think quite good enough for them.

TRENCH. But I assure you my people arnt a bit snobbish. Blanche is a lady: thatll be good enough for them.

SARTORIUS [*moved*] I am glad you think so. [*He offers his hand. Trench, astonished, takes it*]. I think so myself. [*He presses Trench's hand gratefully and releases it*]. And now, Dr Trench, since you have acted handsomely, you shall have no cause to complain of me. There shall be no difficulty about money: you shall entertain as much as you please: I will guarantee all that. But I must have a guarantee on my side that she will be received on equal terms by your family.

TRENCH. Guarantee!

SARTORIUS. Yes, a reasonable guarantee. I shall expect you to write to your relatives explaining your intention, and adding what you think proper as to my daughter's fitness for the best society. When you can shew me a few letters from the principal members of your family, congratulating you in a fairly cordial way, I shall be satisfied. Can I say more?

TRENCH [*much puzzled, but grateful*] No indeed. You are really very good. Many thanks. Since you wish it, I'll write to my people. But I assure you youll find them as jolly as possible over it. I'll make them write by return.

SARTORIUS. Thank you. In the meantime, I must ask you not to regard the matter as settled.

TRENCH. Oh! Not to regard the—I see. You mean between Blanche and—

SARTORIUS. I mean between you and Miss Sartorius. When I interrupted your conversation here some time ago, you and she were evidently regarding it as settled. In case difficulties arise, and the match—you see I call it a match—is broken off, I should not wish Blanche to think that she had allowed a gentleman to— to— [*Trench nods sympathetically*] Quite so. May I depend on you to keep a fair distance, and so spare me the necessity of having to restrain an intercourse which promises to be very pleasant to us all?

TRENCH. Certainly; since you prefer it. [*They shake hands on it*].

SARTORIUS [*rising*] You will write today, I think you said?

TRENCH [*eagerly*] I'll write now, before I leave here: straight off.

SARTORIUS. I will leave you to yourself then. [*He hesitates, the conversation having made him self-conscious and embarrassed; then recovers himself with an effort, and adds with dignity, as he turns to go*] I am pleased to have come to an understanding with you. [*He goes into the hotel; and Cokane, who has been hanging about inquisitively, emerges from the shrubbery*].

TRENCH [*excitedly*] Billy, old chap: youre just in time to do me a favor. I want you to draft a letter for me to copy out.

COKANE. I came with you on this tour as a friend, Trench: not as a secretary.

TRENCH. Well, youll write as a friend. It's to my Aunt Maria, about Blanche and me. To tell her, you know.

COKANE. Tell her about Blanche and you! Tell her about your conduct! Betray you, my friend; and forget that I am writing to a lady? Never!

TRENCH. Bosh, Billy: dont pretend you dont understand. We're engaged: engaged, my boy! what do you think of that? I must write by tonight's post. You are the man to tell me what to say. Come, old chap [*coaxing him to sit down at one of the tables*]: heres a pencil. Have you a bit of—oh, here: thisll do: write it on the back of the map. [*He tears the map out of his Baedeker and spreads it face downwards on the table. Cokane takes the pencil and prepares to write*]. Thats right. Thanks awfully, old chap. Now fire away. [*Anxiously*] Be careful how you word it though, Cokane.

COKANE [*putting down the pencil*] If you doubt my ability to express myself becomingly to Lady Roxdale—

TRENCH [*propitiating him*] All right, old fellow, all right: theres not a man alive who could do it half so well as you. I only wanted to explain. You see, Sartorius has got it into his head, somehow, that my people will snub Blanche; and he wont consent unless they send letters and invitations and congratulations and the deuce knows what not. So just put it in such a way that Aunt Maria will write by return saying she is delighted, and asking us—Blanche and me, you know—to stay with her, and so forth. You know what I mean. Just tell her all about it in a chatty way; and—

COKANE [*crushingly*] If you will tell me all about it in a chatty way, I daresay I can communicate it to Lady Roxdale with becoming delicacy. What is Sartorius?

TRENCH [*taken aback*] I dont know: I didnt ask. It's a sort of question you cant very well put to a man—at least a man like him. Do you think you could word the letter so as to pass all that over? I really dont like to ask him.

COKANE. I can pass it over if you wish. Nothing easier. But if you think Lady Roxdale will pass it over, I differ from you. I may be wrong: no doubt I am. I generally am wrong, I believe; but that is my opinion.

TRENCH [*much perplexed*] Oh, confound it! What the deuce am I to do? Cant you say he's a gentleman: that wont commit us to anything. If you dwell on his being well off, and Blanche an only child, Aunt Maria will be satisfied.

COKANE. Henry Trench: when will you begin to get a little sense? This is a serious business. Act responsibly, Harry: act responsibly.

TRENCH. Bosh! Dont be moral!

COKANE. I am not moral, Trench. At least I am not a moralist: that is the expression I should have used. Moral, but not a moralist. If you are going to get money with your wife, doesnt it concern your family to know how that money was made? Doesnt it concern you—you, Harry? [*Trench looks at him helplessly, twisting his fingers nervously. Cokane throws down the pencil and leans back with ostentatious indifference*]. Of course it is no business of mine: I only throw out the suggestion. Sartorius may be a retired burglar for all I know. [*Sartorius and Blanche, ready for dinner, come from the hotel*].

TRENCH. Sh! Here they come. Get the letter finished before dinner, like a good old chappie: I shall be awfully obliged to you.

COKANE [*impatiently*] Leave me, leave me: you disturb me. [*He waves him off, and begins to write*].

TRENCH [*humbly and gratefully*] Yes, old chap. Thanks awfully. [*By this time Blanche has left her father, and is strolling off towards the riverside. Sartorius comes down the garden, Baedeker in hand, and sits near Cokane, reading. Trench addresses him*]. You wont mind my taking Blanche in to dinner, I hope, sir?

SARTORIUS. By all means, Dr Trench. Pray do so. [*He graciously waves him off to join Blanche. Trench hurries after her through the gate. The light reddens as the Rhenish sunset begins. Cokane, making wry faces in the agonies of composition, is disconcerted to find Sartorius's eye upon him*].

SARTORIUS. I do not disturb you, I hope, Mr Cokane.

COKANE. By no means. Our friend Trench has entrusted me with a difficult and delicate task. He has requested me, as a friend of the family, to write to them on a subject that concerns you.

SARTORIUS. Indeed, Mr Cokane! Well, the communication could not be in better hands.

COKANE [*with an air of modesty*] Ah, that is going too far, my dear sir, too far. Still, you see what Trench is. A capital fellow in his way, Mr Sartorius, an excellent young fellow. But family communications like these require good manners. They require tact; and tact is Trench's weak point. He has an excellent heart, but no tact: none whatever. Everything depends on the way the matter is put to Lady Roxdale. But as to that, you may rely on me. I understand the sex.

SARTORIUS. Well, however she may receive it—and I care as little as any man, Mr Cokane, how people may choose to receive me—I trust I may at least have the pleasure of seeing you sometimes at my house when we return to England.

COKANE [*overwhelmed*] My dear sir! You express yourself in the true spirit of an English gentleman.

SARTORIUS. Not at all. You will always be most welcome. But I fear I have disturbed you in the composition of your letter. Pray resume it. I shall leave you to yourself. [*He pre-*

tends to rise, but checks himself to add] Unless indeed I can assist you in any way? by clearing up any point on which you are not informed, for instance? or even, if I may so far presume on my years, giving you the benefit of my experience as to the best way of wording the matter? [*Cokane looks a little surprised at this. Sartorius looks hard at him, and continues deliberately and meaningly*] I shall always be happy to help any friend of Dr Trench's, in any way, to the best of my ability and of my means.

COKANE. My dear sir: you are really very good. Trench and I were putting our heads together over the letter just now; and there certainly were one or two points on which we were a little in the dark. [*Scrupulously*] But I would not permit Harry to question you. No. I pointed out to him that, as a matter of taste, it would be more delicate to wait until you volunteered the necessary information.

SARTORIUS. Hm! May I ask what you have said, so far?

COKANE. "My dear Aunt Maria." That is, Trench's dear Aunt Maria, my friend Lady Roxdale. You understand that I am only drafting a letter for Trench to copy.

SARTORIUS. Quite so. Will you proceed; or would it help you if I were to suggest a word or two?

COKANE [*effusively*] Your suggestions will be most valuable, my dear sir, most welcome.

SARTORIUS. I think I should begin in some such way as this. "In travelling with my friend Mr Cokane up the Rhine—"

COKANE [*murmuring as he writes*] Invaluable, invaluable. The very thing. "—my friend Mr Cokane up the Rhine—"

SARTORIUS. "I have made the acquaintance of"—or you may say "picked up," or "come across," if you think that would suit your friend's style better. We must not be too formal.

COKANE. "Picked up"! oh no: too dégagé, Mr Sartorius, too dégagé. I should say "had the privilege of becoming acquainted with."

SARTORIUS [*quickly*] By no means: Lady Roxdale must

judge of that for herself. Let it stand as I said. "I have made the acquaintance of a young lady, the daughter of—" [*He hesitates*].

COKANE [*writing*] "acquaintance of a young lady, the daughter of"—yes?

SARTORIUS. "of"—you had better say "a gentleman."

COKANE [*surprised*] Of course.

SARTORIUS [*with sudden passion*] It is not of course, sir. [*Cokane, startled, looks at him with dawning suspicion. Sartorius recovers himself somewhat shamefacedly*]. Hm! "—of a gentleman of considerable wealth and position—"

COKANE [*echoing him with a new note of coldness in his voice as he writes the last words*] "—and position"

SARTORIUS. "which, however, he has made entirely for himself." [*Cokane, now fully enlightened, stares at him instead of writing*]. Have you written that?

COKANE [*expanding into an attitude of patronage and encouragement*] Ah, indeed. Quite so, quite so. [*He writes*] "—entirely for himself." Just so. Proceed, Sartorius, proceed. Very clearly expressed.

SARTORIUS. "The young lady will inherit the bulk of her father's fortune, and will be liberally treated on her marriage. Her education has been of the most expensive and complete kind obtainable; and her surroundings have been characterized by the strictest refinement. She is in every essential particular—"

COKANE [*interrupting*] Excuse the remark; but dont you think this is rather too much in the style of a prospectus of the young lady? I throw out the suggestion as a matter of taste.

SARTORIUS [*troubled*] Perhaps you are right. I am of course not dictating the exact words;—

COKANE. Of course not: of course not.

SARTORIUS. —but I desire that there may be no wrong impression as to my daughter's—er—breeding. As to myself—

COKANE. Oh, it will be sufficient to mention your profession, or pursuits, or— [*He pauses; and they look pretty hard at one another*].

SARTORIUS [*very deliberately*] My income, sir, is derived from the rental of a very extensive real estate in London. Lady Roxdale is one of the head landlords; and Dr Trench holds a mortgage from which, if I mistake not, his entire income is derived. The truth is, Mr Cokane, I am quite well acquainted with Dr Trench's position and affairs; and I have long desired to know him personally.

COKANE [*again obsequious, but still inquisitive*] What a remarkable coincidence! In what quarter is the estate situated, did you say?

SARTORIUS. In London, sir. Its management occupies as much of my time as is not devoted to the ordinary pursuits of a gentleman. [*He rises and takes out his card case*]. The rest I leave to your discretion. [*He leaves a card on the table*]. That is my address at Surbiton. If it should unfortunately happen, Mr Cokane, that this leads to nothing but a disappointment for Blanche, probably she would rather not see you afterwards. But if all turns out as we hope, Dr Trench's best friends will then be our best friends.

COKANE [*rising and confronting Sartorius confidently, pencil and paper in hand*] Rely on me, Mr Sartorius. The letter is already finished here [*pointing to his brain*]. In five minutes it will be finished there [*He points to the paper; nods to emphasize the assertion; and begins to pace up and down the garden, writing, and tapping his forehead from time to time as he goes, with every appearance of severe intellectual exertion*].

SARTORIUS [*calling through the gate after a glance at his watch*] Blanche.

BLANCHE [*replying in the distance*] Yes?

SARTORIUS. Time, my dear. [*He goes into the table d'hôte*].

BLANCHE [*nearer*] Coming. [*She comes back through the gate, followed by Trench*].

TRENCH [*in a half whisper, as Blanche goes towards the table d'hôte*] Blanche: stop. One moment. [*She stops*]. We must be careful when your father is by. I had to promise him not to regard anything as settled until I hear from my people at home.

BLANCHE [*chilled*] Oh, I see. Your family may object to me; and then it will be all over between us. They are almost sure to.

TRENCH [*anxiously*] Dont say that, Blanche: it sounds as if you didnt care. I hope you regard it as settled. You havnt made any promise, you know.

BLANCHE [*earnestly*] Yes, I have: *I* promised papa too. But I have broken my promise for your sake. I suppose I am not so conscientious as you. And if the matter is not to be regarded as settled, family or no family, promise or no promise, let us break it off here and now.

TRENCH [*intoxicated with affection*] Blanche: on my most sacred honor, family or no family, promise or no promise— [*The waiter reappears at the table d'hôte entrance, ringing his bell*]. Damn that noise!

COKANE [*as he comes to them, flourishing the letter*] Finished, dear boy, finished. Done to a turn, punctually to the second. C'est fini, mon cher garçon, c'est fini. [*Sartorius returns*].

SARTORIUS. Will you take Blanche in, Dr Trench? [*Trench takes Blanche in to the table d'hôte*]. Is the letter finished, Mr Cokane?

COKANE [*with an author's pride, handing his draft to Sartorius*] There! [*Sartorius reads it, nodding gravely over it with complete approval*].

SARTORIUS [*returning the draft*] Thank you, Mr Cokane. You have the pen of a ready writer.

COKANE [*as they go in together*] Not at all, not at all. A little tact, Mr Sartorius, a little knowledge of the world, a little experience of women— [*They disappear into the annexe*].

ACT II

IN the library of a handsomely appointed villa at Surbiton on a sunny forenoon in September. Sartorius is busy at a writing table littered with business letters. The fireplace, decorated for summer, is close behind him: the window is in the opposite wall. Between the table and the window Blanche, in her prettiest frock, sits reading The Queen. The door is in the middle. All the walls are lined with shelves of smartly tooled books, fitting into their places like bricks.

SARTORIUS. Blanche.

BLANCHE. Yes, papa.

SARTORIUS. I have some news here.

BLANCHE. What is it?

SARTORIUS. I mean news for you—from Trench.

BLANCHE [*with affected indifference*] Indeed?

SARTORIUS. "Indeed?"! Is that all you have to say to me? Oh, very well.

He resumes his work. Silence.

BLANCHE. What do his people say, papa?

SARTORIUS. His people? I dont know. [*Still busy*].

Another pause.

BLANCHE. What does he say?

SARTORIUS. He! He says nothing. [*He folds a letter leisurely, and looks for the envelope*]. He prefers to communicate the result of his—where did I put?—oh, here. Yes: he perfers to communicate the result in person.

BLANCHE [*springing up*] Oh, papa! When is he coming?

SARTORIUS. If he walks from the station, he may arrive in the course of the next half-hour. If he drives, he may be here at any moment.

BLANCHE [*making hastily for the door*] Oh!

SARTORIUS. Blanche.

BLANCHE. Yes, papa.

SARTORIUS. You will of course not meet him until he has spoken to me.

BLANCHE [*hypocritically*] Of course not, papa. I shouldnt have thought of such a thing.

SARTORIUS. That is all. [*She is going, when he puts out his hand, and says with fatherly emotion*] My dear child. [*She responds by going over to kiss him. A tap at the door*]. Come in.

Lickcheese enters, carrying a black handbag. He is a shabby, needy man, with dirty face and linen, scrubby beard and whiskers, going bald. A nervous, wiry, pertinacious human terrier, judged by his mouth and eyes, but miserably apprehensive and servile before Sartorius. He bids Blanche "Good morning, miss"; *and she passes out with a slight and contemptuous recognition of him.*

LICKCHEESE. Good morning, sir.

SARTORIUS [*harsh and peremptory*] Good morning.

LICKCHEESE [*taking a little sack of money from his bag*] Not much this morning, sir. I have just had the honor of making Dr Trench's acquaintance, sir.

SARTORIUS [*looking up from his writing, displeased*] Indeed?

LICKCHEESE. Yes, sir. Dr Trench asked his way of me, and was kind enough to drive me from the station.

SARTORIUS. Where is he, then?

LICKCHEESE. I left him in the hall, with his friend, sir. I should think he is speaking to Miss Sartorius.

SARTORIUS. Hm! What do you mean by his friend?

LICKCHEESE. There is a Mr Cokane with him, sir.

SARTORIUS. I see you have been talking to him, eh?

LICKCHEESE. As we drove along: yes, sir.

SARTORIUS [*sharply*] Why did you not come by the nine o'clock train?

LICKCHEESE. I thought—

SARTORIUS. It cannot be helped now; so never mind what you thought. But do not put off my business again to the last moment. Has there been any further trouble about the St Giles property?

LICKCHEESE. The Sanitary Inspector has been complaining again about No. 13 Robbins's Row. He says he'll bring it before the vestry.

SARTORIUS. Did you tell him that I am on the vestry?

LICKCHEESE. Yes, sir.

SARTORIUS. What did he say to that?

LICKCHEESE. Said he supposed so, or you wouldnt dare to break the law so scand'lous. I only tell you what he said.

SARTORIUS. Hm! Do you know his name?

LICKCHEESE. Yes, sir. Speakman.

SARTORIUS. Write it down in the diary for the day of the next meeting of the Health Committee. I will teach Mr Speakman his duty to members of the vestry.

LICKCHEESE [*doubtfully*] The vestry cant hurt him, sir. He's under the Local Government Board.

SARTORIUS. I did not ask you that. Let me see the books. [*Lickcheese produces the rent book, and hands it to Sartorius; then makes the desired entry in the diary on the table, watching Sartorius with misgiving as the rent book is examined. Sartorius rises, frowning*]. One pound four for repairs to number thirteen! What does this mean?

LICKCHEESE. Well, sir, it was the staircase on the third floor. It was downright dangerous: there werent but three whole steps in it, and no handrail. I thought it best to have a few boards put in.

SARTORIUS. Boards! Firewood, sir, firewood! They will burn every stick of it. You have spent twenty-four shillings of my money on firewood for them.

LICKCHEESE. There ought to be stone stairs, sir: it would be a saving in the long run. The clergyman says—

SARTORIUS. What! Who says?

LICKCHEESE. The clergyman, sir, only the clergyman. Not that I make much account of him; but if you knew how he has worried me over that staircase—

SARTORIUS. I am an Englishman; and I will suffer no priest to interfere in my business. [*He turns suddenly on Lickcheese*]. Now look here, Mr Lickcheese! This is the third time this year that you have brought me a bill of over a pound for repairs. I have warned you repeatedly against dealing with these tenement houses as if they were mansions in a West-End square. I have had occasion to warn you too against discussing my affairs with strangers. You have chosen to disregard my wishes. You are discharged.

LICKCHEESE [*dismayed*] Oh, sir, dont say that.

SARTORIUS [*fiercely*] You are discharged.

LICKCHEESE. Well, Mr Sartorius, it is hard, so it is. No man alive could have screwed more out of them poor destitute devils for you than I have, or spent less in doing it. I have dirtied my hands at it until theyre not fit for clean work hardly; and now you turn me—

SARTORIUS [*interrupting him menacingly*] What do you mean by dirtying your hands? If I find that you have stepped an inch outside the letter of the law, Mr Lickcheese, I will prosecute you myself. The way to keep your hands clean is to gain the confidence of your employers. You will do well to bear that in mind in your next situation.

THE PARLORMAID [*opening the door*] Mr Trench and Mr Cokane.

Cokane and Trench come in: Trench festively dressed and in buoyant spirits: Cokane highly self-satisfied.

SARTORIUS. How do you do, Dr Trench? Good morning, Mr Cokane. I am pleased to see you here. Mr Lickcheese: you will place your accounts and money on the table: I will examine them and settle with you presently.

Lickcheese retires to the table, and begins to arrange his accounts, greatly depressed. The parlormaid withdraws.

TRENCH [*glancing at Lickcheese*] I hope we're not in the way.

SARTORIUS. By no means. Sit down, pray. I fear you have been kept waiting.

TRENCH [*taking Blanche's chair*] Not at all. Weve only just come in. [*He takes out a packet of letters, and begins untying them*].

COKANE [*going to a chair nearer the window, but stopping to look admiringly round before sitting down*] You must be happy here with all these books, Mr Sartorius. A literary atmosphere.

SARTORIUS [*resuming his seat*] I have not looked into

them. They are pleasant for Blanche occasionally when she wishes to read. I chose the house because it is on gravel. The death-rate is very low.

TRENCH [*triumphantly*] I have any amount of letters for you. All my people are delighted that I am going to settle. Aunt Maria wants Blanche to be married from her house. [*He hands Sartorius a letter*].

SARTORIUS. Aunt Maria?

COKANE. Lady Roxdale, my dear sir: he means Lady Roxdale. Do express yourself with a little more tact, my dear fellow.

TRENCH. Lady Roxdale, of course. Uncle Harry—

COKANE. Sir Harry Trench. His godfather, my dear sir, his godfather.

TRENCH. Just so. The pleasantest fellow for his age you ever met. He offers us his house at St Andrews for a couple of months, if we care to pass our honeymoon there. [*He hands Sartorius another letter*]. It's the sort of house nobody can live in, you know; but it's a nice thing for him to offer. Dont you think so?

SARTORIUS [*dissembling a thrill at the titles*] No doubt. These seem very gratifying, Dr Trench.

TRENCH. Yes, arnt they? Aunt Maria has really behaved like a brick. If you read the postscript youll see she spotted Cokane's hand in my letter. [*Chuckling*] He wrote it for me.

SARTORIUS [*glancing at Cokane*] Indeed! Mr Cokane evidently did it with great tact.

COKANE [*returning the glance*] Dont mention it.

TRENCH [*gleefully*] Well, what do you say now, Mr Sartorius? May we regard the matter as settled at last?

SARTORIUS. Quite settled. [*He rises and offers his hand. Trench, glowing with gratitude, rises and shakes it vehemently, unable to find words for his feelings*].

COKANE [*coming between them*]. Allow me to congratulate you both. [*He shakes hands with the two at the same time*].

SARTORIUS. And now, gentlemen, I have a word to say to my daughter. Dr Trench: you will not, I hope, grudge me the pleasure of breaking this news to her: I have had to disappoint her more than once since I last saw you. Will you excuse me for ten minutes?

COKANE [*in a flush of friendly protest*] My dear sir: can you ask?

TRENCH. Certainly.

SARTORIUS. Thank you. [*He goes out*].

TRENCH [*chuckling again*] He wont have any news to break, poor old boy: she's seen all the letters already.

COKANE. I must say your behavior has been far from straightforward, Harry. You have been carrying on a clandestine correspondence.

LICKCHEESE [*stealthily*] Gentlemen—

TRENCH, COKANE [*turning: they had forgotten his presence*] Hallo!

LICKCHEESE [*coming between them very humbly, but in mortal anxiety and haste*] Look here, gentlemen. [*To Trench*] You, sir, I address myself to more particlar. Will you say a word in my favor to the guvnor? He's just given me the sack; and I have four children looking to me for their bread. A word from you, sir, on this happy day, might get him to take me on again.

TRENCH [*embarrassed*] Well, you see, Mr Lickcheese, I dont see how I can interfere. I'm very sorry, of course.

COKANE. Certainly you cannot interfere. It would be in the most execrable taste.

LICKCHEESE. Oh, gentlemen, youre young; and you dont know what loss of employment means to the like of me. What harm would it do you to help a poor man? Just listen to the circumstances, sir. I only—

TRENCH [*moved, but snatching at an excuse for taking a high tone in avoiding the unpleasantness of helping him*] No: I had rather not. Excuse my saying plainly that I think Mr Sartorius is not a man to act hastily or harshly. I have always found him very fair and generous; and I believe he is a better judge of the circumstances than I am.

COKANE [*inquisitive*] I think you ought to hear the circumstances, Harry. It can do no harm. Hear the circumstances by all means.

LICKCHEESE. Never mind, sir: it aint any use. When I hear that man called generous and fair!—well, never mind.

TRENCH [*severely*] If you wish me to do anything for you, Mr Lickcheese, let me tell you that you are not going the right way about it in speaking ill of Mr Sartorius.

LICKCHEESE. Have I said one word against him, sir? I leave it to your friend: have I said a word?

COKANE. True: true. Quite true. Harry: be just.

LICKCHEESE. Mark my words, gentlemen: he'll find what a man he's lost the very first week's rents the new man'll bring him. Youll find the difference yourself, Dr Trench, if you or your children come into the property. Ive took money there when no other collector alive would have wrung it out. And this is the thanks I get for it! Why, see here, gentlemen! Look at that bag of money on the table. Hardly a penny of that but there was a hungry child crying for the bread it would have bought. But I got it for him—screwed and worried and bullied it out of them. I—look here, gentlemen: I'm pretty seasoned to the work; but theres money there that I couldnt have taken if it hadnt been for the thought of my own children depending on me for giving him satisfaction. And because I charged him four-and-twenty shillin to mend a staircase that three women have been hurt on, and that would have got him prosecuted for manslaughter if it had been let go much longer, he gives me the sack. Wouldnt listen to a word, though I would have offered to make up the money out of my own pocket: aye, and am willing to do it still if you will only put in a word for me.

TRENCH [*aghast*] You took money that ought to have fed starving children! Serve you right! If I had been the father of one of those children, I'd have given you something worse than the sack. I wouldnt say a word to save your soul, if you have such a thing. Mr Sartorius was quite right.

LICKCHEESE [*staring at him, surprised into contemptuous amusement in the midst of his anxiety*] Just listen to this! Well, you are an innocent young gentleman. Do you suppose he sacked me because I was too hard? Not a bit on it: it was because I wasnt hard enough. I never heard him say he was satisfied yet: no, nor he wouldnt, not if I skinned em alive. I dont say he's the worst landlord in London: he couldnt be worse than some; but he's no better than the worst I ever had to do with. And, though I say it, I'm better than the best collector he ever done business with. Ive screwed more and spent less on his properties than anyone would believe that knows what such properties are. I know my merits, Dr Trench, and will speak for myself if no one else will.

COKANE. What description of properties? Houses?

LICKCHEESE. Tenement houses, let from week to week by the room or half room: aye, or quarter room. It pays when you know how to work it, sir. Nothing like it. It's been calculated on the cubic foot of space, sir, that you can get higher rents letting by the room than you can for a mansion in Park Lane.

TRENCH. I hope Mr Sartorius hasnt much of that sort of property, however it may pay.

LICKCHEESE. He has nothing else, sir; and he shews his sense in it, too. Every few hundred pounds he could scrape together he bought old houses with: houses that you wouldnt hardly look at without holding your nose. He has em in St Giles's: he has em in Marylebone: he has em in Bethnal Green. Just look how he lives himself, and youll see the good of it to him. He likes a low death-rate and a gravel soil for himself, he does. You come down with me to Robbins's Row; and I'll shew you a soil and a death-rate, I will! And, mind you, it's me that makes it pay him so well. Catch him going down to collect his own rents! Not likely!

TRENCH. Do you mean to say that all his property—all his means—come from this sort of thing?

LICKCHEESE. Every penny of it, sir.

Trench, overwhelmed, has to sit down.

COKANE [*looking compassionately at him*] Ah, my dear fellow, the love of money is the root of all evil.

LICKCHEESE. Yes, sir; and we'd all like to have the tree growing in our garden.

COKANE [*revolted*] Mr Lickcheese: I did not address myself to you. I do not wish to be severe with you; but there is something peculiarly repugnant to my feelings in the calling of a rent collector.

LICKCHEESE. It's no worse than many another. I have my children looking to me.

COKANE. True: I admit it. So has our friend Sartorius. His affection for his daughter is a redeeming point—a redeeming point, certainly.

LICKCHEESE. She's a lucky daughter, sir. Many another daughter has been turned out upon the streets to gratify his affection for her. Thats what business is, sir, you see. Come, sir: I think your friend will say a word for me now he knows I'm not in fault.

TRENCH [*rising angrily*] I will not. It's a damnable business from beginning to end; and you deserve no better luck for helping in it. Ive seen it all among the out-patients at the hospital; and it used to make my blood boil to think that such things couldnt be prevented.

LICKCHEESE [*his suppressed spleen breaking out*] Oh indeed, sir. But I suppose youll take your share when you marry Miss Blanche, all the same. [*Furiously*] Which of us is the worse, I should like to know? me that wrings the money out to keep a home over my children, or you that spend it and try to shove the blame on to me?

COKANE. A most improper observation to address to a gentleman, Mr Lickcheese! A most revolutionary sentiment!

LICKCHEESE. Perhaps so. But then Robbins's Row aint a school for manners. You collect a week or two there—youre welcome to my place if I cant keep it for myself—and youll hear a little plain speaking, you will.

COKANE [*with dignity*] Do you know to whom you are speaking, my good man?

LICKCHEESE [*recklessly*] I know well enough who I'm

speaking to. What do I care for you, or a thousand such? I'm poor: thats enough to make a rascal of me. No consideration for me! nothing to be got by saying a word for me! [*Suddenly cringing to Trench*] Just a word, sir! It would cost you nothing. [*Sartorius appears at the door, unobserved*]. Have some feeling for the poor.

TRENCH. I'm afraid you have shewn very little, by your own confession.

LICKCHEESE [*breaking out again*] More than your precious father-in-law, anyhow. I—[*Sartorius's voice, striking in with deadly coldness, paralyzes him*].

SARTORIUS. You will come here tomorrow not later than ten, Mr Lickcheese, to conclude our business. I shall trouble you no further today. [*Lickcheese, cowed, goes out amid dead silence. Sartorius continues, after an awkward pause*] He is one of my agents, or rather was; for I have unfortunately had to dismiss him for repeatedly disregarding my instructions. [*Trench says nothing. Sartorius throws off his embarrassment, and assumes a jocose, rallying air, unbecoming to him under any circumstances, and just now almost unbearably jarring*]. Blanche will be down presently, Harry [*Trench recoils*] —I suppose I must call you Harry now. What do you say to a stroll through the garden, Mr Cokane? We are celebrated here for our flowers.

COKANE. Charmed, my dear sir, charmed. Life here is an idyll—a perfect idyll. We were just dwelling on it.

SARTORIUS [*slyly*] Harry can follow with Blanche. She will be down directly.

TRENCH [*hastily*] No. I cant face her just now.

SARTORIUS [*rallying him*] Indeed! Ha, ha!

The laugh, the first they have heard from him, sets Trench's teeth on edge. Cokane is taken aback, but instantly recovers himself.

COKANE. Ha! ha! ha! Ho! ho!

TRENCH. But you dont understand.

SARTORIUS. Oh, I think we do, I think we do. Eh, Mr Cokane? Ha! ha!

COKANE. I should think we do. Ha! ha! ha!

They go out together, laughing at him. He collapses into a chair, shuddering in every nerve. Blanche appears at the door. Her face lights up when she sees that he is alone. She trips noiselessly to the back of his chair and clasps her hands over his eyes. With a convulsive start and exclamation he springs up and breaks away from her.

BLANCHE [*astonished*] Harry!

TRENCH [*with distracted politeness*] I beg your pardon. I was thinking—wont you sit down?

BLANCHE [*looking suspiciously at him*] Is anything the matter? [*She sits down slowly near the writing table. He takes Cokane's chair*].

TRENCH. No. Oh no.

BLANCHE. Papa has not been disagreeable, I hope.

TRENCH. No: I have hardly spoken to him since I was with you.[*He rises; takes up his chair; and plants it beside hers. This pleases her better. She looks at him with her most winning smile. A sort of sob breaks from him; and he catches her hands and kisses them passionately. Then, looking into her eyes with intense earnestness, he says*] Blanche: are you fond of money?

BLANCHE [*gaily*] Very. Are you going to give me any?

TRENCH [*wincing*] Dont make a joke of it: I'm serious. Do you know that we shall be very poor?

BLANCHE. Is that what made you look as if you had neuralgia?

TRENCH [*pleadingly*] My dear: it's no laughing matter. Do you know that I have a bare seven hundred a year to live on?

BLANCHE. How dreadful!

TRENCH. Blanche: it's very serious indeed: I assure you it is.

BLANCHE. It would keep me rather short in my housekeeping, dearest boy, if I had nothing of my own. But papa has promised me that I shall be richer than ever when we are married.

TRENCH. We must do the best we can with seven hundred. I think we ought to be self-supporting.

BLANCHE. Thats just what I mean to be, Harry. If I were to eat up half your seven hundred, I should be making you twice as poor; but I'm going to make you twice as rich instead. [*He shakes his head*]. Has papa made any difficulty?

TRENCH [*rising with a sigh and taking his chair back to its former place*] No. None at all. [*He sits down dejectedly. When Blanche speaks again her face and voice betray the beginning of a struggle with her temper*].

BLANCHE. Harry: are you too proud to take money from my father?

TRENCH. Yes, Blanche: I am too proud.

BLANCHE [*after a pause*] That is not nice to me, Harry.

TRENCH. You must bear with me, Blanche. I—I cant explain. After all, it's very natural.

BLANCHE. Has it occurred to you that I may be proud, too?

TRENCH. Oh, thats nonsense. No one will accuse you of marrying for money.

BLANCHE. No one would think the worse of me if I did, or of you either. [*She rises and begins to walk restlessly about*]. We really cannot live on seven hundred a year, Harry; and I dont think it quite fair of you to ask me merely because you are afraid of people talking.

TRENCH. It's not that alone, Blanche.

BLANCHE. What else is it, then?

TRENCH. Nothing. I—

BLANCHE [*getting behind him, and speaking with forced playfulness as she bends over him, her hands on his shoulders*] Of course it's nothing. Now dont be absurd, Harry: be good; and listen to me: I know how to settle it. You are too proud to owe anything to me; and I am too proud to owe anything to you. You have seven hundred a year. Well, I will take just seven hundred a year from papa at first; and then we shall be quits. Now, now, Harry, you know youve not a word to say against that.

TRENCH. It's impossible.

BLANCHE. Impossible!

TRENCH. Yes, impossible. I have resolved not to take any money from your father.

BLANCHE. But he'll give the money to me, not to you.

TRENCH. It's the same thing. [*With an effort to be sentimental*] I love you too well to see any distinction. [*He puts up his hand half-heartedly: she takes it over his shoulder with equal indecision. They are both trying hard to conciliate one another*].

BLANCHE. Thats a very nice way of putting it, Harry; but I'm sure theres something I ought to know. Has papa been disagreeable?

TRENCH. No: he has been very kind—to me, at least. It's not that. It's nothing you can guess, Blanche. It would only pain you—perhaps offend you. I dont mean, of course, that we shall live always on seven hundred a year. I intend to go at my profession in earnest, and work my fingers to the bone.

BLANCHE [*playing with his fingers, still over his shoulder*] But I shouldnt like you with your fingers worked to the bone, Harry. I must be told what the matter is. [*He takes his hand quickly away: she flushes angrily; and her voice is no longer even an imitation of the voice of a lady as she exclaims*] I hate secrets; and I dont like to be treated as if I were a child.

TRENCH [*annoyed by her tone*] Theres nothing to tell. I dont choose to trespass on your father's generosity: thats all.

BLANCHE. You had no objection half an hour ago, when you met me in the hall, and shewed me all the letters. Your family doesnt object. Do you object?

TRENCH [*earnestly*] I do not indeed. It's only a question of money.

BLANCHE [*imploringly, the voice softening and refining for the last time*] Harry: theres no use in our fencing in this way. Papa will never consent to my being absolutely dependent on you; and I dont like the idea of it myself. If you even mention such a thing to him you will break off the match: you will indeed.

TRENCH [*obstinately*] I cant help that.

BLANCHE [*white with rage*] You cant help—! Oh, I'm beginning to understand. I will save you the trouble. You can tell papa that *I* have broken off the match; and then there will be no further difficulty.

TRENCH [*taken aback*] What do you mean, Blanche? Are you offended?

BLANCHE. Offended! How dare you ask me?

TRENCH. Dare!

BLANCHE. How much more manly it would have been to confess that you were trifling with me that time on the Rhine! Why did you come here today? Why did you write to your people?

TRENCH. Well, Blanche, if you are going to lose your temper—

BLANCHE. Thats no answer. You depended on your family to get you out of your engagement; and they did not object: they were only too glad to be rid of you. You were not mean enough to stay away, and not manly enough to tell the truth. You thought you could provoke me to break the engagement: thats so like a man—to try to put the woman in the wrong. Well, you have your way: I release you. I wish youd opened my eyes by downright brutality; by striking me; by anything rather than shuffling as you have done.

TRENCH [*hotly*] Shuffling! If I'd thought you capable of turning on me like this, I'd never have spoken to you. Ive a good mind never to speak to you again.

BLANCHE. You shall not—not ever. I will take care of that [*going to the door*].

TRENCH [*alarmed*] What are you going to do?

BLANCHE. To get your letters: your false letters, and your presents: your hateful presents, to return them to you. I'm very glad it's all broken off; and if—[*as she puts her hand to the door it is opened from without by Sartorius, who enters and shuts it behind him*].

SARTORIUS [*interrupting her severely*] Hush, pray, Blanche: you are forgetting yourself: you can be heard all over the house. What is the matter?

BLANCHE [*too angry to care whether she is overheard or not*] You had better ask him. He has some excuse about money.

SARTORIUS. Excuse! Excuse for what?

BLANCHE. For throwing me over.

TRENCH [*vehemently*] I declare I never—

BLANCHE [*interrupting him still more vehemently*] You did. You did. You are doing nothing else—

TRENCH }
BLANCHE } *together: each trying to shout down the other*

{I am doing nothing of the sort. You know very well that
{What else is it but throwing me over? But I dont care for
{what you are saying is disgracefully untrue. It's a damned
{you. I hate you. I always hated you. Beastly—dirty—
{lie. I wont stand—
{vile—

SARTORIUS [*in desperation at the noise*] Silence! [*Still more formidably*] Silence!! [*They obey. He proceeds firmly*] Blanche: you must control your temper: I will not have these repeated scenes within hearing of the servants. Dr Trench will answer for himself to me. You had better leave us. [*He opens the door, and calls*] Mr Cokane: will you kindly join us here.

COKANE [*in the conservatory*] Coming, my dear sir, coming. [*He appears at the door*].

BLANCHE. I'm sure I have no wish to stay. I hope I shall find you alone when I come back. [*An inarticulate exclamation bursts from Trench. She goes out, passing Cokane resentfully. He looks after her in surprise; then looks questioningly at the two men. Sartorius shuts the door with an angry stroke, and turns to Trench*].

SARTORIUS [*aggressively*] Sir—

TRENCH [*interrupting him more aggressively*] Well, sir?

COKANE [*getting between them*] Gently, dear boy, gently. Suavity, Harry, suavity.

SARTORIUS [*mastering himself*] If you have anything to say to me, Dr Trench, I will listen to you patiently. You will then allow me to say what I have to say on my part.

TRENCH [*ashamed*] I beg your pardon. Of course, yes. Fire away.

SARTORIUS. May I take it that you have refused to fulfil your engagement with my daughter?

TRENCH. Certainly not: your daughter has refused to fulfil her engagement with me. But the match is broken off, if thats what you mean.

SARTORIUS. Dr Trench: I will be plain with you. I know that Blanche has a quick temper. It is part of her strong character and her physical courage, which is greater than that of most men, I can assure you. You must be prepared for that. If this quarrel is only Blanche's temper, you may take my word for it that it will be over before tomorrow. But I understood from what she said just now that you have made some difficulty on the score of money.

TRENCH [*with renewed excitement*] It was Miss Sartorius who made the difficulty. I shouldnt have minded that so much, if it hadnt been for the things she said. She shewed that she doesnt care that [*snapping his fingers*] for me.

COKANE [*soothingly*] Dear boy—

TRENCH. Hold your tongue, Billy: it's enough to make a man wish he'd never seen a woman. Look here, Mr Sartorius: I put the matter to her as delicately and considerately as possible, never mentioning a word of my reasons, but just asking her to be content to live on my own little income; and yet she turned on me as if I'd behaved like a savage.

SARTORIUS. Live on your income! Impossible: my daughter is accustomed to a proper establishment. Did I not expressly undertake to provide for that? Did she not tell you I promised her to do so?

TRENCH. Yes, I know all about that, Mr Sartorius; and I'm greatly obliged to you; but I'd rather not take anything from you except Blanche herself.

SARTORIUS. And why did you not say so before?

TRENCH. No matter why. Let us drop the subject.

SARTORIUS. No matter! But it does matter, sir. I insist on an answer. Why did you not say so before?

TRENCH. I didnt know before.

SARTORIUS [*provoked*] Then you ought to have known your own mind on a point of such vital importance.

TRENCH [*much injured*] I ought to have known! Cokane: is this reasonable? [*Cokane's features are contorted by an air of judicial consideration; but he says nothing; and Trench again addresses Sartorius, this time with a marked diminution of respect*]. How the deuce could I have known? You didnt tell me.

SARTORIUS. You are trifling with me, sir. You said that you did not know your own mind before.

TRENCH. I said nothing of the sort. I say that I did not know where your money came from before.

SARTORIUS. That is not true, sir. I—

COKANE. Gently, my dear sir. Gently, Harry, dear boy. Suaviter in modo: fort—

TRENCH. Let him begin, then. What does he mean by attacking me in this fashion?

SARTORIUS. Mr Cokane: you will bear me out. I was explicit on the point. I said I was a self-made man; and I am not ashamed of it.

TRENCH. You are nothing of the sort. I found out this morning from your man—Lickcheese, or whatever his confounded name is—that your fortune has been made out of a parcel of unfortunate creatures that have hardly enough to keep body and soul together—made by screwing, and bullying, and threatening, and all sorts of pettifogging tyranny.

SARTORIUS [*outraged*] Sir! [*They confront one another threateningly*].

COKANE [*softly*] Rent must be paid, dear boy. It is inevitable, Harry, inevitable. [*Trench turns away petulantly. Sartorius looks after him reflectively for a moment; then resumes his former deliberate and dignified manner, and addresses Trench with studied consideration, but with a perceptible condescension to his youth and folly*].

SARTORIUS. I am afraid, Dr Trench, that you are a very young hand at business; and I am sorry I forgot that for a moment or so. May I ask you to suspend your judgment until we have had a little quiet discussion of this sentimental notion of yours? if you will excuse me for calling it so. [*He takes a chair, and motions Trench to another on his right*].

COKANE. Very nicely put, my dear sir. Come, Harry: sit down and listen; and consider the matter calmly and judicially. Dont be headstrong.

TRENCH. I have no objection to sit down and listen; but I dont see how that can make black white; and I am tired of being turned on as if I were in the wrong. [*He sits down*].

Cokane sits at Trench's elbow, on his right. They compose themselves for a conference.

SARTORIUS. I assume, to begin with, Dr Trench, that you are not a Socialist, or anything of that sort.

TRENCH. Certainly not. I'm a Conservative. At least, if I ever took the trouble to vote, I should vote for the Conservative and against the other fellow.

COKANE. True blue, Harry, true blue!

SARTORIUS. I am glad to find that so far we are in perfect sympathy. I am, of course, a Conservative. Not a narrow or prejudiced one, I hope, nor at all opposed to true progress. Still, a sound Conservative. As to Lickcheese, I need say no more about him than that I have dismissed him from my service this morning for a breach of trust; and you will hardly accept his testimony as friendly or disinterested. As to my business, it is simply to provide homes suited to the small means of very poor people, who require roofs to shelter them just like other people. Do you suppose I can keep up those roofs for nothing?

TRENCH. Yes: thats all very fine; but the point is, what sort of homes do you give them for their money? People must live somewhere, or else go to jail. Advantage is taken of that to make them pay for houses that are not fit for dogs. Why dont you build proper dwellings, and give fair value for the money you take?

SARTORIUS [*pitying his innocence*] My young friend: these poor people do not know how to live in proper dwellings:

they would wreck them in a week. You doubt me: try it for yourself. You are welcome to replace all the missing banisters, handrails, cistern lids and dusthole tops at your own expense; and you will find them missing again in less than three days: burnt, sir, every stick of them. I do not blame the poor creatures: they need fires, and often have no other way of getting them. But I really cannot spend pound after pound in repairs for them to pull down, when I can barely get them to pay me four and sixpence a week for a room, which is the recognized fair London rent. No, gentlemen: when people are very poor, you cannot help them, no matter how much you may sympathize with them. It does them more harm than good in the long run. I prefer to save my money in order to provide additional houses for the homeless, and to lay by a little for Blanche. [*He looks at them. They are silent: Trench unconvinced, but talked down; Cokane humanely perplexed. Sartorius bends his brows; comes forward in his chair as if gathering himself for a spring; and addresses himself, with impressive significance, to Trench*]. And now, Dr Trench, may I ask what your income is derived from?

TRENCH [*defiantly*] From interest: not from houses. My hands are clean as far as that goes. Interest on a mortgage.

SARTORIUS [*forcibly*] Yes: a mortgage on my property. When I, to use your own words, screw, and bully, and drive these people to pay what they have freely undertaken to pay me, I cannot touch one penny of the money they give me until I have first paid you your seven hundred a year out of it. What Lickcheese did for me, I do for you. He and I are alike intermediaries: you are the principal. It is because of the risks I run through the poverty of my tenants that you exact interest from me at the monstrous and exorbitant rate of seven per cent, forcing me to exact the uttermost farthing in my turn from the tenants. And yet, Dr Trench, you, who have never done a hand's turn of work in connection with the place, you have not hesitated to speak contemptuously of me because I have applied my industry and forethought to the management of our property, and am maintaining it by the same honorable means.

COKANE [*greatly relieved*] Admirable, my dear sir, excellent! I felt instinctively that Trench was talking unpractical nonsense. Let us drop the subject, my dear boy: you only make an ass of yourself when you meddle in business matters. I told you it was inevitable.

TRENCH [*dazed*] Do you mean to say that I am just as bad as you are?

COKANE. Shame, Harry, shame! Grossly bad taste! Be a gentleman. Apologize.

SARTORIUS. Allow me, Mr Cokane. [*To Trench*] If, when you say you are just as bad as I am, you mean that you are just as powerless to alter the state of society, then you are unfortunately quite right.

Trench does not at once reply. He stares at Sartorius, and then hangs his head and gazes stupidly at the floor, morally beggared, with his clasped knuckles between his knees, a living picture of disillusion. Cokane comes sympathetically to him and puts an encouraging hand on his shoulder.

COKANE [*gently*] Come, Harry, come! Pull yourself together. You owe a word to Mr Sartorius.

TRENCH [*still stupefied, slowly unlaces his fingers; puts his hands on his knees, and lifts himself upright; pulls his waistcoat straight with a tug; and tries to take his disenchantment philosophically as he says, turning to Sartorius*] Well, people who live in glass houses have no right to throw stones. But, on my honor, I never knew that my house was a glass one until you pointed it out. I beg your pardon. [*He offers his hand*].

SARTORIUS. Say no more, Harry: your feelings do you credit: I assure you I feel exactly as you do, myself. Every man who has a heart must wish that a better state of things was practicable. But unhappily it is not.

TRENCH [*a little consoled*] I suppose not.

COKANE. Not a doubt of it, my dear sir: not a doubt of it. The increase of the population is at the bottom of it all.

SARTORIUS [*to Trench*] I trust I have convinced you that you need no more object to Blanche sharing my fortune, than I need object to her sharing yours.

TRENCH [*with dull wistfulness*] It seems so. We're all in the same swim, it appears. I hope youll excuse my making such a fuss.

SARTORIUS. Not another word. In fact, I thank you for refraining from explaining the nature of your scruples to Blanche: I admire that in you, Harry. Perhaps it will be as well to leave her in ignorance.

TRENCH [*anxiously*] But I must explain now. You saw how angry she was.

SARTORIUS. You had better leave that to me. [*He looks at his watch, and rings the bell*]. Lunch is nearly due: while you are getting ready for it I can see Blanche; and I hope the result will be quite satisfactory to us all. [*The parlormaid answers the bell: he addresses her with his habitual peremptoriness*]. Tell Miss Blanche I want her.

THE PARLORMAID [*her face falling expressively*] Yes, sir. [*She turns reluctantly to go*].

SARTORIUS [*on second thoughts*] Stop. [*She stops*]. My love to Miss Blanche; and I am alone here and would like to see her for a moment if she is not busy.

THE PARLORMAID [*relieved*] Yes, sir. [*She goes out*].

SARTORIUS. I will shew you your room, Harry. I hope you will soon be perfectly at home in it. You also, Mr Cokane, must learn your way about here. Let us go before Blanche comes. [*He leads the way to the door*].

COKANE [*cheerily, following him*] Our little discussion has given me quite an appetite.

TRENCH [*moodily*] It's taken mine away.

The two friends go out, Sartorius holding the door for them. He is following when the parlormaid reappears. She is a snivelling sympathetic creature, and is on the verge of tears.

SARTORIUS. Well: is Miss Blanche coming?

THE PARLORMAID. Yes, sir. I think so, sir.

SARTORIUS. Wait here until she comes; and tell her that I will be back in a moment. I have to shew Dr Trench his room.

THE PARLORMAID. Yes, sir. [*She comes into the room. A sound between a sob and a sniff escapes her*].

Sartorius looks suspiciously at her. He half closes the door.

SARTORIUS [*lowering his voice*] Whats the matter with you?

THE PARLORMAID [*whimpering*] Nothing, sir.

SARTORIUS [*at the same pitch, more menacingly*] Take care how you behave yourself when there are visitors present. Do you hear?

THE PARLORMAID. Yes, sir. [*Sartorius goes out*].

SARTORIUS [*outside*] Excuse me: I had a word to say to the servant.

Trench is heard replying "Not at all," *and Cokane* "Dont mention it, my dear sir."

Their voices pass out of hearing. The parlormaid sniffs; dries her eyes; and takes some brown paper and a ball of string from a cupboard under the bookcase. She puts them on the table, and wrestles with another sob. Blanche comes in, with a jewel box in her hands. Her expression is that of a strong and determined woman in an intense passion. The maid looks at her with abject wounded affection and bodily terror.

BLANCHE [*looking round*] Wheres my father?

THE PARLORMAID [*tremulously propitiatory*] He left word he'd be back directly, miss. I'm sure he wont be long. Heres the paper and string all ready, miss. [*She spreads the paper on the table*]. Can I do the parcel for you, miss?

BLANCHE. No. Mind your own business. [*She empties the box on the sheet of brown paper. It contains a packet of letters and some jewellery. She plucks a ring from her finger and throws it down on the heap so angrily that it rolls away and falls on the carpet. The maid submissively picks it up and puts it on the table, again sniffing and drying her eyes*]. What are you crying for?

THE PARLORMAID [*plaintively*] You speak so brutal to me, Miss Blanche; and I do love you so. I'm sure no one else would stay and put up with what I have to put up with.

BLANCHE. Then go. I dont want you. Do you hear. Go.

THE PARLORMAID [*piteously, falling on her knees*] Oh no,

Miss Blanche. Dont send me away from you: dont—

BLANCHE [*with fierce disgust*] Agh! I hate the sight of you. [*The maid, wounded to the heart, cries bitterly*]. Hold your tongue. Are those two gentlemen gone?

THE PARLORMAID [*weeping*] Oh, how could you say such a thing to me, Miss Blanche: me that—

BLANCHE [*seizing her by the hair and throat*] Stop that noise, I tell you, unless you want me to kill you.

THE PARLORMAID [*protesting and imploring, but in a carefully subdued voice*] Let me go, Miss Blanche: you know youll be sorry: you always are. Remember how dreadfully my head was cut last time.

BLANCHE [*raging*] Answer me, will you. Have they gone?

THE PARLORMAID. Lickcheese has gone, looking dreadf—[*she breaks off with a stifled cry as Blanche's fingers tighten furiously on her*].

BLANCHE. Did I ask you about Lickcheese? You beast: you know who I mean: youre doing it on purpose.

THE PARLORMAID [*in a gasp*] Theyre staying to lunch.

BLANCHE [*looking intently into her face*] He?

THE PARLORMAID [*whispering with a sympathetic nod*] Yes, miss. [*Blanche lets her drop, and stands forlorn, with despair in her face. The parlormaid, recognizing the passing of the crisis of passion, and fearing no further violence, sits discomfitedly on her heels, and tries to arrange her hair and cap, whimpering a little with exhaustion and soreness*]. Now youve set my hands all trembling; and I shall jingle the things on the tray at lunch so that everybody will notice me. It's too bad of you, Miss Bl— [*Sartorius coughs outside*].

BLANCHE [*quickly*] Sh! Get up. *The parlormaid hastily rises, and goes out as demurely as she can. Sartorius glances sternly at her and comes to Blanche.*

SARTORIUS [*mournfully*] My dear: can you not make a little better fight with your temper?

BLANCHE [*panting with the subsidence of her fit*] No I cant. I wont. I do my best. Nobody who really cares for me gives me up because of my temper. I never shew my temper to any of the servants but that girl; and she is the only one that will stay with us.

SARTORIUS. But, my dear, remember that we have to meet our visitors at luncheon presently. I have run down before them to say that I have arranged that little difficulty with Trench. It was only a piece of mischief made by Lickcheese. Trench is a young fool; but it is all right now.

BLANCHE. I dont want to marry a fool.

SARTORIUS. Then you will have to take a husband over thirty, Blanche. You must not expect too much, my child. You will be richer than your husband, and, I think, cleverer too. I am better pleased that it should be so.

BLANCHE [*seizing his arm*] Papa.

SARTORIUS. Yes, my dear.

BLANCHE. May I do as I like about this marriage; or must I do as you like?

SARTORIUS [*uneasily*] Blanche—

BLANCHE. No, papa: you must answer me.

SARTORIUS [*abandoning his self-control, and giving way recklessly to his affection for her*] You shall do as you like now and always, my beloved child. I only wish to do as my own darling pleases.

BLANCHE. Then I will not marry him. He has played fast and loose with me. He thinks us beneath him: he is ashamed of us: he dared to object to being benefited by you—as if it were not natural for him to owe you everything; and yet the money tempted him after all. [*She throws her arms hysterically about his neck*] Papa: I dont want to marry: I only want to stay with you and be happy as we have always been. I hate the thought of being married: I dont care for him: I dont want to leave you. [*Trench and Cokane come in; but she can hear nothing but her own voice and does not notice them*]. Only send him away: promise me that you will send him away and keep me here with you as we have always— [*seeing Trench*] Oh! [*She hides her face on her father's breast*].

TRENCH [*nervously*] I hope we are not intruding.

SARTORIUS [*formidably*] Dr Trench: my daughter has

changed her mind.

TRENCH [*disconcerted*] Am I to understand—

COKANE [*striking in in his most vinegary manner*] I think, Harry, under the circumstances, we have no alternative but to seek luncheon elsewhere.

TRENCH. But, Mr Sartorius, have you explained?

SARTORIUS [*straight in Trench's face*] I have explained, sir. Good morning. [*Trench, outraged, advances a step. Blanche sinks away from her father into a chair. Sartorius stands his ground rigidly*].

TRENCH [*turning away indignantly*] Come on, Cokane.

COKANE. Certainly, Harry, certainly. [*Trench goes out, very angry. The parlormaid, with a tray jingling in her hands, passes outside*]. You have disappointed me, sir, very acutely. Good morning. [*He follows Trench*].

ACT III

THE drawing-room in Sartorius's house in Bedford Square, London. Winter evening: fire burning, curtains drawn, and lamps lighted. Sartorius and Blanche are sitting glumly near the fire. The parlormaid, who has just brought in coffee, is placing it on a small table between them. There is a large table in the middle of the room. Looking from it towards the two windows, the pianoforte, a grand, is on the right, with a photographic portrait of Blanche on a miniature easel on a sort of bedspread which covers the top, shewing that the instrument is seldom, if ever, opened. There are two doors: one on the left, further forward than the fireplace, leading to the study; the other by the corner nearest the right hand window, leading to the lobby. Blanche has her workbasket at hand, and is knitting. Sartorius, closer to the fire, has a newspaper. The parlormaid goes out.

SARTORIUS. Blanche, my love.

BLANCHE. Yes.

SARTORIUS. I had a long talk to the doctor today about our going abroad.

BLANCHE [*impatiently*] I am quite well; and I will not go abroad. I loathe the very thought of the Continent. Why will you bother me so about my health?

SARTORIUS. It was not about your health, Blanche, but about my own.

BLANCHE [*rising*] Yours! [*She goes anxiously to him*]. Oh, papa, theres nothing the matter with you, I hope?

SARTORIUS. There will be: there must be, Blanche, long before you begin to consider yourself an old woman.

BLANCHE. But theres nothing the matter now?

SARTORIUS. Well, my dear, the doctor says I need change, travel, excitement—

BLANCHE. Excitement! You need excitement! [*She laughs joylessly, and sits down on the rug at his feet*]. How is it, papa, that you, who are so clever with everybody else, are not a bit clever with me? Do you think I cant see through your little plan to take me abroad? Since I will not be the invalid and allow you to be the nurse, you are to be the invalid and I am to be the nurse.

SARTORIUS. Well, Blanche, if you will have it that you are well and have nothing preying on your spirits, I must insist on being ill and have something preying on mine. And indeed, my girl, there is no use in our going on as we have for the last four months. You have not been happy; and I have been very far from comfortable. [*Blanche's face clouds: she turns away from him, and sits dumb and brooding. He waits in vain for some reply; then adds in a lower tone*] Need you be so inflexible, Blanche?

BLANCHE. I thought you admired inflexibility: you have always prided yourself on it.

SARTORIUS. Nonsense, my dear, nonsense! I have had to give in often enough. And I could shew you plenty of soft fellows who have done as well as I, and enjoyed themselves more, perhaps. If it is only for the sake of inflexibility that you are standing out—

BLANCHE. I am not standing out. I dont know what you mean. [*She tries to rise and go away*].

SARTORIUS [*catching her arm and arresting her on her knees*] Come, my child! you must not trifle with me as if I were a stranger. You are fretting because—

BLANCHE [*violently twisting herself free and speaking as she rises*] If you say it, papa, I will kill myself. It is not true. If he were here on his knees tonight, I would walk out of the house sooner than endure it. [*She goes out excitedly*].

Sartorius, greatly troubled, turns again to the fire with a heavy sigh.

SARTORIUS [*gazing gloomily into the glow*] Now if I fight it out with her, no more comfort for months! I might as well live with my clerk or my servant. And if I give in now, I shall have to give in always. Well! I cant help it. I have stuck to having my own way all my life; but there must be an end to that drudgery some day. She is young: let her have her turn at it.

The parlormaid comes in, evidently excited.

THE PARLORMAID. Please, sir, Mr Lickcheese wants to see you very particlar. On important business. Your business, he told me to say.

SARTORIUS. Mr Lickcheese! Do you mean Lickcheese who used to come here on my business?

THE PARLORMAID. Yes, sir. But indeed, sir, youd scarcely know him.

SARTORIUS [*frowning*] Hm! Starving, I suppose. Come to beg?

THE PARLORMAID [*intensely repudiating the idea*] O-o-o-o-h NO, sir. Quite the gentleman, sir! Sealskin overcoat, sir! Come in a hansom, all shaved and clean! I'm sure he's come into a fortune, sir.

SARTORIUS. Hm! Shew him up.

Lickcheese, who has been waiting at the door, instantly comes in. The change in his appearance is dazzling. He is in evening dress, with an overcoat lined throughout with furs presenting all the hues of the tiger. His shirt is fastened at the breast with a single diamond stud. His silk hat is of the glossiest black; a handsome gold watch-chain hangs like a garland on his filled-out waistcoat; he has shaved his whiskers and grown a moustache, the ends of which are waxed and pointed. As Sartorius stares speechless at him, he stands, smiling, to be admired, intensely enjoying the effect he is producing. The parlormaid, hardly less pleased with her own share in this coup-de-théâtre, goes out beaming, full of the news for the kitchen. Lickcheese clinches the situation by a triumphant nod at Sartorius.

SARTORIUS [*bracing himself: hostile*] Well?

LICKCHEESE. Quite well, Sartorius, thankee.

SARTORIUS. I was not asking after your health, sir, as you know, I think, as well as I do. What is your business?

LICKCHEESE. Business that I can take elsewhere if I meet with less civility than I please to put up with, Sartorius. You and me is man and man now. It was money that used to be my master, and not you: dont think it. Now that I'm independent in respect of money—

SARTORIUS [*crossing determinedly to the door, and holding it open*] You can take your independence out of my house, then. I wont have it here.

LICKCHEESE [*indulgently*] Come, Sartorius: dont be stiff-necked. I come here as a friend to put money in your pocket. No use your lettin on to me that youre above money. Eh?

SARTORIUS [*hesitates, and at last shuts the door, saying guardedly*] How much money?

LICKCHEESE [*victorious, going to Blanche's chair and taking off his overcoat*] Ah! there you speak like yourself, Sartorius. Now suppose you ask me to sit down and make myself comfortable?

SARTORIUS [*coming from the door*] I have a mind to put you downstairs by the back of your neck, you infernal blackguard.

LICKCHEESE [*not a bit ruffled, hangs his overcoat on the back of Blanche's chair, pulling a cigar case out of one of the pockets as he does so*] You and me is too much of a pair for me to take anything you say in bad part, Sartorius. Ave a cigar?

SARTORIUS. No smoking here: this is my daughter's room. However, sit down, sit down. [*They sit*].

LICKCHEESE. I' bin gittin on a little since I saw you last.

SARTORIUS. So I see.

LICKCHEESE. I owe it partly to you, you know. Does that surprise you?

SARTORIUS. It doesnt concern me.

LICKCHEESE. So you think, Sartorius; because it never did concern you how *I* got on, so long as I got y o u on by bringin in the rents. But I picked up something for myself down at Robbins's Row.

SARTORIUS. I always thought so. Have you come to make restitution?

LICKCHEESE. You wouldnt take it if I offered it to you, Sartorius. It wasnt money: it was knowledge: knowledge of the great public question of the Ousing of the Working Classes. You know theres a Royal Commission on it, dont you?

SARTORIUS. Oh, I see. Youve been giving evidence.

LICKCHEESE. Giving evidence! Not me. What good would that do me? Only my expenses; and that not on the professional scale, neither. No: I gev no evidence. But I'll tell you what I did. I kep it back, jast to oblige one or two people whose feelins would 'a bin urt by seein their names in a bluebook as keepin a fever den. Their Agent got so friendly with me over it that he put his name on a bill of mine to the tune of—well, no matter: it gev me a start; and a start was all I ever wanted to get on my feet. Ive got a copy of the first report of the Commission in the pocket of my overcoat. [*He rises and gets at his overcoat, from a pocket of which he takes a bluebook*]. I turned down the page to shew you: I thought youd like to see it. [*He doubles the book back at the place indicated, and hands it to Sartorius*].

SARTORIUS. So blackmail is the game, eh? [*He puts the book on the table without looking at it, and strikes it emphatically with his fist*]. I dont care t h a t for my name being in bluebooks. My friends dont read them; and I'm neither a Cabinet Minister nor a candidate for Parliament. Theres nothing to be got out of me on that lay.

LICKCHEESE [*shocked*] Blackmail! Oh, Mr Sartorius, do you think I would let out a word about your premises? Round on an old pal! no: that aint Lickcheese's way. Besides, they know all about you already. Them stairs that you and me quarrelled about, they was a whole arternoon examinin the clergyman that made such a fuss—you remember?—about the women that was urt on it. He made the worst he could of it, in an ungentlemanly, unchristian spirit. I wouldnt have that clergyman's disposition for worlds. Oh no: thats not what was in my thoughts.

SARTORIUS. Come, come, man! what w a s in your thoughts? Out with it.

LICKCHEESE [*with provoking deliberation, smiling and looking mysteriously at him*] You aint spent a few hundreds in repairs since we parted, ave you? [*Sartorius, losing patience, makes a threatening movement*]. Now dont fly out at me. I know a landlord that owned as beastly a slum as you could find in London, down there by the Tower. By my advice that man put half the houses into first-class repair, and let the other half to a new Company: the North Thames Iced Mutton Depot Company, of which I hold a few shares: promoters' shares. And what was the end of it, do you think?

SARTORIUS. Smash, I suppose.

LICKCHEESE. Smash! not a bit of it. Compensation, Mr Sartorius, compensation. Do you understand that?

SARTORIUS. Compensation for what?

LICKCHEESE. Why, the land was wanted for an extension of the Mint; and the Company had to be bought out, and the buildings compensated for. Somebody has to know these things beforehand, you know, no matter how dark theyre kept.

SARTORIUS [*interested, but cautious*] Well?

LICKCHEESE. Is that all you have to say to me, Mr Sartorius? "Well"! as if I was next door's dog! Suppose I'd got wind of a new street that would knock down Robbins's Row and turns Burke's Walk into a frontage worth thirty pound a foot! would you say no more to me than [*mimicking*] "Well"? [*Sartorius hesitates, looking at him in great doubt. Lickcheese rises and exhibits himself*]. Come! look at my get-up, Mr Sartorius. Look at this watch-chain! Look at the corporation Ive got on me! Do you think all that came from keeping my mouth shut? No: it came from keeping my ears and eyes open.

Blanche comes in, followed by the parlormaid, who has a silver tray on which she collects the coffee cups. Sartorius, impatient at the interruption, rises and motions Lickcheese to the door of the study.

SARTORIUS. Sh! We must talk this over in the study. There is a good fire there; and you can smoke. Blanche: an old friend of ours.

LICKCHEESE. And a kind one to me. I hope to see you well, Miss Blanche.

BLANCHE. Why, it's Mr Lickcheese! I hardly knew you.

LICKCHEESE. I find you a little changed yourself, miss.

BLANCHE [*hastily*] Oh, I am the same as ever. How are Mrs Lickcheese and the chil—

SARTORIUS [*impatiently*] We have business to transact, Blanche. You can talk to Mr Lickcheese afterwards. Come on.

Sartorius and Lickcheese go into the study. Blanche, surprised at her father's abruptness, looks after them for a moment. Then, seeing Lickcheese's overcoat on her chair, she takes it up, amused, and looks at the fur.

THE PARLORMAID. Oh, we are fine, aint we, Miss Blanche? I think Mr Lickcheese must have come into a legacy. [*Confidentially*] I wonder what he can want with the master, Miss Blanche! He brought him this big book. [*She shews the bluebook to Blanche*].

BLANCHE [*her curiosity aroused*] Let me see. [*She takes the book and looks at it*]. Theres something about papa in it. [*She sits down and begins to read*].

THE PARLORMAID [*folding the tea-table and putting it out of the way*] He looks ever s'much younger, Miss Blanche, dont he? I couldnt help laughing when I saw him with his whiskers shaved off: it do look so silly when youre not accustomed to it. [*No answer from Blanche*]. You havnt finished your coffee, miss: I suppose I may take it away? [*No answer*]. Oh, you are interested in Mr Lickcheese's book, miss.

Blanche springs up. The parlormaid looks at her face, and instantly hurries out of the room on tiptoe with her tray.

BLANCHE. So that was why he would not touch the money. [*She tries to tear the book across. Finding this impossible she throws it violently into the fireplace. It falls into the fender*]. Oh, if only a girl could have no father, no family, just as I have no mother! Clergyman! beast! "The worst slum landlord in London." "Slum landlord." Oh! [*She covers her face with her hands, and sinks shuddering into the chair on which the overcoat lies. The study door opens*].

LICKCHEESE [*in the study*] You just wait five minutes: I'll fetch him. [*Blanche snatches a piece of work from her basket, and sits erect and quiet, stitching at it. Lickcheese comes back, speak-*

ing to Sartorius, who follows him]. He lodges round the corner in Gower Street; and my private ansom's at the door. By your leave, Miss Blanche [*pulling gently at his overcoat*].

BLANCHE [*rising*] I beg your pardon. I hope I havnt crushed it.

LICKCHEESE [*gallantly, as he gets into the coat*] Youre welcome to crush it again now, Miss Blanche. Dont say good evenin to me, miss: I'm comin back presently: me and a friend or two. Ta ta, Sartorius: I shant be long. [*He goes out*].

Sartorius looks about for the bluebook.

BLANCHE. I thought we were done with Lickcheese.

SARTORIUS. Not quite yet, I think. He left a book here for me to look over: a large book in a blue paper cover. Has the girl put it away? [*He sees it in the fender; looks at Blanche; and adds*] Have you seen it?

BLANCHE. No. Yes. [*Angrily*] No: I have not seen it. What have I to do with it?

Sartorius picks the book up and dusts it; then sits down quietly to read. After a glance up and down the columns, he nods assentingly, as if he found there exactly what he expected.

SARTORIUS. It's a curious thing, Blanche, that the Parliamentary gentlemen who write such books as these should be so ignorant of practical business. One would suppose, to read this, that we are the most grasping, grinding, heartless pair in the world, you and I.

BLANCHE. Is it not true? About the state of the houses, I mean?

SARTORIUS [*calmly*] Oh, quite true.

BLANCHE. Then it is not our fault?

SARTORIUS. My dear: if we made the houses any better, the rents would have to be raised so much that the poor people would be unable to pay, and would be thrown homeless on the streets.

BLANCHE. Well, turn them out and get in a respectable class of people. Why should we have the disgrace of harboring such wretches?

SARTORIUS [*opening his eyes*] That sounds a little hard on them, doesnt it, my child?

BLANCHE. Oh, I hate the poor. At least, I hate those dirty, drunken, disreputable people who live like pigs. If they must be provided for, let other people look after them. How can you expect any one to think well of us when such things are written about us in that infamous book?

SARTORIUS [*coldly and a little wistfully*] I see I have made a real lady of you, Blanche.

BLANCHE [*defiantly*] Well? Are you sorry for that?

SARTORIUS. No, my dear: of course not. But do you know, Blanche, that my mother was a very poor woman, and that her poverty was not her fault?

BLANCHE. I suppose not; but the people we want to mix with now dont know that. And it was not my fault; so I dont see why *I* should be made to suffer for it.

SARTORIUS [*enraged*] Who makes you suffer for it, miss? What would you be now but for what your grandmother did for me when she stood at her wash-tub for thirteen hours a day and thought herself rich when she made fifteen shillings a week?

BLANCHE [*angrily*] I suppose I should have been down on her level instead of being raised above it, as I am now. Would you like us to go and live in that place in the book for the sake of grandmamma? I hate the idea of such things. I dont want to know about them. I love you because you brought me up to something better. [*Half aside, as she turns away from him*] I should hate you if you had not.

SARTORIUS [*giving in*] Well, my child, I suppose it is natural for you to feel that way, after your bringing up. It is the ladylike view of the matter. So dont let us quarrel, my girl. You shall not be made to suffer any more. I have made up my mind to improve the property, and get in quite a new class of tenants. There! does that satisfy you? I am only waiting for the consent of the ground landlord, Lady Roxdale.

BLANCHE. Lady Roxdale!

SARTORIUS. Yes. But I shall expect the mortgagee to take his share of the risk.

BLANCHE. The mortgagee! Do you mean— [*She cannot finish the sentence: Sartorius does it for her*].

SARTORIUS. Harry Trench. Yes. And remember, Blanche: if he consents to join me in the scheme, I shall have to be friends with him.

BLANCHE. And to ask him to the house?

SARTORIUS. Only on business. You need not meet him unless you like.

BLANCHE [*overwhelmed*] When is he coming?

SARTORIUS. There is no time to be lost. Lickcheese has gone to ask him to come round.

BLANCHE [*in dismay*] Then he will be here in a few minutes! What shall I do?

SARTORIUS. I advise you to receive him as if nothing had happened, and then go out and leave us to our business. You are not afraid to meet him?

BLANCHE. Afraid! No: most certainly not. But—

LICKCHEESE'S VOICE [*without*] Straight in front of you, doctor. You never bin here before; but I know the house better than my own.

BLANCHE. Here they are. Dont say I'm here, papa. [*She rushes away into the study*].

Lickcheese comes in with Trench and Cokane. Both are in evening dress. Cokane shakes hands effusively with Sartorius. Trench, who is coarsened and sullen, and has evidently not been making the best of his disappointment, bows shortly and resentfully. Lickcheese covers the general embarrassment by talking cheerfully until they are all seated round the large table: Trench nearest the fireplace; Cokane nearest the piano; and the other two between them, with Lickcheese next Cokane].

LICKCHEESE. Here we are, all friends round St Paul's You remember Mr Cokane? he does a little business for me now as a friend, and gives me a help with my correspondence: sekketerry we call it. Ive no litery style, and thats the truth; so Mr Cokane kindly puts it into my letters and draft prospectuses and advertisements and the like. Dont you, Cokane? Of course you do: why shouldnt you? He's been helping me to persuade his old friend, Dr Trench, about the matter we were speaking of.

COKANE [*austerely*] No, Mr Lickcheese, not trying to persuade him. No: this is a matter of principle with me. I say it is your duty, Henry—your d u t y—to put those abominable buildings into proper and habitable repair. As a man of science you owe it to the community to perfect the sanitary arrangements. In questions of duty there is no room for persuasion, even from the oldest friend.

SARTORIUS [*to Trench*] I certainly feel, as Mr Cokane puts it, that it is our duty: one which I have perhaps too long neglected out of regard for the poorest class of tenants.

LICKCHEESE. Not a doubt of it, gents: a dooty. I can be as sharp as any man when it's a question of business; but dooty's another pair o' shoes.

TRENCH. Well, I dont see that it's any more my duty now than it was four months ago. I look at it simply as a question of so much money.

COKANE. Shame, Harry, shame! Shame!

TRENCH. Oh, shut up, you fool. [*Cokane springs up*].

LICKCHEESE [*catching his coat and holding him*] Steady! steady! Mr Sekketerry. Dr Trench is only joking.

COKANE. I insist on the withdrawal of that expression. I have been called a fool.

TRENCH [*morosely*] So you are a fool.

COKANE. Then you are a damned fool. Now, sir!

TRENCH. All right. Now weve settled that. [*Cokane, with a snort, sits down*]. What I mean is this. Dont lets have any nonsense about this job. As I understand it, Robbins's Row is to be pulled down to make way for the new street into the Strand; and the straight tip now is to go for compensation.

LICKCHEESE [*chuckling*] That'so, Dr Trench. Thats it.

TRENCH [*continuing*] Well, it appears that the dirtier a place is the more rent you get; and the decenter it is, the more compensation you get. So we're to give up dirt and go in for decency.

SARTORIUS. I should not put it exactly in that way; but—

COKANE. Quite right, Mr Sartorius, quite right. The case could not have been stated in worse taste or with less tact.

LICKCHEESE. Sh-sh-sh-sh!

SARTORIUS. I do not quite go with you there, Mr Cokane. Dr Trench puts the case frankly as a man of business. I take the wider view of a public man. We live in a progressive age; and humanitarian ideas are advancing and must be taken into account. But my practical conclusion is the same as his. I should hardly feel justified in making a large claim for compensation under existing circumstances.

LICKCHEESE. Of course not; and you wouldnt get it if you did. You see, it's like this, Dr Trench. Theres no doubt that the Vestries has legal powers to play old Harry with slum properties, and spoil the houseknacking game if they please. That didnt matter in the good old times, because the Vestries used to be us ourselves. Nobody ever knew a word about the election; and we used to get ten of us into a room and elect one another, and do what we liked. Well, that cock wont fight any longer; and, to put it short, the game is up for men in the position of you and Mr Sartorius. My advice to you is, take the present chance of getting out of it. Spend a little money on the block at the Cribbs Market end: enough to make it look like a model dwelling, you know; and let the other block to me on fair terms for a depot of the North Thames Iced Mutton Company. Theyll be knocked down inside of two year to make room for the new north and south main thoroughfare; and youll be compensated to the tune of double the present valuation, with the cost of the improvements thrown in. Leave things as they are; and you stand a good chance of being fined, or condemned, or pulled down before long. Now's your time.

COKANE. Hear, hear! Hear, hear! Hear, hear! Admirably put from the business point of view! I recognize the uselessness of putting the moral point of view to you,

Trench; but even you must feel the cogency of Mr Lickcheese's business statement.

TRENCH. But why cant you act without me? What have I got to do with it? I'm only a mortgagee.

SARTORIUS. There is a certain risk in this compensation investment, Dr Trench. The County Council may alter the line of the new street. If that happens, the money spent in improving the houses will be thrown away: simply thrown away. Worse than thrown away, in fact; for the new buildings may stand unlet or half let for years. But you will expect your seven per cent as usual.

TRENCH. A man must live.

COKANE. Je n'en vois pas la nécessité.

TRENCH. Shut up, Billy; or else speak some language you understand. No, Mr Sartorius: I should be very glad to stand in with you if I could afford it; but I cant; so you may leave me out of it.

LICKCHEESE. Well, all I can say is that youre a very foolish young man.

COKANE. What did I tell you, Harry?

TRENCH. I dont see that it's any business of yours, Mr Lickcheese.

LICKCHEESE. It's a free country: every man has a right to his opinion.

COKANE. Hear, hear!

LICKCHEESE. Come! wheres your feelins for them poor people, Dr Trench? Remember how it went to your heart when I first told you about them. What! are you going to turn hard?

TRENCH. No: it wont do: you cant get over me that way. You proved to me before that there was no use in being sentimental over that slum shop of ours; and it's no good your turning round on the philanthropic tack now that you want me to put my capital into your speculation. Ive had my lesson; and I'm going to stick to my present income. It's little enough for me as it is.

SARTORIUS. It really matters nothing to me, Dr Trench,

how you decide. I can easily raise the money elsewhere and pay you off. Then, since you are resolved to run no risks, you can invest your ten thousand pounds in Consols and get two hundred and fifty pounds a year for it instead of seven hundred.

Trench, completely outwitted, stares at them in consternation. Cokane breaks the silence.

COKANE. This is what comes of being avaricious, Harry. Two thirds of your income gone at one blow. And I must say it serves you right.

TRENCH. Thats all very fine; but I dont understand it. If you can do this to me, why didnt you do it long ago?

SARTORIUS. Because, as I should probably have had to borrow at the same rate, I should have saved nothing; whereas you would have lost over four hundred a year: a very serious matter for you. I had no desire to be unfriendly; and even now I should be glad to let the mortgage stand, were it not that the circumstances mentioned by Mr Lickcheese force my hand. Besides, Dr Trench, I hoped for some time that our interests might be joined by closer ties even than those of friendship.

LICKCHEESE [*jumping up, relieved*] There! Now the murder's out. Excuse me, Dr Trench. Ex-cuse me, Mr Sartorius: excuse my freedom. Why not Dr Trench marry Miss Blanche, and settle the whole affair that way?

Sensation. Lickcheese sits down triumphant.

COKANE. You forget, Mr Lickcheese, that the young lady, whose taste has to be considered, decisively objected to him.

TRENCH. Oh! Perhaps you think she was struck with you.

COKANE. I do not say so, Trench. No man of any delicacy would suggest such a thing. You have an untutored mind, Trench, an untutored mind.

TRENCH. Well, Cokane: Ive told you my opinion of you already.

COKANE [*rising wildly*] And I have told you my opinion

of you. I will repeat it if you wish. I am ready to repeat it.

LICKCHEESE. Come, Mr Sekketerry: you and me, as married men, is out of the unt as far as young ladies is concerned. I know Miss Blanche: she has her father's eye for business. Explain this job to her; and she'll make it up with Dr Trench. Why not have a bit of romance in business when it costs nothing? We all have our feelins: we aint mere calculatin machines.

SARTORIUS [*revolted*] Do you think, Lickcheese, that my daughter is to be made part of a money bargain between you and these gentlemen?

LICKCHEESE. Oh come, Sartorius! dont talk as if you was the only father in the world. I have a daughter too; and my feelins in that matter is just as fine as yours. I propose nothing but what is for Miss Blanche's advantage and Dr Trench's.

COKANE. Lickcheese expresses himself roughly, Mr Sartorius; but his is a sterling nature; and what he says is to the point. If Miss Sartorius can really bring herself to care for Harry, I am far from desiring to stand in the way of such an arrangement.

TRENCH. Why, what have you got to do with it?

LICKCHEESE. Easy, Dr Trench, easy. We want your opinion. Are you still on for marrying Miss Blanche if she's agreeable?

TRENCH [*shortly*] I dont know that I am. [*Sartorius rises indignantly*].

LICKCHEESE. Easy one moment, Mr Sartorius. [*To Trench*] Come now, Dr Trench! you say you dont know that you are. But do you know that you aint? thats what we want to know.

TRENCH [*sulkily*] I wont have the relations between Miss Sartorius and myself made part of a bargain. [*He rises to leave the table*].

LICKCHEESE [*rising*] Thats enough: a gentleman could say no less. [*Insinuatingly*] Now, would you mind me and Cokane and the guvnor steppin into the study to arrange about the lease to the North Thames Iced Mutton Company?

TRENCH. Oh, *I* dont mind. I'm going home. Theres nothing more to say.

LICKCHEESE. No: dont go. Only just a minute: me and Cokane will be back in no time to see you home. Youll wait for us, wont you?

TRENCH. Oh well, if you wish, yes.

LICKCHEESE [*cheerily*] Didnt I know you would!

SARTORIUS [*at the study door, to Cokane*] After you, sir.

Cokane bows formally and goes into the study.

LICKCHEESE [*at the door, aside to Sartorius*] You never ad such a managin man as me, Sartorius. [*He goes into the study chuckling, followed by Sartorius*].

Trench, left alone, looks round carefully and listens a moment. Then he goes on tiptoe to the piano and leans upon it with folded arms, gazing at Blanche's portrait. Blanche herself appears presently at the study door. When she sees how he is occupied, she closes it softly and steals over to him, watching him intently. He rises from his leaning attitude, and takes the portrait from the easel, and is about to kiss it when, taking a second look round to reassure himself that nobody is watching him, he finds Blanche close upon him. He drops the portrait, and stares at her without the least presence of mind.

BLANCHE [*shrewishly*] Well? So you have come back here. You have had the meanness to come into this house again. [*He flushes and retreats a step. She follows him up remorselessly*]. What a poor spirited creature you must be! Why dont you go? [*Red and wincing, he starts huffily to get his hat from the table; but when he turns to the door with it she deliberately stands in his way; so that he has to stop*]. *I* dont want you to stay. [*For a moment they stand face to face, quite close to one another, she provocative, taunting, half defying, half inviting him to advance, in a flush of undisguised animal excitement. It suddenly flashes on him that all this ferocity is erotic: that she is making love to him. His eye lights up: a cunning expression comes into the corners of his mouth: with a heavy assumption of indifference he walks straight back to his chair, and plants himself in it with his arms folded. She comes down the room after him*]. But I forgot: you have found that there is some money to be made here. Lickcheese told you. You, who were so disinterested, so independent, that you could not accept anything from my father! [*At the end of every sentence she waits to see what execution she has done*]. I suppose you will try to persuade me that you have come down here on a great philanthropic enterprise—to befriend the poor by having those houses rebuilt, eh? [*Trench maintains his attitude and makes no sign*]. Yes: when my father makes you do it. And when Lickcheese has discovered some way of making it profitable. Oh, I know papa; and I know you. And for the sake of that, you come back here—into the house where you were refused—ordered out. [*Trench's face darkens: her eyes gleam as she sees it*]. Aha! you remember that. You know it's true: you cant deny it. [*She sits down, and softens her tone a little as she affects to pity him*]. Well, let me tell you that you cut a poor figure, a very, very poor figure, Harry. [*At the word Harry he relaxes the fold of his arms; and a faint grin of anticipated victory appears on his face*]. And you, too, a gentleman! so highly connected! with such distinguished relations! so particular as to where your money comes from! I wonder at you. I really wonder at you. I should have thought that if your fine family gave you nothing else, it might at least have given you some sense of personal dignity. Perhaps you think you look dignified at present: eh? [*No reply*]. Well, I can assure you that you dont: you look most ridiculous—as foolish as a man could look—you dont know what to say; and you dont know what to do. But after all, I really dont see what any one could say in defence of such conduct. [*He looks straight in front of him, and purses up his lips as if whistling. This annoys her; and she becomes affectedly polite*]. I am afraid I am in your way, Dr Trench. [*She rises*]. I shall not intrude on you any longer. You seem so perfectly at home that I need make no apology for leaving you to yourself. [*She makes a feint of going to the door; but he does not budge; and she returns and comes behind his chair*]. Harry. [*He does not turn. She comes a step nearer*]. Harry: I want you to answer me a question. [*Earnestly, stooping over him*] Look me in the face [*No reply*]. Do you hear? [*Seizing his cheeks and twisting his head round*] Look—me—in—the—face. [*He shuts his eyes tight and grins. She suddenly kneels down beside him with her breast against his shoulder*]. Harry: what were you doing with my photograph just now, when you thought you were alone? [*He opens his eyes: they are full of delight. She flings her arms round him, and crushes him in an ecstatic embrace as she adds, with furious tenderness*] How dare you touch anything belonging to me?

The study door opens and voices are heard.

TRENCH. I hear some one coming.

She regains her chair with a bound, and pushes it back as far as possible. Cokane, Lickcheese and Sartorius come from the study. Sartorius and Lickcheese come to Trench. Cokane crosses to Blanche in his most killing manner.

COKANE. How do you do, Miss Sartorius? Nice weather for the return of l'enfant prodigue, eh?

BLANCHE. Capital, Mr Cokane. So glad to see you. [*She gives him her hand, which he kisses with gallantry*].

LICKCHEESE [*on Trench's left, in a low voice*] Any noos for us, Dr Trench?

TRENCH [*to Sartorius, on his right*] I'll stand in, compensation or no compensation. [*He shakes Sartorius's hand*].

The parlormaid has just appeared at the door.

THE PARLORMAID. Supper is ready, miss.

COKANE. Allow me.

Exeunt omnes: Blanche on Cokane's arm; Lickcheese jocosely taking Sartorius on one arm, and Trench on the other.

GREAT CATHERINE

A THUMBNAIL SKETCH OF RUSSIAN COURT LIFE
IN THE XVIII CENTURY (WHOM GLORY STILL ADORES)

Written in 1913

First Performed London 1913

THE AUTHOR'S APOLOGY FOR GREAT CATHERINE

EXCEPTION has been taken to the title of this seeming tomfoolery on the ground that the Catherine it represents is not Great Catherine, but the Catherine whose gallantries provide some of the lightest pages of modern history. Great Catherine, it is said, was the Catherine whose diplomacy, whose campaigns and conquests, whose plans of Liberal reform, whose correspondence with Grimm and Voltaire enabled her to cut such a magnificent figure in the XVIII century. In reply, I can only confess that Catherine's diplomacy and her conquests do not interest me. It is clear to me that neither she nor the statesmen with whom she played this mischievous kind of political chess had any notion of the real history of their own times, or of the real forces that were moulding Europe. The French Revolution, which made such short work of Catherine's Voltairean principles, surprised and scandalized her as much as it surprised and scandalized any provincial governess in the French chateaux.

The main difference between her and our modern Liberal Governments was that whereas she talked and wrote quite intelligently about Liberal principles before she was frightened into making such talking and writing a flogging matter, our Liberal ministers take the name of Liberalism in vain without knowing or caring enough about its meaning even to talk and scribble about it, and pass their flogging Bills, and institute their prosecutions for sedition and blasphemy and so forth, without the faintest suspicion that such proceedings need any apology from the Liberal point of view.

It was quite easy for Patiomkin to humbug Catherine as to the condition of Russia by conducting her through sham cities run up for the occasion by scenic artists; but in the little world of European court intrigue and dynastic diplomacy which was the only world she knew she was more than a match for him and for all the rest of her contemporaries. In such intrigue and diplomacy, however, there was no romance, no scientific political interest, nothing that a sane mind can now retain even if it can be persuaded to waste time in reading it up. But Catherine as a woman, with plenty of character and (as we should say) no morals, still fascinates and amuses us as she fascinated and amused her contemporaries. They were great sentimental comedians, these Peters, Elizabeths, and Catherines who played their Tsarships as eccentric character parts, and produced scene after scene of furious harlequinade with the monarch as clown, and of tragic relief in the torture chamber with the monarch as pantomime demon committing real atrocities, not forgetting the indispensable love interest on an enormous and utterly indecorous scale. Catherine kept this vast Guignol Theatre open for nearly half a century, not as a Russian, but as a highly domesticated German lady whose household routine was not at all so unlike that of Queen Victoria as might be expected from the difference in their notions of propriety in sexual relations.

In short, if Byron leaves you with an impression that he said very little about Catherine, and that little not what was best worth saying, I beg to correct your impression by assuring you that what Byron said was all there really is to say that is worth saying. His Catherine is my Catherine and everybody's Catherine. The young man who gains her favor is a Spanish nobleman in his version. I have made him an English country gentleman, who gets out of his rather dangerous scrape by simplicity, sincerity, and the courage of these qualities. By this I have given some offence to the many Britons who see themselves as heroes: what they mean by heroes being theatrical snobs of superhuman pretensions which, though quite groundless, are admitted with awe by the rest of the human race. They say I think an Englishman a fool. When I do, they have themselves to thank.

I must not, however, pretend that historical portraiture was the motive of a play that will leave the reader as ignorant of Russian history as he may be now before he has turned the page. Nor is the sketch of Catherine complete even idiosyncratically, leaving her politics out of the question. For example, she wrote bushels of plays. I confess I have not yet read any of them. The truth is, this play grew out of the relations which inevitably exist in the theatre between authors and actors. If the actors have sometimes to use their skill as the author's puppets rather than in full self-expression, the author has sometimes to use his skill as the actors' tailor, fitting them with parts written to display the virtuosity of the performer rather than to solve problems of life, character, or history. Feats of this kind may tickle an author's technical vanity; but he is bound on such occasions to admit that the performer for whom he writes is "the onlie begetter" of his work, which must be regarded critically as an addition to the debt dramatic literature owes to the art of acting and its exponents. Those who have seen Miss Gertrude Kingston play the part of Catherine will have no difficulty in believing that it was her talent rather than mine that brought the play into existence. I once recommended Miss Kingston professionally to play queens. Now in the modern drama there were no queens for her to play; and as to the older literature of our stage, did it not provoke the veteran actress in Sir Arthur Pinero's Trelawny of the Wells to declare that, as parts, queens are not worth a tinker's oath? Miss Kingston's comment on my suggestion, though more elegantly worded, was to the same effect; and it ended in my having to make good my advice by writing Great Catherine. History provided no other queen capable of standing up to our joint talents.

In composing such bravura pieces, the author limits himself only by the range of the virtuoso, which by definition far transcends the modesty of nature. If my Russians seem more Muscovite than any Russian, and my English people more insular than any Briton, I will not plead, as I honestly might, that the fiction has yet to be written that can exaggerate the reality of such subjects; that the apparently outrageous Patiomkin is but a timidly bowdlerized ghost of the original; and that Captain Edstaston is no more than a miniature that might hang appropriately on the walls of nineteen out of twenty English country houses to this day. An artistic presentment must not condescend to justify itself by a comparison with crude nature; and I prefer to admit that in this kind my *dramatis personae* are, as they should be, of the stage stagey, challenging the actor to act up to them or beyond them, if he can. The more heroic the overcharging, the better for the performance.

In dragging the reader thus for a moment behind the scenes, I am departing from a rule which I have hitherto imposed on myself so rigidly that I never permit myself, even in a stage direction, to let slip a word that could bludgeon the imagination of the reader by reminding him of the boards and the footlights and the sky borders and the rest of the theatrical scaffolding, for which nevertheless I have to plan as carefully as if I were the head carpenter as well as the author. But even at the risk of talking shop, an honest playwright should take at least one opportunity of acknowledging that his art is not only limited by the art of the actor, but often stimulated and developed by it. No sane and skilled author writes plays that present impossibilities to the actor or to the stage engineer. If, as occasionally happens, he asks them to do things that they have never done before and cannot conceive as presentable or possible (as Wagner and Thomas Hardy have done, for example), it is always found that the difficulties are not really insuperable, the author having foreseen unsuspected possibilities both in the actor and in the audience, whose will-to-make-believe can perform the quaintest miracles. Thus may authors advance the arts of acting and of staging plays. But the actor also may enlarge the scope of the drama by displaying powers not previously discovered by the author. If the best available actors are only Horatios, the authors will have to leave Hamlet out, and be content with Horatios for heroes. Some of the difference between Shakespear's Orlandos and Bassanios and Bertrams and his Hamlets and Macbeths must have been due not only to his development as a dramatic poet, but to the development of Burbage as an actor. Playwrights do not write for ideal actors when their livelihood is at stake: if they did, they would write parts for heroes with twenty arms like an Indian god. Indeed the actor often influences the author too much; for I can remember a time (I am not implying that it is yet wholly past) when the art of writing a fashionable play had become very largely the art of writing it "round" the personalities of a group of fashionable performers of whom Burbage would certainly have said that their parts needed no acting. Everything has its abuse as well as its use.

It is also to be considered that great plays live longer than great actors, though little plays do not live nearly so long as the worst of their exponents. The consequence is that the great actor, instead of putting pressure on contemporary authors to supply him with heroic parts, falls back on the Shakespearean repertory, and takes what he needs from a dead hand. In the nineteenth century, the careers of Kean, Macready, Barry Sullivan, and Irving, ought to have produced a group of heroic plays comparable in intensity to those of Æschylus, Sophocles, and Euripides; but nothing of the kind happened: these actors played the works of dead authors, or, very occasionally, of live poets who were hardly regular professional playwrights. Sheridan Knowles, Bulwer Lytton, Wills, and Tennyson produced a few glaringly artificial high horses for the great actors of their time; but the playwrights proper, who really kept the theatre going, and were kept going by the theatre, did not cater for the great actors: they could not afford to compete with a bard who was not of an age but for all time, and who had, moreover, the overwhelming attraction for the actor-managers of not charging author's fees. The result was that the playwrights and the great actors ceased to think of themselves as having any concern with one another: Tom Robertson, Ibsen, Pinero, and Barrie might as well have belonged to a different solar system as far as Irving was concerned; and the same was true of their respective predecessors.

Thus was established an evil tradition; but I at least can plead that it does not always hold good. If Forbes Robertson had not been there to play Caesar, I should not have written Caesar and Cleopatra. If Ellen Terry had never been born, Captain Brassbound's conversion would never have been effected. The Devil's Disciple, with which I won my *cordon bleu* in America as a potboiler, would have had a different sort of hero if Richard Mansfield had been a different sort of actor, though the actual commission to write it came from an English actor, William Terriss, who was assassinated before he recovered from the dismay into which the result of his rash proposal threw him. For it must be said that the actor or actress who inspires or commissions a play as often as not regards it as a Frankenstein's monster, and will none of it. That does not make him or her any the less parental in the fecundity of the playwright.

To an author who has any feeling of his business there is a keen and whimsical joy in divining and revealing a side of an actor's genius overlooked before, and unsuspected even by the actor himself. When I snatched Mr Louis Calvert from Shakespear, and made him wear a frock coat and silk hat on the stage for perhaps the first time in his life, I do not think he expected in the least that his performance would enable me to boast of his Tom Broadbent as a genuine stage classic. Mrs Patrick Campbell was famous before I wrote for her, but not for playing illiterate cockney flower-maidens. And in the case which is provoking me to all these impertinences, I am quite sure that Miss Gertrude Kingston, who first made her reputation as an impersonator of the most delightfully feather-headed and inconsequent ingenues, thought me more than usually mad when I persuaded her to play the Helen of Euripides, and then launched her on a queenly career as Catherine of Russia.

It is not the whole truth that if we take care of the actors the plays will take care of themselves; nor is it any truer that if we take care of the plays the actors will take care of themselves. There is both give and take in the business. I have seen plays written for actors that made me exclaim, "How oft the sight of means to do ill deeds makes deeds ill done!" But Burbage may have flourished the prompt copy of Hamlet under Shakespear's nose at the tenth rehearsal and cried, "How oft the sight of means to do great deeds makes playwrights great!" I say the tenth because I am convinced that at the first he denounced his part as a rotten one; thought the ghost's speech ridiculously long; and wanted to play the king. Anyhow, whether he had the wit to utter it or not, the boast would have been a valid one. The best conclusion is that every actor should say, "If I create the hero in myself, God will send an author to write his part." For in the long run the actors will get the authors, and the authors the actors, they deserve.

GREAT CATHERINE

THE FIRST SCENE

1776. *Patiomkin in his bureau in the Winter Palace, St Petersburgh. Huge palatial apartment: style, Russia in the XVIII century imitating the Versailles du Roi Soleil. Extravagant luxury. Also dirt and disorder.*

Patiomkin, gigantic in stature and build, his face marred by the loss of one eye and a marked squint in the other, sits at the end of a table littered with papers and the remains of three or four successive breakfasts. He has supplies of coffee and brandy at hand sufficient for a party of ten. His coat, encrusted with diamonds, is on the floor. It has fallen off a chair placed near the other end of the table for the convenience of visitors. His court sword, with its attachments, is on the chair. His three-cornered hat, also bejewelled, is on the table. He himself is half dressed in an unfastened shirt and an immense dressing-gown, once gorgeous, now food-splashed and dirty, as it serves him for towel, handkerchief, duster, and every other use to which a textile fabric can be put by a slovenly man. It does not conceal his huge hairy chest, nor his half-buttoned knee breeches, nor his legs. These are partly clad in silk stockings, which he occasionally hitches up to his knees, and presently shakes down to his shins, by his restless movements. His feet are thrust into enormous slippers, worth, with their crust of jewels, several thousand roubles apiece.

Superficially Patiomkin is a violent, brutal barbarian, an upstart despot of the most intolerable and dangerous type, ugly, lazy, and disgusting in his personal habits. Yet ambassadors report him the ablest man in Russia, and the one who can do most with the still abler Empress Catherine II, who is not a Russian but a German, by no means barbarous or intemperate in her personal habits. She not only disputes with Frederick the Great the reputation of being the cleverest monarch in Europe, but may even put in a very plausible claim to be the cleverest and most attractive individual alive. Now she not only tolerates Patiomkin long after she has got over her first romantic attachment to him, but esteems him highly as a counsellor and a good friend. His love letters are among the best on record. He has a wild sense of humor, which enables him to laugh at himself as well as at everybody else. In the eyes of the English visitor now about to be admitted to his presence he may be an outrageous ruffian. In fact he actually is an outrageous ruffian, in no matter whose eyes; but the visitor will find out, as everyone else sooner or later finds out, that he is a man to be reckoned with even by those who are not intimidated by his temper, bodily strength, and exalted rank.

A pretty young lady, Varinka, his favorite niece, is lounging on an ottoman between his end of the table and the door, very sulky and dissatisfied, perhaps because he is preoccupied with his papers and his brandy bottle, and she can see nothing of him but his broad back.

There is a screen behind the ottoman.

An old soldier, a Cossack sergeant, enters.

THE SERGEANT [*softly to the lady, holding the door handle*] Little darling honey: is his Highness the prince very busy?

VARINKA. His Highness the prince is very busy. He is singing out of tune; he is biting his nails; he is scratching his head; he is hitching up his untidy stockings; he is making himself disgusting and odious to everybody; and he is pretending to read state papers that he does not understand because he is too lazy and selfish to talk and be companionable.

PATIOMKIN [*growls; then wipes his nose with his dressing-gown*]!!

VARINKA. Pig. Ugh! [*She curls herself up with a shiver of disgust and retires from the conversation*].

THE SERGEANT [*stealing across to the coat, and picking it up to replace it on the back of the chair*] Little Father: the English captain, so highly recommended to you by old Fritz of Prussia, by the English ambassador, and by Monsieur Voltaire (whom [*crossing himself*] may God in his infinite mercy damn eternally!), is in the antechamber and desires audience.

PATIOMKIN [*deliberately*] To hell with the English captain; and to hell with old Fritz of Prussia; and to hell with the English ambassador; and to hell with Monsieur Voltaire; and to hell with you too!

THE SERGEANT. Have mercy on me, Little Father. Your head is bad this morning. You drink too much French brandy and too little good Russian kvass.

PATIOMKIN [*with sudden fury*] Why are visitors of consequence announced by a sergeant? [*Springing at him and seizing him by the throat*] What do you mean by this, you hound? Do you want five thousand blows of the stick? Where is General Volkonsky?

THE SERGEANT [*on his knees*] Little Father: you kicked his Highness downstairs.

PATIOMKIN [*flinging him down and kicking him*] You lie, you dog. You lie.

THE SERGEANT. Little Father: life is hard for the poor. If you say it is a lie, it is a lie. He fell downstairs. I picked him up; and he kicked me. They all kick me when you kick them. God knows that is not just, Little Father!

PATIOMKIN [*laughs ogreishly; then returns to his place at the table, chuckling*]!!!

VARINKA. Savage! Boor! It is a disgrace. No wonder the French sneer at us as barbarians.

THE SERGEANT [*who has crept round the table to the screen, and insinuated himself between Patiomkin's back and Varinka*] Do you think the Prince will see the Captain, little darling?

PATIOMKIN. He will not see any captain. Go to the devil!

THE SERGEANT. Be merciful, Little Father. God knows it is your duty to see him! [*To Varinka*] Intercede for him and for me, beautiful little darling. He has given me a rouble.

PATIOMKIN. Oh, send him in, send him in; and stop pestering me. Am I never to have a moment's peace?

The Sergeant salutes joyfully and hurries out, divining that Patiomkin has intended to see the English captain all along, and has played this comedy of fury and exhausted impatience to conceal his interest in the visitor.

VARINKA. Have you no shame? You refuse to see the most exalted persons. You kick princes and generals downstairs. And then you see an English captain merely because he has given a rouble to that common soldier. It is scandalous.

PATIOMKIN. Darling beloved, I am drunk; but I know what I am doing. I wish to stand well with the English.

VARINKA. And you think you will impress an Englishman by receiving him as you are now, half drunk?

PATIOMKIN [*gravely*] It is true: the English despise men who cannot drink. I must make myself wholly drunk. [*He takes a huge draught of brandy*].

VARINKA. Sot!

The Sergeant returns ushering a handsome strongly built young English officer in the uniform of a Light Dragoon. He is evidently on fairly good terms with himself, and very sure of his social position. He crosses the room to the end of the table opposite Patiomkin's, and awaits the civilities of that statesman with confidence. The Sergeant remains prudently at the door.

THE SERGEANT [*paternally*] Little Father: this is the English captain, so well recommended to her sacred Majesty the Empress. God knows, he needs your countenance and protec—[*he vanishes precipitately, seeing that Patiomkin is about to throw a bottle at him. The Captain contemplates these preliminaries with astonishment, and with some displeasure, which is not allayed when Patiomkin, hardly condescending to look at his visitor, of whom he nevertheless takes stock with the corner of his one eye, says gruffly*] Well?

EDSTASTON. My name is Edstaston: Captain Edstaston of the Light Dragoons. I have the honor to present to your Highness this letter from the British ambassador, which will give you all necessary particulars. [*He hands Patiomkin the letter*].

PATIOMKIN [*tearing it open and glancing at it for about a second*] What do you want?

EDSTASTON. The letter will explain to your Highness who I am.

PATIOMKIN. I dont want to know who you are. What do you want?

EDSTASTON. An audience of the Empress. [*Patiomkin contemptuously throws the letter aside. Edstaston adds hotly*] Also some civility, if you please.

PATIOMKIN [*with derision*] Ho!

VARINKA. My uncle is receiving you with unusual civility, Captain. He has just kicked a general downstairs.

EDSTASTON. A Russian general, madam?

VARINKA. Of course.

EDSTASTON. I must allow myself to say, madam, that your uncle had better not attempt to kick an English officer downstairs.

PATIOMKIN. You want me to kick you upstairs: eh? You want an audience of the Empress.

EDSTASTON. I have said nothing about kicking, sir. If it comes to that, my boots shall speak for me. Her Majesty has signified a desire to have news of the rebellion in America. I have served against the rebels; and I am instructed to place myself at the disposal of her Majesty, and to describe the events of the war to her, as an eye-witness, in a discreet and agreeable manner.

PATIOMKIN. Psha! I know. You think if she once sets eyes on your face and your uniform your fortune is made. You think that if she could stand a man like me, with only one eye, and a cross eye at that, she must fall down at your feet at first sight, eh?

EDSTASTON [*shocked and indignant*] I think nothing of the sort; and I'll trouble you not to repeat it. If I were a Russian subject and you made such a boast about my queen, I'd strike you across the face with my sword. [*Patiomkin, with a yell of fury, rushes at him*]. Hands off, you swine! [*As Patiomkin, towering over him, attempts to seize him by the throat, Edstaston, who is a bit of a wrestler, adroitly backheels him. He falls, amazed, on his back*].

VARINKA [*rushing out*] Help! Call the guard! The Englishman is murdering my uncle! Help! Help!

The guard and the Sergeant rush in. Edstaston draws a pair of small pistols from his boots, and points one at the Sergeant and the other at Patiomkin, who is sitting on the floor, somewhat sobered. The soldiers stand irresolute.

EDSTASTON. Stand off. [*To Patiomkin*] Order them off, if

you dont want a bullet through your silly head.

THE SERGEANT. Little Father: tell us what to do. Our lives are yours; but God knows you are not fit to die.

PATIOMKIN [*absurdly self-possessed*] Get out.

THE SERGEANT. Little Father—

PATIOMKIN [*roaring*] Get out. Get out, all of you. [*They withdraw, much relieved at their escape from the pistol. Patiomkin attempts to rise and rolls over*]. Here! help me up, will you? Dont you see that I'm drunk and cant get up?

EDSTASTON [*suspiciously*] You want to get hold of me.

PATIOMKIN [*squatting resignedly against the chair on which his clothes hang*] Very well, then: I shall stay where I am, because I'm drunk and youre afraid of me.

EDSTASTON. I'm not afraid of you, damn you!

PATIOMKIN [*ecstatically*] Darling: your lips are the gates of truth. Now listen to me. [*He marks off the items of his statement with ridiculous stiff gestures of his head and arms, imitating a puppet*] You are Captain Whathisname; and your uncle is the Earl of Whatdyecallum; and your father is Bishop of Thingummybob; and you are a young man of the highest spr-promise (I told you I was drunk), educated at Cambridge, and got your step as captain in the field at the GLORIOUS battle of Bunker's Hill. Invalided home from America at the request of Aunt Fanny, Lady-in-Waiting to the Queen. All right, eh?

EDSTASTON. How do you know all this?

PATIOMKIN [*crowing fantastically*] In er lerrer, darling, darling, darling, darling. Lerrer you shewed me.

EDSTASTON. But you didnt read it.

PATIOMKIN [*flapping his fingers at him grotesquely*] Only one eye, darling. Cross eye. Sees everything. Read lerrer ince-ince-istastaneously. Kindly give me vinegar borle. Green borle. On'y to sober me. Too drunk to speak proply. If you would be so kind, darling. Green borle. [*Edstaston, still suspicious, shakes his head and keeps his pistols ready*]. Reach it myself. [*He reaches behind him up to the table, and snatches at the green bottle, from which he takes a copious draught.*

Its effect is appalling. His wry faces and agonized belchings are so heartrending that they almost upset Edstaston. When the victim at last staggers to his feet, he is a pale fragile nobleman, aged and quite sober, extremely dignified in manner and address, though shaken by his recent convulsions]. Young man: it is not better to be drunk than sober; but it is happier. Goodness is not happiness. That is an epigram. But I have overdone this. I am too sober to be good company. Let me redress the balance. [*He takes a generous draught of brandy, and recovers his geniality*]. Aha! Thats better. And now listen, darling. You must not come to court with pistols in your boots.

EDSTASTON. I have found them useful.

PATIOMKIN. Nonsense. I'm your friend. You mistook my intention because I was drunk. Now that I am sober—in moderation—I will prove that I am your friend. Have some diamonds. [*Roaring*] Hullo there! Dogs, pigs: hullo!

The Sergeant comes in.

THE SERGEANT. God be praised, Little Father: you are still spared to us.

PATIOMKIN. Tell them to bring some diamonds. Plenty of diamonds. And rubies. Get out. [*He aims a kick at the Sergeant, who flees*]. Put up your pistols, darling. I'll give you a pair with gold handgrips. I am your friend.

EDSTASTON [*replacing the pistols in his boots rather unwillingly*] Your Highness understands that if I am missing, or if anything happens to me, there will be trouble.

PATIOMKIN [*enthusiastically*] Call me darling.

EDSTASTON. It is not the English custom.

PATIOMKIN. You have no hearts, you English! [*Slapping his right breast*] Heart! Heart!

EDSTASTON. Pardon, your Highness: your heart is on the other side.

PATIOMKIN [*surprised and impressed*] Is it? You are learned! You are a doctor! You English are wonderful! We are barbarians, drunken pigs. Catherine does not know it; but we are. Catherine's a German. But I have given her a Russian heart [*he is about to slap himself again*].

EDSTASTON [*delicately*] The other side, your Highness.

PATIOMKIN [*maudlin*] Darling: a true Russian has a heart on both sides.

The Sergeant enters carrying a goblet filled with precious stones.

PATIOMKIN. Get out. [*He snatches the goblet and kicks the Sergeant out, not maliciously but from habit, indeed not noticing that he does it*]. Darling: have some diamonds. Have a fistful. [*He takes up a handful and lets them slip back through his fingers into the goblet, which he then offers to Edstaston*].

EDSTASTON. Thank you: I dont take presents.

PATIOMKIN [*amazed*] You refuse!

EDSTASTON. I thank your Highness; but it is not the custom for English gentlemen to take presents of that kind.

PATIOMKIN. Are you really an Englishman?

EDSTASTON [*bows*]!

PATIOMKIN. You are the first Englishman I ever saw refuse anything he could get. [*He puts the goblet on the table; then turns again to Edstaston*]. Listen, darling. You are a wrestler: a splendid wrestler. You threw me on my back like magic, though I could lift you with one hand. Darling: you are a giant, a paladin.

EDSTASTON [*complacently*] We wrestle rather well in my part of England.

PATIOMKIN. I have a Turk who is a wrestler: a prisoner of war. You shall wrestle with him for me. I'll stake a million roubles on you.

EDSTASTON [*incensed*] Damn you! do you take me for a prize-fighter? How dare you make me such a proposal?

PATIOMKIN [*with wounded feeling*] Darling: there is no pleasing you. Dont you like me?

EDSTASTON [*mollified*] Well, in a sort of way I do; though I dont know why I should. But my instructions are that I am to see the Empress; and—

PATIOMKIN. Darling: you shall see the Empress. A glorious woman, the greatest woman in the world. But lemme give you piece 'vice—pah! still drunk. They water my vinegar. [*He shakes himself; clears his throat; and resumes soberly*]. If Catherine takes a fancy to you, you may ask for roubles, diamonds, palaces, titles, orders, anything! and you may aspire to everything: field-marshal, admiral, minister, what you please—except Tsar.

EDSTASTON. I tell you I dont want to ask for anything. Do you suppose I am an adventurer and a beggar?

PATIOMKIN [*plaintively*] Why not, darling? *I* was an adventurer. *I* was a beggar.

EDSTASTON. Oh, you!

PATIOMKIN. Well: whats wrong with me?

EDSTASTON. You are a Russian. Thats different.

PATIOMKIN [*effusively*] Darling: I am a man; and you are a man; and Catherine is a woman. Woman reduces us all to the common denominator. [*Chuckling*]. Again an epigram! [*Gravely*] You understand it, I hope. Have you had a college education, darling? *I* have.

EDSTASTON. Certainly. I am a Bachelor of Arts.

PATIOMKIN. It is enough that you are a bachelor, darling: Catherine will supply the arts. Aha! Another epigram? I am in the vein today.

EDSTASTON [*embarrassed and a little offended*] I must ask your Highness to change the subject. As a visitor in Russia, I am the guest of the Empress; and I must tell you plainly that I have neither the right nor the disposition to speak lightly of her Majesty.

PATIOMKIN. You have conscientious scruples?

EDSTASTON. I have the scruples of a gentleman.

PATIOMKIN. In Russia a gentleman has no scruples. In Russia we face facts.

EDSTASTON. In England, sir, a gentleman never faces any facts if they are unpleasant facts.

PATIOMKIN. In real life, darling, all facts are unpleasant. [*Greatly pleased with himself*] Another epigram! Where is my accursed chancellor? these gems should be written down and recorded for posterity. [*He rushes to the table; sits down; and snatches up a pen. Then, recollecting himself,*] But I have not asked you to sit down. [*He rises and goes to the other chair*].

I am a savage: a barbarian. [*He throws the shirt and coat over the table on to the floor and puts his sword on the table*]. Be seated, Captain.

EDSTASTON. Thank you.

They bow to one another ceremoniously. Patiomkin's tendency to grotesque exaggeration costs him his balance: he nearly falls over Edstaston, who rescues him and takes the proffered chair.

PATIOMKIN [*resuming his seat*] By the way, what was the piece of advice I was going to give you?

EDSTASTON. As you did not give it, I dont know. Allow me to add that I have not asked for your advice.

PATIOMKIN. I give it to you unasked, delightful Englishman. I remember it now. It was this. Dont try to become Tsar of Russia.

EDSTASTON [*in astonishment*] I havnt the slightest intention—

PATIOMKIN. Not now; but you will have: take my word for it. It will strike you as a splendid idea to have conscientious scruples—to desire the blessing of the Church on your union with Catherine.

EDSTASTON [*rising in utter amazement*] My union with Catherine! Youre mad.

PATIOMKIN [*unmoved*] The day you hint at such a thing will be the day of your downfall. Besides, it is not lucky to be Catherine's husband. You know what happened to Peter?

EDSTASTON [*shortly: sitting down again*] I do not wish to discuss it.

PATIOMKIN. You think she murdered him?

EDSTASTON. I know that people have said so.

PATIOMKIN [*thunderously: springing to his feet*] It is a lie: Orloff murdered him. [*Subsiding a little*] He also knocked my eye out; but [*sitting down placidly*] I succeeded him for all that. And [*patting Edstaston's hand very affectionately*] I'm sorry to say, darling, that if you become Tsar, *I* shall murder you.

EDSTASTON [*ironically returning the caress*] Thank you. The occasion will not arise. [*Rising*] I have the honor to wish your Highness good morning.

PATIOMKIN [*jumping up and stopping him on his way to the door*] Tut tut! I'm going to take you to the Empress now, this very instant.

EDSTASTON. In these boots? Impossible! I must change.

PATIOMKIN. Nonsense! You shall come just as you are. You shall shew her your calves later on.

EDSTASTON. But it will take me only half an hour to—

PATIOMKIN. In half an hour it will be too late for the *petit lever*. Come along. Damn it, man, I must oblige the British ambassador, and the French ambassador, and old Fritz, and Monsieur Voltaire and the rest of them. [*He shouts rudely to the door*] Varinka! [*To Edstaston, with tears in his voice*] Varinka shall persuade you: nobody can refuse Varinka anything. My niece. A treasure, I assure you. Beautiful! devoted! fascinating! [*Shouting again*] Varinka: where the devil are you?

VARINKA [*returning*] I'll not be shouted for. You have the voice of a bear, and the manners of a tinker.

PATIOMKIN. Tsh-sh-sh. Little angel Mother: you must behave yourself before the English captain. [*He takes off his dressing-gown and throws it over the papers and the breakfasts; picks up his coat; and disappears behind the screen to complete his toilette*].

EDSTASTON. Madam! [*He bows*].

VARINKA [*curtseying*] Monsieur le Capitaine!

EDSTASTON. I must apologize for the disturbance I made, madam.

PATIOMKIN [*behind the screen*] You must not call her madam. You must call her Little Mother, and beautiful darling.

EDSTASTON. My respect for the lady will not permit it.

VARINKA. Respect! How can you respect the niece of a savage?

EDSTASTON [*deprecating*] Oh, madam!

VARINKA. Heaven is my witness, Little English Father, we need someone who is not afraid of him. He is so strong!

I hope you will throw him down on the floor many, many, many times.

PATIOMKIN [*behind the screen*] Varinka!

VARINKA. Yes?

PATIOMKIN. Go and look through the keyhole of the Imperial bed-chamber; and bring me word whether the Empress is awake yet.

VARINKA. Fi donc! I do not look through keyholes.

PATIOMKIN [*emerging, having arranged his shirt and put on his diamonded coat*] You have been badly brought up, little darling. Would any lady or gentleman walk unannounced into a room without first looking through the keyhole? [*Taking his sword from the table and putting it on*] The great thing in life is to be simple; and the perfectly simple thing is to look through keyholes. Another epigram: the fifth this morning! Where is my fool of a chancellor? Where is Popof?

EDSTASTON [*choking with suppressed laughter*] !!!!

PATIOMKIN [*gratified*] Darling: you appreciate my epigram.

EDSTASTON. Excuse me. Pop off! Ha! ha! I cant help laughing. Whats his real name, by the way, in case I meet him?

VARINKA [*surprised*] His real name? Popof, of course. Why do you laugh, Little Father?

EDSTASTON. How can anyone with a sense of humor help laughing? Pop off! [*He is convulsed*].

VARINKA [*looking at her uncle, taps her forehead significantly*] !!

PATIOMKIN [*aside to Varinka*] No: only English. He will amuse Catherine. [*To Edstaston*] Come! you shall tell the joke to the Empress: she is by way of being a humorist. [*He takes him by the arm, and leads him towards the door*].

EDSTASTON [*resisting*] No, really. I am not fit—

PATIOMKIN. Persuade him, Little angel Mother.

VARINKA [*taking his other arm*] Yes, yes, yes, Little English Father: God knows it is your duty to be brave and wait on the Empress. Come.

EDSTASTON. No. I had rather—

PATIOMKIN [*hauling him along*] Come.

VARINKA [*pulling him and coaxing him*] Come, little love: you cant refuse me.

EDSTASTON. But how can I?

PATIOMKIN. Why not? She wont eat you.

VARINKA. She will; but you must come.

EDSTASTON. I assure you—it is quite out of the question —my clothes.

VARINKA. You look perfect.

PATIOMKIN. Come along, darling.

EDSTASTON [*struggling*] Impossible—

VARINKA. Come, come, come.

EDSTASTON. No. Believe me—I dont wish—I—

VARINKA. Carry him, uncle.

PATIOMKIN [*lifting him in his arms like a father carrying a little boy*] Yes: I'll carry you.

EDSTASTON. Dash it all, this is ridiculous!

VARINKA [*seizing his ankles and dancing as he is carried out*] You must come. If you kick you will blacken my eyes.

PATIOMKIN. Come, baby, come.

By this time they have made their way through the door and are out of hearing.

THE SECOND SCENE

THE Empress's petit lever. The central doors are closed. Those who enter through them find on their left, on a dais of two broad steps, a magnificent curtained bed. Beyond it a door in the panelling leads to the Empress's cabinet. Near the foot of the bed, in the middle of the room, stands a gilt chair, with the Imperial arms carved and the Imperial monogram embroidered.

The Court is in attendance, standing in two melancholy rows down the side of the room opposite to the bed, solemn, bored, waiting for the Empress to awaken. The Princess Dashkoff, with two ladies, stands a little in front of the line of courtiers, by the Imperial chair. Silence, broken only by the yawns and whispers of the courtiers. Naryshkin, the Chamberlain, stands by the head of the bed.

A loud yawn is heard from behind the curtains.

NARYSHKIN [*holding up a warning hand*] Ssh!

The courtiers hastily cease whispering; dress up their lines; and stiffen. Dead silence. A bell tinkles within the curtains. Naryshkin and the Princess solemnly draw them and reveal the Empress.

Catherine turns over on her back, and stretches herself.

CATHERINE [*yawning*] Heigho—ah—yah—ah—ow—what o'clock is it? [*Her accent is German*].

NARYSHKIN [*formally*] Her Imperial Majesty is awake. [*The Court falls on its knees*].

ALL. Good morning to your Majesty.

NARYSHKIN. Half-past ten, Little Mother.

CATHERINE [*sitting up abruptly*] Potztausend! [*Contemplating the kneeling courtiers*] Oh, get up, get up. [*All rise*]. Your etiquette bores me. I am hardly awake in the morning before it begins. [*Yawning again, and relapsing sleepily against her pillows*] Why do they do it, Naryshkin?

NARYSHKIN. God knows it is not for your sake, Little Mother. But you see if you were not a great queen they would all be nobodies.

CATHERINE [*sitting up*] They make me do it to keep up

their own little dignities? So?

NARYSHKIN. Exactly. Also because if they didnt you might have them flogged, dear Little Mother.

CATHERINE [*springing energetically out of bed and seating herself on the edge of it*] Flogged! I! A Liberal Empress! A philosopher! You are a barbarian, Naryshkin. [*She rises and turns to the courtiers*] And then, as if I cared! [*She turns again to Naryshkin*] You should know by this time that I am frank and original in character, like an Englishman. [*She walks about restlessly*]. No: what maddens me about all this ceremony is that I am the only person in Russia who gets no fun out of my being Empress. You all glory in me: you bask in my smiles: you get titles and honors and favors from me: you are dazzled by my crown and my robes: you feel splendid when you have been admitted to my presence; and when I say a gracious word to you, you talk about it to everyone you meet for a week afterwards. But what do *I* get out of it? Nothing. [*She throws herself into the chair. Naryshkin deprecates with a gesture: she hurls an emphatic repetition at him*] Nothing!! I wear a crown until my neck aches: I stand looking majestic until I am ready to drop: I have to smile at ugly old ambassadors and frown and turn my back on young and handsome ones. Nobody gives me anything. When I was only an Archduchess, the English ambassador used to give me money whenever I wanted it—or rather whenever he wanted to get anything out of my sacred predecessor Elizabeth [*the Court bows to the ground*]; but now that I am Empress he never gives me a kopek. When I have headaches and colics I envy the scullerymaids. And you are not a bit grateful to me for all my care of you, my work, my thought, my fatigue, my sufferings.

THE PRINCESS DASHKOFF. God knows, Little Mother, we all implore you to give your wonderful brain a rest. That is why you get headaches. Monsieur Voltaire also has headaches. His brain is just like yours.

CATHERINE. Dashkoff: what a liar you are! [*Dashkoff curtsies with impressive dignity*]. And you think you are flattering me! Let me tell you I would not give a rouble to have the brains of all the philosophers in France. What is our business for today?

NARYSHKIN. The new museum, Little Mother. But the model will not be ready until tonight.

CATHERINE [*rising eagerly*] Yes: the museum. An enlightened capital should have a museum. [*She paces the chamber with a deep sense of the importance of the museum*]. It shall be one of the wonders of the world. I must have specimens: specimens, specimens, specimens.

NARYSHKIN. You are in high spirits this morning, Little Mother.

CATHERINE [*with sudden levity*] I am always in high spirits, even when people do not bring me my slippers. [*She runs to the chair and sits down, thrusting her feet out*].

The two ladies rush to her feet, each carrying a slipper. Catherine, about to put her feet into them, is checked by a disturbance in the antechamber.

PATIOMKIN [*carrying Edstaston through the antechamber*] Useless to struggle. Come along, beautiful baby darling. Come to Little Mother. [*He sings*]

March him baby,
Baby, baby,
Lit-tle ba-by bumpkins.

VARINKA [*joining in to the same doggerel in canon, a third above*] March him, baby, etc., etc.

EDSTASTON [*trying to make himself heard*] No, no. This is carrying a joke too far. I must insist. Let me down! Hang it, will you let me down! Confound it! No, no. Stop playing the fool, will you? We dont understand this sort of thing in England. I shall be disgraced. Let me down.

CATHERINE [*meanwhile*] What a horrible noise! Naryshkin: see what it is.

Naryshkin goes to the door.

CATHERINE [*listening*] That is Prince Patiomkin.

NARYSHKIN [*calling from the door*] Little Mother: a stranger.

Catherine plunges into bed again and covers herself up. Patiomkin, followed by Varinka, carries Edstaston in; dumps him down on the foot of the bed; and staggers past it to the cabinet door. Varinka joins the courtiers at the opposite side of the room. Catherine, blazing with wrath, pushes Edstaston off her bed on to the floor; gets out of bed; and turns on Patiomkin with so terrible an expression that all kneel down hastily except Edstaston, who is sprawling on the carpet in angry confusion.

CATHERINE. Patiomkin: how dare you? [*Looking at Edstaston*] What is this?

PATIOMKIN [*on his knees: tearfully*] I dont know. I am drunk. What is this, Varinka?

EDSTASTON [*scrambling to his feet*] Madam: this drunken ruffian—

PATIOMKIN. Thas true. Drungn ruffian. Took dvantage of my being drunk. Said: take me to Lil angel Mother. Take me to beaufl Empress. Take me to the grea'st woman on earth. Thas whas he said. I took him. I was wrong. I am not sober.

CATHERINE. Men have grown sober in Siberia for less, Prince.

PATIOMKIN. Serve em right! Sgusting habit. Ask Varinka.

Catherine turns her face from him to the Court. The courtiers see that she is trying not to laugh, and know by experience that she will not succeed. They rise, relieved and grinning.

VARINKA. It is true. He drinks like a pig.

PATIOMKIN [*plaintively*] No: not like pig. Like prince. Lil Mother made poor Patiomkin prince. Whas use being prince if I maynt drink?

CATHERINE [*biting her lips*] Go. I am offended.

PATIOMKIN. Dont scold, Ll Mother.

CATHERINE [*imperiously*] Go.

PATIOMKIN [*rising unsteadily*] Yes: go. Go bye bye. Very sleepy. Berr go bye bye than go Siberia. Go bye bye in Lil Mother's bed. [*He pretends to make an attempt to get into the bed*].

CATHERINE [*energetically pulling him back*] No, no! Patiomkin! What are you thinking of? [*He falls like a log on the floor, apparently dead drunk*].

THE PRINCESS DASHKOFF. Scandalous! An insult to your Imperial Majesty!

CATHERINE. Dashkoff: you have no sense of humor. [*She steps down to the floor level and looks indulgently at Patiomkin. He gurgles brutishly. She has an impulse of disgust*]. Hog. [*She kicks him as hard as she can*]. Oh! You have broken my toe. Brute. Beast. Dashkoff is quite right. Do you hear?

PATIOMKIN. If you ask my pi-pinion of Dashkoff, my pipinion is that Dashkoff is drunk. Scanlous. Poor Patiomkin go bye bye. [*He relapses into drunken slumbers*].

Some of the courtiers move to carry him away.

CATHERINE [*stopping them*] Let him lie. Let him sleep it off. If he goes out it will be to a tavern and low company for the rest of the day. [*Indulgently*] There! [*She takes a pillow from the bed and puts it under his head; then turns to Edstaston; surveys him with perfect dignity; and asks, in her queenliest manner*] Varinka: who is this gentleman?

VARINKA. A foreign captain: I cannot pronounce his name. I think he is mad. He came to the Prince and said he must see your Majesty. He can talk of nothing else. We could not prevent him.

EDSTASTON [*overwhelmed by this apparent betrayal*] Oh! Madam: I am perfectly sane: I am actually an Englishman. I should never have dreamt of approaching your Majesty without the fullest credentials. I have letters from the English ambassador, from the Prussian ambassador. [*Naively*]. But everybody assured me that Prince Patiomkin is all-powerful with your Majesty; so I naturally applied to him.

PATIOMKIN [*interrupts the conversation by an agonized wheezing groan, as of a donkey beginning to bray*]!!!

CATHERINE [*like a fishfag*] Schweig, du Hund. [*Resuming her impressive Royal manner*] Have you never been taught, sir, how a gentleman should enter the presence of a sovereign.

EDSTASTON. Yes, Madam; but I did not enter your presence: I was carried.

CATHERINE. But you say you asked the Prince to carry you.

EDSTASTON. Certainly not, Madam. I protested against it with all my might. I appeal to this lady to confirm me.

VARINKA [*pretending to be indignant*] Yes: you protested. But, all the same, you were very very v e r y anxious to see her Imperial Majesty. You blushed when the Prince spoke of her. You threatened to strike him across the face with your sword because you thought he did not speak enthusiastically enough of her. [*To Catherine*] Trust me: he has seen your Imperial Majesty before.

CATHERINE [*to Edstaston*] You have seen us before?

EDSTASTON. At the review, Madam.

VARINKA [*triumphantly*] Aha! I knew it. Your Majesty wore the hussar uniform. He saw how radiant! how splendid! your Majesty looked. Oh! he has dared to admire your Majesty. Such insolence is not to be endured.

EDSTASTON. All Europe is a party to that insolence, Madam.

THE PRINCESS DASHKOFF. All Europe is content to do so at a respectful distance. It is possible to admire her Majesty's policy and her eminence in literature and philosophy without performing acrobatic feats in the Imperial bed.

EDSTASTON. I know nothing about her Majesty's eminence in policy or philosophy: I dont pretend to understand such things. I speak as a practical man. And I never knew that foreigners had any policy. I always thought that policy was Mr Pitt's business.

CATHERINE [*lifting her eyebrows*] So?

VARINKA. What else did you presume to admire her Majesty for, pray?

EDSTASTON [*addled*] Well, I—I—I—that is, I—[*He stammers himself dumb*].

CATHERINE [*after a pitiless silence*] We are waiting for your answer.

EDSTASTON. But I never said I admired your Majesty. The lady has twisted my words.

VARINKA. You dont admire her, then?

EDSTASTON. Well, I—naturally—of course, I cant deny that the uniform was very becoming—perhaps a little unfeminine—still—

Dead silence. Catherine and the Court watch him stonily. He is wretchedly embarrassed.

CATHERINE [*with cold majesty*] Well, sir: is that all you have to say?

EDSTASTON. Surely there is no harm in noticing that er—that er—[*He stops again*].

CATHERINE. Noticing that er—? [*He gazes at her, speechless, like a fascinated rabbit. She repeats fiercely*] That er—?

EDSTASTON [*startled into speech*] Well, that your Majesty was—was—[*Soothingly*] Well, let me put it this way: that it was rather natural for a man to admire your Majesty without being a philosopher.

CATHERINE [*suddenly smiling and extending her hand to him to be kissed*] Courtier!

EDSTASTON [*kissing it*] Not at all. Your Majesty is very good. I have been very awkward; but I did not intend it. I am rather stupid, I am afraid.

CATHERINE. Stupid! By no means. Courage, Captain: we are pleased. [*He falls on his knee. She takes his cheeks in her hands; turns up his face; and adds*] We are greatly pleased. [*She slaps his cheek coquettishly: he bows almost to his knee*]. The *petit lever* is over. [*She turns to go into the cabinet, and stumbles against the supine Patiomkin*]. Ach! [*Edstaston springs to her assistance, seizing Patiomkin's heels and shifting him out of the Empress's path*]. We thank you, Captain.

He bows gallantly, and is rewarded by a very gracious smile. Then Catherine goes into her cabinet, followed by the Princess Dashkoff, who turns at the door to make a deep curtsey to Edstaston.

VARINKA. Happy Little Father! Remember: *I* did this for you. [*She runs out after the Empress*].

Edstaston, somewhat dazed, crosses the room to the courtiers, and is received with marked deference, each courtier making him a profound bow or curtsey before withdrawing through the central doors. He returns each obeisance with a nervous jerk, and turns away from it, only to find another courtier bowing at the other side. The process finally reduces him to distraction, as he bumps into one in the act of bowing to another and then has to bow his apologies. But at last they are all gone except Naryshkin.

EDSTASTON. Ouf!

PATIOMKIN [*jumping up vigorously*] You have done it, darling. Superbly! Beautifully!

EDSTASTON [*astonished*] Do you mean to say you are not drunk?

PATIOMKIN. Not dead drunk, darling. Only diplomatically drunk. As a drunken hog, I have done for you in five minutes what I could not have done in five months as a sober man. Your fortune is made. She likes you.

EDSTASTON. The devil she does!

PATIOMKIN. Why? Arnt you delighted?

EDSTASTON. Delighted! Gracious heavens, man, I am engaged to be married.

PATIOMKIN. What matter? She is in England, isnt she?

EDSTASTON. No. She has just arrived in St Petersburg.

THE PRINCESS DASHKOFF [*returning*] Captain Edstaston: the Empress is robed, and commands your presence.

EDSTASTON. Say I was gone before you arrived with the message. [*He hurries out. The other three, too taken aback to stop him, stare after him in the utmost astonishment*].

NARYSHKIN [*turning from the door*] She will have him knouted. He is a dead man.

THE PRINCESS DASHKOFF. But what am *I* to do? I cannot take such an answer to the Empress.

PATIOMKIN. P-P-P-P-P-P-W-W-W-W-W-rrrrrr [*a long puff, turning into a growl*]! [*He spits*]. I must kick somebody.

NARYSHKIN [*flying precipitately through the central doors*] No, no. Please.

THE PRINCESS DASHKOFF [*throwing herself recklessly in front of Patiomkin as he starts in pursuit of the Chamberlain*] Kick me. Disable me. It will be an excuse for not going back to her. Kick me hard.

PATIOMKIN. Yah! [*He flings her on the bed and dashes after Naryshkin*].

THE THIRD SCENE

IN a terrace garden overlooking the Neva. Claire, a robust young English lady, is leaning on the river wall. She turns expectantly on hearing the garden gate opened and closed. Edstaston hurries in. With a cry of delight she throws her arms round his neck.

CLAIRE. Darling!

EDSTASTON [*making a wry face*] Dont call me darling.

CLAIRE [*amazed and chilled*] Why?

EDSTASTON. I have been called darling all the morning.

CLAIRE [*with a flash of jealousy*] By whom?

EDSTASTON. By everybody. By the most unutterable swine. And if we do not leave this abominable city now: do you hear? now: I shall be called darling by the Empress.

CLAIRE [*with magnificent snobbery*] She would not dare. Did you tell her you were engaged to me?

EDSTASTON. Of course not.

CLAIRE. Why?

EDSTASTON. Because I didnt particularly want to have you knouted, and to be hanged or sent to Siberia myself.

CLAIRE. What on earth do you mean?

EDSTASTON. Well, the long and short of it is—dont think me a coxcomb, Claire: it is too serious to mince matters—I have seen the Empress; and—

CLAIRE. Well: you wanted to see her.

EDSTASTON. Yes; but the Empress has seen me.

CLAIRE. She has fallen in love with you.

EDSTASTON. How did you know?

CLAIRE. Dearest: as if anyone could help it.

EDSTASTON. Oh, dont make me feel like a fool. But, though it does sound conceited to say it, I flatter myself I'm better looking than Patiomkin and the other hogs she is accustomed to. Anyhow, I darent risk staying.

CLAIRE. What a nuisance! Mamma will be furious at having to pack, and at missing the Court ball this evening.

EDSTASTON. I cant help that. We havnt a moment to lose.

CLAIRE. May I tell her she will be knouted if we stay?

EDSTASTON. Do, dearest.

He kisses her and lets her go, expecting her to run into the house.

CLAIRE [*pausing thoughtfully*] Is she—is she good-looking when you see her close?

EDSTASTON. Not a patch on you, dearest.

CLAIRE [*jealous*] Then you did see her close?

EDSTASTON. Fairly close.

CLAIRE. Indeed! How close? No: thats silly of me: I will tell mamma. [*She is going out when Naryshkin enters with the Sergeant and a squad of soldiers*]. What do you want here?

The Sergeant goes to Edstaston; plumps down on his knees; and takes out a magnificent pair of pistols with gold grips. He proffers them to Edstaston, holding them by the barrels.

NARYSHKIN. Captain Edstaston: his Highness Prince Patiomkin sends you the pistols he promised you.

THE SERGEANT. Take them, Little Father; and do not forget us poor soldiers who have brought them to you; for God knows we get but little to drink.

EDSTASTON [*irresolutely*] But I cant take these valuable things. By Jiminy, though, theyre beautiful! Look at them, Claire.

As he is taking the pistols the kneeling Sergeant suddenly drops them; flings himself forward; and embraces Edstaston's hips to prevent him from drawing his own pistols from his boots.

THE SERGEANT. Lay hold of him there. Pin his arms. I have his pistols. [*The soldiers seize Edstaston*].

EDSTASTON. Ah, would you, damn you! [*He drives his knee into the Sergeant's epigastrium, and struggles furiously with his captors*].

THE SERGEANT [*rolling on the ground, gasping and groaning*] Owgh! Murder! Holy Nicholas! Owwwgh!

CLAIRE. Help! help! They are killing Charles. Help!

NARYSHKIN [*seizing her and clapping his hand over her mouth*] Tie him neck and crop. Ten thousand blows of the stick if you let him go. [*Claire twists herself loose; turns on him; and cuffs him furiously*] Yow—ow! Have mercy, Little Mother.

CLAIRE. You wretch! Help! Help! Police! We are being murdered. Help!

The Sergeant, who has risen, comes to Naryshkin's rescue, and grasps Claire's hands, enabling Naryshkin to gag her again. By this time Edstaston and his captors are all rolling on the ground together. They get Edstaston on his back and fasten his wrists together behind his knees. Next they put a broad strap round his ribs. Finally they pass a pole through this breast strap and through the wrist strap and lift him by it, helplessly trussed up, to carry him off. Meanwhile he is by no means suffering in silence.

EDSTASTON [*gasping*] You shall hear more of this. Damn you, will you untie me? I will complain to the ambassador. I will write to the Gazette. England will blow your trumpery little fleet out of the water and sweep your tinpot army into Siberia for this. Will you let me go? Damn you! Curse you! What the devil do you mean by it? I'll—I'll—I'll—[*he is carried out of hearing*].

NARYSHKIN [*snatching his hands from Claire's face with a scream, and shaking his finger frantically*] Agh! [*The Sergeant, amazed, lets go her hands*]. She has bitten me, the little vixen.

CLAIRE [*spitting and wiping her mouth disgustedly*] How dare you put your dirty paws on my mouth? Ugh! Psha!

THE SERGEANT. Be merciful, Little angel Mother.

CLAIRE. Do not presume to call me your little angel mother. Where are the police?

NARYSHKIN. We are the police in St Petersburg, little spitfire.

THE SERGEANT. God knows we have no orders to harm you, Little Mother. Our duty is done. You are well and strong; but I shall never be the same man again. He is a mighty and terrible fighter, as stout as a bear. He has broken my sweetbread with his strong knees. God knows poor folk should not be set upon such dangerous adversaries!

CLAIRE. Serve you right! Where have they taken Captain

Edstaston to?

NARYSHKIN [*spitefully*] To the Empress, little beauty. He has insulted the Empress. He will receive a hundred and one blows of the knout. [*He laughs and goes out, nursing his bitten finger*].

THE SERGEANT. He will feel only the first twenty; and he will be mercifully dead long before the end, little darling.

CLAIRE [*sustained by an invincible snobbery*] They dare not touch an English officer. I will go to the Empress myself: she cannot know who Captain Edstaston is—who we are.

THE SERGEANT. Do so in the name of the Holy Nicholas, little beauty.

CLAIRE. Dont be impertinent. How can I get admission to the palace?

THE SERGEANT. Everybody goes in and out of the palace, little love.

CLAIRE. But I must get into the Empress's presence. I must speak to her.

THE SERGEANT. You shall, dear Little Mother. You shall give the poor old Sergeant a rouble; and the blessed Nicholas will make your salvation his charge.

CLAIRE [*impetuously*] I will give you [*she is about to say fifty roubles, but checks herself cautiously*]—Well: I dont mind giving you two roubles if I can speak to the Empress.

THE SERGEANT [*joyfully*] I praise Heaven for you, Little Mother. Come. [*He leads the way out*]. It was the temptation of the devil that led your young man to bruise my vitals and deprive me of breath. We must be merciful to one another's faults.

THE FOURTH SCENE

A TRIANGULAR recess communicating by a heavily curtained arch with the huge ballroom of the palace. The light is subdued by red shades on the candles. In the wall adjoining that pierced by the arch is a door. The only piece of furniture is a very handsome chair on the arch side. In the ballroom they are dancing a polonaise to the music of a brass band.

Naryshkin enters through the door, followed by the soldiers carrying Edstaston, still trussed to the pole. Exhausted and dogged, he makes no sound.

NARYSHKIN. Halt. Get that pole clear of the prisoner. [*They dump Edstaston on the floor, and detach the pole. Naryshkin stoops over him and addresses him insultingly*]. Well! are you ready to be tortured? This is the Empress's private torture chamber. Can I do anything to make you quite comfortable? You have only to mention it.

EDSTASTON. Have you any back teeth?

NARYSHKIN [*surprised*] Why?

EDSTASTON. His Majesty King George the Third will send for six of them when the news of this reaches London; so look out, damn your eyes!

NARYSHKIN [*frightened*] Oh, I assure you I am only obeying my orders. Personally I abhor torture, and would save you if I could. But the Empress is proud; and what woman would forgive the slight you put upon her?

EDSTASTON. As I said before: Damn your eyes!

NARYSHKIN [*almost in tears*] Well, it isnt my fault. [*To the soldiers, insolently*] You know your orders? You remember what you have to do when the Empress gives you the word? [*The soldiers salute in assent*].

Naryshkin passes through the curtains, admitting a blare of music and a strip of the brilliant white candle-light from the chandeliers in the ballroom as he does so. The white light vanishes and the music is muffled as the curtains fall together behind him. Presently the band stops abruptly; and Naryshkin comes back through the curtains. He makes a warning gesture to the soldiers, who stand at attention. Then he moves the curtain to allow

Catherine to enter. She is in full Imperial regalia, and stops sternly just where she has entered. The soldiers fall on their knees.

CATHERINE. Obey your orders.

The soldiers seize Edstaston, and throw him roughly at the feet of the Empress.

CATHERINE [*looking down coldly on him*] Also [*the German word*], you have put me to the trouble of sending for you twice. You had better have come the first time.

EDSTASTON [*exsufflicate, and pettishly angry*] I havnt come either time. Ive been carried. I call it infernal impudence.

CATHERINE. Take care what you say.

EDSTASTON. No use. I daresay you look very majestic and very handsome; but I cant see you; and I am not intimidated. I am an Englishman; and you can kidnap me; but you cant bully me.

NARYSHKIN. Remember to whom you are speaking.

CATHERINE [*violently, furious at his intrusion*] Remember that dogs should be dumb. [*He shrivels*]. And do you, Captain, remember that famous as I am for my clemency, there are limits to the patience even of an Empress.

EDSTASTON. How is a man to remember anything when he is trussed up in this ridiculous fashion? I can hardly breathe. [*He makes a futile struggle to free himself*]. Here: dont be unkind, your Majesty: tell these fellows to unstrap me. You know you really owe me an apology.

CATHERINE. You think you can escape by appealing, like Prince Patiomkin, to my sense of humor?

EDSTASTON. Sense of humor! Ho! Ha, ha! I like that. Would anybody with a sense of humor make a guy of a man like this, and then expect him to take it seriously? I say: do tell them to loosen these straps.

CATHERINE [*seating herself*] Why should I, pray?

EDSTASTON. Why! Why!! Why, because theyre hurting me.

CATHERINE. People sometimes learn through suffering. Manners, for instance.

EDSTASTON. Oh, well, of course, if youre an ill-natured

woman, hurting me on purpose, I have nothing more to say.

CATHERINE. A monarch, sir, has sometimes to employ a necessary and salutary severity—

EDSTASTON [*interrupting her petulantly*] Quack! quack! quack!

CATHERINE. Donnerwetter!

EDSTASTON [*continuing recklessly*] This isnt severity: it's tomfoolery. And if you think it's reforming my character or teaching me anything, youre mistaken. It may be a satisfaction to you; but if it is, all I can say is that it's not an amiable satisfaction.

CATHERINE [*turning suddenly and balefully on Naryshkin*] What are you grinning at?

NARYSHKIN [*falling on his knees in terror*] Be merciful, Little Mother. My heart is in my mouth.

CATHERINE. Your heart and your mouth will be in two separate parts of your body if you again forget in whose presence you stand. Go. And take your men with you. [*Naryshkin crawls to the door. The soldiers rise*]. Stop. Roll that [*indicating Edstaston*] nearer. [*The soldiers obey*]. Not so close. Did I ask you for a footstool? [*She pushes Edstaston away with her foot*].

EDSTASTON [*with a sudden squeal*] Agh!!! I must really ask your Majesty not to put the point of your Imperial toe between my ribs. I am ticklesome.

CATHERINE. Indeed? All the more reason for you to treat me with respect, Captain. [*To the others*] Begone. How many times must I give an order before it is obeyed?

NARYSHKIN. Little Mother: they have brought some instruments of torture. Will they be needed?

CATHERINE [*indignantly*] How dare you name such abominations to a Liberal Empress? You will always be a savage and a fool, Naryshkin. These relics of barbarism are buried, thank God, in the grave of Peter the Great. My methods are more civilized. [*She extends her toe towards Edstaston's ribs*].

EDSTASTON [*shrieking hysterically*] Yagh! Ah! [*Furiously*] If your Majesty does that again I will write to the London Gazette.

CATHERINE [*to the soldiers*] Leave us. Quick! do you hear? Five thousand blows of the stick for the soldier who is in the room when I speak next. [*The soldiers rush out*]. Naryshkin: are you waiting to be knouted? [*Naryshkin backs out hastily*].

Catherine and Edstaston are now alone. Catherine has in her hand a sceptre or baton of gold. Wrapped round it is a new pamphlet, in French, entitled L'Homme aux Quarante Écus. She calmly unrolls this and begins to read it at her ease as if she were quite alone. Several seconds elapse in dead silence. She becomes more and more absorbed in the pamphlet, and more and more amused by it.

CATHERINE [*greatly pleased by a passage, and turning over the leaf*] Ausgezeichnet!

EDSTASTON. Ahem!

Silence. Catherine reads on.

CATHERINE. Wie komisch!

EDSTASTON. Ahem! ahem!

Silence.

CATHERINE [*soliloquizing enthusiastically*] What a wonderful author is Monsieur Voltaire! How lucidly he exposes the folly of this crazy plan for raising the entire revenue of the country from a single tax on land! how he withers it with his irony! how he makes you laugh whilst he is convincing you! how sure one feels that the proposal is killed by his wit and economic penetration: killed never to be mentioned again among educated people!

EDSTASTON. For Heaven's sake, Madam, do you intend to leave me tied up like this while you discuss the blasphemies of that abominable infidel? Agh!! [*She has again applied her toe*]. Oh! Oo!

CATHERINE [*calmly*] Do I understand you to say that Monsieur Voltaire is a great philanthropist and a great philosopher as well as the wittiest man in Europe?

EDSTASTON. Certainly not. I say that his books ought to

be burnt by the common hangman [*her toe touches his ribs*]. Yagh! Oh dont. I shall faint. I cant bear it.

CATHERINE. Have you changed you opinion of Monsieur Voltaire?

EDSTASTON. But you cant expect me as a member of the Church of England [*she tickles him*]—Agh! Ow! Oh Lord! he is anything you like. He is a philanthropist, a philosopher, a beauty: he ought to have a statue, damn him! [*she tickles him*] No! bless him! save him victorious, happy and glorious! Oh, let eternal honors crown his name: Voltaire thrice worthy on the rolls of fame! [*Exhausted*]. Now will you let me up? And look here! I can see your ankles when you tickle me: it's not ladylike.

CATHERINE [*sticking out her toe and admiring it critically*] Is the spectacle so disagreeable?

EDSTASTON. It's agreeable enough; only [*with intense expression*] for heaven's sake dont touch me in the ribs.

CATHERINE [*putting aside the pamphlet*] Captain Edstaston: why did you refuse to come when I sent for you?

EDSTASTON. Madam: I cannot talk tied up like this.

CATHERINE. Do you still admire me as much as you did this morning?

EDSTASTON. How can I possibly tell when I cant see you? Let me get up and look. I cant see anything now except my toes and yours.

CATHERINE. Do you still intend to write to the London Gazette about me?

EDSTASTON. Not if you will loosen these straps. Quick: loosen me. I'm fainting.

CATHERINE. I dont think you are [*tickling him*].

EDSTASTON. Agh! Cat!

CATHERINE. What [*she tickles him again*]!

EDSTASTON [*with a shriek*] No: angel, angel!

CATHERINE [*tenderly*] Geliebter!

EDSTASTON. I dont know a word of German; but that sounded kind. [*Becoming hysterical*] Little Mother, beautiful little darling angel mother: dont be cruel: untie me. Oh,

I beg and implore you. Dont be unkind. I shall go mad.

CATHERINE. You are expected to go mad with love when an Empress deigns to interest herself in you. When an Empress allows you to see her foot you should kiss it. Captain Edstaston: you are a booby.

EDSTASTON [*indignantly*] I am nothing of the kind. I have been mentioned in dispatches as a highly intelligent officer. And let me warn your Majesty that I am not so helpless as you think. The English Ambassador is in that ballroom. A shout from me will bring him to my side; and then where will your Majesty be?

CATHERINE. I should like to see the English Ambassador or anyone else pass through that curtain against my orders. It might be a stone wall ten feet thick. Shout your loudest. Sob. Curse. Scream. Yell [*she tickles him unmercifully*].

EDSTASTON [*frantically*] Ahowyow!!!! Agh! Ooh! Stop! Oh Lord! Ya-a-a-ah! [*A tumult in the ballroom responds to his cries*].

VOICES FROM THE BALLROOM. Stand back. You cannot pass. Hold her back there. The Empress's orders. It is out of the question. No, little darling, not in there. Nobody is allowed in there. You will be sent to Siberia. Dont let her through there, on your life. Drag her back. You will be knouted. It is hopeless, Mademoiselle: you must obey orders. Guard there! Send some men to hold her.

CLAIRE'S VOICE. Let me go. They are torturing Charles in there. I will go. How can you all dance as if nothing was happening? Let me go, I tell you. Let—me—go. [*She dashes through the curtain. No one dares follow her*].

CATHERINE [*rising in wrath*] How dare you?

CLAIRE [*recklessly*] Oh, dare your grandmother! Where is my Charles? What are they doing to him?

EDSTASTON [*shouting*] Claire: loosen these straps, in Heaven's name. Quick.

CLAIRE [*seeing him and throwing herself on her knees at his side*] Oh, how dare they tie you up like that! [*To Catherine*] You wicked wretch! You Russian savage! [*She pounces on the straps, and begins unbuckling them*].

CATHERINE [*conquering herself with a mighty effort*] Now self-control. Self-control, Catherine. Philosophy. Europe is looking on. [*She forces herself to sit down*].

EDSTASTON. Steady, dearest: it is the Empress. Call her your Imperial Majesty. Call her Star of the North, Little Mother, Little Darling: thats what she likes; but get the straps off.

CLAIRE. Keep quiet, dear: I cannot get them off if you move.

CATHERINE [*calmly*] Keep quite still, Captain [*she tickles him*].

EDSTASTON. Ow! Agh! Ahowyow!

CLAIRE [*stopping dead in the act of unbuckling the straps and turning sick with jealousy as she grasps the situation*] Was that what I thought was your being tortured?

CATHERINE [*urbanely*] That is the favorite torture of Catherine the Second, Mademoiselle. I think the Captain enjoys it very much.

CLAIRE. Then he can have as much more of it as he wants. I am sorry I intruded. [*She rises to go*].

EDSTASTON [*catching her train in his teeth and holding on like a bull-dog*] Dont go. Dont leave me in this horrible state. Loosen me. [*This is what he is saying; but as he says it with the train in his mouth it is not very intelligible*].

CLAIRE. Let go. You are undignified and ridiculous enough yourself without making me ridiculous. [*She snatches her train away*].

EDSTASTON. Ow! Youve nearly pulled my teeth out: youre worse than the Star of the North. [*To Catherine*] Darling Little Mother: you have a kind heart, the kindest in Europe. Have pity. Have mercy. I love you. [*Claire bursts into tears*]. Release me.

CATHERINE. Well, just to shew you how much kinder a Russian savage can be than an English one (though I am sorry to say I am a German) here goes! [*She stoops to loosen the straps*].

CLAIRE [*jealously*] You neednt trouble, thank you. [*She pounces on the straps; and the two set Edstaston free between them*]. Now get up, please; and conduct yourself with some dignity if you are not utterly demoralized.

EDSTASTON. Dignity! Ow! I cant. I'm stiff all over. I shall never be able to stand up again. Oh Lord! how it hurts! [*They seize him by the shoulders and drag him up*]. Yah! Agh! Wow! Oh! Mmmmmm! Oh, Little Angel Mother, dont ever do this to a man again. Knout him; kill him; roast him; baste him; head, hang, and quarter him; but dont tie him up like that and tickle him.

CATHERINE. Your young lady still seems to think that you enjoyed it.

CLAIRE. I know what I think. I will never speak to him again. Your Majesty can keep him, as far as I am concerned.

CATHERINE. I would not deprive you of him for worlds; though really I think he's rather a darling [*she pats his cheek*].

CLAIRE [*snorting*] So I see, indeed.

EDSTASTON. Dont be angry, dearest: in this country everybody's a darling. I'll prove it to you. [*To Catherine*] Will your Majesty be good enough to call Prince Patiomkin?

CATHERINE [*surprised into haughtiness*] Why?

EDSTASTON. To oblige me.

Catherine laughs good-humoredly and goes to the curtains and opens them. The band strikes up a Redowa.

CATHERINE [*calling imperiously*] Patiomkin! [*The music stops suddenly*]. Here! To me! Go on with your music there, you fools. [*The Redowa is resumed*].

The sergeant rushes from the ballroom to relieve the Empress of the curtain. Patiomkin comes in dancing with Varinka.

CATHERINE [*to Patiomkin*] The English captain wants you, little darling.

Catherine resumes her seat as Patiomkin intimates by a grotesque bow that he is at Edstaston's service. Varinka passes behind Edstaston and Claire, and posts herself on Claire's right.

EDSTASTON. Precisely. [*To Claire*] You observe, my love: "little darling." Well, if her Majesty calls him a darling, is it my fault that she calls me one too?

CLAIRE. I dont care: I dont think you ought to have done it. I am very angry and offended.

EDSTASTON. They tied me up, dear. I couldnt help it. I fought for all I was worth.

THE SERGEANT [*at the curtains*] He fought with the strength of lions and bears. God knows I shall carry a broken sweetbread to my grave.

EDSTASTON. You cant mean to throw me over, Claire. [*Urgently*] Claire. Claire.

VARINKA [*in a transport of sympathetic emotion, pleading with clasped hands to Claire*] Oh, sweet little angel lamb, he loves you: it shines in his darling eyes. Pardon him, pardon him.

PATIOMKIN [*rushing from the Empress's side to Claire and falling on his knees to her*] Pardon him, pardon him, little cherub! little wild duck! little star! little glory! little jewel in the crown of heaven!

CLAIRE. This is perfectly ridiculous.

VARINKA [*kneeling to her*] Pardon him, pardon him, little delight, little sleeper in a rosy cradle.

CLAIRE. I'll do anything if youll only let me alone.

THE SERGEANT [*kneeling to her*] Pardon him, pardon him, lest the mighty man bring his whip to you. God knows we all need pardon!

CLAIRE [*at the top of her voice*] I pardon him! I pardon him!

PATIOMKIN [*springing up joyfully and going behind Claire, whom he raises in his arms*] Embrace her, victor of Bunker's Hill. Kiss her till she swoons.

THE SERGEANT. Receive her in the name of the holy Nicholas.

VARINKA. She begs you for a thousand dear little kisses all over her body.

CLAIRE [*vehemently*] I do not. [*Patiomkin throws her into Edstaston's arms*]. Oh! [*The pair, awkward and shamefaced, recoil from one another, and remain utterly inexpressive*].

CATHERINE [*pushing Edstaston towards Claire*] There is no help for it, Captain. This is Russia, not England.

EDSTASTON [*plucking up some geniality, and kissing Claire ceremoniously on the brow*] I have no objection.

VARINKA [*disgusted*] Only one kiss! and on the forehead! Fish. See how I kiss, though it is only my horribly ugly old uncle [*she throws her arms round Patiomkin's neck and covers his face with kisses*].

THE SERGEANT [*moved to tears*] Sainted Nicholas: bless your lambs!

CATHERINE. Do you wonder now that I love Russia as I love no other place on earth?

NARYSHKIN [*appearing at the door*] Majesty: the model for the new museum has arrived.

CATHERINE [*rising eagerly and making for the curtains*] Let us go. I can think of nothing but my museum. [*In the archway she stops and turns to Edstaston, who has hurried to lift the curtain for her*]. Captain: I wish you every happiness that your little angel can bring you. [*For his ear alone*] I could have brought you more; but you did not think so. Farewell.

EDSTASTON [*kissing her hand, which, instead of releasing, he holds caressingly and rather patronizingly in his own*] I feel your Majesty's kindness so much that I really cannot leave you without a word of plain wholesome English advice.

CATHERINE [*snatching her hand away and bounding forward as if he had touched her with a spur*] Advice!!!

PATIOMKIN. Madman: take care!

NARYSHKIN. Advise the Empress!!

THE SERGEANT. Sainted Nicholas!

VARINKA. Hoohoo! [*a stifled splutter of laughter*].

[*exclaiming simultaneously*].

EDSTASTON [*following the Empress and resuming kindly but*

judicially] After all, though your Majesty is of course a great queen, yet when all is said, I am a man; and your Majesty is only a woman.

CATHERINE. Only a wo—[*she chokes*].

EDSTASTON [*continuing*] Believe me, this Russian extravagance will not do. I appreciate as much as any man the warmth of heart that prompts it; but it is overdone: it is hardly in the best taste: it is—really I must say it—it is not proper.

CATHERINE [*ironically, in German*] So!

EDSTASTON. Not that I cannot make allowances. Your Majesty has, I know, been unfortunate in your experience as a married woman—

CATHERINE [*furious*] Alle Wetter!!!

EDSTASTON [*sentimentally*] Dont say that. Dont think of him in that way. After all, he was your husband; and whatever his faults may have been, it is not for you to think unkindly of him.

CATHERINE [*almost bursting*] I shall forget myself.

EDSTASTON. Come! I am sure he really loved you; and you truly loved him.

CATHERINE [*controlling herself with a supreme effort*] No, Catherine. What would Voltaire say?

EDSTASTON. Oh, never mind that vile scoffer. Set an example to Europe, Madam, by doing what I am going to do. Marry again. Marry some good man who will be a strength and a support to your old age.

CATHERINE. My old—[*she again becomes speechless*].

EDSTASTON. Yes: we must all grow old, even the handsomest of us.

CATHERINE [*sinking into her chair with a gasp*] Thank you.

EDSTASTON. You will thank me more when you see your little ones round your knee, and your man there by the fireside in the winter evenings—by the way, I forgot that you have no firesides here in spite of the coldness of the climate; so shall I say by the stove?

CATHERINE. Certainly, if you wish. The stove, by all

means.

EDSTASTON [*impulsively*] Ah, Madam, abolish the stove: believe me, there is nothing like the good old open grate. Home! duty! happiness! they all mean the same thing; and they all flourish best on the drawing room hearthrug. [*Turning to Claire*] And now, my love, we must not detain the Queen: she is anxious to inspect the model of her museum, to which I am sure we wish every success.

CLAIRE [*coldly*] *I* am not detaining her.

EDSTASTON. Well, goodbye [*wringing Patiomkin's hand*], goo-oo-oodbye, Prince: come and see us if ever you visit England. Spire View, Deepdene, Little Mugford, Devon, will always find me. [*To Varinka, kissing her hand*] Goodbye, Mademoiselle: goodbye, Little Mother, if I may call you that just once. [*Varinka puts her up face to be kissed*]. Eh? No, no, no, no: you dont mean that, you know. Naughty! [*To the Sergeant*] Goodbye, my friend. You will drink our healths with this [*tipping him*].

THE SERGEANT. The blessed Nicholas will multiply your fruits, Little Father.

EDSTASTON. Goodbye, goodbye, goodbye, goodbye, goodbye, goodbye.

He goes out backwards bowing, with Claire curtseying, having been listened to in utter dumfoundedness by Patiomkin and Naryshkin, in childlike awe by Varinka, and with quite inexpressible feelings by Catherine. When he is out of sight she rises with clinched fists and raises her arms and her closed eyes to Heaven. Patiomkin, rousing himself from his stupor of amazement, springs to her like a tiger, and throws himself at her feet.

PATIOMKIN. What shall I do to him for you? Skin him alive? Cut off his eyelids and stand him in the sun? Tear his tongue out? What shall it be?

CATHERINE [*opening her eyes*] Nothing. But oh, if I could only have had him for my—for my—for my—

PATIOMKIN [*in a growl of jealousy*] For your lover?

CATHERINE [*with an ineffable smile*] No: for my museum.

TOO TRUE TO BE GOOD

(A POLITICAL EXTRAVAGANZA)

Written in 1931

First Performed Boston 1932

PREFACE

MONEY AND HAPPINESS

SOMEHOW my play, Too True To Be Good, has in performance excited an animosity and an enthusiasm which will hardly be accounted for by the printed text. Some of the spectators felt that they had had a divine revelation, and overlooked the fact that the eloquent gentleman through whose extremely active mouth they had received it was the most hopeless sort of scoundrel: that is, one whose scoundrelism consists in the absence of conscience rather than in any positive vices, and is masked by good looks and agreeable manners. The less intellectual journalist critics sulked as they always do when their poverty but not their will consents to their witnessing a play of mine; but over and above the resultant querulousness to which I have long been accustomed I thought I detected an unusual intensity of resentment, as if I had hit them in some new and unbearably sore spot.

Where, then, was the offence that so exceedingly disgruntled these unhappy persons? I think it must have been the main gist and moral of the play, which is not, as usual, that our social system is unjust to the poor, but that it is cruel to the rich. Our revolutionary writers have dwelt on the horrors of poverty. Our conventional and romantic writers have ignored those horrors, dwelling pleasantly on the elegances of an existence free from pecuniary care. The poor have been pitied for miseries which do not, unfortunately, make them unbearably miserable. But who has pitied the idle rich or really believed that they have a worse time of it than those who have to live on ten shillings a day or less, and earn it? My play is a story of three reckless young people who come into possession of, for the moment, unlimited riches, and set out to have a thoroughly good time with all the modern machinery of pleasure to aid them. The result is that they get nothing for their money but a multitude of worries and a maddening dissatisfaction.

I doubt whether this state of things is ever intentionally produced. We see a man apparently slaving to place his children in the position of my three adventurers; but on closer investigation we generally find that he does not care twopence of his children, and is wholly wrapped up in the fascinating game of making money. Like other games it is enjoyable only by people with an irresistible and virtually exclusive fancy for it, and enough arithmetical ability and flair for market values to play it well; but with these qualifications the poorest men can make the most astounding fortunes. They accumulate nothing but powers of extracting money every six months from their less acquisitive neighbors; and their children accumulate nothing but obligations to spend it. As between these two processes of bleeding and being bled, bleeding is the better fun. The vampire has a better time than the calf hung up by the heels with its throat cut. The money-getter spends less on his food, clothes, and amusements than his clerks do, and is happy. His wife and sons and daughters, spending fabulous sums on themselves, are no happier than their housemaids, if so happy; for the routine of fashion is virtually as compulsory as the routine of a housemaid, its dressing is as much dictated as her uniform, its snubbings are as humiliating, and its monotony is more tedious because more senseless and useless, not to mention that it must be pleasanter to be tipped than to tip. And, as I surmise, the housemaid's day off or evening off is really off: in those hard earned hours she ceases to be a housemaid and can be herself; but the lady of fashion never has a moment off: she has to be fashionable even in her little leisure, and dies without ever having had any self at all. Here and there you find rich ladies taking up occupations and interests which keep them so busy doing professional or public work that they might as well have five hundred a year as fifty thousand "for all the good it does them" as the poor say in their amazement when they see people who could afford to be fashionable and extravagant working hard and dressing rather plainly. But that requires a personal endowment of tastes and talents quite out of the common run.

I remember a soldier of the old never-do-well type drifting into a little Socialist Society which I happened to be addressing more than fifty years ago. As he had evidently blundered into the wrong shop and was half drunk, some of the comrades began to chaff him, and finally held me up to him as an example of the advantages of teetotalism. With the most complete conviction he denounced me as a hypocrite and a liar, affirming it to be a well-known and inexorable law of nature that no man with money in his pocket could pass a public house without going in for a drink.

THE OLD SOLDIER AND THE PUBLIC HOUSE

I have never forgotten that soldier, because his delusion, in less crude forms, and his conception of happiness, seem to afflict everybody in England more or less. When I say less crude forms I do not mean truer forms; for the soldier, being half drunk, was probably happier than he would have been if quite sober, whereas the plutocrat who has spent a hundred pounds in a day in the search for pleasure is not happier than if he had spent only five shillings. For it must be admitted that a private soldier, outside that surprising centre of culture, the Red Army of Russia, has so little to be happy about when sober that his case is hardly a fair one. But it serves to illustrate the moral of my play, which is, that our capitalistic system, with its golden exceptions of idle richery and its leaden rule of anxious poverty, is as desperate a failure from the point of view of the rich as of the poor. We are all amazed and incredulous, like the soldier, when we hear of the multimillionaire passing the public house without going in and drinking himself silly; and we envy his sons and daughters who do go in and drink themselves silly. The vulgar pub may be in fact a Palace Hotel, and the pints of beer or glasses of whisky an elaborate dinner with many courses and wines culminating in cigars and liqueurs; but the illusion and the results are cognate.

I therefore plead for a science of happiness to cure us of the miserable delusion that we can achieve it by becoming richer than our neighbors. Modern colossal fortunes have demonstrated its vanity. When country parsons were "passing rich with forty pounds a year" there was some excuse for believing that to be rich was to be happy, as the conception of riches did not venture beyond enough to pay for the necessities of a cultivated life. A hundred years ago Samuel Warren wrote a famous novel about a man who became enormously rich. The title of the novel was Ten Thousand a Year; and this, to any resident Irish family in my boyhood, represented an opulence beyond which only Lords Lieutenant and their like could aspire. The scale has changed since then. I have just seen in the papers a picture of the funeral of a shipping magnate whose income, if the capital value of the property left by him be correctly stated, must have been over four thousand pounds a day or a million and a half a year. If happiness is to be measured by riches he must have been fourteen thousand times as happy as the laborer lucky enough to be earning two pounds a week. Those who believe that riches are the reward of virtue are bound to conclude that he was also fourteen thousand times as sober, honest, and industrious, which would lead to the quaint conclusion that if he drank a bottle of wine a day the laborer must have drunk fourteen thousand.

THE UNLOADING MILLIONAIRES

This is so obviously monstrous that it may now be dismissed as an illusion of the poor who know nothing of the lives of the rich. Poverty, when it involves continual privation and anxiety, is, like toothache, so painful that the victim can desire nothing happier than the cessation of the pain. But it takes no very extraordinary supply of money to enable a humble person to say "I want for nothing"; and when that modest point is reached the power of money to produce happiness vanishes, and the trouble which an excess of it brings begins to assert itself, and finally reaches a point at which the multimillionaires are seen frantically unloading on charitable, educational, scientific, religious, and even (though rarely) artistic and political "causes" of all kinds, mostly without stopping to examine whether the causes produce any effects, and if so what effects. And far from suffering a loss of happiness every time they give away a thousand pounds, they find themselves rather in the enviable state of mind of the reveller in The Pilgrim's Progress with his riddle "There was a man, though some did think him mad, the more he gave away the more he had."

DELUSIONS OF POVERTY

The notion that the rich must be happy is complemented by the delusion that the poor must be miserable. Our society is so constituted that most people remain all their lives in the condition in which they were born, and have to depend on their imagination for their notions of what it is like to be in the opposite condition. The upstarts and the downstarts, though we hear a great deal about them either as popular celebrities or criminals, are exceptional. The rich, it is said, do not know how the poor live; but nobody insists on the more mischievous fact that the poor do not know how the rich live. The rich are a minority; and they are not consumed with envy of the poor. But the poor are a huge majority and they are so demoralized by the notion that they would be happy if only they were rich, that they make themselves poorer, if hopefuller, by backing horses and buying sweepstake tickets on the chance of realizing their daydreams of unearned fortunes. Our penny newspapers now depend for their circulation, and consequently for their existence, on the sale of what are virtually lottery coupons. The real opposition to Socialism comes from the fear (well founded) that it would cut off the possibilities of becoming rich beyond those dreams of avarice which our capitalist system encourages. The odds against a poor person becoming a millionaire are of astronomical magnitude; but they are sufficient to establish and maintain the Totalisator as a national institution, and to produce unlimited daydreams of bequests from imaginary long lost uncles in Australia or a lucky ticket in the Calcutta or Irish Sweeps.

TRYING IT FOR AN HOUR

Besides, even quite poor people save up for holidays during which they can be idle and rich, if not for life, at least for an hour, an afternoon, or even a week. And for the poor these moments derive such a charm from the change from the monotony of daily toil and servitude, that the most intolerable hardships and discomforts and fatigues in excursion trains and overcrowded lodgings seem delightful, and leave the reveller with a completely false notion of what a lifetime of such revelry would be.

I maintain that nobody with a sane sense of values can feel that the sole prize which our villainous capitalist system has to offer, the prize of admission to the ranks of the idle rich, can possibly confer either happiness or health or freedom on its winner. No one can convict me of crying sour grapes; for during the last thirty-five years I have been under no compulsion to work, nor had any material privation or social ostracism to fear as a consequence of not working. But, like all the intelligent rich people of my acquaintance, I have worked as hard, ate and drunk no more, and dressed no better than when I had to work or starve. When my pockets were empty I did not buy any of the luxuries in the London shops because I had no money to buy them with. When, later on, I had enough to buy anything that London could tempt me with, the result was the same: I returned home day after day without having made a single purchase. And I am no ascetic: no man alive is freer than I from the fancy that selfmortification will propitiate a spiteful deity or increase my balance in a salvation bank in a world beyond the grave. I would and could live the life of the idle rich if I liked it; and my sole reason for not living it is that I dont like it. I have every opportunity of observing it both in its daily practice and its remoter results; and I know that a year of it would make me more unhappy than anything else of an accepted kind that I can imagine. For, just as the beanfeaster can live like a lord for an afternoon, and the Lancashire factory operative have a gorgeous week at Blackpool when the wakes are on, so I have had my afternoon as an idle rich man, and know only too well what it is like. It makes me feel suicidal.

You may say that I am an exceptional man. So I am, in respect of being able to write plays and books; but as everybody is exceptional in respect of being able to do something that most other people cannot do, there is nothing in that. Where I am really a little exceptional is in respect of my having experienced both poverty and riches, servitude and selfgovernment, and also having for some reason or other (possibly when I was assured in my infancy that some nasty medicine was delicious) made up my mind early in life never to let myself be persuaded that I am enjoying myslf gloriously when I am, as a matter of fact, being bored and pestered and plundered and worried and tired. You cannot humbug me on this point: I understand perfectly why Florence Nightingale fled from fashionable society in London to the horrors of the Crimean hospitals rather than behave like a lady, and why my neighbor Mr Apsley Cherry-Garrard, the sole survivor of what he calls with good reason "the worst journey in the world" through the Antarctic winter, was no poor sailorman driven by his need for daily bread to make a hard living before the mast, but a country gentleman opulent enough to choose the best that London society could offer him if he chose. Better the wards of the most terrible of field hospitals than a drawingroom in Mayfair: better the South Pole at its blackest six months winter night and its most murderous extremities of cold than Sunday by the Serpentine in the height of the season.

CONSOLATIONS OF THE LANDED GENTRY

To some extent this misery of riches is a new thing. Anyone who has the run of our country houses, with their great parks and gardens, their staffs of retainers, indoor and outdoor, and the local public work that is always available for the resident landed gentry, will at once challenge the unqualified assertion that the rich, in a lump, are miserable. Clearly they are nothing of the sort, any more than the poor in a lump. But then they are neither idle nor free. A lady with a big house to manage, and the rearing of a family to supervise, has a reasonably busy time of it even without counting her share in the routine of sport and entertainment and occasional travel which to people brought up to it is a necessary and important part of a well ordered life. The landed gentry have enough exercise and occupation and sense of social importance and utility to keep them on very good terms with themselves and their neighbors. If you suddenly asked them whether they really enjoyed their routine and whether they would not rather be Communists in Russia they would be more sincerely scandalized than if you had turned to them in church and asked them whether they really believed every clause in the Apostles' Creed. When one of their ugly ducklings becomes a revolutionist it is not because countryhouse life is idle, but because its activities are uncongenial and because the duckling has tastes or talents which it thwarts, or a faculty for social criticism which discovers that the great country house is not built on the eternal rock but on the sandy shore of an ocean of poverty which may at any moment pass from calm to tempest. On the whole, there is no reason why a territorial lady should not be as happy as her dairymaid, or her husband be as happy as his gamekeeper. The riches of the county families are attached to property; and the only miserable county people are those who will not work at their job.

PREFACE
MISERIES OF THE VAGRANT ROOTLESS RICH

But the new thing is riches detached from real property: that is, detached from work, from responsibility, from tradition, and from every sort of prescribed routine, even from the routine of going to the village church every Sunday, paying and receiving calls, and having every month set apart for the killing of some particular bird or animal. It means being a tramp without the daily recurrent obligation to beg or steal your dinner and the price of your bed. Instead, you have the daily question "What shall I do? Where shall I go?" and the daily answer "Do what you please: go where you like: it doesnt matter what you do or where you go." In short, the perfect liberty of which slaves dream because they have no experience of its horrors. Of course the answer of outraged Nature is drowned for a time by the luxury merchants shouting "Come and shop, whether you need anything or not. Come to our palace hotels. Come round the world in our liners. Come and wallow in our swimming pools. Come and see our latest model automobile: we have changed the inventor's design for-better-for-worse solely to give you an excuse for buying a new one and selling your old one at scrap iron prices. Come and buy our latest fashions in dress: you cannot possibly be seen in last season's garments." And so on and so forth. But the old questions come home to the rich tourists in the palace hotels and luxury liners just as they do to the tramps on the highroad. They come up when you have the latest car and the latest wardrobe and all the rest of it. The only want that money can satisfy without satiating for more than a few hours is the need for food and drink and sleep. So from one serious meal a day and two very minor ones you go on to three serious meals a day and two minor ones. Then you work another minor one between breakfast and lunch "to sustain you"; and you soon find that you cannot tackle any meal without a cocktail, and that you cannot sleep. That obliges you to resort to the latest soporific drug, guaranteed in the advertisements to have none of the ruinous effects of its equally guaranteed forerunner. Then comes the doctor, with his tonics, which are simply additional cocktails, and his sure knowledge that if he tells you the truth about yourself and refuses to prescribe the tonics and the drugs, his children will starve. If you indulge in such a luxury as a clerical spiritual adviser it is his duty to tell you that what is the matter with you is that you are an idle useless glutton and drunkard and that you are going to hell; but alas! he, like the doctor, cannot afford this, as he may have to ask you for a subscription tomorrow to keep his church going. And that is "Liberty: thou choicest treasure."

This sort of life has been made possible, and indeed inevitable, by what William Cobbett, who had a sturdy sense of vital values, denounced as The Funding System. It was a product of war, which obliged belligerent governments to obtain enormous sums from all and sundry by giving them in exchange the right to live for nothing on the future income of the country until their money was returned: a system now so popular among people with any money to spare that they can be induced to part with it only on condition that the Government promises not to repay it before a certain more or less remote day. When joint stock companies were formed to run big industrial concerns with money raised on the still more tempting terms that the money is never to be repaid, the system became so extensive that the idle upstart rich became a definitely mischievous and miserable class quite different in character from the old feudal rich.

THE REDEMPTION FROM PROPERTY

When I propose the abolition of our capitalistic system to redeem mankind from the double curse of poverty and riches, loud wailings arise. The most articulate sounds in the hubbub are to the effect that the wretched slaves of the curse will lose their liberty if they are forced to earn their living honorably. The retort that they have nothing to lose but their chains, with the addition that the gold chains are as bad as the iron ones, cannot silence them, because they think they are free, and have been brought up to believe that unless the country remains the private property of irresponsible owners maintaining a parliament to make any change impossible, with churches schools and universities to inculcate the sacredness of private property and party government disguised as religion education and democracy, civilization must perish. I am accused of every sort of reactionary extravagance by the people who think themselves advanced, and of every sort of destructive madness by people who thank God they are no wiser than their fathers.

Now I cannot profitably discuss politics religion and economics with terrified ignoramuses who understand neither what they are defending nor what they are attacking. But it happens that Mr Gilbert Chesterton, who is not an ignoramus and not in the least terrified, and whose very interesting conversion to Roman Catholicism has obliged him to face the problem of social organization fundamentally, discarding the Protestant impostures on English history which inspired the vigorous Liberalism of his salad days, has lately taken me to task for the entirely imaginary offence of advocating government by a committee of celebrities. To clear up the matter I have replied to Mr Chesterton very fully and in Catholic terms. Those who have read my reply in the magazines in which it appeared need read no further, unless they wish, as I should advise, to read it twice. For the benefit of the rest, and to put it on permanent record, here it is.

FUNDAMENTAL NATURAL CONDITIONS OF HUMAN SOCIETY

1. Government is necessary wherever two or three are gathered together—or two or three billions—for keeps.

2. Government is neither automatic nor abstract: it must be performed by human rulers and agents as best they can.

3. The business of the rulers is to check disastrously selfish or unexpected behavior on the part of individuals in social affairs.

4. This business can be done only by devizing and enforcing rules of social conduct codifying the greatest common measure of agreement as to the necessary sacrifice of individual liberty to the good of the community.

5. The paradox of government is that as the good of the community involves a maximum of individual liberty for all its members the rulers have at the same time to enslave everyone ruthlessly and to secure for everyone the utmost possible freedom.

6. In primitive communities people feed and lodge themselves without bothering the Government. In big civilizations this is impossible; so the first business of the Government is to provide for the production and distribution of wealth from day to day and the just sharing of the labor and leisure involved. Thus the individual citizen has to be compelled not only to behave himself properly, but to work productively.

7. The moral slavery of the compulsion to behave properly is a whole-time compulsion admitting of no liberty; but the personal slavery of the compulsion to work lasts only as many hours daily as suffice to discharge the economic duties of the citizen, the remaining hours (over and above those needed for feeding, sleeping, locomotion, etc.) being his leisure.

8. Leisure is the sphere of individual liberty: labor is the sphere of slavery.

9. People who think they can be honestly free all the time are idiots: people who seek whole-time freedom by putting their share of productive work on others are thieves.

10. The use of the word slavery to denote subjection to public government has grown up among the idiots and thieves, and is resorted to here only because it is expedient to explain things to fools according to their folly.

So much for the fundamental natural conditions of social organization. They are as completely beyond argument as the precession of the equinoxes; but they present different problems to different people. To the thief, for instance, the problem is how to evade his share in the labor of production, to increase his share in the distribution of the product, and to corrupt the Government so that it may protect and glorify his chicaneries instead of liquidating him. To Mr Chesterton the Distributist (or Extreme Left Communist) and Catholic (or Equalitarian Internationalist) it is how to select rulers who will govern righteously and impartially in accordance with the fundamental natural conditions.

The history of civilization is the history of the conflict between these rival views of the situation. The Pirate King, the Robber Baron, and the Manchester Man produced between them a government which they called the Empire, the State, the Realm, the Republic, or any other imposing name that did not give away its central purpose. The Chestertonians produced a government which they called The Church; and in due time the Last of the Chestertons joined this Catholic Church, like a very large ship entering a very small harbor, to the great peril of its many rickety old piers and wharves, and the swamping of all the small craft in its neighborhood. So let us see what the Catholic Church made of its governmental problem.

THE CATHOLIC SOLUTION

To begin with, the Church, being catholic, was necessarily democratic to the extent that its aim was to save the souls of all persons without regard to their age, sex, nationality, class or color. The nobleman who felt that God would not lightly damn a man of his quality received no countenance from the Church in that conviction. Within its fold all souls were equal before God.

But the Church did not draw the ridiculous conclusion that all men and women are equally qualified or equally desirous to legislate, to govern, to administer, to make decisions, to manage public affairs or even their own private affairs. It faced the fact that only about five per cent. of the population are capable of exercising these powers, and are certain to be corrupted by them unless they have an irresistible religious vocation for public work and a faith in its beneficence which will induce them to take vows to abstain from any profit that is not shared by all the rest, and from all indulgences which might blunt their consciences or subject them to the family influences so bitterly deprecated by Jesus.

This natural "called" minority was never elected in the scandalous way we call democratic. Its members were in the first instance self-elected: that is, they voluntarily lived holy lives and devoted themselves to the public welfare in obedience to the impulse of the Holy Ghost within them. This impulse was their vocation. They were called from above, not chosen by the uncalled. To protect themselves and obtain the necessary power, they organized themselves, and called their organization The Church. After that, the genuineness and sufficiency of the vocation of the new recruits were judged by The Church. If the judgment was favorable, and the candidates took certain vows, they were admitted to the official priesthood and set to govern as priests in the parish and spiritual directors in the family, all of them being eligible, if they had the requisite ability, for promotion to the work of governing the Church itself as bishops or cardinals, or to the supreme rank of Pope or Vicar of Christ on earth. And all this without the smallest reference to the opinions of the uncalled and unordained.

NEED FOR A COMMON FAITH

Now comes the question, why should persons of genuine vocation be asked to take vows before being placed in authority? Is not the vocation a sufficient guarantee of their wisdom?

No. Before priests can govern they must have a common faith as to the fundamental conditions of a stable human society. Otherwise the result might be an assembly of random men of genius unable to agree on a single legislative measure or point of policy. An ecumenical council consisting of Einstein and Colonel Lynch, Aquinas and Francis Bacon, Dante and Galileo, Lenin and Lloyd George, could seldom come to a unanimous decision, if indeed to any decision except in the negative against a minority of one, on any point beyond the capacity of a coroner's jury. The Pope must not be an eccentric genius presiding over a conclave of variously disposed cardinals: he must have an absolutely closed mind on what Herbert Spencer called Social Statics; and in this the cardinals must resemble and agree with him. What is more, they must to some extent represent the conscience of the common people; for it is evident that if they made laws and gave personal directions which would produce general horror or be taken as proofs of insanity their authority would collapse. Hence the need for vows committing all who take them to definite articles of faith on social statics, and to their logical consequences in law and custom. Such vows automatically exclude revolutionary geniuses, who, being uncommon, are not representative, more especially scientific geniuses, with whom it is a point of honor to have unconditionally open minds even on the most apparently sacred subjects.

RUSSIA REDISCOVERS THE CHURCH SYSTEM

A tremendous importance is given to a clear understanding of the Catholic system at this moment by the staggering fact that the biggest State in the modern world, having made a clean sweep of its Church by denouncing its religion as dope, depriving its priests and bishops of any greater authority than a quack can pick up at a fair, encouraging its most seriously minded children to form a League of the Godless, shooting its pious Tsar, turning its cathedrals into historical museums illustrating the infamies of ecclesiastical history and expressly entitling them anti-religious: in short, addressing itself solemnly and implacably to a root-and-branch extermination of everything that we associate with priesthood, has, under pressure of circumstances, unconsciously and spontaneously established as its system of government an as-close-as-possible reproduction of the hierarchy of the Catholic Church. The nomenclature is changed, of course: the Church is called the Communist Party; and the Holy Office and its familiars are known as the Komintern and the Gay Pay Oo. There is the popular safeguard of having the symptoms of the priestly vocation verified in the first instance by the group of peasants or industrial workers with whom the postulant's daily life has been passed, thus giving a genuine democratic basis to the system; and the hierarchy elected on this basis is not only up to date for the moment, but amenable to the daily lessons of trial and error in its practical operations and in no way pledged against change and innovation as such. But essentially the system is that of the old Christian Catholic Church, even to its fundamental vow of Communism and the death penalty on Ananias and Sapphira for violating it.

If our newspapers knew what is really happening in the world, or could discriminate between the news value of a bicycle accident in Clapham and that of a capsize of civilization, their columns would be full of this literally epoch-making event. And the first question they would address to Russia would be "Why, seeing that the Christian system has been such a hopeless failure, do you go back to it, and invite us to go back to it?"

WHY THE CHRISTIAN SYSTEM FAILED

The answer is that the Christian system failed, not because it was wrong in its psychology, its fundamental postulate of equality, or its anticipation of Lenin's principle that the rulers must be as poor as the ruled so that they can raise themselves only by raising their people, but because the old priests' ignorance of economics and political science blinded them to the mischief latent in the selfishness of private property in the physical earth. Before the

Church knew where it was (it has not quite located itself yet) it found itself so prodigiously rich that the Pope was a secular Italian prince with armies and frontiers, enjoying not only the rent of Church lands, but selling salvation on such a scale that when Torquemada began burning Jews instead of allowing them to ransom their bodies by payments to the Roman treasury, and leaving their souls to God, a first-rate quarrel between the Church and the Spanish Inquisition was the result.

But the riches of the Church were nothing compared to the riches of the Church's great rival, the Empire. And the poverty of the priest was opulence compared to the poverty of the proletarian. Whilst the Church was being so corrupted by its own property, and by the influence on it of the lay proprietors, that it lost all its moral prestige, the warriors and robbers of the Empire had been learning from experience that a pirate ship needs a hierarchy of officers and an iron discipline even more than police boats, and that the work of robbing the poor all the time involves a very elaborate system of government to ensure that the poor shall, like bees, continue to produce not only their own subsistence but the surplus that can be robbed from them without bringing on them the doom of the goose that lays the golden eggs. Naked coercion is so expensive that it became necessary to practise on the imaginations of the poor to the extent of making them believe that it is a pious duty to be robbed, and that their moment of life in this world is only a prelude to an eternity in which the poor will be blest and happy, and the rich horribly tortured.

Matters at last reached a point at which there was more law and order in the Empire than in The Church. Emperor Philip of Spain was enormously more respectable and pious, if less amiable, than Pope Alexander Borgia. The Empire gained moral prestige as The Church lost it until the Empire, virtuously indignant, took it on itself to reform The Church, all the more readily as the restoration of priestly poverty was a first-rate excuse for plundering it.

Now The Church could not with any decency allow itself to be reformed by a plutocracy of pirate kings, robber barons, commercial adventurers, moneylenders, and deserters from its own ranks. It reformed itself from within by its own saints and the Orders they founded, and thus "dished" the Reformation; whilst the Reformers set up national Churches and free Churches of their own under the general definition of Protestants, and thereby found themselves committed to a curious adulteration of their doctrine of Individualism, or the right of private judgment, with most of the ecclesiastical corruptions against which they had protested. And as neither Church nor Empire would share the government of mankind with the other nor allow the common people any say in the matter, the Catholics and Protestants set to work to exterminate one another with rack and stake, fire, sword, and gunpowder, aided by the poison gas of scurrilous calumny, until the very name of religion began to stink in the nostrils of all really charitable and faithful people.

GOVERNMENT BY EVERYBODY

The moral drawn from all this was that as nobody could be trusted to govern the people the people must govern themselves, which was nonsense. Nevertheless it was assumed that by inscribing every man's name on a register of voters we could realize the ideal of every man his own Solon and his own Plato, as to which one could only ask why not every man his own Shakespear and his own Einstein? But this assumption suited the plutocrats very well, as they had only to master the easy art of stampeding elections by their newspapers to do anything they liked in the name of the people. Votes for everybody (called for short, Democracy) ended in government neither of the best nor of the worst, but in an official government which could do nothing but talk, and an actual government of landlords, employers, and financiers at war with an Opposition of trade unionists, strikers, pickets, and —occasionally—rioters. The resultant disorder, indiscipline, and breakdown of distribution, produced a reaction of pure disappointment and distress in which the people looked wildly round for a Savior, and were ready to give a hopeful trial to anyone bold enough to assume dictatorship and kick aside the impotent official government until he had completely muzzled and subjugated it.

FAILURE ALL ROUND

That is the history of Catholicism and Protestantism. Church and Empire, Liberalism and Democracy, up to date. Clearly a ghastly failure, both positively as an attempt to solve the problem of government and negatively as an attempt to secure freedom of thought and facility of change to keep pace with thought.

Now this does not mean in the least that the original Catholic plan was wrong. On the contrary, all the disasters to which it has led have been demonstrations of the eternal need for it. The alternative to vocational government is a mixture of a haporth of very incompetent official government with an intolerable deal of very competent private tyranny. Providence, or Nature if you prefer that expression, has not ordained that all men shall have a vocation for being "servants of all the rest" as saints or rulers. Providence knows better than to provide armies consisting exclusively of commanders-in-chief or factories staffed exclusively with managing directors; and to that inexorable natural fact we shall always have to come back, just as the Russian revolutionists, who were reeking with Protestant Liberal superstitions at the beginning, have had to come back to it. But we have now thought out much more carefully than St Peter the basic articles of faith, without which the vocation of the priest is inevitably pushed out by the vocation of the robbers and the racketeers, self-elected as gentlemen and ladies. We know that private property distributes wealth, work, and leisure so unevenly that a wretchedly poor and miserably overworked majority are forced to maintain a minority inordinately rich and passionately convinced that labor is so disgraceful to them that they dare not be seen carrying a parcel down Bond Street. We know that the strains set up by such a division of interests also destroy peace, justice, religion, good breeding, honor, reasonable freedom, and everything that government exists to secure, and that all this iniquity arises automatically when we thoughtlessly allow a person to own a thousand acres of land in the middle of London much more completely than he owns the pair of boots in which he walks over it; for he may not kick me out of my house into the street with his boots; but he may do so with his writ of ejectment. And so we are driven to the conclusion that the modern priesthood must utterly renounce, abjure, abhor, abominate and annihilate private property as the very worst of all the devil's inventions for the demoralization and damnation of mankind. Civilized men and women must live by their ordered and equal share in the work needed to support the community, and must find their freedom in their ordered and equal share of the leisure produced by scientific economy in producing that support. It still takes some conviction to repudiate an institution so well spoken of as private property; but the facts must be faced: our clandestine methods of violating it by income tax and surtax, which mean only "What a thief stole steal thou from the thief," will no longer serve; for a modern government, as the Russians soon found out, must not take money, even from thieves, until it is ready to employ it productively. To throw it away in doles as our governing duffers do, is to burn the candle at both ends and precipitate the catastrophe they are trying to avert.

OBSOLETE VOWS

As to the vows, some of the old ones must go. The Catholic Church and our Board of Education insist on celibacy, the one for priests and the other for schoolmistresses. That is a remnant of the cynical superstition of original sin. Married people have a right to married rulers; mothers have a right to have their children taught and handled by mothers; and priests and pastors who meddle with family affairs should know what they are talking about.

Another important modern discovery is that government is not a whole-time job for all its agents. A council of peasants derives its ancient wisdom from its normal day's work on the land, without which it would be a council of tramps and village idiots. It is not desirable that an ordinary parish priest should have no other occupation, nor an abnormal occupation, even that of a scholar. Nor is it desirable that his uniform should be too sacerdotal; for that is the method of idolatry, which substitutes for rational authority the superstitious awe produced by a contrived singularity. St Vincent de Paul knew thoroughly well what he was about when he constituted his Sisterhood of Charity on the rule that the sister should not be distinguishable from an ordinary respectable woman. Unfortunately, the costume prescribed under this rule has in the course of the centuries become as extraordinary as that of the Bluecoat boy; and St Vincent's idea is consequently lost; but modern industrial experience confirms it; for the latest rediscovery of the Vincentian principle has been made by Mr Ford, who has testified that if you want a staff of helpful persons who will turn their hands to anything at need you must not give them either title, rank, or uniform, as the immediate result will be their partial disablement by the exclusion from their activities of many of the most necessary jobs as beneath their dignity.

Another stipulation made by St Vincent, who already in the sixteenth century was far ahead of us, was that no sister may pledge herself for longer than a year at a time, however often she may renew her vows. Thus the sisters can never lose their freedom nor suffer from cold feet. If he were alive today St Vincent would probably propose a clean sweep of all our difficulties about marriage and divorce by forbidding people to marry for longer than a year, and make them renew their vows every twelve months. In Russia the members of the Communist Party cannot dedicate themselves eternally: they can drop out into the laity when they please, and if they do not please and nevertheless have become slack in their ministry, they are pushed out.

SUPERNATURAL PRETENSIONS

Furthermore, modern priests must not make supernatural pretensions. They must not be impostors. A vocation for politics, though essentially a religious vocation, must be on the same footing as a vocation for music or mathematics or cooking or nursing or acting or architecture or farming or billiards or any other born aptitude. The authority which must attach to all public officials and councils must rest on their ability and efficiency. In the Royal Navy every mishap to a ship involves a court martial on the responsible officer: if the officer makes a mistake he forfeits his command unless he can convince the court that he is still worthy it. In no other way can our hackneyed phrase "responsible government" acquire any real meaning. When a Catholic priest goes wrong (or too right) he is silenced: when a Russian Commissar goes wrong, he is expelled from the Party. Such responsibility necessarily makes official authority very authoritative and frightens off the unduly nervous. Stalin and Mussolini are the most responsible statesmen in Europe because they have no hold on their places except their efficiency; and their authority is consequently greater than that of any of the monarchs, presidents, and prime ministers who have to deal with them. Stalin is one of the higher functionaries with whom governing is necessarily a whole-time job. But he is no richer than his neighbors, and can "better himself" only by bettering them, not by bettering them like a British demagogue.

ECLECTIC DEMOCRACY

I think my views on intellectual aristocracy and democracy and all the rest of it are now plain enough. As between the intentions of The Church and the intentions of The Empire (unrealized ideals both) I am on the side of The Church. As to the evil done by The Church with the best intentions and the good done by The Empire with the worst, I am an Eclectic: there is much to be learnt from each. I harp on Russia because the Moscow experiment is the only really new departure from Tweedledum and Tweedledee: Fascism is still wavering between Empire and Church, between private property and Communism. Years ago, I said that what democracy needed was a trustworthy anthropometric machine for the selection of qualified rulers. Since then I have elaborated this by demanding the formation of panels of tested persons eligible for the different grades in the governmental hierarchy. Panel A would be for diplomacy and international finance, Panel B for national affairs, Panel C for municipal and county affairs, Panel D for the village councils, and so forth. Under such a panel system the voters would lose their present liberty to return such candidates as the late Horatio Bottomley to parliament by enormous majorities; but they would gain the advantage of at least knowing that their rulers know how to read and write, which they do not enjoy at present.

Nobody ventured to disagree with me when I urged the need for such panels; but when I was challenged to produce my anthropometric machine or my endocrine or phrenological tests, I was obliged to confess that they had not yet been invented, and that such existing attempts at them as competitive examinations are so irrelevant and misleading as to be worse than useless as tests of vocation. But the Soviet system, hammered out under the sternest pressure of circumstances, supplies an excellent provisional solution, which turns out to be the solution of the old Catholic Church purged of supernatural pretension, assumption of final perfection, and the poison of private property with its fatal consequences. Mr Stalin is not in the least like an Emperor, nor an Archbishop, nor a Prime Minister, nor a Chancellor; but he would be strikingly like a Pope, claiming for form's sake an apostolic succession from Marx, were it not for his frank method of Trial and

Error, his entirely human footing, and his liability to removal at a moment's notice if his eminence should upset his mental balance. At the other end of the scale are the rank and file of the Communist Party, doing an ordinary day's work with the common folk, and giving only their leisure to the Party. For their election as representatives of the commons they must depend on the votes of their intimate and equal neighbors and workmates. They have no incentive to seek election except the vocational incentive; for success, in the first instance, means, not release from the day's ordinary work, but the sacrifice of all one's leisure to politics, and, if promotion to the whole-time-grades be achieved, a comparatively ascetic discipline and virtually no pecuniary gain.

If anyone can suggest a better practically tested plan, now is the time to do it; for it is all up with the old Anarchist-Liberal parliamentary systems in the face of thirty millions of unemployed, and World Idiotic Conferences at which each nation implores all the others to absorb its unemployed by a revival of international trade. Mr Chesterton says truly that a government, if it is to govern, "cannot select one ruler to do something and another to undo it, one intellectual to restore the nation and another to ruin the nation." But that is precisely what our parliamentary party system does. Mr Chesterton has put it in a nutshell; and I hope he will appreciate the sound Catholicism with which I have cracked it.

AYOT ST LAWRENCE,
1933.

TOO TRUE TO BE GOOD

ACT I

NIGHT. One of the best bedrooms in one of the best suburban villas in one of the richest cities in England. A young lady with an unhealthy complexion is asleep in the bed. A small table at the head of the bed, convenient to her right hand, and crowded with a medicine bottle, a measuring glass, a pill box, a clinical thermometer in a glass of water, a half read book with the place marked by a handkerchief, a powder puff and hand-mirror, and an electric bell handle on a flex, shews that the bed is a sick bed and the young lady an invalid.

The furniture includes a very handsome dressing table with silver-backed hairbrushes and toilet articles, a dainty pincushion, a stand of rings, a jewel box of black steel with the lid open and a rope of pearls heaped carelessly half in and half out, a Louis Quinze writing table and chair with inkstand, blotter, and cabinet of stationery, a magnificent wardrobe, a luxurious couch, and a tall screen of Chinese workmanship which, like the expensive carpet and everything else in the room, proclaims that the owner has money enough to buy the best things at the best shops in the best purchaseable taste.

The bed is nearly in the middle of the room, so that the patient's nurses can pass freely between the wall and the head of it. If we contemplate the room from the foot of the bed, with the patient's toes pointing straight at us, we have the door (carefully sandbagged lest a draught of fresh air should creep underneath) level with us in the righthand wall, the couch against the same wall farther away, the window (every ray of moonlight excluded by closed curtains and a dark green spring blind) in the middle of the left wall with the wardrobe on its right and the writing table on its left, the screen at right angles to the wardrobe, and the dressing table against the wall facing us half way between the bed and the couch.

Besides the chair at the writing table there is an easy

chair at the medicine table, and a chair at each side of the dressing table.

The room is lighted by invisible cornice lights, and by two mirror lights on the dressing table and a portable one on the writing table; but these are now switched off; and the only light in action is another portable one on the medicine table, very carefully subdued by a green shade.

The patient is sleeping heavily. Near her, in the easy chair, sits a Monster. In shape and size it resembles a human being; but in substance it seems to be made of a luminous jelly with a visible skeleton of short black rods. It droops forward in the chair with its head in its hands, and seems in the last degree wretched.

THE MONSTER. Oh! Oh!! Oh!!! I am so ill! so miserable! Oh, I wish I were dead. Why doesnt she die and release me from my sufferings? What right has she to get ill and make me ill like this? Measles: thats what she's got. Measles! German measles! And she's given them to me, a poor innocent microbe that never did her any harm. And she says that *I* gave them to her. Oh, is this justice? Oh, I feel so rotten. I wonder what my temperature is: they took it from under her tongue half an hour ago. [*Scrutinizing the table and discovering the thermometer in the glass*]. Here's the thermometer: theyve left it for the doctor to see instead of shaking it down. If it's over a hundred I'm done for: I darent look. Oh, can it be that I'm dying? I must look. [*It looks, and drops the thermometer back into the glass with a gasping scream*]. A hundred and three! It's all over. [*It collapses*].

The door opens; and an elderly lady and a young doctor come in. The lady steals along on tiptoe, full of the deepest concern for the invalid. The doctor is indifferent, but keeps up his bedside manner carefully, though he evidently does not think the case so serious as the lady does. She comes to the bedside on the invalid's left. He comes to the other side of the bed and looks attentively at his patient.

THE ELDERLY LADY [*in a whisper sibillant enough to wake the dead*] She is asleep.

THE MONSTER. I should think so. This fool here, the doctor, has given her a dose of the latest fashionable opiate that would keep a cock asleep til half past eleven on a May morning.

THE ELDERLY LADY. Oh doctor, do you think there is any chance? Can she possibly survive this last terrible complication?

THE MONSTER. Measles! He mistook it for influenza.

THE ELDERLY LADY. It was so unexpected! such a crushing blow! And I have taken such care of her. She is my only surviving child: my pet: my precious one. Why do they all die? I have never neglected the smallest symptom of illness. She has had doctors in attendance on her almost constantly since she was born.

THE MONSTER. She has the constitution of a horse or she'd have died like the others.

THE ELDERLY LADY. Oh, dont you think, dear doctor—of course you know best; but I am so terribly anxious—dont you think you ought to change the prescription? I had such hopes of that last bottle; but you know it was after that that she developed measles.

THE DOCTOR. My dear Mrs. Mopply, you may rest assured that the bottle had nothing to do with the measles. It was merely a gentle tonic—

THE MONSTER. Strychnine!

THE DOCTOR. —to brace her up.

THE ELDERLY LADY. But she got measles after it.

THE DOCTOR. That was a specific infection: a germ, a microbe.

THE MONSTER. Me! Put it all on me.

THE ELDERLY LADY. But how did it get in? I keep the windows closed so carefully. And there is a sheet steeped in carbolic acid always hung over the door.

THE MONSTER [*in tears*] Not a breath of fresh air for me!

THE DOCTOR. Who knows? It may have lurked here since the house was built. You never can tell. But you must not worry. It is not serious: a light rubeola: you can hardly call it measles. We shall pull her through, believe me.

THE ELDERLY LADY. It is such a comfort to hear you say so, doctor. I am sure I shall never be able to express my gratitude for all you have done for us.

THE DOCTOR. Oh, that is my profession. We do what we can.

THE ELDERLY LADY. Yes; but some doctors are dreadful. There was that man at Folkstone: he was impossible. He tore aside the curtain and let the blazing sunlight into the room, though she cannot bear it without green spectacles. He opened the windows and let in all the cold morning air. I told him he was a murderer; and he only said "One guinea, please". I am sure he let in that microbe.

THE DOCTOR. Oh, three months ago! No: it was not that.

THE ELDERLY LADY. Then what was it? Oh, are you quite quite sure that it would not be better to change the prescription?

THE DOCTOR. Well, I have already changed it.

THE MONSTER. Three times!

THE ELDERLY LADY. Oh, I know you have, doctor: nobody could have been kinder. But it really did not do her any good. She got worse.

THE DOCTOR. But, my dear lady, she was sickening for measles. That was not the fault of my prescription.

THE ELDERLY LADY. Oh, of course not. You mustnt think that I ever doubted for a moment that everything you did was for the best. Still—

THE DOCTOR. Oh, very well, very well: I will write another prescription.

THE ELDERLY LADY. Oh, thank you, thank you: I felt sure you would. I have so often known a change of medicine work wonders.

THE DOCTOR. When we have pulled her through this

attack I think a change of air—

THE ELDERLY LADY. Oh no: dont say that. She must be near a doctor who knows her constitution. Dear old Dr Newland knew it so well from her very birth.

THE DOCTOR. Unfortunately, Newland is dead.

THE ELDERLY LADY. Yes; but you bought his practice. I should never be easy in my mind if you were not within call. You persuaded me to take her to Folkstone; and see what happened! No: never again.

THE DOCTOR. Oh, well! [*He shrugs his shoulders resignedly, and goes to the bedside table*]. What about the temperature?

THE ELDERLY LADY. The day nurse took it. I havnt dared to look.

THE DOCTOR [*looking at the thermometer*] Hm!

THE ELDERLY LADY [*trembling*] Has it gone up? Oh, doctor!

THE DOCTOR [*hastily shaking the mercury down*] No. Nothing. Nearly normal.

THE MONSTER. Liar.

THE ELDERLY LADY. What a relief!

THE DOCTOR. You must be careful, though. Dont fancy she's well yet: she isnt. She must not get out of bed for a moment. The slightest chill might be serious.

THE ELDERLY LADY. Doctor: are you sure you are not concealing something from me? Why does she never get well in spite of the fortune I have spent on her illnesses? There must be some deep-rooted cause. Tell me the worst: I have dreaded it all my life. Perhaps I should have told you the whole truth; but I was afraid. Her uncle's stepfather died of an enlarged heart. Is that what it is?

THE DOCTOR. Good gracious, NO! What put that into your head?

THE ELDERLY LADY. But even before this rash broke out there were pimples.

THE MONSTER. Boils! Too many chocolate creams.

THE DOCTOR. Oh, that! Nothing. Her blood is not quite

what it should be. But we shall get that right.

THE ELDERLY LADY. You are sure it is not her lungs?

THE DOCTOR. My good lady, her lungs are as sound as a seagull's.

THE ELDERLY LADY. Then it must be her heart. Dont deceive me. She has palpitations. She told me the other day that it stopped for five minutes when that horrid nurse was rude to her.

THE DOCTOR. Nonsense! She wouldnt be alive now if her heart had stopped for five seconds. There is nothing constitutionally wrong. A little below par: that is all. We shall feed her up scientifically. Plenty of good fresh meat. A half bottle of champagne at lunch and a glass of port after dinner will make another woman of her. A chop at breakfast, rather underdone, is sometimes very helpful.

THE MONSTER. I shall die of overfeeding. So will she too: thats one consolation.

THE DOCTOR. Dont worry about the measles. It's really quite a light case.

THE ELDERLY LADY. Oh, you can depend on me for that. Nobody can say that I am a worrier. You wont forget the new prescription?

THE DOCTOR. I will write it here and now [*he takes out his pen and book, and sits down at the writing table*].

THE ELDERLY LADY. Oh, thank you. And I will go and see what the new night nurse is doing. They take so long with their cups of tea [*she goes to the door and is about to go out when she hesitates and comes back*]. Doctor: I know you dont believe in inoculations; but I cant help thinking she ought to have one. They do so much good.

THE DOCTOR [*almost at the end of his patience*] My dear Mrs Mopply: I never said that I dont believe in inoculations. But it is no use inoculating when the patient is already fully infected.

THE ELDERLY LADY. But I have found it so necessary myself. I was inoculated against influenza three years ago; and I have had it only four times since. My sister has it every February. Do, to please me, give her an inoculation. I feel such a responsibility if anything is left undone to cure her.

THE DOCTOR. Oh very well, very well: I will see what can be done. She shall have both an inoculation and a new prescription. Will that set your mind at rest?

THE ELDERLY LADY. Oh, thank you. You have lifted such a weight from my conscience. I feel sure they will do her the greatest good. And now excuse me a moment while I fetch the nurse. [*She goes out*].

THE DOCTOR. What a perfectly maddening woman!

THE MONSTER [*rising and coming behind him*] Yes: aint she?

THE DOCTOR [*staring*] What! Who is that?

THE MONSTER. Nobody but me and the patient. And you have dosed her so that she wont speak again for ten hours. You will overdo that some day.

THE DOCTOR. Rubbish! She thought it was an opiate; but it was only an aspirin dissolved in ether. But who am I talking to? I must be drunk.

THE MONSTER. Not a bit of it.

THE DOCTOR. Then who are you? What are you? Where are you? Is this a trick?

THE MONSTER. I'm only an unfortunate sick bacillus.

THE DOCTOR. A sick bacillus!

THE MONSTER. Yes. I suppose it never occurs to you that a bacillus can be sick like anyone else.

THE DOCTOR. Whats the matter with you?

THE MONSTER. Measles.

THE DOCTOR. Rot! The microbe of measles has never been discovered. If there is a microbe it cannot be measles: it must be parameasles.

THE MONSTER. Great Heavens! what are parameasles?

THE DOCTOR. Something so like measles that nobody can see any difference.

THE MONSTER. If there is no measles microbe why did you tell the old girl that her daughter caught measles from a microbe?

THE DOCTOR. Patients insist on having microbes nowadays. If I told her there is no measles microbe she wouldnt believe me; and I should lose my patient. When there is no microbe I invent one. Am I to understand that you are the missing microbe of measles, and that you have given them to this patient here?

THE MONSTER. No: she gave them to me. These humans are full of horrid diseases: they infect us poor microbes with them; and you doctors pretend that it is we that infect them. You ought all to be struck off the register.

THE DOCTOR. We should be, if we talked like that.

THE MONSTER. Oh, I feel so wretched! Please cure my measles.

THE DOCTOR. I cant. I cant cure any disease. But I get the credit when the patients cure themselves. When she cures herself she will cure you too.

THE MONSTER. But she cant cure herself because you and her mother wont give her a dog's chance. You wont let her have even a breath of fresh air. I tell you she's naturally as strong as a rhinoceros. Curse your silly bottles and inoculations! Why dont you chuck them and turn faith healer?

THE DOCTOR. I am a faith healer. You dont suppose I believe the bottles cure people? But the patient's faith in the bottle does.

THE MONSTER. Youre a humbug: thats what you are.

THE DOCTOR. Faith is humbug. But it works.

THE MONSTER. Then why do you call it science?

THE DOCTOR. Because people believe in science. The Christian Scientists call their fudge science for the same reason.

THE MONSTER. The Christian Scientists let their patients cure themselves. Why dont you?

THE DOCTOR. I do. But I help them. You see, it's easier to believe in bottles and inoculations than in oneself and in that mysterious power that gives us our life and that none of us knows anything about. Lots of people believe in the bottles and wouldnt know what you were talking about if you suggested the real thing. And the bottles do the trick. My patients get well as often as not. That is, unless their number's up. Then we all have to go.

THE MONSTER. No girl's number is up until she's worn out. I tell you this girl could cure herself and cure me if youd let her.

THE DOCTOR. And I tell you that it would be very hard work for her. Well, why should she work hard when she can afford to pay other people to work for her? She doesnt black her own boots or scrub her own floors. She pays somebody else to do it. Why should she cure herself, which is harder work than blacking boots or scrubbing floors, when she can afford to pay the doctor to cure her? It pays her and it pays me. That's logic, my friend. And now, if you will excuse me, I shall take myself off before the old woman comes back and provokes me to wring her neck. [*Rising*] Mark my words: someday somebody will fetch her a clout over the head. Somebody who can afford to. Not the doctor. She has driven me mad already: the proof is that I hear voices and talk to them. [*He goes out*].

THE MONSTER. Youre saner than most of them, you fool. They think I have the keys of life and death in my pocket; but I have nothing but a horrid headache. Oh dear! oh dear!

The Monster wanders away behind the screen. The patient, left alone, begins to stir in her bed. She turns over and calls querulously for somebody to attend to her.

THE PATIENT. Nurse! Mother! Oh, is anyone there? [*Crying*] Selfish beasts! to leave me like this. [*She snatches angrily at the electric bell which hangs within her reach and presses the button repeatedly*].

The Elderly Lady and the night nurse come running in. The nurse is young, quick, active, resolute, and decidedly pretty. Mrs Mopply goes to the bedside table, the nurse going to the patient's left.

THE ELDERLY LADY. What is it, darling? Are you awake? Was the sleeping draught no good? Are you worse? What has happened? What has become of the doctor?

THE PATIENT. I am in the most frightful agony. I have been lying here ringing for ages and ages, and no one has come to attend to me. Nobody cares whether I am alive or dead.

THE ELDERLY LADY. Oh, how can you say such things, darling? I left the doctor here. I was away only for a minute. I had to receive the new night nurse and give her her instructions. Here she is. And oh, do cover up your arm, darling. You will get a chill; and then it will be all over. Nurse: see that she is never uncovered for a moment. Do you think it would be well to have another hot water bottle against her arm until it is quite warm again? Do you feel it cold, darling?

THE PATIENT [*angrily*] Yes, deadly cold.

THE ELDERLY LADY. Oh, dont say that. And there is so much pneumonia about. I wish the doctor had not gone. He could sound your lungs—

NIGHT NURSE [*feeling the patient's arm*] She is quite warm enough.

THE PATIENT [*bursting into tears*] Mother: take this hateful woman away. She wants to kill me.

THE ELDERLY LADY. Oh no, dear: she has been so highly recommended. I cant get a new nurse at this hour. Wont you try, for my sake, to put up with her until the day nurse comes in the morning?

THE NURSE. Come! Let me arrange your pillows and make you comfortable. You are smothered with all this bedding. Four thick blankets and an eiderdown! No wonder you feel irritable.

THE PATIENT [*screaming*] Dont touch me. Go away. You want to murder me. Nobody cares whether I am alive or dead.

THE ELDERLY LADY. Oh, darling, dont keep on saying that. You know it's not true; and it does hurt me so.

THE NURSE. You must not mind what a sick person says, madam. You had better go to bed and leave the patient to me. You are quite worn out. [*She comes to Mrs Mopply and takes her arm coaxingly but firmly*].

THE ELDERLY LADY. I know I am: I am ready to drop. How sympathetic of you to notice it! But how can I leave her at such a moment?

THE NURSE. She ought not to have more than one person in the room at a time. You see how it excites and worries her.

THE ELDERLY LADY. Oh, thats very true. The doctor said she was to be kept as quiet as possible.

THE NURSE [*leading her to the door*] You need a good night's sleep. You may trust me to do what is right and necessary.

THE ELDERLY LADY [*whispering*] I will indeed. How kind of you! You will let me know if anything—

THE NURSE. Yes, yes. I promise to come for you and wake you if anything happens. Good night, madam.

THE ELDERLY LADY [*sotto voce*] Good night. [*She steals out*].

The nurse, left alone with her patient, pays no attention to her, but goes to the window. She opens the curtains and raises the blind, admitting a flood of moonlight. She unfastens the sash and throws it right up. She then makes for the door, where the electric switch is.

THE PATIENT [*huddling herself up in the bedclothes*] What are you doing? Shut that window and pull down that blind and close those curtains at once. Do you want to kill me?

The nurse turns all the lights full on.

THE PATIENT [*hiding her eyes*] Oh! Oh! I cant bear it: turn it off.

The nurse switches the lights off.

THE PATIENT. So inconsiderate of you!

The nurse switches the lights on again.

THE PATIENT. Oh, please, please. Not all that light.

The nurse switches off.

THE PATIENT. No, no. Leave me something to read by. My bedside lamp is not enough, you stupid idiot.

The nurse switches on again, and calmly returns to the bedside.

THE PATIENT. I cant imagine how anyone can be so thoughtless and clumsy when I am so ill. I am suffering horribly. Shut that window and switch off half those lights at once: do you hear?

The nurse snatches the eiderdown and one of the pillows rudely from the bed, letting the patient down with a jerk, and arranges them comfortably in the bedside chair.

THE PATIENT. How dare you touch my pillow? The audacity!

The nurse sits down; takes out a leaf cut from an illustrated journal; and proceeds to study it attentively.

THE PATIENT. Well! How much longer are you going to sit there neglecting me? Shut that window instantly.

THE NURSE [*insolently, in her commonest dialect*] Oh go to—to sleep [*she resumes her study of the document*].

THE PATIENT. Dont dare address me like that. I dont believe you are a properly qualified nurse.

THE NURSE [*calmly*] I should think not. I wouldnt take five thousand a year to be a nurse. But I know how to deal with you and your like, because I was once a patient in a hospital where the women patients were a rough lot, and the nurses had to treat them accordingly. I kept my eyes open there, and learnt a little of the game. [*She takes a paper packet from her pocket and opens it on the bedside table. It contains about half a pound of kitchen salt*]. Do you know what that is and what it's for?

THE PATIENT. Is it medicine?

THE NURSE. Yes. It's a cure for screaming and hysterics and tantrums. When a woman starts making a row, the first thing she does is to open her mouth. A nurse who knows her business just shoves a handful of this into it.

Common kitchen salt. No more screaming. Understand?

THE PATIENT [*hardily*] No I dont [*she reaches for the bell*].

THE NURSE [*intercepting her quickly*] No you dont. [*She throws the bell cord with its button away on the floor behind the bed*]. Now we shant be disturbed. No bell. And if you open your mouth too wide, youll get the salt. See?

THE PATIENT. And do you think I am a poor woman in a hospital whom you can illtreat as you please? Do you know what will happen to you when my mother comes in the morning?

THE NURSE. In the morning, darling, I shall be over the hills and far away.

THE PATIENT. And you expect me, sick as I am, to stay here alone with you!

THE NURSE. We shant be alone. I'm expecting a friend.

THE PATIENT. A friend!

THE NURSE. A gentleman friend. I told him he might drop in when he saw the lights switched off twice.

THE PATIENT. So that was why—

THE NURSE. That was why.

THE PATIENT. And you calmly propose to have your young man here in my room to amuse yourself all night before my face.

THE NURSE. You can go to sleep.

THE PATIENT. I shall do nothing of the sort. You will have to behave yourself decently before me.

THE NURSE. Oh, dont worry about that. He's coming on business. He's my business partner, in fact: not my best boy.

THE PATIENT. And can you not find some more suitable place for your business than in my room at night?

THE NURSE. You see, you dont know the nature of the business yet. It's got to be done here and at night. Here he is, I think.

A burglar, well dressed, wearing rubber gloves and a small white mask over his nose, clambers in. He is still in his early thirties, and quite goodlooking. His voice is dis-

armingly pleasant.

THE BURGLAR. All right, Sweetie?

THE NURSE. All right, Popsy.

The burglar closes the window softly; draws the curtains; and comes past the nurse to the bedside.

THE BURGLAR. Damn it, she's awake. Didn't you give her a sleeping draught?

THE PATIENT. Do you expect me to sleep with you in the room? Who are you? and what are you wearing that mask for?

THE BURGLAR. Only so that you will not recognize me if we should happen to meet again.

THE PATIENT. I have no intention of meeting you again. So you may just as well take it off.

THE NURSE. I havent broken to her what we are here for, Popsy.

THE PATIENT. I neither know nor care what you are here for. All I can tell you is that if you dont leave the room at once and send my mother to me, I will give you both measles.

THE BURGLAR. We have both had them, dear invalid. I am afraid we must intrude a little longer. [*To the nurse*] Have you found out where it is?

THE NURSE. No: I havent had time. The dressing table's over there. Try that.

The burglar crosses to the other side of the bed, coming round by the foot of it, and is making for the dressing table when—

THE PATIENT. What do you want at my dressing table?

THE BURGLAR. Obviously, your celebrated pearl necklace.

THE PATIENT [*escaping from her bed with a formidable bound and planting herself with her back to the dressing table as a bulwark for the jewel case*] Not if I know it, you shant.

THE BURGLAR [*approaching her*] You really must allow me.

THE PATIENT. Take that.

Holding on to the table edge behind her, she lifts her foot vigorously waist high, and shoots it hard into his solar plexus. He curls up on the bed with an agonized groan and rolls off on to the carpet at the other side. The nurse rushes across behind the head of the bed and tackles the patient. The patient swoops at her knees, lifts her; and sends her flying. She comes down with a thump flat on her back on the couch. The patient pants hard; sways giddily; staggers to the bed and falls on it, exhausted. The nurse, dazed by the patient's very unexpected athleticism, but not hurt, springs up.

THE NURSE. Quick, Popsy: tie her feet. She's fainted.

THE BURGLAR [*utters a lamentable groan and rolls over on his face*]!!

THE NURSE. Be quick, will you?

THE BURGLAR [*trying to rise*] Ugh! Ugh!

THE NURSE [*running to him and shaking him*] My God, you are a fool, Popsy. Come and help me before she comes to. She's too strong for me.

THE BURGLAR. Ugh! Let me die.

THE NURSE. Are you going to lie there for ever? Has she killed you?

THE BURGLAR [*rising slowly to his knees*] As nearly as doesnt matter. Oh, Sweetiest, why did you tell me that this heavyweight champion was a helpless invalid?

THE NURSE. Shut up. Get the pearls.

THE BURGLAR [*rising with difficulty*] I dont seem to want any pearls. She got me just in the wind. I am sorry to have been of so little assistance; but oh, my Sweetie-Weetie, Nature never intended us to be burglars. Our first attempt has been a hopeless failure. Let us apologize and withdraw.

THE NURSE. Fathead! Dont be such a coward. [*Looking closely at the patient*] I say, Popsy: I believe she's asleep.

THE BURGLAR. Let her sleep. Wake not the lioness's

wrath.

THE NURSE. You maddening fool, dont you see that we can tie her feet and gag her before she wakes, and get away with the pearls. It's quite easy if we do it quick together. Come along.

THE BURGLAR. Do not deceive yourself, my pet: we should have about as much chance as if we tried to take a female gorilla to the Zoo. No: I am not going to steal those jewels. Honesty is the best policy. I have another idea, and a much better one. You leave this to me. [*He goes to the dressing table. She follows him*].

THE NURSE. Whatever have you got into your silly head now?

THE BURGLAR. You shall see. [*Handling the jewel case*] One of these safes that open by a secret arrangement of letters. As they are as troublesome as an automatic telephone nobody ever locks them. Here is the necklace. By Jove! If they are all real, it must be worth about twenty thousand pounds. Gosh! here's a ring with a big blue diamond in it. Worth four thousand pounds if it's worth a penny. Sweetie: we are on velvet for the rest of our lives.

THE NURSE. What good are blue diamonds to us if we dont steal them?

THE BURGLAR. Wait. Wait and see. Go and sit down in that chair and look as like a nice gentle nurse as you can.

THE NURSE. But—

THE BURGLAR. Do as you are told. Have faith—faith in your Popsy.

THE NURSE [*obeying*] Well, I give it up. Youre mad.

THE BURGLAR. I was never saner in my life. Stop. How does she call people? Hasnt she an electric bell? Where is it?

THE NURSE [*picking it up*] Here. I chucked it out of her reach when she was grabbing at it.

THE BURGLAR. Put it on the bed close to her hand.

THE NURSE. Popsy: youre off your chump. She—

THE BURGLAR. Sweetie: in our firm I am the brains:

you are the hand. This is going to be our most glorious achievement. Obey me instantly.

THE NURSE [*resignedly*] Oh, very well. [*She places the handle of the bell as desired*]. I wash my hands of this job. [*She sits down doggedly*].

THE BURGLAR [*coming to the bedside*] By the way, she is hardly a success as The Sleeping Beauty. She has a wretched complexion; and her breath is not precisely ambrosial. But if we can turn her out to grass she may put up some good looks. And if her punch is anything like her kick she will be an invaluable bodyguard for us two weaklings—if I can persuade her to join us.

THE NURSE. Join us! What do you mean?

THE BURGLAR. Shshshshsh. Not too much noise: we must wake her gently. [*He stoops to the patient's ear and whispers*] Miss Mopply.

THE PATIENT [*in a murmur of protest*] Mmmmmmm-mmmmmmmmm.

THE NURSE. What does she say?

THE BURGLAR. She says, in effect, "You have waked me too soon: I must slumber again." [*To the patient, more distinctly*] It is not your dear mother, Miss Mopply: it is the burglar. [*The patient springs half up, threateningly. He falls on his knees and throws up his hands.*] Kamerad, Miss Mopply: Kamerad! I am utterly at your mercy. The bell is on your bed, close to your hand: look at it. You have only to press the button to bring your mother and the police in upon me [*she seizes the handle of the bell*] and be a miserable invalid again for the rest of your life. [*She drops the bell thoughtfully*]. Not an attractive prospect, is it? Now listen. I have something to propose to you of the greatest importance: something that may make another woman of you and change your entire destiny. You can listen to me in perfect security: at any moment you can ring your bell, or throw us out of the window if you prefer it. I ask you for five minutes only.

THE PATIENT [*still dangerously on guard*] Well?

THE BURGLAR [*rising*] Let me give you one more proof of my confidence. [*He takes off his mask*]. Look. Can you be afraid of such a face? Do I look like a burglar?

THE PATIENT [*relaxing, and even shewing signs of goodhumor*] No: you look like a curate.

THE BURGLAR [*a little hurt*] Oh, not a curate. I hope I look at least like a beneficed clergyman. But it is very clever of you to have found me out. The fact is, I am a clergyman. But I must ask you to keep it a dead secret; for my father, who is an atheist, would disinherit me if he knew. I was secretly ordained when I was up at Oxford.

THE PATIENT. Oh, this is ridiculous. I'm dreaming. It must be that new sleeping draught the doctor gave me. But it's delicious, because I'm dreaming that I'm perfectly well. Ive never been so happy in my life. Go on with the dream, Pops: the nicest part of it is that I am in love with you. My beautiful Pops, my own, my darling, you are a perfect film hero, only more like an English gentleman. [*She waves him a kiss*].

THE NURSE. Well I'll be da—

THE BURGLAR. Shshshshsh. Break not the spell.

THE PATIENT [*with a deep sigh of contentment*] Let nobody wake me. I'm in heaven. [*She sinks back blissfully on her pillows*]. Go on, Pops. Tell me another.

THE BURGLAR. Splendid. [*He takes a chair from beside the dressing table and seats himself comfortably at the bedside*]. We are going to have an ideal night. Now listen. Picture to yourself a heavenly afternoon in July: a Scottish loch surrounded by mirrored mountains, and a boat—may I call it a shallop?—

THE PATIENT [*ecstatically*] A shallop! Oh, Popsy!

THE BURGLAR.—with Sweetie sitting in the stern, and I stretched out at full length with my head pillowed on Sweetie's knees.

THE PATIENT. You can leave Sweetie out, Pops. Her amorous emotions do not interest me.

THE BURGLAR. You misunderstand. Sweetie's thoughts

were far from me. She was thinking about you.

THE PATIENT. Just like her impudence! How did she know about me?

THE BURGLAR. Simply enough. In her lily hand was a copy of The Lady's Pictorial. It contained an illustrated account of your jewels. Can you guess what Sweetie said to me as she gazed at the soft majesty of the mountains and bathed her soul in the beauty of the sunset?

THE PATIENT. Yes. She said "Popsy: we must pinch that necklace."

THE BURGLAR. Exactly. Word for word. But now can you guess what *I* said?

THE PATIENT. I suppose you said "Right you are, Sweetie" or something vulgar like that.

THE BURGLAR. Wrong. I said, "If that girl had any sense she'd steal the necklace herself."

THE PATIENT. Oh! This is getting interesting. How could I steal my own necklace?

THE BURGLAR. Sell it; and have a glorious spree with the price. See life. Live. You dont call being an invalid living, do you?

THE PATIENT. Why shouldnt I call it living? I am not dead. Of course when I am awake I am terribly delicate—

THE BURGLAR. Delicate! It's not five minutes since you knocked me out, and threw Sweetie all over the room. If you can fight like that for a string of pearls that you never have a chance of wearing, why not fight for freedom to do what you like, with your pocket full of money and all the fun in the wide world at your command? Hang it all, dont you want to be young and goodlooking and have a sweet breath and be a lawn tennis champion and enjoy everything that is to be enjoyed instead of frowsting here and being messed about by your silly mother and all the doctors that live on her folly? Have you no conscience, that you waste God's gifts so shamefully? You think you are in a state of illness. Youre not: youre in a state of sin. Sell the necklace and buy your salvation with the proceeds.

THE PATIENT. Youre a clergyman all right, Pops. But I dont know how to sell the necklace.

THE BURGLAR. I do. Let me sell it for you. You will of course give us a fairly handsome commission on the transaction.

THE PATIENT. Theres some catch in this. If I trust you with it how do I know that you will not keep the whole price for yourself?

THE BURGLAR. Sweetie: Miss Mopply has the makings of a good business woman in her. [*To the patient*] Just reflect, Mops (Let us call one another Mops and Pops for short). If I steal that necklace, I shall have to sell it as a burglar to a man who will know perfectly well that I have stolen it. I shall be lucky if I get a fiftieth of its value. But if I sell it on the square, as the agent of its lawful owner, I shall be able to get its full market value. The payment will be made to you; and I will trust you to pay me the commission. Sweetie and I will be more than satisfied with fifty per cent.

THE PATIENT. Fifty! Oh!

THE BURGLAR [*firmly*] I think you will admit that we deserve it for our enterprise, our risk, and the priceless boon of your emancipation from this wretched home. Is it a bargain, Mops?

THE PATIENT. It's a monstrous overcharge; but in dreamland generosity costs nothing. You shall have your fifty. Lucky for you that I'm asleep. If I wake up I shall never get loose from my people and my social position. It's all very well for you two criminals: you can do what you like. If you were ladies and gentlemen, youd know how hard it is not to do what everybody else does.

THE BURGLAR. Pardon me; but I think you will feel more at ease with us if I inform you that we are ladies and gentlemen. My own rank—not that I would presume on it for a moment—is, if you ask Burke or Debrett, higher than your own. Your people's money was made in trade: my people have always lived by owning property or governing Crown Colonies. Sweetie would be a woman of the highest position but for the unfortunate fact that her parents, though united in the sight of Heaven, were not legally married. At least so she tells me.

THE NURSE [*hotly*] I tell you what is true. [*To the patient*] Popsy and I are as good company as ever you kept.

THE PATIENT. No, Sweetie: you are a common little devil and a liar. But you amuse me. If you were a real lady you wouldnt amuse me. Youd be afraid to be so unladylike.

THE BURGLAR. Just so. Come! confess! we are better fun than your dear anxious mother and the curate and all the sympathizing relatives, arent we? Of course we are.

THE PATIENT. I think it perfectly scandalous that you two, who ought to be in prison, are having all the fun while I, because I am respectable and a lady, might just as well be in prison.

THE BURGLAR. Dont you wish you could come with us?

THE PATIENT [*calmly*] I fully intend to come with you. I'm going to make the most of this dream. Do you forget that I love you, Pops? The world is before us. You and Sweetie have had a week in the land of the mountain and the flood for seven guineas, tips included. Now you shall have an eternity with your Mops in the loveliest earthly paradise we can find, for nothing.

THE NURSE. And where do I come in?

THE PATIENT. You will be our chaperone.

THE NURSE. Chaperone! Well, you have a nerve, you have.

THE PATIENT. Listen. You will be a Countess. We shall go abroad, where nobody will know the difference. You shall have a splendid foreign title. The Countess Valbrioni: doesnt that tempt you?

THE NURSE. Tempt me hell! I'll see you further first.

THE BURGLAR. Stop. Sweetie: I have another idea. A regular dazzler. Let's stage a kidnap.

THE NURSE. What do you mean? stage a kidnap.

THE BURGLAR. It's quite simple. We kidnap Mops:

that is, we shall hide her in the mountains of Corsica or Istria or Dalmatia or Greece or in the Atlas or where you please that is out of reach of Scotland Yard. We shall pretend to be brigands. Her devoted mother will cough up five thousand to ransom her. We shall share the ransom fifty-fifty: fifty for Mops, twentyfive for you, twentyfive for me. Mops: you will realize not only the value of the pearls, but of yourself. What a stroke of finance!

THE PATIENT [*excited*] Greece! Dalmatia! Kidnapped! Brigands! Ransomed! [*Collapsing a little*] Oh, dont tantalize me, you two fools: you have forgotten the measles.

The Monster suddenly reappears from behind the screen. It is transfigured. The bloated moribund Caliban has become a dainty Ariel.

THE MONSTER [*picking up the last remark of the patient*] So have you. No more measles: that scrap for the jewels cured you and cured me. Ha ha! I am well, I am well, I am well. [*It bounds about ecstatically, and finally perches on the pillows and gets into bed beside the patient*].

THE NURSE. If you could jump out of bed to knock out Popsy and me you can jump out to dress yourself and hop it from here. Wrap yourself up well: we have a car waiting.

THE BURGLAR. It's no worse than being taken to a nursing home, Mops. Strike for freedom. Up with you!

They pull her out of bed.

THE PATIENT. But I cant dress myself without a maid.

THE NURSE. Have you ever tried?

THE BURGLAR. We will give you five minutes. If you are not ready we go without you [*he looks at his watch*].

The patient dashes at the wardrobe and tears out a fur cloak, a hat, a walking dress, a combination, a pair of stockings, black silk breeches, and shoes, all of which she flings on the floor. The nurse picks up most of them; the patient snatches up the rest; the two retire behind the screen. Meanwhile the burglar comes forward to the foot of the bed and comments oratorically, half auctioneer, half clergyman.

THE BURGLAR. Fur cloak. Seal. Old fashioned but worth forty-five guineas. Hat. Quiet and ladylike. Tailor made frock. Combination: silk and wool. Real silk stockings without ladders. Knickers: how daringly modern! Shoes: heels only two inches but no use for the mountains. What a theme for a sermon! The well brought up maiden revolts against her respectable life. The aspiring soul escapes from home, sweet home, which, as a wellknown author has said, is the girl's prison and the woman's workhouse. The intrusive care of her anxious parents, the officious concern of the family clergyman for her salvation and of the family doctor for her health, the imposed affection of uninteresting brothers and sisters, the outrage of being called by her Christian name by distant cousins who will not keep their distance, the invasion of her privacy and independence at every turn by questions as to where she has been and what she has been doing, the whispering behind her back about her chances of marriage, the continual violation of that sacred aura which surrounds every living soul like the halo surrounding the heads of saints in religious pictures: against all these devices for worrying her to death the innermost uppermost life in her rises like milk in a boiling saucepan and cries "Down with you! away with you! henceforth my gates are open to real life, bring what it may. For what sense is there in this world of hazards, disasters, elations and victories, except as a field for the adventures of the life everlasting? In vain do we disfigure our streets with scrawls of Safety First: in vain do the nations clamor for Security, security, security. They who cry Safety First never cross the street: the empires which sacrifice life to security find it in the grave. For me Safety Last; and Forward, Forward, always For—"

THE NURSE [*coming from behind the screen*] Dry up, Popsy: she's ready.

The patient, cloaked, hatted, and shoed, follows her breathless, and comes to the burglar, on his left.

THE PATIENT. Here I am, Pops. One kiss; and then—Lead on.

THE BURGLAR. Good. Your complexion still leaves something to be desired; but [*kissing her*] your breath is sweet: you breathe the air of freedom.

THE MONSTER. Never mind her complexion: look at mine!

THE BURGLAR [*releasing the patient and turning to the nurse*] Did you speak?

THE NURSE. No. Hurry up, will you.

THE BURGLAR. It must have been your mother snoring, Mops. It will be long before you hear that music again. Drop a tear.

THE PATIENT. Not one. A woman's future is not with her mother.

THE NURSE. If you are going to start preaching like Popsy, the milkman will be here before we get away. Remember, I have to take off this uniform and put on my walking things downstairs. Popsy: there may be a copper on his beat outside. Spy out and see. Safety First [*she hurries out*].

THE BURGLAR. Well, for just this once, safety first [*he makes for the window*].

THE PATIENT [*stopping him*] Idiot: the police cant touch you if I back you up. It's I who run the risk of being caught by my mother.

THE BURGLAR. True. You have an unexpectedly powerful mind. Pray Heaven that in kidnapping you I am not biting off more than I can chew. Come along. [*He runs out*].

THE PATIENT. He's forgotten the pearls!!! Thank Heaven he's a fool, a lovely fool: I shall be able to do as I like with him. [*She rushes to the dressing table; bundles the jewels into their case; and carries it out*].

THE MONSTER [*sitting up*] The play is now virtually over; but the characters will discuss it at great length for two acts more. The exit doors are all in order. Goodnight. [*It draws up the bedclothes round its neck and goes to sleep*].

ACT II

A *SEA beach in a mountainous country. Sand dunes rise to a brow which cuts off the view of the plain beyond, only the summits of the distant mountain range which bounds it being visible. An army hut on the hither side, with a klaxon electric horn projecting from a board on the wall, shews that we are in a military cantoonment. Opposite the hut is a particolored canvas bathing pavilion with a folding stool beside the entrance. As seen from the sand dunes the hut is on the right and the pavilion on the left. From the neighborhood of the hut a date palm throws a long shadow; for it is early morning.*

In this shadow sits a British colonel in a deck chair, peacefully reading the weekly edition of The Times, but with a revolver in his equipment. A light cane chair for use by his visitors is at hand by the hut. Though well over fifty, he is still slender, handsome, well set up, and every inch a commanding officer. His full style and title is Colonel Tallboys V.C., D.S.O. He won his cross as a company-officer, and has never looked back since then.

He is disturbed by a shattering series of explosions announcing the approach of a powerful and very imperfectly silenced motor bicycle from the side opposite to the huts.

TALLBOYS. Damn that noise!

The unseen rider dismounts and races his engine with a hideous clatter.

TALLBOYS [*angrily*] Stop that motorbike, will you?

The noise stops; and the bicyclist, having hoiked his machine up on to its stand, taken off his goggles and gloves, and extracted a letter from his carrier, comes past the pavilion into the colonel's view with the letter in his hand.

He is an insignificant looking private soldier, dusty as to his clothes and a bit gritty as to his windbeaten face. Otherwise there is nothing to find fault with: his tunic and puttees are smart and correct, and his speech ready and rapid. Yet the colonel, already irritated by the racket of the bicycle and the interruption to his newspaper, con-

templates him with stern disfavor; for there is something exasperatingly and inexplicably wrong about him. He wears a pith helmet with a pagri; and in profile this pagri suggests a shirt which he has forgotten to tuck in behind, whilst its front view as it falls on his shoulders gives him a feminine air of having ringlets and a veil which is in the last degree unsoldierly. His figure is that of a boy of seventeen; but he seems to have borrowed a long head and Wellingtonian nose and chin from somebody else for the express purpose of annoying the colonel. Fortunately for him these are offences which cannot be stated on a charge sheet and dealt with by the provo-marshal; and of this the colonel is angrily aware. The dispatch rider seems conscious of his incongruities; for, though very prompt, concise, and soldierly in his replies, he somehow suggests that there is an imprescriptible joke somewhere by an invisible smile which unhappily produces at times an impression of irony.

He salutes; hands the letter to the colonel; and stands at attention.

TALLBOYS [*taking the letter*] Whats this?

THE RIDER. I was sent with a letter to the headman of native village in the mountains, sir. That is his answer, sir.

TALLBOYS. I know nothing about it. Who sent you?

THE RIDER. Colonel Saxby, sir.

TALLBOYS. Colonel Saxby has just returned to the base, seriously ill. I have taken over from him. I am Colonel Tallboys.

THE RIDER. So I understand, sir.

TALLBOYS. Well, is this a personal letter to be sent on to him, or is it a dispatch?

THE RIDER. Dispatch, sir. Service document, sir. You may open it.

TALLBOYS [*turning in his chair and concentrating on him with fierce sarcasm*] Thank you. [*He surveys him from his instep to his nose*]. What is your name?

THE RIDER. Meek, sir.

TALLBOYS [*with disgust*] What!

THE RIDER. Meek, sir. M, double e, k.

The colonel looks at him with loathing, and tears open the letter. There is a painful silence whilst he puzzles over it.

TALLBOYS. In dialect. Send the interpreter to me.

MEEK. It's of no consequence, sir. It was only to impress the headman.

TALLBOYS. INNdeed. Who picked you for this duty?

MEEK. Sergeant, sir.

TALLBOYS. He should have selected a capable responsible person, with sufficient style to impress the native headman to whom Colonel Saxby's letter was addressed. How did he come to select you?

MEEK. I volunteered, sir.

TALLBOYS. Did you indeed? You consider yourself an impressive person, eh? You think you carry about with you the atmosphere of the British Empire, do you?

MEEK. No, sir. I know the country. I can speak the dialects a little.

TALLBOYS. Marvellous! And why, with all these accomplishments, are you not at least a corporal?

MEEK. Not educationally qualified, sir.

TALLBOYS. Illiterate! Are you not ashamed?

MEEK. No, sir.

TALLBOYS. Proud of it, eh?

MEEK. Cant help it, sir.

TALLBOYS. Where did you pick up your knowledge of the country?

MEEK. I was mostly a sort of tramp before I enlisted, sir.

TALLBOYS. Well, if I could get hold of the recruiting sergeant who enlisted you, I'd have his stripes off. Youre a disgrace to the army.

MEEK. Yessir.

TALLBOYS. Go and send the interpreter to me. And dont come back with him. Keep out of my sight.

MEEK [*hesitates*] Er—

TALLBOYS [*peremptorily*] Now then! Did you hear me give you an order? Send me the interpreter.

MEEK. The fact is, Colonel—

TALLBOYS [*outraged*] How dare you say Colonel and tell me that the fact is? Obey your order and hold your tongue.

MEEK. Yessir. Sorry, sir. *I* am the interpreter.

Tallboys bounds to his feet; towers over Meek, who looks smaller than ever; and folds his arms to give emphasis to a terrible rejoinder. On the point of delivering it, he suddenly unfolds them again and sits down resignedly.

TALLBOYS [*wearily and quite gently*] Very well. If you are the interpreter you had better interpret this for me. [*He proffers the letter*].

MEEK [*not accepting it*] No need, thank you, sir. The headman couldnt compose a letter, sir. I had to do it for him.

TALLBOYS. How did you know what was in Colonel Saxby's letter?

MEEK. I read it to him, sir.

TALLBOYS. Did he ask you to?

MEEK. Yessir.

TALLBOYS. He had no right to communicate the contents of such a letter to a private soldier. He cannot have known what he was doing. You must have represented yourself as being a responsible officer. Did you?

MEEK. It would be all the same to him, sir. He addressed me as Lord of the Western Isles.

TALLBOYS. You! You worm! If my letter was sent by the hands of an irresponsible messenger it should have contained a statement to that effect. Who drafted it?

MEEK. Quartermaster's clerk, sir.

TALLBOYS. Send him to me. Tell him to bring his note of Colonel Saxby's instructions. Do you hear? Stop making idiotic faces; and get a move on. Send me the quartermaster's clerk.

MEEK. The fact is—

TALLBOYS [*thundering*] Again!!

MEEK. Sorry, sir. *I* am the quartermaster's clerk.

TALLBOYS. What! You wrote both the letter and the headman's answer?

MEEK. Yessir.

TALLBOYS. Then either you are lying now or you were lying when you said you were illiterate. Which is it?

MEEK. I don't seem to be able to pass the examination when they want to promote me. It's my nerves, sir, I suppose.

TALLBOYS. Your nerves! What business has a soldier with nerves? You mean that you are no use for fighting, and have to be put to do anything that can be done without it.

MEEK. Yessir.

TALLBOYS. Well, next time you are sent with a letter I hope the brigands will catch you and keep you.

MEEK. There are no brigands, sir.

TALLBOYS. No brigands! Did you say no brigands?

MEEK. Yessir.

TALLBOYS. You are acquainted with the Articles of War, are you not?

MEEK. I have heard them read out, sir.

TALLBOYS. Do you understand them?

MEEK. I think so, sir.

TALLBOYS. You think so! Well, do a little more thinking. You are serving on an expeditionary force sent out to suppress brigandage in this district and to rescue a British lady who is being held for ransom. You know that. You dont think it: you know it, eh?

MEEK. So they say, sir.

TALLBOYS. You know also that under the Articles of War any soldier who knowingly does when on active service any act calculated to imperil the success of his Majesty's forces or any part thereof shall be liable to suffer death. Do you understand? Death!

MEEK. Yessir. Army Act, Part One, Section Four, Number Six. I think you mean Section Five, Number Five, sir.

TALLBOYS. Do I? Perhaps you will be good enough to quote Section Five, Number Five.

MEEK. Yessir. "By word of mouth spreads reports calculated to create unnecessary alarm or despondency."

TALLBOYS. It is fortunate for you, Private Meek, that the Act says nothing about private soldiers who create despondency by their personal appearance. Had it done so your life would not be worth half an hour's purchase.

MEEK. No, sir. Am I to file the letter and the reply with a translation, sir?

TALLBOYS [*tearing the letter to pieces and throwing them away*] Your folly has made a mockery of both. What did the headman say?

MEEK. Only that the country has very good roads now, sir. Motor coaches ply every day all the year round. The last active brigand retired fifteen years ago, and is ninety years old.

TALLBOYS. The usual tissue of lies. That headman is in league with the brigands. He takes a turn himself occasionally, I should say.

MEEK. I think not, sir. The fact is—

TALLBOYS. Did I hear you say "The fact is"?

MEEK. Sorry, sir. That old brigand was the headman himself. He is sending you a present of a sheep and six turkeys.

TALLBOYS. Send them back instantly. Take them back on your damned bicycle. Inform him that British officers are not orientals, and do not accept bribes from officials in whose districts they have to restore order.

MEEK. He wont understand, sir. He wont believe you have any authority unless you take presents. Besides, they havnt arrived yet.

TALLBOYS. Well, when his messengers arrive pack them

back with their sheep and their turkeys and a note to say that my favor can be earned by honesty and diligence, but not purchased.

MEEK. They wont dare take back either the presents or the note, sir. Theyll steal the sheep and turkeys and report gracious messages from you. Better keep the meat and the birds, sir: they will be welcome after a long stretch of regulation food.

TALLBOYS. Private Meek.

MEEK. Yessir.

TALLBOYS. If you should be at any future time entrusted with the command of this expedition you will no doubt give effect to your own views and moral standards. For the present will you be good enough to obey my orders without comment?

MEEK. Yessir. Sorry, sir.

As Meek salutes and turns to go, he is confronted by the nurse, who, brilliantly undressed for bathing under a variegated silk wrap, comes from the pavilion, followed by the patient in the character of a native servant. All traces of the patient's illness have disappeared: she is sunburnt to the color of terra cotta; and her muscles are hard and glistening with unguent. She is disguised en belle sauvage *by headdress, wig, ornaments, and girdle proper to no locality on earth except perhaps the Russian ballet. She carries a sun umbrella and a rug.*

TALLBOYS [*rising gallantly*] Ah, my dear Countess, delighted to see you. How good of you to come!

THE COUNTESS [*giving him her finger tips*] How do, Colonel? Hot, isn't it? [*Her dialect is now a spirited amalgamation of the foreign accents of all the waiters she has known*].

TALLBOYS. Take my chair. [*He goes behind it and moves it nearer to her*].

THE COUNTESS. Thanks. [*She throws off her wrap, which the patient takes, and flings herself with careless elegance into the chair, calling*] Mr. Meek. Mr.

Mee-e-e-eek!

Meek returns smartly, and touches the front of his cap.

THE COUNTESS. My new things from Paris have arrived at last. If you would be so very sweet as to get them to my bungalow somehow. Of course I will pay anything necessary. And could you get a letter of credit cashed for me. I'd better have three hundred pounds to go on with.

MEEK [*quite at his ease: unconsciously dropping the soldier and assuming the gentleman*] How many boxes, Countess?

THE COUNTESS. Six, I am afraid. Will it be a lot of trouble?

MEEK. It will involve a camel.

THE COUNTESS. Oh, strings of camels if necessary. Expense is no object. And the letter of credit?

MEEK. Sorry, Countess: I have only two hundred on me. You shall have the other hundred tomorrow. [*He hands her a roll of notes; and she gives him the letter of credit*].

THE COUNTESS. You are never at a loss. Thanks. So good of you.

TALLBOYS. Chut! Dismiss.

Meek comes to attention, salutes, left-turns, and goes out at the double.

TALLBOYS [*who has listened to this colloquy in renewed stupefaction*] Countess: that was very naughty of you.

THE COUNTESS. What have I done?

TALLBOYS. In camp you must never forget discipline. We keep it in the background; but it is always there and always necessary. That man is a private soldier. Any sort of social relation—any hint of familiarity with him—is impossible for you.

THE COUNTESS. But surely I may treat him as a human being.

TALLBOYS. Most certainly not. Your intention is natural and kindly; but if you treat a private soldier as a human being the result is disastrous to himself. He presumes. He takes liberties. And the consequence of that is that he gets into trouble and has a very bad time of it until he is taught his proper place by appropriate disciplinary measures. I must ask you to be particularly careful with this man Meek. He is only half-witted: he carries all his money about with him. If you have occasion to speak to him, make him feel by your tone that the relation between you is one of a superior addressing a very distant inferior. Never let him address you on his own initiative, or call you anything but "my lady." If there is anything we can do for you we shall be delighted to do it; but you must always ask me.

The patient, greatly pleased with the colonel for snubbing Sweetie, deposits her rug and umbrella on the sand, and places a chair for him on the lady's right with grinning courtesy. She then seats herself on the rug, and listens to them, hugging her knees and her umbrella, and trying to look as indigenous as possible.

TALLBOYS. Thank you. [*He sits down*].

THE COUNTESS. I am so sorry. But if I ask anyone else they only look helpless and say "You had better see Meek about it."

TALLBOYS. No doubt they put everything on the poor fellow because he is not quite all there. Is it understood that in future you come to me, and not to Meek?

THE COUNTESS. I will indeed, Colonel. I am so sorry, and I thoroughly understand. I am scolded and forgiven, arnt I?

TALLBOYS [*smiling graciously*] Admonished, we call it. But of course it is not your fault: I have no right to scold you. It is I who must ask your forgiveness.

THE COUNTESS. Granted.

THE PATIENT [*in waiting behind them, coughs significantly*]!!

THE COUNTESS [*hastily*] A vulgar expression, Colonel, isnt it? But so simple and direct. I like it.

TALLBOYS. I didnt know it was vulgar. It is concise.

THE COUNTESS. Of course it isnt really vulgar. But a little lower middle class, if you follow me.

THE PATIENT [*pokes the chair with the sun umbrella*]!

THE COUNTESS [*as before*] Any news of the brigands, Colonel?

TALLBOYS. No; but Miss Mopply's mother, who is in a distracted condition—very naturally of course, poor woman!—has actually sent me the ransom. She implores me to pay it and release her child. She is afraid that if I make the slightest hostile demonstration the brigands will cut off the girl's fingers and send them in one by one until the ransom is paid. She thinks they may even begin with her ears, and disfigure her for life. Of course that is a possibility: such things have been done; and the poor lady points out very justly that I cannot replace her daughter's ears by exterminating the brigands afterwards, as I shall most certainly do if they dare lay a hand on a British lady. But I cannot countenance such a concession to deliberate criminality as the payment of a ransom. [*The two conspirators exchange dismayed glances*]. I have sent a message to the old lady by wireless to say that payment of a ransom is out of the question, but that the British Government is offering a substantial reward for information.

THE COUNTESS [*jumping up excitedly*] Wotjesoy? A reward on top of the ransom?

THE PATIENT [*pokes her savagely with the umbrella*]!!!

TALLBOYS [*surprised*] No. Instead of the ransom.

THE COUNTESS [*recollecting herself*] Of course. How silly of me! [*She sits down and adds, reflectively*] If this native girl could find out anything would she get the reward?

TALLBOYS. Certainly she would. Good idea that: what?

THE COUNTESS. Yes, Colonel, isn't it?

TALLBOYS. By the way, Countess, I met three people yesterday who know you very well.

THE PATIENT [*forgetting herself and scrambling for-*

ward to her knees] But you—

THE COUNTESS [*stopping her with a backhanded slap on the mouth*] Silence, girl. How dare you interrupt the colonel? Go back to your place and hold your tongue.

The patient obeys humbly until the Colonel delicately turns his head away, when she shakes her fist threateningly at the smiter.

TALLBOYS. One of them was a lady. I happened to mention your brother's name; and she lit up at once and said "Dear Aubrey Bagot! I know his sister intimately. We were all three children together."

THE COUNTESS. It must have been dear Florence Dorchester. I hope she wont come here. I want to have an absolute holiday. I dont want to see anybody—except you, Colonel.

TALLBOYS. Haw! Very good of you to say so.

The burglar comes from the bathing tent, very elegant in black and white bathing costume and black silken wrap with white silk lapels: a clerical touch.

TALLBOYS [*continuing*] Ah, Bagot! Ready for your dip? I was just telling the Countess that I met some friends of yours yesterday. Fancy coming on them out here of all places! Shews how small the world is, after all. [*Rising*] And now I am off to inspect stores. There is a shortage of maroons that I dont understand.

THE COUNTESS. What a pity! I love maroons. They have such nice ones at that confectioner's near the Place Vendôme.

TALLBOYS. Oh, youre thinking of marrons glacés. No: maroons are fireworks: things that go off with a bang. For signalling.

THE COUNTESS. Oh! the things they used to have in the war to warn us of an air raid?

TALLBOYS. Just so. Well, au revoir.

THE COUNTESS. Au revoir. Au revoir.

The Colonel touches his cap gallantly and bustles off past the hut to his inspection.

THE PATIENT [*rising vengefully*] You dare smack me in the face again, my girl, and I'll lay you out flat, even if I have to give away the whole show.

THE COUNTESS. Well, you keep that umbrella to yourself next time. What do you suppose I'm made of? Leather?

AUBREY [*coming between them*] Now! now! now! Children! children! Whats wrong?

THE PATIENT. This silly bitch—

AUBREY. Oh no, no, no, Mops. Damn it, be a lady. Whats the matter, Sweetie?

THE COUNTESS. You shouldnt talk like that, dearie. A low girl might say a thing like that; but youre expected to know better.

AUBREY. Mops: youve shocked Sweetie.

THE PATIENT. Well: do you think she never shocks me? She's a walking earthquake. And now what are we to do if these people the colonel has met turn up? There must be a real Countess Valbrioni.

THE COUNTESS. Not much there isnt. Do you suppose we three are the only liars in the world? All you have to do is to give yourself a swell title, and all the snobs within fifty miles will swear that you are their dearest friend.

AUBREY. The first lesson a crook has to learn, darling, is that nothing succeeds like lying. Make any statement that is so true that it has been staring us in the face all our lives, and the whole world will rise up and passionately contradict you. If you dont withdraw and apologize, it will be the worse for you. But just tell a thundering silly lie that everyone knows is a lie, and a murmur of pleased assent will hum up from every quarter of the globe. If Sweetie had introduced herself as what she obviously is: that is, an ex-hotel chambermaid who became a criminal on principle through the preaching of an ex-army chaplain —me!—with whom she fell in love deeply but transitorily, nobody would have believed her. But she has no sooner made the impossible statement that she is a countess, and that the ex-chaplain is her half step-brother the Honorable Aubrey Bagot, than clouds of witnesses spring up to assure Colonel Tallboys that it is all gospel truth. So have no fear of exposure, darling; and do you, my Sweetie, lie and lie and lie until your imagination bursts.

THE PATIENT [*throwing herself moodily into the deck chair*] I wonder are all crooks as fond of preaching as you are.

AUBREY [*bending affectionately over her*] Not all, dearest. I dont preach because I am a crook, but because I have a gift—a divine gift—that way.

THE PATIENT. Where did you get it? Is your father a bishop?

AUBREY [*straightening himself up to declaim*] Have I not told you that he is an atheist, and, like all atheists, an inflexible moralist? He said I might become a preacher if I believed what I preached. That, of course, was nonsense: my gift of preaching is not confined to what I believe: I can preach anything, true or false. I am like a violin, on which you can play all sorts of music, from jazz to Mozart. [*Relaxing*] But the old man never could be brought to see it. He said the proper profession for me was the bar. [*He snatches up the rug; replaces it on the patient's left; and throws himself down lazily on it*].

THE COUNTESS. Aint we going to bathe?

AUBREY. Oh, dash it, dont lets go into the water. Lets sun-bathe.

THE COUNTESS. Lazy devil! [*She takes the folding stool from the pavilion, and sits down discontentedly*].

THE PATIENT. Your father was right. If you have no conscience about what you preach, your proper job is at the bar. But as you have no conscience about what you do, you will probably end in the dock.

AUBREY. Most likely. But I am a born preacher, not a pleader. The theory of legal procedure is that if you set two liars to expose one another, the truth will emerge. That would not suit me. I greatly dislike being contradicted; and the only place where a man is safe from contradiction is in the pulpit. I detest argument: it is unmannerly, and obscures the preacher's message. Besides, the law is too much concerned with crude facts and too little with spiritual things; and it is in spiritual things that I am interested: they alone call my gift into full play.

THE PATIENT. You call preaching things you dont believe spiritual, do you?

AUBREY. Put a sock in it, Mops. My gift is divine: it is not limited by my petty personal convictions. It is a gift of lucidity as well as of eloquence. Lucidity is one of the most precious of gifts: the gift of the teacher: the gift of explanation. I can explain anything to anybody; and I love doing it. I feel I must do it if only the doctrine is beautiful and subtle and exquisitely put together. I may feel instinctively that it is the rottenest nonsense. Still, if I can get a moving dramatic effect out of it, and preach a really splendid sermon about it, my gift takes possession of me and obliges me to sail in and do it. Sweetie: go and get me a cushion for my head: there's a dear.

THE PATIENT. Do nothing of the kind, Sweetie. Let him wait on himself.

THE COUNTESS [*rising*] He'd only mess everything about looking for it. I like to have my rooms left tidy. [*She goes into the pavilion*].

THE PATIENT. Isn't that funny, Pops? She has a conscience as a chambermaid and none as a woman.

AUBREY. Very few people have more than one point of honor, Mops. And lots of them havnt even one.

THE COUNTESS [*returning with a silk cushion, which she hurls hard at Aubrey's head*] There! And now I give you both notice. I'm getting bored with this place.

AUBREY [*making himself comfortable with his cushion*] Oh, you are always getting bored.

THE PATIENT. I suppose that means that you are tired of Tallboys.

THE COUNTESS [*moving restlessly about*] I am fed up

with him to that degree that I sometimes feel I could almost marry him, just to put him on the list of the inevitables that I must put up with willynilly, like getting up in the morning, and washing and dressing and eating and drinking: things you darent let yourself get tired of because if you did theyd drive you mad. Lets go and have a bit of real life somewhere.

THE PATIENT. Real life! I wonder where thats to be found! Weve spent nearly six thousand pounds in two months looking for it. The money we got for the necklace wont last for ever.

AUBREY. Sweetie: you will have to stick it in this spot until we touch that ransom; and that's all about it.

THE COUNTESS. I'll do as I like, not what you tell me. And I tell you again—the two of you—you can take a week's notice. I'm bored with this business. I need a change.

AUBREY. What are we to do with her, Mops? Always change! change! change!

THE COUNTESS. Well, I like to see new faces.

AUBREY. I could be happy as a Buddha in a temple, eternally contemplating my own middle and having the same old priest to polish me up every day. But Sweetie wants a new face every fortnight. I have known her fall in love with a new face twice in the same week. [*Turning to her*] Woman: have you any sense of the greatness of constancy?

COUNTESS. I might be constant if I were a real countess. But I'm only a hotel chambermaid; and a hotel chambermaid gets so used to new faces that at last they become a necessity. [*She sits down on the stool*].

AUBREY. And the oftener the faces change the more the tips come to, eh?

COUNTESS. Oh, it's not that, though of course that counts. The real secret of it is that though men are awfully nice for the first few days, it doesnt last. You get the best out of men by having them always new. What I say is that a love affair should always be a honeymoon. And the only way to make sure of that is to keep changing the man; for the same man can never keep it up. In all my life I have known only one man that kept it up til he died.

THE PATIENT [*interested*] Ah! Then the thing is possible?

COUNTESS. Yes: it was a man that married my sister: that was how I came to know about it.

AUBREY. And his ardor never palled? Day in and day out, until death did them part, he was the same as on the wedding day? Is that really true, Sweetie?

THE COUNTESS. It is. But then he beat her on their wedding day; and he beat her just as hard every day afterwards. I made her get a separation order; but she went back to him because nobody else paid her any attention.

AUBREY. Why didn't you tell me that before? I'd have beaten you black and blue sooner than lose you. [*Sitting up*] Would you believe it, Mops, I was in love with this woman: madly in love with her. She was not my intellectual equal; and I had to teach her table manners. But there was an extraordinary sympathy between our lower centres; and when after ten days she threw me over for another man I was restrained from murder and suicide only by the most resolute exercise of my reasoning powers, my determination to be a civilized man, and fear of the police.

THE COUNTESS. Well, I gave you a good time for the ten days, didnt I? Lots of people dont get that much to look back on. Besides, you know it was for your own good, Popsy. We werent really suited, were we?

AUBREY. You had acquired an insatiable taste for commercial travellers. You could sample them at the rate of three a week. I could not help admiring such amazing mobility of the affections. I had heard operatic tenors bawling Woman Is Fickle; but it always seemed to me that what was to be dreaded in women was their inplacable constancy. But you! Fickle! I should think so.

THE COUNTESS. Well, the travellers were just as bad,

you know.

AUBREY. Just as bad! Say just as good. Fickleness means simply mobility, and mobility is a mark of civilization. You should pride yourself on it. If you dont you will lose your self-respect; and I cannot endure a woman who has no self-respect.

THE COUNTESS. Oh, whats the use of us talking about self-respect? You are a thief and so am I. I go a little further than that, myself; and so would you if you were a woman. Dont you be a hypocrite, Popsy: at least not with me.

AUBREY. At least not with you! Sweetie: that touch of concern for my spiritual welfare almost convinces me that you still love me.

THE COUNTESS. Not me. Not much. I'm through with you, my lad. And I cant quite fancy the colonel: he's too old, and too much the gentleman.

AUBREY. He's better than nobody. Who else is there?

THE COUNTESS. Well, there's the sergeant. I daresay I have low tastes; but he's my sort, and the colonel isnt.

THE PATIENT. Have you fallen in love with Sergeant Fielding, Sweetie?

THE COUNTESS. Well, yes; if you like to call it that.

AUBREY. May I ask have you sounded him on the subject?

THE COUNTESS. How can I? I'm a countess; and he's only a sergeant. If I as much as let on that I'm conscious of his existence I give away the show to the colonel. I can only look at him. And I cant do even that when anyone else is looking. And all the time I want to hug him [*she breaks down in tears*].

AUBREY. Oh for Heaven's sake dont start crying.

THE PATIENT. For all you know, Sweetie, the sergeant may be a happily married man.

THE COUNTESS. What difference does that make to my feelings? I am so lonely. The place is so dull. No pictures. No dances. Nothing to do but be ladylike. And the one really lovable man going to waste! I'd rather be dead.

THE PATIENT. Well, it's just as bad for me.

THE COUNTESS. No it isnt. Youre a real lady: youre broken in to be dull. Besides, you have Popsy. And youre supposed to be our servant. That gives you the run of the whole camp when youre tired of him. You can pick up a private when you like. Whats to prevent you?

THE PATIENT. My ladylike morals, I suppose.

THE COUNTESS. Morals your grandmother! I thought youd left all that flapdoodle behind you when you came away with us.

THE PATIENT. I meant to. Ive tried to. But you shock me in spite of myself every second time you open your mouth.

THE COUNTESS. Dont you set up to be a more moral woman than I am, because youre not.

THE PATIENT. I dont pretend to be. But I may tell you that my infatuation for Popsy, which I now see was what really nerved me to this astonishing breakaway, has been, so far, quite innocent. Can you believe that, you clod?

THE COUNTESS. Oh yes I can: Popsy's satisfied as long as you let him talk. What I mean is—and I tell it to you straight—that with all my faults I'm content with one man at a time.

THE PATIENT. Do you suggest that I am carrying on with two men?

THE COUNTESS. I dont suggest anything. I say what I mean straight out; and if you dont like it you can lump it. You may be in love with Popsy; but youre interested in Private Meek, though what you see in that dry little worm beats me.

THE PATIENT. Have you noticed, my Sweetie, that your big strapping splendid sergeant is completely under the thumb of that dry little worm?

THE COUNTESS. He wont be when I get him under my thumb. But you just be careful. Take this tip from me: one man at a time. I am advising you for your good, because youre only a beginner; and what you think is love, and interest, and all that, is not real love at all: three quarters of it is only unsatisfied curiosity. Ive lived at that address myself; and I know. When I love a man now it's all love and nothing else. It's the real thing while it lasts. I havnt the least curiosity about my lovely sergeant: I know just what he'll say and what he'll do. I just want him to do it.

THE PATIENT [*rising, revolted*] Sweetie: I really cannot bear any more of this. No doubt it's perfectly true. It's quite right that you should say it frankly and plainly. I envy and admire the frightful coolness with which you plump it all out. Perhaps I shall get used to it in time. But at present it knocks me to pieces. I shall simply have to go away if you pursue the subject. [*She sits down in the cane chair with her back to them*].

AUBREY. Thats the worst of Sweetie. We all have—to put it as nicely as I can—our lower centres and our higher centres. Our lower centres act: they act with a terrible power that sometimes destroys us; but they dont talk. Speech belongs to the higher centres. In all the great poetry and literature of the world the higher centres speak. In all respectable conversation the higher centres speak, even when they are saying nothing or telling lies. But the lower centres are there all the time: a sort of guilty secret with every one of us, though they are dumb. I remember asking my tutor at college whether, if anyone's lower centres began to talk, the shock would not be worse than the one Balaam got when his donkey began talking to him. He only told me half a dozen improper stories to shew how openminded he was. I never mentioned the subject again until I met Sweetie. Sweetie is Balaam's ass.

THE COUNTESS. Keep a civil tongue in your head, Popsy. I—

AUBREY [*springing to his feet*] Woman: I am paying you a compliment: Balaam's ass was wiser than Balaam. You should read your Bible. That is what makes Sweetie almost superhuman. Her lower centres speak. Since the war the lower centres have become vocal. And the effect is that of an earthquake. For they speak truths that have never been spoken before—truths that the makers of our domestic institutions have tried to ignore. And now that Sweetie goes shouting them all over the place, the institutions are rocking and splitting and sundering. They leave us no place to live, no certainties, no workable morality, no heaven, no hell, no commandments, and no God.

THE PATIENT. What about the light in our own souls that you were so eloquent about the day before yesterday at lunch when you drank a pint of champagne?

AUBREY. Most of us seem to have no souls. Or if we have them, they have nothing to hang on to. Meanwhile, Sweetie goes on shouting. [*He takes refuge in the deck chair*].

THE COUNTESS [*rising*] Oh, what are you gassing about? I am not shouting. I should be a good woman if it wasnt so dull. If youre goodnatured, you just get put upon. Who are the good women? Those that enjoy being dull and like being put upon. Theyve no appetites. Life's thrown away on them: they get nothing out of it.

THE PATIENT. Well, come, Sweetie! What do you get out of it?

THE COUNTESS. Excitement: thats what I get out of it. Look at Popsy and me! We're always planning robberies. Of course I know it's mostly imagination; but the fun is in the planning and the expectation. Even if we did them and were caught, there would be the excitement of being tried and being in all the papers. Look at poor Harry Smiler that murdered the cop in Croydon! When he came and told us what he'd done Popsy offered to go out and get him some cyanide to poison himself; for it was a dead sure thing that he'd be caught and bumped off. "What!" says Harry; "and lose the excitement of being tried for my life! I'd rather be hanged" he says; and hanged he was. And I say it must have been almost worth it. After all, he'd have died anyhow: perhaps of something really painful. Harry wasnt a bad man really; but he couldnt bear dullness. He had a wonderful collection of pistols that he had begun as a boy: he picked up a lot in the war. Just for the romance of it, you know: he meant no harm. But he'd never shot anyone with them; and at last the temptation was too great and he went out and shot the cop. Just for nothing but the feeling that he'd fired the thing off and done somebody in with it. When Popsy asked him why he'd done it, all he could say was that it was a sort of fulfilment. But it gives you an idea, doesnt it, of what I mean? [*She sits down again, relieved by her outburst*].

AUBREY. All it means is a low vitality. Here is a man with all the miracles of the universe to stagger his imagination and all the problems of human destiny to employ his mind, and he goes out and shoots an innocent policeman because he can think of nothing more interesting to do. Quite right to hang him. And all the people who can find nothing more exciting to do than to crowd into the court to watch him being sentenced to death should have been hanged too. You will be hanged someday, Sweetie, because you have not what people call a richly stored mind. I have tried to educate you—

THE COUNTESS. Yes: you gave me books to read. But I couldnt read them: they were as dull as ditchwater. Ive tried crossword puzzles to occupy my mind and keep me off planning robberies; but what crossword puzzle is half the fun and excitement of picking somebody's pocket, let alone that you cant live by it? You wanted me to take to drink to keep me quiet. But I dont like being drunk; and what would become of my good looks if I did? Ten bottles of champagne couldnt make you feel as you do when you walk past a policeman who has only to stop you and search you to put you away for three years.

THE PATIENT. Pops: did you really try to set her drinking? What a thoroughpaced blackguard you are!

AUBREY. She is much better company when she's half drunk. Listen to her now, when she is sober!

THE PATIENT. Sweetie: are you really having such a jolly time after all? You began by threatening to give up our exciting enterprise because it is so dull.

AUBREY. She is free. There is the sergeant. And there is always the hope of something turning up and the sense of being ready for it without having to break all the shackles and throw down all the walls that imprison a respectable woman.

THE PATIENT. Well, what about me?

AUBREY [*puzzled*] Well, what about you? You are free, arnt you?

THE PATIENT [*rising very deliberately, and going behind him to his left hand, which she picks up and fondles as she sermonizes, seated on the arm of his chair*] My angel love, you have rescued me from respectability so completely that I have for a month past been living the life of a mountain goat. I have got rid of my anxious worrying mother as completely as a weaned kid, and I no longer hate her. My slavery to cooks stuffing me with long meals of fish, flesh, and fowl is a thing of the miserable past: I eat dates and bread and water and raw onions when I can get them; and when I cant get them I fast, with the result that I have forgotten what illness means; and if I ran away from you two neither of you could catch me; and if you did I could fight the pair of you with one hand tied behind me. I revel in all your miracles of the universe: the delicious dawns, the lovely sunsets, the changing winds, the cloud pictures, the flowers, the animals and their ways, the birds and insects and reptiles. Every day is a day of adventure with its cold and heat, its light and darkness, its cycles of exultant vigor and exhaustion, hunger and satiety, its longings for action that change into a longing for sleep, its thoughts of heavenly things that change so suddenly into a need for food.

AUBREY. What more could any mortal desire?

THE PATIENT [*seizing him by the ears*] Liar.

AUBREY. Thank you. You mean, I presume, that these

things do not satisfy you: you want me as well.

THE PATIENT. You!! You!!! you selfish lazy sugary tongued blackguard. [*Releasing him*] No: I included you with the animals and their ways, just as I included Sweetie and the sergeant.

THE COUNTESS. You let Sweetie and her sergeant alone: d'y'hear? I have had enough of that joke on me.

THE PATIENT [*rising and taking her by the chin to turn her face up*] It is no joke, Sweetiest: it is the dead solemn earnest. I called Pops a liar, Sweetie, because all this is not enough. The glories of nature dont last any decently active person a week, unless theyre professional naturalists or mathematicians or a painter or something. I want something sensible to do. A beaver has a jolly time because it has to build its dam and bring up its family. I want my little job like the beaver. If I do nothing but contemplate the universe there is so much in it that is cruel and terrible and wantonly evil, and so much more that is oppressively astronomical and endless and inconceivable and impossible, that I shall just go stark raving mad and be taken back to my mother with straws in my hair. The truth is, I am free; I am healthy; I am happy; and I am utterly miserable. [*Turning on Aubrey*] Do you hear? Utterly miserable.

AUBREY [*losing his temper*] And what do you suppose I am? Here with nothing to do but drag about two damn' silly women and talk to them.

THE COUNTESS. It's worse for them. They have to listen to you.

THE PATIENT. I despise you. I hate you. You—you—you—you gentleman thief. What right has a thief to be a gentleman? Sweetie is bad enough, heaven knows, with her vulgarity and her low cunning: always trying to get the better of somebody or to get hold of a man; but at least she's a woman; and she's real. Men are not real: theyre all talk, talk, talk—

THE COUNTESS [*half rising*] You keep a civil tongue in

your head: do you hear?

THE PATIENT. Another syllable of your cheek, Sweetie; and I'll give you a hiding that will keep you screaming for half an hour. [*Sweetie subsides*]. I want to beat somebody: I want to kill somebody. I shall end by killing the two of you. What are we, we three glorious adventurers? Just three inefficient fertilizers.

AUBREY. What on earth do you mean by that?

THE PATIENT. Yes: inefficient fertilizers. We do nothing but convert good food into bad manure. We are walking factories of bad manure: thats what we are.

THE COUNTESS [*rising*] Well, I am not going to sit here and listen to that sort of talk. You ought to be ashamed of yourself.

AUBREY [*rising also, shocked*] Miss Mopply: there are certain disgusting truths that no lady would throw in the teeth of her fellow creatures—

THE PATIENT. I am not a lady: I am free now to say what I please. How do you like it?

THE COUNTESS [*relenting*] Look here, dearie. You mustnt go off at the deep end like this. You— [*The patient turns fiercely on her: she screams*] Ah-a-a-ah! Popsy: she's mad. Save me [*She runs away, out past the pavilion*].

AUBREY. What is the matter with you? Are you out of your senses? [*He tries to hold her; but she sends him sprawling*].

THE PATIENT. No. I am exercising my freedom. The freedom you preached. The freedom you made possible for me. You dont like to hear Sweetie's lower centres shouting. Well, now you hear my higher centres shouting. You dont seem to like it any better.

AUBREY. Mops: youre hysterical. You felt splendid an hour ago; and you will feel splendid again an hour from now. You will always feel splendid if you keep yourself fit.

THE PATIENT. Fit for what? A lost dog feels fit: thats what makes him stray; but he's the unhappiest thing alive.

I am a lost dog: a tramp, a vagabond. Ive got nothing to do. Ive got nowhere to go. Sweetie's miserable; and youre miserable; and I'm miserable; and I shall just kick you and beat you to a jelly.

She rushes at him. He dodges her and runs off past the hut. At that moment Tallboys returns with Meek past the other side of the hut; and the patient, unable to check herself, crashes into his arms.

TALLBOYS [*sternly*] Whats this? What are you doing here? Why are you making this noise? Dont clench your fists in my presence. [*She droops obsequiously*]. Whats the matter?

THE PATIENT [*salaaming and chanting*] Bmal elttil a dah yram, Tuan.

TALLBOYS. Can you speak English?

THE PATIENT. No Engliss.

TALLBOYS. Or French?

THE PATIENT. No Frennss, Tuan. Wons sa etihw saw eceelf sti.

TALLBOYS. Very well: dont do it again. Now off with you.

She goes out backward into the pavilion, salaaming. Tallboys sits down in the deck chair.

TALLBOYS [*To Meek*] Here, you. You say youre the interpreter. Did you understand what that girl said to me?

MEEK. Yessir.

TALLBOYS. What dialect was it? It didnt sound like what the natives speak here.

MEEK. No sir. I used to speak it at school. English back slang, sir.

TALLBOYS. Back slang? What do you mean?

MEEK. English spelt backwards. She reversed the order of the words too, sir. That shews that she has those two little speeches off by heart.

TALLBOYS. But how could a native girl do such a thing? I couldnt do it myself.

MEEK. That shews that she's not a native girl, sir.

TALLBOYS. But this must be looked into. Were you able to pick up what she said?

MEEK. Only bmal elttil, sir. That was quite easy. It put me on to the rest.

TALLBOYS. But what does bmal elttil mean?

MEEK. Little lamb, sir.

TALLBOYS. She called me a little lamb!

MEEK. No sir. All she said was "Mary had a little lamb." And when you asked her could she speak French she said, of course, "Its fleece was white as snow."

TALLBOYS. But that was insolence.

MEEK. It got her out of her difficulty, sir.

TALLBOYS. This is very serious. The woman is passing herself off on the Countess as a native servant.

MEEK. Do you think so, sir?

TALLBOYS. I dont think so: I know so. Dont be a fool, man. Pull yourself together, and dont make silly answers.

MEEK. Yessir. No sir.

TALLBOYS [*angrily bawling at him*] "Ba Ba black sheep: have you any wool? Yes sir, no sir, three bags full." Dont say yessir no sir to me.

MEEK. No sir.

TALLBOYS. Go and fetch that girl back. Not a word to her about my finding her out, mind. When I have finished with her you will explain to me about those maroons.

MEEK. Yessir. [*He goes into the pavilion*].

TALLBOYS. Hurry up. [*He settles himself comfortably and takes out his cigaret case*].

The Countess peers round the corner of the pavilion to see whether she may safely return. Aubrey makes a similar reconnaissance round the corner of the hut.

THE COUNTESS. Here I am again, you see. [*She smiles fascinatingly at the Colonel and sits down on her stool*].

AUBREY. Moi aussi. May I— [*he stretches himself on the rug*].

TALLBOYS [*sitting up and putting the cigaret case back in his pocket*] Just in the nick of time. I was about to send for you. I have made a very grave discovery. That native servant of yours is not a native. Her lingo is a ridiculous fraud. She is an English-woman.

AUBREY. You dont say so!

THE COUNTESS. Oh, impossible.

TALLBOYS. Not a doubt of it. She's a fraud: take care of your jewels. Or else—and this is what I suspect—she's a spy.

AUBREY. A spy! But we are not at war.

TALLBOYS. The League of Nations has spies everywhere. [*To the Countess*] You must allow me to search her luggage at once, before she knows that I have found her out.

THE COUNTESS. But I have missed nothing. I am sure she hasnt stolen anything. What do you want to search her luggage for?

TALLBOYS. For maroons.

THE COUNTESS } [*together*] { Maroons!
AUBREY } { Maroons!

TALLBOYS. Yes, maroons. I inspected the stores this morning; and the maroons are missing. I particularly wanted them to recall me at lunch time when I go sketching. I am rather a dab at water-colors. And there is not a single maroon left. There should be fifteen.

AUBREY. Oh, I can clear that up. It's one of your men: Meek. He goes about on a motor bicycle with a sack full of maroons and a lot of wire. He said he was surveying. He was evidently very anxious to get rid of me; so I did not press my inquiries. But that accounts for the maroons.

TALLBOYS. Not at all. This is very serious. Meek is a half witted creature who should never have been enlisted. He is like a child: this woman could do anything she pleases with him.

THE COUNTESS. But what could she possibly want with maroons?

TALLBOYS. I dont know. This expedition has been sent out without the sanction of the League of Nations. We always forget to consult it when there is anything serious in hand. The woman may be an emissary of the League. She may be working against us.

THE COUNTESS. But even so, what harm can she do us?

TALLBOYS [*tapping his revolver*] My dear lady, do you suppose I am carrying this for fun? Dont you realize that the hills here are full of hostile tribes who may try to raid us at any moment? Look at that electric horn there. If it starts honking, look out; for it will mean that a body of tribesmen has been spotted advancing on us.

THE COUNTESS [*alarmed*] If I'd known that, you wouldnt have got me here. Is that so, Popsy?

AUBREY. Well, yes; but it doesnt matter: they're afraid of us.

TALLBOYS. Yes, because they dont know that we are a mere handful of men. But if this woman is in communication with them and has got hold of that idiot Meek, we may have them down on us like a swarm of hornets. I dont like this at all. I must get to the bottom of it at once. Ah! here she comes.

Meek appears at the entrance to the pavilion. He stands politely aside to let the patient pass him, and remains there.

MEEK. The colonel would like a word with you, Miss.

AUBREY. Go easy with her, Colonel. She can run like a deer. And she has muscles of iron. You had better turn out the guard before you tackle her.

TALLBOYS. Pooh! Here, you!

The patient comes to him past the Countess with an air of disarming innocence; falls on her knees; lifts her palms; and smites the ground with her forehead.

TALLBOYS. They tell me you can run fast. Well, a bullet can run faster. [*He taps his revolver*]. Do you understand that?

THE PATIENT [*salaaming*] Bmal elttil a dah yram wons sa etihwa saw eceelf tsi—

TALLBOYS [*tomitruant*] And everywhere that Mary went—

THE PATIENT [*adroitly cutting in*] That lamb was sure to go. Got me, Colonel. How clever of you! Well, what of it?

TALLBOYS. That is what I intend to find out. You are not a native.

THE PATIENT. Yes, of Somerset.

TALLBOYS. Precisely. Well, why are you disguised? Why did you try to make me believe that you dont understand English?

THE PATIENT. For a lark, Colonel.

TALLBOYS. Thats not good enough. Why have you passed yourself off on this lady as a native servant? Being a servant is no lark. Answer me. Dont stand there trying to invent a lie. Why did you pretend to be a servant?

THE PATIENT. One has so much more control of the house as a servant than as a mistress nowadays, Colonel.

TALLBOYS. Very smart, that. You will tell me next that one controls a regiment much more effectively as a private than as a colonel, eh?

The klaxon sounds stridently. The Colonel draws his revolver and makes a dash for the top of the sandhill, but is outraced by Meek, who gets there first and takes the word of command with irresistible authority, leaving him stupent. Aubrey, who has scrambled to his feet, moves towards the sand dunes to see what is happening. Sweetie clutches the patient's arm in terror and drags her towards the pavilion. She is fiercely shaken off; and Mops stands her ground defiantly and runs towards the sound of the guns when they begin.

MEEK. Stand to. Charge your magazines. Stand by the maroons. How many do you make them, sergeant? How far off?

SERGEANT FIELDING [*invisible*] Forty horse. Nine hundred yards, about, I make it.

MEEK. Rifles at the ready. Cut-offs open. Sights up to eighteen hundred, right over their heads: no hitting. Ten rounds rapid: fire. [*Fusillade of rifles*]. How is that?

SERGEANT'S VOICE. Theyre coming on, sir.

MEEK. Number one maroons: ready. Contact. [*Formidable explosions on the right*]. How is that?

SERGEANT'S VOICE. Theyve stopped.

MEEK. Number two maroons ready. Contact. [*Explosions on the left*]. How is that?

SERGEANT'S VOICE. Bolted, sir, every man of them.

Meek returns from the hill in the character of an insignificant private, followed by Aubrey, to the Colonel's left and right respectively.

MEEK. Thats all right, sir. Excuse interruption.

TALLBOYS. Oh! You call this an interruption?

MEEK. Yessir: theres nothing in it to trouble you about. Shall I draw up the report, sir? Important engagement: enemy routed: no British casualties. D.S.O. for you, perhaps, sir.

TALLBOYS. Private Meek: may I ask—if you will pardon my presumption—who is in command of this expedition, you or I?

MEEK. You, sir.

TALLBOYS [*repouching the revolver*] You flatter me. Thank you. May I ask, further, who the devil gave you leave to plant the entire regimental stock of maroons all over the hills and explode them in the face of the enemy?

MEEK. It was the duty of the intelligence orderly, sir. I'm the intelligence orderly. I had to make the enemy believe that the hills are bristling with British cannon. They think that now, sir. No more trouble from them.

TALLBOYS. Indeed! Quartermaster's clerk, interpreter, intelligence orderly. Any further rank of which I have not been informed?

MEEK. No sir.

TALLBOYS. Quite sure youre not a fieldmarshal, eh?

MEEK. Quite sure, sir. I never was anything higher than a colonel.

TALLBOYS. You a colonel? What do you mean?

MEEK. Not a real colonel, sir. Mostly a brevet, sir, to save appearances when I had to take command.

TALLBOYS. And how do you come to be a private now?

MEEK. I prefer the ranks, sir. I have a freer hand. And the conversation in the officers' mess doesnt suit me. I always resign a commission and enlist again.

TALLBOYS. Always! How many commissions have you held?

MEEK. I dont quite remember, sir. Three, I think.

TALLBOYS. Well, I am dashed!

THE PATIENT. Oh, Colonel! And you mistook this great military genius for a half wit!!!

TALLBOYS [*with aplomb*] Naturally. The symptoms are precisely the same. [*To Meek*] Dismiss.

Meek salutes and trots smartly out past the hut.

AUBREY. By Jove!!

THE COUNTESS. Well I ne— [*Correcting herself*] Tiens, tiens, tiens, tiens!

THE PATIENT. What are you going to do about him, Colonel?

TALLBOYS. Madam: the secret of command, in the army and elsewhere, is never to waste a moment doing anything that can be delegated to a subordinate. I have a passion for sketching in watercolors. Hitherto the work of commanding my regiment has interfered very seriously with its gratification. Henceforth I shall devote myself almost entirely to sketching, and leave the command of the expedition to Private Meek. And since you all seem to be on more intimate terms with him than I can claim, will you be good enough to convey to him—casually, you understand—that I already possess the D.S.O. and that what I am out for at present is a K.C.B. Or rather, to be strictly accurate, that is what my wife is out for. For myself, my sole concern for the moment is whether I should paint that sky with Prussian blue or with cobalt.

THE COUNTESS. Fancy you wasting your time on painting pictures!

TALLBOYS. Countess: I paint pictures to make me feel sane. Dealing with men and women makes me feel mad. Humanity always fails me: Nature never.

ACT III

A *NARROW gap leading down to the beach through masses of soft brown sandstone, pitted with natural grottoes. Sand and big stones in the foreground. Two of the grottoes are accessible from the beach by mounting from the stones, which make rough platforms in front of them. The soldiers have amused themselves by hewing them into a rude architecture and giving them fancy names. The one on your right as you descend the rough path through the gap is taller than it is broad, and has a natural pillar and a stone like an altar in it, giving a Gothic suggestion which has been assisted by knocking the top of the opening into something like a pointed arch, and surmounting it with the inscription* ST PAULS. *The grotto to the left is much wider. It contains a bench long enough to accommodate two persons; its recesses are illuminated rosily by bulbs wrapped in pink paper; and some scholarly soldier has carved above it in Greek characters the word* Αγαπεμονε, *beneath which is written in red chalk* THE ABODE OF LOVE, *under which again some ribald has added in white chalk,* NO NEED TO WASTE THE ELECTRIC LIGHT.

For the moment The Abode of Love has been taken possession of by the sergeant, a wellbuilt handsome man, getting on for forty. He is sitting on the bench, and is completely absorbed in two books, comparing them with rapt attention.

St Pauls is also occupied. A very tall gaunt elder, by his dress and bearing a well-to-do Englishman, sits on a stone at the altar, resting his elbows on it with his chin in his hands. He is in the deepest mourning; and his attitude is one of hopeless dejection.

Sweetie, now fully and brilliantly dressed, comes slowly down the path through the gap, moody and bored. On the beach she finds nothing to interest her until the sergeant unconsciously attracts her notice by finding some remarkable confirmation or contradiction between his two books, and smiting one of them appreciatively with his fist. She instantly brightens up; climbs to the mouth of the grotto eagerly; and posts herself beside him, on his right. But he is so rapt in his books that she waits in vain to be noticed.

SWEETIE [*contemplating him ardently*] Ahem!

The sergeant looks up. Seeing who it is, he springs to his feet and stands to attention.

SWEETIE [*giving herself no airs*] You neednt stand up for me, you know.

THE SERGEANT [*stiffly*] Beg pardon, your ladyship. I was not aware of your ladyship's presence.

SWEETIE. Can all that stuff, Sergeant. [*She sits on the bench on his right*]. Dont lets waste time. This place is as dull for me as it is for you. Dont you think we two could amuse ourselves a bit if we were friends?

THE SERGEANT [*with stern contempt*] No, my lady, I dont. I saw a lot of that in the war: pretty ladies brightening up the hospitals and losing their silly heads, let alone upsetting the men; and I dont hold with it. Keep to your class: I'll keep to mine.

SWEETIE. My class! Garn! I'm no countess; and I'm fed up with pretending to be one. Didnt you guess?

THE SERGEANT [*resuming his seat and treating her as one of his own class*] Why should I trouble to start guessing about you? Any girl can be a countess nowadays if she's goodlooking enough to pick up a count.

SWEETIE. Oh! You think I'm goodlooking, do you?

THE SERGEANT. Come! If youre not a countess what are you? Whats the game, eh?

SWEETIE. The game, darling, is that youre my fancy. I love you.

THE SERGEANT. Whats that to me? A man of my figure can have his pick.

SWEETIE. Not here, dear. Theres only one other white woman within fifty miles; and she's a real lady. She wouldn't look at you.

THE SERGEANT. Well, thats a point. Thats a point, certainly.

SWEETIE [*snuggling to him*] Yes, isnt it?

THE SERGEANT [*suffering the advance but not responding*] This climate plays the devil with a man, no matter how serious minded he is.

SWEETIE [*slipping her arm through his*] Well, isnt it natural? Whats the use of pretending.

THE SERGEANT. Still, I'm not a man to treat a woman as a mere necessity. Many soldiers do: to them a woman is no more than a jar of marmalade, to be consumed and put away. I dont take that view. I admit that there is that side to it, and that for people incapable of anything better—mere animals as you might say—thats the beginning and the end of it. But to me thats only the smallest part of it. I like getting a woman's opinions. I like to explore her mind as well as her body. See these two little books I was deep in when you accosted me? I carry them with me wherever I go. I put the problems they raise for me to every woman I meet.

SWEETIE [*with growing misgiving*] What are they?

THE SERGEANT [*pointing to them successively*] The Bible. The Pilgrim's Progress from this world to that which is to come.

SWEETIE [*dismayed, trying to rise*] Oh, my God!

SERGEANT [*holding her ruthlessly in the crook of his elbow*] No you dont. Sit quiet; and dont take the name of the Lord your God in vain. If you believe in him, it's blasphemy: if you dont, it's nonsense. You must learn to exercise your mind: what is a woman without an active mind to a man but a mere convenience?

SWEETIE. I have plenty to exercise my mind looking after my own affairs. What I look to you for, my lad, is a bit of fun.

THE SERGEANT. Quite. But when men and women pick one another up just for a bit of fun, they find theyve picked up more than they bargained for, because men and women have a top storey as well as a ground floor; and you cant have the one without the other. Theyre always trying to; but it doesnt work. Youve picked up my mind as well as my body; and youve got to explore it. You thought you could have a face and a figure like mine with the limitations of a gorilla. Youre finding out your mistake: thats all.

SWEETIE. Oh, let me go: I have had enough of this. If I'd thought you were religious I'd have given you a wide berth, I tell you. Let me go, will you?

THE SERGEANT. Wait a bit. Nature may be using me as a sort of bait to draw you to take an interest in things of the mind. Nature may be using your pleasant animal warmth to stimulate my mind. I want your advice. I dont say I'll take it; but it may suggest something to me. You see, I'm in a mess.

SWEETIE. Well, of course. Youre in the sergeants' mess.

THE SERGEANT. Thats not the mess I mean. My mind's in a mess—a muddle. I used to be a religious man; but I'm not so clear about it as I was.

SWEETIE. Thank goodness for that, anyhow.

THE SERGEANT. Look at these two books. I used to believe every word of them because they seemed to have nothing to do with real life. But war brought those old stories home quite real; and then one starts asking questions. Look at this bit here [*he points to a page of The Pilgrim's Progress*]. It's on the very first page of it. "I am for certain informed that this our city will be burned with fire from heaven, in which fearful overthrow both myself, with thee my wife, and you my sweet babes, shall miserably come to ruin, except some way of escape can be found whereby we may be delivered." Well, London and Paris and Berlin and Rome and the rest of them will be burned with fire from heaven all right in the next war: thats certain. Theyre all Cities of Destruction. And our Government chaps are running about with a great burden of corpses and debts on their backs, crying "What must we do to be saved?" There it is: not a story in a book as it used to be, but God's truth in the real actual world. And all the comfort they get is "Flee from the wrath to come." But where are they to flee to? There they are, meeting at Geneva or hobnobbing at Chequers over the weekend, asking one another, like the man in the book, "Whither must we flee?" And nobody can tell them. The man in the book says "Do you see yonder shining light?" Well, today the place is blazing with shining lights: shining lights in parliament, in the papers, in the churches, and in the books that they call Outlines—Outlines of History and Science and what not—and in spite of all their ballyhoo here we are waiting in the City of Destruction like so many sheep for the wrath to come. This uneducated tinker tells me the way is straight before us and so narrow that we cant miss it. But he starts by calling the place the wilderness of this world. Well, theres no road in a wilderness: you have to make one. All the straight roads are made by soldiers; and the soldiers didnt get to heaven along them. A lot of them landed up in the other place. No, John: you could tell a story well; and they say you were a soldier; but soldiers that try to make storytelling do for service end in the clink; and thats where they put you. Twelve years in Bedford Gaol, he got. He used to read the Bible in gaol; and—

SWEETIE. Well, what else was there to read there? It's all they give you in some gaols.

THE SERGEANT. How do you know that?

SWEETIE. Never you mind how I know it. It's nothing to do with you.

THE SERGEANT. Nothing to do with me! You dont know me, my lass. Some men would just order you off; but to me the most interesting thing in the world is the experience of a woman thats been shut up in a cell for years at a time with nothing but a Bible to read.

SWEETIE. Years! What are you talking about? The longest I ever did was nine months; and if anyone says I ever did a day longer she's a liar.

THE SERGEANT [*laying his hand on the Bible*] You could read that book from cover to cover in nine months.

SWEETIE. Some of it would drive you melancholy mad. It only got me into trouble: it did. The chaplain asked me what I was in for. Spoiling the Egyptians, I says; and heres chapter and verse for it. He went and reported me, the swine; and I lost seven days remission for it.

THE SERGEANT. Serves you right! I dont hold with spoiling the Egyptians. Before the war, spoiling the Egyptians was something holy. Now I see plainly it's nothing but thieving.

SWEETIE [*shocked*] Oh, you shouldnt say that. But what I say is, if Moses might do it why maynt I?

THE SERGEANT. If thats the effect it had on your mind, it's a bad effect. Some of this scripture is all right. Do justice; love mercy; and walk humbly before your God. That appeals to a man if only it could be set out in plain army regulations. But all this thieving, and slaughtering your enemies without giving quarter, and offering up human sacrifices, and thinking you can do what you like to other people because youre the chosen people of God, and you are in the right and everyone else is in the wrong: how does that look when you have had four years of the real thing instead of merely reading about it. No: damn it, we're civilized men; and though it may have gone down with those old Jews it isnt religion. And, if it isnt, where are we? Thats what I want to know.

SWEETIE. And is this all you care about? Sitting here and thinking of things like that?

THE SERGEANT. Well, somebody must think about them, or whats going to become of us all? The officers wont think about them. The colonel goes out sketching: the lootnants go out and kill the birds and animals, or play polo. They wont flee from the wrath to come, not they. When they wont do their military duties I have to do them. It's the same with our religious duties. It's the chaplain's job, not mine; but when you get a real religious chaplain you find he doesnt believe any of the old stuff; and if you get a gentleman, all he cares about is to shew you that he's a real sport and not a mealy mouthed parson. So I have to puzzle it out for myself.

SWEETIE. Well, God help the woman that marries you: thats all I have to say to you. I dont call you a man. [*She rises quickly to escape from him*].

THE SERGEANT [*also rising, and seizing her in a very hearty embrace*] Not a man, eh? [*He kisses her*]. How does that feel, Judy?

SWEETIE [*struggling, but not very resolutely*] You let me go, will you. I dont want you now.

THE SERGEANT. You will if I kiss you half a dozen times, more than you ever wanted anything in your life before. Thats a hard fact of human nature; and it's one of the facts that religion has to make room for.

SWEETIE. Oh, well, kiss me and have done with it. You cant kiss and talk about religion at the same time.

THE ELDER [*springing from his cell to the platform in front of it*] Forbear this fooling, both of you. You, sir, are not an ignorant man: you know that the universe is wrecked.

SWEETIE [*clinging to the sergeant*] He's mad.

THE ELDER. I am sane in a world of lunatics.

THE SERGEANT [*putting Sweetie away*] It's a queer thing, isn't it, that though there is a point at which I'd rather kiss a woman than do anything else in the world, yet I'd rather be shot than let anyone see me doing it?

THE ELDER. Sir: women are not, as they suppose, more interesting than the universe. When the universe is crumbling let women be silent; and let men rise to something nobler than kissing them.

The Sergeant, interested and overawed, sits down quietly and makes Sweetie sit beside him as before. The Elder continues to declaim with fanatical intensity.

THE ELDER. Yes, sir: the universe of Isaac Newton,

which has been an impregnable citadel of modern civilization for three hundred years, has crumbled like the walls of Jericho before the criticism of Einstein. Newton's universe was the stronghold of rational Determinism: the stars in their orbits obeyed immutably fixed laws; and when we turned from surveying their vastness to study the infinite littleness of the atoms, there too we found the electrons in their orbits obeying the same universal laws. Every moment of time dictated and determined the following moment, and was itself dictated and determined by the moment that came before it. Everything was calculable: everything happened because it must: the commandments were erased from the tables of the law; and in their place came the cosmic algebra: the equations of the mathematicians. Here was my faith: here I found my dogma of infallibility: I, who scorned alike the Catholic with his vain dream of responsible Free Will, and the Protestant with his pretence of private judgment. And now—now—what is left of it? The orbit of the electron obeys no law: it chooses one path and rejects another: it is as capricious as the planet Mercury, who wanders from his road to warm his hands at the sun. All is caprice: the calculable world has become incalculable: Purpose and Design, the pretexts for all the vilest superstitions, have risen from the dead to cast down the mighty from their seats and put paper crowns on presumptuous fools. Formerly, when differences with my wife, or business worries, tried me too hard, I sought consolation and reassurance in our natural history museums, where I could forget all common cares in wondering at the diversity of forms and colors in the birds and fishes and animals, all produced without the agency of any designer by the operation of Natural Selection. Today I dare not enter an aquarium, because I can see nothing in those grotesque monsters of the deep but the caricatures of some freakish demon artist: some Zeus-Mephistopheles with paintbox and plasticine, trying to surpass himself in the production of fantastic and laughable creatures to people a Noah's ark for his baby. I have to rush from the building lest I go mad, crying, like the man in your book, "What must I do to be saved?" Nothing can save us from a perpetual headlong fall into a bottomless abyss but a solid footing of dogma; and we no sooner agree to that than we find that the only trustworthy dogma is that there is no dogma. As I stand here I am falling into that abyss, down, down, down. We are all falling into it; and our dizzy brains can utter nothing but madness. My wife has died cursing me. I do not know how to live without her: we were unhappy together for forty years. My son, whom I brought up to be an incorruptible Godfearing atheist, has become a thief and a scoundrel; and I can say nothing to him but "Go, boy: perish in your villainy; for neither your father nor anyone else can now give you a good reason for being a man of honor."

He turns from them and is rushing distractedly away when Aubrey, in white tropicals, comes strolling along the beach from the St Pauls side, and hails him nonchalantly.

AUBREY. Hullo, father, is it really you? I thought I heard the old trombone: I couldnt mistake it. How the dickens did you turn up here?

THE ELDER [*to the sergeant*] This is my prodigal son.

AUBREY. I am not a prodigal son. The prodigal son was a spendthrift and neer-do-well who was reduced to eating the husks that the swine did eat. I am not ruined: I am rolling in money. I have never owed a farthing to any man. I am a model son; but I regret to say that you are very far from being a model father.

THE ELDER. What right have you to say that, sir? In what way have I fallen short?

AUBREY. You tried to thwart my manifest destiny. Nature meant me for the Church. I had to get ordained secretly.

THE ELDER. Ordained! You dared to get ordained without my knowledge!

AUBREY. Of course. You objected. How could I have

done it with your knowledge? You would have stopped my allowance.

THE ELDER [*sitting down on the nearest stone, overwhelmed*] My son a clergyman! This will kill me.

AUBREY [*coolly taking another stone, on his father's right*] Not a bit of it: fathers are not so easily killed. It was at the university that I became what was then called a sky pilot. When the war took me it seemed natural that I should pursue that avocation as a member of the air force. As a flying ace I won a very poorly designed silver medal for committing atrocities which were irreconcilable with the profession of a Christian clergyman. When I was wounded and lost my nerve for flying, I became an army chaplain. I then found myself obliged to tell mortally wounded men that they were dying in a state of grace and were going straight to heaven when as a matter of fact they were dying in mortal sin and going elsewhere. To expiate this blasphemy I kept as much under fire as possible; but my nerve failed again: I had to take three months leave and go into a nursing home. In that home I met my doom.

THE ELDER. What do you mean by your doom? You are alive and well, to my sorrow and shame.

AUBREY. To be precise, I met Sweetie. Thats Sweetie.

SWEETIE. Very pleased to meet Popsy's father, I'm sure.

THE ELDER. My son was called Popsy in his infancy, I put a stop to it, on principle, when he entered on his sixth year. It is strange to hear the name from your lips after so long an interval.

SWEETIE. I always ask a man what his mother called him, and call him that. It takes the starch out of him, somehow.

AUBREY [*resuming his narrative*] Sweetie was quite the rottenest nurse that ever raised the mortality of a hospital by ten per cent. But—

SWEETIE. Oh, what a lie! It was the other nurses that

killed the men: waking them up at six in the morning and washing them! Half of them died of chills.

AUBREY. Well, you will not deny that you were the prettiest woman in the place.

SWEETIE. You thought so, anyhow.

THE ELDER. Oh, cease—cease this trifling. I cannot endure this unending sex appeal.

AUBREY. During the war it was found that sex appeal was as necessary for wounded or shellshocked soldiers as skilled nursing; so pretty girls were allowed to pose as nurses because they could sit about on beds and prevent the men from going mad. Sweetie did not prevent me going mad: on the contrary, she drove me mad. I saw in Sweetie not only every charm, but every virtue. And she returned my love. When I left that nursing home, she left it too. I was discharged as cured on the third of the month: she had been kicked out on the first. The trained staff could stand a good deal; but they could not stand Sweetie.

SWEETIE. They were jealous; and you know it.

AUBREY. I daresay they were. Anyhow, Sweetie and I took the same lodgings; and she was faithful to me for ten days. It was a record for her.

SWEETIE. Popsy: are you going to give the whole show away, or only part of it? The Countess Valbrioni would like to know.

AUBREY. We may as well be frank up to the point at which we should lose money by it. But perhaps I am boring the company.

THE ELDER. Complete your confession, sir. You have just said that you and this lady took the same lodging. Am I to understand that you are husband and wife?

SWEETIE. We might have been if we could have depended on you for a good time. But how could I marry an army chaplain with nothing but his pay and an atheist for his father?

AUBREY. So that was the calculation, Sweetie, was it? I never dreamt that the idea of marriage had occurred to either of us. It certainly never occurred to me. I went to live with you quite simply because I felt I could not live without you. The improbability of that statement is the measure of my infatuation.

SWEETIE. Dont you be so spiteful. Did I give you a good time or did I not?

AUBREY. Heavenly. That also seems improbable; but it is gospel truth.

THE ELDER. Wretched boy: do not dare to trifle with me. You said just now that you owe no man anything, and that you are rolling in money. Where did you get that money?

AUBREY. I stole a very valuable pearl necklace and restored it to the owner. She rewarded me munificently. Hence my present opulence. Honesty is the best policy—sometimes.

THE ELDER. Worse even than a clergyman! A thief!

AUBREY. Why make such a fuss about nothing?

THE ELDER. Do you call the theft of a pearl necklace nothing?

AUBREY. Less than nothing, compared to the things I have done with your approval. I was hardly more than a boy when I first dropped a bomb on a sleeping village. I cried all night after doing that. Later on I swooped into a street and sent machine gun bullets into a crowd of civilians: women, children, and all. I was past crying by that time. And now you preach to me about stealing a pearl necklace! Doesnt that seem a little ridiculous?

THE SERGEANT. That was war, sir.

AUBREY. It was me, Sergeant: ME. You cannot divide my conscience into a war department and a peace department. Do you suppose that a man who will commit murder for political ends will hesitate to commit theft for personal ends? Do you suppose you can make a man the mortal enemy of sixty millions of his fellow creatures without making him a little less scrupulous about his next door neighbor?

THE ELDER. I did not approve. Had I been of military age I should have been a conscientious objector.

AUBREY. Oh, you were a conscientious objector to everything, even to God. But my mother was an enthusiast for everything: that was why you never could get on with her. She would have shoved me into the war if I had needed any shoving. She shoved my brother into it, though he did not believe a word of all the lies we were stuffed with, and didnt want to go. He was killed; and when it came out afterwards that he was right, and that we were all a parcel of fools killing one another for nothing, she lost the courage to face life, and died of it.

THE SERGEANT. Well, sir, I'd never let a son of mine talk to me like that. Let him have a bit of your Determinism, sir.

THE FATHER [*rising impulsively*] Determinism is gone, shattered, buried with a thousand dead religions, evaporated with the clouds of a million forgotten winters. The science I pinned my faith to is bankrupt: its tales were more foolish than all the miracles of the priests, its cruelties more horrible than all the atrocities of the Inquisition. Its spread of enlightenment has been a spread of cancer: its counsels that were to have established the millennium have led straight to European suicide. And I—I who believed in it as no religious fanatic has ever believed in his superstition! For its sake I helped to destroy the faith of millions of worshippers in the temples of a thousand creeds. And now look at me and behold the supreme tragedy of the atheist who has lost his faith—his faith in atheism, for which more martyrs have perished than for all the creeds put together. Here I stand, dumb before my scoundrel of a son; for that is what you are, boy, a common scoundrel and nothing else.

AUBREY. Well, why not? If I become an honest man I shall become a poor man; and then nobody will respect me: nobody will admire me; nobody will say thank you to me. If on the contrary I am bold, unscrupulous, acquisitive, successful and rich, everyone will respect me, admire me, court me, grovel before me. Then no doubt I shall be able to afford the luxury of honesty. I learnt that from my religious education.

THE ELDER. How dare you say that you had a religious education. I shielded you from that, at least.

AUBREY. You thought you did, old man; but you reckoned without my mother.

THE ELDER. What!

AUBREY. You forbad me to read the Bible; but my mother made me learn three verses of it every day, and whacked me if I could not repeat them without misplacing a word. She threatened to whack me still worse if I told you.

THE ELDER [*thunderstruck*] Your mother!!!

AUBREY. So I learnt my lesson. Six days on the make, and on the seventh shalt thou rest. I shall spend another six years on the make, and then I shall retire and be a saint.

THE ELDER. A saint! Say rather the ruined son of an incorrigibly superstitious mother. Retire now—from the life you have dishonored. There is the sea. Go. Drown yourself. In that graveyard there are no lying epitaphs. [*He mounts to his chapel and again gives way to utter dejection*].

AUBREY [*unconcerned*] I shall do better as a saint. A few thousands to the hospitals and the political party funds will buy me a halo as large as Sweetie's sun hat. That is my program. What have any of you to say against it?

THE SERGEANT. Not the program of a gentleman, as I understand the word, sir.

AUBREY. You cannot be a gentleman on less than fifty thousand a year nowadays, sergeant.

THE SERGEANT. You can in the army, by God.

AUBREY. Yes: because you drop bombs on sleeping villages. And even then you have to be an officer. Are you a gentleman?

THE SERGEANT. No, sir: it wouldnt pay me. I couldnt

afford it.

Disturbance. A voice is heard in complaint and lamentation. It is that of the Elderly Lady, Mrs Mopply. She is pursuing Colonel Tallboys down the path through the gap, the lady distracted and insistent, the colonel almost equally distracted: she clutching him and stopping him: he breaking loose and trying to get away from her. She is dressed in black precisely as if she were in Cheltenham, except that she wears a sun helmet. He is equipped with a box of sketching materials slung over his shoulder, an easel, which he has tucked under his left arm, and a sun umbrella, a substantial affair of fawn lined with red, podgily rolled up, which he carries in his right hand.

MRS MOPPLY. I wont be patient. I wont be quiet. My child is being murdered.

TALLBOYS. I tell you she is not being murdered. Will you be good enough to excuse me whilst I attend to my business.

MRS MOPPLY. Your business is to save my child. She is starving.

TALLBOYS. Nonsense. Nobody starves in this country. There are plenty of dates. Will you be good enough—

MRS MOPPLY. Do you think my child can live on dates? She has to have a sole for breakfast, a cup of nourishing soup at eleven, a nice chop and a sweetbread for lunch, a pint of beef-tea with her ordinary afternoon tea, and a chicken and some lamb or veal—

TALLBOYS. Will you be good enough—

MRS MOPPLY. My poor delicate child with nothing to eat but dates! And she is the only one I have left: they were all delicate—

TALLBOYS. I really must— [*He breaks away and hurries off along the beach past the Abode of Love*].

MRS MOPPLY [*running after him*] Colonel, Colonel: you might have the decency to listen to a distracted mother for a moment. Colonel: my child is dying. She may be dead for all I know. And nobody is doing anything: nobody cares. Oh dear, wont you listen— [*Her voice is lost in the distance*].

Whilst they are staring mutely after the retreating pair, the patient, still in her slave girl attire, but with some brilliant variations, comes down the path.

THE PATIENT. My dream has become a nightmare. My mother has pursued me to these shores. I cannot shake her off. No woman can shake off her mother. There should be no mothers: there should be only women, strong women able to stand by themselves, not clingers. I would kill all the clingers. Mothers cling: daughters cling: we are all like drunken women clinging to lamp posts: none of us stands upright.

THE ELDER. There is great comfort in clinging, and great loneliness in standing alone.

THE PATIENT. Hallo! [*She climbs to the St Pauls platform and peers into the cell*]. A sententious anchorite! [*To Aubrey*]. Who is he?

AUBREY. The next worst thing to a mother: a father.

THE ELDER. A most unhappy father.

AUBREY. My father, in fact.

THE PATIENT. If only I had had a father to stand between me and my mother's care. Oh, that I had been an orphan!

THE SERGEANT. You will be, miss, if the old lady drives the colonel too hard. She has been at him all the morning, ever since she arrived; and I know the colonel. He has a temper; and when it gives way, it's a bit of high explosive. He'll kill her if she pushes him too far.

THE PATIENT. Let him kill her. I am young and strong: I want a world without parents: there is no room for them in my dream. I shall found a sisterhood.

AUBREY. All right, Mops. Get thee to a nunnery.

THE PATIENT. It need not be a nunnery if men will come in without spoiling everything. But all the women must be rich. There must be no chill of poverty. There are plenty of rich women like me who hate being devoured by parasites.

AUBREY. Stop. You have the most disgusting mental pictures. I really cannot stand intellectual coarseness. Sweetie's vulgarity I can forgive and even enjoy. But you say perfectly filthy things that stick in my mind, and break my spirit. I can bear no more of it. [*He rises angrily and tries to escape by the beach past the Abode of Love*].

SWEETIE. Youre dainty, arnt you? If chambermaids were as dainty as you, youd have to empty your own slops.

AUBREY [*recoiling from her with a yell of disgust*] You need not throw them in my teeth, you beast. [*He sits in his former place, sulking*].

THE ELDER. Silence, boy. These are home truths. They are good for you. [*To the patient*]. May I ask, young woman, what are the relations between you and my son, whom you seem to know.

THE PATIENT. Popsy stole my necklace, and got me to run away with him by a wonderful speech he made about freedom and sunshine and lovely scenery. Sweetie made me write it all down and sell it to a tourist agency as an advertisement. And then I was devoured by parasites: by tourist agencies, steamboat companies, railways, motor car people, hotel keepers, dressmakers, servants, all trying to get my money by selling me things I dont really want; shoving me all over the globe to look at what they call new skies, though they know as well as I do that it is only the same old sky everywhere; and disabling me by doing all the things for me that I ought to do for myself to keep myself in health. They preyed on me to keep themselves alive: they pretended they were making me happy when it was only by drinking and drugging—cocktails and cocaine—that I could endure my life.

AUBREY. I regret to have to say it, Mops; but you have not the instincts of a lady. [*He sits down moodily on a stone a little way up the path*].

THE PATIENT. You fool, there is no such thing as a lady. I have the instincts of a good housekeeper: I want to clean up this filthy world and keep it clean. There must be other women who want it too. Florence Nightingale had the same instinct when she went to clean up the Crimean war. She wanted a sisterhood; but there wasnt one.

THE ELDER. There were several. But steeped in superstition, unfortunately.

THE PATIENT. Yes, all mixed up with things that I dont believe. Women have to set themselves apart to join them. I dont want to set myself apart. I want to have every woman in my sisterhood, and to have all the others strangled.

THE ELDER. Down! down! down! Even the young, the strong, the rich, the beautiful, feel that they are plunging into a bottomless pit.

THE SERGEANT. Your set, miss, if you will excuse me saying so, is only a small bit of the world. If you dont like the officers' mess, the ranks are open to you. Look at Meek! That man could be an emperor if he laid his mind to it: but he'd rather be a private. He's happier so.

THE PATIENT. I dont belong to the poor, and dont want to. I always knew that there were thousands of poor people; and I was taught to believe that they were poor because God arranged it that way to punish them for being dirty and drunken and dishonest, and not knowing how to read and write. But I didnt know that the rich were miserable. I didnt know that I was miserable. I didnt know that our respectability was uppish snobbery and our religion gluttonous selfishness, and that my soul was starving on them. I know now. I have found myself out thoroughly—in my dream.

THE ELDER. You are young. Some good man may cure you of this for a few happy years. When you fall in love, life will seem worth living.

THE PATIENT. I did fall in love. With that thing. And though I was never a hotel chambermaid I got tired of him sooner than Sweetie did. Love gets people into difficulties, not out of them. No more lovers for me: I want a sisterhood. Since I came here I have been wanting to join the army, like Joan of Arc. It's a brotherhood, of a sort.

THE SERGEANT. Yes, miss: that is so; and there used to be a peace of mind in the army that you could find nowhere else. But the war made an end of that. You see, miss, the great principle of soldiering, I take it, is that the world is kept going by the people who want the right thing killing the people who want the wrong thing. When the soldier is doing that, he is doing the work of God, which my mother brought me up to do. But thats a very different thing from killing a man because he's a German and he killing you because youre an Englishman. We were not killing the right people in 1915. We werent even killing the wrong people. It was innocent men killing one another.

THE PATIENT. Just for the fun of it.

THE SERGEANT. No, miss: it was no fun. For the misery of it.

THE PATIENT. For the devilment of it, then.

THE SERGEANT. For the devilment of the godless rulers of this world. Those that did the killing hadnt even the devilment to comfort them: what comfort is there in screwing on a fuse or pulling a string when the devilment it makes is from three to forty miles off, and you dont know whether you have only made a harmless hole in the ground or blown up a baby in its cradle that might have been your own? That wasnt devilment: it was damnation. No, miss: the bottom has come out of soldiering. What the gentleman here said about our all falling into a bottomless pit came home to me. I feel like that too.

THE ELDER. Lost souls, all of us.

THE PATIENT. No: only lost dogs. Cheer up, old man: the lost dogs always find their way home. [*The voice of the Elderly Lady is heard returning*]. Oh! here she comes again!

Mrs Mopply is still pursuing the colonel, who is walking doggedly and steadily away from her, with closed lips and a dangerous expression on his set features.

MRS MOPPLY. You wont even speak to me. It's a disgrace. I will send a cable message home to the Government about it. You were sent out here to rescue my daughter from these dreadful brigands. Why is nothing being done? What are the relations between yourself and that disgraceful countess who ought to have her coronet stripped off her back? You are all in a conspiracy to murder my poor lost darling child. You are in league with the brigands. You are—

The colonel turns at bay, and brings down his umbrella whack on poor Mrs Mopply's helmet.

MRS MOPPLY. Oh! Oh! Oh! Oh! [*With a series of short, dry, detached screams she totters and flutters back along the beach out of sight like a wounded bird*].

General stupefaction. All stare at the colonel aghast. The sergeant rises in amazement, and remains standing afterwards as a matter of military etiquette.

THE PATIENT. Oh, if only someone had done that to her twenty years ago, how different my childhood would have been! But I must see to the poor old dear. [*She runs after her mother*].

AUBREY. Colonel: you have our full, complete, unreserved sympathy. We thank you from the bottom of our hearts. But that does not alter the fact that the man who would raise his hand to a woman, save in the way of kindness, is unworthy the name of Briton.

TALLBOYS. I am perfectly aware of that, sir. I need no reminder. The lady is entitled to an apology. She shall have it.

THE ELDER. But have you considered the possibility of a serious injury—

TALLBOYS [*cutting him short*] My umbrella is quite uninjured, thank you. The subject is now closed. [*He sits down on the stone below St Pauls recently vacated by Aubrey. His manner is so decisive that nobody dares carry the matter further*].

As they sit uneasily seeking one another's eyes and

avoiding them again, dumbfounded by the violence of the catastrophe, a noise like that of a machine gun in action reaches their ears from afar. It increases to shattering intensity as it approaches. They all put their fingers to their ears. It diminishes slightly, then suddenly rises to a climax of speed and uproar, and stops.

TALLBOYS. Meek.

AUBREY. Meek.

SWEETIE. Meek.

THE ELDER. What is this? Why do you all say Meek?

Meek, dusty and gritty, but very alert, comes down the path through the gap with a satchel of papers.

TALLBOYS. My dear Meek, can you not be content with a motor cycle of ordinary horse power? Must you always travel at eighty miles an hour?

MEEK. I have good news for you, Colonel; and good news should travel fast.

TALLBOYS. For me?

MEEK. Your K.C.B., sir. [*Presenting a paper*] Honors list by wireless.

TALLBOYS [*rising joyously to take the paper*] Ah! Congratulate me, my friends. My dear Sarah is Lady Tallboys at last. [*He resumes his seat and pores over the paper*].

AUBREY	[*together*]	Splendid!
THE SERGEANT		You deserve it, sir, if I may say so.
SWEETIE		Delighted, I am sure.

THE ELDER. May I crave to know the nature of the distinguished service which has won this official recognition, sir?

TALLBOYS. I have won the battle of the maroons. I have suppressed brigandage here. I have rescued a British lady from the clutches of the brigands. The Government is preparing for a general election, and has had to make the most of these modest achievements.

THE ELDER. Brigands! Are there any here?

TALLBOYS. None.

THE ELDER. But—? The British lady? In their clutches?

TALLBOYS. She has been in my clutches, and perfectly safe, all the time.

THE ELDER [*more and more puzzled*] Oh! Then the battle of the—

TALLBOYS. Won by Private Meek. I had nothing whatever to do with it.

AUBREY. I invented the brigands and the British lady. [*To Tallboys*] By the way, Colonel, the impressive old party in the shrine is my father.

TALLBOYS. Indeed! Happy to meet you, sir, though I cannot congratulate you on your son, except in so far as you have brought into the world the most abandoned liar I have ever met.

THE ELDER. And may I ask, sir, is it your intention not only to condone my son's frauds, but to take advantage of them to accept a distinction which you have in no way earned?

TALLBOYS. I have earned it, sir, ten times over. Do you suppose, because the brigandage which I am honored for suppressing has no existence, that I have never suppressed real brigands? Do you forget that though this battle of which I am crowned victor was won by a subordinate, I, too, have won real battles, and seen all the honors go to a brigadier who did not even know what was happening? In the army these things average themselves out: merit is rewarded in the long run. Justice is none the less justice though it is always delayed, and finally done by mistake. My turn today: Private Meek's tomorrow.

THE FATHER. And meanwhile Mr Meek—this humble and worthy soldier—is to remain in obscurity and poverty whilst you are strutting as a K.C.B.

TALLBOYS. How I envy him! Look at me and look at him! I, loaded with responsibilities whilst my hands are tied, my body disabled, my mind crippled because a colonel must not do anything but give orders and look significant and profound when his mind is entirely vacant! he, free to turn his hand to everything and to look like an idiot when he feels like one! I have been driven to sketching in watercolors because I may not use my hands in life's daily useful business. A commanding officer must not do this, must not do that, must not do the other, must not do anything but tell other men to do it. He may not even converse with them. I see this man Meek doing everything that is natural to a complete man: carpentering, painting, digging, pulling and hauling, fetching and carrying, helping himself and everybody else, whilst I, with a bigger body to exercise and quite as much energy, must loaf and loll, allowed to do nothing but read the papers and drink brandy and water to prevent myself going mad. I should have become a drunkard had it not been for the colors.

THE SERGEANT. Ah yes, sir, the colors. The fear of disgracing them has kept me off the drink many a time.

TALLBOYS. Man: I do not mean the regimental colors, but the watercolors. How willingly would I exchange my pay, my rank, my K.C.B., for Meek's poverty, his obscurity!

MEEK. But, my dear Colonel—sorry, sir: what I mean to say is that you can become a private if you wish. Nothing easier: I have done it again and again. You resign your commission; take a new and very common name by deed poll; dye your hair and give your age to the recruiting sergeant as twenty-two, and there you are! You can select your own regiment.

TALLBOYS. Meek: you should not tantalize your commanding officer. No doubt you are an extraordinary soldier. But have you ever passed the extreme and final test of manly courage?

MEEK. Which one is that, sir?

TALLBOYS. Have you ever married?

MEEK. No, sir.

TALLBOYS. Then do not ask me why I do not resign my

commission and become a free and happy private. My wife would not let me.

THE COUNTESS. Why dont you hit her on the head with your umbrella?

TALLBOYS. I dare not. There are moments when I wish some other man would. But not in my presence. I should kill him.

THE ELDER. We are all slaves. But at least your son is an honest man.

TALLBOYS. Is he? I am glad to hear it. I have not spoken to him since he shirked military service at the beginning of the war and went into trade as a contractor. He is now so enormously rich that I cannot afford to keep up his acquaintance. Neither need you keep up that of your son. By the way, he passes here as the half step-brother of this lady, the Countess Valbrioni.

SWEETIE. Valbrioni be blowed! My name is Susan Simpkins. Being a countess isnt worth a damn. There's no variety in it: no excitement. What I want is a month's leave for the sergeant. Wont you give it to him, Colonel?

TALLBOYS. What for?

SWEETIE. Never mind what for. A fortnight might do; but I dont know for certain yet. There's something steadying about him; and I suppose I will have to settle down some day.

TALLBOYS. Nonsense! The sergeant is a pious man, not your sort. Eh, Sergeant?

SERGEANT. Well, sir, a man should have one woman to prevent him from thinking too much about women in general. You cannot read your Bible undisturbed if visions and wandering thoughts keep coming between you and it. And a pious man should not marry a pious woman: two of a trade never agree. Besides, it would give the children a onesided view of life. Life is very mixed, sir: it is not all piety and it is not all gaiety. This young woman has no conscience; but I have enough for two. I have no money; but she seems to have enough for two. Mind: I am not committing myself; but I will go so far as to say that I am not dead set against it. On the plane of this world and its vanities—and weve got to live in it, you know, sir—she appeals to me.

AUBREY. Take care, Sergeant. Constancy is not Sweetie's strong point.

THE SERGEANT. Neither is it mine. As a single man and a wandering soldier I am fair game for every woman. But if I settle down with this girl she will keep the others off. I'm a bit tired of adventures.

SWEETIE. Well, if the truth must be told, so am I. We were made for one another, Sergeant. What do you say?

THE SERGEANT. Well, I dont mind keeping company for a while, Susan, just to see how we get along together.

The voice of Mrs Mopply is again heard. Its tone is hardy and even threatening; and its sound is approaching rapidly.

MRS MOPPLY'S VOICE. You just let me alone, will you? Nobody asked you to interfere. Get away with you.

General awe and dismay. Mrs Mopply appears striding resolutely along the beach. She walks straight up to the colonel, and is about to address him when he rises firmly to the occasion and takes the word out of her mouth.

TALLBOYS. Mrs Mopply: I have a duty to you which I must discharge at once. At our last meeting, I struck you.

MRS MOPPLY. Struck me! You bashed me. Is that what you mean?

TALLBOYS. If you consider my expression inadequate I am willing to amend it. Let us put it that I bashed you. Well, I apologize without reserve, fully and amply. If you wish, I will give it to you in writing.

MRS MOPPLY. Very well. Since you express your regret, I suppose there is nothing more to be said.

TALLBOYS [*darkening ominously*] Pardon me. I apologized. I did not express my regret.

AUBREY. Oh, for heaven's sake, Colonel, dont start her again. Dont qualify your apology in any way.

MRS MOPPLY. You shut up, whoever you are.

TALLBOYS. I do not qualify my apology in the least. My apology is complete. The lady has a right to it. My action was inexcusable. But no lady—no human being—has a right to impose a falsehood on me. I do not regret my action. I have never done anything which gave me more thorough and hearty satisfaction. When I was a company officer I once cut down an enemy in the field. Had I not done so he would have cut me down. It gave me no satisfaction: I was half ashamed of it: I have never before spoken of it. But this time I struck with unmixed enjoyment. In fact I am grateful to Mrs Mopply. I owe her one of the very few delightfully satisfactory moments of my life.

MRS MOPPLY. Well, thats a pretty sort of apology, isnt it?

TALLBOYS [*firmly*] I have nothing to add, madam.

MRS MOPPLY. Well, I forgive you, you peppery old blighter.

Sensation. They catch their breaths, and stare at one another in consternation. The patient arrives.

THE PATIENT. I am sorry to say, Colonel Tallboys, that you have unsettled my mother's reason. She wont believe that I am her daughter. She's not a bit like herself.

MRS MOPPLY. Isnt she? What do you know about myself? my real self? They told me lies; and I had to pretend to be somebody quite different.

TALLBOYS. Who told you lies, madam? It was not with my authority.

MRS MOPPLY. I wasnt thinking of you. My mother told me lies. My nurse told me lies. My governess told me lies. Everybody told me lies. The world is not a bit like what they said it was. I wasnt a bit like what they said I ought to be. I thought I had to pretend. And I neednt have pretended at all.

THE ELDER. Another victim! She, too, is falling through the bottomless abyss.

MRS MOPPLY. I dont know who you are or what you think you mean; but you have just hit it: I dont know my head from my heels. Why did they tell me that children couldnt live without medicine and three meat meals a day? Do you know that I have killed two of my children because they told me that? My own children! Murdered them, just!

THE ELDER. Medea! Medea!

MRS MOPPLY. It isn't an idea: it's the truth. I will never believe anything again as long as I live. I'd have killed the only one I had left if she hadnt run away from me. I was told to sacrifice myself—to live for others; and I did it if ever a woman did. They told me that everyone would love me for it; and I thought they would; but my daughter ran away when I had sacrificed myself to her until I found myself wishing she would die like the others and leave me a little to myself. And now I find it was not only my daughter that hated me but that all my friends, all the time they were pretending to sympathize, were just longing to bash me over the head with their umbrellas. This poor man only did what all the rest would have done if theyd dared. When I said I forgave you I meant it: I am greatly obliged to you. [*She kisses him*]. But now what am I to do? How am I to behave in a world thats just the opposite of everything I was told about it?

THE PATIENT. Steady, mother! steady! steady! Sit down. [*She picks up a heavy stone and places it near the Abode of Love for Mrs Mopply to sit on*].

MRS MOPPLY [*seating herself*] Dont you call me mother. Do you think my daughter could carry rocks about like that? she that had to call the nurse to pick up her Pekingese dog when she wanted to pet it! You think you can get round me by pretending to be my daughter; but that just shews what a fool you are; for I hate my daughter and my daughter hates me, because I sacrificed myself to her. She was a horrid selfish girl, always ill and complaining, and never satisfied, no matter how much you did for her. The only sensible thing she ever did was to steal her own necklace and sell it and run away to spend the money on herself. I expect she's in bed somewhere with a dozen nurses and six doctors all dancing attendance on her. Youre not a bit like her, thank goodness: thats why Ive taken a fancy to you. You come with me, darling. I have lots of money, and sixty years of a misspent life to make up for; so you will have a good time with me. Come with me as my companion; and lets forget that there are such miserable things in the world as mothers and daughters.

THE PATIENT. What use shall we be to one another?

MRS MOPPLY. None, thank God. We can do without one another if we dont hit it off.

THE PATIENT. Righto! I'll take you on trial until Ive had time to look about me and see what I'm going to do. But only on trial, mind.

MRS MOPPLY. Just so, darling. We'll both be on trial. So thats settled.

THE PATIENT. And now, Mr Meek, what about the little commission you promised to do for me? Have you brought back my passport?

THE COUNTESS. Your passport! Whatever for?

AUBREY. What have you been up to, Mops? Are you going to desert me?

Meek advances and empties a heap of passports from his satchel on the sand, kneeling down to sort out the patient's.

TALLBOYS. What is the meaning of this? Whose passports are these? What are you doing with them? Where did you get them?

MEEK. Everybody within fifty miles is asking me to get a passport visa'd.

TALLBOYS. Visa'd! For what country?

MEEK. For Beotia, sir.

TALLBOYS. Beotia?

MEEK. Yessir. The Union of Federated Sensible Societies, sir. The U.F.S.S. Everybody wants to go there now, sir.

THE COUNTESS. Well I never!

THE ELDER. And what is to become of our unhappy country if all its inhabitants desert it for an outlandish place in which even property is not respected?

MEEK. No fear, sir: they wont have us. They wont admit any more English, sir: they say their lunatic asylums are too full already. I couldn't get a single visa, except [*to the Colonel*] for you, sir.

TALLBOYS. For me! Damn their impudence! I never asked for one.

MEEK. No, sir; but their people have so much leisure that they are at their wits' end for some occupation to keep them out of mischief. They want to introduce the only institution of ours that they admire.

THE ELDER. And pray which one is that?

MEEK. The English school of watercolor painting, sir. Theyve seen some of the Colonel's work; and theyll make him head of their centres of repose and culture if he'll settle there.

TALLBOYS. This cannot be true, Meek. It indicates a degree of intelligence of which no Government is capable.

MEEK. It's true, sir, I assure you.

TALLBOYS. But my wife—

MEEK. Yessir: I told them. [*He repacks his satchel*].

TALLBOYS. Well, well: there is nothing for it but to return to our own country.

THE ELDER. Can our own country return to its senses, sir? that is the question.

TALLBOYS. Ask Meek.

MEEK. No use, sir: all the English privates want to be colonels: there's no salvation for snobs. [*To Tallboys*] Shall I see about getting the expedition back to England, sir?

TALLBOYS. Yes. And get me two tubes of rose madder

and a big one of Chinese White, will you?

MEEK [*about to go*] Yessir.

THE ELDER. Stop. There are police in England. What is to become of my son there?

SWEETIE [*rising*] Make Popsy a preacher, old man. But dont start him until weve gone.

THE ELDER. Preach, my son, preach to your heart's content. Do anything rather than steal and make your military crimes an excuse for your civil ones. Let men call you the reverend. Let them call you anything rather than thief.

AUBREY [*rising*] If I may be allowed to improve the occasion for a moment—

General consternation. All who are seated rise in alarm, except the patient, who jumps up and claps her hands in mischievous encouragement to the orator.

MRS MOPPLY	[*together*]	You hold your tongue, young man.
SWEETIE		Oh Lord! we're in for it now.
THE ELDER		Shame and silence would better become you, sir.
THE PATIENT		Go on, Pops. It's the only thing you do well.

AUBREY [*continuing*]—it is clear to me that though we seem to be dispersing quietly to do very ordinary things: Sweetie and the sergeant to get married [*the sergeant hastily steals down from his grotto, beckoning to Sweetie to follow him. They both escape along the beach*] the colonel to his wife, his watercolors, and his K.C.B. [*the colonel hurries away noiselessly in the opposite direction*] Napoleon Alexander Trotsky Meek to his job of repatriating the expedition [*Meek takes to flight up the path through the gap*] Mops, like Saint Teresa, to found an unladylike sisterhood with her mother as cook-housekeeper [*Mrs Mopply hastily follows the sergeant, dragging with her the patient, who is listening to Aubrey with signs of becoming rapt in his discourse*] yet they are all, like my father here, falling, falling, falling endlessly and hopelessly through a void in which they can find no footing. [*The Elder vanishes into the recesses of St Pauls, leaving his son to preach in solitude.*] There is something fantastic about them, something unreal and perverse, something profoundly unsatisfactory. They are too absurd to be believed in; yet they are not fictions: the newspapers are full of them: what storyteller, however reckless a liar, would dare to invent figures so improbable as men and women with their minds stripped naked? Naked bodies no longer shock us: our sunbathers, grinning at us from every illustrated summer number of our magazines, are nuder than shorn lambs. But the horror of the naked mind is still more than we can bear. Throw off the last rag of your bathing costume; and I shall not blench nor expect you to blush. You may even throw away the outer garments of your souls: the manners, the morals, the decencies. Swear; use dirty words; drink cocktails; kiss and caress and cuddle until girls who are like roses at eighteen are like battered demireps at twenty-two: in all these ways the bright young things of the victory have scandalized their dull old prewar elders and left nobody but their bright young selves a penny the worse. But how are we to bear this dreadful new nakedness: the nakedness of the souls who until now have always disguised themselves from one another in beautiful impossible idealisms to enable them to bear one another's company. The iron lightning of war has burnt great rents in these angelic veils, just as it has smashed great holes in our cathedral roofs and torn great gashes in our hillsides. Our souls go in rags now; and the young are spying through the holes and getting glimpses of the reality that was hidden. And they are not horrified: they exult in having found us out: they expose their own souls; and when we their elders desperately try to patch our torn clothes with scraps of the old material, the young lay violent hands on us and tear from us even the rags that were left to us. But when they have stripped themselves and us utterly naked, will they be able to bear the spectacle? You have seen me try to strip my soul before my father; but when these two young women stripped themselves more boldly than I—when the old woman had the mask struck from her soul and revelled in it instead of dying of it—I shrank from the revelation as from a wind bringing from the unknown regions of the future a breath which may be a breath of life, but of a life too keen for me to bear, and therefore for me a blast of death. I stand midway between youth and age like a man who has missed his train: too late for the last and too early for the next. What am I to do? What am I? A soldier who has lost his nerve, a thief who at his first great theft has found honesty the best policy and restored his booty to its owner. Nature never intended me for soldiering or thieving: I am by nature and destiny a preacher. I am the new Ecclesiastes. But I have no Bible, no creed: the war has shot both out of my hands. The war has been a fiery forcing house in which we have grown with a rush like flowers in a late spring following a terrible winter. And with what result? This: that we have outgrown our religion, outgrown our political system, outgrown our own strength of mind and character. The fatal word NOT has been miraculously inserted into all our creeds: in the desecrated temples where we knelt murmuring "I believe" we stand with stiff knees and stiffer necks shouting "Up, all! the erect posture is the mark of the man: let lesser creatures kneel and crawl: we will not kneel and we do not believe." But what next? Is NO enough? For a boy, yes: for a man, never. Are we any the less obsessed with a belief when we are denying it than when we were affirming it? No: I must have affirmations to preach. Without them the young will not listen to me; for even the young grow tired of denials. The negative-monger falls before the soldiers, the men of action, the fighters, strong in the old uncompromising affirmations which give them status, duties, certainty of consequences; so that the pugnacious spirit of man in them can reach out and strike deathblows with steadfastly closed minds. Their way is straight and sure; but it is the way of death; and the preacher must preach the way of life. Oh, if I could only find it! [*A white sea fog swirls up from the beach to his feet, rising and thickening round him*]. I am ignorant: I have lost my nerve and am intimidated: all I know is that I must find the way of life, for myself and all of us, or we shall surely perish. And meanwhile my gift has possession of me: I must preach and preach and preach no matter how late the hour and how short the day, no matter whether I have nothing to say—

The fog has enveloped him; the gap with its grottoes is lost to sight; the ponderous stones are wisps of shifting white cloud; there is left only fog: impenetrable fog; but the incorrigible preacher will not be denied his peroration, which, could we only hear it distinctly, would probably run—

—or whether in some pentecostal flame of revelation the Spirit will descend on me and inspire me with a message the sound whereof shall go out unto all lands and realize for us at last the Kingdom and the Power and the Glory for ever and ever. Amen.

The audience disperses (or the reader puts down the book) impressed in the English manner with the Pentecostal flame and the echo from the Lord's Prayer. But fine words butter no parsnips. A few of the choicer spirits will know that the Pentecostal flame is always alight at the service of those strong enough to bear its terrible intensity. They will not forget that it is accompanied by a rushing mighty wind, and that any rascal who happens to be also a windbag can get a prodigious volume of talk out of it without ever going near enough to be shrivelled up. The author, though himself a professional talk maker, does not believe that the world can be saved by talk alone. He has given the rascal the last word; but his own favorite is the woman of action, who begins by knocking the wind out of the rascal, and ends with a cheerful conviction that the lost dogs always find their way home. So they will, perhaps, if the women go out and look for them.

PREFACE: TRIFLES AND TOMFOOLERIES

Containing:

TRIFLES AND TOMFOOLERIES

ALL playwrights and all actors tomfool sometimes if they can. The practice needs no apology if it amuses them and their audiences harmlessly. Irresponsible laughter is salutary in small quantities. One throws off these things as Beethoven threw off a few bagatelles, and Mozart a few senseless bravura pieces for friends who were violinists. Besides, tomfoolery is as classic as tragedy. High comedy seldom achieves a whole act without revealing traces of its origin in the altercations and topical discussions of the circus clown with the ringmaster: what else indeed are the passages between Monsieur Jourdain and his philosophers and fencing masters in Molière's most famous comedy? I could cite many examples from plays of my own which pretend to be highly serious. The following playlets are tomfooleries pure and simple, except the tragedietta, which is only a trifle. I do not mean that their words are utterly void of wit and wisdom, or their figures characterless; for this kind of work would be unbearable if it added deficiency to folly. I mean just what I say: they are tomfooleries.

On their topical side they are more or less out of date; but as the world continues to excite itself over the same sort of scandal they can always be adapted to the cries of the moment. They may disgust the admirers of my more pretentious work; but these highbrows must remember that there is a demand for little things as well as for big things, and that as I happen to have a few little things in my shop I may as well put them in the window with the rest.

AYOT ST LAWRENCE, *July* 1926.

THE GLIMPSE OF REALITY

A TRAGEDIETTA

Written in 1909

First Performed Glasgow 1927

See Preface: Trifles and Tomfooleries (*page 721*)

THE GLIMPSE OF REALITY
A TRAGEDIETTA

IN the fifteenth century A.D. Gloaming. An inn on the edge of an Italian lake. A stone cross with a pedestal of steps. A very old friar sitting on the steps. The angelus rings. The friar prays and crosses himself. A girl ferries a boat to the shore and comes up the bank to the cross.

THE GIRL. Father: were you sent here by a boy from—

THE FRIAR [*in a high, piping, but clear voice*] I'm a very old man. Oh, very old. Old enough to be your great grandfather, my daughter. Oh, very v e r y old.

THE GIRL. But were you sent here by a boy from—

THE FRIAR. Oh yes, yes, yes, yes, yes. Quite a boy, he was. Very young. And I'm very old. Oh, very very old, dear daughter.

THE GIRL. Are you a holy man?

THE FRIAR [*ecstatically*] Oh, very holy. Very, very, very, v e r y holy.

THE GIRL. But have you your wits still about you, father? Can you absolve me from a great sin?

THE FRIAR. Oh yes, yes, yes. A very great sin. I'm very old; but Ive my wits about me. I'm one hundred and thirteen years old, by the grace of Our Lady; but I still remember all my Latin; and I can bind and loose; and I'm very very wise; for I'm old and have left far behind me the world, the flesh, and the devil. You see I am blind, daughter; but when a boy told me that there was a duty for me to do here, I came without a guide, straight to this spot, led by St Barbara. She led me to this stone, daughter. It's a comfortable stone to me: she has blessed it for me.

THE GIRL. It's a cross, father.

THE FRIAR [*piping rapturously*] Oh blessed, blessed, ever blessed be my holy patroness for leading me to this sacred spot. Is there any building near this, daughter? The boy mentioned an inn.

THE GIRL. There is an inn, father, not twenty yards away. It's kept by my father, Squarcio.

THE FRIAR. And is there a barn where a very very old man may sleep and have a handful of peas for his supper?

THE GIRL. There is bed and board both for holy men who will take the guilt of our sins from us. Swear to me on the cross that you are a very holy man.

THE FRIAR. I'll do better than that, daughter. I'll prove my holiness to you by a miracle.

THE GIRL. A miracle!

THE FRIAR. A most miraculous miracle. A wonderful miracle! When I was only eighteen years of age I was already famous for my devoutness. When the hand of the blessed Saint Barbara, which was chopped off in the days when the church was persecuted, was found at Viterbo, I was selected by the Pope himself to carry it to Rome for that blessed lady's festival there; and since that my hand has never grown old. It remains young and warm and plump whilst the rest of my body is withered almost to dust, and my voice is cracked and become the whistling you now hear.

THE GIRL. Is that true? Let me see. [*He takes her hand in his. She kneels and kisses it fervently*] Oh, it's true. You are a saint. Heaven has sent you in answer to my prayer.

THE FRIAR. As soft as your neck, is it not? [*He caresses her neck*].

THE GIRL. It thrills me: it is wonderful.

THE FRIAR. It thrills me also, daughter. That, too, is a miracle at my age.

THE GIRL. Father—

THE FRIAR. Come closer, daughter. I'm very very old and very very very deaf: you must speak quite close to my ear if you speak low. [*She kneels with her breast against his arm and her chin on his shoulder*]. Good. Good. Thats better. Oh, I'm very very old.

THE GIRL. Father: I am about to commit a deadly sin.

THE FRIAR. Do, my daughter. Do, do, do, do, do.

THE GIRL [*discouraged*] Oh, you do not hear what I say.

THE FRIAR. Not hear! Then come closer, daughter. Oh, much, much closer. Put your arm round my shoulders, and speak in my ear. Do not be ashamed, my daughter: I'm only a sack of old bones. You can hear them rattle. [*He shakes his shoulders and makes the beads of his rosary rattle at the same time*]. Listen to the old man's bones rattling. Oh, take the old old man to heaven, Blessed Barbara.

THE GIRL. Your wits are wandering. Listen to me. Are you listening?

THE FRIAR. Yes yes yes yes yes yes. Remember: whether I hear or not, I can absolve. All the better for you perhaps if I do not hear the worst. He! He! He! Well well. When my wits wander, squeeze my young hand; and the blessed Barbara will restore my faculties. [*She squeezes his hand vigorously*]. Thats right. Tha-a-a-ats right. Now I remember what I am and who you are. Proceed, my child.

THE GIRL. Father, I am to be married this year to a young fisherman.

THE FRIAR. The devil you are, my dear.

THE GIRL [*squeezing his hand*] Oh listen, listen; you are wandering again.

THE FRIAR. Thats right: hold my hand tightly. I understand, I understand. This young fisherman is neither very beautiful nor very brave; but he is honest and devoted to you; and there is something about him different to all the other young men.

THE GIRL. You know him, then!

THE FRIAR. No no no no no. I'm too old to remember people. But Saint Barbara tells me everything.

THE GIRL. Then you know why we cant marry yet.

THE FRIAR. He is too poor. His mother will not let him unless his bride has a dowry—

THE GIRL [*interrupting him impetuously*] Yes, yes: oh blessed be Saint Barbara for sending you to me! Thirty crowns—thirty crowns from a poor girl like me: it is wicked —monstrous. I must sin to earn it.

THE FRIAR. That will not be your sin, but his mother's.

THE GIRL. Oh, that is true: I never thought of that. But

will she suffer for it?

THE FRIAR. Thousands of years in purgatory for it, my daughter. The worse the sin, the longer she will suffer. So let her have it as hot as possible. [*The girl recoils*]. Do not let go my hand: I'm wandering. [*She squeezes his hand*]. Thats right, darling. Sin is a very wicked thing, my daughter. Even a mother-in-law's sin is very expensive; for your husband would stint you to pay for masses for her soul.

THE GIRL. That is true. You are very wise, father.

THE FRIAR. Let it be a venial sin: an amiable sin. What sin were you thinking of, for instance?

THE GIRL. There is a young Count Ferruccio [*the Friar starts at the name*], son of the tyrant of Parma—

THE FRIAR. An excellent young man, daughter. You could not sin with a more excellent young man. But thirty crowns is too much to ask from him. He cant afford it. He is a beggar: an outcast. He made love to Madonna Brigita, the sister of Cardinal Poldi, a Cardinal eighteen years of age, a nephew of the Holy Father. The Cardinal surprised Ferruccio with his sister; and Ferruccio's temper got the better of him. He threw that holy young Cardinal out of the window and broke his arm.

THE GIRL. You know everything.

THE FRIAR. Saint Barbara, my daughter, Saint Barbara. *I* know nothing. But where have you seen Ferruccio? Saint Barbara says that he never saw you in his life, and has not thirty crowns in the world.

THE GIRL. Oh, why does not Saint Barbara tell you that I am an honest girl who would not sell herself for a thousand crowns.

THE FRIAR. Do not give way to pride, daughter. Pride is one of the seven deadly sins.

THE GIRL. I know that, father; and believe me, I'm humble and good. I swear to you by Our Lady that it is not Ferruccio's love that I must take, but his life. [*The Friar, startled, turns powerfully on her*]. Do not be angry, dear father: do not cast me off. What is a poor girl to do? We are very poor, my father and I. And I am not to kill him. I am only to decoy him here; for he is a devil for women; and once he is in the inn, my father will do the rest.

THE FRIAR [*in a rich baritone voice*] Will he, by thunder and lightning and the flood and all the saints, will he? [*He flings off his gown and beard, revealing himself as a handsome youth, a nobleman by his dress, as he springs up and rushes to the door of the inn, which he batters with a stone*]. Ho there, Squarcio, rascal, assassin, son of a pig: come out that I may break every bone in your carcass.

THE GIRL. You are a young man!

THE FRIAR. Another miracle of Saint Barbara. [*Kicking the door*] Come out, whelp: come out, rat. Come out and be killed. Come out and be beaten to a jelly. Come out, dog, swine, animal, mangy hound, lousy— [*Squarcio comes out, sword in hand*]. Do you know who I am, dog?

SQUARCIO [*impressed*] No, your excellency.

THE FRIAR. I am Ferruccio, Count Ferruccio, the man you are to kill, the man your devil of a daughter is to decoy, the man who is now going to cut you into forty thousand pieces and throw you into the lake.

SQUARCIO. Keep your temper, Signor Count.

FERRUCCIO. I'll not keep my temper. Ive an uncontrollable temper. I get blinding splitting headaches if I do not relieve my temper by acts of violence. I'll relieve it now by pounding you to jelly, assassin that you are.

SQUARCIO [*shrugging his shoulders*] As you please, Signor Count. I may as well earn my money now as another time. [*He handles his sword*].

FERRUCCIO. Ass: do you suppose I have trusted myself in this territory without precautions? My father has made a wager with your feudal lord here about me.

SQUARCIO. What wager, may it please your excellency?

FERRUCCIO. What wager, blockhead! Why, that if I am assassinated, the murderer will not be brought to justice.

SQUARCIO. So that if I kill you—

FERRUCCIO. Your Baron will lose ten crowns unless you

are broken on the wheel for it.

SQUARCIO. Only ten crowns, Excellency! Your father does not value your life very highly.

FERRUCCIO. Dolt. Can you not reason? If the sum were larger your Baron would win it by killing me himself and breaking somebody else on the wheel for it: you, most likely. Ten crowns is just enough to make him break you on the wheel if you kill me, but not enough to pay for all the masses that would have to be said for him if the guilt were his.

SQUARCIO. That is very clever, Excellency. [*Sheathing his sword*] You shall not be slain: I will take care of that. If anything happens, it will be an accident.

FERRUCCIO. Body of Bacchus! I forgot that trick. I should have killed you when my blood was hot.

SQUARCIO. Will your Excellency please to step in? My best room and my best cooking are at your Excellency's disposal.

FERRUCCIO. To the devil with your mangy kennel! You want to tell every traveller that Count Ferruccio slept in your best bed and was eaten by your army of fleas. Take yourself out of my sight when you have told me where the next inn is.

SQUARCIO. I'm sorry to thwart your Excellency; but I have not forgotten your father's wager; and until you leave this territory I shall stick to you like your shadow.

FERRUCCIO. And why, pray?

SQUARCIO. Someone else might kill your Excellency; and, as you say, my illustrious Baron might break me on the wheel for your father's ten crowns. I must protect your Excellency, whether your Excellency is willing or not.

FERRUCCIO. If you dare to annoy me, I'll handle your bones so that there will be nothing left for the hangman to break. Now what do you say?

SQUARCIO. I say that your Excellency over-rates your Excellency's strength. You would have no more chance against me than a grasshopper. [*Ferruccio makes a demonstration*]. Oh, I know that your Excellency has been taught by fencers and wrestlers and the like; but I can take all you can give me without turning a hair, and settle the account when you are out of breath. That is why common men are dangerous, your Excellency: they are inured to toil and endurance. Besides, I know all the tricks.

THE GIRL. Do not attempt to quarrel with my father, Count. It must be as he says. It is his profession to kill. What could you do against him? If you want to beat somebody, you must beat me. [*She goes into the inn*].

SQUARCIO. I advise you not to try that, Excellency. She also is very strong.

FERRUCCIO. Then I shall have a headache: thats all. [*He throws himself ill-humoredly on a bench at the table outside the inn. Giulia returns with a tablecloth and begins preparing the table for a meal*].

SQUARCIO. A good supper, Excellency, will prevent that. And Giulia will sing for you.

FERRUCCIO. Not while theres a broomstick in the house to break her ugly head with. Do you suppose I'm going to listen to the howling of a she-wolf who wanted me to absolve her for getting me killed?

SQUARCIO. The poor must live as well as the rich, sir. Giulia is a good girl. [*He goes into the inn*].

FERRUCCIO [*shouting after him*] Must the rich die that the poor may live?

GIULIA. The poor often die that the rich may live.

FERRUCCIO. What an honor for them! But it would have been no honor for me to die merely that you might marry your clod of a fisherman.

GIULIA. You are spiteful, Signor.

FERRUCCIO. I am no troubadour, Giuliaccia, if that is what you mean.

GIULIA. How did you know about my Sandro and his mother? How were you so wise when you pretended to be an old friar? you that are so childish now that you are yourself!

FERRUCCIO. I take it that either Saint Barbara inspired me, or else that you are a great fool.

GIULIA. Saint Barbara will surely punish you for that wicked lie you told about her hand.

FERRUCCIO. The hand that thrilled you?

GIULIA. That was blasphemy. You should not have done it. You made me feel as if I had had a taste of heaven; and then you poisoned it in my heart as a taste of hell. That was wicked and cruel. You nobles are cruel.

FERRUCCIO. Well! do you expect us to nurse your babies for you? Our work is to rule and to fight. Ruling is nothing but inflicting cruelties on wrongdoers: fighting is nothing but being cruel to one's enemies. You poor people leave us all the cruel work, and then wonder that we are cruel. Where would you be if we left it undone? Outside the life I lead all to myself—the life of thought and poetry—I know only two pleasures: cruelty and lust. I desire revenge: I desire women. And both of them disappoint me when I get them.

GIULIA. It would have been a good deed to kill you, I think.

FERRUCCIO. Killing is always sport, my Giuliaccia.

SANDRO'S VOICE [*on the lake*] Giulietta! Giulietta!

FERRUCCIO [*calling to him*] Stop that noise. Your Giulietta is here with a young nobleman. Come up and amuse him. [*To Giulietta*] What will you give me if I tempt him to defy his mother and marry you without a dowry?

GIULIA. You are tempting me. A poor girl can give no more than she has. I should think you were a devil if you were not a noble, which is worse. [*She goes out to meet Sandro*].

FERRUCCIO [*calling after her*] The devil does evil for pure love of it: he does not ask a price: he offers it. [*Squarcio returns*]. Prepare supper for four, bandit.

SQUARCIO. Is your appetite so great in this heat, Signor?

FERRUCCIO. There will be four to supper. You, I, your daughter, and Sandro. Do not stint yourselves: I pay for all. Go and prepare more food.

SQUARCIO. Your order is already obeyed, Excellency.

FERRUCCIO. How?

SQUARCIO. I prepared for four, having you here to pay. The only difference your graciousness makes is that we shall have the honor to eat with you instead of after you.

FERRUCCIO. Dog of a bandit: you should have been born a nobleman.

SQUARCIO. I was born noble, signor; but as we had no money to maintain our pretensions, I dropped them. [*He goes back into the inn*].

Giulia returns with Sandro.

GIULIA. This is the lad, Excellency. Sandro: this is his lordship Count Ferruccio.

SANDRO. At your lordship's service.

FERRUCCIO. Sit down, Sandro. You, Giulia, and Squarcio are my guests. [*They sit*].

GIULIA. Ive told Sandro everything, Excellency.

FERRUCCIO. And what does Sandro say? [*Squarcio returns with a tray*].

GIULIA. He says that if you have ten crowns in your purse, and we kill you, we can give them to the Baron. It would be the same to him as if he got it from your illustrious father.

SQUARCIO. Stupid: the Count is cleverer than you think. No matter how much money you give the Baron he can always get ten crowns more by breaking me on the wheel if the Count is killed.

GIULIA. That is true. Sandro did not think of that.

SANDRO [*with cheerful politeness*] Oh! what a head I have! I am not clever, Excellency. At the same time you must know that I did not mean my Giulietta to tell you. I know my duty to your Excellency better than that.

FERRUCCIO. Come! You are dear people: charming people. Let us get to work at the supper. You shall be the mother of the family and give us our portions, Giulietta. [*They take their places*]. Thats right. Serve me last, Giulietta. Sandro is hungry.

SQUARCIO [*to the girl*] Come come! do you not see that his Excellency will touch nothing until we have had some first.

[*He eats*]. See, Excellency! I have tasted everything. To tell you the truth, poisoning is an art I do not understand.

FERRUCCIO. Very few professional poisoners do, Squarcio. One of the best professionals in Rome poisoned my uncle and aunt. They are alive still. The poison cured my uncle's gout, and only made my aunt thin, which was exactly what she desired, poor lady, as she was losing her figure terribly.

SQUARCIO. There is nothing like the sword, Excellency.

SANDRO. Except the water, Father Squarcio. Trust a fisherman to know that. Nobody can tell that drowning was not an accident.

FERRUCCIO. What does Giulietta say?

GIULIA. I should not kill a man if I hated him. You cannot torment a man when he is dead. Men kill because they think it is what they call a satisfaction. But that is only fancy.

FERRUCCIO. And if you loved him? Would you kill him then?

GIULIA. Perhaps. If you love a man you are his slave: everything he says—everything he does—is a stab to your heart: every day is a long dread of losing him. Better kill him if there be no other escape.

FERRUCCIO. How well you have brought up your family, Squarcio! Some more omelette, Sandro?

SANDRO [*very cheerfully*] I thank your Excellency. [*He accepts and eats with an appetite*].

FERRUCCIO. I pledge you all. To the sword and the fisherman's net: to love and hate! [*He drinks: they drink with him*].

SQUARCIO. To the sword!

SANDRO. To the net, Excellency, with thanks for the honor.

GIULIA. To love, signor.

FERRUCCIO. To hate: the noble's portion!

SQUARCIO. The meal has done you good, Excellency. How do you feel now?

FERRUCCIO. I feel that there is nothing but a bait of ten crowns between me and death, Squarcio.

SQUARCIO. It is enough, Excellency. And enough is always enough.

SANDRO. Do not think of that, Excellency. It is only that we are poor folk, and have to consider how to make both ends meet as one may say. [*Looking at the dish*] Excellency—?

FERRUCCIO. Finish it, Sandro. Ive done.

SANDRO. Father Squarcio?

SQUARCIO. Finish it, finish it.

SANDRO. Giulietta?

GIULIA [*surprised*] Me? Oh no. Finish it, Sandro: it will only go to the pig.

SANDRO. Then, with your Excellency's permission—[*he helps himself*].

SQUARCIO. Sing for his Excellency, my daughter.

Giulia turns to the door to fetch her mandoline.

FERRUCCIO. I shall jump into the lake, Squarcio, if your cat begins to miaowl.

SANDRO [*always cheerful and reassuring*] No, no, Excellency: Giulietta sings very sweetly: have no fear.

FERRUCCIO. I do not care for singing: at least not the singing of peasants. There is only one thing for which one woman will do as well as another, and that is lovemaking. Come, Father Squarcio: I will buy Giulietta from you: you can have her back for nothing when I am tired of her. How much?

SQUARCIO. In ready money, or in promises?

FERRUCCIO. Old fox. Ready money.

SQUARCIO. Fifty crowns, Excellency.

FERRUCCIO. Fifty crowns! Fifty crowns for that black-faced devil! I would not give fifty crowns for one of my mother's ladies-in-waiting. Fifty pence, you must mean.

SQUARCIO. Doubtless your Excellency, being a younger son, is poor. Shall we say five and twenty crowns?

FERRUCCIO. I tell you she is not worth five.

SQUARCIO. Oh, if you come to what she is worth, Excellency, what are any of us worth? I take it that you are a gentleman, not a merchant.

GIULIA. What are you worth, Signorino?

FERRUCCIO. I am accustomed to be asked for favors, Giuliaccia, not to be asked impertinent questions.

GIULIA. What would you do if a strong man took you by the scruff of your neck, or his daughter thrust a knife in your throat, Signor?

FERRUCCIO. It would be many a year, my gentle Giuliaccia, before any baseborn man or woman would dare threaten a nobleman again. The whole village would be flayed alive.

SANDRO. Oh no, Signor. These things often have a great air of being accidents. And the great families are well content that they should appear so. It is such a great trouble to flay a whole village alive. Here by the water, accidents are so common.

SQUARCIO. We of the nobility, Signor, are not strict enough. I learnt that when I took to breeding horses. The horses you breed from thoroughbreds are not all worth the trouble: most of them are screws. Well, the horsebreeder gets rid of his screws for what they will fetch: they go to labor like any peasant's beast. But our nobility does not study its business so carefully. If you are a screw, and the son of a baron, you are brought up to think yourself a little god, though you are nothing, and cannot rule yourself, much less a province. And you presume, and presume, and presume—

GIULIA. And insult, and insult, and insult.

SQUARCIO. Until one day you find yourself in a strange place with nothing to help you but your own hands and your own wits—

GIULIA. And you perish—

SANDRO. Accidentally—

GIULIA. And your soul goes crying to your father for vengeance—

SQUARCIO. If indeed, my daughter, there be any soul left when the body is slain.

FERRUCCIO [*crossing himself hastily*] Dog of a bandit: do you dare doubt the existence of God and the soul?

SQUARCIO. I think, Excellency, that the soul is so precious

a gift that God will not give it to a man for nothing. He must earn it by being something and doing something. I should not like to kill a man with a good soul. Ive had a dog that had, I'm persuaded, made itself something of a soul; and if anyone had murdered that dog, I would have slain him. But shew me a man with no soul: one who has never done anything or been anything; and I will kill him for ten crowns with as little remorse as I would stick a pig.

SANDRO. Unless he be a nobleman, of course—

SQUARCIO. In which case the price is fifty crowns.

FERRUCCIO. Soul or no soul?

SQUARCIO. When it comes to a matter of fifty crowns, Excellency, business is business. The man who pays me must square the account with the devil. It is for my employer to consider whether the action be a good one or no: it is for me to earn his money honestly. When I said I should not like to kill a man with a good soul, I meant killing on my own account: not professionally.

FERRUCCIO. Are you such a fool then as to spoil your own trade by sometimes killing people for nothing?

SQUARCIO. One kills a snake for nothing, Excellency. One kills a dog for nothing sometimes.

SANDRO [*apologetically*] Only a mad dog, Excellency, of course.

SQUARCIO. A pet dog, too. One that eats and eats and is useless, and makes an honest man's house dirty. [*He rises*]. Come, Sandro, and help me to clean up. You, Giulia, stay and entertain his Excellency.

He and Sandro make a hammock of the cloth, in which they carry the wooden platters and fragments of the meal indoors. Ferruccio is left alone with Giulia. The gloaming deepens.

FERRUCCIO. Does your father do the house work with a great girl like you idling about? Squarcio is a fool, after all.

GIULIA. No, Signor: he has left me here to prevent you from escaping.

FERRUCCIO. There is nothing to be gained by killing me, Giuliaccia.

GIULIA. Perhaps; but I do not know. I saw Sandro make a sign to my father: that is why they went in. Sandro has something in his head.

FERRUCCIO [*brutally*] Lice, no doubt.

GIULIA [*unmoved*] That would only make him scratch his head, Signor, not make signs with it to my father. You did wrong to throw the Cardinal out of the window.

FERRUCCIO. Indeed: and pray why?

GIULIA. He will pay thirty crowns for your dead body. Then Sandro could marry me.

FERRUCCIO. And be broken on the wheel for it.

GIULIA. It would look like an accident, Signor. Sandro is very clever; and he is so humble and cheerful and good-tempered that people do not suspect him as they suspect my father.

FERRUCCIO. Giulietta: if I reach Sacromonte in safety, I swear to send you thirty crowns by a sure messenger within ten days. Then you can marry your Sandro. How does that appeal to you?

GIULIA. Your oath is not worth twenty pence, Signor.

FERRUCCIO. Do you think I will die here like a rat in a trap—[*his breath fails him*].

GIULIA. Rats have to wait in their traps for death, Signor. Why not you?

FERRUCCIO. I'll fight.

GIULIA. You are welcome, Signor. The blood flows freeest when it is hot.

FERRUCCIO. She devil! Listen to me, Giulietta—

GIULIA. It is useless, Signor. Giulietta or Giuliaccia: it makes no difference. If they two in there kill you it will be no more to me—except for the money—than if my father trod on a snail.

FERRUCCIO. Oh, it is not possible that I, a nobleman, should die by such filthy hands.

GIULIA. You have lived by them, Signor. I see no sign of any work on your own hands. We can bring death as well as life, we poor people, Signor.

FERRUCCIO. Mother of God, what shall I do?

GIULIA. Pray, Signor.

FERRUCCIO. Pray! With the taste of death in my mouth? I can think of nothing.

GIULIA. It is only that you have forgotten your beads, Signor [*she picks up the Friar's rosary*]. You remember the old man's bones rattling. Here they are [*she rattles them before him*].

FERRUCCIO. That reminds me. I know of a painter in the north that can paint such beautiful saints that the heart goes out of one's body to look at them. If I get out of this alive I'll make him paint St Barbara so that every one can see that she is lovelier than St Cecilia, who looks like my washerwoman's mother in her Chapel in our cathedral. Can you give St Cecilia a picture if she lets me be killed?

GIULIA. No; but I can give her many prayers.

FERRUCCIO. Prayers cost nothing. She will prefer the picture unless she is a greater fool than I take her to be.

GIULIA. She will thank the painter for it, not you, Signor. And I'll tell her in my prayers to appear to the painter in a vision, and order him to paint her just as he sees her if she really wishes to be painted.

FERRUCCIO. You are devilishly ready with your answers. Tell me, Giulietta: is what your father told me true? Is your blood really noble?

GIULIA. It is red, Signor, like the blood of the Christ in the picture in Church. I do not know if yours is different. I shall see when my father kills you.

FERRUCCIO. Do you know what I am thinking, Giulietta?

GIULIA. No, Signor.

FERRUCCIO. I am thinking that if the good God would oblige me by taking my fool of an elder brother up to heaven, and his silly doll of a wife with him before she has time to give him a son, you would make a rare duchess for me. Come! Will you help me to outwit your father and Sandro if I marry you afterwards?

GIULIA. No, Signor: I'll help them to kill you.

FERRUCCIO. My back is to the wall, then?

GIULIA. To the precipice, I think, Signor.

FERRUCCIO. No matter, so my face is to the danger. Did you notice, Giulia, a minute ago? I was frightened.

GIULIA. Yes, Signor. I saw it in your face.

FERRUCCIO. The terror of terrors.

GIULIA. The terror of death.

FERRUCCIO. No: death is nothing. I can face a stab just as I faced having my tooth pulled out at Faenza.

GIULIA [*shuddering with sincere sympathy*] Poor Signorino! That must have hurt horribly.

FERRUCCIO. What! You pity me for the tooth affair, and you did not pity me in that hideous agony of terror that is not the terror of death nor of anything else, but pure grim terror in itself.

GIULIA. It was the terror of the soul, Signor. And I do not pity your soul: you have a wicked soul. But you have pretty teeth.

FERRUCCIO. The toothache lasted a week; but the agony of my soul was too dreadful to last five minutes: I should have died of it if it could have kept its grip of me. But you helped me out of it.

GIULIA. I, Signor!

FERRUCCIO. Yes: you. If you had pitied me: if you had been less inexorable than death itself, I should have broken down and cried and begged for mercy. But now I have come up against something hard: something real: something that does not care for me. I see now the truth of my excellent uncle's opinion that I was a spoilt cub. When I wanted anything I threatened men or ran crying to women; and they gave it to me. I dreamed and romanced: imagining things as I wanted them, not as they really are. There is nothing like a good look into the face of death: close up: right on you: for shewing you how little you really believe and how little you really are. A priest said to me once, "In your last hour everything will fall away from you except your religion."

But I have lived through my last hour; and my religion was the first thing that fell away from me. When I was forced at last to believe in grim death I knew at last what belief was, and that I had never believed in anything before: I had only flattered myself with pretty stories, and sheltered myself behind Mumbo Jumbo, as a soldier will shelter himself from arrows behind a clump of thistles that only hide the shooters from him. When I believe in everything that is real as I believed for that moment in death, then I shall be a man at last. I have tasted the water of life from the cup of death; and it may be now that my real life began with this [*he holds up the rosary*] and will end with the triple crown or the heretic's fire: I care not which. [*Springing to his feet*] Come out, then, dog of a bandit, and fight a man who has found his soul. [*Squarcio appears at the door, sword in hand. Ferruccio leaps at him and strikes him full in the chest with his dagger. Squarcio puts back his left foot to brace himself against the shock. The dagger snaps as if it had struck a stone wall*].

GIULIA. Quick, Sandro.

Sandro, who has come stealing round the corner of the inn with a fishing net, casts it over Ferruccio, and draws it tight.

SQUARCIO. Your Excellency will excuse my shirt of mail. A good home blow, nevertheless, Excellency.

SANDRO. Your Excellency will excuse my net: it is a little damp.

FERRUCCIO. Well, what now? Accidental drowning, I suppose.

SANDRO. Eh, Excellency, it is such a pity to throw a good fish back into the water when once you have got him safe in your net. My Giulietta: hold the net for me.

GIULIA [*taking the net and twisting it in her hands to draw it tighter round him*] I have you very fast now, Signorino, like a little bird in a cage.

FERRUCCIO. You have my body, Giulia. My soul is free.

GIULIA. Is it, Signor? I think Saint Barbara has got that in her net too. She has turned your jest into earnest.

SANDRO. It is indeed true, sir, that those who come under

the special protection of God and the Saints are always a little mad; and this makes us think it very unlucky to kill a madman. And since from what Father Squarcio and I overheard, it is clear that your Excellency, though a very wise and reasonable young gentleman in a general way, is somewhat cracked on the subject of the soul and so forth, we have resolved to see that no harm comes to your Excellency.

FERRUCCIO. As you please. My life is only a drop falling from the vanishing clouds to the everlasting sea, from finite to infinite, and itself part of the infinite.

SANDRO [*impressed*] Your Excellency speaks like a crazy but very holy book. Heaven forbid that we should raise a hand against you! But your Excellency will notice that this good action will cost us thirty crowns.

FERRUCCIO. Is it not worth it?

SANDRO. Doubtless, doubtless. It will in fact save us the price of certain masses which we should otherwise have had said for the souls of certain persons who—ahem! Well, no matter. But we think it dangerous and unbecoming that a nobleman like your Excellency should travel without a retinue, and unarmed; for your dagger is unfortunately broken, Excellency. If you would therefore have the condescension to accept Father Squarcio as your man-at-arms —your servant in all but the name, to save his nobility—he will go with you to any town in which you will feel safe from His Eminence the Cardinal, and will leave it to your Excellency's graciousness as to whether his magnanimous conduct will not then deserve some trifling present: say a wedding gift for my Giulietta.

FERRUCCIO. Good: the man I tried to slay will save me from being slain. Who would have thought Saint Barbara so full of irony!

SANDRO. And if the offer your Excellency was good enough to make in respect of Giulietta still stands—

FERRUCCIO. Rascal: have you then no soul?

SANDRO. I am a poor man, Excellency: I cannot afford these luxuries of the rich.

FERRUCCIO. There is a certain painter will presently make a great picture of St Barbara; and Giulia will be his model. He will pay her well. Giulia: release the bird. It is time for it to fly.

She takes the net from his shoulders.

COOLE PARK, *Summer*, 1909.

PASSION, POISON, AND PETRIFACTION,

or

THE FATAL GAZOGENE

(A BRIEF TRAGEDY FOR BARNS AND BOOTHS)

Written in 1905

First Performed London 1905

See Preface: Trifles and Tomfooleries (*page 721*)

PASSION, POISON, AND PETRIFACTION
OR
THE FATAL GAZOGENE

IN a bed-sitting room in a fashionable quarter of London a lady sits at her dressing-table, with her maid combing her hair. It is late; and the electric lamps are glowing. Apparently the room is bedless; but there stands against the opposite wall to that at which the dressing-table is placed a piece of furniture that suggests a bookcase without carrying conviction. On the same side is a chest of drawers of that disastrous kind which, recalcitrant to the opener until she is provoked to violence, then suddenly come wholly out and defy all her efforts to fit them in again. Opposite this chest of drawers, on the lady's side of the room, is a cupboard. The presence of a row of gentleman's boots beside the chest of drawers proclaims that the lady is married. Her own boots are beside the cupboard. The third wall is pierced midway by the door, above which is a cuckoo clock. Near the door a pedestal bears a portrait bust of the lady in plaster. There is a fan on the dressing-table, a hatbox and rug strap on the chest of drawers, an umbrella and a bootjack against the wall near the bed. The general impression is one of brightness, beauty, and social ambition, damped by somewhat inadequate means. A certain air of theatricality is produced by the fact that though the room is rectangular it has only three walls. Not a sound is heard except the overture and the crackling of the lady's hair as the maid's brush draws electric sparks from it in the dry air of the London midsummer.

The cuckoo clock strikes sixteen.

THE LADY. How much did the clock strike, Phyllis?

PHYLLIS. Sixteen, my lady.

THE LADY. That means eleven o'clock, does it not?

PHYLLIS. Eleven at night, my lady. In the morning it means half-past two; so if you hear it strike sixteen during your slumbers, do not rise.

THE LADY. I will not, Phyllis. Phyllis: I am weary. I will go to bed. Prepare my couch.

Phyllis crosses the room to the bookcase and touches a button.

The front of the bookcase falls out with a crash and becomes a bed. A roll of distant thunder echoes the crash.

PHYLLIS [*shuddering*] It is a terrible night. Heaven help all poor mariners at sea! My master is late. I trust nothing has happened to him. Your bed is ready, my lady.

THE LADY. Thank you, Phyllis. [*She rises and approaches the bed*]. Goodnight.

PHYLLIS. Will your ladyship not undress?

THE LADY. Not tonight, Phyllis. [*Glancing through where the fourth wall is missing*] Not under the circumstances.

PHYLLIS [*impulsively throwing herself on her knees by her mistress's side, and clasping her round the waist*] Oh, my beloved mistress, I know not why or how; but I feel that I shall never see you alive again. There is murder in the air. [*Thunder*]. Hark!

THE LADY. Strange! As I sat there methought I heard angels singing, Oh, wont you come home, Bill Bailey? Why should angels call me Bill Bailey? My name is Magnesia Fitztollemache.

PHYLLIS [*emphasizing the title*] L a d y Magnesia Fitztollemache.

LADY MAGNESIA. In case we should never again meet in this world, let us take a last farewell.

PHYLLIS [*embracing her with tears*] My poor murdered angel mistress!

LADY MAGNESIA. In case we should meet again, call me at half-past eleven.

PHYLLIS. I will, I will.

Phyllis withdraws, overcome by emotion. Lady Magnesia switches off the electric light, and immediately hears the angels quite distinctly. They sing Bill Bailey so sweetly that she can attend to nothing else, and forgets to remove even her boots as she draws the coverlet over herself and sinks to sleep, lulled by celestial harmony. A white radiance plays on her pillow, and lights up her beautiful face. But the thunder growls again; and a lurid red glow concentrates itself on the door, which is presently flung open, revealing a saturnine figure in evening dress, partially concealed by a crimson cloak. As he steals towards the bed the unnatural glare in his eyes and the broad-bladed dagger nervously gripped in his right hand bode ill for the sleeping lady. Providentially she sneezes on the very brink of eternity; and the tension of the murderer's nerves is such that he bolts precipitately under the bed at the sudden and startling Atscha! *A dull, heavy, rhythmic thumping—the beating of his heart—betrays his whereabouts. Soon he emerges cautiously and raises his head above the bed coverlet level.*

THE MURDERER. I can no longer cower here listening to the agonized thumpings of my own heart. She but snoze in her sleep. I'll do't. [*He again raises the dagger. The angels sing again. He cowers*] What is this? Has that tune reached Heaven?

LADY MAGNESIA [*waking and sitting up*] My husband! [*All the colors of the rainbow chase one another up his face with ghastly brilliancy*]. Why do you change color? And what on earth are you doing with that dagger?

FITZ [*affecting unconcern, but unhinged*] It is a present for you: a present from mother. Pretty, isnt it? [*he displays it fatuously*].

LADY MAGNESIA. But she promised me a fish slice.

FITZ. This is a combination fish slice and dagger. One day you have salmon for dinner. The next you have a murder to commit. See?

LADY MAGNESIA. My sweet mother-in-law! [*Someone knocks at the door*]. That is Adolphus's knock. [*Fitz's face turns a dazzling green*]. What has happened to your complexion? You have turned green. Now I think of it, you always do when Adolphus is mentioned. Arnt you going to let him in?

FITZ. Certainly not. [*He goes to the door*]. Adolphus: you cannot enter. My wife is undressed and in bed.

LADY MAGNESIA [*rising*] I am not. Come in, Adolphus [*she switches on the electric light*].

ADOLPHUS [*without*] Something most important has happened. I must come in for a moment.

FITZ [*calling to Adolphus*] Something important happened? What is it?

ADOLPHUS [*without*] My new clothes have come home.

FITZ. He says his new clothes have come home.

LADY MAGNESIA [*running to the door and opening it*] Oh, come in, come in. Let me see.

Adolphus Bastable enters. He is in evening dress, made in the latest fashion, with the right half of the coat and the left half of the trousers yellow and the other halves black. His silver-spangled waistcoat has a crimson handkerchief stuck between it and his shirt front.

ADOLPHUS. What do you think of it?

LADY MAGNESIA. It is a dream! a creation! [*she turns him about to admire him*].

ADOLPHUS [*proudly*] I shall never be mistaken for a waiter again.

FITZ. A drink, Adolphus?

ADOLPHUS. Thanks.

Fitztollemache goes to the cupboard and takes out a tray with tumblers and a bottle of whisky. He puts them on the dressing-table.

FITZ. Is the gazogene full?

LADY MAGNESIA. Yes: you put in the powders yourself today.

FITZ [*sardonically*] So I did. The special powders! Ha! ha! ha! ha! ha! [*his face is again strangely variegated*].

LADY MAGNESIA. Your complexion is really going to pieces. Why do you laugh in that silly way at nothing?

FITZ. Nothing! Ha, ha! Nothing! Ha, ha, ha!

ADOLPHUS. I hope, Mr Fitztollemache, you are not laughing at my clothes. I warn you that I am an Englishman. You may laugh at my manners, at my brains, at my national institutions; but if you laugh at my clothes, one of us must die.

Thunder.

FITZ. I laughed but at the irony of Fate [*he takes a gazogene from the cupboard*].

ADOLPHUS [*satisfied*] Oh, that! Oh, yes, of course!

FITZ. Let us drown all unkindness in a loving cup. [*He puts the gazogene on the floor in the middle of the room*]. Pardon the absence of a table: we found it in the way and pawned it. [*He takes the whisky bottle from the dressing-table*].

LADY MAGNESIA. We picnic at home now. It is delightful.

She takes three tumblers from the dressing-table and sits on the floor, presiding over the gazogene, with Fitz and Adolphus squatting on her left and right respectively. Fitz pours whisky into the tumblers.

FITZ [*as Magnesia is about to squirt soda into his tumbler*] Stay! No soda for me. Let Adolphus have it all—all. I will take mine neat.

LADY MAGNESIA [*proffering tumbler to Adolphus*] Pledge me, Adolphus.

FITZ. Kiss the cup, Magnesia. Pledge her, man. Drink deep.

ADOLPHUS. To Magnesia!

FITZ. To Magnesia! [*The two men drink*] It is done. [*Scrambling to his feet*] Adolphus: you have but ten minutes to live—if so long.

ADOLPHUS. What mean you?

MAGNESIA [*rising*] My mind misgives me. I have a strange feeling here [*touching her heart*].

ADOLPHUS. So have I, but lower down [*touching his stomach*]. That gazogene is disagreeing with me.

FITZ. It was poisoned!

Sensation.

ADOLPHUS [*rising*] Help! Police!

FITZ. Dastard! you would appeal to the law! Can you not die like a gentleman?

ADOLPHUS. But so young! when I have only worn my new clothes once.

MAGNESIA. It is too horrible. [*To Fitz*] Fiend! what drove you to this wicked deed?

FITZ. Jealousy. You admired his clothes: you did not admire mine.

ADOLPHUS. My clothes [*his face lights up with heavenly radiance*]! Have I indeed been found worthy to be the first clothes-martyr? Welcome, death! Hark! angels call me. [*The celestial choir again raises its favorite chant. He listens with a rapt expression. Suddenly the angels sing out of tune; and the radiance on the poisoned man's face turns a sickly green*] Yah—ah! Oh—ahoo! The gazogene is disagreeing extremely. Oh! [*he throws himself on the bed, writhing*].

MAGNESIA [*to Fitz*] Monster: what have you done? [*She points to the distorted figure on the bed*]. That was once a Man, beautiful and glorious. What have you made of it? A writhing, agonized, miserable, moribund worm.

ADOLPHUS [*in a tone of the strongest remonstrance*] Oh, I say! Oh, come! No: look here, Magnesia! Really!

MAGNESIA. Oh, is this a time for petty vanity? Think of your misspent life—

ADOLPHUS [*much injured*] Whose misspent life?

MAGNESIA [*continuing relentlessly*] Look into your conscience: look into your stomach. [*Adolphus collapses in hideous spasms. She turns to Fitz*] And this is your handiwork!

FITZ. Mine is a passionate nature, Magnesia. I must have your undivided love. I must have your love: do you hear? LOVE! LOVE!! LOVE!!! LOVE!!!! LOVE!!!!!

He raves, accompanied by a fresh paroxysm from the victim on the bed.

MAGNESIA [*with sudden resolution*] You shall have it.

FITZ [*enraptured*] Magnesia! I have recovered your love! Oh, how slight appears the sacrifice of this man compared to so glorious a reward! I would poison ten men without a thought of self to gain one smile from you.

ADOLPHUS [*in a broken voice*] Farewell, Magnesia: my last hour is at hand. Farewell, farewell, farewell!

MAGNESIA. At this supreme moment, George Fitztollemache, I solemnly dedicate to you all that I formerly dedicated to poor Adolphus.

ADOLPHUS. Oh, please not poor Adolphus yet. I still live, you know.

MAGNESIA. The vital spark but flashes before it vanishes. [*Adolphus groans*]. And now, Adolphus, take this last comfort from the unhappy Magnesia Fitztollemache. As I have dedicated to George all that I gave to you, so I will bury in your grave—or in your urn if you are cremated—all that I gave to him.

FITZ. I hardly follow this.

MAGNESIA. I will explain. George: hitherto I have given Adolphus all the romance of my nature—all my love—all my dreams—all my caresses. Henceforth they are yours!

FITZ. Angel!

MAGNESIA. Adolphus: forgive me if this pains you.

ADOLPHUS. Dont mention it. I hardly feel it. The gazogene is so much worse. [*Taken bad again*] Oh!

MAGNESIA. Peace, poor sufferer: there is still some balm. You are about to hear what I am going to dedicate to you.

ADOLPHUS. All I ask is a peppermint lozenge, for mercy's sake.

MAGNESIA. I have something far better than any lozenge: the devotion of a lifetime. Formerly it was George's. I kept his house, or rather, his lodgings. I mended his clothes. I darned his socks. I bought his food. I interviewed his creditors. I stood between him and the servants. I administered his domestic finances. When his hair needed cutting or his countenance was imperfectly washed, I pointed it out to him. The trouble that all this gave me made him prosaic in my eyes. Familiarity bred contempt. Now all that shall end. My husband shall be my hero, my lover, my perfect knight. He shall shield me from all care and trouble. He shall ask nothing in return but love—boundless, priceless, rapturous, soul-enthralling love, LOVE! LOVE!! LOVE!!! [*she raves and flings her arms about Fitz*]. And the duties I formerly discharged shall be replaced by the one supreme duty of duties: the duty of weeping at Adolphus's tomb.

FITZ [*reflectively*] My ownest, this sacrifice makes me feel that I have perhaps been a little selfish. I cannot help feeling that there is much to be said for the old arrangement. Why should Adolphus die for my sake?

ADOLPHUS. I am not dying for your sake, Fitz. I am dying because you poisoned me.

MAGNESIA. You do not fear to die, Adolphus, do you?

ADOLPHUS. N-n-no, I dont exactly fear to die. Still—

FITZ. Still, if an antidote—

ADOLPHUS [*bounding from the bed*] Antidote!

MAGNESIA [*with wild hope*] Antidote!

FITZ. If an antidote would not be too much of an anti-climax.

ADOLPHUS. Anti-climax be blowed! Do you think I am going to die to please the critics? Out with your antidote. Quick!

FITZ. The best antidote to the poison I have given you is lime, plenty of lime.

ADOLPHUS. Lime! You mock me! Do you think I carry lime about in my pockets?

FITZ. There is the plaster ceiling.

MAGNESIA. Yes, the ceiling. Saved, saved, saved!

All three frantically shy boots at the ceiling. Flakes of plaster rain down which Adolphus devours, at first ravenously, then with a marked falling off in relish.

MAGNESIA [*picking up a huge slice*] Take this, Adolphus: it is the largest [*she crams it into his mouth*].

FITZ. Ha! a lump off the cornice! Try this.

ADOLPHUS [*desperately*] Stop! stop!

MAGNESIA. Do not stop. You will die. [*She tries to stuff him again*].

ADOLPHUS [*resolutely*] I prefer death.

MAGNESIA and FITZ [*throwing themselves on their knees on either side of him*] For our sakes, Adolphus, persevere.

ADOLPHUS. No: unless you can supply lime in liquid form, I must perish. Finish that ceiling I cannot and will not.

MAGNESIA. I have a thought—an inspiration. My bust. [*She snatches it from its pedestal and brings it to him*].

ADOLPHUS [*gazing fondly at it*] Can I resist it?

FITZ. Try the bun.

ADOLPHUS [*gnawing the knot of hair at the back of the bust's head: it makes him ill*]. Yah, I cannot. I cannot. Not even your bust, Magnesia. Do not ask me. Let me die.

FITZ [*pressing the bust on him*] Force yourself to take a mouthful. Down with it, Adolphus!

ADOLPHUS. Useless. It would not stay down. Water! Some fluid! Ring for something to drink [*he chokes*].

MAGNESIA. I will save you [*she rushes to the bell and rings*].

Phyllis, in her night-gown, with her hair prettily made up into a chevaux de frise of crocuses with pink and yellow curl papers, rushes in straight to Magnesia.

PHYLLIS [*hysterically*] My beloved mistress, once more we meet. [*She sees Fitztollemache and screams*] Ah! ah! ah! A man! [*She sees Adolphus*] Men!! [*She flies; but Fitztollemache seizes her by the night-gown just as she is escaping*]. Unhand me, villain!

FITZ. This is no time for prudery, girl. Mr Bastable is dying.

PHYLLIS [*with concern*] Indeed, sir? I hope he will not think it unfeeling of me to appear at his deathbed in curl papers.

MAGNESIA. We know you have a good heart, Phyllis. Take this [*giving her the bust*]; dissolve it in a jug of hot water; and bring it back instantly. Mr Bastable's life depends on your haste.

PHYLLIS [*hesitating*] It do seem a pity, dont it, my lady, to spoil your lovely bust?

ADOLPHUS. Tush! This craze for fine art is beyond all bounds. Off with you [*he pushes her out*]. Drink, drink, drink! My entrails are parched. Drink! [*he rushes deliriously to the gazogene*].

FITZ [*rushing after him*] Madman, you forget! It is poisoned.

ADOLPHUS. I dont care. Drink, drink! [*They wrestle madly for the gazogene. In the struggle they squirt all its contents away, mostly into one another's face. Adolphus at last flings Fitztollemache to the floor, and puts the spout into his mouth*]. Empty!

empty! [*with a shriek of despair he collapses on the bed, clasping the gazogene like a baby, and weeping over it*].

FITZ [*aside to Magnesia*] Magnesia: I have always pretended not to notice it; but you keep a siphon for your private use in my hat-box.

MAGNESIA. I use it for washing old lace; but no matter: he shall have it [*she produces a siphon from the hat-box, and offers a tumbler of soda-water to Adolphus*].

ADOLPHUS. Thanks, thanks, oh, thanks! [*he drinks. A terrific fizzing is heard. He starts up screaming*] Help! help! The ceiling is effervescing! I am BURSTING! [*He wallows convulsively on the bed*].

FITZ. Quick! the rug strap! [*They pack him with blankets and strap him*]. Is that tight enough?

MAGNESIA [*anxiously*] Will you hold, do you think?

ADOLPHUS. The peril is past. The soda-water has gone flat.

MAGNESIA and FITZ. Thank heaven!

Phyllis returns with a washstand ewer, in which she has dissolved the bust.

MAGNESIA [*snatching it*] At last!

FITZ. You are saved. Drain it to the dregs.

Fitztollemache holds the lip of the ewer to Adolphus's mouth and gradually raises it until it stands upside down. Adolphus's efforts to swallow it are fearful, Phyllis thumping his back when he chokes, and Magnesia loosening the straps when he moans. At last, with a sigh of relief, he sinks back in the women's arms. Fitz shakes the empty ewer upside down like a potman shaking the froth out of a flagon.

ADOLPHUS. How inexpressibly soothing to the chest! A delicious numbness steals through all my members. I would sleep.

MAGNESIA, FITZ, PHYLLIS [*whispering*] Let him sleep.

He sleeps. Celestial harps are heard; but their chords cease on the abrupt entrance of the landlord, a vulgar person in pyjamas.

THE LANDLORD. Eah! Eah! Wots this? Wots all this noise? Ah kin ennybody sleep through it? [*Looking at the floor and ceiling*] Ellow! wot you bin doin te maw ceilin?

FITZ. Silence, or leave the room. If you wake that man he dies.

THE LANDLORD. If e kin sleep through the noise you three mikes e kin sleep through ennythink.

MAGNESIA. Detestable vulgarian: your pronunciation jars on the finest chords of my nature. Begone!

THE LANDLORD [*looking at Adolphus*] Aw downt blieve eze esleep. Aw blieve eze dead. [*Calling*] Pleece! Pleece! Merder! [*A blue halo plays mysteriously on the door, which opens and reveals a policeman. Thunder*]. Eah, pleecmin: these three's bin an merdered this gent between em, an naw tore moy ahse dahn.

THE POLICEMAN [*offended*] Policeman, indeed! Wheres your manners?

FITZ. Officer—

THE POLICEMAN [*with distinguished consideration*] Sir?

FITZ. As between gentlemen—

THE POLICEMAN [*bowing*] Sir: to you.

FITZ [*bowing*] I may inform you that my friend had an acute attack of indigestion. No carbonate of soda being available, he swallowed a portion of this man's ceiling. [*Pointing to Adolphus*] Behold the result!

THE POLICEMAN. The ceiling was poisoned! Well, of all the artful— [*he collars the landlord*]. I arrest you for wilful murder.

THE LANDLORD [*appealing to the heavens*] Ow, is this jestice! Ah could aw tell e wiz gowin te eat moy ceilin?

THE POLICEMAN [*releasing him*] True. The case is more complicated than I thought. [*He tries to lift Adolphus's arm but cannot*]. Stiff already.

THE LANDLORD [*trying to lift Adolphus's leg*] An' precious evvy. [*Feeling the calf*] Woy, eze gorn ez awd ez niles.

FITZ [*rushing to the bed*] What is this?

MAGNESIA. Oh, say not he is dead. Phyllis: fetch a doctor.

[*Phyllis runs out. They all try to lift Adolphus; but he is perfectly stiff, and as heavy as lead*]. Rouse him. Shake him.

THE POLICEMAN [*exhausted*] Whew! Is he a man or a statue? [*Magnesia utters a piercing scream*]. Whats wrong, Miss?

MAGNESIA [*to Fitz*] Do you not see what has happened?

FITZ [*striking his forehead*] Horror on horror's head!

THE LANDLORD. Wotjemean?

MAGNESIA. The plaster has set inside him. The officer was right: he is indeed a living statue.

Magnesia flings herself on the stony breast of Adolphus. Fitztollemache buries his head in his hands; and his chest heaves convulsively. The policeman takes a small volume from his pocket and consults it.

THE POLICEMAN. This case is not provided for in my book of instructions. It dont seem no use trying artificial respiration, do it? [*To the landlord*] Here! lend a hand, you. We'd best take him and set him up in Trafalgar Square.

THE LANDLORD. Aushd pat im in the cestern an worsh it aht of im.

Phyllis comes back with a Doctor.

PHYLLIS. The medical man, my lady.

THE POLICEMAN. A poison case, sir.

THE DOCTOR. Do you mean to say that an unqualified person! a layman! has dared to administer poison in my district?

THE POLICEMAN [*raising Magnesia tenderly*] It looks like it. Hold up, my lady.

THE DOCTOR. Not a moment must be lost. The patient must be kept awake at all costs. Constant and violent motion is necessary.

He snatches Magnesia from the Policeman, and rushes her about the room.

FITZ. Stop! That is not the poisoned person!

THE DOCTOR. It is you, then. Why did you not say so before?

He seizes Fitztollemache and rushes him about.

THE LANDLORD. Naow, naow, thet ynt im.

THE DOCTOR. What, you!

He pounces on the Landlord and rushes him round.

THE LANDLORD. Eah! chack it. [*He trips the Doctor up. Both fall*]. Jest owld this leoonatic, will you, Mister Horficer?

THE POLICEMAN [*dragging both of them to their feet*] Come out of it, will you. You must all come with me to the station.

Thunder.

MAGNESIA. What! In this frightful storm!

The hail patters noisily on the window.

PHYLLIS. I think it's raining.

The wind howls.

THE LANDLORD. It's thanderin and lawtnin.

FITZ. It's dangerous.

THE POLICEMAN [*drawing his baton and whistle*] If you wont come quietly, then—

He whistles. A fearful flash is followed by an appalling explosion of heaven's artillery. A thunderbolt enters the room, and strikes the helmet of the devoted constable, whence it is attracted to the waistcoat of the doctor by the lancet in his pocket. Finally it leaps with fearful force on the landlord, who, being of a gross and spongy nature, absorbs the electric fluid at the cost of his life. The others look on horror-stricken as the three victims, after reeling, jostling, cannoning through a ghastly quadrille, at last sink inanimate on the carpet.

MAGNESIA [*listening at the doctor's chest*] Dead!

FITZ [*kneeling by the landlord, and raising his hand, which drops with a thud*] Dead!

PHYLLIS [*seizing the looking-glass and holding it to the Policeman's lips*] Dead!

FITZ [*solemnly rising*] The copper attracted the lightning.

MAGNESIA [*rising*] After life's fitful fever they sleep well. Phyllis: sweep them up.

Phyllis replaces the looking-glass on the dressing-table; takes up the fan; and fans the Policeman, who rolls away like a leaf before the wind to the wall. She disposes similarly of the land-

lord and doctor.

PHYLLIS. Will they be in your way if I leave them there until morning, my lady? Or shall I bring up the ashpan and take them away?

MAGNESIA. They will not disturb us. Goodnight, Phyllis.

PHYLLIS. Goodnight, my lady. Goodnight, sir.

She retires.

MAGNESIA. And now, husband, let us perform our last sad duty to our friend. He has become his own monument. Let us erect him. He is heavy; but love can do much.

FITZ. A little leverage will get him on his feet. Give me my umbrella.

MAGNESIA. True.

She hands him the umbrella, and takes up the bootjack. They get them under Adolphus's back, and prize him up on his feet.

FITZ. Thats done it! Whew!

MAGNESIA [*kneeling at the left hand of the statue*] For ever and for ever, Adolphus.

FITZ [*kneeling at the right hand of the statue*] The rest is silence.

The Angels sing Bill Bailey. The statue raises its hands in an attitude of blessing, and turns its limelit face to heaven as the curtain falls. National Anthem.

ATTENDANTS [*in front*] All out for the next performance. Pass along, please, ladies and gentlemen: pass along.

THE FASCINATING FOUNDLING

(A DISGRACE TO THE AUTHOR)

Written in 1909

First Performed 1909

See Preface: Trifles and Tomfooleries (*page 721*)

THE FASCINATING FOUNDLING

MORNING. Office of the Lord Chancellor. Door on the right leading to his private room, near the fireplace. Door on the left leading to the public staircase. Mercer, an elderly clerk, seated at work. Enter, to him, through the public door, Horace Brabazon, a smart and beautiful young man of nineteen, dressed in the extremity of fashion, with a walking stick.

BRABAZON. I want to see the Lord Chancellor.

MERCER. Have you an appointment?

BRABAZON. No.

MERCER. Then you cant see the Lord Chancellor.

BRABAZON. I tell you I must see him.

MERCER. I tell you you cant. Look here: do you think the Lord Chancellor's a palmist or a hair doctor that people can rush in out of the street and see him whenever they want to?

BRABAZON. That speech was meant to insult and humiliate me. I make it a rule to fight people who attempt to insult and humiliate me. [*Throwing away his stick*] Put up your hands. [*He puts up his own*].

MERCER. Here: you let me alone. You leave this office, d'ye hear; or I'll have the police in on you.

BRABAZON. You are face to face with your destiny; and your destiny is to fight me. Be quick: I'm going to begin. Dont look pale: I scorn to take you by surprise. I shall lead off with my left on your right eye. Put them up.

MERCER. I aint going to fight you. Let me alone, will you? I said nothing to you.

BRABAZON. Liar and slave. Fight, I tell you: fight.

MERCER. Oh, was there ever the like of this? Dont make such a noise.

BRABAZON. I'm making it on purpose. I want you to fight because itll make more noise than anything else. The Lord Chancellor will come to see what the noise is about if only it's loud enough. Time! [*he spars*].

MERCER [*retreating to the fireplace and snatching up the poker*] Ah, would you? You come near me, and I'll split your head open, I will.

BRABAZON [*snatching up the tongs, and engaging him in a stage fight of the noisiest*] Lay on, Macduff; and damned be he that first cries Hold! Enough!

The Lord Chancellor enters indignantly.

THE LORD CHANCELLOR. Whats this? Who is this gentleman?

BRABAZON. The Lord Chancellor. Good. [*To Mercer*] Hence, horrible shadow: unreal mockery, hence. My lord, I have called on professional business. In the matter of Brabazon, an infant.

THE LORD CHANCELLOR. If you are a solicitor, sir, you must be aware that this is not the proper way to approach the Court.

BRABAZON. I approach you as the father of all the orphans in Chancery.

THE LORD CHANCELLOR. Sir—

BRABAZON. Dont fly out: I'll explain everything. You remember the matter of Brabazon, an infant. Come, now! frankly as man to man you do remember the matter of Brabazon, an infant.

THE LORD CHANCELLOR. There is such a case, I believe.

BRABAZON. Of course there is. Well, I'm the infant. I'm Brabazon. I'll call thee Hamlet! King! father! Royal Dane: wilt thou not answer me? [*Prosaically*] Now you see, dont you?

THE LORD CHANCELLOR. You are young Horace Brabazon, are you?

BRABAZON. I am, my lord. Such is life!

THE LORD CHANCELLOR. You are a ward of the Court; and you have systematically disobeyed every order made in your case.

BRABAZON. The orders were unreasonable. Fatuous, in fact.

THE LORD CHANCELLOR. Sir—

BRABAZON. Let me explain. One of the orders was that I was to go into the Church.

THE LORD CHANCELLOR. At your own desire.

BRABAZON. Exactly. But I should not have been indulged. I was too young. How did I know what was good for me? I put it to you as one man to another: do I look like an archbishop?

THE LORD CHANCELLOR. Stuff, sir.

BRABAZON. As you say, nothing could have been more idiotic. You ought to have known better. No: the Church is not in my line. Nature intended me for the stage. The Unreal Mockery here was practising Macduff with me when you came in. Now what I want to know is, can you get me an engagement? As your ward, I have a right to expect that of you. You must know lots of people who could give me a start. And theres another thing: very important. I—Oh, by the way, wont you sit down? Excuse me keeping you standing all this time. Macduff: a chair.

THE LORD CHANCELLOR [*with ironic politeness*] You are too good. [*He sits down*].

BRABAZON. Dont mention it. Well, you know: I want some good home influence to steady me. You see you cant steady me: youre too much occupied here with your shop: besides, you may shake a loose leg yourself occasionally for all the public knows, eh? Even if you are virtuous, I should probably lead you astray. No: what I want is a wife. Not a young woman, you know. Someone old enough to be my mother: say thirty or so. I adore a mature woman. Not old enough to be *your* mother, you understand: old enough to be my mother. I attach some importance to that distinction; so be good enough to bear it in mind. One mustnt overdo these notions.

THE LORD CHANCELLOR. Mr Mercer, will you be good enough to make a careful note of this gentleman's requirements: an engagement at a leading theatre to play Macbeth, and a wife of quiet habits and grave disposition. Anything else, Mr Brabazon?

BRABAZON. Nothing today, thank you. And now, I know better than to take up the time of a busy man. Happy to have made your acquaintance. So long! Ta, ta, Macduff.

He goes out.

THE LORD CHANCELLOR. What do you mean by letting this lunatic in, Mr Mercer? I'm extremely annoyed.

MERCER. I didnt let him in, my lord. He came in. I was keeping him from you at the risk of my life when you came in to ask what the noise was.

THE LORD CHANCELLOR [*with emotion*] My faithful Mercer.

MERCER. My honored master. [*They shake hands, weeping*].

THE LORD CHANCELLOR. We were happy together until this man came between us.

MERCER. Let us try to forget him, my lord. [*Turns to his desk and sees Brabazon's walking stick on the floor*] My lord, he has left his walking stick behind. He will return for it. Let us fly. [*He picks it up and puts it on the desk*].

THE LORD CHANCELLOR. Nonsense, Mercer: we have no aeroplane; and if we had we shouldnt know how to use it. Hark! A visitor at the door. [*They both rush to it. The handle is turned*]. Tell him we have both gone out.

MERCER. Useless, my lord: he is a man of strong reasoning powers: he would conclude, on hearing our voices, that we were both within.

A WOMAN'S VOICE. Is anybody there? Let me in. [*She rattles the door*].

THE LORD CHANCELLOR. That is the voice of a young and probably beautiful woman.

MERCER. It is, my lord.

THE LORD CHANCELLOR. Then why the dickens dont you open the door instead of striking melodramatic attitudes? How dare you keep the lady waiting? I'm very much annoyed.

MERCER. I'm sorry, my lord. [*He opens the door*].

Anastasia Vulliamy enters.

ANASTASIA [*to Mercer*] Is this the Lord Chancellor's?

MERCER. Yes.

ANASTASIA. Sir Cardonius Boshington's?

MERCER. Yes, maam.

ANASTASIA. Are you the Lord Chancellor?

MERCER. No, maam. Leastways, not yet.

ANASTASIA. What are you?

MERCER. I'm the Lord Chancellor's—

ANASTASIA. Secretary?

MERCER. Well, hardly that, maam. If you ask me, I should say I was a sort of what you might call a clerk-valet to his lordship.

ANASTASIA. Are you a gentleman?

MERCER [*staggered*] Well, thats a poser, Miss, really. I'm in a manner of speaking a gentleman.

ANASTASIA. In what manner of speaking are you a gentleman?

MERCER. Well, Miss, I'm a gentleman to my tobacconist. Every man is a gentleman to his tobacconist. The parliamentary candidate for Hornsey always addresses me as a gentleman. But then he aint particular: leastways, not at election times. You see, Miss, there are three classes of gentry in this country.

ANASTASIA. Only three?

MERCER. Only three, maam.

ANASTASIA. How do you tell one from the other?

MERCER. You tell by the railway porters, Miss. The real upper class gives them a shilling; the upper middle class sixpence; and the lower middle, tuppence. I give tuppence myself.

ANASTASIA. And which particular class of gentleman is it, pray, that gives a lady a chair?

MERCER. Oh, I'm sure I beg your pardon, Miss. [*He places a chair for her*].

ANASTASIA. Thanks. And now will you be good enough to tell Sir Cardonius Boshington that Miss Anastasia Vulliamy wishes to see him?

MERCER [*to the Lord Chancellor*] Miss Anaesthesia Vulliamy, my lord, to see you.

ANASTASIA [*springing up*] Do you mean to tell me that this old man in livery is the great Chancellor?

THE LORD CHANCELLOR. At your service, Miss Vulliamy.

ANASTASIA [*producing a newspaper*] Quite impossible. I have here an article on Sir Cardonius, headed Our Great Chancellor; and the description does not correspond in the least. [*Reading*] "No man of our time has succeeded in tempering the awe inspired by a commanding stature and majestic presence with a love and confidence which even the youngest and most timid ward of the Court feels at the sound of his kindly voice and the encouraging beam, twinkling with humor, of his tender grey eyes." Do you mean to tell me that thats you?

THE LORD CHANCELLOR. It is not for me to say how far the description is an accurate or a happy one, madam; but I believe I am the person intended by the writer.

MERCER [*producing another paper*] Perhaps youd recognize this better, Miss. Sir Cardonius and me is on opposite sides in politics.

ANASTASIA [*taking the paper and reading at the place he indicates* "How much longer will the nation allow this despicable pantaloon to occupy the woolsack—" Whats the woolsack?

MERCER. What the Lord Chancellor sits on in the House of Lords, Miss.

ANASTASIA [*continuing her reading*] "whose contents only too strongly resemble those of his own head." Thats a nasty one, you know: isnt it? It means that your brains are woolly, doesnt it?

THE LORD CHANCELLOR. Its meaning is entirely beneath my notice. I'm surprised, Mercer, to find you in possession of a scurrilous rag of this character. We may differ in our opinions; but if any paper taken in by me were to speak of you in such unbecoming terms, I should never open it again.

MERCER. Well, my lord; politics is politics; and after all, what is politics if it isnt shewing up the other side? When I pay a penny for a paper Ive a right to get value for my money the same as any other man.

ANASTASIA. But I dont understand [*To the Chancellor*] Are you a despicable pantaloon? The other paper says your name will be cherished by the warm hearts of the English people when Eldon and Sir Thomas More are forgotten. I thought that whatever is in the papers must be true. How do you explain being a great Chancellor and a despicable pantaloon at the same time?

THE LORD CHANCELLOR. I take it that the excellent journal from which you first quoted has put all considerations of party aside, and simply endeavored to place before you a dispassionate estimate of such modest services as I have been able to render to my country. The other paper gives you nothing but the vituperative ravings of an illiterate penny-a-liner blinded by party passion.

MERCER. You should never read more than one paper, Miss. It unsettles the mind, let alone the waste of a penny.

ANASTASIA. Well, it's a great relief to me to hear that the Great Chancellor paper is the right one. [*To the Lord Chancellor*] You think I may believe everything it says?

THE LORD CHANCELLOR. I trust I shall not disappoint any favorable opinion you may have founded on it.

ANASTASIA. It says here that though you are stern with the worthless and merciless to the impostor, yet your mature wisdom and unparalleled legal knowledge are freely at the service of all deserving persons, and that no distressed suitor has ever been turned empty away from your door.

THE LORD CHANCELLOR. That refers to my private house, madam. I dont keep food here.

MERCER. I have a sandwich for my lunch, Miss. Sooner than send you empty away, I would give it to you, Miss, most joyfully.

ANASTASIA. I ask, not charity, but justice.

THE LORD CHANCELLOR. Madam: I must request you to speak like a lady and not like a procession of the unemployed. The House of Lords always gives charity and never gives justice.

MERCER. The House of Lords will find itself unemployed one of these days, if you ask me.

THE LORD CHANCELLOR. Silence, Mercer. Have the goodness to keep your Radicalism to yourself in the presence of this lady.

ANASTASIA. Why do you allow your clerk to be a Radical?

THE LORD CHANCELLOR. Well, madam, to make him a Conservative and an Imperialist I should have to raise his salary very considerably; and I prefer to save money and put up with a Radical.

ANASTASIA. Youll excuse me asking you all these questions; but as Ive decided, after what the paper says, that you are the man to advise me and be a father to me, it's very important that you should be quite all right, isnt it?

THE LORD CHANCELLOR. But it's not my business to be a father to every young lady who walks into my office.

ANASTASIA. Not your business! Why, Whitaker's Almanack says you get £10,000 a year. You dont get that for nothing, I suppose. [*To Mercer*] By the way, Whitaker doesnt say how much you get.

MERCER. I get one-fifty.

ANASTASIA. One-fifty into £10,000 goes about 66 times. Why does he get 66 times as much as you? Is he sixty-six times as good?

MERCER. He thinks so.

THE LORD CHANCELLOR. I set up no such ridiculous pretension, Mercer.

ANASTASIA [*to the Lord Chancellor*] Perhaps youre 66 times as sober. How much do you drink every day?

THE LORD CHANCELLOR. I am almost a teetotaller. A single bottle of burgundy is quite sufficient for me.

ANASTASIA [*to Mercer*] Then I suppose you drink 66 bottles of burgundy a day.

MERCER. 66 bottles of burgundy a day on one-fifty a year! Not me. It hardly runs to beer on Sundays.

ANASTASIA. Well, there must be something awfully wrong about you, you know, if you get only the sixty-sixth of what he gets.

THE LORD CHANCELLOR. No, madam. Mercer is an excellent man in his proper place.

ANASTASIA. Then there must be something awfully right about you.

THE LORD CHANCELLOR. I hope so.

ANASTASIA. I dont see the difference myself.

MERCER. He's better fed.

ANASTASIA. Is he? I should have thought he was too red about the nose to be quite healthy. It's the burgundy, I expect. However, I didnt come here to talk about you two. Call it selfish if you will; but I came to talk about myself. The fact is, I'm an orphan. At least, I think I am.

THE LORD CHANCELLOR. Dont you know?

ANASTASIA. No. I was brought up in what you might politely call a sort of public institution. They found me on the doorstep, you know. Might have happened to anybody, mightnt it?

MERCER [*scandalized*] And you have the audacity to come here and talk up to us as if you was a lady. Be off with you; and be ashamed of yourself, you hussy.

THE LORD CHANCELLOR. Gently, Mercer, gently. It is not the poor girl's fault.

MERCER. Not her fault! Why, she aint anybody's daughter: she's only an offspring.

ANASTASIA. Perhaps I'm his daughter, my lord.

MERCER. Oh, you wicked girl! Oh, you naughty story, you! Oh, that I should have lived to have this accusation brought against me: me! a respectable man!

ANASTASIA. I had a feeling the moment I saw you.

THE LORD CHANCELLOR. The voice of Nature! Oh, Mercer, Mercer!

MERCER. I'll have the law of you for this, I will. Oh, say you dont believe her, my lord. Dont drive me mad. Say you dont believe her.

THE LORD CHANCELLOR. I cant disregard the voice of Nature, Mercer. The evidence against you is very black.

MERCER. Me the father of a common girl found on a workhouse doorstep!

ANASTASIA [*rising most indignantly*] How dare you presume to say such a thing? A workhouse doorstep indeed! I was found on the doorstep of one of the very best houses in Park Lane.

THE LORD CHANCELLOR [*overwhelmed*] My dear young lady, how can I apologize—

MERCER [*crushed*] I'm sure I beg your pardon most humbly, Miss.

THE LORD CHANCELLOR. Forget the rudeness of my clerk: he knows no better. Resume your seat, I beg.

MERCER. If I had only known, Miss! Park Lane! I could bite my tongue out for my bad manners, I do assure you.

ANASTASIA. Say no more. Of course you could not know my social position.

MERCER. Dont say that, Miss. You have Park Lane in every feature.

THE LORD CHANCELLOR [*effusively*] In your manners.

MERCER. In your accent.

THE LORD CHANCELLOR. In your tone—

MERCER. Address—

THE LORD CHANCELLOR. A je ne sais quoi—

MERCER. A tout ensemble—

ANASTASIA. You speak French?

MERCER. Not a word, Miss; but at the sight of that hat of yours the French fairly burst out of me.

ANASTASIA. You are very good—

THE LORD CHANCELLOR. } Oh, not at all.
MERCER. } Dont mention it.

ANASTASIA. Dont begin again. I forgive you both. Now, attention! I'm a good-hearted but somewhat flighty girl; and I require some serious interest in life to steady me. As I had an ungovernable appetite, and was naturally rather inclined to be stout, I tried politics. For you, a man, politics meant the House of Lords. For me, a woman, politics meant Holloway Gaol and the hunger strike. I refused to take food until I was so frightfully hungry that when the Governor—who was a plump, chubby, tempting sort of man, you know—came into my cell and remonstrated with me, I attempted to devour him.

THE LORD CHANCELLOR. Pardon me. I thought you Suffragist lambs prided yourselves on acting always on principle. On what principle, may I ask, do you justify an attempt to devour an estimable public official?

ANASTASIA. On the Cat and Mouse principle, my lord. That is a part of the law of England.

MERCER. Never. Not when the woman is the cat.

THE LORD CHANCELLOR. May I ask, madam, what the unfortunate mouse did on this occasion?

ANASTASIA. He got quite angry, and said he wouldnt have me in his prison another minute—not if I went down on my knees and begged him to let me stay. Of course I refused to go; but I had to let the poor man have his way at last, though it took ten wardresses to persuade me to do it. I left them simply in ribbons, poor things. Prison made a great change in me. Before I went in I felt a great want of something to love; but when I came out I felt nothing but a great want of something to eat. There were two public houses near the prison. One had a placard up "Sausage and Mashed," the other "Sandwich and Small Lloyd George." I visited both in succession, and had two goes of each delicacy. I then drove to the Holborn Restaurant and had a five shilling lunch, stopping at three Pearce and Plentys on the way to sustain exhausted nature. At the Holborn they refused to serve me with a second lunch; so I went on to the Carlton. Of my subsequent experiences at the Savoy, Pagani's, Frascati's, Gatti's, five baked potato men, and a coffee stall, I shall say nothing. Suffice it that when at last the craving for food was stilled, the craving for love returned in all its original force. I felt I must have something to cherish, to sacrifice myself for. You no doubt hold that self-sacrifice is a woman's chief amusement.

THE LORD CHANCELLOR. Certainly I do.

ANASTASIA. Any man would. Well, what was I to love? My friends recommended marriage: a man, in fact. But I hesitated to rush at once to so expensive and troublesome an extreme. I tried a pet dog; but when it had been stolen for the sixth time by the man I bought it from, I refused to pay any more rewards, and we were parted for ever. I tried a cat; but its conduct was so disreputable that I really could not live in the same house with it. I adopted the orphan child of a crossing sweeper who was run over; but when its aunt learnt that I had no parents she would not permit it to stay. Glad as I must confess I was to get rid of the little beast, my starved heart still ached, my empty arms still longed to gather some beloved object to my breast.

THE LORD CHANCELLOR. If I can be of any service to you, madam—

ANASTASIA. You? You are married, are you not?

THE LORD CHANCELLOR. Well, er, yes, I er—am married.

MERCER [*catching her eye*] I'm sorry, miss; but so am I. Still, a divorce would be a matter of only eighty pound or so if we made it a fairly straight case.

ANASTASIA. Never shall it be said that Anastasia Vulliamy built her happiness on the ruin of another woman's home. There are younger and handsomer men than you, my lord: there are more genteel characters than Mercer. Neither of you, if I may be allowed the expression, is precisely what I should call a peach. And I want—oh, I want a peach. He must be a young peach. Not that I am to be seduced by the fleeting charms of a smooth cheek and a slim figure. But it's a necessity of my position as a woman that I should marry someone whom I can bully, because if a woman cant bully her husband, her husband generally bullies her.

You, my lord, you will, you can,
Find me a young and foolish man.
Into my arms: under my thumb
Let him come, let him come.

I fear I am almost dropping into poetry; but the tumult of my emotions carries me away. I implore you not to keep me waiting. My soul, my soul is thrilling as it never thrilled before. My arms, my arms are longing as they never longed before. My heart, my heart is beating as it never bet before. Every nerve in my body, every fibre in my heart—

Brabazon enters.

BRABAZON. Excuse me: I left my stick, I think—

ANASTASIA [*throwing herself into his arms*] He has come: he has come: the very thing I want.

BRABAZON. Quite out of the question, my dear lady. Sir Cardonius will tell you that you are too young, too irresponsible, too impulsive to be anything more to me than an extremely agreeable object of contemplation, and a charming hostess. With that object may I venture to propose a marriage to you?

ANASTASIA. Silly! that is exactly what *I* am proposing to you.

BRABAZON. Not marriage to the same person, I think. You, as I understand it, propose to marry m e. *I* propose that you should marry one of my friends. You can then invite me to your house, and put on your best company manners for my benefit. He will have the privilege of paying for your hats, and enjoying your no-company manners.

MERCER. My lord: this man has a giant intellect.

THE LORD CHANCELLOR. It will avail him as little as if he were the biggest fool in creation. Young man: you are lost. I argued as you do. I tried to get out of it.

MERCER. I moved all the way from Gospel Oak to Islington to escape; but it was no use.

THE LORD CHANCELLOR. Beware how you anger her by shewing any reluctance. Remember: "Hell hath no fury like a woman scorned."

MERCER. Whats the good of that nowadays? When that was written a woman would take no for an answer. She wont now.

ANASTASIA. You will begin walking out with me at once. You are only on approval, of course; but if you suit, you may consider next Friday three weeks named as the day.

BRABAZON. But where does the merit come in for me? Where is the moral discipline? Where is the self-sacrifice? You are an agreeable person: to marry you would be an act of pure selfishness.

ANASTASIA. So you think now, dearest. You wont think that a year hence. I'll take care of that for my own boy.

BRABAZON. Yes, but look here, you know. Have you any money?

ANASTASIA. Not a rap.

BRABAZON. And you expect to get a slave for nothing. What cheek!

ANASTASIA. I'm richer than you think, darling. It's true that I'm a poor penniless orphan. Doesnt that touch you?

BRABAZON. Not in the least.

ANASTASIA. Thoughtless boy. Have you forgotten that the women who have money always belong to some family or other?

BRABAZON. Well?

ANASTASIA. Well, a family means relations. You cant call your house your own. The brothers borrow money. The sisters come and stay for months. The mother quarrels with your mother.

MERCER. Gospel truth, every word of it.

THE LORD CHANCELLOR. Undeniable. [*He sighs deeply*].

ANASTASIA. I, my love, am not perfect. I am a weak woman: I have nothing to cling to but your love, nor any place to rest except your very becoming fancy waistcoat. But at least I'm a foundling.

BRABAZON [*excited and hopeful*] A foundling?

ANASTASIA. I havnt a relation in the world.

BRABAZON [*clasping her*] Mine! m i n e!! MINE!!!

AYOT ST LAWRENCE, 10*th August* 1909.

CYMBELINE REFINISHED

(A VARIATION ON SHAKESPEAR'S ENDING)

Written in 1937

First Performed London 1937

FOREWORD

THE practice of improving Shakespear's plays, more especially in the matter of supplying them with what are called happy endings, is an old established one which has always been accepted without protest by British audiences. When Mr Harley Granville-Barker, following up some desperate experiments by the late William Poel, introduced the startling innovation of performing the plays in the West End of London exactly as Shakespear wrote them, there was indeed some demur; but it was expressed outside the theatre and led to no rioting. And it set on foot a new theory of Shakespearean representation. Up to that time it had been assumed as a matter of course that everyone behind the scenes in a theatre must know much better than Shakespear how plays should be written, exactly as it is believed in the Hollywood studios today that everyone in a film studio knows better than any professional playwright how a play should be filmed. But the pleasure given by Mr Granville-Barker's productions shook that conviction in the theatre; and the superstition that Shakespear's play as written by him are impossible on the stage, which had produced a happy ending to King Lear, Cibber's Richard III, a love scene in the tomb of the Capulets between Romeo and Juliet before the poison takes effect, and had culminated in the crude literary butcheries successfully imposed on the public and the critics as Shakespear's plays by Henry Irving and Augustin Daly at the end of the last century, is for the moment heavily discredited. It may be asked then why I, who always fought fiercely against that superstition in the days when I was a journalist-critic, should perpetrate a spurious fifth act to Cymbeline, and do it too, not wholly as a literary *jeu d'esprit*, but in response to an actual emergency in the theatre when it was proposed to revive Cymbeline at no less sacred a place than the Shakespear Memorial Theatre at Stratford-upon-Avon.

Cymbeline, though one of the finest of Shakespear's

later plays now on the stage, goes to pieces in the last act. In fact I mooted the point myself by thoughtlessly saying that the revival would be all right if I wrote a last act for it. To my surprise this blasphemy was received with acclamation; and as the applause, like the proposal, was not wholly jocular, the fancy began to haunt me, and persisted until I exorcised it by writing the pages which ensue.

I had a second surprise when I began by reading the authentic last act carefully through. I had not done so for many years, and had the common impression about it that it was a cobbled-up affair by several hands, including a vision in prison accompanied by scraps of quite ridiculous doggerel.

For this estimate I found absolutely no justification nor excuse. I must have got it from the last revival of the play at the old Lyceum theatre, when Irving, as Iachimo, a statue of romantic melancholy, stood dumb on the stage for hours (as it seemed) whilst the others toiled through a series of *dénouements* of crushing tedium, in which the characters lost all their vitality and individuality, and had nothing to do but identify themselves by moles on their necks, or explain why they were not dead. The vision and the verses were cut out as a matter of course; and I ignorantly thanked Heaven for it.

When I read the act as aforesaid I found that my notion that it is a cobbled-up *pasticcio* by other hands was an unpardonable stupidity. The act is genuine Shakespear to the last full stop, and late phase Shakespear in point of verbal workmanship.

The doggerel is not doggerel: it is a versified masque, in Shakespear's careless woodnotes wild, complete with Jupiter as *deus ex machina*, eagle and all, introduced, like the Ceres scene in The Tempest, to please King Jamie, or else because an irresistible fashion had set in, just as at all the great continental opera houses a ballet used to be *de rigueur*. Gounod had to introduce one into his Faust, and Wagner into his Tannhäuser, before they could be staged at the Grand Opera in Paris. So, I take it, had Shakespear to stick a masque into Cymbeline. Performed as such, with suitable music and enough pictorial splendor, it is not only entertaining on the stage, but, with the very Shakespearean feature of a comic jailor which precedes it, just the thing to save the last act.

Without it the act is a tedious string of unsurprising *dénouements* sugared with insincere sentimentality after a ludicrous stage battle. With one exception the characters have vanished and left nothing but dolls being moved about like the glass balls in the game of solitaire until they are all got rid of but one. The exception is the hero, or rather the husband of the heroine, Leonatus Posthumus. The late Charles Charrington, who with his wife Janet Achurch broke the ice for Ibsen in England, used to cite Posthumus as Shakespear's anticipation of his Norwegian rival. Certainly, after being theatrically conventional to the extent of ordering his wife to be murdered, he begins to criticize, quite on the lines of Mrs Alving in Ghosts, the slavery to an inhuman ideal of marital fidelity which led him to this villainous extremity. One may say that he is the only character left really alive in the last act; and as I cannot change him for the better I have left most of his part untouched. I make no apology for my attempt to bring the others back to dramatic activity and individuality.

I should like to have retained Cornelius as the exponent of Shakespear's sensible and scientific detestation of vivisection. But as he has nothing to say except that the Queen is dead, and nobody can possibly care a rap whether she is alive or dead, I have left him with her in the box of puppets that are done with.

I have ruthlessly cut out the surprises that no longer surprise anybody. I really could not keep my countenance over the identification of Guiderius by the mole on his neck. That device was killed by Maddison Morton, once a famous farce writer, now forgotten by everyone save Mr Gordon Craig and myself. In Morton's masterpiece, Box and Cox, Box asks Cox whether he has a strawberry mark on his left arm. "No" says Cox. "Then you are my long lost brother" says Box as they fall into one another's arms and end the farce happily. One could wish that Guiderius had anticipated Cox.

Plot has always been the curse of serious drama, and indeed of serious literature of any kind. It is so out-of-place there that Shakespear never could invent one. Unfortunately, instead of taking Nature's hint and discarding plots, he borrowed them all over the place and got into trouble through having to unravel them in the last act, especially in The Two Gentlemen of Verona and Cymbeline. The more childish spectators may find some delight in the revelation that Polydore and Cadwal are Imogen's long lost brothers and Cymbeline's long lost sons; that Iachimo is now an occupant of the penitent form and very unlike his old self; and that Imogen is so dutiful that she accepts her husband's attempt to have her murdered with affectionate docility. I cannot share these infantile joys. Having become interested in Iachimo, in Imogen, and even in the two long lost princes, I wanted to know how their characters would react to the *éclaircissement* which follows the battle. The only way to satisfy this curiosity was to rewrite the act as Shakespear might have written it if he had been post-Ibsen and post-Shaw instead of post-Marlowe.

In doing so I had to follow the Shakespearean verse pattern to match the 89 lines of Shakespear's text which I retained. This came very easily to me. It happened when I was a child that one of the books I delighted in was an illustrated Shakespear, with a picture and two or three lines of text underneath it on every third or fourth page. Ever since, Shakespearean blank verse has been to me as natural a form of literary expression as the Augustan English to which I was brought up in Dublin, or the latest London fashion in dialogue. It is so easy that if it were possible to kill it it would have been burlesqued to death by Tom Thumb, Chrononhotonthologos, and Bombastes Furioso. But Shakespear will survive any possible extremity of caricature.

I shall not deprecate the most violent discussion as to the propriety of meddling with masterpieces. All I can say is that the temptation to do it, and sometimes the circumstances which demand it, are irresistible. The results are very various. When a mediocre artist tries to improve on a great artist's work the effect is ridiculous or merely contemptible. When the alteration damages the original, as when a bad painter repaints a Velasquez or a Rembrandt, he commits a crime. When the changed work is sold or exhibited as the original, the fraud is indictable. But when it comes to complete forgery, as in the case of Ireland's Vortigern, which was much admired and at last actually performed as a play by Shakespear, the affair passes beyond the sphere of crime and becomes an instructive joke.

But what of the many successful and avowed variations? What about the additions made by Mozart to the score of Handel's Messiah? Elgar, who adored Handel, and had an unbounded contempt for all the lesser meddlers, loved Mozart's variations, and dismissed all purist criticism of them by maintaining that Handel must have extemporized equivalents to them on the organ at his concerts. When Spontini found on his visit to Dresden that Wagner had added trombone parts to his choruses, he appropriated them very gratefully. Volumes of variations on the tunes of other composers were published as such by Mozart and Beethoven, to say nothing of Bach and Handel, who played Old Harry with any air that amused them. Would anyone now remember Diabelli's vulgar waltz but for Beethoven's amazing variations, one of which is also a variation on an air from Don Giovanni?

And now consider the practice of Shakespear himself. Tolstoy declared that the original Lear is superior to Shakespear's rehandling, which he abhorred as immoral. Nobody has ever agreed with him. Will it be contended that Shakespear had no right to refashion Hamlet? If he had spoiled both plays, that would be a reason for reviving them without Shakespear's transfigurations, but not for challenging Shakespear's right to remake them.

Accordingly, I feel no qualm of conscience and have no apology to make for indulging in a variation on the last act of Cymbeline. I stand in the same time relation to Shakespear as Mozart to Handel, or Wagner to Beethoven. Like Mozart, I have not confined myself to the journeyman's job of writing "additional accompaniments": I have luxuriated in variations. Like Wagner dealing with Gluck's overture to *Iphigenia in Aulis* I have made a new ending for its own sake. Beethoven's Ninth Symphony towers among the classic masterpieces; but if Wagner had been old enough in his Dresden days not only to rescore the first and greatest movement as he did, but to supply the whole work with a more singable ending I should not have discouraged him; for I must agree with Verdi that the present ending, from the change to six-four onward, though intensely Beethovenish, is in performance usually a screaming voice destroying orgy.

I may be asked why all my instances are musical instead of literary. Is it a plot to take the literary critics out of their depth? Well, it may have that good effect; but I am not aiming at it. It is, I suppose, because music has succeeded to the heroic rank taken by literature in the sixteenth century. I cannot pretend to care much about what Nat Lee did in his attempts to impart Restoration gentility to Shakespear, or about Thomas Corneille's bowdlerization of Molière's *Festin de Pierre*, or any of the other literary precedents, though I am a little ashamed of being found in the company of their perpetrators. But I do care a good deal about what Mozart did to Handel, and Wagner to Gluck; and it seems to me that to discuss the artistic morality of my alternative ending without reference to them would be a waste of time. Anyhow, what I have done I have done; and at that I must leave it.

FOREWORD

I shall not press my version on managers producing Cymbeline if they have the courage and good sense to present the original word-for-word as Shakespear left it, and the means to do justice to the masque. But if they are halfhearted about it, and inclined to compromise by leaving out the masque and the comic jailor and mutilating the rest, as their manner is, I unhesitatingly recommend my version. The audience will not know the difference; and the few critics who have read Cymbeline will be too grateful for my shortening of the last act to complain.

G. B. S.

Ayot Saint Lawrence
December 1945

CYMBELINE REFINISHED

ACT V

A ROCKY defile. A wild evening. Philario, in armor, stands on a tall rock, straining his eyes to see into the distance. In the foreground a Roman captain, sword in hand, his helmet badly battered, rushes in panting. Looking round before he sits down on a rock to recover his breath, he catches sight of Philario.

CAPTAIN. Ho there, signor! You are in danger there.
You can be seen a mile off.

PHILARIO [*hastening down*] Whats your news?
I am sent by Lucius to find out how fares
Our right wing led by General Iachimo.

CAPTAIN. He is outgeneralled. There's no right wing now.
Broken and routed, utterly defeated,
Our eagles taken and the few survivors
In full flight like myself. And you?

PHILARIO. My news
Is even worse. Lucius, I fear, is taken.
Our centre could not stand the rain of arrows.

CAPTAIN. Someone has disciplined these savage archers.
They shoot together and advance in step:
Their horsemen trot in order to the charge
And then let loose th' entire mass full speed.
No single cavaliers but thirty score
As from a catapult four hundred tons
Of horse and man in one enormous shock
Hurled on our shaken legions. Then their chariots
With every axle furnished with a scythe
Do bloody work. They made us skip, I promise you. Their slingers! [*He points to his helmet*].
—Well: see their work! Two inches further down
I had been blind or dead. The crackbrained Welshmen
Raged like incarnate devils.

PHILARIO. Yes: they thought
We were the Britons. So our prisoners tell us.

CAPTAIN. Where did these bumpkins get their discipline?

PHILARIO. Ay: thats the marvel. Where?

CAPTAIN. Our victors say
Cassivelaunus is alive again.
But thats impossible.

PHILARIO. Not so impossible
As that this witless savage Cymbeline,
Whose brains were ever in his consort's head,
Could thus defeat Roman-trained infantry.

CAPTAIN. 'Tis my belief that old Belarius,
Banned as a traitor, must have been recalled.
That fellow knew his job. These fat civilians
When we're at peace, rob us of our rewards
By falsely charging us with this or that;
But when the trumpet sounds theyre on their knees to us.

PHILARIO. Well, Captain, I must hasten back to Lucius
To blast his hopes of any help from you.
Where, think you, is Iachimo?

CAPTAIN. I know not.
And yet I think he cannot be far off.

PHILARIO. He lives then?

CAPTAIN. Perhaps. When all was lost he fought
Like any legionary, sword in hand.
His last reported word was "Save yourselves:
Bid all make for the rocks; for there
Their horsemen cannot come". I took his counsel;
And here I am.

PHILARIO. You were best come with me.
Failing Iachimo, Lucius will require
Your tale at first hand.

CAPTAIN. Good. But we shall get
No laurel crowns for what we've done today.

Exeunt together. Enter Posthumus dressed like a peasant, but wearing a Roman sword and a soldier's iron cap. He has in his hand a bloodstained handkerchief.

POSTHUMUS. Yea, bloody cloth, I'll keep thee; for I

wish'd
Thou shouldst be colour'd thus. You married ones,
If each of you should take this course, how many
Must murder wives much better than themselves
For wrying but a little? O Pisanio!
Every good servant does not all commands:
No bond, but to do just ones. Gods, if you
Should have ta'en vengeance on my faults, I ne'er
Had liv'd to put on this: so had you sav'd
The noble Imogen to repent, and struck
Me (wretch) more worth your vengeance. But, alack,
You snatch some hence for little faults: that's love,
To have them fall no more. You some permit
To second ills with ills, each elder worse,
And make them dread it, to the doers' thrift;
But Imogen is your own: do your best wills,
And make me blest to obey! I am brought hither
Among the Italian gentry, and to fight
Against my lady's kingdom: 'tis enough
That, Britain, I have kill'd thy mistress. Peace!
I'll give no wound to thee. I have disrobed me
Of my Italian weeds, and drest myself
As does a Briton peasant; so I've fought
Against the part I came with; so I'll die
For thee, O Imogen, even for whom my life
Is every breath a death; and thus unknown,
Pitied nor hated, to the face of peril
Myself I'll dedicate. Let me make men know
More valour in me than my habits shew.
Gods, put the strength o' the Leonati in me!
To shame the guise o' the world, I'll begin
The fashion, less without and more within.

He is hurrying off when he is confronted with Iachimo, battle stained, hurrying in the opposite direction. Seeing a British enemy he draws his sword.

POSTHUMUS. Iachimo! Peace, man: 'tis I, Posthumus.

IACHIMO. Peace if you will. The battle's lost and won.

Pass on.

POSTHUMUS. Do you not know me?

IACHIMO. No.

POSTHUMUS. Look closer.
You have some reason to remember me
And I to hate you. Yet we're sworn friends.

IACHIMO. By all the gods, Leonatus!

POSTHUMUS. At your service,
Seducer of my wife.

IACHIMO. No more of that.
Your wife, Posthumus, is a noble creature.
I'll set your mind at rest upon that score.

POSTHUMUS. At rest! Can you then raise her from the grave?
Where she lies dead to expiate our crime?

IACHIMO. Dead! How? Why? When? And expiate! What mean you?

POSTHUMUS. This only: I have had her murdered, I.
And at my best am worser than her worst.

IACHIMO. We are damned for this. [*On guard*] Let's cut each other's throats.

POSTHUMUS [*drawing*] Ay, let us.

They fight furiously. Enter Cymbeline, Belarius, Guiderius, Arviragus, Pisanio, with Lucius and Imogen as Fidele: both of them prisoners guarded by British soldiers.

BELARIUS [*taking command instinctively*] Part them there. Make fast the Roman.

Guiderius pounces on Iachimo and disarms him. Arviragus pulls Posthumus back.

ARVIRAGUS. In the King's presence sheath your sword, you lout.

IACHIMO. In the King's presence I must yield perforce;
But as a person of some quality
By rank a gentleman, I claim to be
You royal highness's prisoner, not this lad's.

LUCIUS. His claim is valid, sir. His blood is princely.

POSTHUMUS. 'Tis so: he's noble.

CYMBELINE. What art thou?

POSTHUMUS. A murderer.

IMOGEN. His voice! His voice! Oh, let me see his face.
[*She rushes to Posthumus and puts her hand on his face*].

POSTHUMUS. Shall's have a play with this? There lies thy part [*he knocks her down with a blow of his fist*].

GUIDERIUS. Accursed churl: take that. [*He strikes Posthumus and brings him down on one knee*].

ARVIRAGUS. You dog, how dare you [*threatening him*].

POSTHUMUS. Soft, soft, young sirs. One at a time, an 't please you. [*He springs up and stands on the defensive*].

PISANIO [*interposing*] Hands off my master! He is kin to the king.

POSTHUMUS. [*to Cymbeline*] Call off your bulldogs, sir. Why all this coil
About a serving boy?

CYMBELINE. My son-in-law!

PISANIO. Oh, gentlemen, your help. My lord Posthumus:
You ne'er killed Imogen till now. Help! help!

IMOGEN. Oh, let me die. I heard my husband's voice
Whom I thought dead; and in my ecstasy,
The wildest I shall ever feel again,
He met me with a blow.

POSTHUMUS. Her voice. 'Tis Imogen
Oh, dearest heart, thou livest. Oh, you gods,
What sacrifice can pay you for this joy?

IMOGEN. You dare pretend you love me.

POSTHUMUS. Sweet, I dare
Anything, everything. Mountains of mortal guilt
That crushed me are now lifted from my breast.
I am in heaven that was but now in hell.
You may betray me twenty times again.

IMOGEN. Again! And pray, when have I e'er betrayed you?

POSTHUMUS. I had the proofs. There stands your para-

mour.
Shall's have him home? I care not, since thou liv'st.

IMOGEN. My paramour! [*To Iachimo*] Oh, as you are a gentleman,
Give him the lie.

IACHIMO. He knows no better, madam.
We made a wager, he and I, in Italy
That I should spend a night in your bedchamber.

IMOGEN [*to Posthumus*] You made this wager! And I'm married to you!

POSTHUMUS. I did. He won it.

IMOGEN. How? He never came
Within my bedchamber.

IACHIMO. I spent a night there.
It was the most uncomfortable night
I ever passed.

IMOGEN. You must be mad, signor.
Or else the most audacious of all liars
That ever swore away a woman's honor.

IACHIMO. I think, madam, you do forget that chest.

IMOGEN. I forget nothing. At your earnest suit
Your chest was safely houséd in my chamber;
But where were you?

IACHIMO. I? I was in the chest [*Hilarious sensation*].
And on one point I do confess a fault.
I stole your bracelet while you were asleep.

POSTHUMUS. And cheated me out of my diamond ring!

IACHIMO. Both ring and bracelet had some magic in them
That would not let me rest until I laid them
On Mercury's altar. He's the god of thieves.
But I can make amends. I'll pay for both
At your own price, and add one bracelet more
For the other arm.

POSTHUMUS. With ten thousand ducats
Due to me for the wager you have lost.

IMOGEN. And this, you think, signors, makes good to me
All you have done, you and my husband there!

IACHIMO. It remedies what can be remedied.
As for the rest, it cannot be undone.
We are a pitiable pair. For all that
You may go further and fare worse; for men
Will do such things to women.

IMOGEN. You at least
Have grace to know yourself for what you are.
My husband thinks that all is settled now
And this a happy ending!

POSTHUMUS. Well, my dearest,
What could I think? The fellow did describe
The mole upon your breast.

IMOGEN. And thereupon
You bade your servant kill me.

POSTHUMUS. It seemed natural.

IMOGEN. Strike me again; but do not say such things.

GUIDERIUS. An if you do, by Thor's great hammer stroke
I'll kill you, were you fifty sons-in-law.

BELARIUS. Peace, boy: we're in the presence of the king.

IMOGEN. Oh, Cadwal, Cadwal, you and Polydore,
My newfound brothers, are my truest friends.
Would either of you, were I ten times faithless,
Have sent a slave to kill me?

GUIDERIUS [*shuddering*] All the world
Should die first.

ARVIRAGUS. Whiles we live, Fidele,
Nothing shall harm you.

POSTHUMUS. Child: hear me out.
Have I not told you that my guilty conscience
Had almost driven me mad when heaven opened
And you appeared? But prithee, dearest wife,
How did you come to think that I was dead?

IMOGEN. I cannot speak of it: it is too dreadful.
I saw a headless man drest in your clothes.

GUIDERIUS. Pshaw! That was Cloten: son, he said, to the king.
I cut his head off.

CYMBELINE. Marry, the gods forefend!
I would not thy good deeds should from my lips
Pluck a hard sentence: prithee, valiant youth,
Deny 't again.

GUIDERIUS. I have spoke it, and I did it.

CYMBELINE. He was a prince.

GUIDERIUS. A most incivil one: the wrongs he did me
Were nothing prince-like; for he did provoke me
With language that would make me spurn the sea
If it could so roar to me. I cut off 's head;
And am right glad he is not standing here
To tell this tale of mine.

CYMBELINE. I am sorry for thee:
By thine own tongue thou art condemn'd, and must
Endure our law: thou 'rt dead. Bind the offender,
And take him from our presence.

BELARIUS. Stay, sir king:
This man is better than the man he slew,
As well descended as thyself, and hath
More of thee merited than a band of Clotens
Had ever scar for. [*To the Guard*] Let his arms alone,
They were not born for bondage.

CYMBELINE. Why, old soldier,
Wilt thou undo the worth thou art unpaid for,
By tasting of our wrath? How of descent
As good as we?

GUIDERIUS. In that he spake too far.

CYMBELINE. And thou shalt die for 't.

BELARIUS. We will die all three:
But I will prove that two on 's are as good
As I have given out him.

CYMBELINE. Take him away.
The whole world shall not save him.

BELARIUS. Not so hot.

First pay me for the nursing of thy sons;
And let it be confiscate all so soon
As I've received it.

CYMBELINE. Nursing of my sons!

BELARIUS. I am too blunt and saucy: here's my knee.
Ere I arise I will prefer my sons.
Then spare not the old father. Mighty sir:
These two young gentlemen that call me father,
And think they are my sons, are none of mine.
They are the issue of your loins, my liege,
And blood of your begetting.

CYMBELINE. How? my issue?

BELARIUS. So sure as you your father's. These your princes
(For such and so they are) these twenty years
Have I train'd up: those arts they have as I
Could put into them; my breeding was, sir, as
Your highness knows. Come hither, boys, and pay
Your loves and duties to your royal sire.

GUIDERIUS. We three are fullgrown men and perfect strangers.
Can I change fathers as I'd change my shirt?

CYMBELINE. Unnatural whelp! What doth thy brother say?

ARVIRAGUS. I, royal sir? Well, we have reached an age
When fathers' helps are felt as hindrances.
I am tired of being preached at.

CYMBELINE [*to Belarius*] So, sir, this
Is how you have bred my puppies.

GUIDERIUS. He has bred us
To tell the truth and face it.

BELARIUS. Royal sir:
I know not what to say: not you nor I
Can tell our children's minds. But pardon him.
If he be overbold the fault is mine.

GUIDERIUS. The fault, if fault there be, is in my Maker.
I am of no man's making. I am I:

Take me or leave me.

IACHIMO [*to Lucius*] Mark well, Lucius, mark.
There spake the future king of this rude island.

GUIDERIUS. With you, Sir Thief, to tutor me? No, no:
This kingly business has no charm for me.
When I lived in a cave methought a palace
Must be a glorious place, peopled with men
Renowned as councillors, mighty as soldiers,
As saints a pattern of holy living,
And all at my command were I a prince.
This was my dream. I am awake today.
I am to be, forsooth, another Cloten,
Plagued by the chatter of his train of flatterers,
Compelled to worship priest invented gods,
Not free to wed the woman of my choice,
Being stopped at every turn by some old fool
Crying "You must not", or, still worse, "You must".
Oh no, sir: give me back the dear old cave
And my unflattering four footed friends.
I abdicate, and pass the throne to Polydore.

ARVIRAGUS. Do you, by heavens? Thank you for nothing, brother.

CYMBELINE. I'm glad you're not ambitious. Seated monarchs
Do rarely love their heirs. Wisely, it seems.

ARVIRAGUS. Fear not, great sir: we two have never learnt
To wait for dead men's shoes, much less their crowns.

GUIDERIUS. Enough of this. Fidele: is it true
Thou art a woman, and this man thy husband?

IMOGEN. I am a woman, and this man my husband.
He would have slain me.

POSTHUMUS. Do not harp on that.

CYMBELINE. God's patience, man, take your wife home to bed.
You're man and wife: nothing can alter that.
Are there more plots to unravel? Each one here,

It seems, is someone else. [*To Imogen*] Go change your dress
For one becoming to your sex and rank.
Have you no shame?

IMOGEN. None.

CYMBELINE. How? None!

IMOGEN. All is lost.
Shame, husband, happiness, and faith in Man.
He is not even sorry.

POSTHUMUS. I'm too happy.

IACHIMO. Lady: a word. When you arrived just now
I, as you saw, was hot on killing him.
Let him bear witness that I drew on him
To avenge your death.

IMOGEN. Oh, do not make me laugh.
Laughter dissolves too many just resentments,
Pardons too many sins.

IACHIMO. And saves the world
A many thousand murders. Let me plead for him.
He has his faults; but he must suffer yours.
You are, I swear, a very worthy lady;
But still, not quite an angel.

IMOGEN. No, not quite,
Nor yet a worm. Subtle Italian villain!
I would that chest had smothered you.

IACHIMO. Dear lady
It very nearly did.

IMOGEN. I will not laugh.
I must go home and make the best of it
As other women must.

POSTHUMUS. Thats all I ask. [*He clasps her*].

BELARIUS. The fingers of the powers above do tune
The harmony of this peace.

LUCIUS. Peace be it then.
For by this gentleman's report and mine
I hope imperial Cæsar will reknit
His favour with the radiant Cymbeline,

Which shines here in the west.

CYMBELINE. Laud we the gods,
And let our crooked smokes climb to their nostrils
From our blest altars. Publish we this peace
To all our subjects. Set we forward: let
A Roman and a British ensign wave
Friendly together: so through Lud's town march,
And in the temple of great Jupiter
Our peace we'll ratify; seal it with feasts.
Set on there! Never was a war did cease,
Ere bloody hands were wash'd, with such a peace.

[*Curtain*

THE END

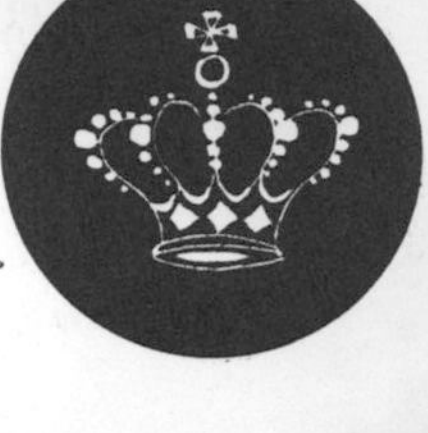

INDEX OF PLAYS